HATSHEPSUT THE WOMAN WHO WAS PHARAOH

Author

NELY EMILIANI

ISBN: 978-0-692-09019-0

Before I decided to publish my book, I wanted the opinion of my dear friends who I trust, and these are their thoughts:

September 30, 2017.

HATSHEPSUT THE WOMAN WHO WAS PHARAOH, is a riveting and intriguing book, so much so, that I can't put it down. This is a book of Hatshepsut's life, from the beginning up until her death. It tells of her love, bravery, trials, sorrows and death.

This book keeps you rapt with its excitement, sorrows, drama, quests and achievements. It is a truly spectacular read.

I highly recommend this book! You will not be disappointed.

Geri Hart.

March 28, 2018

Reading HATSHEPSUT, THE WOMAN WHO WAS PHARAOH made me wonder about our existence. I have always been a believer of life and death, meaning I didn't have any room for a gray area.

I went into this with an open mind, and I kept going back and forth between the book and historic information about Egypt and its governance.

The things written in this book intertwine with historic Egypt so much, that I began to wonder… It's a must read!!! I could not put it down. I was on it while everyone slept. It was so different, and I wanted to know more.

It's a book about love, first and foremost, and reincarnation.

Uzezi Augustine.

Only Love is Real

Sen-Mut

Know, therefore, that from the greater silence, I shall return.

Forget not that I shall come back to you…

A little while, a moment of rest upon the wind, and another woman should bear me…

Hatshepsut

by Kahlil Gibran

Dedication

To God Almighty, for making it possible for me to return to Earth. I love you, Father.

To Sen-Mut, for being the inspiration of my book. Our love transcends space and time.

Acknowledgements

I want to thank my son Jonathan and my daughter Michelle for their support and encouragement in writing my life story since 1995. I want to thank my godson Joshua A. Carretero for his love and support.

I want to thank James L. Sinsel, my ex-husband. He has believed me since the very beginning when I told him that I lived in Egypt 3,500 years ago.

I must thank my father, Ramon Emiliani (R.I.P), for not putting me in a mental institution when I was a small child and told him that he was not my father and that Egypt was my home. I narrated my life story to him when I was 35 years old, and his words were, “Thank God I didn’t listen to people when they told me to put you in a mental institution.”

I want to thank Ofelia Rodriguez de Emiliani (R.I.P), my mother in this life, for always being there and putting up with me during my childhood when I was driving her crazy.

I especially want to thank psychologist Leo Sprinkle, Ph.D. and his wife, Marilyn Sprinkle, for helping me to remember fully my past life, so that I may relate the truth to the public and explain events as they really happened. I want to thank Leo for bearing with me and for listening patiently every time I had an emotional crisis of the past. He listened patiently to my cries until I calmed down. He encouraged me to write this manuscript. Leo also researched his records and clarified that our first meeting was in 1978 and not in 1974, as I first thought.

I want to also thank my brothers and sisters, Ramon, Romulo, David, Carmen Nelly, Nelva Emiliani, and my cousin Merle Buendia, who always believed who I was since we were children.

I want to thank Joseph H. Hubbard, who has been my dearest friend forever. I hold him close to my heart.

I want to thank to my friends Carol Robinson and Geraldine Hart, who were always there for me. Thank you for your support.

I would like to thank Edna Castillo, my book cover designer, who worked so hard to create the marvelous book cover exactly as I wanted. Thank you so much! (edna.castillo1@gmail.com).

I want to thank my childhood best friend, Roberto Perez (Robby), for the years of friendship.

Thanks to Lance Windle for all the help he gave me in terms of technical support during these five years. Genius!

I want to thank Howard G. Slade, my editor, who worked very hard and did a superb job in editing my book, since English is my second language. I could not have done it without him. I would hire him again and highly recommend him! (hgslade75@gmail.com).

Also, I want to thank my dear friend Uzetti who proof read my book.

I want to apologize to a dear friend, Queen Ati from Punt, for the misinformation published as my opinion of her and her family. I firmly refuse such publications. I personally did not express myself in that way, nor did Sen-Mut. I am sure that Sen-Mut would not have permitted such way to be written anywhere in the palace, nor in my temple. My father, the Great Maat, taught me many things, and one of them was that I must love my people and respect them for my people to respect me and love me back. I became friends with Queen Ati then, and I will always remember her sweetness and her kindness.

TABLE OF CONTENTS

CHAPTER 1 **Page-1**

MY BIRTH 1949 A.D.

CHAPTER 2 **Page-3**

SIX TO NINE MONTHS OLD

CHAPTER 3 **Page-4**

FIVE YEARS OLD

CHAPTER 4 **Page-8**

SEVEN YEARS OLD

CHAPTER 5 **Page-10**

NINE YEARS OLD

CHAPTER 6 **Page-14**

ELEVEN YEARS OLD – FIFTEEN YEARS OLD

CHAPTER 7 **Page-18**

HIGH SCHOOL

CHAPTER 8 **page-20**

FIRST REGRESSION, CHEYENNE, WYOMING

1978 A.D.

CHAPTER 9 **Page-23**

VIENNA, AUSTRIA 1750 A.D.

CHAPTER 10 **Page-26**

REGRESSION – INTERMISSION

CHAPTER 11 **Page-27**

THEBES, EGYPT 1450 B.C.

CHAPTER 12 **Page-30**

THUTMOSES II'S BIRTH

CHAPTER 13 **Page-32**

LITTLE HORUS OF EGYPT

CHAPTER 14 **Page-47**

SEN-MUT, A FARM BOY

CHAPTER 15 **Page-49**

LITTLE HORUS

CHAPTER 16 **Page-55**

CRETE, GREECE

CHAPTER 17 **Page-64**

TEACHING AAKHEPEREN-RE

TO BE BRAVE (Thutmoses II)

CHAPTER 18 **Page-113**

NEFERU-BITY

CHAPTER 19 **Page-124**

MEETING SEN-MUT

CHAPTER 20 **Page-169**

PHARAOH'S HUNTING TRIP

CHAPTER 21 **Page-173**

CELEBRATION

CHAPTER 22 **Page-197**

ISLAND OF PHILAE

CHAPTER 23 **Page-231**

FATHER'S WARNINGS

CHAPTER 24 **Page-240**

MOTHER'S DEATH

CHAPTER 25 **Page-249**

QUEEN OF EGYPT

CHAPTER 26 **Page-278**

PHARAOH'S DEATH

CHAPTER 27 **Page-284**

MARRIAGE TO THUTMOSES II

& CORONATION

CHAPTER 28 **Page-304**

NEFERU-RE'S BIRTH

CHAPTER 29 **Page-333**

PRINCESS HATSHEPSET'S BIRTH

CHAPTER 30 **Page-337**

MENKHEP-RE'S BIRTH

CHAPTER 31 **Page-343**

WAR

CHAPTER 32 **Page-380**

PRINCESS NEFERU-RE'S DEATH

CHAPTER 33 **Page-394**

THUTMOSES II'S DEATH

CHAPTER 34 **Page-498**

CROWN PHARAOH OF EGYPT

CHAPTER 35 **Page-568**

OBELISKS

CHAPTER 36 **Page-592**

EXPEDITION TO PUNT

CHAPTER 37 **Page-626**

SEN-MUT

CHAPTER 38 **Page-636**

T'QUETA

CHAPTER 39 **Page-644**

MESSAGE FROM SEN-MUT

CHAPTER 40 **Page-656**

SEN-MUT'S VICTORIOUS RETURN

CHAPTER 41 **Page-708**

QUEEN ATI

CHAPTER 42 **Page-718**

COUP D' ETAT

CHAPTER 43 **Page-757**

AKHELA

CHAPTER 44 **Page-767**

MENKHEP-RE

CHAPTER 45 **Page 782**

DEATH

FORWARD

On Sep. 24, 2001, I met with Ms. Nely Emiliani for a psychological counseling session. She reminded me that we had met earlier, at a Reincarnation Workshop, which was conducted by me and my wife, Marilyn. The session in 2001 was devoted to her explorations of a POL (Possible Another Lifetime) in Ancient Egypt. Ms. Emiliani described her memories of being a royal woman, HATSHEPSUT. She recalled names and places, as well as many experiences in that lifetime.

Nely was pleased to learn that many people have participated in Workshops on Reincarnation, based upon the work of a psychologist, Dr. Helen Wambach, Ph. D, and her books:

Reliving Past Lives: The Evidence Under Hypnosis. 1978. NY: Harper & Row.

Life Before Life. 1979. NY: Bantam.

Earlier work had been conducted by a psychiatrist, Dr. Ian Stevenson, MD, at the University of Virginia. (Stevenson, I. 1966. Twenty Cases Suggestive of Reincarnation. NY: American Society of Psychical Research.)

At the time of our 2001 session, I viewed Nely as intelligent and educated, with a pleasant smile and courteous manner. I viewed her as somewhat obsessive/compulsive in her focus – partly because English is her second language – and partly because of her desire to be accurate. I did not view her as pathological in her behavior. Indeed, I viewed her as courageous in continuing her explorations. She has been willing to consult with scholars and historical authorities about her memories.

As a retired psychologist, I do not have the knowledge of an anthropologist or historian of Ancient Egypt. Thus, I am not able to confirm or deny what Ms. Emiliani has written. However, I can confirm her sincerity and her desire to record accurately what she remembers from that lifetime.

I am providing my support for her. I am hopeful that she can gain editorial and historical evaluation of her manuscript, and professional assistance in the publishing of her book.

Respectfully Submitted,

R. Leo Sprinkle, Ph. D. Professor Emeritus,

Counseling Services, University of Wyoming.[1]

---

[1] We meet for the first time in Cheyenne Wyoming in 1978. When I sought his help, and he regressed me back in time to 1450 B.C. That is when everything began to fall in place.

PREFACE

I want to thank with all my heart the Only One who could have made it possible for me to return to this life, **GOD ALMIGHTY**!

FATHER, I THANK YOU WITH ALL MY HEART FOR LOVING ME THE WAY THAT YOU DO.

For months, I have battled with all the pros and cons of what I might encounter if I published my life story because of my religious upbringing. I was afraid that I would be called a heretic by my church, and I am NOT a heretic. Will I lose the few friends I have? Especially my dear ones and the ones who know who they were in my past life. After they read what happened in the past, will they still love me and continue to be my friends? I say this because I know some of them will be angry at me. But I must tell it as it happened.

Few knew the degree of my love for my Lord Jesus Christ and GOD ALMIGHTY, as Fr. Timothy A. Hopkins R.I.P. and Fr. Gunther Richter (R.I.P.)[2] and those who are closest to me and my family. In the last chapter of my book, there is a section about the end of my life when I meet with my creator, and while I was writing it, I remembered the scripture, John 1:1 which says:

"IN THE BEGINNING WAS THE WORD, AND THE WORD WAS WITH GOD; AND THE WORD WAS GOD. He was in the beginning with GOD. All things were made through Him, and without Him was made nothing that has been made. In Him was life, and the life

---

[2] They were Traditional Catholic Priest, very strict in the Catholic teachings, and they were my greatest friends. They knew of my memories of the past. Father Gunther Richter once said to me, "The brain is the blueprint of the soul." I love them and miss them terribly.

was the light of men. And the light shines in the darkness; and the darkness grasped it not."

When I came into His presence, I threw myself at His feet. (Yes! At his feet.) He was already in the form of a man and was so bright that I could only see His feet, and they were not yet speared. Then, writing my book, I remembered GOD'S words: "HE CREATED MAN IN HIS OWN IMAGE!" With a face, body, and feelings. He created all of us the way He looks and feels.

I want the world to know that a terrible deed was done to me and to the man I was in love with and whom I still love. I needed desperately to come back to the Earth and find Sen-Mut and tell him the truth of what happened that terrible day! I begged God Almighty to let me come back. I felt as if I already knew that I could come back again, and within me, I also know that people who commit murders do not return to Earth, nor do evil people.

I want to thank Sen-Mut, the one I love, a love that transcends space, time, and eternity. He is the inspiration for my book.

For many years, I searched for Sen-Mut, believing that if I was alive, he must be too. But where? I became exhausted in my desperate search for him. In 1980, I sought the help of a fortune teller but feared that she might say he may not exist in this life. I walked into a tarot card reading store, and the fortuneteller greeted me.

"Welcome, Queen of Egypt! I have been waiting for you for the last three months," she said.

I was startled, because she was right. I had been thinking about it for that long. Then I thought that maybe she greeted everyone in the same way.

Then she said, "Please wear this crown on your head. Otherwise, I will not be able to do the reading for you."

I took the crown and put it on my head, then she said, "I've been waiting for you, as I said, for the last three months!"

I did not know what to say, and she said, "You don't believe that you are Queen of Egypt?"

"Yes, I know that I am Queen of Egypt, and actually Pharaoh of Egypt!" I replied.

She looked at me with surprise, nodding her head and smiling, and I smiled back at her.

"Please sit down, Queen of Egypt," she said, then she stared to shuffle the tarot cards and divided the deck into three stacks.

"Choose one of the three stacks of cards and touch it with your finger," she said.

I touched the center stack, and she pulled one card from the top and turned it over. She placed it on the center of the red tablecloth.

"There is a dark-headed, Anglo man who you are going to meet, but you already know him," she said.

I was surprised and happy, and I asked her, "How am I going to meet a man that I already know?"

"I don't know but you know him from the past. And you are going to fall in love with him all over again!" she said.

It's him! I will find him! I will find him! My heart became very happy, for I knew now that he was alive in this life and that I would find him. At that moment, however, I also became anxious.

"How will I recognize him?" I asked.

"As I said, he is a dark-haired Anglo. And he is a Libra!" she said.

"When I will meet him?"

"Soon. The tarot cards don't say what day, time, or month. But he is in your path, and you will recognize him," she said.

I stopped her from reading anything else, for I had heard what I had come for. After that day, I looked for him in the streets of Denver, Colorado, in the face of every man who walked by me, every man who talked to me. And on February 19, 1982, I found him.

“For those who believe, no proof is necessary.

For those who don’t believe, no proof is possible.”

Kahlil Gibram

INTRODUCTION

The first time I sought the help of a professional in the field of regression, I did so because I had a morbid fear of snakes and had been having episodes of blacking out every time I saw a snake in a magazine, in a newspaper, or on the television.

The last fainting episode occurred in 1978 when my ex-husband Jim held me close to him and forced me to look at a picture of a python in the Cheyenne, newspaper. After this scare, Jim read an editorial regarding people who had fears they couldn't explain, fears for which the cause was unknown. The editorial discussed a famous psychologist, Professor R. Leo Sprinkle, Ph.D. of the University of Wyoming, who practiced regression therapy on his patients to help them discover what was causing their fears and to help them with a regression to stop those fears. After Jim read this editorial on Dr. Sprinkle, he suggested that I place a call to him and make an appointment, which I did.

After meeting with Dr. Sprinkle, who was a very nice person, we had a session, and he hypnotized me. I was regressed in time, a process which helped me to rediscover who I was in Egypt and why, as a child, I told my parents that they were not my parents, that our home was not my home, and why I had the deepest feelings and love for Egypt, a country I had never visited. And why I was so terrified of snakes.

Dr. Sprinkle told me that over the years, I would remember more and more, and I did. I eventually remembered my entire life in Egypt. I remembered who I was, who my loved ones were, the man I was in love with, my dearest friend, my parents, and my daughters. I also remembered the people who were faithful to me and loved me, the people who were my enemies, and the way in which I was killed.

I don't remember dates. I have only vivid memories of events. I could have written my life story using the dates and the narrative written by some archeologists, but it would not be the truth and would not coincide with what I remember.

I am writing my life story as I remember it, explaining what happened to me, to my beloved Sen-Mut, and to Hapuseneb.

I want to clarify that Menkhep-Re (Thutmoses III) was never Pharaoh during my lifetime, and I never married him. Also, let me clarify to you the readers, historians, archeologists, and Egyptologists who believe that I usurped my throne, for Thutmoses III to have become Pharaoh of Egypt, he would have had to have been of full royal blood, and he was NOT.

Before my brother Thutmoses II's (Aakheperen-Re) death, he wanted Menkhep-Re to become Thutmoses III, his successor, but there was a problem: he was not of full royal blood, as I was. I had the birthright to rule my kingdom as Pharaoh because I had already held the Crown of Horus since the early age of five summers for being brave and passing the test of the foreseeing. Also, those were the wishes of my father, the Great Maat, from the very beginning of my life, and he crowned me Prince of

Egypt in the presence of all the gods and all the priests of the Temple of Amun-Ra. He also placed the Double Crown of Pharaohs on my head when I became Queen of Egypt. I was trained as a warrior at a very young age to defend my kingdom.

Becoming Prince of Egypt gave me the control of all my land and the duties that are part of such a responsibility, and I was not about to give the control of my kingdom or my birthright to a three-year-old whose mother was desperate for power, a power that was rightfully mine.

The only way for him to become Pharaoh was for us to get married, which we did not, or for my daughter Hatshepset to be Queen and marry him to transfer the full royal blood to him (she was not Queen during my lifetime). Or I had to be dead.

We utilized Menkhep-Re's (Thutmoses III's) name for political reasons only until I could transition into the position of Pharaoh of Egypt. He usurped the throne after he murdered me, Sen-Mut, and Hapuseneb. He should be known to history as a murderer.

It gives me great satisfaction that Thutmoses III never wore the original Double Crown of Egypt nor any of the other crowns of Pharaoh, nor did his decedents, because Sen-Mut kept them hidden in a secret place where he could never find them. Even though I raised him as my own son and loved him as one, I always doubted him to be my brother's child. I had strong feelings and believe that he was not. Isis spent too much time in the Temple of Amun talking with Puyem-Re, Second Prophet of Amun. Rumors spread, and the gossip was that Menkhep-Re was perhaps the son of Puyem-Re.

At that time, I could not prove my suspicions, but according to a publication by S B Wire on March 19, 2012, recent DNA tests suggest that Thutmoses III is not related to my brother Thutmoses II.

It has taken 3,500 years for the truth to surface, and I am alive to see it. And I was right all along. I am relating all my memories and events as they happened 3,500 years ago.

In 1979, I found my dearest and beloved friend, Hapuseneb. He no longer had gray eyes or wavy black hair. He had sandy-blond hair and blue eyes but the same facial features. One day in 1979, I said to him "Would you think that I am crazy if I tell you that I know you from another life, a past life in Egypt?" I was afraid of his response, but to my surprise, he lowered his head, and thought about it, and said, "No, I would not think that you are crazy. I believe that It could be possible." Was his heart speaking to him?

CHAPTER 1

MY BIRTH

1949 A.D.

My soul was floating above a woman's body. She was in labor pain, and she was about to give birth to a child. Then I saw the woman giving birth. It was a girl, and when the baby took her first breath, my ka (soul) was pulled into the body of the child. And I was born again.

I was born in a small town called Dolega, in the province of Chiriqui, in the Republic of Panama on July 25, 1949 at 12:00 PM, and, according to the astrologers, on that day the planets were all aligned.

"It's dark, and I feel hot, very hot. I must be sick," I thought, and I started to cry. Then I heard steps; a woman came close to me and gave me something to drink. It was warm milk. I shook my head several times; "I don't want it!" I thought. Then the women left. I thought she must be a new slave because I didn't recognize her. In a short time, the women returned and brought me water. I drank the water, for I was very thirsty, and when I was finished drinking the water, the women left. I thought, "I must be very sick, and I should sleep for a while so that I may get well again."

When I was thirty-two years old, my mother Ofelia came to visit me from Panama. One day after work, I asked her, "Mother, how old was I when you brought me the baby bottle and it was warm milk, and I shook my head several times refusing to take it, because I wanted water. Then you left and came back and brought me water, and I drank it all because I was feeling very hot."

She looked at me, startled, because she was surprised by what I was asking her.

Then she said, "Do you remember that?!"

"Yes, Mom, I do!" I said.

"You really remember that? she asked again.

"You were only a week old, and I cannot believe that you can remember that!" she said very surprised.

She was shocked and realized that I could remember my life that far back.

CHAPTER 2

SIX TO NINE MONTHS OLD

"Why is it that I cannot stand up and walk as before?" I remember asking myself and then looking at a pale green wall. I thought, "If I can crawl to that wall and lean my back against it, the wall will hold me up, and I will be able to stand up and walk again."

I saw a woman sitting on a couch to my left and watching what I was doing. She was doing something with her hands, but I didn't know who she was.

It was my mother in the present time.

Later in life, my mother told me that when I was between six and nine-month-old, I did that. And I remembered.

CHAPTER 3

FIVE YEARS OLD

One night, my parents, brothers and sisters, and I were having dinner at the dining table, and I looked at my father straight in his eye, and with a calm voice, I said, "You are not my father!" And looking at my mother and pointing at her, I said, "And she is not my mother either! My father and mother are on the other side of the sea, very far away! And this is not my home. My home is big! Very big! And I want to go home! I want to go home!"

My father Ramon looked at me startled, and Ofelia (my mother) said to my dad, "See what I told you? Something is wrong with her. You need to take her to see a psychiatrist and see what is wrong with her head!"

By this time, she probably had seen things that were not normal for a child of my age. I had a mind of my own, and she could not control me in any way.

My father kept his silence, looking at me and caressing my head with his right hand. He loved me so much that he could not bear to think that something could be wrong with me.

Sometimes on the weekends we would visit an uncle. He lived in the small town of Chorrera, about a forty-five-minute drive from the city of Panama. One time, as we were approaching his home, I noticed that he had a bull's eye in his back yard, and after all of the usual greetings, I said, "Uncle Nicanor, can I throw the javelin? I know how! Please, please!"

And after I had nagged at him many times, he said, "You are too small for this, and it's going to be heavy for you."

"No, it's not!" I replied. "Come, come, give it to me!" I was pulling his arm.

After I insisted and persisted for a while, he gave up. He said, "Okay, let's go." He was laughing all the way to the back yard. Then he said, "Here it is. Don't fall down." He was laughing hard.

I took the javelin, and he was right. It was very heavy, and I noticed that it was too long for me?

"Why?" I asked myself, and I was puzzled because it was not like this before. The distance between me and the bull's eye was about twenty or twenty-five feet. I took a deep breath, took a few steps back and then forward, and aiming at the center of bull's eye, I threw it as hard as I could and hit the center of the target. A bull's eye! I was jumping up and down, up and down, screaming, "See, see? I told you! I know how to do it!"

My uncle looked at me, surprised, and brought his right hand to his head and said, "Yes! You did it! Who taught you how to throw it?"

I replied, "No one. I just knew how!"

My father was laughing and patted my head, while saying, "Good girl!"

My uncle told my dad that he had been trying to hit the bull's eye of the target for the longest time and had not been able to do it, but here comes this five-year-old girl and hit the bull's eye! They started to laugh together and walked away.

That same year, we went on vacation for three months, as we did every year, to the town where I was born, Dolega, Chiriqui in Panama. I was playing with my childhood friends, Tito Perez and his brother Tabo, when we saw a man riding a white horse. He came closer to us, and I asked him, "Senor, can I ride your horse?"

He looked at me and at my friends, and smiling, he asked, "Do you know how to ride a horse, young lady?"

I smiled. "Yes, I do!" I was quick to reply.

Then he asked, "Where are your mother and father?"

I replied, "You know my mother. She is Ofelia Rodriguez de Emiliani." I was hoping he knew my mother since everyone knew each other in that small town.

"Oh! Yeah, we grow up together," he said with a smile, then continued, "Okay, I am going to put you on top of the horse, but you must walk him slowly, do you understand?"

"Okay, okay, I will!" Then when I was on top of the horse, I noticed that the horse was big, too big and I was puzzled. I could not comprehend why this horse was so big. I had ridden horses before, and they were not as large as this one. And I couldn't reach the stirrups, so I did not have any choice but to ride the horse slowly. If I could have reached the stirrups, I would have urged the horse into a gallop.

While I was riding the horse slowly, I saw my mom walking very fast towards me, and she saw me on the horse. "Oh! Shoot!" I thought.

She said, "Get down, from that horse right now!"

"Why?" I asked.

"You are going to fall and hurt yourself! And you don't know how to ride a horse!"

"Yes, I do!" I shouted at her. "I know how! I've done it before!"

Her friend came running and said to her, "She said that she knows how to ride a horse!"

"She's never ridden a horse before!" she told him.

"Yes, I have!" I shouted at her again.

The horse's owner got me off the horse's back, and my mother grabbed my hand. As we started to walk away, she said, "Wait until your father comes home. I am going to tell him what you just did, putting yourself in danger!"

"But I know how to ride a horse, Mother! I've done it before."

"No! You never have!"

I didn't understand why she didn't believe me. When my dad came home, she told him what I had done. He came close to me, caressed my head twice and said, "So, you rode a horse today? What a brave girl!"

Oh boy, he was not mad at me! But then I thought back and wondered: why was that horse so big?

My father never spanked me. I was his little princess, and he always said, "You are the most beautiful girl in the world. Don't let anyone tell you otherwise!" And I knew that I was.

At this early age, I used to get up very early in the morning and wash my face and hands and face east, the point at which the sun rises. I knelt and bowed to the floor several times to give thanks to God Almighty for bringing us safely to the beginning of the day.

No one else in my family was doing this, just me.

CHAPTER 4

SEVEN YEARS OLD

My brother, sisters, and I, along with our friends, used to play cowboys and Indians. I liked to play the Indian because I could use the bow and arrow, but inside of me, I knew that I was not an Indian. But what was I? The bow did not have enough strength to shoot as far as I wanted it to, so I decided to make my own. I looked for a branch of a tree, looked for one that was hard enough that I could bend it a bit. Then I used twine to hold the two ends. After I had finished it, I tried shooting the arrow, but it still was not shooting as far as I was used to, so I gave up.

One night, I was playing with my brother and sisters in the living room, and I got up from the floor and went to my mother's bedroom. I pulled off the bed covers, took off the white sheets, and wrapped them around my body. Oh boy! The sheets were so long, and I walked to the living room, dragging the sheets behind me. I felt like a queen. I saw my mother sitting on the sofa at the end of the living room.

When she saw me, she had a surprised face, "What are you doing?" she asked.

I was dragging the long white sheets, barely able to walk, and I said, "I am a *queen*!" My brother and sisters looked at me, and they started to laugh.

My mother started to laugh, too, and she asked, "Queen of Sheba?"

"No! Queen of Egypt!" I screamed.

My mother continued laughing and said, "So, you are Cleopatra?"

I did not recognize that name and shouted at her "No! Queen of Egypt!" I was very angry because she did not believe me, that I was Queen of Egypt. And she did not realize that the word Egypt[3] had never been mentioned in my house before.

---

[3]The movie *Cleopatra* was released in 1963, and in 1963 I was fourteen years old. Before that, I had never seen a movie based on Egypt, nor even knew that Egypt existed at the age of seven. (Thebes was Waset and Kemet is now known as Egypt, and for the readers I am using the name "Egypt.")

CHAPTER 5

NINE YEARS OLD

I used to go around the house in my underwear since my mother was not able to make me wear any clothing. I also used to look at myself in the bathroom mirror and pull all my hair back and wonder, "What would I look like if I shaved my hair off?" Then I would run to my mother and say, "Mom, I want you to shave the hair off my head. All of it!"

She would sigh, turn around and look at me, and roll her eyes and shake her head several times as if I were driving her crazy.

My father came home daily for lunch, and I always waited for him at the door. I was very happy when I saw him because he would dance with me. He would lift me and stand me up on top of his shoes.

One day, he came home, and we did not do that because he had brought home a very large magazine. I don't remember if it was *Life* or *Time* magazine. He sat down on the chair at the dining room table and opened this large magazine. I came near him and leaned on his left arm as he was flipping pages. Suddenly, something caught my eye, and I re-acted by slamming both of my hands-on top of the page. I started to scream, "That is my home! That is my home! See? I told you before that this house is not my home! This house is too small!"

I became very happy. I was seeing the Temple of Karnak in Egypt. It was Thebes (now Luxor). I became agitated and started to scream, "I want to go home! I want to go home! This is not my home. This house is too small!"

My father was startled with all my screaming. He turned around and looked at my mother, and so did I. We were about ten or fifteen feet from her. She said to him, "Ramon, I told you before that something is wrong with her mind, and you need to take her to the Manicomio to see a psychiatrist to see what is wrong with her!"

My father then told her, "I would never, never take my daughter to a place like that! That is a horrible place for a child!" By this time, I probably really was driving my mother crazy.

My father became angry at my mother for suggesting what she said, and he got up from the chair. As he was walking toward the front door, I went up behind him and asked, "Dad, can I keep the magazine?"

He said, "Yes, you can," and gave me a kiss on the head and left. I felt sad for my father, and I wondered what "Manicomio" meant. I later found out it was an institution for the mentally ill.

I grabbed the big magazine with my two hands and ran to my bedroom which I shared with my sister Baby. I closed the door behind me and locked it. Then I sat on my bed and put the large magazine on my lap and turned the pages slowly. I could see how beautiful Karnak was. It was good to see my home again. I caressed the pages and brought the magazine to my chest and held it tight and closed my eyes, breathing deeply.

"Why is it that I cannot go back home?" I wondered. I wanted the sand of Egypt to run through my veins. I wanted to hug the pillars of the Temple of Karnak and I wanted to feel Egypt inside of me.

I tore out the first page and rubbed it so hard on my face and throat and arms until the page was almost in pieces. Then I tried to straighten the page and lifted my mattress and lay the page under it, so I could sleep in my home that night. I tore a second page out, took off my pale-yellow dress, and rubbed the page all over my chest, belly, and back as far as I could reach with my hand. I tried to straighten the page again as much as I could and placed it under the mattress. Then I tore out a third page and rubbed it on my legs, front and back. Oh! You don't know how much I wanted Egypt inside of me and the sands to run in my veins! Then I straightened the page again as much as I could and put it under my mattress with the other ones. I tore a fourth page out and rubbed it on the bottom of my feet, so I might feel that I was walking in my home, my beloved Egypt. Then whatever was left of the page, I tried to straighten and put it with the rest of the pages. I knew, I would sleep in my beloved home, Thebes, that night.

I remember sitting on my bed for a long time in silence, and I wondered why the Temple of Karnak looked so old. It did not look as fresh as when I was there… I felt as it was only few days ago.[4] Then I got up from the bed, got dressed, and ran out of my bedroom to go outside and play. My mother saw me as I was opening the front door to go out. "Where are, you are going to?" she asked.

I turned around, and she looked at me and yelled, "What did you do to yourself?!"

"Nothing," I said.

She shook her head and sighed, then snapped at me, "Go and look at yourself in the mirror. And take a shower!"

I ran to the bathroom and did as she said. I looked at myself in the bathroom mirror, and my face was full of dark ink from the pages of

---

[4] My eyes are full of tears right now, just remembering that moment, wanting to go home and having no one to take me home. 7/19/2014.

the magazine, as were my arms, legs, and belly. I sat on the bathroom floor for a long time thinking that if I took a shower, my home would go away and that I did not want to wash my home away. I did not want Egypt to go away from me. Never.

****

We used to walk to the beach every afternoon with my mother and friends whom I grew up with. The walk to the beach was about thirty minutes from my home. I always walked with Robby, my best friend since childhood. We had been constantly in each other's presence since the age of four or five. People would say that he was my boyfriend because we were always together. He and I were inseparable. We took walks together on the beach and sat in the sand and watched the waves going back and forth.

I remember I used to look far away across the sea, and then sadness would invade me. I would remember my father Maat and mother Ahmose with sadness. I would wonder, "Why is it that they don't come for me? Don't they love me anymore?" Then we would get up and run into the water to play.

CHAPTER 6

ELEVEN YEARS OLD - FIFTEEN YEARS OLD

ne, day, when I was eleven years old, Robby asked me, “What are you doing?”

“What do you mean?” I said.

“Why are you turning something with your fingers? I see you doing that all the time.” he said.

“Oh, because I feel that I have two rings, one on each hand, and I like to feel that I am turning them around as I walk.” I was not wearing any rings.

****

Across the street from our house, an apartment building was being built. Several months passed, and I wanted to go and see it up close. I got dressed to do that, putting on white shorts, a pink shirt, and white tennis shoes. I got my bike to go, but my mother saw me.

“Where are you going? And don’t you get any ideas like you always do. I mean it!” Mother said.

"I'm just going for a ride on my bike, Mother," I told her.

Before I could leave, she said, "I don't want to see you around that construction site. You can get hurt. Do you understand?"

"Okay, I won't," I said. I rode my bike various places at first. Eventually, though, hoping my mother would not see me, I went to the building site and went around to the back of the building. I was looking at the walls of the construction when, suddenly, I hit a rock with the front tire and lost my balance. To avoid falling, I put my right foot down, and I felt a very sharp pain on the arch of my foot. I had stepped onto a large construction nail, and it had punctured the arch of my foot. I could see the nail almost four inches above my shoelaces, and my white tennis shoes were filling with blood. But the worst part about it was that the nail was attached to a heavy, twelve-foot-long piece of construction lumber. I could not move my foot, it was too painful. I felt terrible pain, but then I thought about the pain that our Lord Jesus Christ experienced when the Romans soldiers crucified him with nails.

I could not scream, for there was no one at the construction site. I could not call my mother, brothers or sisters because I was across the street, and the street was a busy avenue with tons of cars passing. They would not be able to hear me even if I screamed, so I had to take the pain because I was "Brave! The bravest of all brave," I thought.

I stayed sitting on the seat of the bike wondering how I was going to release my foot from the nail. By this time, the white tennis shoe was soaked in blood. I thought to myself, "I will scream very hard to give me the strength like in Karate classes. AHHH!" I screamed hard and pulled up my foot as hard as I could, and guess what? My foot was not released from the nail. I still could see about an inch of the nail above the shoelaces. My leg was getting tired, and I could not lean on my foot because the nail would go back in again. I said to myself, "I am the bravest of all!" And I screamed hard again, "AHHH!" And I pulled my leg as hard as I could. The pain was horrible, but I noticed that I had released my foot from the nail.

I was happy, but now my foot was swollen. I needed to walk the bike out of the construction site, and I could see the same type of nails on the lumber everywhere. I walked out very carefully and crossed the busy street.

My mother was already looking for me everywhere. When she saw me limping and the tennis shoe full of blood, she screamed and ran to me, crying. My father was home, and he was screaming, "What happened, what happened?" He lifted me up in his arms, and I was rushed to the ER.

The doctor had to cut off my tennis shoe. The medical staff washed and scrubbed my feet very hard. Everything they did was painful, but I shed not one tear. The doctor asked me how I gotten injured, and I related the whole event in front of my father and mother.

He said, "You are a very brave girl. Other children would have cried and stayed there. You could have bled to death." He was nodding his head.

He looked at my father and said, "Now the bad part is that the tests show that she is allergic to the tetanus immune globulin."

Looking at me, he said, "We must give you several injections in your belly." By this time, I was burning up with a high fever.

My mother said, "She can take it, Doctor. She never cries for anything except when she is blamed for something that she has not done. That makes her cry!"

So, I took the pain of the injections. Of course, I could take it. I was a brave soldier.

****

One day when I was fifteen years old, I was walking with my best friend Robby on the beach at sunset. As the sun was fading away and everything was looking orange, red, and blue (a very lovely sight), suddenly an immense sadness invaded me. Tears were pouring down my face, and I started to cry so hard I had to stop walking. I did not know what was happening to me. There was a terrible feeling inside me in the middle of my chest. The pain was unbearable, as if I had lost someone whom I loved with my whole heart, and I cried for a long time.

Robby did not know what to do or how to help me. I had to sit in the sand because I could not stop crying. This feeling stayed with me for many years. I cried at the same time every day at sunset, feeling the same feeling of loss, and Robby always asked me, "Why do you cry at the same time?"

"I really don't know what this terrible feeling inside of me is that makes me cry at sunset," I said.

The sunset always made me sad and made me cry, and when I cried, I always looked across the sea to the east.

CHAPTER 7

HIGH SCHOOL

When, I was fifteen years old, I went to my biology class, and at the beginning of the class, the teacher said, "Today we will learn about reptiles. Let's open our books."

He mentioned a page number, and I was about to open the book when I noticed the cover included pictures of several reptiles, including a snake. I froze. I could not move. I was short of breath. I jumped out of my chair extremely fast and went to my teacher, shaking, and I said, "Teacher, I cannot open the book. I am terrified of snakes!"

Looking at me, he said, "Emiliani, yes, you can."

"No! I cannot!" I shouted at him. My heart was pounding very hard, and I was shaking. I could see that he had the same book on his desk, and I didn't want to look at it. He pulled me beside him. Holding me with his left arm, he opened a page with pictures of so many types of snakes that I could not breathe. Again, I froze, and then I blacked out. I had fainted.

I remember that they were using the smell of alcohol to revive me. Then I heard someone say, "She is going to be okay."

My teacher was very worried, and after a while, he said, "Don't worry, Emiliani. You can get another book and learn about crocodiles or other types of reptiles."

I always tried to avoid snakes in every magazine, television program, newspaper, or anything else that had pictures of snakes or discussed them. Why I was so afraid of snakes? I did not know.

And why did I feel that I loved someone so much, but I didn't know who? I always asked myself that question. Then the years passed, and I could not fall in love with anyone. Why? I still felt that I loved this person so much, but who was he?

At the age of nineteen, falling in love was hard for me. My friends kept reminding me that I had never had a boyfriend, and that I should have been married by this time. I felt pressured. I had many, many suitors, but I was not interested in anyone. I only wanted to be with my closest friend Robby with whom I felt comfortable and could trust.

CHAPTER 8

FIRST REGRESSION 1978 A.D.

In 1973, I was twenty-four years old, almost twenty-five, when I married James L. S. He was a very nice twenty-nine-year-old man from Minden, Nebraska. We met in Cheyenne, Wyoming.

I had mentioned to him how terrified I was of snakes.

One day in 1978, Jim was reading the Cheyenne newspaper, and he called me to sit down next to him. I did, and he opened the newspaper to a page where there was a picture of a python. I tried to get up, but he held me fast and said, "Yes, you can look at it!" I blacked out.

The next thing I remember was that he was standing there, holding something in his hand, and the look on his face was one of fear. I heard him saying, "Are you okay? Are you okay?" Fainting this time was strange. It was different, worse than before. Maybe because I was closer to someone I knew from my past?

About a week later, he was reading the newspaper again, as he always did, and he came across an article regarding regressions by Psychologist R. Leo Sprinkle. He was a professor of Psychology at the University of Wyoming. The article discussed people who were afraid of something and didn't know why. It also explained that, with regression, they could be cured of their fears. My husband showed me the article and said, “Call him and ask him how much he charges for the regression.” So, I did.

I dialed Dr. Sprinkle’s telephone number, and at the end of the line I heard a pleasant voice. I said, “Hello, may I please speak to Professor Leo Sprinkle?”

“Yes, this is he,” he said.

I mentioned his article in the newspaper. I identified myself and told him of my fear of snakes from a very young age, and I asked him if I could make an appointment to see him and how much he charged. He said that the process would sometimes require several regressions to find out the cause of the fear. He then explained how much it was per hour, and I excused myself for a moment and told Jim how much it was.

Jim said that it was okay, so I asked him when I could see him. We made an appointment for the following Thursday at seven in the morning in Laramie, Wyoming, about a forty-five-minute drive from Cheyenne. I gave him my telephone number.

A few days later, the telephone rang. It was Dr. Sprinkle.

“Hello, Nely. I am calling because I am going to have a workshop on regression this coming Saturday, October the 21st. Several other people are going to participate in the regression, and I was wondering if you would like to participate. It will only be twenty-five dollars and will be held from 7:00 a.m. to about 7:00 p.m.”

“Sure,” I told him.

He said, “You need to bring several blankets and pillows because under a regression the body temperature drops to almost a death stage.”

He gave me an address in Cheyenne where we would be meeting. Then we said our goodbyes until we could meet each other on that Saturday. I was anxious, for I did not know what to expect. I had never had a regression done before.

Finally, the day arrived. I left home very early in the morning, about 5:00 a.m. I arrived at the meeting place early. It was a large house. There were already about ten cars parked in front of it. I knocked on the door, and a pleasant man answered. It was Dr. Sprinkle. We smiled at each other, and I introduced myself to him. He followed and introduced me to everyone in the living room. I remember it was a very large living room. He explained to all of us what was going to happen in the regression and that if we reached another life, we would not feel frightened, nor feel any kind of pain in the hour of our deaths.

"You will only listen to my voice," he said. "And the regression is going to take about twelve hours. But at noon we will break for a light lunch, and afterwards, we will continue."

We all found our places on the floor and placed the blankets and pillows there. Then he said, "Everybody, lay down and cover your selves with the blankets." We all did as he said.

"Now I want all of you to listen to my voice. Breathe deep and exhale, and let your body relax, starting from your feet up. You'll feel that your body is getting as light as a feather and is being carried on a cloud. 99, 98, 97, 96... 5, 4, 3, 2, 1…1900, 1850, 1800, 1750."

CHAPTER 9

VIENNA, AUSTRIA

1750 A.D.

Suddenly, I was arguing with an Anglo man who was my father. He was a very tall, slender man with black hair, and he was wearing a white long-sleeved shirt, with black pants. I was wearing a long, gray satin dress with white lace in front and on my sleeves. I was yelling at him and telling him that I would NOT marry the man he had chosen for me to marry, another aristocrat as we were. He grabbed me by my arm and shook me hard, and said, "You are NOT going to see that stableman whom you have been seeing any more. Do you understand? People are talking. He is a stableman. I prefer to kill you than to have you continue to offend my honor."

I saw myself struggling with him. Then I got my arms free, and I was running out of the palace in Austria. It was raining very hard. I ran down the steps, went to the stables, got on top of a horse, and rode so very fast away from him. The rain was pouring, the night was approaching, and it was getting cold.

"I will not marry anyone else. Only the one I love!" I said to myself as I was riding. I arrived at the stables, and he was there, waiting for me. We ran into each other's arms and hugged each other tightly and kissed. I was crying, and looking at him, I said, "My father wants me to marry (I don't remember his name), and he has already arranged the marriage. He said if I don't get married, he will kill me!"

Suddenly, the stable doors swung open. There were six men. Two grabbed me by my arms. I fought hard, and I bit one of them on the hand. The other four grabbed Sebastian, my beloved, and they were beating him up. I was screaming, "Stop! Stop!"

I tried to get loose to help him, but they dragged me out of the stables in the mud, as I was kicking and screaming. They put me inside of a coach, and the coach started to move. By now it was raining very hard. In the coach, I fought and kicked as hard as I could, and I was screaming at them, "What are you going to do with him? Tell me!"

I was so terrified for his life, and I kept screaming at them. But they did not answer me or say anything. I knew who they were. They were my father's men.

By this time, it was dark, and we had arrived at the palace. I saw my father waiting for us, holding a lamp in his hand, at the bottom of the stairs. He came out to meet us at the coach in the rain, and they told him that I was with Sebastian.

He said, "Take her to the stable and tie her to the pole." I started to scream, and as I was screaming, they took me to the stable and tied me to the pole. My father told them, "Tear the back of her dress." He had a whip in his right hand.

They tore the back of my dress, and he started to whip me very hard. I screamed in pain. He hit me so many times that I passed out. The next thing I remember is that I was in my bed, and the maids were around me crying. I was lying on my stomach, and they were tending to my open wounds which hurt very badly.

Then I remembered what had happened. "Sebastian!" I turned to the maids.

"Oh, help me. I need to speak with my father," I said and got up with the help of the maids. I could barely walk and could barely breathe, both were painful. We walked to my father's office and I could see through the large windows that the rain had stopped, and that it was morning. The sun was shining outside.

"Father, what did you do with Sebastian?" I asked.

He looked at me and said in anger, "Didn't you learn the lesson?"

I yelled, "Tell me first what has happened to Sebastian. Tell me!"

"He got a severe beating for you, and I can assure you that the next time, I will kill him. Whether or not that happens is up to you. No matter what, you are going to marry (don't remember the name)."

Sebastian was twenty years old, had wavy black hair and brown eyes. He was tall with a gorgeous body. I was seventeen years old at the time. We loved each other very much, and we made love all the time when we were together. I didn't care what my father thought about him. Really, I was a brat with my father. I was his only child, and I did not respect him at all. I wasn't going to do what he told me to do.[5]

I never saw Sebastian again, even though I always thought about him and wondered if he ever thought about me as well. Or if he was even alive.

---

[5] Many years have passed since the regression. I now firmly believe that Dr. Sprinkle was my father in Austria. I felt that I had to apologize to him because I was a terrible child. I was a brat, and I gave him terrible headaches. Now I understand why he whipped me so hard that day at the stables. He was getting all his anger out of his chest for everything that I had made him go through. 2014

CHAPTER 10

REGRESSION – INTERMISSION

I heard the voice of Prof. Sprinkle again saying, "On the count of three, you will wake up, 3, 2, 1." I woke up and he said that it was 12:00 p.m. I remember saying it felt as if it had been only fifteen minutes, and he answered, "Yes, most of the time it does feel like only fifteen minutes have passed, but it is longer than that. In a regression, it's a lifetime in that time, and over the years you will remember your full life story, and all will come back to you." He said. I was puzzle because it has been five hours, and it felt that it was only fifteen minutes under hypnosis.

We had a light lunch and started again at 1:00 p.m.

"99, 98, 97…50, 40, 30…3, 2, 1, the year A.D. 1650,

1600, 1550, 1500…1000…0…B.C…1, 2, 3, 4…1000…1450 B.C."

CHAPTER 11

THEBES, EGYPT

1450 B.C.

I saw myself arguing with my half-brother, Thutmoses II, in the palace. We were arguing about Isis. He was tall, fair, and very handsome and was wearing a white kilt.

I was slim with a golden tan, and wearing a plaited see-through sheath, with a long black braided wig intertwined with gold. It hung down to the middle of my back.

I could see the tall columns of the palace behind him, and around me the wind was blowing. I could feel my sheath softly flowing at my ankles. Around us were tall, sand-colored pillars, carved from the bottom up with painted lotus flowers. I was standing in the open entrance of the palace, the Nile at my left, and the water was as blue as the sky. I could see far across the Nile where dirt and sand were the only things you could see. I could see the slow current of the Nile running north, and all the colors were vivid and fresh.

Suddenly, I saw a black asp slither about ten feet behind Thutmoses. I screamed, "Asp!" He jumped, running towards me.

Abruptly I sat down, and I was trying to wake up. I saw a man sitting on my right about ten feet away from me. I saw this tall man get up from his chair and walk towards me, and he was strangely dressed. I didn't know who he was. (It was Dr. Sprinkle.)

"Where am I?" I asked myself. I looked around at my surroundings, but I did not recognize this place. I was just arguing with Thutmoses, and now I am in this strange place!

The man approached me and touched my shoulder. Gently, he laid me down on my back, and with a kind voice, he said, "Go back to sleep, and go back to a younger age."

I went back in time, and I saw myself as a five-year-old boy and was puzzled by that. I was bald and wearing a kilt. I was on top of a litter being carried by slaves, and I was racing against the other children of the palace. I was trying to stand up and not lose my balance and fall. I wanted to stand as I did when I rode the chariots with my father. I was yelling at the slaves to hurry to make it to the finish line, and I was laughing a lot. But we lost. I got down from the litter, laughing hard, and noticed that on the left side of my waist was the golden seal of the Eye of Horus, the royal seal. But I am a girl, why was I seeing myself as a boy?

I heard again the voice of Dr. Sprinkle. "Go back to an older age."

I did, and I saw myself as a seventeen-year-old woman being bathed by my slaves. I was submerged in a large pool, and rose petals were floating on the water. I looked at the walls of the bathing room. They were painted light blue, with drawings of slaves holding large jars on their shoulders, pouring water into a pool. Others were playing music.

I realized that I was not a boy, but a girl with a bald head. I was helped by the slaves out of the pool. The bathroom was surrounded by lighted torches and burning incense. The delicious smell of the rose petals mixed with the smell of the burning incense. It was nice. I stood there with my arms extended and my eyes closed, lost in thought. They were patting my body and feet dry with fine white linen.

Again, I heard the voice of the professor. “Go back to your older years.”

Suddenly, I saw a queen whipping a woman who I believe was a slave. The whipping was severe and was done in a rage, and I did not like that. Then I realized that I was the queen.

Again, I heard the voice of Dr. Sprinkle. “Go back to later years.”

I saw myself walking beside the Nile at sunset, crying, with the most profound pain in my heart. The pain was unbearable. I saw myself collapsing to the ground, sobbing terribly as the sun faded away.

“Now,” he said. “Go back to the day of your death. Don’t be afraid. You won’t feel any pain.”

But I really did.

CHAPTER 12

THUTMOSES II'S BIRTH

reat Maat! Great Maat!" Hesemh was running across the palace yard and calling the Pharaoh. "Mutnofret, thy secondary wife, is about to have the child," the servant said.

"Let us hope it is a boy!" the Great Maat said as he walked across the yard towards Mutnofret's quarters. "Summon the High Priest Khety and the priestesses of the Temple of Amun, and my dear friend the great architect Ineni to Mutnofret's quarters," he said.

It was very late afternoon, and the rays of Ra, the sun god, were almost gone. A fresh breeze blew across the palace yards. And seven high priests of the Temple of Amun-Ra were walking across the yard of the palace. the rays of Ra are gone, and Mother Nut had covered the kingdom with her darkness. The stars were starting to shine.

All of them were inside Mutnofret's quarters as the midwife held her on a stool to bear the child. The priests started to chant. Then the cry of the newborn child echoed through the palace walls.

The First Prophet of Amun Khety raised the child above his shoulders and said with pride, "Your Majesty, it is a boy, AAKHEPEREN-RE!" he shouted.

He presented the boy to His Majesty, Pharaoh of Egypt. The face of the Pharaoh lit up with happiness. As he held his son in his arms, he whispered, "Finally, a royal boy. Aakheperen-Re!"

All of the priests started to shout, "AAKHEPEREN-RE! AAKHEPEREN-RE! AAKHEPEREN-RE!"

There was great joy in the palace that night, and the news of the newborn prince reached across the land and across the whole kingdom.

Later that night, Pharaoh, the First Prophet of Amun, and the rest of the high priests of the temple gathered together with the Oracle to foresee the future of the new royal child. The priestesses and priests started to chant the incantation words. Then the Book of Life was opened. The room was full of incense, an aromatic sweet smell, and they started to move their hands in a circle on top of a round pool full of sacred water.

The face of Khety, the First Prophet of Amun, became somber and looked at His Majesty with a serious face. The Pharaoh brought his hand to his chest, as if a spear had gone through his heart.

Khety walked to His Majesty and said, "Sorry, Your Majesty. The child will not live long. How many summers, we do not know. Maybe he will reach fifteen or twenty summers. He is a very sick child. You must have another child."

The Great Maat became silent, turned around, and left with a broken heart. He walked slowly in the silence of the night. He did not want anyone to see his tears.

****

Ten years later…

CHAPTER 13

LITTLE HORUS OF EGYPT

The festivities of Shomu had started, and the harvest had begun. It was a month of celebration. The sky was blue, not one cloud in the sky. I was standing on top of a litter, and I was screaming at my litter-bearers to hurry. "I want to win this race. I will give you gold for your wives if I win this race. Hurry, hurry!" I screamed at them.

But I lost. I could see my father and mother siting together. Also, there were Ineni; Khety; my uncle Thutmoses; and several other generals of the different armed forces. I could see how the wind was blowing on the different banners of the armies. Everyone was gathered around Father, and all were laughing at us as they watched the children of the palace racing against one another. I heard my father, the Great Maat Thutmoses I, calling me. I could see food everywhere, as I rushed to him.

"Little one, sit beside me," Father said. Ahmose, my mother, the Queen, was looking at me with a smile. I sat down beside my father.

"Dear little one, tonight I must have a long talk with you, and you must listen attentively to everything that I am going to tell you," my father said to me.

Looking at him, I said, "Yes, Father."

The games were over, and I walked to my quarters and was bathed by Sitre-In, my wet nurse. Afterwards, my mother and father walked into my quarters when I was about to eat and sat down beside me. They both smiled at me.

My father said, "As you know that nine summers ago, the Oracle and the stars foretold the fate of your brother Aakheperen-re when he was born. He was born very fragile, and we don't know the day when Anubis[6] will come for him. On that same night, I was told by Khety that I must have another child to rule my kingdom when I am gone. And one night, the mighty Amun-Ra visited me, took my form, and covered your mother with his seed. And so, you were fashioned in her womb, and you are the daughter of Amun-Ra. I am going to crown you Prince of Egypt. You will be trained as a warrior and learn how the government is run and the politics of the kingdom. You will have ears to listen, and eyes like a hawk to see, and you will be aware of every plot and every enemy that is out there against you in this kingdom, when I and your mother are gone.

"I have spoken to Khety, First Prophet of Amun, and he agrees that you must be prepared to rule Egypt. But you must pass a test, a test that is going to be very hard for you, but it must be done. I had to pass this test before I became Pharaoh, but I was a full-grown man and a soldier when I passed the test. The test lasted seven days for me. I had to prove to my father that I would do everything in my power to defend this kingdom, and that I had the wisdom and the knowledge of how to do it. I had to learn everything about how to run my kingdom, and now you must learn all of it as well.

"The day that you were born, Khety and I consulted the Oracle and the stars. The Oracle speaks of your greatness. Your birth coincided with the stars, and this meant that you would rule the kingdom with a firm

---

[6] Anubis was the god of the underworld.

hand. Now, I must prepare you for it. You are of full royal blood, and your brother Aakheperen-Re is not. Listen well, if I am gone and your mother is still alive, she must marry him, for him to become full royal blood and become Pharaoh. And if she goes to the other side and I am still alive, I must marry you for you to become Queen. When I am gone, if Aakheperen-Re is still alive, you must marry him and transfer the royal blood to him so that he can be full royal blood and become Pharaoh, thus continuing the linage of the royal bloodline. No half-blooded Prince can be Pharaoh if he does not marry a full royal Queen first. But if he has gone to the underworld, you will become Pharaoh and rule Egypt. I have already spoken to all of the priests of the Temple of Amun-Ra, and we all agree that you must reach the throne."

I was listening very attentively, and as young as I was, I understood everything Father was telling me.

He continued. "Khety will see to it that you become Pharaoh of Upper and Lower Egypt. I will give you only one bit of advice: trust no one. I mean no one, not even a high priest. Now, you can speak and ask me any questions."

I responded, "Great Maat, what about Aakheperen-Re? He will be very hurt if you crown me Prince of Egypt and not him, and what about Neferu-Knib? She is older than me, almost three summers, and she is a princess like me."

"She is soft, and she doesn't have any interest right now in anything. But you are different. We have been observing you and all that you do, the way you act when you come with me to see the soldiers train, and your eagerness to learn everything too. Look at you! Five summers, and you can ride a horse as well as the members of the cavalry. The army admires you and loves you. The charioteers love you. The archers love you. Everyone loves you! As does your brother Aakheperen-Re, but the dust makes him ill when he rides his horse or when he is in the chariots. I have tried not to strain him too much. A Pharaoh cannot be constantly ill. He would not be able to stand up in a war against the Hyksos or Kadesh or any other enemy in battle if he is sick. We must prepare you well for the tests of strength, wisdom, knowledge, and foresight."

"What is foresight?" I asked.

"Foresight is knowledge, a knowledge of the future. It allows you to sense danger around you. You will be able to feel the presence of anything dangerous, including a scarab walking or a cobra slithering, even when you cannot see them with your own eyes," Father said.

"Great Maat, I have a few mongooses in my room, so no cobras can come in. They will protect me!" I said.

"Yes, but they won't always be with you wherever you go. We must prepare you. The test will be given on the next full moon. Now you must eat. You are going to need all of your strength."

"Can you tell me what this test is about?" My mother asked.

"It's better for her not to know now. It's better for her to know on the day of the test. Otherwise, the knowledge will frighten her." The word "frighten" lingered in my mind until the next moon.

For the next several weeks, we went to the temple every morning to be in the presence of Amun-Ra and make offerings. We presented myrrh, the sweet incense, to him, hoping he would give me fortitude, strength, wisdom, knowledge, and finally, foresight.

As I prostrated myself on the floor in the presence of the gold statue of Amun, I whispered very low, "Great and Almighty God are you there? Can you hear me?" It was my first time being alone in the darkness with the Highest.

The dim light of the oil candle shined on his face. I said in a whisper, "I am your daughter, Hatshepset. I come to thee with a request. Please, give me the strength and the courage to pass this test that I must take, that I may protect my kingdom when the Great Maat is gone. Bless me with kindness that I may treat everyone fairly and with love. Please insure that

I will never have enemies, that happiness will cover my land, and that there will always be peace. But if there is a threat to my kingdom, insure that I might have no mercy on my enemies. I will crush their heads with my heel. Pharaoh said that you fashioned me, and I am your daughter. And I promise that when I am grown, I will build for you the most beautiful shrines, and your name will resound all over the land. Father, can you help me?"

Suddenly, I felt a great peace in my heart and inside of me. The Great Amun-Ra had answered me, and I knew that I would succeed.

****

"Princess, Princess!" I heard the soft voice of Sitre-In calling me. "Wake, up dear. Today is the day of the big test, and the mighty one sent word for you to be ready. I must bathe you well and dress you quickly."

It was dark outside, and Mother Nut still covered the land with her mantle, and the rays of Amun-Ra would not show themselves for several hours. I got up right away and went to be bathed. I was excited and anxious to find out about the test. Great Maat had said that he would tell me about it today.

Sitre-In started to wash my body well with warm water, and I could see the worry in her eyes.

"Sitre-In, do you know anything about this test?" I asked.

"No, my little one, but I will go to the Temple of Amun-Ra every day, and I will make offerings for your wellbeing and for your safe return to me. Her Majesty the Queen is waiting for you now. She must speak with you before you leave to take that test," she said.

I rushed through the hallways of the palace until I reached my mother's quarters. The guards opened the golden doors as I approached them.

My mother was waiting for me with open arms and held me tight against her chest. She said with a sweet voice, "My beloved little one, may

Amun-Ra protect you in this test and guide and bless you and provide you with all of the wisdom that you seek, and return you to me alive with the greatest triumph! But if you believe that you cannot succeed, yell very hard and abandon this test. Do you understand me? The Great Maat was a warrior when he took this test, and he was a full-grown man. But you are just a child of five summers. I can tell you that he has faith that you will succeed. But remember, don't be afraid. The High Priest will be there, and the Great Maat will be there, too. Now, my love, fare well. Remember that Amun-Ra walks with you and that the rays of Ra will always be at your back until we see each other again in three nights."

She kissed me with love and hugged me very tightly.

"Mother, will you take care of my little Bastet[7] until I come back?"

"Yes, I will, my little one."

"Don't forget to kiss them and hug them for me, okay?"

"I will take care of your cats, I promise," she said and smiled at me.

There was a knock on the golden doors. A guard came in and said, "Prince, the Pharaoh is waiting."

"I must go now, Mother."

I looked at her. In response, she hugged me very tightly, kissed my forehead several times and smiled. Then I turned around and walked quickly to the doors.

The golden doors closed behind me as I walked away to meet with my father the Great Maat. It was still dark outside, and five guards walked

---

[7] Cats

with me holding torches in their hands. We walked across the palace yard, and I could see Mother Nut and the stars.

"Guard, what is your name?" I asked.

"D'Jed, Princess!"

"Very well, D'Jed. I am hungry. Does Father plan to feed me before we go?"

"I don't know, Princess," he answered me as we were walking. I could see hundreds of torches far ahead in the darkness, waiting for me. As we came near them, I could see Father talking with his general and several other priests.

"Father, I am hungry. Will I get to eat before we go?"

"No!" Khety the High Priest said, but Father immediately responded, "Yes! You will, my beloved one."

We walked to the edge of Hopi[8] and got into a large barge. Father clapped his hands, and slaves came with many fruits, wine, sweet breads, and my favorite hot drink[9]. I could feel the barge move as it started to sail. We were followed by two other large barges as we sailed across the Nile to whatever place we were going to.

The Great Maat began, "Dear one, this is the moment that we have being waiting for. I must tell you about the test. I don't want you to be afraid because we will be with you at all times."

"What is it, Father?"

"When we arrive at the Valley of the Dead, we will go into an empty tomb, and you will be placed inside of an empty coffin. The lid will

---

[8] The Egyptian name for the Nile River.

[9] It tasted like cocoa.

be closed on top of you, and you will remain in there for three days, without food or water."

"How will I breathe, Father?" I asked. My heart was pounding hard.

"You will be able to breathe. The coffin was made special for the test. It has tiny holes that will enable you to breathe, but the room will be in total darkness and in silence, so that in the darkness, you will be able to feel your surroundings and obtain knowledge, wisdom, and foresight. From that day forward, you will be able to foresee danger and know who your enemies are, to hear anything far away, to hear when people are talking about you or thinking about you, even if they are very far away from you, and to see and feel when your loved ones are in danger or are happy. This is a knowledge that you will appreciate the rest of your life and in the after-life. Now, I must ask you, do you believe that you will want to continue with this test?" I saw worry in his eyes as he finished.

I thought about it. I had been in the darkness many times, and I was not afraid or scared.

"Yes, Father, I will, so that one day I might rule Egypt," I said.

With a big smile on his face, he said, "Then, let's do it."

I could feel the barge touching the edge of the bank of the other side of the Nile. "I am not hungry anymore," I thought.

We arrived at our destination and could see that hundreds and hundreds of soldiers with torches were waiting for us there. As we got down from the barge, I was lifted by my father's general who set me on top of a horse. Father was beside me, and we rode side by side together in the darkness with his generals. I could see hundreds of torches riding in front of us. The night was warm and full of stars. We rode for about forty-five minutes, then from far away, I could see more torches in a camp set up for us. By then the wind was blowing, and I was happy that there were no mosquitos tonight.

Arriving at the camp, the soldiers were aligned. They gave a firm salute and then knelt for their Pharaoh.

The tent was light blue with gold accents. In the center was a very large rug, and many cushions of different colors and oil lamps were scattered everywhere.

I needed to answer the call of nature, so I ran out and took care of my bodily functions. I could hear the Great Maat talking with the High Priest as I waited.

"Khety, are you sure she is going to be alright?" the Great Maat was asking the First Prophet of Amun-Ra.

"Yes, Your Majesty. The Oracle and the stars were all consulted. They foresaw that she would have your strength and that she would be victorious. She will rule Egypt after You and Aakheperen-Re are gone!"

I could see the first rays of Amun in the east, and we all knelt at the same time. The high priests incensed the area and chanted the morning prayers.

"Beloved one, it is time," the Great Maat said. We started to walk towards the rocky hills, guarded by fifty soldiers. They were carrying torches in their hands, and after a while, we entered an opening in the hills and walked down rocky stairs. It was very dark, with only the light of the torch to lead us. I could hardly stand in the loose pile of rocks, and I stumbled several times. The air was thick and heavy and smelled musty and dusty. We walked for a while, descending those rocky stairs. I could see that further ahead, there were more torches at the end of the passage, and we stopped in front of the two guards by the door. We walked inside of this dark tomb with a few guards holding torches. Inside the tomb lay a large, empty coffin on a pedestal, as Father indicated. I was silent. I did not know what to think at this point, but I knew that I could not let Egypt or Father down. I knew that I must finish the test ahead of me.

The Great Maat picked me up. I noticed that his arms were very strong. He lifted me as though I were as light as a feather. He laid me inside of the empty coffin. I was calm and unafraid, but I wondered about the unknown. But then suddenly I knew what I would do! I would sleep for three days. However, then I realized that I couldn't, that I must ask for the gods' help, especially that of Amun-Ra.

Father was holding my hand and said, "If at any time you think you do not want to continue, just call out. The guard will come to get you out immediately. Otherwise, I will come on the third day and get you out myself. Don't be afraid." He kissed my forehead and helped the guards to close the lid.

I was in complete darkness. I stayed still. I don't know how long I was in there before I started to feel hot, but I was sweating and felt short of breath. The Great Maat had said that this would happen. I must stay still.

"Oh!" I thought, "I can't breathe." I started to summon the great god Konso, the god of all creation, and my eternal Father Amun-Ra. In a low voice, I said, "In thy presence, I come to you, beloved God, to ask for your help to obtain wisdom, understanding, kindness, knowledge, discernment, and judgment, these abilities so that I might judge correctly the affairs of my kingdom, that I might help the less fortunate, and treat everyone equally with love. Give me the wisdom of foresight, that I might recognize danger, hear the thoughts of the good people, hear the bad plotting against me, feel danger around me, and recognize friend and enemy. Give me the strength to finish this test."

I could barely breathe. Then I felt myself floating. My Ka was leaving my body. I was above the sarcophagus, there was no more darkness, and I was not afraid. I could see the guards at the door and the torches on the entrance to the tomb. My Ka went through the wall of the rocky mountain, and I could see Amun-Ra shining in its full majesty. I could see the tent and the horses. My Ka was flying, flying to the palace, and I could see my mother wearing a yellow sheath, and in her arms, were many white flowers. She was followed by my wet nurse, Sitre-In. They were walking into the Temple of Amun to make offerings for my well-being. I continued floating on the air, and I could see the flowing waters of the Nile. Then my Ka came back, and darkness surrounded me again. This time, I was cold, very cold, and I slipped into darkness again. I had the sensation of floating, and my Ka left my body again. This time, as my Ka resumed flying, I saw Aakheperen-Re and Mutnofret, his mother, walking to the temple to make offerings for my well-being. Then my Ka was flying faster. Suddenly, I was in the middle of all the stars. It was completely silent, and I could see the entire universe. I was amazed by the beauty of it. "I must be dead," I thought.

"Hatshepset! Hatshepset! Wake up!" I could hear a voice calling me urgently from very, very far away. It was Great Maat, and he was getting me out of the coffin and carrying me in his arms out of the empty tomb in a hurry. I was weak, unable to speak. I could not open my eyes or lift my head as he was carrying me out of the mountain. I slowly opened my eyes, and I could see that the full moon, Thoth, was bathing us with its rays.

The Great Maat laid me on cushions, and I could hear him screaming for water.

"Hatshepset, beloved one, wake up!" he said. I could barely open my eyes, but I looked at him and could see tears rolling down his face.

"Fa…ther…did…I…pass…the…test?"

"Yes, Little Horus, yes! You did! Don't talk!"

"I can fly, Father! I can fly," I whispered, and then I closed my eyes.

I heard Father's voice saying, "Drink. Drink." He was giving me water to drink and cover me with a warm galabia. I was barely able to swallow, my throat hurt so bad. Father was holding me in his arms the whole time, and he never left my side. I sipped the water little by little.

The slaves came and rubbed my body and feet with herbs and cover me again. The High Priest was burning incense and chanting prayers for my health. I was given lentil warm soup to drink by my father, and I sipped small amounts because my throat was really hurting. Then I fell asleep.

I don't know how long I was asleep, but they kept waking me up to sip more warm soup. Eventually, I could swallow better. My father was with me every single moment I opened my eyes.

"Beloved one, don't worry. Mother is here now," I heard my mother's voice. I opened my eyes again, though I was still weak. She smiled at me. She was holding me in her arms on her lap. With a faint voice, I whispered, "Mother, I am a little Horus now. I passed the test."

She gave me a big smile and said, "Yes, beloved one, you did! The whole kingdom knows that you did, and we must celebrate after we get you better. Now, don't talk, and you must rest. You must get your full strength back." And she rocked me in her arms.

I saw Neferu-Knib, my sister. She was holding my hand with sweetness and kindness, as she always did. Sitre-In, my wet nurse, was kneeling beside me and smiled at me. She started to rub my body and feet. I still felt stiff and cold.

"Mother, I am very cold!" I said. I looked around for Aakheperen-Re, my brother. I could not see him. "Where is Aakheperen-Re?" I asked. Sitre-In came and cover me with another warm galabia[10].

"He must remain in the palace with the Vizier as long as your father and I are here, but he sends his love, certainly," Mother replied.

"Mother, I know that he is too sick to take the test, but can I make him Horus?"

---

[10] An Egyptian robe made of camel hair or cotton.

Father was listening to my question. He said, "Yes, maybe someday, you can."

"Father, when are we going home?" I asked.

"As soon as you get your strength back. We must celebrate, for I know this truth: Horus will rule Egypt when the time comes," he said. He was happy. I could see it on his face.

I could feel the happiness around the camp. I was getting stronger. Now I could walk and eat all my favorite foods, especially duck in sweet honey, as well as sweet bread with dates and fruit.

On the first day that I was able to walk out of the tent, the two royal guards opened the royal blue curtains of the tent, and I walked out. To my surprise, the army cheered and roared their approval, saluting me as their brave Little Horus.

My mother was wearing the yellow sheath, and she looked radiant with happiness. She was smiling at me. My father walked beside me and held my hand.

Now that the test was over, I felt different. I felt as if I had grown older and was now able to see things differently.

Eventually, I was able to recover from the test. We headed back to Thebes. I could hardly wait to see my brother and tell him all about the test and that I could fly. I would tell him that he didn't need to worry and need not take the test because I would make him Horus of Egypt someday.

"Neferu-Knib, ride with me," I said.

"How can you ride a horse, when only seven days ago you were weak and could barely talk?" she asked.

"Well, I feel great now. I am Horus, and the Great Maat said that yes, I could ride if I wanted to, but that if I get tired, we must stop and rest."

"Very well, but let's not ride too fast, since I could fall," she said.

"Okay. Neferu-Knib, let's ride beside Mother. Would you like that?"

"Yes, Hatshepset, I think it would be better, and when are you going to start calling me by my correct name? You know that it is Neferu-Bity. You are growing older now, and you are no longer a baby. You used to call me that when you couldn't say my name correctly. Now, say it," she said.

"Neferu-Bity. I said it. Are you happy now?" I asked her.

"Well, that doesn't sound like you. Okay, you can still call me Neferu-Knib," she said and smiled.

"Neferu-Knib, did Aakheperen-Re worry about me?"

"Yes, he was beside the Nile when the guard arrived with the news that you passed the test but were so weak, and Father sent for our mother and your nurse, Sitre-In. He was very worried about you, but he said that you were strong, and he knew you would be all right. He wanted to come, but he had to remain in the palace with the Vizier. I saw him walking towards the temple with Mutnofret, his mother, when we left. I gather they went to make an offering to Amun-Ra for you."

"I wish he was not sick all the time!" I said. "Neferu-Knib, you will be eight summers soon, and when you reach twelve summers you are going to be betrothed to Aakheperen-Re and some day you will be Queen!"

"Yes, that is the law of the palace. Don't you see, the Great Maat married his half-sister because she was a full royal blood. We are full royal blood, but Aakheperen-Re is a half-blood royal. If one of us were to marry him, it would make him a full royal. Let's not talk about it anymore. We are children talking about marriage," she said.

After our long ride, we arrived at the edge of the Nile. The guards and part of the army were waiting for us beside the barge. We sailed back to Thebes, and I stood in the front of the barge and let the breeze blow on my face. I closed my eyes and enjoyed the breeze of the Nile. I loved to sail the waters of Hopi.

CHAPTER 14

SEN-MUT, A FARM BOY

On the other side of the Nile, fifteen miles south of Thebes in the farming town of Luny where the peasants farmed their lands and brought their goods to be sold in the market of Thebes, lived a child of the name Sen-Mut, he was seven summers and lived with his parents Ramose and Hatnufer and his brothers and sisters. He helped his father with the minor chores of the farm, such as feeding the geese and the chickens.

He had heard the big commotion about the Little Horus, and asked his father, "Father, what is a little Horus?"

His father answered, "Horus is the god of the sky who takes different forms. He has the face of the falcon, who can see everything from above. He is divine. His right eye is the sun, and his left eye is the moon. The speckled feathers on his breast are the stars, and the wings are the sky. Every morning, he bathes us and the land with his rays because he is the giver of life, and we must always worship him every morning and in the evening before Ra fades away. He is the son of Osiris and Isis. The divine child, the little Hatshepset, who is only five summers, has passed a test and become the little goddess Horus!"

“Father, can she be Horus since she is a girl?” Sen-Mut asked his father.

“Yes, little Sen-Mut. Our Pharaoh is a god, and she is the daughter of Horus.”

“She must have been a very brave child,” his father told him. “We must get ready to leave after you milk the goats, since we have been invited to go to Thebes. My great friend Ineni has invited us to come to celebrate the festivities in the name of the little Horus.”

“Will I be able to meet Little Horus?” Sen-Mut asked his father.

“I really don’t know,” was the reply.

They got ready, and Sen-Mut was very happy to go to Thebes. They crossed the Nile in a felucca[11]. Sen-Mut marveled as they approached Thebes. He had never seen the temple nor the palace this close, only from at afar. It was afternoon when they arrived at Thebes. Music was playing everywhere, and everyone was happy!

[11] An Egyptian sailing boats.

CHAPTER 15

LITTLE HORUS

In the distance, I could see the tall Pillars of Karnak under the blue sky as we approached Thebes on the barge returning home from the Valley of the Dead.

"How magnificent Thebes looks! And I wonder if Aakheperen-Re is waiting for me since he has always been good to me," I thought. I could see him and his mother Mutnofret waiting for us. She tried to hold his hand, but he refused to do it. I gathered that he had become a big boy.

As the boat docked, the Great Maat said, "Little Horus, you will walk first in front of us." As I walked down the ramp, I could see the different colors of banners of the royal armed forces, and to my surprise, all of the armed forces knelt in front of me, and then they rose and started to shout, "Hail, Little Horus of Egypt! Hail, Little Horus of Egypt!" I was full of joy and pride. I felt very happy. I had never seen anything as beautiful as this.

I walked to Aakheperen-Re who was smiling at me, and I said, "I am Little Horus now. And someday, I will make you Horus of Egypt." And he hugged me tightly. Looking up at him, I said, "The Great Maat said that I could do it!"

"I heard that you were a very brave girl. Now you are a goddess, and the kingdom loves you. I wish I could have taken that test, too. I wish I was not sick all the time and I could do all the things the other children of the palace do," he said.

"I will tell you all that I saw during the test. I was even able to fly!"

With a surprised look, he said, "You could fly? And how is that? Have you told the Great Maat all of this?"

"Not yet. He wants to hear all of it tonight during the feast in the banquet hall."

"Little Horus and Aakheperen-Re!" I heard our father calling us.

We started to walk to the Temple of Amun to present offerings of gratitude to Amun-Ra and the god Konso. We were walking through the avenue of soldiers, and the people of Thebes who were cheering me on. As I walked beside them, I was smiling at them.

"Oh, how much I love thee, Thebes!" I thought. On both sides of our path, people were throwing white petals of flowers. I took a deep breath at the aroma of the blue lotus flowers. The fragrance was soft and delicious to my nostrils. We arrived at the Temple of Amun-Ra. All the priests and priestesses were aligned along the long corridor of the temple, all wearing fine white linen sheaths, except for Khety, the High Priest, who was wearing his long white kilt, golden belt, and a leopard skin over his shoulders.

They held in their hands incense censers, and I could smell the sweet perfume of myrrh. The large doors were opened, and we entered the Hall of Halls. I proceeded walking by myself and entered the narrow door of the inner shrine of the sanctuary and came into the presence of the god of gods, Amun-Ra, and prostrated myself completely on the floor. The doors of the inner sanctuary were closed behind me, and the smell of burning myrrh inundated the sanctuary.

"Oh! Greatest of all the greatest of all gods, I come into thy presence to give thee thanks for all the blessings you have bestowed upon me. You gave me the strength to surpass this test. With my hands elevated up to the heavens, I want to thank you with all my heart for the wisdom you have bestowed upon your daughter Hatshepset. Thank you for the wisdom of foresight. Now, I understand what Father meant when he said that I would see everything clearly, but you went further. You showed me that I could fly and that I could see the universe. It was the most beautiful thing that I have ever seen. It was wonderful to fly. Thank you for the wisdom of knowledge and love. I love you, Father."

That night I related my full experience to everyone in the banquet hall. Father was amazed, as were Mother and the High Priest, when I told them that my Ka came out of my body and I was flying and could see every one of them and what they were wearing on that day. I continued and told them that I saw my mother, wearing a yellow sheath, carrying white flowers in her arms, and walking with Sitre-In into the temple of Amun-Ra, to make offerings for my well-being.

Mother was stunned upon hearing what I had say.

"Yes!" she said. "I wore the yellow sheath and brought flowers to the temple with Sitre-In!"

Then the Great Maat said, "She went further than I did." Then he stood up and said, "I crown you Prince Horus of Egypt!"

Everyone shouted, "Hail, Horus of Egypt! Hail, Horus of Egypt!"

And he placed a small gold coronet on my head. It was the body of Horus in gold, with open wings on the front of the coronet, and he tied it on the back of my head with leather string. Then there was an explosion of applause. Everyone was shouting, "Little Horus of Egypt!" I was so very happy, and I walked off to the garden, looking for my Bastet Month-It. She was my cat, and my cats were usually around here. I continued looking for her and reached the entrance of the large garden, and I found her. I picked her up in my arms and was going back to the banquet hall, when I saw Ineni talking to a man. There were four children with them. I saw a boy who was around my age, and I ran to look for Sitre-In.

"Sitre-In!" I called.

"Yes, child," she said.

"Send the slaves to prepare a large basket with food and drinks, and a lot of date cakes, and send it to the entrance of the palace. There is a family with children talking to Master Ineni. And let's get some Bastet's to give them as a gift for coming to my celebration." I said.

"Will do, sweetheart."

I saw Sitre-In talking to one of my slaves, and the slave ran to the kitchen. Sitre-In and I went looking for my little cats, and we found them. I carried two in my arms, and Sitre-In also carried two. We arrived at the entrance of the palace with the slaves carrying baskets of food and drinks, but they were gone. I became sad because I wanted to share my little Bastet's with them. I took them back to the inner gardens and let them loose. I walked back with my cat Month-It in my arms and went looking for Ineni.

"Good evening, Master Builder!" I said.

"Good evening, young Horus. Congratulations on passing the foresight test. You are a brave Prince." He said.

I smiled at him. He was always kind to me and sweet.

"Ineni, earlier I saw you speaking to a family with four children. I sent for a basket with food and lots of date cakes to be prepared, and I have four Bastet to give to them as a gift. When I came back they were gone. Where did they go?"

"How sweet and kind of you young Horus. I invited them to come to Thebes to celebrate you becoming Horus. They just stopped by to say hello. Ramose is my best friend since childhood and they live in Luny, a farming town not far from Thebes. They came earlier to celebrate and enjoyed the festivities."

"Ineni, will they come back? I was hoping they would," I said.

"No, Your Majesty, I don't believe so," he said.

"Then I want you to send them all the baskets prepared with food and date cakes. With each basket, take a small kitten for each child as a gift from me for coming to my celebration of me becoming Horus," I said.

I clapped my hands and my slaves came running me.

"Bring all the baskets here and four small kittens and follow the orders of Master Ineni." And looking at Ineni, I said, "I am pretty sure they are going to love my little Bastet's."

"I am sure that they will, Your Majesty. If you excuse me, I will try to reach them before they go back to Luny. Otherwise, I will send a messenger with your gifts to them." He said.

I clapped my hands in happiness and smiled. He bowed his head and turned around and left. I saw the slaves walking behind him carrying the baskets on their shoulders and the cats in their hands. I walked to where mother and father were sitting and sat beside her. I was very tired and leaned on my mother's shoulder and fell asleep.

It was morning when I was awakened. I didn't know how long I had slept.

Sitre-In said to me, "Little one, the Pharaoh has sent for you. Let me bathe you so that you will be presentable to your father. How do you feel this morning? I always knew that you would succeed, though I was very worried about you during that test. The Queen was terribly worried, and I heard that the Pharaoh was, too."

"But you see, Sitre-In, how strong and brave I was. I had the blessing of the greatest of all the gods, Amun-Ra. I am his daughter," I told her.

“Yes, you are my child.” she finished dressing me and placed the golden coronet of Horus on my bald head. As I walked through my golden doors, the guards threw themselves at my feet.

I walked past them, to see my father and his guards did the same.

“Good morning, Father.”

“Hatshepset, I have a nice surprise for you!” Father said.

“What is it, Father?”

“I am taking you on a long trip to see the Great Pyramids of Giza, and we will visit several other cities along the way. Also, we will visit one of our cities next to the green sea, before going to a very far off city that is in an island in the blue sea. You are going to be so happy and will be impressed with the beauty of the sea. Also, I will bring back a scriber who is also a cantor and who knows other languages. With his knowledge and abilities, we have continued to trade with these far-off lands,” he said.

“When do we leave Father?” I asked.

“In two moons, in the month of Akhet, which is when the monsoon season starts. The rains will flood Hopi, and it will fill its banks for us to be able to sail the river,” he answered.

“Father, can we go to Philae, too? I love to go there. It is my favorite place other than home!” I told him.

“That is in the opposite direction. Maybe when we come back from this trip. It’s going to be a very long journey because we are going very far away. And we will have plenty of time to go to Philae when we return.” He said.

CHAPTER 16

CRETE, GREECE

The current of Hopi was strong, and it was good for sailing, and the time had arrived to set sail north. I was excited about the trip to the unknown land that father had told me about. We set sail at the first rays of Ra in the month of ATHYR. We sailed north, and the strong current of Hopi helped us along. We stopped to visit every shrine along the way, and we paid homage to every god along the river for our safe trip. The mosquitos were active and were eating me alive. I felt sorry for Sitre-In. She spent most of the night awake watching over me, so I would not be bitten by them. I saw small towns along the way. We sailed northwest to Memphis, and I liked Father's white palace. We were greeted by Father's Vizier Rekhemire and paid homage to the Triad of Memphis; Ptah, the god of architecture, Sekhmet, his wife, the lioness, and Nefer-Tum, his son. We had a wonderful time there, but we only remained there for a week. We also stopped in Saqqara and saw the step pyramid built by the Pharaoh Djoser.

Then we continued our journey to the north on our way to Giza. Then our ship turned to the left into a wide-open branch of the Nile. I could see greenery along the Nile and palm trees as we approached the small pyramid. I could see the small pyramid from our ship at my right. The ship stopped at sun down. Early the following morning, the horses were unloaded.

Father, Neferu-Knib, and I rode with the soldiers to the Pyramids. Mother remained on the ship. She believed that it was too hot to ride or walk on the sand under the hot sun. We rode to see the smaller Pyramid first and then rode until we reached the middle Pyramid. Next, we rode to the larger Pyramid of Pharaoh Cheops, it was magnificent, and the stones used to build it were larger than me. Father and the soldiers helped us climb up the stones of the pyramid. I tried to see Thebes from up there, but I could not. Then I saw the large Sphinx and was amazed, as was Neferu-Knib. I liked the Sphinx. Father said that it was built by Pharaoh Cheops. I was very impressed by the enormous size of the Sphinx and the three pyramids. Mother was right, it was terribly hot. I thought I was going to faint from the heat.

After the sight-seeing, we returned to the ship, and the oarsmen started rowing in reverse until we reached the Nile again. The oarsmen turned to the left and were rowing north with the help of the strong current of the Nile to the city of Heliopolis. We arrived at Heliopolis two or three days later, and we remained on the ship to prepare the offerings for the following morning.

At sunrise, we started to walk to the beautiful, large Temple of Heliopolis. Heliopolis was the city of all the gods of Upper and Lower Egypt, and we must pay homage to all the gods in the temple. Those were long hours making offerings to them. It was tiring for all of us. Khety was exhausted too. Then early in the morning the following day we set sail to the north again, until we reached the green sea[12]. I'd never seen green waters before. The sea was immense and beautiful, and we docked in a city with many people, including many children like me, playing and running everywhere. From the ship, I could see a little girl about my age, who kept looking at me and smiling, and I liked her.

"Father, come, can you see that little girl over there? Can you give her to me? The one with pale skin and long black hair? Can you see her,

[12] The Mediterranean Sea

the one who is looking at me? She and I can play in the palace, and she can play with me all the time. And when she grows up, she can serve me, too," I said.

"If she is here on our return from Crete, I will give her to you," Father said.

We sailed the green sea. It was beautiful, but the rocking of the ship made me sick. It made me dizzy, and I vomited many times. I could not hold food in my stomach.

I was given something to chew to alleviate my nausea. It helped a little, but not that much. I was pale yellow, Mother said, from throwing up so much. I did not have fun on this trip, being sick all the time. We finally arrived on the island of Crete. It felt strange to stand on firm land again, but at least I could finally eat and hold food in my stomach.

I saw so many beautiful things. I was impressed with so many flowers, especially the pink roses that had a beautiful smell.

The people of Crete wore different clothing from us. Some of them wore kilts, but most of them wore long fabrics over their shoulders. The women had long hair, and the men didn't shave their heads as men in Egypt did.

"Father, why do they dress in that way? Why don't the men shave their hair, and why do all the women have long hair?" I ask.

"Because this country is cooler than ours. We dress the way we do to accommodate ourselves to our climate, and they dress that way to accommodate to theirs."

I nodded, then said, "This city is beautiful, and the sea is beautiful, too. Mother, can we take some of these flowers home with us? They smell beautiful."

Mother smelled them. "Oh yes, they smell beautiful. I will tell your father to purchase them for your garden, and they can be replanted."

“Why don’t we take them? Doesn’t all this belong to us?” I asked.

“No, this country is not ours. We trade with them,” she said.

“What does trade mean?” I asked her.

“I will explain it to you later. Look, there are so many beautiful and colorful material for sheaths. They have every color,” she said.

The merchants had a lot of material. They had a lot of everything, but what I liked most was the flowers and the oils that made my skin smell delicious.

We spent lots of time swimming in the sea. Its water tasted different than Hopi. The waves had a strong undertow that could drag people into the sea and cause them to drown.

We spent a very long time in Crete. Then it was time to return home. I was glad that we were going back home. I missed my bed. One day before departing on the voyage home, I was standing close to the ramp of the ship. I saw a man boarding our ship with a child and his wife. I looked at the little boy, who was about eight summers.

Father came forward and the three members of the family knelt at my father’s feet. In fact, they seemed to know him.

Later, Mother told me that they were Greeks, but that they had been in Egypt for a long time. Father had sent the man to trade for him, for the man knew both languages. He was a scriber for him.

The child’s name was Hapuseneb, and they called him Hapu. Neferu-Knib was the one who talked to him first. I didn’t care to talk to him.

On our return voyage, I started throwing up again, and the child approached me and gave me something to chew. It really helped. After my stomach was settled, I asked him, “Hapu, what kind of name is that?”

"My name is from a Greek god."

"So, you are a god? Like my father?"

"I don't know. That is what I have been told," he said.

"That you are a god, or you don't know if you are a god?" I said.

"Leave him alone," Neferu-Knib snapped at me. Looking at him, she said, "You speak my tongue well."

"Well, my father has spoken to me in Egyptian since I was a little boy, and I can read and write also."

"Why are you coming with us?" I asked.

"Father said that it is time to come back home, and my grandparents are still in Thebes."

"How old are you?" she asked him.

"I am almost nine summers."

"I am almost eight," she told him.

I left them there talking and went to Mother. "Mother, I don't feel sick to my stomach anymore. The child gave me, something to chew and it helped. His name is Hapu, and he said that it is the name of a Greek god. Is he a god?"

"No, child. He is just a wealthy child returning to Thebes with his parents."

"I've never seen gray eyes like his before," I said.

"I have. There are many people who come to our kingdom to trade. I've seen green, blue, and gray eyes."

“Mother, why are you fair, while father is dark? Why is his hair not like the Nubians? And why am I golden tan, while Neferu-Knib is fair like you?”

“Because my mother was fair-skinned, as was my father, but your father’s mother was a dark tan Egyptian, but not a Nubian. See, you are not as dark as your father, but between both of our colors. Your skin is golden. It is a beautiful color, I can tell you that,” she said.

“Mother, how long will it be before we get to the next port? Father promised me that I would have the little girl to play with.”

“Yes, he told me that if she is there, he will give her to you as a present.”

“Good.” I jumped in happiness. “Maat is the most loving father,” I thought.

We continued sailing and arrived at the port, and I could not see the little girl. I sat there for a while, looking for her. Then Father asked me if I wanted to come down with him, and I told him yes. As we did, everyone was prostrating themselves at my father’s feet as we walked past them with our guards.

I found her. She was standing in a corner. She was a homeless child, and she lived on the streets. She became very happy when she saw me. I walked to where she was standing with my father.

“Do you want to come with me to my palace and live there with us?” I asked.

She looked happy and said, “Yes.”

“Come with me to my ship. We are going on a long trip because it’s a long way home, and you are going to like it. We have lots of food. Are you hungry now?”

“Yes.”

"Father, let's go. She is hungry. Let's go now!"

We walked to the ship and standing there were Neferu-Knib and Hapu. I passed without looking at them.

I came close to my mother and said, "Mother, she is the little girl I was telling you about, and she is very hungry. We must feed her now."

Mother clapped her hands, and several slaves came forward. Mother ordered for her to be taken away, given food and bathed. She further ordered that during the bath, they were to look for lice in her hair and on her body. She also said that the child would be raised by a nursemaid and that she would be allowed to play with me all the time.

They took the little girl by the hand. She was gone for five hours. Then I saw the slaves bringing her back to us. They had cut off her hair and shave completely. Now she was bald like me.

"Your Majesty," the slave said. My mother turned and looked at the slave and the child. "The child's hair was infested with lice, as was her body. We had to burn her clothing and bathe her well. Though she had already eaten, she was still very hungry. It seems that she had not eaten for several days. I think she will be very happy in the palace." she said with a smile.

"Child, come close to me," Mother told her, and she did. My mother held her by the hand and looked at her. She did not look like the child who first boarded the ship. She was no longer covered in dirt. She was fair-skinned, like Mother. She had slanted brown eyes, and she was now without hair.

"What is your name, child, and where are you parents?" my mother asked her.

"I don't know," she said simply. "My name is T'Queta."

"Do you have a mother, child?"

"No, I sleep on the street."

I felt like crying for her, and I came closer. "Now, you are going to have a home and a mother and plenty to eat. Does that make you happy?" I asked her.

"Yes," she said with a smile.

"Come with me." I held her hand, ready to go play.

"Wait!" Mother said, and she looked at the young girl. "Is she completely clean to play with the Prince of Egypt?"

"Yes, Your Majesty, she is."

"Hat, go ahead and play with her." I held her hand and started to run around the ship. I was so happy now that I had someone to play with. It wouldn't be so boring.

Hapu and Neferu-Knib came to play with us, too. We played until I became very tired.

"Mother, can she sleep with me?"

Mother clapped her hands, and the slave came running. "Prepare a place for her to sleep beside Hat." Afterwards, we ate again. I was very happy now that I had a friend of my own age to play with. I was bathed by Sitre-In, and my new friend stood there as I was being bathed. I asked her if she was hungry again, and she said yes. I sent for more food, and she ate again.

"She will never go hungry again," I thought. It was a long journey back home, and we played every day and into the night. We lay in the bow of the ship, and saw the stars, even many falling stars. We laughed a lot.

I was very happy, and I started to be friendlier with Hapu. The long hours on the ship seemed to last forever, but my stomach never bothered me again with what he had given me to chew.

T'Queta gained weight. Her hair was growing, and she was becoming quite pretty. She was impressed with everything that she saw along the way. She was no longer sleeping in my quarters because she was being raised by some of the slaves from the kitchen, and they all loved her. I was very happy for her, because she had gained several mothers.

The trip to Crete and the return home took a total of four summers. Finally, I could see the pillars of the Temple of Karnak from far away. I was relieved when we finally arrived home. Aakheperen-Re was waiting with the palace court to welcome us from our return.

I reached my ninth summer during our return trip from Crete. We did not know how old T'Queta was, but Mother thought that she was a few months younger than I was. She came to play with me sometimes. I spent most of my time with Maat in the arena practicing with my bow and arrows and throwing spears. I also practiced driving a chariot with the charioteers.

T'Queta would start serving me when she reached the age of twelve summers. She needed to learn everything about the kitchen first and then everything about the palace.

Her black hair had grown very long. It was down to her waist, and she washed it all the time. She came to visit me and tell me the gossip from the kitchen, and we laughed a lot together.

CHAPTER 17

NINE SUMMERS

TEACHING THUTMOSES II

HOW TO BE BRAVE

I was looking at my brother Aakheperen-Re from my balcony. He was in front of the waters of Hopi throwing stones. I ran down the stairs to reach him. As I came closer, I called, "Aakheperen-Re! I have not seen you for several days. Are you sick?" I asked.

"No, I'm just bored, and I'm tired of the fact that Maat won't even look at me. I know he wishes that he had a very healthy, strong, and brave son, but what can I do when most of the time I am sick? And he has you. And nothing else matters to him but you," he told me.

"Do you want to be as brave as the warriors of our armies?" I asked him. "Because I know what to do, and I can teach you, and you can become brave as they are. And that will make Father happy and proud of you."

Father had taken me several times to see the test that every future warrior must take so that they could prove to him that they were brave enough to serve in his army.

“It’s a very scary test,” I continued, “but I can teach you how to be very fast because I know how our warriors train, and I know that you can do it. You can show Father that you are brave enough to command his army, and the children of the palace will stop teasing you. And Ursaramun will stop telling you that I am Horus and that you are still in the nest. Get it? Please, I want you to become Horus, and I don’t want you to wait until I can make you Horus of Egypt,” I told him.

“What is this test about? Do I need to go inside of a tomb like you did for three days?” he asked.

“No, but if you have to do it, you will be inside of the coffin for a whole week and not three days like I was. No, this is a different test,” I said, and looking at him, I wondered if it was a good idea to be telling him now what this test was about.

“Okay, I am going to tell you now.” I was looking at him attentively, and he was seriously looking at me and listening “The test you will have to pass is one in which you must put a trap made of hard bamboo inside the mouth of the Sobek[13], pull out your hand quickly, and take off running before the crocodiles eats you!”

The look on his face changed. He was stone. “No! I would not do that!” He became flush and looked terrified “What if he eats me?”

“Well, that would be a problem. Hmm… Maat would be very angry at me for a while,” I was thinking with my finger on my mouth. “But he probably would say that you were very brave for even trying!”

I was looking at him very seriously then I said, “But that will not happen because we will go in the middle of the night when Thoth is full. We’ll go very quietly and find a smaller Sobek that is asleep with its mouth open, because the rest of the crocodiles are in the water since the water is

[13] An Egyptian god associated with the crocodile.

warm at night. I will hold the torch and you will do it. How about that?" I asked him.

"Hmm... I really don't know, Hat. Let me think about it," he said.

"Don't tell Ursaramun, OK! Because he will run and tell his father Amethu, and his father will tell our father. But if you say OK, we can start practicing by running every day to make you faster, and we can start tomorrow early in the morning. Anyway, the next full moon will be next month, so we have a whole month of summer to prepare before Shomu is over.

"OK, but I must think about this first," he said.

"OK," I said. "Give me your answer tomorrow morning, and let's meet in my quarters for breakfast. Now, let's run into the waters of the Nile, and you can try to catch me. I took off running and laughing with him trailing me. We were laughing hard, and I could see Hapuseneb and Neferu-Knib running to join us. We started to swim and throw water at each other.

Then I turned around, and Aakhep' was gone. I saw him standing at the edge of the Nile looking at us. "Come back, Aakhep'! Come back!" I called him. He shook his head and left. I saw him leave, and I felt very sad for him. He could not stay in the water for long, or he would get sick and be unable to breathe. I hoped he would be alright tonight.

It was very early the following morning when I went to his quarters.

"Prince of Egypt, what are you doing in our quarters so early in the morning?" Mutnofret, my aunt, asked me.

"I came to see if my brother is okay. We were playing in the water of the Nile a little bit yesterday, and I thought I'd come to see if he was alright this morning."

"Oh, he slept very well last night," she said.

"Good. Tell him that I will be waiting for him in my quarters to have breakfast together as we agreed. I will send my slave to bring our favorites: eggs, sweet bread, fruit, and our delicious hot drink[14]. Tell him that Hapuseneb and Neferu-Knib are coming, too."

"Sure, I will tell him, Hatshepset," Mutnofret said.

Then I turned around and left his quarters. I went into my quarters and walked to the dining area and sat impatiently at the breakfast table waiting for him. When the double doors opened, I thought it would be him, but it was Mother. She came closer and kissed me.

"My precious daughter, did you sleep well last night? I could see you and your sister with some of the children of the palace playing in the waters for long time. Why don't you have dinner with us tonight in the banquet hall?" she asked.

"Mother, I have been thinking and wondering the best way to teach Aakheperen-Re how to be brave. I want Father to love him more. He thinks Father doesn't love him because he doesn't take him to the warrior's practice fields or riding with him. He does not do anything with him, only with me. And I feel that my brother wants to be strong and brave for Father."

My mother hugged me and looked at me; then she said, "How sweet of you to try to make your brother brave and strong. I wish he were not such a sick child. My poor sister Mutnofret has suffered for him so much. I will talk to Maat about it and see if he can do more with him."

"Oh, Mother, that will make him very happy! And me, too," I said.

"Are you coming to have breakfast with us?" she asked.

---

[14] Like hot cocoa

"No, Mother, I am waiting for Aakheperen-Re, Hapuseneb, and Neferu-Knib to have breakfast here with me."

There was a knock on the doors.

"Enter," I said. It was Hapuseneb. He walked toward us.

"Your Majesty." He knelt on one knee at my mother's feet.

"Rise, Hapuseneb, and you don't have to genuflect anymore. You are family," she said and smiled at him.

He rose from the floor and smiled at me. "Good morning, Flower of Egypt."

"Good morning to you, too, Hapu." I smiled back at him.

My mother called to him, "Hapuseneb, come here, that I may see those beautiful gray eyes again."

"Mother! You are making him blush. Don't you see how red he is?"

Mother started to laugh. "Very well. I will leave you two alone." By the time she turned around, the doors were opened again for Neferu-Knib who looked very happy.

"Good morning, Mother. It is wonderful to see you here. Are you having breakfast with us too?"

"No, darling. I will be meeting with Maat to have breakfast with him this glorious morning. I came to invite you all, but you guys have other plans."

"Mother, please tell Father what I told you. Please!" I said.

"I certainly will, and now I will leave you, my loved ones." She then kissed Neferu-Knib and me. She looked at Hapuseneb and smiled. He kneeled, and she came closer to him, pulled his face up with her right hand

and looked in to his eyes. "Beautiful eyes, beautiful eyes. When you grow up, you are going to drive the women of the palace crazy with love for you. You are very, very handsome. Your black hair goes well with your gray eyes and long black eyelashes." She was smiling at him, and he was blushing again.

He smiled back at her. I could see the face of Neferu-Knib light up with a smile. Then mother was leaving, and as she was crossing the double doors, when Aakheperen-Re walk in. We all said hello. He sat beside me, and we started to eat.

"Aakheperen-Re, do you have an answer for me?"

He looked at me in surprise. "I thought it was between you and me only," he said.

"Yes, it is. You only have to say 'yes' or 'no.'"

Hapuseneb and Neferu-Knib looked at me and at Aakheperen-Re.

"Didn't you sleep, Hatshepset?" he snapped at me. "My mother said that you came early this morning. Couldn't you have waited for my answer? Couldn't you?"

"You are so ungrateful!" I shouted at him. "I only wanted to see if you were alright because yesterday we played in the waters of Hopi, and I was afraid that you might have become ill, like the other times; and it would have been my fault."

I pressed for his answer. "Answer me! Yes or no?" Aakheperen-Re looked worried. I could tell he was thinking about it; then he said, "Yes. We will do it!"

"Aren't we going to finish eating?" Hapuseneb asked.

"Let's eat," I said.

Looking at me, Hapu asked, "Now can you tell us what is going on, Flower of Egypt?"

"I am going to teach him how to be brave like the warriors of our armies," I said.

Hapuseneb and Neferu-Knib exchanged looks. Neferu-Knib looked at me and asked, "How will you do that?"

"It's only between me and Aakhep'," I told them.

Then it was Hapu and Aakhep' who were exchanging glances.

"But you guys can help by running with us every morning," I said.

"I will help," Hapu said.

"How early must we be here? Neferu-Knib asked.

"Very early in the morning and after the blessings of the doors. And after running, we can have breakfast!" I told them.

She thought about it, and then she said, "That is for men only. I am not a man, so I'll just watch the three of you do it from under the sycamore tree after I have my breakfast."

Then I remember what Father said, that she was not interested in anything. Well, she was a girl, I thought to myself.

"Aakhep' and Hapu, I will tell you what to do every day," I said. "And let's go now! Let's run beside Hopi, but for now, we must go slowly so that he doesn't become too tired. When he starts picking up speed, we will do it faster, OK?" I told them.

We ran at the edge of Hopi, ran as far as we could, but Aakhep' was trailing us. Hapu and I slowed down until he caught up with us. Eventually, he did.

"I am so thirsty," Aakhep' said.

“We are also thirsty.” I told him.

“Hat, why didn’t you have your slaves bring water for us when we finish?” Aakhep’ asked.

“I forgot. Tomorrow I will.” We had run far, and we were a long way from the palace. “Let’s stop for today, because it’s very hot right now,” I told them, and we started to walk back.

I could see my father far away looking at us from his balcony. Then Mother joined him and stood next to him. She was looking at us. I could see them even at this distance. I knew I would make him proud of Aakhep’. I wanted so much for Father to take him hunting with him, and I wanted us to join the battlefield practices together.

“Ahmose, I like seeing them play together in harmony,” my father said.

“They are not playing. Hatshepset is teaching Aakheperen-Re how to be brave,” she told him.

He quickly turned around and looked at her. “What did you say? And who told you that?” he asked.

“She told me so herself, just this morning. She wants you to love Aakheperen-Re more. She believes that if she can make him brave, you will take him hunting with you, and he would be able to practice with the warriors in the field, as you practice with her. Also, she has mentioned to me before that she is tired of hearing in the classroom that he is weak and that he is going to be a real falcon in the nest. Get it? It means that he will never be brave and will instead remain in the palace, doing nothing. I also heard that he gets very angry when they tease him about the fact that she is a girl, yet she is Horus, and he is not.”

“Well, the stars foretold her strength and bravery and predicted that she would have the capacity to rule Thebes and command an army. She also has a great heart. I do love my son, but he gets sick so quickly. I am hesitant to take him far away in case he becomes sick, and I cannot make it to Thebes in time to save his life," he said.

We continued walking beside the Nile. Hapu said to me, "Lotus of Egypt, tomorrow I must be in the temple before sunrise. I must continue with my priestly learnings, and I missed the chanting and the services for Amun-Ra this morning. And I missed Khety's classes. I can already hear the voice of the First Prophet of Amun scolding me tomorrow."

"Tell Khety that I ordered you to come to my quarters early this morning and do not expect you to return for one whole month, and I can guarantee that he would not say anything to you again," I said, with a smile, which he returned with one of his own sweet smiles.

"Let's jump in the water of Hopi!" I yelled, and we ran to the waters. We spent a happy and fun day swimming and playing in the waters and laughing a great deal.

Afterward, we began to walk homeward until we reached the palace. The slaves were waiting with water, food, fruit drinks, and fresh fruits, and under the very large sycamore trees sat Maat and my mother Ahmose. Mutnofret, Aakheperen-Re's mother, was also there and had a big smile on her face while she was looking at me and Aakheperen-Re. I smiled at them, though it seemed a bit strange that my father, mother, and aunt were all sitting together on a hot day.

"Father, you came. What a surprise seeing you and Mother here. And Mutnofret. Did you come to see us play? Don't you think it's too hot for all of you to be here?" I asked.

I saw Mother turn around and look behind her. Hapu, the scriber and father of Hapuseneb, was walking beside Ineni, who was my father's architect and builder. Trailing behind them was Neferu-Knib. She had a beautiful smile on her face, as always.

I could hear the musicians playing soft music, and I decided that one day I would compose a poem to this lovely music. I was surprised when I saw Khety and Puyem-Re coming to join us. “What is going on?” I asked myself.

Father and Mother were happy, as was Aakheperen-Re’s mother who had the biggest smile on her face. I had never seen her so happy before today, and I thought the whole situation was odd. We all ate and were laughing when Father stood up and called Neferu-Knib, who was talking to Hapu, to come to his left side. She did so smiling. He called Aakheperen-Re to be at his side, and he walked to my father’s right side. The face of Neferu-Knib changed. She became pale as she looked at me and at Hapuseneb.

Father took her right hand and place it on Aakheperen-Re left hand.

Then he said, “Neferu-Bity, Princess of Egypt, in the presence of Khety, First Prophet of Amun-Ra, and Puyem-Re, Second Prophet of Amun-Ra, I betroth you to Aakheperen-Re on this day. And when you reach the age of fifteen summers, the wedding will take place in the Hall of the Holiest.”

Neferu-Knib was in shock. She was pale and on the verge of crying. Aakheperen-re was also in shock. I was in shock, and Hapuseneb was in shock. All of us looked at each other in disbelief. Except our parents, and Mutnofret, who was full of joy, as her son would likely one day be THUTMOSES II Pharaoh of Egypt.

But Neferu-Knib didn’t want to marry him. She was only twelve summers, and her blood had not come yet. She wasn’t ready to marry anybody, I thought.

The High Priest of Amun-Ra started to bless their hands using incense. The smoke of the incense was passed over their hands. It was done.

“In two and a half or three summers, the wedding will be held,” Father said.

My dear sister was stone. She was frozen and could not move, could not run away from Maat. I saw the desperate look on her face. It was clear she wanted to cry and run away, as did I. I did not know what to do, so I just reacted.

"Father, are you finished? Can we go play now?" He pulled me up and sat me on his lap.

"In just a few minutes. Be patient. I heard from your mother that you are teaching your brother to be brave?"

"Yes, Father, so that you can take him hunting with you, and then the three of us, including Hapuseneb, can go to the arena and practice with you. I have been teaching him how to shoot the bow and arrows for a while now, so now he knows how to shoot them. And when we target practice, he does well. Soon, you will have a brave warrior! Can we show you how well he shoots? Can we do that now?" I asked.

"Yes, you can," he said.

"Neferu-Knib, Hapuseneb, come with me. Aakhep', send for an archer to bring your bow and arrows and send for the practice marker. I am going to my quarters to get my bow and arrows as well," I said.

"Hatshepset, send your slave to get it for you," Father said.

I looked at T'Queta. "No, Father. I want to go myself. Neferu-Knib and Hapuseneb, come with me." I started to run right away before he could say anything else. They were running behind me. When we were close to the palace, I stopped and turned around. I could see that she had stopped a good distance behind me and that Hapu was talking to her.

I walked back, looking at her sadly. She was crying, and it broke my heart. I had never seen my sister cry before.

"I am so sorry, Neferu-Knib. I was shocked by what Father just did. Maybe in two and a half summers, things will be different, and you will learn how to love him like I do."

"Why don't you marry him instead?!" she shouted at me.

I became quiet. I did not know what else to say. She would not stop crying and sobbing, and it brought tears to my eyes. I could see Hapuseneb's face. He was blushing and sad as well. He must be thinking how sad life was for us the royal women, that we could not choose and marry for love.

"I will tell Father that I will marry him, for you! But please don't cry anymore." I had tears in my eyes, and there were tears rolling down her face.

Looking at me, she said, "There is no point anymore. It's done. He betrothed me to him, even though I told Mother that I do not want to marry him! I want to choose the one that my heart desires, and I will kill myself if he forces me to marry Aakhep'. I will kill myself!"

We walked slowly to the palace. She was still crying. I stopped and hugged her. To be honest, I didn't understand why she thought it was such a bad idea to marry him. He was getting handsome, except for the prominent teeth, and he is only a boy of thirteen summers and still had to grow into a man, I thought.

We continued walking until we arrived at the palace. Once we got there, I saw her walk towards her quarters. "Aren't you coming back with us?" I asked her.

"No, I am not going back!" she shouted at me again.

I turned to Hapu. "Hapu, are you coming back with me?"

He looked at her and said, "Yes, but Neferu-Bity don't cry anymore. It makes me very sad, too."

She looked at him. "It makes you sad, too?" she asks.

"Yes, come back with us please." he said.

He held her hand. She looked at him, shook her head, "No," then turned around and walked off to her quarters. I stood there sad, looking at her as she moved away.

Hapu and I went back to my quarters and picked up my bow and arrows. Then we were running back to Father, when, suddenly, Hapu stopped.

"Flower of Egypt, I feel terribly bad for Neferu-Bity right now, and it saddens my heart." He said.

"It hurts mine, too. I wish I could spare her grief. I don't mind marrying Aakheperen-Re for her."

"No!" he reacted. "It's the law of the royal blood. She is the oldest, and she must marry Aakheperen-re," he said. Then we continue walking.

We got to Father, and they had already installed the targets. And Aakhep' was hitting the markers, and Hapu walked and joined him.

"Where is Neferu-Bity?" Mother asked.

I looked at her and said, "Mother, why does she have to marry Aakhep'? She does not want to marry him, and I told her that I would marry him."

Father was listening to our conversation. He turned around, and looked at me, and said, "Because I have other plans for you. Aakheperen-Re is like Neferu-Bity: calm and soft. They do not have your strength, and they don't have the willpower to run this country. You do! And she will get over it within a few months." He turned around and noticed how well Aakhep' hit his targets. "He is indeed good, very good!"

"Yes, Father. I told you that he is good like me," I said.

"Let's go and hit our markers like your brother. I know that you are good, very good," he told me. "Come with me. Let's make this a joyful day. Let's shoot at the targets and see who wins. Guard!" he shouted.

A guard came running to him. "Summon the generals of the charioteers, the archers, General D'Jehuty, and Amethu and his son Ursaramun so that they might all enjoy this wonderful day with us."

He was laughing as we walked toward Aakheperen-Re and Hapuseneb who were shooting arrows at the markers.

There was a big commotion, and the servants run to see Pharaoh participating in the target shooting. I could see them running with their white sheaths, some of them half naked, running to cheer us on as we shot with our arrows and hit our targets.

I came closer to Father and whispered, very low in his ear, "Father, should I let you win?"

He was startled at my question and look at me and started to laugh.

"Hat, should I let you win?" By now he really was laughing hard.

"OK, Father, should we let Aakhep' win?"

"Of course not. In a real battle, we are not going to be beside him to hold his hand or fight his battle. He must prove that he has what it takes to be Pharaoh. You don't need to do that; you have already proved it."

Watching him shoot, I was amazed at how fast and good Father was, He was hitting the target right at the center every single time. Aakhep' was good, too. Hapu was not bad either, but of course, I taught them both.

All the generals and commanders were participating. All of them were good. I wondered how anyone could lose. No one is going to lose? I wondered. There was a lot of beer and wine drinking. Mother was enjoying the day, as we all were. T'Queta was constantly smiling and cheering me on, though she sometimes cheered for Hapuseneb. Mother did as well because he was her favorite.

Father came to me, pushing at me with his left elbow, and said, "What do you think now? Do you think I need help?" He started to laugh.

Aakhep' came closer and said, "Father, what do you think about what I can do? Do you think we can go hunting soon?"

Father put his right hand over his shoulder, shook him with a sign of approval, and, with a smile on his face, said, "Yes, son, soon. After I come back from the north. I am going on a military campaign, for there are rumors of unrest in that part of the country."

I became worried.

"Father, are you going to war?" I asked.

"We can hope there is no war," he replied.

Father won the tournament. I could see that he was very good. Of course, he was Pharaoh and was a god! He came close to me and said, "You are good, *very good,* for a little girl!"

"Well, Father, isn't that what the Captain of the Archers tells you all the time? Of course, I am good. And I am brave like you. One day I will be Pharaoh, and I have to be good!"

He started to laugh. "Yes, you will be!" Then he knelt on one knee, and looking in to my eyes, he hugged me very tight. "I love you, Hatshepset."

"I love you, too, Father. Tomorrow morning, we must go to the Temple of Amun-Ra to make an offering for your wellbeing on your coming campaign. We will do so if its's okay with you."

"We will do it," he said nodding his head. We walked to the palace holding hands.

I woke up very early the next morning. Ra was not showing its rays yet. Sitre-In bathed me and dressed me.

"Child, where are you going so early in the morning, and in a rush?" she asked.

"I am going to my father's quarters to see Ra rise, to say the morning prayers, and to chant with him. From there we are going to the temple to make offerings to Amun-Ra for his wellbeing in case there's war!"

"War!" She became agitated.

"Yes, war!"

"May Amun-Ra protect him and all our warriors and all of us!" she said.

"Don't worry, Sitre-In. I will protect you with my bow and arrows. They will feel the power of my left arm and my arrows. I shoot as fast as Father, and he is a mighty one!"

"Yes, he is, my child." She said and smiled.

"You can go back to sleep. It is still dark, and I will be with Father all day, and we will probably go to the audience hall to meet with all his generals. I believe he will speak of the possibility of war."

"Very well, my child. May Amun be always with you." She said.

I rushed out and ran to Father's quarters where the guards opened the golden doors. I saw Father sleeping, and I was surprised to see Mother beside him.

I touched his arms, and he opened his eyes and smiled. "Hatshepset what are you doing here so early?"

"I came to wait for the first rays of Ra to rise and chant the morning prayers with you."

He smiled at me.

"Then we will do it. We will wait for Ra together to bless us," he said.

I walked to my mother's side. "Mother, wake up!" I moved her arm, and she awakened and sat up.

"My child, what are you doing here so early? Ra is not even out yet."

"No but he will be soon. I came to wait for Ra with Father and chant the morning prayers with him."

"Then the three of us will do so," she said. Then she pulled me up into the bed beside her. I did not close my eyes because I wanted to be sure that I would see the first rays of Ra. Ra started to show his first rays, and I saw Father get up and wash his hands and face, then Mother and I did. After that, the three of us knelt facing Ra to the east, and Father started to chant the morning prayers. Mother and I prostrated ourselves on the light limestone floors beside Father. I joined him in the chanting, which was only for Father and the priest. I had heard it so many times, and he did not mind when I chanted with him. In the meantime, on the other side of the golden doors, I could hear the priest chanting the prayers for Pharaoh and incensing the golden doors.

We had breakfast together, and then we walked to the temple of Amun-Ra. After we entered the shrine, we said many prayers, poured pure blessed oil, and burned incense over the golden statute of Amun-Ra. Suddenly, I felt the urge to prostrate myself completely in front of Amun-Ra, and I did.

"Father Almighty, do you remember me, Hatshepset, your daughter? I come to thee with a request that there be no war. I want my father here with me and safe. Please keep our kingdom safe. I promise that when I grow up, I will build monuments and shrines for you, and shower you with gold, precious stones, and myrrh," I said.

I remained prostrate on the limestone floor. Suddenly, peace invaded me and filled my heart. God had spoken: there would be no war! We finished our worship.

“Father, Amun-Ra has spoken to me, and there will be no war!”

“I believe you, my sweet daughter. I am waiting on a message from the garrison of the north, and we will know soon if we will go to war. I will be meeting with all the generals and the commanders of the armed forces about the possibility of war in the audience hall.”

“There will be no war, Father!” I told him. We were walking back to the palace when three soldiers from the garrison of the north dismounted from their horses.

“Your Majesty.” They knelt, each on one knee at my father’s feet.

“Rise,” Father told them.

“Your Majesty, it was a small revolt, and we contained them all. There were no more than five hundred insurgents, and we brought you all their heads and hands.

I started to jump up and down in happiness and screamed, “Father, Father, I told you! Amun-Ra told me that there would be no war.” The soldiers look at me startled as I was shouting at my father. I was jumping up and down like a frog. “I told you. I told you, Father.” I was elated with this news, as was Mother.

“Father! I want to see the heads and hands of the insurgents.”

“No! You are too young to see that. It’s a horrible sight, too horrible for a child,” Mother said.

I hear Father said, “I want the army to put their heads and hands on poles and display them all over the borders. They will not reckon with me again!” Father told the warriors.

“Yes, Majesty.” They mounted their horses and left.

“See, Father? Amun-Ra listened to my plea.”

“Yes, my daughter, I can see that he listens to your prayers.” Mother was very happy, as were we, and she hugged the two of us. Then we continued walking to the hall of audience, and Father let every general know that there would not be war.

The next day, I woke up early in the morning and was bathed by Sitre-In. “Now, child, where are you are going so early in the morning?”

“I am going to Aakhep’ quarters. We must continue with his training. He must be trained to be a brave warrior like me!”

“Well now, you better not get hurt yourself trying to make him brave,” she said.

I walked to Aakhep’ quarters, and the doors were opened by the guards.

“Good morning, Aakhep’.”

“What are you doing here so early?” he snapped at me.

I became angry and yelled at him: “I am a brave soldier, and you are not! Do you still want to be a brave soldier or not?”

He lowered his head. “Yes, but it’s so early to start.”

“Well, all of our soldiers wake up even earlier in the morning and start training by the first rays of Ra.

“If you want, I’ll just leave, but don’t come back looking for me!”

Then there was a knock at the door. The doors were opened and in walked Hapuseneb.

“Good morning, Hapu,” I greeted him.

“Good morning, Flower of Egypt. Are we ready?”

“No, I must finish my breakfast,” Aakhep’ said.

"Then send your slave for more breakfast, and we will have breakfast with you," Hapu told him.

Aakhep' clapped his hands to summon his slaves.

"Bring more breakfast," I told the slave who arrived, and she left to get it. "We must make a raft," I told them.

"A raft for what?" Aakhep' asked.

"Because we must cross the Nile like our soldiers do. Once, Father took me to see the test that is done to determine if a soldier is brave enough and ready for battle, and to get to that place we must cross Hopi," I said.

"Why don't we cross in the barge?" Hapu asked.

"Because Father will know what we are we doing," I said.

We continued to practice every day, early in the mornings. Aakhep' had become a faster runner with the daily practice. Now he ran faster than both of us. "I had better start running faster too, in case the Sobek comes after me," I thought.

"Okay, it has been almost a month since we started. Now we must build the raft and the bamboo ladder to reach our balcony," I told them. I saw Neferu-Knib coming closer. "Don't say anything in front of her. I don't want her to tell Mother, because Mother will tell Maat." They both agreed not to say anything.

I knew how I could get rid of her quickly. I started to ask her about the wedding, and she got angry and took off. She still didn't want to talk to Aakhep' since the day of the betrothal. He didn't care since he didn't want to marry her either.

"Wait what did you say about the ladder?" Hapu asked.

"Let me tell you that this is when we are going to need your help. We need for you to put the ladder on my balcony first, and when I am down, I need your help to put the ladder in Aakhep' balcony. I will help you. We cannot go out through the golden doors because the guards will not let us leave." I said.

"Okay, I will help you, but I will not go with you two. I'm not going anywhere in the dark!"

"Okay, you don't have to come with us, because if something happens, Father can put you to death."

"Death!" Hapu shouted. "What are you going to do Hatshepset? Is it dangerous?"

"Yes, well, a little bit, but everything is going to be fine, you will see. If something happens, I will take all the blame for it. I promise," I said.

Aakhep' gave me a look that seemed to say, "What?"

"And you will not tell anyone that you helped us with the ladder. That is an order, understand? You cannot tell your parents. Promise!"

"Okay, I promise," he said.

Aakhep' was quiet. I wondered if he was going to back out.

"Aakhep', are you changing your mind now?" I demanded.

"I must rethink this," he said.

"Okay, you have until tomorrow. We don't have too much time. Let's start cutting the bamboo anyway. We can use the raft for playing even if we don't use it for the plan," I said.

"I agree," Aakhep' said.

The bamboo was very hard to cut. I called several guards and put them to cutting bamboo. We hid the bamboo in a place where Father could not see them and know what we were doing.

One day, a guard came up to us. "Your Majesty! The Great Maat is calling you."

"Go away! And tell him that I will be there in a few minutes," I said.

"No. He said you were to come to his quarters right away," he replied, not convinced by my commanding tone.

"Aakhep' and Hapuseneb, stay here. I will go alone."

I ran to my father's quarters. I saw him sitting in a chair in his chambers. I smiled at him and went to hug him.

"What are you doing, Hat? Why are you ordering the guards to cut bamboo for you?" He was looking straight into my eyes.

"I am starting to make a raft to help teach Aakhep' to be brave. Remember, I know how to make a raft. I was with you when the soldiers were making them before."

"Are you sure you know how to make one? I am going to order one to be made for you. Now, what do you want a raft for?" he asks.

"So that we can sail Hopi while standing without losing our balances. Please order three large poles. One for Aakhep', one for Hapu, and one for me so that we can steer the raft," I said.

I was telling him the truth, but not all the truth, and I hoped he didn't notice.

"Hatshepset, when you are going to use the raft, promise that you will tell me. I will send soldiers to follow you. Do you understand? I feel that you are not telling me the whole truth."

"Do you want to ask me anything else, Father?"

"Hatshepset, you must take care of yourself. You are the Prince of Egypt, and we cannot lose you!"

"You won't, Father. I will let you know when I plan to use the raft. Can I go now?"

"Yes, but remember, don't be disobedient to me!"

"I won't, Father." I close my fist hard behind my back, for the gods not to punish me for not telling him the truth.

I rushed out of his presence. I ordered long bamboo shoots, with some to be cut and made into small pieces for the ladder. A guard came to see what we were doing.

"Out!" I shouted at him. "You are not to come here!" The raft would be done, probably today or the day after. We had to finish the ladder in a hurry, so we could practice for few days with the soldiers to be sure we could manage the raft.

I woke up early the next day, bathed, and had my breakfast. I was called by Maat to his quarters.

"Yes, Father?"

"The raft is ready. Do you want to practice today?" he said.

"Yes, Father, can you come with us?"

"Yes, I will. I will have one of my soldiers show you how to steer with the poles."

I was excited that he was coming. We all went to the waters of Hopi. Father followed us up the Nile. I could see Father looking at me. The soldiers taught us how to use the poles while standing, and Aakhep', Hapu, and I mastered the poles. We were having fun for few days. We had already finished the ladder, and no one had discovered what we were about to do. The next day was a full moon, and we would be able to see very clearly. I already knew where the Sobek were. The training I was getting from the soldiers showed me how far up the Nile the Sobeks were. They were not too far from the palace, and that was good, very good.

During the day, I met with Aakhep', and Hapu. "Remember, to-night is the night. And Aakhep', you're only going to have one shot at the Sobek. You must put the trap in his jaws and wait for his jaw to drop."

"Whaaat!" Hapu screamed.

"Wait, Hapu, let me finish!" "Then you must run as fast as you can, as he is trying to spit out the bamboo trap from his jaws. Once he does, he will start chasing after you. Remember, you must run fast, as if someone is burning your butt. I will be waiting with the torch." I said.

"Hat, what are you talking about? Is he going to put his hand in-side of the crocodile's jaw? Why didn't you tell me that? This is very dan-gerous. I don't know if I can let you do that," Hapu said.

"You must! Otherwise, I will never, and I mean never, talk to you again," I said.

Looking at him, Hapu asked, "Aakhep', do you really want to do this?"

Aakhep' was silent and thought for a minute. "Yes! I must. This is the only way Father will love me, and I want for him to believe in me, that I am brave enough to defend our kingdom."

"OK, I will do it, but I will go with you and carry my bow and arrows, just in case," Hapu said.

"No, you must stay. If you don't see us coming back, you must tell Pharaoh in a hurry," I said.

"Where should I wait?"

"Wait outside the palace. Don't let the soldiers see you. Go to sleep early and wake up close to midnight. You too, Aakhep'. I will be waiting for you and the ladder."

"Okay," Hapu said.

"After dinner in the banquet hall, I will tell them good night, and after I leave, you two will go as well. Hapu, don't go home. It is too far away. You, Aakhep', you go to your quarters, and Hapu, don't let anyone see you, but come to the back of the palace. You know where the ladder is. It's hidden in the shrubs of the papyri. Don't forget that." I said.

"I won't!"

We said our goodbyes until midnight. Before anything could happen, I went to the temple and prayed that everything would go well and visited the shrine of Mother Hathor and asked for her protection as well. I didn't visit the shrine of Amun-Ra and ask for approval because I didn't want Him to say no. The night came, and I left the banquet as I said I would. That was the signal. I kissed my parents, and Father gave me a look.

I left and went to my quarters. In the meantime, Father called a guard and told him to keep an eye on me and to be sure that the guards kept their eyes open and, on my doors, and not to let me come out of my quarters.

I walked into my quarters. "Child, why don't you stay with your parents?" Sitre-In asked.

"No, I am tired. Bathe me now. I want to sleep."

"Aren't you feeling well?"

"I feel fine, just tired."

She bathed me, and I got into my bed and lay there. I could not sleep but lay there waiting. Once Sitre-In started to snore, I got up and put on my kilt. I took my bow and arrows and hung the quiver on my back, waiting for the bamboo ladder on my balcony. Then I saw the ladder moving. I looked down, and there was Hapu. Thoth was bright and shining on him, and I could see everything clearly. This was good for what we were going to do.

I climbed up the balcony and onto the ladder. The ladder was unstable, moving from side to side. I could not stand on it or control it with my feet. I thought I was going to fall and hung on to my balcony as hard as I could, thinking that if I fell, Maat would kill everyone. I knew he would.

Finally, Hapu could hold it straight, and I could secure my sandals on the ladder and come down.

"You almost let me fall!"

"Sorry. I tried to keep it straight."

"Let's go!"

"Wait, Flower of Egypt, I want to tell you something."

I waited. He was quiet, and then he finally said, "Please come back alive."

I looked at his eyes. I saw that he was worried for me, and my heart moved. I smiled. "I will! Hurry, the time is upon us!"

We carried the ladder to Aakhep' balcony. He was waiting for us. We both held the ladder, and Aakhep' came right down with no problem. We rushed to the raft, careful not to let the palace guards see us.

I looked at Aakhep'. "Aakhep'! This is it! Let's show Father that you are as brave a soldier as I am!" I was giving him encouragement.

"You are not a soldier!" he snapped at me. "And you have never taken this test."

"But I will, and I will do it when I am your age or sooner if Maat lets me!" I said.

We continued walking in the dark until we got to the raft. We pulled the raft into the water. The night was so clear and warm.

"Did you bring the torch?" I asked Hapu.

"Yes, I did."

"And I brought our bows and arrows," I told Aakhep'.

"You two better come back alive. Otherwise, your father is going to kill me," Hapu said.

I looked at him and smiled. "We will, I promise. Just say a prayer since you are a young priest."

Aakhep' and I steered to the north in the serene waters of Hopi. It was easy with the current flowing north. The night was clear and so beautiful and peaceful. We were not too far from the palace. We crossed the Nile to an islet. Then we saw some Sobeks in the water, and I saw one on the shore with the open jaw.

"Look there's one, all alone. And it's not that big, so let's do it now!"

"What! It is big! How can you say that it's not that big?" Aakhep' said.

"Well, that one is small compared to the ones I have seen with the soldiers chasing after them."

We stopped just a little way up.

"Aakhep', light the torch," I told him, and he did. I carried the bows and arrows for both of us and the mouth trap that I had taken from the practice field a few weeks before. We walked a little bit between the tall grass and the papyri plants. My heart was pounding so hard, and I can imagine how Aakhep' must feel.

Then we stopped when we came close to the one that was alone. We were silent and stood there looking at the Sobek, and I was thinking that Aakhep' was right. It was not that small at all.

I whispered to him, “Tell me when you are ready. Take the mouth trap, hold it straight up like this, and hold it very tight in your hand. Remember to walk quietly to where he is, and trust me, he is still asleep. Just put it at the edge of the front teeth on its mouth and wait until he snaps his jaw. Otherwise, he will go after you. I will be aiming with my arrows. Go now!”

He thought for a second, looking at the Sobek.

“Uh-uh,” he said and shook his head.

“What?! Aren’t you going to do it?” I hissed.

“Uh-uh,” he said, shaking his head again.

He said no?! I got angry and grabbed the mouth trap from his hand in anger. I started to walk slowly, praying, “Amun, please don’t let him eat me! I will be good with Maat, I promise, and I will never lie to him again. Well, I did not lie to him I just did not tell him the whole truth. Please! I am brave, I must do this. I am brave,” I kept repeating to myself.

Slowly, I walked closer and closer. Then I was in front of his open jaws, and it was huge. I was so scared. I was shaking very badly, afraid that he would wake up and see me. I put the trap just behind his front teeth, and he snapped his jaw extremely fast.

I took off running, screaming, “He is going to eat me! He is going to eat me!!!”

I was looking for the torch; but Aakhep’ was gone, and there was no torch. I continued running and screaming, “He is going to eat me!” I was terrified, running through the tall grass, but I did not know where to run. I was running faster than I ever had before. “He is going to eat me!” I kept thinking. “He is going to eat me.”

I continued running until I slammed into something very hard. “Ahhhh!” I screamed. I had slammed into a Sobek, I thought.

No, it was a palace soldier. He lifted me up in the air very quickly and put me on his shoulder. I was shaking. Then hundreds of lighted torches encircled the Sobek which was still trying to get the trap out of his mouth. The soldier carried me on his shoulder away.

"Your Majesty, what a brave Prince you are. I never thought that such a young Prince could be this brave. I will fight beside you any time!" he said.

"Where is Aakhep'?" I was looking around for him "Where is Aakhep'?" I was still shaking and worried that a Sobek might have eaten him.

"He is waiting beside the raft on the river, and His Majesty is waiting, too. Wait until His Majesty hears how brave you were. I must warn you, he is also very angry, but he will be very proud of you tonight," the soldier said.

We got to the edge of the Nile, and from there I could see that on the roof of the palace soldiers were sending signals with torches to the soldiers here on the islet. The ones on the ground were sending them messages that we were alright. I saw Aakhep' he was waiting beside the Nile. The warrior put me down, and I charged upon Aakhep'. I started to punch him in anger with my fist closed, screaming, "You left me there! Without any torches to see where I was running to!"

I was still shaking.

"No! I did not!" he screamed at me. "The soldier covered my mouth and doused the torch. "I saw when you put the trap in the Sobek's jaws and you started to run screaming. By then one of the soldiers was carrying me to the raft in a hurry."

"He is telling the truth, Your Majesty. I covered his mouth and extinguished the torch so that he wouldn't make any noise or put your life in danger," the soldier said.

I turned around and looked at the warrior "How did you know that we were here?"

"His Majesty, your father, alerted us when your wet nurse did not find you in your bed or in your quarters. She ran to your father's quarters, and he was not asleep yet. Then everyone was on alert. You still had not gone that far, so we jumped into several rafts and moved as fast as we could to catch you. Then I saw where you two were going. In that moment, I realized what you were about to do, and I started to pray to the gods to reach you before anything bad happened. We got here and encircled the Sobek, and I started to pray to the gods again when I saw you walking towards it. When you were almost in front of it; I had to cover Aakhep' mouth and extinguish his torch. I whispered to him not to make a noise or move or else the Sobek might wake up and attack you. We had to wait. You know that the Sobek is a god, and we cannot kill his incarnated form, but this time we almost had to kill him because your life was in danger. But thanks to all the gods, you were brave and ran so swiftly away from him that we did not have to kill him."

I could see that now all the soldiers were coming to the place where I was standing. They encircled me with torches in their hands and knelt at my feet. They shouted, "Hail, brave Prince of Egypt! Hail, brave Prince of Egypt!"

I was so happy because I knew that now I was one of them and that I didn't have to wait until I was thirteen summers to take the test. Yes, I did it. I was as brave as my soldiers.

The raft started back toward the palace. I felt a huge sense of accomplishment. I could hardly wait to tell Maat how brave I was I knew how proud he would be.

Before too long we neared the palace. I saw Hapu waiting, standing at the edge of the Nile with his eyes wide open. I rushed to him and whispered, "Go now! I don't want father to know that you helped us."

“Hatshepset!” There was a commotion in the entire palace, and my father and a guard found me at the edge of the Nile.

“Now that they know that I helped you and Aakhep’, I am going to get a licking like you and Aakhep’,” he told me. He also said that it was going to be done by my father and not by a guard.

“Hapu, I did it! I put the mouth trap in the Sobek’s jaw.”

“What? You did what!”

“Aakhep’ backed out at the last minute, so I did it myself. But I was terrified, and I was worried that I was going to be eaten by the Sobek.”

“Wait here. No, you had better you go home now.” I told him.

“I cannot go home now, Hat! I came to the banks to warn you and Aakhep’. I must walk back with you two and wait outside of your father’s quarters. My father is inside with Pharaoh right now.”

“Then wait here until I come out,” I told him.

Aakhep’ and I walked inside of my father’s quarters with the two soldiers. Father stood up from his chair like a lightning bolt when he saw me. Mother was clearly very nervous and was shaking her head.

“Hat!” Father screamed at me so loudly that I could feel his voice resounding inside of me like thunder, and I started to tremble. “Come in front of me you two,” he said, pointing his finger at his feet.

We walked slowly into his presence, and I was trembling. I imagined that Aakhep’ was, too. He looked at me with anger in his eyes, and I could hear a sob. I looked to my right, and there was Sitre-In crying. “Why is she crying?” I wondered.

“Do you know what you did? You lied to me!” my father shouted at me and his voice resounded inside of me again.

“Father!”

"Be quiet!" he continued, shouting at me. He looked at Aakhep'. "Why did you let her go there to be surrounded by Sobeks? You should have said no, said no from the very beginning. You are four summers older than she is!"

"Father, it's not his fault. It's all my fault!" I said quickly.

"Shut up, Hatshepset!" Father screamed at me again. He was steaming with anger.

I lowered my eyes.

"That was part of the training," I said quickly.

"Shut up, Hatshepset!" he screamed harder again. He continued, "For that, he is going to get a whipping from a soldier's hand, and now I've changed my mind about Hapuseneb. He is going to get the same whipping from a solider as Aakhep', and you will be whipped by Sitre-In. And none of you are allowed outside of your quarters for a month! Sitre-In! Take her to her quarters. I want to see that you whip her thoroughly. Otherwise, I will give the order for you to be whipped yourself for not having your eyes on her all night!" And looking straight into my eyes, he said, "I knew you were up to something. Take her from me now!" he shouted at Sitre-In.

I looked at my mother. "It's your own fault," she said, shaking her head.

The two soldiers remained with Father. As I was walking off with Sitre-In through the golden doors, I heard Father scream, "What?! She did what?!"

I smiled. "Now Father knows what I did," I thought. I walked towards my quarters, happy in that knowledge. When I got to my quarters, my two guards were not there, and I stopped. I look at Sitre-In. "Where are my guards?"

I turned around, and ran to father's quarters, very afraid. I stormed rapidly through the golden doors.

"Father!" I shouted. "I came out by way of the balcony, down a ladder. Aakhep' did, too. Look for the ladders. Please do not kill my guards! Please!" I shouted.

He looked at one of the soldiers. "Look for the ladders," he said. "Go away from me now! Nothing is going to save you from your beating. Go!" he shouted at me again.

I walked to my quarters, feeling sad. I thought that my father would be happy that I was as brave as a soldier. I walked into my quarters, and Sitre-In was crying.

"Why are you crying?" I snapped at her.

"I have never spanked you before, and my heart is hurting."

"Take off my kilt!" I ordered her. "You had better start the whipping right now. Remember what Father told you. If you don't, you will be whipped, and it will hurt very much!"

I stood there, waiting for the whip to fall on my butt when I heard Aakhep' screaming in an incredibly loud voice. His whipping had already started. Since it was a soldier inflicting the punishment, I'm sure it really hurt.

I felt the first lash. It felt like rose petals were falling on me. I turned around and looked at Sitre-In, who was crying.

"If you don't hit me harder, you are going to get the whipping and from a soldier's hand like the one who is whipping Aakhep' right now," I shouted at her.

I could hear Aakhep' screams again. They were extremely loud. I turned around and closed my eyes. This time she hit me very hard, enough to sting my leg.

"Harder!" I shouted.

She whipped me again, and with every strike, she cried harder. "Get it over with!" I yelled at her. She whipped my backside and legs, this time very forcefully, and it hurts.

She must have given me the ten lashes as my father commanded. I did not cry. I was a warrior. I could take it. Brave warriors didn't cry. She finished with the punishment and was still crying. We walked to my tub, and she bathed me. The water stung my skin.

Seeing that her tears were continuing, I said, "Sitre-In, I am a brave warrior now. I put the mouth trap into the Sobek's jaws."

She screamed, "You did what? Oh, child, you did deserve this whipping. I should have whipped you harder. You know what would have happened if a Sobek had eaten you? And what that would have done to your father? I believe it would have killed him with the most terrible pain and grief. And it would have killed your mother on top of that. And me, too!"

I became silent because I had not realized until now how much danger I had put myself and Aakheperen-Re in. I walked to my bed, but I could not sit down because the whipping was still smarting. I lay on my stomach as she put healing ointment on my bottom and legs. I could see that far away, Ra was starting to rise. I still could hear Sitre-In crying in her bed. I got up and went to her. I hugged her and kissed her cheek.

She held me tightly in her arms. "I am so sorry, sweetheart, that I had to spank you."

I kissed her cheek again. "Sitre-In, don't cry anymore, or you are going to make me cry. And warriors don't cry. You don't have to get up from the bed this morning. Let's rest all day and let the other slaves serve us today," I told her, and I went back to my bed.

"My child, what would you like to eat today? I will make it myself for you, and everything will be very special, just for you."

"Sitre-In, I will tell you later. Now, let me sleep. The rays of Ra are starting to show, and I am very tired." I said and fell asleep.

I was awakened later by a soft caress on my bald head. I opened my eyes and saw that it was my mother who was stroking me. She was sitting beside me in my bed.

"Mother." I sat up quickly, but my behind hurt from the whipping. I had to lie on the left side of my body.

"Hatshepset," she said softly. "Do you know how much you have hurt your father by lying to him?"

I started to cry because I felt very bad that I had done that. I had never lied to him before.

"Mother, I did not lie to him. I just did not tell him the whole truth. If I had told Father, he would have stopped me from helping Aakhep' to be brave. I only wanted to help Akheperen-Re. I wanted Father to love him like he loves me. And Aakhep' wants to please him very badly. He wants Father to be proud of him and to trust him."

"I was in shock when I heard from the soldier what you did, and your father was too. I could not believe it either, but now he knows how really brave you are," Mother said.

She was looking at me and caressing my right arm. "I know he is dying to come here and hug you and kiss you and tell you that he is so proud of you. But he is Pharaoh, and he is not coming. Why did you do it? Wasn't Aakheperen-Re the one who was supposed to do it?"

"Yes, but he backed out at the last minute, and I got angry at him and took the trap from his hand and went and did it myself."

"Well, I am also very proud of you, but never do such a thing again. You will talk it over with your father first or with me. Is that understood? If the Sobek had killed you, the pain would have killed your father and me. Thanks be to the gods that you weren't hurt in any way. Imagine, it could have eaten your hand or your whole arm. I hear that it was not a small crocodile and that the soldiers were so proud of you. They've never seen such a brave Prince. I mean a little girl like you doing something like that. But you are not an ordinary child, you are the daughter of Amun-Ra."

"Mother, my guards! Where are my guards? Did Father kill them?"

"No, but they were dreadfully close to being killed because of you. What saved them was that you escaped through the balcony as you told your father. They couldn't have been expected to catch you at that. Very well. Rest the rest of the week. Your father is not going to come, as I said, and he is very hurt. But he is also proud of you. Whatever you need, tell Sitre-In. I also want you to know that you put her life in danger. Your father almost ordered her death as well," she said.

"I am so sorry, Mother. Can you tell Father that I really did not lie to him, that I just did not tell him the whole truth? Please, Mother, tell him that I love him very much, and I promise never to do that again. How are Aakhep' and Hapuseneb?"

"Both got a very good licking by the guard. They will probably not want to speak to you for a while."

"Probably, but I want to be clear that Hapuseneb did not want to help with the test, Mother. Aakhep' said that he wanted to do it, and Hapu was forced to help us because, as you know, they are the best of friends."

"The three of you are the best of friends," she said.

"Mother, tell me what the guard told Father."

"That they had just gotten there as you were walking to the Sobek, and he started to pray. He said that he covered Aakhep' mouth in a hurry and put out the torch because the light would have awakened the crocodile, and that he did not move. All the soldiers were terrified when they saw you walking toward the Sobek and then standing in front of him. Everyone was holding their breath. Then you put the trap in his mouth, and the Sobek snapped his jaw lightning fast. They said that they had never seen a child run so fast. You were screaming, 'Run, it's going to eat me!' But the Sobek stayed behind, trying to get the trap out of his mouth. All the soldiers were ready to kill him if he had charged after you. And by now, the whole army and the whole kingdom knows what you did. We all are very proud of you." She smiled and kissed my head, then kissed me again. "The last kiss is from your father." And she smiles.

I started to cry again, and she rock me in her arms.

"I want you to know that I am very proud of you and so is your father, but he is Pharaoh, and you are the one who needs to go to him and ask for forgiveness. Now, you are a brave warrior," she said and smiled at me, and I smiled at her. Then she got up and went to talk to Sitre-In. I could hear Sitre-In crying again. Mother hugged her, then turned around, and smiled at me again, and left.

"Sitre! Bathe me. I am going to see my father to ask for his forgiveness," I said.

She started to cry as she bathed me.

"Now why are you crying?"

"I really hurt you badly, and your body is all marked from the whipping I inflicted upon you."

"Did you see me crying while you were whipping me? Well, I cried because Father is angry at me, but now I'm going to fix that," I said.

"Yes, my child, you must go so that your father may trust you again."

She dressed me in the kilt, and I ran to the double doors and opened them. I was about to cross the threshold when I noticed that my two guards were back. I was elated to see them again, but as I was about to leave they crossed their spears in front of me and would not let me continue.

"Move. I order you to let me pass!" I shouted.

But they would not let me pass. I screamed at them, "I saved your lives. Let me pass!" But they would not move. I tried to stomp their toes with my heel but could not reach them, and they did not move. I started to kick the backs of their legs and heels until I got tired and my toes were hurting. I turned around and walked back to where Sitre-In was standing.

"Sitre-In, can you go and tell Father that I need to speak to him and that my guards are not letting me leave my quarters. And that I am very sorry. Please! I know he will listen to you!"

"I will, my child, right away." She left, and I walked behind her. The guards moved the spears away to allow her to exit, and I pushed her hard out of the way. I took off running rapidly through the hallway to Father's quarters. The guards were running after me. One caught me and picked me up by my waist. He started to carry me on the side of his hip back to my quarters. I was kicking in the air and screaming, "Maat, Maat!" I was calling my father at the top of my lungs, but there was no response.

Then I heard Father's voice. "Calm down, calm down, Hat! Put her down," he said to the soldier carrying me.

"Yes, Your Majesty!"

"Let's walk to your quarters," Father said, and we did. He stood there with both fists resting on his hips and his legs spread apart, looking at me very seriously. Seeing him, tears started to roll down my face, and I started to cry. "

"You wanted to talk to me? Speak!" His tone of voice was hard and harsh.

I knelt at his feet. I was having trouble speaking, but I said, "Forgive me, Father, please! Now I know how badly I behaved. I did not lie to you. I just did not tell you everything."

He responded, "Was he brave enough to do it? No! So, you went and did it yourself, without thinking that Sobek could have eaten you!" He was shouting. "And you almost killed me, Hatshepset! You don't know how worried I was for you. I rushed to the roof of the palace, and when I saw the lone torch in the area where the Sobeks are, I became terrified for you, and I knew what you two were about to do. I started to pray to Amun-Ra and all the gods for your safety. When I saw that torch extinguish its fire, my heart pounded so hard that it finally stopped. At least that's how it felt. I couldn't breathe. Time was moving as slow as eternity. I thought you were dead. Then I saw all the torches becoming lit, and my warriors started to send signals to me that both of you were alright. At that moment, I was shaking extremely hard, and I thought I was going to collapse right on that spot."

I saw Father's tears rolling down his face. I ran to him, and he hugged me very tightly. We cried together. I did not know how much I had hurt him until that moment. Sobbing, I said, "Father, forgive me please!"

Then he pulled me away from him, and looking at me, he said, "I love you so much, daughter, and I forgive you. However, you will remain punished for the entire month."

I smiled at him "Yes, Father." Then he kissed my bald head and embraced me again. He turned around to leave. As he was leaving, I told him "I love you, Father."

Then he smiled back. "And I love you, too." Then he left.

My heart was still sad. I still felt bad about what I did, but I was happy that I spoke to my father and asked him to forgive me.[15]

****

The month of punishment was over, and I was glad that I was free again. I ran to see how Aakhep' was doing. The guard opened the doors, and I walked in. Standing there was my aunt Mutnofret.

"Good morning, Horus of Egypt. If you came looking for your brother, he doesn't want to see you or speak to you for a long, long time, he told me that, and I suggest that you come back when his anger is over. You know that he was whipped very hard by a soldier, as was Hapuseneb right!"

After she said that, I pulled up my kilt and showed her my bare buttocks and legs, to demonstrate that I was also whipped harshly.

"Look at me! I was whipped hard, too, so tell him that and tell him that I came to see him. I know Hapu will speak to me," I said.

"He doesn't want to see you either." It was Aakhep' voice. I turned around, but I could not see him. He was behind the linen curtains "And don't come back here. You heard me!" He was shouting at me.

---

[15] Writing this part of my memories makes me cry, just remembering how good my father was with me and how much he loved me then. I feel sorry for what I did. As a child, I did not understand the consequences of my actions. I miss him greatly, and I miss my mother Ahmose, Sitre-In, and others as well. In fact, I miss everyone who loved me then and the ones whom I loved. I miss sailing the Nile every afternoon, I miss the palace, and I especially miss Thebes.

"Of course, he will see me!" I told him. "Let me see you," I said softly.

He came out from behind the white linen curtains. I could see that the guards really had whipped him brutally. My heart broke. I felt awful, and tears started to roll down my face.

"I don't want to see you ever again. Don't come back here anymore," he said.

He turned around and left. I walked out of his quarters quite quickly, tears rolling down my face, and ran to Hapuseneb's home. I wondered if he would see me.

I walked into his house without being announced. His mother saw me come in. "Your Majesty," she said and knelt.

"Rise! I want to see Hapuseneb! And I am ordering it!"

"Yes, Your Majesty." His mother left and came back with him.

She was standing behind him with her hands on his shoulders. "Leave us alone," I ordered her, and she left. Oh! The guards had punished him terribly, I thought. Looking at him, I started cry.

"I am so sorry Hapu. Will you forgive me?" I asked softly.

"I don't think I can forgive you! And go away from me!" he shouted at me.

I moved closer to him. "Please walk with me?" I was about to hold his hand, but he pulled his hand away from mine.

"No! You had better go away. I can hardly walk or sit down because of you. I had to stand there and watch the guard whip Aakhep' first and hear him scream at the top of his lungs as the whip fell on him, and then it was my turn. I was so scared. He had to watch me, too. I yelled just as loudly as he did as I was being whipped."

Hearing him tell me of his pain made me feel just terribly. I bent down, pulled up my kilt, and showed him my bare behind and legs so that he could see that I was whipped as well.

Looking at him, I said, "I could not sit or lay down either."

"Leave now! I really don't care. And I really don't want to see you at all. Go!" he shouted at me.

My eyes became full of tears, and I started to cry. I turned around and walked off. I wept as I realized how many people I had hurt with my actions. I should have used my wisdom before I did all of that. I did not go to offer prayers to Amun before I did it because I was afraid that he would forbid it.

I had walked a little way down the path crying, when I heard, "Hat! Hat, wait!"

I turned around. It was Hapu, walking slowly until he reached the spot where I was standing.

"I cannot be angry at you for more than two minutes," he said.

We smiled at each other. My heart was happy again.

"Hapu, you must speak to Aakhep' for me. Please, he is very angry at me right now, but he was the one who wanted to do it. And in the end, I was the one who did it! Hapu does its hurt a lot?"

"Of course, it does! We got a severe beating. I was so scared when the guard made Aakhep' take off his kilt and started to whip him. His screams were terrible. Then it was my turn. Scared, I took off my kilt, and the first lash fell on me. It was horrible. I screamed so hard."

"I remember that. I could hear the screaming all the way to my quarters, and I thought it was Aakhep' who was alone when he was being whipped. How many lashes did each of you get?" I said.

"Five and I thought it would never end. Do you know how they do it? The whip has several strings of hard leather hanging and they dip it in water. The guard strikes you once, then he waits until the wound really starts hurting to give you the next one. He does the same with every strike until he is finished."

"That sounds awful. Now I know why Aakhep' doesn't want to talk to me, but I was whipped ten times."

"What? Ten? Maat really wanted you to feel his anger, I believe," he said.

"Well, it was Sitre-In who whipped me. I had to tell her to do it harder. Otherwise, she was going to be whipped by a soldier. And the poor thing cried every time she hit me, but I did not cry at all. I am a warrior, and warriors don't cry!"

"You would have cried like we did if the guard had done it."

"This is my first time being spanked by anyone. How about you?" I asked him.

"Well, I can say the same. I'd never been spanked either. I have not seen Neferu-Bity. Have you?" he asked.

"No, and she has not come to my quarters to see me either, not even to say hello. Maybe she was not allowed to come and see me. But we could go now and look for her. Do you want to do that?" I said.

"OK, but we must walk slowly. How can you sleep, Flower of Egypt, with your butt hurting?"

"I sleep on my side. Maat forgave me, and I realized that what I did was very dangerous, and I will never do it again. I could have killed my father and mother with grief if I have been eaten by the Sobek."

We became silent and we walked slowly, and I was looking at the current of Hopi. Suddenly, I felt a hard bang on my back that really hurt, and I was left without air. I was trying to catch my breath. Hapu had punched me incredibly hard, and I was startled by it. I turned around quickly and looked at him with hatred.

"That is for my beating!" he shouted. He was still standing there with his closed fist.

I was about to punch him back, but instead I remained still and quiet because I realized that I deserved it.

"You hit me very hard, and it did hurt!" I shouted at him.

"That is not hard or painful. Hard and painful was the beating I got because of you!"

I became quiet again and turned around. I was saddened because he had punched me very hard. I started to walk slowly, without saying anything, and he followed me at a distance. I believe that he was afraid that I was going to punch him back. And he knew that I could kick his ass. Instead, I stopped and without looking at him, I asked, "Are you going to see Aakhep' today? If you do, tell him that I am sorry for his licking and that I will let him hit me one time like you just did, but only one time! OK? But please don't be angry at me anymore."

"OK, I will tell him," he said.

I continued walking beside the Nile. He was still trailing behind me, and I saw Neferu-Knib standing alone looking at the Nile. We both called to her, and she came running to meet us. She had a very bright smile on her face. I guessed that she had gotten over her anger regarding her betrothal to Aakhep'.

"Hi, Neferu-Knib. Why didn't you come to visit me in those days that I was stuck in my quarters?" I ask.

"Hi, Hapu." She was looking at him and ignoring me. Then she looked at me. "You deserved the beating. Look at what you did. You almost killed everyone, including Sitre-In and your guards. Hapu got a harsh beating, as did Aakhep'. I could hear Aakhep' screaming as the whip fell on him. And I didn't know that Hapu was in the same room with Aakhep' waiting to be whipped. I found out later by Mother that he was. And I probably would have gotten a whipping like them too if I had listened to you. And now there is a big commotion in the palace, and I don't know what it's all about." She finally finished barking at me.

"I did not tell you to help us!" I yelled at her. "Because you would probably go to Father with all of this gossip!" I screamed at her as I ran off, leaving them standing there. I ran to the palace to see what commotion she was talking about, hoping desperately that it wasn't about war. I ran to Father's quarters.

"Father! I hear that there is a big commotion in the palace. Is there going to be war?" I was agitated.

"No, Hatshepset. Everything is fine, but tomorrow is going to be a big day. There will be a gathering of all the soldiers and the armed forces. I want you to come with me. Everyone is coming. You must be ready very early in the morning, as we must cross Hopi and go far away to meet with all of them," he said.

"I will be ready, Father. You said that everyone is coming, including Aakheperen-Re?"

"Including him," he said, nodding his head.

"I want Hapuseneb to come with us also."

"He will. His father knows to have him ready, and his father will be there too. Ursaramun is also coming with his father Amethu."

"I don't think Hapu knows about it," I said.

"He will know soon," Father said.

I kissed my father, turned around, and started to walk away.

"Hat!" Father screamed, and I turned back around fast, startled.

"What happened to your back? Why is it bruised?" he asked sternly.

I was caught off guard and needed to think of something quick.

"I saw a small turtle, and I tried to catch it before she got to the water, and I lost my balance and fell on my back," I said. I didn't want to lie, but what would happen to Hapu if I told him the truth, I wondered. He looked at me doubtfully.

"I hope you are telling me the truth, Hat."

"Yes, Father, I am. And I love you," I said, and I smiled at my father and walked off in a hurry.

As I walked to my quarters, I felt terribly bad for not telling the truth. It would not happen again, I told myself. I walked to my quarters in a hurry. I was hungry. I ate fast and was bathed. Father must be planning a war game. He did that from time to time.

Then I remembered how hard Hapu had punched me on my back. It still hurt.

I was awakened very early the next morning by Sitre-In and was bathed. She dressed me with the white kilt and leather sandals.

"I am hungry this morning, Sitre-In," I told her.

"I have ordered some breakfast for you, my child."

Then the double doors opened, and it was my breakfast. I was eating hastily since I was hungry, and there was a knock on my doors.

"Enter!"

A soldier walked into my quarters. "Your Majesty," he said and knelt. He had a smile on his face.

"Rise!"

"His Majesty is waiting for you."

I wiped my mouth with the back of my hand and drank more of my favorite hot drink, then wiped my mouth again as I finished. I left to go to Father's quarters. When I reached the guards at Father's doors, they looked at me and smiled. They were probably happy because I saved my guards' lives, I thought.

I smiled back at them. I walked into Father's quarters and ran to his arms. Mother was there standing beside him with a big smile, and I noticed that Khety, First Prophet of Amun, and my uncle Thutmoses were also there. I hugged my mother, and I was surprised that she was there. She never came with us to any of the war games before.

"Hatshepset," Father said, "come close to me. I have a gift for you. Today, you are ten summers old, and you are growing too fast."

He opened a large wooden box and pulled a golden coronet of Horus and a golden pectoral that had the Eye of Horus on it. I was puzzled.

"You deserve it. You have won the respect of all the soldiers in my army," Father said.

"Father!" I looked at him with tears in my eyes and hugged him. My mother had tears in her eyes also. She came and embraced us both and kissed me.

Khety took the Horus crown, and I knelt on one knee while he placed it on my shaved head. He said a prayer over my head. It fit better than the other one, which was getting too small for my head. He then placed the pectoral around my neck.

I rose. Father applauded me, as did Mother, Khety, and my uncle.

"I feel like I am a Pharaoh already," I said, and they all laughed. We walked down the stairs together. Everyone was waiting for us, including Hapu. He smiled at me. I looked for my brother. He was there and quite serious. He did not smile at me.

We got into the barge, and two other large barges sailed with us. We crossed Hopi to the Valley of the Dead. Our horses were waiting at the edge of the banks when we arrived. I mounted my horse with my rear still hurting, but I had to take the pain. We rode with hundreds of soldiers, and behind me were Aakhep' and Hapu. I turned around to look at Aakhep', but he was still ignoring me. When we arrived at an open field, there was a wooden platform waiting for us to climb onto with our horses.

Father let me climb the platform first on my horse. When I reached the top, every soldier started to shout, "Warrior! Warrior! Warrior!" I was so surprised and moved that all of this was arranged for me.[16]

In front of us were all the armed forces of my father. Red banners belonging to the brave warriors who guard and protect the palace and our doors; yellow banners for the charioteers; turquoise banners for the royal cavalry; turquoise and gold banners, which signaled my father's presence; yellow, white, and gold banners for the archers; dark blue banners for the navy; and red and black banners for the army's battlefield ground warriors.

The armies were so immense that my eyes could not perceive an edge. That is how far and wide they ranged.

"Now," I thought, "it is my army."

---

[16] Writing this part of my life brings tears to my eyes. It was incredibly emotional for me that day, being in front of all the warriors, and experiencing the love of my father for me, and knowing how proud he was of me for being a brave child.

My father, my uncle, and a general from each branch of the armed forces came up beside me. Then Father said in a loud voice, "I present to you, your army! Now you are one of us."

There was an explosion of cheers from all the members of the armed forces. I was full of joy and felt that I was one of them. Then I thought to myself, "Of course, I am one of them."

My uncle lifted me up to his right shoulder, and the army began to chant, "Hatshepset! Hatshepset! Hatshepset!"

We played war games all day. There was food for everyone, wine and beer. I mingled with the soldiers, and all of them praised me. I raced against them in my chariot and shoot arrows.

Aakhep' also raced his chariot, as did Hapu with Neferu-Knib beside him. She did not want to ride with me, nor with Aakhep'. It was clear that Aakhep' was no longer angry. He beat me in the chariot race, or so he thought. I let him win so that he wouldn't be angry with me anymore.

We had a very large tent, turquoise with gold trimmings. Father participated in every game with us, and all of us were happy all over again. I could see how happy Neferu-Knib was beside Hapu. At least she was no longer mad at me anymore.

It was the first day of Mesori[17], and I was ten summers that day. Father had made it the happiest day of my life.

---

[17] The first day of the month in the Egyptian calendar is on the twenty-fifth day of every month. Mesori is the month of July, and I was born in this life on the same day and the same month, July 25th.

CHAPTER 18

NEFERU-BITY

I had not seen Neferu-Knib for several days after we returned from the Valley of the Dead. I walked into her quarters, and she was lying in bed crying. I came closer, sat beside her in her bed, and looked at her.

"Why are you crying?"

She wiped her tears with both hands. "My blood came, and I did not want it to come. I don't want to marry Aakheperen-Re, and I am scared that Maat will find out and force me to marry him sooner than my fifteen summers. If he does, I swear, I will kill myself! I swear I will! I don't want to live without love. Do they not understand that? Mother came to see me, and she already knew about the blood. I begged her not to tell Father. She was kind. She said that she would not. She said that she understood very well how I felt because she went through the same thing, and that Father would find out sooner or later, and the person who would be hurt very badly would be my wet nurse. This is something that my wet nurse cannot keep from him for too long."

"How will he find out?" I asked.

"Mother said that my breasts will grow more, and my body will start to look like a woman's. And I would look more beautiful."

"Neferu-Knib, listen. Aakhep' must also grow before you are married. And maybe you can learn how to love him," I said.

"I don't want him, and I don't want to marry him! Don't you understand?" she shouted at me. "You are lucky. No one will force you to marry anyone. You will be able to choose whomever you like, but I can't. I am doomed!"

"Do you want to come with me to the Nile? We can walk and talk?" I asked.

"Okay, let me get bathed first. I will go to your quarters." She said.

"I'll see you in my quarters then."

I left and walked to my quarters, which were beside hers. I went to my balcony and stood there and looked as far away to the south as I could. In two months, Akhet would start, and the flood would inundate the land. When that happened, I knew that I would be bored to death, and on top of that, the mosquitoes would eat me alive. I hated them. I didn't know how other people could say the mosquitoes didn't bother them after a few rains. Thank goodness for the net around my bed and the smoke from the burning wood, otherwise I would not be able to come out of my quarters.

The double doors opened, and in walked Neferu-Knib. "Let's go. We will sit beside the waters of Hopi." I said.

"Neferu-Knib, does it hurt?" I asked.

"What?"

"Well, the blood."

"No. I woke up three days ago, and it was there. It doesn't hurt. Today it is gone. I was told that it only lasted three days."

"Do you think I am going to get it?"

"Oh, yes, every woman does. That is part of being a woman and having children. Hat, I've heard that Aakheperen-Re and Hapu are starting to visit the women of the harem every day. Soon he will be fourteen summers, and I hear that he and Hapu are spending a lot of their time together there. I hope Aakhep' finds his women there. I don't want him near me! In two weeks, I will be thirteen summers. Have you seen Hapuseneb?" she asked.

"No, have you?" I said.

"No, I have not," she said.

"Look there he is." I pointed at him. He walked in our direction when he saw us. I saw her face light up and how happy she was. I also felt good to see him.

"Flower of Egypt and Neferu-Bity, where have you two been?"

"I have been sick. Well, kind of," she said.

"And where have you been?" I asked him.

"I have been in the harem with Aakhep'," he said and laughed. "Wow, there are so many beautiful women there." He shook his head with a smile.

"You are too young to visit the harem," she told him.

"Well, I am thirteen and soon I will be fourteen summers, and I was told that I must start young to master lovemaking."

"What is that?" I asked him.

He started to laugh, and Neferu-Knib laughed, too.

"Well, you will hear about it soon enough," Neferu-Knib said.

"Flower of Egypt, where is your friend? I have not seen T'Queta with you since Neferu was betrothed to Aakhep'," he said.

"Shut up!" I shouted at him. "Don't you see, that is going to upset her again!"

He looked at Neferu-Knib and said, "Be at ease. Aakhep' doesn't want to marry you either, nor anyone else. He wants to choose his own wife! He told me himself."

"I am hungry. I am going to my quarters to eat something. You are welcome to join me," I told them.

"No, I want to walk with Neferu-Bity for a while."

"Okay, see you tomorrow then."

"We will," he said.

****

In the days that followed, I was in the arena all day, practicing with my bow and arrows. I had not seen Neferu-Knib or Hapuseneb. I was with Aakhep' and Ursaramun, racing our horses and shooting arrows. The other children of the palace were also in the arena.

A few more days passed, and I did not see Neferu-Knib. "Tomorrow morning, I will go and visit her. We can run and play in the waters," I thought.

I went to the banquet hall that night to eat with Father and Mother. Neferu-Knib was not there, but Hapu was. He smiled at me, but then he started staring at me.

"What's wrong with him? Why is he looking at me in that way?" I thought. He came to sit beside me, as did Aakheperen-Re.

"Have you seen Neferu-Bity?" he asked me.

"No, I have been busy practicing with my warriors. Go to her quarters and talk to her if you want to see her," I told him. I turned to my mother. "Mother, where is Neferu-Knib?"

"She still doesn't want to come out of her room. I thought she was getting over it, about the engagement, but she is still angry about it. And now it will be worse. Your father knows about her blood, and he is going to move the wedding to one summer from now instead of the three summers."

I frown, "Does she know that?" I asked.

"Yes, I told her this morning, and she would not stop crying."

Hapu looked at me. I was afraid for Neferu-Knib.

"Mother, can I talk to you alone, right now?"

"Let's walk in the inner gardens," she said.

While we were strolling through the gardens, I said to her, "Mother, I am very worried about Neferu-Knib. She swears that if Father forces her to marry Aakhep', she will kill herself. This is going to make the whole situation worse, what you just told me."

Mother became silent and lowered her eyes. "I said the same thing when my father forced me to marry your father. She will be fine, you will see."

We went back to the banquet hall.

"Mother, I so hope, that you are right, but I am scared for her!"

She changed the subject. "Let's eat, little one."

I had an uneasy feeling inside of me and was very worried about her, so I left and ran to her quarters.

"Prince of Egypt," her wet nurse greeted me.

"I came to see Neferu-Bity." I found myself saying her full name correctly, like she always wanted me to.

"She has been crying for days now. It became worse today. She has not stopped crying since your mother came and gave her that bad news. Now she is asleep, not surprising considering that she has been crying for days. Everything started a few days ago, but I don't know what she is crying so much for."

"Can you tell her that I was here and that I love her?"

"Yes, I will," she said.

I went back to the banquet hall. Hapu was waiting for me with a grin on his face. He was already fourteen summers. He and Aakhep' believed that they were already grown men, going to the harem like that. I still didn't understand why they liked to go there so much. Who wants to go there and be only with women? Idiots!

Later that night, I was deeply asleep when I was awakened by terrible screaming. I got up and ran to the doors, and I saw my guards running. I could see Neferu's wet nurse screaming, running in the hallway, pulling at her hair. She was running to Mother's quarters. I did not like that.

I froze and could not move. A bad feeling was spreading through me, and I ran to Neferu-Knib's room. My body was shaking as I walked to her bed and stood beside her. I saw that she lay there with her eyes open, and she had white, dried saliva on her lips.

I touched her. She was cold! I shook her hard. "Neferu-Knib, wake up! Please, wake up!" Tears were pouring down my face.

When Father slammed the doors open, Mother was screaming behind him. He moved me out of the way fast and lifted her body into his arms and pressed her lifeless body against his chest, weeping. "My daughter!" He screamed and screamed. Mother was screaming as well. Father held her lifeless body in his lap. Mother was kneeling on the floor beside him, touching her body and crying. "My daughter! My daughter!"

I hugged my mother and cried with her.

"This is horrible, Mother! She did it. I told you last night that she was going to do it! Why did you have to force her to marry Aakheperen-Re?!" I screamed at them.

I got up from the floor, ran to my quarters, and threw myself onto the bed, crying. Sitre-In came close, held me in her arms rocking me, and we cried together. I looked at her.

"Let me go! I need to be with my sister," I said and ran off.

Walking to her room, I saw Aakhep' and Mutnofret running to her quarters. When we saw each other, I ran to Aakhep' and he hugged me, and we cried together. He held me in his arms, as we walked inside her room. Father still was holding her lifeless body in his arms.

After a short time, Khety and the other priests walked in with Puyem-Re and some priestesses. They had brought incense and were chanting prayers for the dead for the princess that had just died. Father carried her body in his arms to the House of the Dead while we walked behind him.

I saw Hapuseneb running in our direction. I ran to him, and we hugged each other very tightly. We cried so hard together and Aakhep' came and embraced us, and we wept together for a long time. He was crying uncontrollably, I kept hearing him say, "Oh, God! Oh, God!"

We walked to the House of the Dead. We were not allowed to go inside. Only Father, Mother, the priest, and priestesses were allowed in.

For the next few weeks, I could feel the silence everywhere, as the whole land was in mourning. After a few weeks had passed, I realized that I had not seen Hapu nor Aakhep'. My mother came to my room every day, held me in her arms, and we cried together. She said that Father was taking it very hard. He was blaming himself for the stupid traditions, and I agreed with him.

"Mother, is he going to betroth me to Aakheperen-Re now?"

"No, I am sure he is not. Not now, with the death of Neferu-Bity."

"I don't mind if he does," I said.

"You are too young to know what you are saying. I know what is in your father's heart. He wants you to be Pharaoh, though I don't know how he is going to do that because only men have held the Double Crown as long as I can remember."

"I will be Pharaoh, Mother, and everyone will be happy in my kingdom. There will be no war, and if I have daughters, they will be pharaohs, too!" In silence, she held me in her arms.

****

Another three weeks had passed, and Hapu had not come back, not even to the banquet hall. He must be hurting very badly, because they were the best of friends.

At night, I dreamt about Neferu-Knib, and she kept telling me to stay with her. I wanted her to stay here with us because we missed her very much. She looked happy where she was, but I could not go with her. I must remain here. I must rule Egypt.

Seventy days after Neferu-Bity went to the underworld, the process of embalming of her body was over, and then the procession for her burial started. We crossed Hopi in five large barges. No bulls, carriages, or horses were used to carry her coffin. The coffin was carried by the palace guards on their shoulders. It was a long procession. The priests were burning incense as they walked in front of her body, and we all walked behind her coffin to the Valley of the Dead. My father and mother were holding my hands. We were followed by Mutnofret, Aakheperen-Re, Hapuseneb, our friends, family, slaves of the palace, as well the military. The people of Thebes grieved with us, and many were present in the burial procession.

I turned around and looked at Aakhep' and Hapuseneb, but I was not able to walk with them. The procession was conducted in complete silence. The only sounds were the crying and the wailing of women. We arrived at her tomb, and all her personal belongings were bought inside We all entered. I had never been to a funeral before, but I was not scared at all because I was a brave warrior. Even though I knew that Anubis, the god of the underworld, would come, I knew that Father would protect me.

Her coffin stood leaning against the wall of the tomb. The chanting began. The priests opened the Book of the Dead to summon Anubis from the underworld. I was shaking and held Mother's hands firmly. I could not breathe. The scent of incense was everywhere. I could see the panic in Hapuseneb's eyes when he saw Anubis. Aakhep' was sweating profusely. Mutnofret was behind him, both hands resting on his shoulders. The chanting continued. I was terribly tired, hungry, and frightened. I kept staring at the face of Anubis, the jackal, and at his eyes, and his jaws, which were waiting to devour me.

I moved closer to my mother's body, put my arms around her waist, and clung tightly to her. Mother looked at me and put her arms around me. She was crying. I looked at my father. His face was somber. I wanted to run away, but I held on to my mother.

I turned around and could not see Hapu because he had run out scared. Father held the adze[18] in his hand. He touched Neferu-Bity's mouth, eyes, and ears, so that she could eat, see, and hear in the afterlife. A while later, I was startled by the screams of a calf being slaughtered. I did not like it all. They cut off the head first.

Eventually, we ate there, and we stayed with her for a while. At one point, I began to look for her wet nurse. I had not seen her since the

---

[18] A ceremonial tool used to allow the dead the use of their senses in the afterlife.

day of Neferu-Bity's death. I figured that she must have been so terribly sad that she avoided the funeral.

Finally, everything was over. Mother and I left, crying uncontrollably. Father remained inside the tomb with her body and the open coffin for a while. To my surprise, a soldier had brought the horses and a litter to carry my mother back to the barge. I was grateful because we were all too tired to walk back. I saw Hapuseneb sitting on a rock talking with Aakhep', and I approached them and sat beside Hapu.

"Hapu, it was terrifying, wasn't it, to see the face of the Anubis?"

"Yes, I'd heard of it in the temple, but I've never been to a funeral before," he said.

"Aakhep, were you frightened as well?" I asked him.

"A little bit. I'd also heard what it's like and how it's done from a priest, and Mother explained it to me last night," he said.

"I am so sorry that she killed herself," I said, and noticed that Hapu turned his face away from me. Then he got up and walked away without looking at me. I got up to go after him, but Aakhep' held my arm.

"Hat, let him be."

"Why, Aakhep'? My heart is also terribly sad, and we all should be together."

"We will, but for now, let him be alone!"

I saw Father coming out of the tomb with Khety and Puyem-Re. I looked more closely at Puyem-Re and noticed that for a priest and physician, he was still young, perhaps five or six years older than Aakhep'. He was followed by many other priests and priestesses. Mother got into a litter. Hapu, Aakhep', and I rode our horses. But Father walked all the way back, I gather he feels guilty for her death and I feel sad for him. The rest would remain and return the next day.

We arrived at the edge of the banks and waited for Father. and sailed home in silence. It was very dark when we arrived at the palace. I said goodnight to Hapu and Aakhep', and we hugged each other. Hapu climbed into a litter and was taken home. Mother and Father hugged me once more.

"Mother, can I sleep with you tonight?" I asked.

Father looked at me and said, "Let's all sleep in my quarters. My bed is large enough for the three of us."

We were bathed, and I could see tears and sadness on the faces of the slaves. We ate. I drank wine and fell asleep.

I missed my sister terribly. I still had dreams in which she was calling me to come with her. She would tell me that she was in a beautiful place. I kept telling her that I didn't want to leave Maat or Mother, and that I must rule Egypt one day.

I did not see Hapu or Aakhep' that much after the funeral. I heard from T'Queta that they spent a lot of time with Ursaramun and their other male friends in the harem. She learned this from the gossip in the kitchen and told me laughing.

One morning I woke up with terrible cramps. I got up to go the bathroom and noticed blood on my sheets. My first blood had come. There was a big celebration, especially by my mother, and she said that I would bloom like a beautiful rose. Father never mentioned the word betroth again. It had been three years since Neferu-Bity went to the heavens.

Hapuseneb became a priest, as did Aakheperen-Re. We didn't see each other as much as before, only from time to time, and only in the banquet hall. I noticed how handsome Hapuseneb had become, and Aakhep' had as well. I also heard that both had the women of the palace going crazy for them. It was as my mother said it would be, and recently I noticed the way Hapu looked at me and smiled.

CHAPTER 19

MEETING SEN-MUT

Every morning, I took my breakfast in my beautiful rose garden. It was in bloom and full of pink roses. I would sit and look at the slow flowing water of Hopi, surrounded by the sweet smell of the roses, a scent that was a delight to my nostrils. We had brought them from that trip to Crete long ago, when I was only five summers, and after I had become Horus of Egypt. Looking at the blue sky, I was thinking how time had passed, and now it was five years since Neferu-Bity died.

I saw Hapuseneb walking into my garden. He had been coming to see me every morning for the last few months. He made me feel nice, and I believed I was starting to fall in love with him.

"Blessed morning to you, Hapuseneb," I said and smiled.

"Blessed morning to you, Flower of Egypt," he replied.

I noticed how much he had changed. He was a very handsome man, tall with beautiful pale skin, gorgeous gray eyes, and wavy black hair that went well with his long, black eyelashes. He was as handsome as Mother had said he would be.

We smiled at each other. "Have some sweet bread and fruit with me, Hapuseneb, and this most delicious hot drink, our favorite!" I said.

"Yes, thank you. I will have some," he replied, showing me his beautiful white teeth when he smiled.

I clapped my hands, and T'Queta came running to me.

"Yes, Majesty?"

"T'Queta, bring more sweet breads, fruits, and the hot drink for the young priest." I smiled at him, and he returned the smile.

"Yes, Your Majesty," T'Queta said as she took off running for the kitchen. I could see the way he looked at her, and a hint of jealousy rushed upon me.

"She has been with you for a long time, right?" he asked.

"Yes, Hapuseneb, she has been with me since we brought you and your family from Crete. We brought her from the land of the green sea when I was five summers, and you were only eight summers. Don't you remember that?"

"Not really."

I could see T'Queta coming with a tray in her hands. As she was coming closer, I noticed the way Hapuseneb looked at her again. He had a look of delight on his face.

I snapped, "Do you like her? I could give her to you!"

He looked at me, and with a big smile on his face said, "Lotus of Egypt, do I note some jealousy in the tone of your voice?"

"Of course not!"

By this time, she was near us, and he was looking at her again while she was serving him. She was naked from the waist up. She had pale skin like his, with almond shaped brown eyes, long black hair with a lotus tucked into the strands on the left side of her head, and well-formed breasts.

I clapped my hands very hard. "You may go now!" I said, and I sent her away. She looked at him as she was turning away to leave. He smiled at her, and she almost gave him a smile in return.

I was about to say something when I saw the Great Maat walking across the garden. Hapuseneb got off his chair and knelt on one knee.

"Rise, Hapuseneb," Father said, and he did.

"Good morning, Father."

"Good morning to you, beloved one. Hat, I would like for you to attend to a matter in the hall of audience for me today. It's a favor for the Great Ineni. As this will be your first audience, you can use the wisdom given to you by Amun-Ra, and I will be able to see how well you make decisions for the future. In exchange, I will be taking these days off to go hunting. Hunting is good for me anyway," he said with a laugh. "I am finally taking your brother with me after all those years of promising him that I would. I will see if we can finally bond."

"Father, who else is going with you?"

"I am going with some of my closest friends, some of my generals, and a large group from my army. Now, remember to use your wisdom wisely. You have been present in my audiences many times, and you know how these events are handled. And remember that today the whole power of this kingdom is in your hands and will someday be yours. I have already left word with the generals who are not coming with me that you are in charge and that they must be ready at your command."

"Father, I'm really glad that you are finally taking Aakhep' hunting with you, and I bet he is, too," I said.

"Aakhep' is happy about it as well, and after all these years, I am finally going to do it." He smiled, nodding his head several times.

"I believe that Aakheperen-Re will like hunting," Father said.

"Your Majesty, where are you going hunting?" Hapu asked.

"We are going down to the Sudan. Hapuseneb, I want you to accompany her to her first audience and guide her if she needs you since you have been in my audiences many times before, and you know how to handle it."

"I will, Your Majesty!" he replied.

"Have fun, my daughter. I shall return a few days before your fifteen summers, in about fifteen days, so I can be here when you become a woman." He smiled.

"Father, I will do as you ask. I want you to be safe and have fun hunting. May Amun-Ra keep you safe until your return. I will say prayers to the gods for you and Aakhep' wellbeing and for everyone's safe return."

"Very well. Hapuseneb, I leave my daughter and my Queen in your care. I shall see you both on my return."

Father came to me and kissed my forehead. After he did so, he turned around, and I saw him leave as he had come in.

By this time, my anger at Hapuseneb had dissipated. We finished breakfast, and it was time to go. We started to walk to the audience hall.

"Are you happy that this is your first audience?" Hapu asked.

"Yes, and I hope I do well. I want Father to know that I can do it."

We continued walking until we arrived at the audience hall. I was wearing a white kilt, my golden belt, and uncomfortable golden sandals. I walked to my father's throne and sat down on it. Hapuseneb stood to my right, about two feet away from me.

On the other side of the doors of the hall of audience was a nervous peasant of about seventeen summers pacing back and forth.

"Don't look at the eyes of Horus. You could be put to death. At all times, keep your eyes cast down, and as you approach Horus, you will prostrate yourself on the floor and remain in that position the whole time until he tells you to rise. You will present your request, but do not look at him. After you hear his decision, you will not turn your back to him. You will retreat by walking without turning your back to Horus," the guard warned him.

"Let the audience begin!" I shouted.

The double doors opened, and in the middle stood a young man who started to walk towards me with his eyes cast down. Then when he was closer to me, about ten feet away, I raised my left hand, and the guard told him to stop.

I looked him over from head to toe. He was a young man about my age with a light golden tan and black hair. He was barefoot. His dingy kilt was faded and worn out and showed signs of use and age. His hair was full of tiny little curls, different from other Egyptians, but he was not Nubian.

Gently, I said to him, "Look at me."

Hapuseneb jumped like a cat. It made me want to laugh. He came close to me and whispered, "Lotus of Egypt, you cannot do that."

In a low voice between my teeth, I said, "Yes! I can."

By this time, the peasant was looking directly into my eyes with admiration. He looked to be no more than seventeen summers.

He did not expect to see a little girl turned into a young woman more beautiful than anyone he had ever seen before, who radiated like Ra, who had grown and was no longer the little girl he saw for the first time in the gardens of the palace on the day she was crowned Little Horus of Egypt, carrying in her arms a little Basted, her cat.[19]

He was almost out of breath and was sweating fearfully.

His eyes were dark brown and looking at him moved me inside. Gently, I said, "This audience with your Prince is at the request of the Great Ineni, who is my father's architect. I will hear the petition as a favor to an old friend. What is your name, and what is it your heart desires?" I asked him softly.

He struggled to get his words out at first, but eventually, I heard his voice, as he held his hands clasped to his kilt.

"My name is Sen-Mut, Your Majesty. I come to request the opportunity to study architecture and become as great as the master, Ineni. This has been my only dream and desire since I was seven summers, when I came to Thebes for the first time and saw the greatest temples of Thebes in person. We were invited by the Great Ineni to join in the celebration for thee, upon the occasion of your becoming Little Horus. I would like very much to build for you the greatest temples in Egypt."

His voice was firm and soft, with a clear, sincere tone. I felt as though I could see through to his heart, a very clean heart. His heart, in fact, moved mine. This feeling, it was a strange one that I had never felt before.

"From what town do you come here?" I asked.

"From the farming town of Luny, Your Majesty," he replied.

"So, you crossed Hopi? How did you cross it?"

---

[19] Those were Sen-Mut's thoughts on that day, as per himself telling me later in life.

"I swam across Hopi, yesterday early in the morning, and walked three hours to get here. Then I slept under a tree and rose early this morning to be here Your Majesty."

His words amazed me. I was impressed by his accomplishments, and I saw in him a real desire to become an architect. How could I possibly say no? How could I not grant him his petition?

"Very well, Sen-Mut from Luny. I will give you this opportunity to become an architect, but first, you must learn how to be a priest and serve in the Temple of Amun-Ra. At the same time, you will learn to read and write, and with Ineni you will learn how to build. When the time comes, you must prove that you are worthy of my trust and my father's trust. So be it!" I decreed, and I smiled at him as I granted his wish.

"Scribe!" I shouted. Without looking at the scribe, I pointed at him without taking my eyes away from the peasant. I said, "Write that in three summers, Sen-Mut from the town of Luny must become first a priest and learn all the rituals and services in the Temple of Amun-Ra. He will learn all that Ineni will teach him about architecture. He must prove that he is worthy of my trust and of my father's trust. He will be faithful to Pharaoh, to me, and to my kingdom. So, let it be written, and let it be done."

"Guard take Sen-Mut from the town of Luny to the Temple of Amun-Ra. You must speak directly to the First Prophet of Amun, Khety, and give him this message: I Prince of Egypt, sending Sen-Mut from the town of Luny to him. He must teach him what he needs to become a priest in the Temple of Amun. Tell him that I said to teach him well and to provide him a separate room from the rest of the priests. He is to provide him with fine food, fine wine, clean linen, new kilts, robes, sandals, and a couch with a goose-down mattress. I don't want him sleeping on a mat on the floor. And he must pass the ritual of cleansing.

"Further, tell him that later he must come to the palace to speak with me after the chanting of the doors and when the last rays of Ra are gone. I will be waiting for him to have dinner with me and the Queen in the banquet hall. Be gone from me now," I said.

I saw the surprised face of the peasant, and I smiled at him.

"Sen-Mut, kneel before me."

Looking straight into my eyes, he said, "May I speak, Your Majesty?"

"Speak, peasant."

"I want to give thee thanks for treating this poor peasant with such kindness. I am deeply in your debt for the rest of my life, and from now on, my life and heart belong to thee!" Then he bowed his head to the floor.

His words warmed my heart, and I smiled at him again. Softly, I said, "You may go now."

He bowed his head again and walked away without turning his back to me, and I saw the double doors closing in front of him. He left me with a warm feeling inside of my heart.

Hapuseneb and I started to leave the hall of audience. I was ready to break into a laugh when he said, "Lotus of Egypt!" I could see anger on his face, he was flush, and he was almost shouting at me.

"What was that all about? You were just about to invite him to sleep in the palace. Not even when I was about to become a priest was I given such special treatment. Especially not a room of my own. And on top of that, a goose-down mattress." He was moving his arms up and down. "And I did not like the way he looked at you!" he said.

By then I was laughing hard at him. "But you were never a peasant, nor swam across the Nile, nor walked for three hours under the hot sun just to have an audience without any certainty that your wish would be granted. Your family have always been well off and served my father. Your father has been the cantor and the special scribe for my father since you crossed the blue sea from that island far away. We grew up together in the palace" I said and continued to laugh, remembering the way he jumped like my cat in the hall of audience.

"What's so funny?" he asked.

I stopped walking because I was laughing so hard.

"It's the way you jumped in the hall of audience, as if someone had bitten your tail. The hair on the back of your neck stood up, like the hackles rising on Basted, my cat." By then, I was really howling with laughter. "The only thing missing from you was the meow. Ha, ha, ha!"

"So, you think this is funny?" He was flush with anger. "Look at what you just did, telling a peasant to look at you, and even worse, to look in to your eyes. I've never seen that before in all of the audiences I have attended with your father," he said, getting even angrier at me.

I continued walking, and with a firm voice, I said, "Well, I am Horus, and I can do whatever I wish!"

"Well then, send T'Queta to my quarters to bathe me and to make me a very happy man today!" he shouted at me.

Biting my tongue, I became angry. I was not laughing now. With a sharp tongue, I said, "She is not ready to have a mate yet! But if you want her for a wife, I will give her to you."

He became silent and stopped. He turned around to face me. Gently, he held me by my shoulders, and softly said, "Lotus of Egypt, you know that my heart only belongs to you. Always."

He was so close to me that I could smell his sweet breath, and I held my breath, closing my eyes, waiting for him to press his lips on mine. He hesitated for a second, and I barely opened my right eye and saw far behind him Khety walking towards Ineni's office. "I bet he is going to talk to Ineni about the peasant," I thought.

I opened my eyes and took a deep breath and sighed, "Very well. Don't you ever forget that. But you know the laws of the palace. Otherwise, I would have given you my heart a long time ago." My words took him by surprise. "Now, do you wish to have lunch with me?" I smiled at him.

"No," he said. That took me by surprise.

"What's wrong? What did I do?" I asked him.

"Nothing, Lotus of Egypt." He shook his head. "I must go now," he said, and I could hear the sadness in his voice.

As he was leaving, I looked at him and said, "Then I will wait for you tonight in the banquet hall for dinner." I believe I was starting to fall in love with him.

He turned to face me and said, "We'll see." Then he walked away.

The banquet hall was in a separate building from the palace. It had the same tall pillars as the palace and could accommodate more than two thousand people because of the many guests the palace could hold.

After Hapu left, I walked to the sycamore tree and sat under its shade. It was getting hot. I clapped my hands, and T'Queta, came running.

"Bring me something fresh to drink and some fruit," I said then became lost in thought.

"Your Majesty?" she said.

"Oh, T'Queta, have you ever been in love?" I asked her.

She remained quiet.

"Speak!"

"Well, Your Majesty, in love? I don't know love. Yes, I like some of the boys here in the palace. But I don't know what love is. Some of the others in the palace talk about it. They talk about how love makes them happy, how they just want to be with the one they love. And how handsome the young priest, Hapuseneb, and His Majesty, the young

Aakheperen-Re, are. I hear them talking about love all the time when I am in the kitchen. They all talk about lovemaking. Some of them have been in the young men's beds more than once. I've heard they are very good in bed. Some of them have been called several times by them. Isis by the young Aakheperen-Re, others by Hapuseneb. Some of them dream of becoming the secondary wife of the young Aakheperen-Re, especially Isis. When she comes back from his bed, she acts like she is a peacock showing off because he has showered her with gifts. But Master Hapuseneb is different. The girls say that he is very kind, gentle, and likes to laugh a lot. But when he is having sex, it is like he is thinking of someone else," she said.

"Stop! I don't want to hear anymore." I looked at her and asked, "Do you like Master Hapuseneb?"

She was startled by my question and became quiet.

"Speak! Nothing is going to happen to you," I told her.

"Who wouldn't, Your Majesty, with those beautiful gray eyes and his wavy black hair?"

She was making me uneasy, and I did not like her answer. "Go! Bring me some fruit, something to eat and drink."

She turned around and ran to the kitchen.

I sat there thinking and noticed that there was no breeze blowing. It seemed as if everything was at a standstill, and silence covered the land. The horn sounded to announce the middle of the day, shaking me out of my reverie.

"Oh, Neferu-Knib, why did you have to kill yourself and condemn me to a life without love? Now, I understand when on your twelfth summer you told me that you did not want to be betrothed to Aakheperen-Re." I felt a flash of memories from the past come rushing toward me. I remembered how happy she looked when she was around Hapuseneb. I just realized she was in love with him, even though she was young. That is why she killed herself. Oh, my god. She was… Beloved sister, why did you have to do that? Tears were pouring down my face. "I miss you so much, dear sister. I have no friends to talk to."

T'Queta came with the tray in her hands. She was preparing to give me my food and handed me the fruit juice.

"Remember that you must taste it first," I said.

"Yes, Your Majesty." And she did.

"Do you remember Neferu-Knib?" I asked.

"Yes, Your Majesty, of course. Who wouldn't remember? It's been only five summers since she went to the underworld."

"Have you heard any gossip in the kitchen about why she did it?"

She became silent, and, looking at me, she said, "Well, Your Majesty, the rumors are that three days before she killed herself, they saw her walking beside the Nile with Master Hapuseneb. Afterward, when she was alone in her quarters and believed her wet nurse and her servants had fallen asleep, she cried herself to sleep."

"What else?"

T'Queta became silent.

"Speak!"

"The rumors are that she killed herself because she was in love with Master Hapuseneb, and she did not want to marry Master Aakheperen-Re."

I became more melancholy thinking about it. "Does Mother know this?"

"I don't believe so," she said.

“Speak of this to no one!” I demanded.

“Yes, Your Majesty.”

I sat there under the sycamore tree for hours thinking that I could not blame him or make him feel guilty for Neferu-Knib’s actions. Tears were pouring down my face, thinking that she probably died because of me. I could feel it inside of me. Then the wind started to blow, and I heard voices in the wind.

“You cannot feel guilty for things that were written before you were born,” they said. Hearing what the voices in the wind were telling me, I felt at ease, and I finished eating.

I thought that I had better talk to Ineni about the peasant, so I hurriedly walked to his house. Master Ineni was sitting under a large sycamore tree in his garden. He was a tall, older man, with a stocky build and strong-looking features, but a pleasant personality. He was wearing a white kilt and leather sandals and was looking at his large pond in front of him. The white edges of the pond made it beautiful with the colorful lotuses floating in the water. At his far right were the slow currents of Hopi, and the orange rays of Amun-Ra were starting to fade away.

“Maatke-Re, in fifteen days it will be your fifteen summers, and you will become a full-grown woman. I have been watching you bloom since you were a little child, and you have become more beautiful than any of us could have imagined. The gods have fashioned you. Today, you have a different look in your eyes and a radiant look on your face,” he said with a smile.

“I thank you, Great Ineni. You must come to my celebration. I came to talk to you about the peasant whom I had the audience with this morning. Sen-Mut, I believe, is his name. Pharaoh said to me that the audience was for you, as a favor to a good friend. The peasant pleases me, the way he talks with sincerity of the heart, and I can tell that he really wants to become a great architect and builder like you. Are you willing to teach him everything so that he will become as great as you are, so that in the future when you are gone, he will build for me?" I asked.

"Yes, I will teach him all about architecture, how to make plans and build. I will be happy to teach him all that I know for him to be as great as I am. I am growing old. I built for your grandfather, Amon-Hotep I, for your father, Thutmoses the Great Maat. I have served many good years in the service of the royal house."

"Yes, indeed. You have served my family very well. My father is grateful for your service and holds your friendship in high esteem. Very well. I will talk to the High Priest Khety tonight during dinner. I have already given him orders to teach the boy how to serve in the house of Amun-Ra, and he will reside there until he becomes a priest. I ordered Khety to provide him with new kilts, linen, a bed, plenty of food and wine, and a room for himself. He will learn with the priests in the temple, and in six month I will determine if he is worthy of my trust before he can become an architect for the house of Horus. My wisdom tells me that he will be worthy of my trust," I said and smiled.

"Send a message to your childhood friend. Tell him that his son has been accepted in the house of Horus. And send a very large basket full of many fine delights, wines, beer, geese, and sweet breads made with dates or raisins, my favorite, for his whole family to enjoy and celebrate the good news," I said.

"Khety has already informed me of the goods you have ordered for Sen-Mut, and he said that Sen-Mut is very happy because he has never had so many nice possessions and that you are the most beautiful Horus he's ever seen," Ineni said.

I smiled. "Sweet," I said. "Ineni, you can begin his lessons, and when will you start?"

"Tomorrow, after he finishes incensing the temple, He must learn how to read and write first." He replied.

As I was leaving, I said with a smile, "Very well, Ineni. Teach him well, and I will be waiting for you tonight at dinner." Then I turned around to leave.

Before I could leave, though, I heard him say, "Maatke-Re, did the floor move under your feet this morning?"

I turned around, looked straight into his eyes, and smiled.

"You, old crocodile!" I said and laughed.

I could hear him laughing as I was walked away. I stopped, turned around, and said, "You must bring your new pupil to dine with us tonight. I want Mother to meet him and to give me her opinion about him and let me know if I've made the right decision."

He smiled and started to laugh out loud. I took off my golden sandals and walked barefoot towards the palace. I loved to feel the soft, cool green grass under my feet.

On the other side of the Temple of Amun-Ra, a room was given to Sen-Mut that day. As he was getting ready to eat, Puyem-Re, the Second Prophet of the Temple of Amun, walked in and yelled, "No, you must be bathed before eating, as Her Majesty ordered."

"But I am so hungry, very well, I will run to the Nile to bathe myself."

"The Nile?" Puyem-Re asked "No, child. You come with me. You will be bathed well in a large pool and shaved by palace slaves."

"Ah? Palace girls bathing me?"

"Yes, and your body will be shaved completely."

"What?! All of it?"

“Yes, as all the priests must be very well shaved and clean when we enter the presence of the Highest in the Temple of Amun-Ra. Now, follow me to the bathing pool,” Puyem-Re said.

Then he followed Puyem-Re and discovered a wonderful place to bathe. It was a very large rectangular pool that could hold hundreds of priests, with large, tall pillars around it. The burning incense spread a beautiful scent that he had never experienced before. He was impressed, as he had never seen a pool before. He had only bathed in the waters of the Nile. He was amazed. There were steps going down at the edge of each side of the pool, and the water was warm and appealing. Three slaves entered, carrying several baskets in their arms. One carried thick, white linens, the second carried toiletry bottles and strings, and the third carried aromatic oils, brought from far-away lands, to smooth his skin.

They set their baskets on a small table at the edge of the pool and started to unroll the thick, white linens beside the pool and spread out all the oil jars and fragrances.

One came closer, looked at him, and started to giggle. Then the rest of them joined in, and they started to remove his old kilt. They noticed that he was circumcised. They guided him into the warm waters of the pool. He never had experienced warm water on his skin before, and he loved it. The women poured water over him and over his hair and began to wash him with soap, scrubbing every part of him well. They looked for signs of infestation of lice in his hair, genitals, and pubic area. Once they had ascertained that he didn’t have any, they scrubbed his skin well, even his feet. When they were finished, he was too embarrassed to leave the pool because brushes against the women’s breasts had caused him to become arouse.

The slaves were giggling at him. Puyem-Re was laughing, too, and said, “Don't worry. They have seen many priests aroused before, so don’t be embarrassed. They are also well-versed in the art of sex.”

Sen-Mut exited from the warm pool and lay on thick linen sheets beside the pool where they started to shave his body with strings, and honey wax, including his pubic area. Then they asked him to turn around so that they could look in the crack of his buttocks for any rashes. He was shocked and looked at Puyem-Re for guidance. He nodded.

Sen-Mut then thought to himself, "I must finish with this. It is for my own good." They finished examining his buttocks and went on to shave the rest of his body. He was told to sit down on a wooden chair. Once he had done so, they proceeded to check for lice again. Again, none were found. Next, they cut his hair, the tiny little curls falling on the floor. They rinsed him well, changed the linens, then laid him on the fresh linens. After this, they began to rub oil all over his body. The hands of the slaves caused him to become aroused again. Seeing it, the attendants started to giggle again. But by then, they were done. When they stepped back to observe their handiwork, they were astonished at the change. They were amazed at how handsome he was. No one would believe that he was the same young man who had entered the bathing pool.

Puyem-Re was pleased with the work that was done. He clapped his hands twice to indicate that the servants could leave.

"Sen-Mut, we must go to the temple now, and in thirty minutes, we must incense the doors of Pharaoh before the last rays of Ra fade away," he said.

"But I am very hungry right now," he said.

"Okay, let's go to your room, and you can eat something. But eat as fast as you can because after the chanting, we are invited to dinner at the palace by the young Horus. Invitations like this one aren't extended every day to priests other than Khety."

Sen-Mut's face registered surprise. He had never expected to be invited to the palace to dine with the goddess, the one whom he could not stop thinking about since that morning. His life was changing for the better, and he couldn't imagine how far he will go.[20]

I was approaching the palace when the breeze began to blow. I could see the long white linen curtains hanging from the tall pillars of the palace. They were moving with the wind. It had been a long day. I needed to bathe and wear a lot of fragrance.

When I entered my quarters, T'Queta was waiting for me as always.

"Prepare my bath, but this time I want lots of the sweet lotus fragrance in the water after my body is rinsed," I said.

"Yes, Your Majesty. Lots of lotus fragrance in the water," T'Queta said.

I sat down in a chair on my balcony and thought of the sweet peasant. I hope he does as well as Ineni, I thought. Maybe he'll be even greater than Ineni.

"Your Majesty, your bath is ready."

"Very well," I said.

I walked barefoot to the bath and stood there as T'Queta undressed me. The bathing room didn't have any incoming light from outside, only the light from my quarters and the large burning oil lamps that gave off just enough to make my surroundings clear. I stepped down to the large,

---

[20] Everything that transpired in the first bathing ritual of Sen-Mut, Puyem-Re, and the slaves...were told to me by Sen-Mut later in life, and how did he feel on that day. Also, Puyem-Re himself told me and T'Queta from the gossip of the kitchen.

square pool filled with fresh, cool water and floating rose petals. I sat down as T'Queta entered the pool and started washing my body.

The tub was large enough for four or five people and surrounded by wall paintings. In the past, I had never really paid any attention to them. Now, looking at the walls, I observed that they were painted a soft turquoise color and decorated with pictures of slaves carrying water jars on their shoulders and pouring them into a tub. The paintings were quite lovely, I thought.

The pool had rose petals floating on the water, and several girls were playing harps.

"Your Majesty, why are there not windows in the bathing rooms of the palace?" one of the slaves asked.

"So that when the sandstorms come, the sand will not enter the bathrooms as it does throughout the rest of the palace. It saves you and the other servants from having to clean and sweep the entire palace to remove the sand and the dust from the couches, clothing, and food. And our wigs," I said.

As T'Queta was washing my back, I thought of Hapuseneb. I hoped he was coming tonight for dinner. I decided to ask her, "Do you know if Hapuseneb is courting any ladies in the palace?"

"Well, Your Majesty, I've personally never seen him with anyone, but…"

"Speak!" I said.

"Well, he has been seen talking to Tepi."

I became silent. I found myself thinking that he belongs to me and he will never love anyone but me. I decided that tonight I would make him melt down with love for me. I stood up and said, "Very well. Rinse my body well, then rinse me again with the fragrance of the sweet lotus." I knew that was his favored fragrance on me.

Maybe T'Queta was wondering why I wanted lots of lotus perfume poured over me. It was the first time I had asked her to do that. Was she wondering if I was in love with Hapuseneb?

I stepped out of the tub and spread my arms as she started to dry my body.

"T'Queta, I will wear the pale-yellow sheath, the gold necklace that Mother gave me, the gold bracelet Father gave me, the gold sandals with turquoise gems, and the long, braided wig," I said.

"Yes, my lady."

"I will finally make my mother happy, wearing the sheath and a wig for the first time," I told her.

We walked into my quarters, and I saw the rays of Ra were fading away and that Mother Nut would soon cover the land, and Thoth the Moon soon would bathe us with its silver rays. The incensing of the golden doors would begin soon. I needed to hurry.

"Bring the pomegranate so that you can rouge my cheeks and my lips."

She brought the makeup case and started to outline my eyes with kohl. I could not remember the last time I wore kohl around my eyes. And I had never worn rouge on my cheeks and lips before. She placed the pale-yellow sheath over my head, and I turned to face her.

She fell to her knees, and with admiration on her face said, "Your Majesty, I have never seen thee so beautiful before. Her Majesty, the Queen, will be proud of thee tonight when she sees how lovely you look. You are the perfect goddess."

"You may rise, T'Queta. Your words are kind. Hurry, let's finish. Place the wig on my head," I said, and she did so.

I could hear the priests chanting outside the doors. I told her, "Let's kneel and face Amun-Ra. We must give thanks for the marvelous day we had today," I said, and we knelt. I waited for the chanting to stop, then walked to my mother's quarters. The guards looked at me with surprise on their faces, and I smiled. They opened Mother's golden doors, and I entered. Her slave was finishing the task of brushing her hair. I waited for her to finish. When her hair was done, she turned around, and with an expression of surprise on her face, she said, "Goddess Hathor! My Little Horus is now a beautiful woman." She opened her arms and said, "Come to me, my little precious Maatke-Re!"

I went into her arms, and she hugged me tightly. "I wish Pharaoh were here to see how beautiful you look tonight."

"Mother, this is how you always wanted to see me, and I thought I would give it a try today."

"Yes, you look precious!"

We left her quarters and walked to the banquet hall. A soft breeze was blowing the long white drapes that were hung high all around the long hallway of the banquet hall. The music was playing, and the court was seated in the hall. We stopped at the entrance and my mother's name was announced. "Ahmose, Queen of Egypt!"

Everyone grew silent when we walked in. All eyes were on me. I could see Ineni standing and talking to the High Priest Khety, and his jaw dropped when he saw me. No one had ever seen me wearing a sheath or dressed like this before. Everyone dropped to their knees in front of the Queen of Egypt, my mother. I searched for Hapuseneb, but I could not see him.

"He must come tonight. He must come tonight," I keep repeating to myself.

Mother had a big smile on her face. I was no longer the little girl wearing a boy's kilt. She clapped her hand and said, "I present you my most beautiful daughter, Maatke-Re." There was an explosion of applause. I smiled. I was happy. But I was still searching for Hapuseneb.

When I saw him standing in there looking gorgeous in his long white linen robe of a priest, adorned in gold thread, I smiled at him, and he came walking towards me. He knelt on one knee and saluted the Queen.

She said, "Rise, Hapuseneb, you are family."

"Thank you, my Queen."

I told the slave to call Ineni, Khety, and Puyem-Re to come. The three of them came and sat down facing us. The scent of lotus flowers was clearly intoxicating to Hapuseneb, who whispered in my ear, "I have never seen such a gorgeous lotus in the whole Egypt like you. Your scent has me intoxicated."

He was interrupted by Ineni. who said, "The Little Horus has grown. She is no longer the Little Horus, but a goddess and the most beautiful woman I have ever seen."

Khety raised his cup and said, "To the most kind and loving goddess in the whole of Egypt!"

Everyone raised their golden goblet, toasted, and drank. Mother was happy. I had never seen her so beautiful, wearing a sky-blue sheath and golden sandals. Mutnofret was smiling at me with a sweet smile. She had never seen me wearing the sheath before either. She had only known me to wear the kilt. She knew that I had always loved my big brother Aakheperen-Re and that he had taken care of me since I was born.

Mother interrupted my thoughts. She said, "Yes, she is! Let the dinner begin."

Then T'Queta came close to me and stood behind me, but this time Hapuseneb did not bother to look at her.

I noticed that she was distracted, looking for a long time at someone, and I looked in the direction of her gaze. There stood the future architect, the new pupil.

"Ineni, you brought the new pupil as I told you! I'm glad. I must bring him to Mother so that she can meet him," I said.

Hapuseneb's face registered shock, and he said, "You must send your servant girl to fetch him." I noticed irritation in his voice.

"I will go myself," and got up from my place. He trailed after me as we walked together to the end of the banquet hall. The whole time he was barking at me, but I ignored him.

I noticed the peasant had changed. He had bathed, and his hair was shorter. He looked very clean and was wearing the new white kilt and new sandals. He looked nothing like he looked this morning. He had changed completely. In fact, he was a very handsome man. I came closer to him and noticed he was a little taller than me. I also noticed his wide and strong chest and well-developed arms.

I became nervous, my stomach full of butterflies. I was even short of breath. What was happening to me? He threw himself at my feet.

"Rise, Sen-Mut from Luny," I told him.

But he had something he needed to tell me.

"Beautiful diadem of the universe, I am deeply grateful for your kind invitation to me, a poor peasant, and to meet the most important people in the kingdom and to dine with thee. You are a goddess with a kind and lovely heart."

I could hear Hapuseneb grinding his teeth as he was listening to Sen-Mut's words.

"Well, Sen-Mut from Luny, your words please me, and the Queen is waiting to meet you. First let me introduce you my dearest friend from childhood and a priest of the Temple of Amun-Ra, Hapuseneb. He will contribute to your teaching in the temple." Hapuseneb nodded, as he was looking at Sen-Mut.

"I hope the two of you become great friends. Shall we walk?" I said.

The look on Sen-Mut's face clearly said that he was amaze, as we walked among the banquet tables loaded with many kinds of foods, fruits, and flowers. It was clear that he had never seen something like this before. I wondered what was on his mind looking at so many oil lamps lighting the banquet hall, as if it was daytime. And seeing so many beautiful serving girls around. His hands were sweating, and I notice how he wiped his hands on his kilt. I also notice that the heat from his body was melting the fragrance of the corn wax on his head and the perfume was dripping down to his firm chest.

"Mother, let me introduce you to Sen-Mut from Luny, Ineni's new pupil and protégé."

Sen-Mut's eyes were cast down. He was not looking at my mother, and he prostrated himself on the floor.

My mother looked at Sen-Mut and me, then she said, "Rise, Sen-Mut, you are welcome in the palace. Whoever is a friend of Ineni is a friend of ours," she said with a smile.

I turned to him and said, "You must sit beside Ineni, Khety, and Puyem-Re." I walked to my place, and Hapuseneb sat beside me. I was facing Sen-Mut. For a moment. I thought about the look Mother gave me and Sen-Mut when I introduced him to her.

"T'Queta, bring wine and food for our guest," I said.

"Yes, Majesty," she said and walked fast as a gazelle. She came back and was pouring wine in his golden goblet and I noticed that she was smiling at him, and he was looking at her.

Then a whisper interrupted me. It was the voice of Hapuseneb. "Lotus of Egypt, after we dine, I would like to talk to you. Let's stroll beside Hopi tonight. It is a full moon tonight, and the night is fresh."

As he was whispering in my ear, the eyes of Sen-Mut were on me. I smiled at him. I noticed he was not eating much. I ignored Hapuseneb and said, "Aren't you hungry tonight?"

With a humble voice, he said, "No, Your Majesty. After the audience and with everything that has happened today, I find that I'm not hungry. I did have some food earlier in my room in a hurry. Everyone has been very generous to me, especially the First Prophet of Amun Khety and the Second Prophet Puyem-Re."

Mother was looking at him, interested in the way he expressed himself. Then she directed another question to Ineni, Khety, and Puyem-Re because she had noticed my interest in the young man.

"Ineni, how long will it take for Sen-Mut to become an architect?" Mother asked.

"Well, Your Majesty, almost three summers, as well as the time it takes to learn to read and write. And the study involved to assume the duties of becoming a priest for Amun-Ra. He must work very hard to become a priest and an architect. I know that since he was very young, he has wanted to become an architect," he replied.

I turned to my mother. "Mother, do you know the small town of Luny, across Hopi? Well, he swam across and walked three hours in the hot desert, barefoot under the heat of Ra just to be heard in the audience this morning. I find it courageous and admirable to try to accomplish his dreams, and I believe that he deserves this opportunity."

"Yes, beloved one, he deserves this opportunity. You are showing good wisdom," she said nodding her head. "You did well," she continued and patted my left hand. Looking at Sen-Mut, she said, "Have you ever come to visit Ineni before?"

"Yes, I have, Your Majesty, once. It was my first time visiting Thebes, and I saw for the first time the great temples that Ineni had built. Since then, I have had the desire to become an architect. I was seven summers then, when Ineni invited us to come for the celebration of the Little Horus. I was very impressed when my father told me of her bravery. Ineni was kind to my family and to me, and I am thankful for the invitation. We were in the beautiful palace garden for a moment. It was my first time here. I saw the Little Horus carrying a little Basted in her arms."

I interrupted him. "I remember you. You were with your family, with your brothers and sisters. You were standing in the outer courtyard of the palace. And then I ran to get little the Basted's. I wanted to give you, and your brothers and sisters a little one because I had plenty of the little ones. As I was putting the cats in the basket, I sent Sitre-In to get a basket with some sweet cakes, fruit, and my favorite drink to give you, but upon my return, you and your family were gone."

Khety was listening to and observing us talking. "Is he the one her destiny will unfold with?" Khety thought. He was remembering the words of the Oracle when I was born.[21]

Ineni was observing both of us as we were speaking, with a half-smile on his face.

"She did not find you on her return, then she spoke to me, wondering if you and your family were coming back. I didn't believe so, so she ordered me to send all those goods to your home in Luny," Ineni, said.

---

[21] Khety, told me what he was thinking on that moment later in life.

"We did receive all those goods and the little Basted's. We were so grateful, and I thank you, Your Majesty," Sen-Mut said with a smile.

Suddenly with a smile on his face, Hapuseneb asked, "Sen-Mut, how did you like the bathing this morning?"

I saw the expression on Sen-Mut's face, which said it all. Everyone laughed very hard. I felt embarrassed for him. Seeing the blush on his face, I refrained from laughing, but Mother didn't. She was laughing like the rest of them. Everyone knew the regimen of bathing and shaving and the search for lice on the body in the pubic hair and in the hiding places.

For the rest of the night, the hours passed very quickly. Everyone had a good time, but then it was time to retire for the night. Mother rose, and as she did, everyone else did as well.

"It's time for me to retire. It was a lovely evening. Please stay, all of you, and enjoy yourselves." She said.

"We must leave as well, as we start early tomorrow morning with the lessons for Sen-Mut," Khety said. "He will be starting his reading and writing lessons with his teachers, who will be waiting for him after the first priestly lesson."

"I will be in the temple to guide you and help you in the service of Amun-Ra, Sen-Mut," Hapuseneb told him with a smile on his face.

Sen-Mut smiled back at him. He turned his eyes to me and knelt on one knee. Lowering his head, he said, "I am deeply grateful to thee, Goddess of Egypt for your kindness and this lovely opportunity, for opening the doors of the palace to me. From now on, thou will always be in my prayers."

The look on his face was as if he wanted to say something more. That he would hold me in his heart, I wondered? He rose and bowed his head to me and to my mother. Why is it that my stomach was full of butterflies all night long when I look and talked to him? He made me nervous.

I smiled at him and said good night, and my mother and I turned around and left. As we were leaving, I heard Ineni, Khety, Puyem-Re, and Sen-Mut leaving. I turned around to look at Sen-Mut, but he was fading away into the darkness.

"Lotus of Egypt! Lotus of Egypt!" Hapuseneb called to me.

I turned around and faced him with a smile. He looked gorgeous tonight, and maybe he will kiss me, I thought. It would be my first kiss.

"Very well. Let's stroll beside Hopi. Maybe Mother Nut and Thoth will bathe us with their rays tonight." I said.

We started to walk when I noticed that the guard was following us. "Stop!" I shouted. "Go. You are not to follow us tonight." The guard turned around and left.

"Hapuseneb, I see you every night strolling beside Hopi."

"Yes, I do. I walk every night just to see you sitting on your balcony," he said with a smile.

We continued to stroll quietly beside the Nile under the silver rays of Thoth. His rays were pouring on us, and the night was clear. The stars were very bright, and they look so closely, and I felt that I could reach up and touch them.

"Lotus of Egypt, we did not finish our conversation from this morning. You hurt me deeply. I could not continue talking because I remembered Neferu-Bity and how much she was hurt by your parents on the day she was betrothed to Aakheperen-Re. And This morning, I remembered the day when she committed suicide. I have felt remorseful since then because…" I covered his lips with my fingers.

He shook his head gently. "No, I must finish. Three days before she died, I strolled with her beside the Nile, and she said she didn't want to marry Aakheperen-Re because she was in love with someone else. She asked me if I was in love with someone, and I said yes. She became silent and smiled. Then she asked me whom I was in love with. Then I said with Lotus of Egypt, and her face fell and became blank. She lowered her eyes and became quiet again as though she didn't know what to say. She finally said that she had to go to her quarters and had some tears in her eyes. In that moment, I just realized that she was in love with me. She ran so quickly away."

As he was speaking, he had tears in his eyes. I wanted him to stop, but he shook his head several times.

"I wanted to run after her to apologize for not noticing her feelings for me, but she ran so quickly that she got away from me. I stood there not knowing what to do. This morning you reminded me that you will face a similar fate. And then what? What will become of the love I have for you, love that I've had for a long time?"

I could see a tear rolling down his face.

"Oh. So that was the reason you kept yourself away from me and the palace for those three weeks after she died?" I asked.

"Yes!" he said.

He had poured his heart out to me, and now I was facing reality. He was right! I was possibly facing the same fate as Neferu-Knib. Thoth was shining on his face, and I could clearly see the tears rolling down. His face was very close to mine. I wanted so badly for him to hold me in his arms and kiss me so that I could make him feel better. I could see his lips coming close to mine, and I closed my eyes and took a deep breath.

"Your Majesty!" A yell came from behind him. We were startled. It came from a guard who was riding a horse and stopped in front of us. "Your Majesty, the Queen has been taken ill!"

I hadn't noticed how far Hapuseneb and I had walked. We were a long way from the palace.

"Get down from the horse!" I yelled at the guard, and he did and knelt before me. I stepped onto his right knee and jumped on the horse's back. "Hapuseneb, jump!" I exclaimed. He jumped behind me, and we rode to the palace as fast as we could.

I was worried about my mother.

The guards were waiting for me and knelt as the horse stopped in front of them. One guard knelt to help us off the horse. Hapuseneb stepped on the guard's knee and dismounted, then pulled me by the waist to help me to the ground. I ran across the palace gardens, and he trailed behind me.

I took large steps up the stairs and sprinted to Mother's quarters. After the guard opened the doors, I walked as fast as I could to reach my mother's couch. The physician Puyem-Re was there sitting beside her, and I knelt beside her and held her hand, observing that it was colder than usual.

With a soft voice, I said, "Mother."

She opened her eyes, looked at me, and smiled, and with her gentle voice, said, "Beloved one, don't worry. I've just had too much excitement tonight, and I laughed more than usual. And if I'm being honest, I had a little too much wine, too."

I looked at Puyem-Re, and he gave me a half smile. He said, "Too much excitement for one night. I just gave her a sleeping potion that will make her sleep for the rest of the night. She will be fine tomorrow."

"Why is it that I don't believe him?" I thought.

He looked directly into my eyes and said, "She must rest."

"I will stay with her all night," I said. Then I looked at Hapuseneb. He nodded his head and said he would stay as well.

"I will be in the next room in case she needs me," Puyem-Re said and walked away. He walked to the room in her quarters for physicians.

I was still kneeling beside her and holding her hands. Then looking into my eyes as if she could read what I held in my heart, she said, "I must speak to you alone."

I looked at Hapu. He nodded his head and said, "I will be outside of the golden doors if you need me," and he left.

"Beloved one, I want to talk to you about your feelings. Whatever we discuss, it will remain between us. Is that understood?"

"Yes, Mother," I said.

"I saw the look in your eyes tonight. They had a special brightness when you were speaking to Sen-Mut. Did he move your heart? Were you nervous anytime you were near him tonight?"

"Yes, Mother, ever since this morning in the audience hall when I first saw his face. He was very dirty, his body covered in sand from the desert. He stood there humbly. He looked hungry. I did not know what was happening to me. My heart moved, and my stomach felt as if I had butterflies inside of it. I still don't know what's happening to me because the same butterflies came back tonight when I saw him and when we were speaking. Mother, one thing I am sure of is that I am in love with Hapuseneb!"

"Well, beloved one, I can assure you that you are not in love with Hapuseneb. The feelings that you had this morning with Sen-Mut, that is love that you are starting to feel. Love is a feeling we cannot fight against, I can tell you that." She became quiet, and I saw sadness in her eyes, as if she were remembering someone. "And we don't get to choose happiness as the peasants do, and as some of the people of the court do," she said.

Her eyes began to close. The medications were beginning to have their effects on her, and she was fighting to keep her eyes open. But she wasn't finished. She continued, "I know you believe you are in love with Hapuseneb now, but I am sure you are not. You are entering an age of discovery, and you want to know what it feels like to be kissed, what it feels like to have sex like everyone else. You've heard about these topics all your life in the palace."

She was right, of course. She didn't speak further and contented herself with holding my hand. In fact, she had fallen asleep. I looked at Tuyii, her slave, and thanked her for her fast thinking. I removed my golden earrings and gave them to her, letting her know that I was grateful.

The next thing I knew, the rays of Ra were shining outside and on my face. I opened my eyes. Apparently, I had fallen asleep beside my mother, holding her hand. I moved slowly, and she opened her eyes.

"Mother, how are you feeling?" I asked.

"A little tired. It must be the medication. Did you sleep here all night?"

"Yes, Mother."

I looked for Tuyii. When I spotted her, I told her, "Go for the physician." She ran to the physician's room to summon Puyem-Re, and he came right away, as did Hapuseneb. I looked at him and thought how sweet it was of him to keep watch all night outside the golden doors.

"Hapuseneb, did you stay all night outside of my doors?" Mother asked him.

"Yes, Your Majesty."

"How kind of you. I'm fine now. Both of you must go and rest," she said.

"Mother, I am not leaving you, not until the physician tells me that you are going to be alright."

The chanting started, and all of us except my mother knelt, and we began to offer prayers to Amun-Ra. Then Puyem-Re started to chant the incantation chants for Mother to get her strength back. After we were done, Hapuseneb and Puyem-Re left to go to the temple to get some sleep. I kissed my mother and walked to my quarters. Once I was there, T'Queta undressed me, and I was bathed before I lay down on my bed. I was tired, but my mother's words about Hapuseneb kept repeating themselves in my mind. It took me a while, but eventually I fell asleep.

Later that day, when Ra was pouring his hot rays over the land, I woke up sweating and hungry. I lay there thinking about Mother's words. Then thoughts of the peasant came rushing back to me.

"Why is it that only thinking of the peasant give me butterflies in my stomach and not the thoughts of Hapuseneb? Is Mother right that I am starting to fall in love with someone else?"

I looked at T'Queta who was sitting on her couch waiting for me to call her. I could see she had already prepared my breakfast of fruit and duck. "Mother!" I thought.

Aloud, I said, "T'Queta, have you heard how my mother is this morning?"

"Yes, I saw her this morning in her garden as usual, laughing with Tuyii, and she looks well," she said.

"Have you heard anything from the Temple of Amun-Ra about the new future architect?"

"Yes, Your Majesty." She started to giggle.

"What are you giggling about? Speak!"

"This morning when I went to the kitchen to prepare your breakfast, the rumors were all about the new future priest, and all the girls were talking about his first bath," she said.

I smiled but hid it from her. "What about his bath?" I asked.

"They talked about how well-built he was. His chest and shoulders are very strong, and when they were bathing his body and washing his chest, it felt like they were washing a hard piece of rock. They became aroused as they were washing his chest, and he did, too. They also noticed that he was circumcised, that his legs were firm and strong, and that he did not have any lice. As they were shaving him, they observed that he is a very clean man, has no skin diseases. And they noticed that he is well-endowed. They could also tell that he is tremendously strong. They realized that they had never bathed a body like his before, and they were wondering which of them he would bed first," she said and started to laugh.

"Do you like him?" I asked, watching her closely. She didn't hesitate to answer.

"Oh! Yes, who would not like him? Handsome, golden tan, and with a glorious body! He's also free to choose whom he wants to take for a wife or to take to his bed."

I did not like what she was saying or her tone of voice. It was as if she was rubbing it, that I was doomed and had to settle for a life without love.

Then the thought of him came back to me and the way she had described him. A rush of hot flashes invaded me, and so did sadness, because love was not for me. I took a deep breath, got up from the bed and went to the bathroom to take care of my daily body necessities and then bathed.

After, I went to breakfast and sat down at the table. I was lost in thought when I heard the voice of T'Queta.

"Your Majesty, are thee wearing a sheath today?" she asked.

"No, I will wear the kilt as always," I said, and I thought, "Why should I wear a sheath today, there's no point for me to try to impress anyone."

"As you wish," she said. She dressed me with the white kilt and the golden belt and leather sandals, then I went to Mother's quarters. Mother was eating her lunch as I walked in.

"Mother, I heard that you are feeling much better this morning, and that you were in the garden laughing, and that makes me very happy. Please, Mother, don't get sick again. You scared me last night, and everyone else, too. I sent word to Father last night," I said with a firm voice.

"But he just left yesterday morning. Now he will cut his hunting trip short because of me," she replied.

"Now that I know that you are better, I will send Father another message telling him so. Maybe this message will reach him in time to continue his hunting trip with Aakheperen-Re, has the physician been here this morning to see you again?"

"Yes, Puyem-Re left not too long ago after the chanting and prayers for the sick," she replied.

Softly, I kissed her on the forehead. "I must go now, Mother. I am going to the temple to make offerings for your wellbeing."

"Are you sure that is the only reason you are going to the temple?" she asked with a smile.

"Yes, Mother, that is the only reason I am going to the temple."

I was trying to convince myself that it was the only reason I was going there. I walked across the inner and outer garden, and everything looked incredibly beautiful. I picked some white flowers from Mother's garden, and I had a sense of happiness in my chest. I walked quickly to reach the temple, hoping to catch a glimpse of the future architect.

I could feel the heat of Ra. He had heated the land in a hurry. I walked past the sacred lake and finally entered the Hall of Halls, walking towards the inner shrine of Amun-Ra. I noticed for the first time, the height of the pylons that lined the hallways as I was walking the path to Amun's shrine. It was as if I had never seen it before. I saw the High Priest Khety crossing the temple yards in the same direction. He saw me, bowed his head, and increased his pace to meet me.

"Your Majesty, how is the Queen this morning? We heard that she became ill late last night." He said.

"She is much better this morning. Puyem-Re believes she had too much excitement last night and too much wine. We did, after all, have a very good time." I smiled. I wanted to ask about the peasant, but I held my tongue.

At the other end of the temple, Sen-Mut was returning from his first reading and writing lesson, when he saw me talking to Khety. His heart started to beat rapidly, and his hands started to sweat. He was very nervous and left in a hurry, wondering why I was making him feel in that way.[22]

"Your Majesty, would you like to enter the shrine and make an offering to Amun?" Khety asked.

"Yes, I would." I said.

We walked together, and he opened the double doors of the inner shrine, closing them behind me. He sent two guards to guard the double doors. I was standing in front of the golden statue of Amun-Ra. I knelt, bowing my head to the floor. I looked at him for a while with love and in silence.

I began my prayer. "Oh, Great God, God of all gods, I come to you to make this offering for the wellbeing of my mother Ahmose, the

---

[22] Sen-Mut later in life he told me how nervous he was and how his heart was beating rapidly was when he saw me in the temple talking to Khety.

great Queen and the great mother of mine. She became ill last night, and I beg of thee, please! Let her be well, that she will be with me until she is very old, like Sitre-In my wet nurse, who has been with me since I was born. I offer you my life in exchange for the life of my mother. See, there is not purpose in my life any longer, and I am condemned to live a life without love. I will never be able to love someone or feel the love of a man or his warm kisses, or his warm arms around me."

As I was speaking, I thought of Sen-Mut.

"Will you condemn me to a life without love? I, your daughter? The one you fashioned in my father body?"

I was imploring with all my heart, and I threw myself on the floor with my arms open, tears pouring down my face.

"Why did you allow Neferu-Bity to die? Why can't we be as happy as other people? Mother had to sacrifice her love for our royal lineage. It is not fair. It is not fair. I don't want this life. I want to be able to feel love, to fall in love," I said.

Suddenly, peace invaded me. It was the same feeling I had when I was five summers and had to pass the test of foresight, and when Father thought that there was going to be war.

"You spoke to my heart, my beloved God. You have heard my plea. Now I can walk away with peace in my heart."

I remained where I was, lying on the floor and conversing with God for I don't know how long. Slowly I rose, and I walked backward without turning my back to the God of gods.

"Open!" I yelled, and the doors were opened.

To my surprise, Sen-Mut was standing right in front of me. We looked at each other and I held my breath, a rush of butterflies invaded my stomach. He was startled. He evidently did not expect for me to be here, for it was dark and late. He apparently believed that I was gone by this time. He was waiting to enter with Hapuseneb, Khety, Puyem-Re, and several other priests to make offerings.

He knelt and bowed his head to the floor.

"Rise!" I said quickly. He arose and nodded his head, saying "Your Majesty."

I walked past him and walked away as fast as I could, holding my breath. I did not want him to notice that he made me nervous. But Khety did notice. "Is he the one in her future?" he wondered again.

Sen-Mut was standing there still looking at me, as I faded away into the darkness with the moonlight shining over me. I rushed to the palace where Mother and T'Queta were waiting for me in the banquet hall. I had not bathed for dinner.

"Mother, I am so sorry. I didn't notice the time, as I was conversing with God Almighty in the shrine all this time. And time had gone by fast, and when I came out it was dark already."

"Did you make your offerings with your heart in it," she asked me.

"Yes, Mother! I did!"

"Then I hope all your wishes will be granted," she responded.

"I really hope so, Mother. Will you excuse me? I must bathe. T'Queta let's go and prepare my bath."

We went to my quarters, and when I entered. My beautiful Basted, Mont-It, was waiting for me. She came to me purring and rubbed herself back and forth on my legs. She was happy to see me, as was Kuma, my great friend the mongoose, and his female companion. If he killed any cobras inside my room, the guards and all their families would be killed, including T'Queta. I thought.

T'Queta finished bathing me, and she dried me fast because Mother was waiting for me. It was likely that Sen-Mut would be invited tonight by Khety or Ineni, and my heart was pounding thinking about it. I rushed out of the doors and hurriedly descended the flight of stairs, hoping that he would be there. I got to the banquet hall and searched for him, but he was not around. I did see Hapuseneb walking towards me. Also present were Khety and Puyem-Re, but not Sen-Mut. I sent T'Queta to invite them to dine with us at our table.

Hapuseneb knelt for my mother. "Your Majesty, how are the feeling tonight?"

As he rose, my mother answered, "Very well, Hapuseneb, and thank you for your company last night and for standing guard all night outside the doors for your Flower of Egypt." She smiled at him. And he gave her a big smile.

He came and sat down beside me, as always on my right. He looked at T'Queta as she ran to get the dishes. He had that same grin on his face as the last time. I was already eating my favorite duck with sweet molasses.

"Lotus of Egypt, what was that at the Temple of Amun-Ra tonight? You did not even look at me at all. And you took off so fast without turning back. I could only see the look on Sen-Mut's face. He clearly was startled as he watched you walking away fast as a gazelle."

I took a sip of wine and chose my words carefully.

"I hadn't noticed how much time had passed, when I was in the temple, and when I came out it was already dark. I had to rush to be bathed for dinner and mother was waiting for me. I really didn't have the time to talk to anyone." There. I had said it, plain and simple.

He noticed a different tone in my voice, but before he could say anything more, Khety and Puyem-Re were almost at our table, so he kept his thoughts to himself.

I saw Ineni walking across the garden by himself, and my heart sank. He approached us and nodded to my mother. She offered him a place to sit in front of her. Mother knew that I could not ask about the peasant, so she did.

"Ineni, how is the new pupil, Sen-Mut? How did he do on his first day of learning?"

"It went very well. His first lesson was very early this morning after he did the chanting at the doors. He has started to learn the letters and symbols to prepare him for the reading lessons. Those lessons will be followed by lessons on numbers. He seems anxious to learn everything, and I will introduce him to arithmetic soon," Ineni said.

"Why didn't you bring him tonight?" she asked.

"He has a lot to study for tomorrow morning, and he must absorb everything as quickly as he can. I left him in my office tonight." He said, then looked at me. "It's better for him, because it is cooler in there than in his room, and he will probably be studying until late tonight trying to learn the symbols."

"Thanks, Mother," I thought.

There was no breeze, and the night had not cooled off at all. I was so glad that there were no mosquitoes. The smoke of the burning wood had kept them away.

"How did the peasant do on his first day in the temple?" I asked Khety.

Khety looked straight into my eyes and said, "As it always is in the beginning. It's confusing, but I am sure he will do well. It all depends on him now," he said.

I wondered why I felt silence everywhere. I wanted to get up and leave my place, but I knew I had to remain there since Mother had not finished eating.

“Lotus of Egypt, tonight I notice that you have hardly eaten anything. Are you okay?” Hapuseneb asked.

“Yes, I am fine. it’s hard for me to eat anything other than fruit when it’s this hot. Though eating fruit does refresh me.” I said.

“Would you like to walk tonight beside Hopi?" Hapu asked me.

But Ineni broke the mood. “Well, I believe that in this time of the night, the mosquitoes are in abundance beside Hopi,” he said.

“You’re right, Ineni. I hate mosquito bites,” I said.

It had been only a few hours since I saw the peasant. Thoth was still bathing the night in its silver rays. I wondered if he would come before too long.

“It’s late, and I must rest,” Mother said as she stood up. Everybody dropped to their knees.

She kissed my forehead as she walked off. “Rest, beloved one,” she said. Everyone roses after she walked off.

“I will also retire for the night,” I said. “Hapuseneb, after your lack of sleep last night, you should retire, too,” I told him. “May Amun-Ra keep you all well,” I said and walked off.

I was hoping that I could sleep tonight in the heat. I went up the stairs. T’Queta got up, and we walked without a word to the bath. She wiped my body with fresh water. I lay on my soft goose feather mattress, and she closed the white net around my bed to protect me from the mosquitoes.

I lay there for a while trying to sleep, but I could not. I got up from the bed and walked to my balcony trying to get relief from a breeze, but there was none. An impulse drove me to put on a long white sheath and walk to the sacred Lake of Mut. There was still a full moon, and the night was full of stars. It was a beautiful walk to the sacred lake of Mut but stifling without a breeze.

I took off my sheath and got into the fresh waters of the sacred lake. It was cool and refreshing to my body and it felt good. Father came here sometimes when it was this hot, he told me secretly. I started to swim when I noticed the shadow of a man behind a pillar of the shrine of Mut.

"Who is there?" I shouted. "Show your face right now, or I will call the guards, and you will be put to death! How long have you been standing there? Show yourself?" I shouted again.

A voice came from the darkness, then a figure walked slowly towards me as the rays of Thoth shined on him.

"I am Sen-Mut, the peasant from Luny, Your Majesty," and knelt.

I froze! I never thought that he would be here. My stomach started to have butterflies again, and for the first time, I felt embarrassed of my naked body.

"Rise! And turn around until I get dressed!" I told him. And he did so.

I got out of the sacred pool quickly and got dressed right away.

"Come here," I told him. He was on the other side of the pool, and I saw him walking around the sacred pool with his eyes cast down. Then he came closer to me. I was so nervous that I could barely breathe. I could see how much he had changed. He was well-groomed as he was last night. He was wearing his new kilt and sandals, and that pleased me. He looked better tonight under the rays of Thoth, then he did the night before.

Sweetly, I told him to look at me. His eyes traveled all over my wet body under the sheath. Then we were close to each other, about two feet apart, and I was trembling. I could see the way he looked at me. I noticed that he was sweating, and his hands were shaking.

"How long have you been standing there?" I asked him softly.

"Not for very long, Your Majesty. I left the office of Ineni because it was too hot and because there was no breeze coming through the windows. I thought that if I came here and sat for a while, maybe the night would become a bit more refreshing, and my body wouldn't be so hot." Then he paused.

"Speak!" I said softly.

"As I was approaching the sacred pool, I saw the silhouette of a beautiful goddess who was being bathed by the silver rays of Thoth in the dark. But then I stopped when I realized it was thee, Your Majesty. I didn't know what to do," he said.

I noticed that he was so nervous his forehead was sweating. The little drops of sweat on his forehead shone under the rays of Thoth as stars.

"I was afraid and thought that if I continued walking, the guards would stop me, and I would be put to death for looking at such a beautiful goddess." He smiled.

Then there was silence between us, as we looked at each other. I could tell that his heart was pounding hard like mine, and he was breathing rapidly. He had noticed my naked body under my wet sheath and the hardness of my nipples, and his eyes scrolled over my body again as the silver rays of Thoth shine on me.

I notice the look on his eyes, as if he wanted to kiss me and made love to me, and I wish he did.[23]

"Very well, Sen-Mut from Luny. Don't tell anyone that you've seen my naked body," I said and smiled. "Otherwise death will fall upon you. Not by my hands, but by the hands of my father." I turned and started to walk away.

Then I heard him say, "I would never do something like that, Your Majesty. These secret dies with me." I heard an honest tone in his voice, and I believed him.

I stopped, and without turning my back, I said softly, "I know. I know," and I smiled because I had seen him again and because I was very happy about it. Then I continued walking quickly away from him toward the palace.

He saw me fading away under the silver rays of Thoth and wondered what to do with the heat in his loins. He sat down at the edge of the sacred lake, thinking that I had left him in ecstasy and with the sweet scent

---

[23] Later in life, he told me about this magic moment. I believe the reader should know how we felt during our encounter in the sacred lake of Mut and how hard was for him to cool off the heat of his loins and what happened after he got to his room.

of lotus lingering behind me. He had not taken a woman yet, and his body was hot and completely aroused. He knew that he could not get into the sacred lake, but he took off the kilt, and got into the pool, and quietly swam until the heat of his loins cooled. After a while he cooled off, and came out of the pool, got dressed, and walked to his room. There, he lay staring at the ceiling, remembering the drops of water rolling from her head down to her lips and down to her wet breasts with hardened nipples. He became aroused again, and it was difficult for him to contain his desire. Nothing would satisfy his desires but her body. He finally fell asleep.

I reach the Palace and run up the stairs, the guards opened the golden doors. And I saw T'Queta asleep. I took off the wet sheath and dried myself. I did not want the magic to fade away. I lay naked in my bed, no longer hot from the heat of the night, but from another kind of heat. I placed a lightweight blanket over me and smiled at the thought of him, seeing him in front of me. Mother was right. It was a different kind of feeling. I wanted him to press his lips on mine tonight, and I had a deep desire to kiss him. Never had I felt such powerful feelings inside of me. It was hard for me to contain myself. My body was trembling, and his words kept playing over and over in my head: "I saw a silhouette of a goddess who was bathed by the silver rays of Thoth." Those words echoed in my head. So, this is how it feels when someone falls in love? I like it. After a while I finally fell asleep.

Father had received my second message and did not return.

CHAPTER 20

PHARAOH'S HUNTING TRIP

Ra, was high in the sky in the Sudan when Aakheperen-Re saw a lion kill the mother of a small gazelle from his position on the back of his horse. The lion was feasting on her body, and the baby gazelle was standing there shaking, not knowing what to do. Then Aakhep' noticed another threat. There was a pack of hyenas heading toward the small gazelle.

"Father, look! Those hyenas are going to eat that baby gazelle. If we don't do anything, she will die," Aakhep' said to his father.

Father called out, "Archer! Aim at the hyenas. Kill them all! I hate them!"

Then Thutmoses galloped away on his horse toward the lion, with more than two hundred soldiers following him. On his way, he aimed his bow and killed the lion. Then he spurred his horse forward to the baby gazelle. When he got to there, he dismounted and picked it up. It was still shaking.

Father followed on his horse, then said, "Quick thinking, son. You saved the life of this poor little baby animal."

He smiled, and with the little gazelle in his arms, he said, "I will give it to my little sister as a gift on her birthday."

"She will like that very much. You know she loves all creatures. The gift will make her very happy," Father said.

The bond between Father and Aakheperen-Re was good, finally. Father had a son who was almost nineteen summers hunting with him for the first time. He had seen him practicing with the charioteers and hitting his marks very well. He knew his son was trying to do his best with his health condition, and he had discovered that he was kind-hearted too.

Aakhep' gave the gazelle to one of the soldiers. "Make a cage for the gazelle and feed it from now on. Right now, you must find milk for it."

"Yes, Your Majesty," the soldier said.

Sunset was approaching, and Ra was fading away. The camp was set, and a fire was burning. The smell of the fire had spread all over the camp. Aakheperen-Re and Father were sitting with the generals around the fire, talking about the battle with the Kadesh.

"Aakheperen-Re, come to my tent later this evening. I must speak with you in private," the Great Maat told him.

"Yes, Father," he replied.

Mother Nut covered the sky and wood was still on the fire. The Great Maat rose, and then all the generals and Aakhep' did as well.

"I am going to retire for the night. Aakheperen-Re, follow me!"

They walked together to Father's tent. Father sat on one of the cushions that were spread all over the tent.

He said, "Aakheperen-Re, make yourself comfortable. I have been meaning to talk to you for several months now. Soon you will be nineteen summers, and I have been thinking of the day when Anubis, the god of the underworld, will come for me. Thinking about that subject makes me realize that you and your sister Hatshepset must marry for you to become Pharaoh of Egypt. This marriage worries me. I don't want your sister to live a life without the real love of a man, a man whom she chooses with her own heart, a man who will love her as she deserves to be loved. We have deprived our queens of the love of their hearts, and that was the reason Neferu-Bity killed herself and since then I have felt guilty because of it. I don't want that same fate for your sister Hatshepset. I've heard rumors that you have been taking to your couch several of the palace girls."

Aakheperen-Re had a grin on his face. Father continued.

"You probably have your favorite, as I did too. No slave woman can ever be taken as a secondary wife if she is not of royal blood. That must be understood by you! You will not impose yourself upon your sister, either. Let her be happy. She knows that one day she must do her duty as Queen or Pharaoh. You know that she has been prepared for many years to rule Egypt. And she knows that she must produce a royal heir for the throne. If she doesn't produce a royal heir, you can have one with one of your numerous concubines. But you must understand that if you are gone to the underworld, it is up to Hatshepset to marry him for him to have the divine blood. If she doesn't, he will never be Pharaoh, and she can choose whomever she wants and start a new linage. But you, you are going to be divine because of her. You must become divine as a god to be Pharaoh, and she is the only one that can make that happen to you. You can have as many children as you want with several concubines, but the children will be just as the other royal children in the palace, the same as your brothers and sisters who have already gone to the underworld. She is the last person of full royal blood left. Without her blood, there will be no more Thutmoses Pharaohs in Egypt, only imposters."

A scream interrupted the conversation. It was coming from outside. Both rushed outside the tent to see a soldier holding a baby cub cheetah by the back of the neck. The cheetah was screaming extremely loudly, his claws ready to attack, as if it were a full-grown animal. Everyone was laughing.

"Where did you find him?" Father asked the soldier.

"Your Majesty, he was looking for food in the kitchen tent," the soldier answered.

"Akheperen-Re, do you think your sister would like him?" Father asked.

"She loves cats. I'm sure she would love this one," he replied, laughing.

"I believe he can be domesticated," Father said.

"I believe it, too," one of his generals agreed.

"If the mother comes for him, you must release him and give him back to her. For now, feed him. Give him milk. He probably doesn't eat meat yet. He is too small. All of you must be aware that if the mother were to come looking for him, we could be in danger," Father said.[24]

---

[24] After Father and Aakheperen-Re's return, both told me all about the hunting trip. And later in life, Aakheperen-Re told me what father spoke to him about me.

CHAPTER 21

CELEBRATION

Almost fifteen days had passed, and the palace was in full preparation for the feast of me becoming a grown woman. I had not seen the peasant since that night at the lake, and I dared not go looking for him. Just the thought of him made me tremble. Mother had noticed the changes in me. She said that I had become happier and that I now laughed all the time. I had a different look on my face, and I began to wear heavy makeup, something I hadn't really done before. I was wearing more kohl around my eyes and rouge on my cheeks. But I hadn't changed the way I dressed. I was still wearing the kilt.

"T'Queta!" I called out, and she came running to me. "Have you heard anything more of Hapuseneb and what's her name?" I ask.

"No, Your Majesty." Her tone of voice was different. What I really wanted to ask her was about the peasant, but I didn't dare ask about him directly.

"Your Majesty" She came closer to where I was sitting on the balcony and knelt at my feet. "I have a petition, a favor to ask. I know thee have a very kind heart." I nodded, letting her know that she could speak.

"I would like your permission to have sex. There is someone that is very much interested in me, and I like him very much, too," she said.

My heart froze! I was trembling inside.

"How do you know that he is interested in you?" I asked her.

"Because he whispered in my ear last night and that I was beautiful and that he would like to bed me," she said.

I was not about to ask her for his name, but I remained silent for I was afraid to hear his name on her lips. I looked at her and noticed that she was very happy.

"Very well. If he desires you, and you desire him. Be aware that if you become with child, he must take you for a wife or concubine until I give you your freedom," I said.

And so, with sadness in my heart, I gave her my permission. Her face lit up with happiness. I could never prevent her happiness. She kissed my feet's.

"Be happy," I said and touched her head with my left hand. Then I sent her away to help in the kitchen. I wanted to be alone. I could hardly hold back my tears as she left. They were quickly pouring down my face. My world had just collapsed in front of me.

I thought of him. I sat there for hours as the last rays of Ra were fading away. Mother Nut would soon cover the land, and the stars would shine. The chanting on the doors started, and I knelt in front of Ra. I was crying over thoughts of love, a love that was not for me.

She came back to bathe me. I walked into the bathing room to the white limestone pool full of lukewarm water. I took a few steps down and said, "Tell Mother that I will not be coming to the banquet hall tonight, that I am not feeling well."

"Aren't thee feeling well tonight?" she asked.

"No, and you may go now. I can finish bathing myself. Bring me my food so that I can eat here in my quarters," I told her.

I wanted to be alone with my sadness.

I bathed myself wondering why my life had to be so sad, and I remembered the words of Neferu-Bity and Hapuseneb: a life without love, and what do I do with this love inside of me? It was happening to me now. It will not happen to me the way it happened to my mother and all the rest of the queens of the past. I will experience love no matter what. I am Horus, and someday I will be Pharaoh of Egypt! Aakheperen-Re will understand that. Why could he love someone, but I could not? My brother loves me very much and will not let me live without love.

I got out of the water and dried myself with white soft linen. I would not wear anything. I would sit on my balcony naked and wait for Mother Nut and the stars to bathe me with their rays.

I could hear T'Queta in the background of the room. She was lighting the oil lamps, and I could see them flickering through the linen net around my bed.

"T'Queta, no more lamps tonight," I said.

She came to me, knelt, and looked at me. "Your Majesty, are you not feeling well? Has your blood come tonight?"

"No, I just want to be alone and quiet for a while and visit with Mother Nut and Mother Hathor tonight," I said. "I want to ask them if they will condemn me to a life without love."

The happy face of T'Queta changed. Her expression turned sad.

"They would never condemn thee to live without love. I will pray for thee, that that will never happen," she said.

"If you love someone more than anything, should you give him up for someone else to be happy?" I asked her.

"Only for thee would I do that," she replied.

I touched her cheeks and smiled at her. "You are very kind. Run to your beloved and be very happy tonight. I will be happy for you."

My lips were trembling, and I could barely hold back my tears.

She kissed my feet's again and rushed out to experience her happiness.

I sat there with the tears pouring down my face. By now Mother Nut had covered the land with her darkness, the stars were shining, and their lights were adorning the dark sky as if Thoth was shining.

"Mother Hathor, will you really condemn me, thy daughter, to a life without love? Now that my heart has started to be awakened by love?" I asked.

I started to sob deeply. Then something caught my eye, a silhouette of someone walking beside Hopi and then stopping. I had the sensation that the person silhouetted was looking at me. I was distracted from my talk with Mother Hathor and Mother Nut. It was Hapuseneb! I stood up, and in a rush, I walked away from my balcony and got dressed. I put on the white sheath and rushed down the stairs, for I was determined that Hapuseneb was going to kiss me tonight! I would not live a life without knowing what it felt like being kissed by a man.

I needed to hurry before he left, so I ran down the stairs fast. I ran beside the Nile in the darkness with only the light of the stars to show me the way to him. By the time I got there, he was gone, but I knew where he was: the banquet hall. I walked as fast as I could to the banquet hall, all the while looking for him. Everyone was there except the peasant, and my eyes were misty with tears again. My heart was pierced. Of course, he was with T'Queta.

"Mother, have you seen Hapuseneb?" I asked her.

She turned and answered me. "I thought you were indisposed tonight. He was here a few minutes ago, but he just left."

Then I heard his laughter across the garden. I rushed out to the garden looking for him.

Oh! I could not believe what I was seeing.

Hapuseneb was holding T'Queta by her waist. And they were walking away laughing.

I leaned against the pillar and covered my mouth with both hands to stifle my cry out of surprise. I realized that it was Hapuseneb she was talking about and not Sen-Mut!

"Oh, Mother Hathor and Mother Nut, I thank you! Thank you!"

A rush of happiness filled my heart and my body. I started to laugh as I walked back to the banquet hall. How silly and stupid I was. I rushed to the banquet hall so very happy that I felt like I could kiss everyone in there. I ran inside and sat down beside Mother.

"Why are you so happy?" She asked me.

I was lost in thought about what I had just seen. I raised my eyes to answer Mother, and I saw Sen-Mut walking in our direction with his eyes fixed on me. A rush of butterflies invaded my stomach again, and I smiled at him. He smiled back at me.

Ineni turned around to see who I was smiling at. When he saw who it was, he smiled too as if he were pleased with Sen-Mut's presence here.

Mother also noticed who I was smiling at as he was approaching. She said, "Sen-Mut from Luny, come and sit with us." He knelt in front of my mother and bowed his head to me. He had a huge smile on his face.

I clapped my hands, and several slaves came rushing to me, and served us wine. I asked them to serve us food and for our guest and they did, and I clapped again, and they were gone again.

"Sen-Mut, it's been almost fifteen days since you came to eat with us?" Mother asked him.

"My Queen, I have been studying day and night and barely have time to eat or sleep. I want to become an architect as soon as I can, so that my Master Ineni…," and turning his eyes towards me, "and the diadem of Egypt will be pleased with me."

"I see, but you must eat so that you will have the health and the strength to become the architect you want to be," Mother told him.

"Yes, Majesty," he said and nodded his head.

"I thought you were not coming tonight," Ineni said to him.

"The night was fresh, and I wanted to refresh myself by walking beside Hopi before coming to the banquet hall. In fact, it did cool me off, and the sound of the current relaxed me."

So, it was him. The silhouette in the dark was him. I had thought it was Hapuseneb. No matter what, I was very happy that he was not the one to bed T'Queta tonight.

"How is your studying coming along? Are you learning a lot?" I asked.

With a wide smile on his lips, looking at me with his dark brown eyes, he said, "Yes, I am Your Majesty, and I am looking forward to going with Master Ineni to the building sights soon."

Building sights? The buildings were far away. In fact, Ineni didn't come back sometimes for several months. I looked at my mother.

"Ineni, when are you leaving?" Mother asked.

"Not for several months. I'm allowing time for Sen-Mut to learn more about numbers and weights and to learn to read before I take him to the building sights," he replied.

"Very well," I said, relieved that it wouldn't be any time soon. "I was thinking you had to be here for my fifteen summers celebration, which is happening in a few days," I said to Ineni and Sen-Mut.

"I wouldn't miss such a wonderful celebration for all the world. I was here when you were born, and I will be here now that you are becoming a woman," Ineni replied.

Several high priests of Amun-Ra had been invited to dinner. Khety was very quiet, observing me and Sen-Mut. Mother was doing the same.

I could hear the music at the end of the hallway and smell the lotus perfume from the oil that poured down from Sen-Mut's head to his chest. Sen-Mut and I exchanged a look, and it felt as if time had stopped, as if no one else existed but us. My heart was racing. His eyes were serene, his face without expression. I wondered what was going on in his mind.

I wanted to dance and sing. I was so very happy just looking at him sitting there in front of me.

Mother stood up and said, "Well, it's late. I must go to my quarters."

At that same moment, everyone else stood up and knelt. I would have loved to have stayed and spoken more to Sen-Mut, but I knew Mother would not agree with it at this moment. I stood up and smiled at everyone and especially at Sen-Mut. He remained kneeling on one knee. He lifted his head and looked straight into my eyes, and I felt as if he was caressing me with his look.

I left the banquet hall full of happiness and walked beside Mother, hanging on to her arm.

She said, "Hatshepset. What was all that about, this burst of happiness after you were looking for Hapuseneb? Did you find him?"

"Yes, I found him, and no, I did not speak to him. I saw him walking away across the inner garden holding a woman by her waist. They both looked very happy."

"Who was she?" she asked. And I smiled.

"T'Queta!"

"T'Queta?" she responded with surprise. "Did she ask your permission to be bedded by Hapuseneb?"

"Yes, she did, but I did not ask her who he was because I was afraid to hear the name of Sen-Mut on her lips. I am happy for her that she found love. And for Hapuseneb."

"And for that reason, you were happy?" she asked.

"Oh yes! Mother, I must tell you everything," I hung to my Mother's arm and we continued walking.

"Then let's go to my quarters. I must hear everything, beloved one," she said.

We got to her quarters where her slaves were waiting. She clapped her hands, and both were gone. She removed her wig and lay it on her make-up table.

"Come and tell everything about it," she said.

I lay beside her on her couch, with my head on my right hand. I told her about the strange nervousness inside my stomach and the lack of breath I experienced every time I was near Sen-Mut. I told her all about T'Queta and Hapuseneb. She was surprised to find out about Hapuseneb and T'Queta, but not about my feelings for Sen-Mut.

"I've noticed the way both of you look at each other. I've also observed a calculated look on the faces of both Khety and Ineni. You must be cautious that this will not get to your father's ears. Sen-Mut is too young to lose his head by your father's hands. Your father will not allow a peasant to be near you. Remember that he must not become too close to you, and he certainly cannot fall in love with you!" she said.

I jumped out of her bed and screamed, "Death! Why?"

She sat at the edge of the bed. "Because you will probably be betrothed to your half-brother so that you can make him Pharaoh of Egypt! Tell me who will rule Egypt when Maat is gone?" she demanded.

"I will! That is why Father made me Horus of Egypt when I was five summers and prepared me to rule Egypt," I said.

"I understand. Your father loves you too much, and he will do whatever is your heart desires. As for ruling Egypt, that is for when the underworld god Anubis comes for you brother. The Oracle of the temple, on the day of his birth, said that he will go to the underworld when he was a child. But many summers have gone by, and now he is going into his twenty summers. Your father and I are still alive. Maybe the gods have other plans for him and you," she said.

"I don't want for him to die, Mother. I don't want Anubis to take him to the underworld yet." I was saddened by the prospect of my brother leaving me.

"If Aakheperen-Re goes to the underworld, will Father let me marry Sen-Mut?" I asked her.

"I really don't know. We must wait and see what the stars tell us. I must advise you to stay away from Sen-Mut and the temple. And from Ineni's office. Remember that your father has eyes and ears all over the palace and on the whole land. When we are in the banquet hall, don't look at him as much as you did tonight. Your father will notice, and you will just create enormous problems for him, a young man whose life is just beginning. I've told you before that love is not for us. Let us see what happens, and if the stars were right and your brother goes to the underworld, I will try to convince your father to allow you to marry Sen-Mut."

She stood up, raised her eyes and hands and said, "Oh, Mother Hathor, help my daughter." Then she turned to me and said, "You must stop this worry for now. Time will tell. Now go to bed."

She came to me, hugged me, and kissed my forehead. "I love you," she said with a smile.

"I love you, too, Mother," I said in return, then walked away to the golden doors. Now I was depressed again. Then I remembered that Sen-Mut was not with T'Queta, and I became happy again.

I will not die without love or the love of a man. I want what other people have, I told myself as I was walking to my quarters. Another slave was waiting to undress me and bathe me. After my bath, I lay in bed thinking of him and how happy I was. Then I remembered that was him who was walking earlier beside the Nile and looking at me.

A few days had passed, and Father and Aakheperen-Re returned from their hunting trip. There was a tremendous amount of commotion in the palace that day. I had not seen Sen-Mut again, as I had done as Mother had advised me to do. I started to be afraid for his life, and I kept away from the temple and Ineni's office. He had not come to the banquet hall either. But late at night when I was sitting on my balcony alone and the stars shone over the land, I could see him far away in the dark, walking beside the Nile, stopping and looking at me. From that day on, I waited for him every night.

Every day I watched T'Queta leave for her rendezvous with Hapuseneb. She was apparently very happy. She still had not told me who is the man she was in love with, and who was making her happy, nor did I ask her for I knew who he was. Hapuseneb had not mentioned her to me either. He was still very loving to me. I wondered if he consoled himself with T'Queta because he could not have me.

On the following day, I would be fifteen summers. It was going to be a very tiring day, beginning with the bathing ritual.

All the viziers, mayors, and governors from the different towns, and dignitaries from all over the land, would be here. I needed to rest all day today. Father had said that he had brought several gifts for me and Aakheperen-Re. I could hardly wait to see what they were.

The chanting prayer begin early in the morning as the new day started with the blessing of Ra, I became a full-grown woman today, and I was very happy.

There was an early knock on the golden doors.

"Enter," I said, and a procession of slaves walked in, carrying in their arms several beautiful and colorful sheaths, gifts from my mother. They laid all of them on my bed. I stood there, looking at them. T'Queta and the other slaves were beside me, all of us emotional looking at so many beautiful sheaths.

"Your Majesty, which of these new sheaths will thou choose to wear today?" T'Queta asked.

"I don't know yet, all are beautiful." I said.

"T'Queta, bring me my jewelry box. Girls, come right here!" I called them, and they rushed to where I was sitting and gathering around me. I opened my jewelry box, and I gave each one a piece of my jewelry as a gift. I could see their happiness as they jumped for joy and looked at each other to see what they got. T'Queta was happy to see them giggle Then I told them, "Tomorrow my cartouche must be removed by the goldsmith. Now, all of you go and enjoy my party. This celebration is for the whole kingdom."

One by one, kissed my feet's and thanked me, and then they left.

"T'Queta, to your question of which I will wear, I will wear the sky-blue. What do you think?" I asked her.

"I believe that is a very good choice. It will go very well with thy lovely honey skin color, but they are all beautiful. Her Majesty, the Queen chooses beautiful colors for thee and all are very nice," she said.

"T'Queta, I would like to give you all my other sheaths so that you can wear one today, that you may look beautiful tonight for your beloved one."

She turned around to face me. "Oh! Your Majesty, how kind of you. But thou have yet to wear them all, and they are all new."

I smiled at her. "All are yours! Enjoy them."

I was sitting at my makeup table, looking at my jewelry box. I was thinking about how happy I felt that I would be able to see and speak to Sen-Mut. No one could stop me tonight.

"T'Queta, come close to me and sit beside me."

She ran and sat beside me on the floor. I looked at her and noted that she was beautiful. I could see the glow of love in her face, and I could see how love had made her more beautiful than she was before.

"Are you happy, T'Queta?"

"Oh yes, Your Majesty, very happy. Lovemaking is wonderful," she said.

"Are you protecting yourself?"

"Yes, I must. That was one of his conditions before he would bed me. I also agreed that it would not be good for me to carry a child without marriage. Your Majesty also warned me about it before," she said.

I pulled a gold bracelet from my jewelry box, one that I had ordered to be made especially for her. She deserved a beautiful gift for being my servant and friend since we were little girls. In a few months, she would be fifteen summers as well.

“T’Queta, I want you to have this gift I ordered to be made for you. I am grateful to you because you have been my companion and friend since we were little girls. Today is a very special day for me, and I wanted to thank you, mostly for being my friend and confidant. And for your kind words to me the other night.” Then I put the gold bracelets on her wrist.

She looked at the bracelet with surprise, and with a lovely smile said, “I did not expect a gift today, Your Majesty. It is so beautiful!” She stood up and then knelt and kissed my feet.

“Your Majesty, Your Majesty! Only a goddess would have such a kind heart,” she exclaimed.

She reminded me of Sen-Mut, and I smiled at the thought of him in the sacred lake.

I touched her head. “Rise, T’Queta,” I said, and she did.

Then she asked, “Your Majesty, when you mentioned ‘Your kind words’ earlier, what words were you referring to?”

“Remember the day I asked you if you would give up the man you love, and you said that you would only do it for me? Remember?”

“Yes, and I would do it. I would give my life for thee and at any time,” she said.

I smiled at her.

“It's not so hot today, and I hope there aren’t any mosquitos to-night. I hate mosquitos,” I said.

The double doors opened, and there was Mother smiling at me. She approached me, clearly very happy.

“Beloved one! The greatest gift that Amun-Ra and Mother Hathor ever gave me was you on this first day of Mesori.” She kissed my forehead. “Today you turn into a woman, and tonight the whole kingdom will be at your feet. All the guests and dignitaries are arriving at the palace. Everyone seems very excited to be here. Have you decided yet which of the new sheaths that you like the most? And which one you will wear tonight?" Mother asked.

"Yes, Mother, it will be the sky-blue one. T'Queta believes it will go well with my skin."

"Great choice. You are going to look marvelous," she said.

"Mother, where's Father?" I asked.

"The Great Maat is at the audience hall, with the Vizier of Heliopolis and the Vizier of Saqqara, Memphis. They have come from far away to celebrate your fifteen summers, and you must bathe soon. T'Queta, please put a lot of fragrance of rose petals in her water," Mother directed. "Then she must be submerged in goat milk for her skin to be smooth and soft. I want her to be as radiant as Ra today. I want every vizier, governor, and dignitary from all over the land to see how beautiful my daughter is. I am sending two other slaves to help you with everything. Beloved, are you happy today?"

"Yes, Mother. I am very happy."

Mother clapped her hands twice. Then T'Queta left my quarters. Mother held up my chin with one hand.

"Tonight, Sen-Mut is going to be there, and Maat is going to meet him. Because this is your day, you may speak all that you want with him. You can even stroll in the garden with him. Only be careful. Don't show too many emotions. Tonight, all eyes will be on you, and we don't want your father to hear rumors and mistrust Sen-Mut. I like him, and we need to let time tell what the future holds," she said and kissed my forehead. "I will be sending the servants right away. I want for you to wear a lot of kohl around your eyes, red rouge on your cheeks, and red lipstick on your mouth."

She clapped her hands again and T'Queta came running. Then Mother commanded, "Tell the jewelry maker to come in."

T'Queta ran to the doors. She reentered with a tall, older man carrying a box in his hands. He was accompanied by two boys, each of whom was also carrying boxes.

The three of them knelt before Mother and me. Mother said to me, "This my gift to you. With all of my love."

The older gentleman opened a jewelry box, and inside was a beautiful necklace made of gold. In the center was a scarab of turquoise stones.

"Oh Mother, how beautiful. Thank you!" I hugged her very firmly and kissed her.

But she wasn't finished. "There is more." One of the children opened a small jewelry box. Inside was a pair of golden earrings with scarabs made of turquoise stones. They matched the necklace.

"Mother, they are gorgeous!"

The other boy came closer and opened another jewelry box, a larger one. Inside was a pair of sandals made of leather, with gold entwined in the leather and a scarab made of turquoise, again the same design as the necklace and the earrings. I was moved by the gifts. I looked at Mother with tears in my eyes. The older man bowed to me, knelt, and put one of the sandals on one foot and then one on the other. I stood up and walked in them. They were very soft and comfortable. "They are very soft where my feet rest. They don't hurt like the others." I said.

"Because they are made with soft leather. We made sure to soften the leather for several months to be able to intertwine it with the gold," he said.

I looked at his eyes and said, "Thank you. You and your family are invited to my celebration today and the feast following in the banquet hall."

Mother clapped her hands, and they were gone.

"Mother, you are the most loving and caring mother, and I love you very much. Thank you for these beautiful gifts and for the beautiful sheaths. Has Father seen them yet?" I asked.

"No, he will see you today at the third hour. I want him to see you radiant like Ra. I must go and start my bath as well. I love you. When you are ready, come to my quarters, and we will go to the audience hall together, where everyone will be waiting for you. Later we'll feast in the banquet hall," she said.

"Very well, Mother. I will meet you in your quarters before the third hour. I'm going to have my bath ritual now."

She turned around and left. I was astounded by her beautiful gifts.

"Oh, Mother Hathor, thank you for sending me a beautiful mother like her," I said.

T'Queta was waiting for me in the bath with two other slaves from the temple. The two slaves were already in the pool when I got in the water, which was full of rose petals and perfume. It was warm, and they started to scrub my entire body. With string and honey wax, they removed the hair from all over my body and exfoliated my face with honey wax. They continued pouring perfumes into the water and dropping in more rose petals. Then I was bathed in goat milk to soften my skin. The scents of incense, lotus, and rose petals were a delight to my nostrils. They continued massaging my body with perfume oils.

About four hours later, I was rinsed again. I had finished with my bath. I exited the tub and extended my arms, so the servants could dry my body. Then we walked to my room, and everything was laid out on top of the bed. I sat at my makeup table, and Mother's makeup artist began to transform me. She outlined my eyes with kohl, emphasized my cheek bones with rouge, and made my mouth a luscious red color with lipstick.

T'Queta dressed me in the sky-blue sheath. I sat back down at the makeup table, and a long, braided wig was carefully placed on my head, each braid entwined with gold thread. Last of all, the Crown of Horus was placed over the wig. The final effect was beautiful.

The girls were in awe of how beautiful I looked. T'Queta put the golden sandals on my feet, and I stood. The four girls fell to their knees.

"Rise," I said, and they did. They started to say how beautiful I looked. I was very happy to hear that, for I had seen myself in my gold hand mirror, and yes, I looked beautiful. I looked different. I looked like a grown woman! I sent each of the girls away with a gold gift, and T'Queta took the gold necklace and put it on my neck. Then she put the very long earrings in my ears.

We walked out my golden doors, and my guards were surprise seeing me with make-up and dress well, and we walk to Mother's quarters. When I got there, the guards looked at me with surprised faces. They smiled and opened my mother's golden doors, and I entered. Mother turned around and looked at me. She got up from her makeup table, and, with her arms in the air, said, "How beautiful. How beautiful is my daughter! Mother Hathor, my daughter is a beautiful woman! May Amun-Ra protect you always. May Mother Nut protect you through the night and bless you with beauty, and may Thoth always make you shine among the stars in the night sky."

"Thank you, Mother. I feel beautiful today. And you certainly look it. The white sheath and the gold necklace compliment your skin tone, Mother."

She turned to T'Queta. "T'Queta, tell the guards to call for Maat. We are ready to walk to the audience hall. Tell him also that we will be waiting for him in my quarters."

T'Queta talked to the guards and returned to us. After a few minutes, the golden doors were opened and in walked my father. He looked majestic, with his red cape, white kilt, and golden belt, and on his neck the golden pectoral with the Eye of Horus on it, and on his head the Double Crown of Egypt. When he saw me, he had the biggest smile I had ever seen on his face.

He rushed to me and said, "Daughter, my beautiful daughter, you have grown to become a beautiful Horus." Smiling, he hugged me tightly and kissed my forehead. Mother and I held his arms. "Let's celebrate!" he said.

Father was proud of me, I could tell. I could see that he was happy. I could smell the wine on his breath, too. He started to walk down the stairs with mother beside him, and I followed behind them.

The palace was full of garlands made up of white flowers. They were strewn across all the balconies, including my own. Aakheperen-Re was waiting at the bottom of the stairs. He smiled when he saw me. Beside him was Hapuseneb, who also smiled at me and looked at me as though he had never seen me before. Aakheperen-Re came and stood at my left, leaving Hapuseneb at my right as always.

T'Queta and Tuyii, Mother's servants walked behind us, and then the rest of the court followed us into the hall of audience. The children of the palace started to throw red and white rose petals into my path. Father called me to his right side, with Mother at his left. I could hear the lovely music the musicians were playing from their place at the front of the room. The hall was full of dignitaries. The smell of incense was sweet and beautiful, and the hall was well decorated.

I searched for Sen-Mut, but I didn't see him at first. After a short time searching, I saw him. He was standing beside Ineni, Khety, Puyem-Re, and the rest of the priests and priestesses of the Temple of Amun- Ra. They were all standing at the entrance of the audience hall. I smiled at him, and he smiled back at me. I turned and smiled at everyone. I was enjoying myself immensely.

Father took his place on his throne, and we sat down beside him. Then Father started to speak. By way of introduction, he said, "To everyone here, I would like to present to you Hatshepset, my daughter, who on this first day of Mesori, July the twenty-fifth, becomes a woman."

The people in the hall of audience exploded with cheerful, loud shouts and applause. Father clapped his hands, and two manservants arrived carrying a full-length gold mirror.

"This is my gift to you, my beautiful daughter." He said.

I took the few steps down from the dais. I looked at his gift and touched it. I could see myself and my full body, and for the first time, I could see what I was wearing, and see that what I was wearing was beautiful, that I looked beautiful in this sheath.

I turned around and looked at Father.

"Thank you, Father. It's such a beautiful gift."

But there was more to come. He mentioned that Aakheperen-Re had two gifts for me, then clapped his hands. When he did, a soldier entered, bringing with him a baby cat and a baby gazelle.

I looked at Aakhep', and I said, "Thank you, it is a beautiful cat."

"It's not a cat. It's a cheetah, a wild cat that will grow very big," he said.

I was observing the animal, fascinated. He was so cute and looked just like a house cat.

Aakheperen-Re continued, "Also I brought you this baby gazelle. I saved her life when she was about to be eaten by hyenas. She also grows to be big. I believe the cheetah can be domesticated, and I know that you like all kind of animals."

"Thank you, big brother. They are beautiful gifts," I told him with sincerity.

Then every vizier, governor, mayor, and dignitary presented their gifts, so many beautiful gifts. I was tired, but happy. From time to time, I looked for Sen-Mut among the many people, but I could not see him for a while. I kept searching everywhere for him, then I finally saw him again.

Wine and fruit were freely distributed to everyone, and the atmosphere was merry. I had few drinks myself. Then after all the gifts were presented, around a thousand, and so much gold jewelry, we started to walk to the banquet hall. Oh! They had made it so beautiful with white flowers hanging all over the hall and encircling its pillars. There were an incredible number of candles, and the long, bright white linen curtains were moving in the breeze. The night was fresh. I felt lovely and happy.

We were all siting together when I noticed that Hapuseneb had sat in front of me, rather than beside me as he always did.

I whispered in Father's ear, "Father, may I bring to the table the peasant I want you to meet, the peasant from Luny? Do you remember the audience you asked me to conduct for you, my first audience? The one when you told me to use my wisdom? That's when I first met him."

"Sure, I would like to meet him. What is his name?" He asked me.

"Sen-Mut," I told him.

I got up and went to look for him. Everyone knelt as I passed them. Finally, he was there, standing and looking at me. He knelt with reverence.

"Your Majesty, there are no words to express how beautiful thou look tonight. More beautiful than any diadem in the universe," he said to me.

"Rise, Sen-Mut," I said, and he did. "Pharaoh would like to meet you. Don't be nervous, for he is a kind god, but don't look him in the eyes." I warn him.

We walked together for a bit. I was not yet ready to reach Father's table, as I wanted to spend more time with him. When we got to my father's table, Sen-Mut knelt before Maat.

"Rise!" Father told him, and he did. "What is your name and from what town do you come from?"

"My name is Sen-Mut, Your Majesty, and I come from the farming town of Luny, Your Majesty." He said it without looking at Father's eyes.

"Ineni has told me that you want to be an architect like him and that you are a fast learner, proof that Hatshepsut made the right decision and knew well how to use her wisdom. I have decided that I will like you if she does. You are most welcome in my palace. Sit with us, and we will all celebrate my beautiful daughter becoming a woman today," he said.

Sen-Mut was sweating, nervous at the sight of Pharaoh. The music was playing, and everyone was dancing.

"Sen-Mut, come and sit beside me," I said, and he came closer. I noticed that Mother, Ineni, and Khety were looking at us. Father was quite joyful and drinking a lot. Hapuseneb had not stopped looking at me and drinking. I notice that his face changed when Sen-Mut sat beside me in his place, the place that he had since we were children.

He stood up and said, "A toast for the most beautiful Lotus of Egypt!" Everyone stood and raised their golden goblets to make a toast to me. I was smiling, pleased with his toast. He looked very masculine and so very handsome. In fact, love had made him more handsome. And I wondered why he did not sit beside me.

The music was loud, and the food was delicious. Sen-Mut and I spoke for the first time face-to-face without any fear. It was as though no one existed but us. He was kind and polite. My stomach was full of butterflies again, and I was nervous, having him so close to me. We spoke for a long time, but the hours passed too fast. From time to time, I looked at Hapuseneb, and I noticed that he had been drinking all night and had had too much to drink. I observed that he was still looking at me, and he was getting drunk.

He came up to me and softly said, "Lotus of Egypt, may I speak with you in the gardens?"

"Yes, you may." I excused myself from Sen-Mut and told him that I would return soon.

Hapuseneb and I walked to the outer edge of the larger garden, away from everyone. Suddenly, he grabbed me by my arms and shook me very hard several times. He would not let me go, and he was hurting me.

"Are you in love with this peasant? Are you?" he asked in anger.

"Let go of my arm. You are hurting me." I tried to free myself from him, but he had a hard grip on my arms. He was strong, and I couldn't set myself free. I did not recognize the man who was in front of me. Finally, he let go off my arm.

"You are drunk!" I screamed at him.

"Yes! but drunk with love for you! You look so beautiful tonight. I've never seen you look so gorgeous before. And I'm angry that I cannot make you mine. It hurts me very deeply. You can't possibly know how much. I cannot bear to see him sitting beside you, cannot bear to see you talking to this peasant. I did not sit beside you tonight because you look so beautiful, and I had too much to drink in the hall of audience. I was afraid that I would not contain myself and would kiss you in front of everybody," he said with some anguish.

I laughed and snapped at him, "But you are well consoled every night, aren't you? You're bedding T'Queta." The expression on his face changed. I had surprised him.

"Who told you?"

"Nobody. I saw you that night when I went running looking for you and determinant for you to kiss me. I didn't care anymore, I was going to ask you to kiss me that night. I saw a man walking beside the Nile as you always do. You looked at me, and I run looking for you, but you were gone. Then I rushed to the banquet hall looking for you. I asked Mother if she had seen you, and she said yes. Then I heard your voice laughing, and I rushed to the inner garden looking for you. But what I saw was you crossing the gardens holding T'Queta by her waist, and you two were laughing and happy. I was quiet so that you two couldn't hear me. Then I knew that you were the man who was going to bed her that night." And that was not you that night beside Hopi.

I turned around and walked off, leaving him standing there. I was holding my arms where he had grabbed me because they were still hurting.

I returned to Sen-Mut who still sitting in his place, where I left him, talking to Ineni, Khety, Puyem-Re, and Father. I was holding my arms across my chest, afraid that Father and Sen-Mut would notice the redness of my arms. I sat beside Sen-Mut, who noticed that I was holding my arms for the rest of the night.

We all talked about my childhood, and what it was like the first time I rode a horse and the chariots with Matt, then later by myself. We talked about how I joined the armed forces to learn how to fight, how I practiced with the charioteers, learned how to shoot the bow and arrow, and about how well I did all of that at a very young age. And everyone laughed very hard when father told of my bravery putting the trap in the Sobek's mouth at the age of nine summers, and running so fast and screaming, "Run! Run! He is going to eat me!"

Sen-Mut was completely surprised, then he remembered when the news spread to his town. "What a brave girl," he said.

Even though the hour got late, we continued to talk until the early part of the morning. When Father rose, everyone else rose and knelt. Then he said that he was retiring because it had been a long day for him.

Mother and I searched for Hapuseneb. I had not seen him come back after our argument. Then I looked at Sen-Mut and said goodnight. He bowed his head.

I walked with my parents, and I thanked them for this beautiful party, told them that I was most happy with their gifts. When we reached our quarters, we said our goodnights. Father and Mother kissed my forehead, and I walked to my quarters.

I would have been willing to stay all night talking to Sen-Mut, even though he was still shy and didn't talk much.

I reached my quarters, and Month-It and my mongoose ran to me, happy to see me. My quarters were full of the presents given to me at the hall audience. There was no space to walk. Two slaves were waiting to undress and to bathe me. I walked to my makeup table, and on it there was a beautiful pink rose. It was quite lovely. I took it in both of my hands and brought it to my nose to inhale its sweet perfume. I wondered who had left it there. Maybe it was T'Queta, who was not here tonight. I had seen her earlier, wearing one of the sheaths I had given her and the bracelet I had given her as a birthday gift. She looked lovely. I thought she was probably consoling Hapuseneb tonight.

The slaves removed the Horus crown and the wig from my head. I walked to the tub to be bathed. As I was being bathed, my thoughts returned to Hapuseneb. I remembered how angry and jealous he was and how hard his grip had been on my arms when he shook me. I looked at my arm, and there were vivid bruises, the marks of his fingers showing black and blue against my skin. I hoped that neither my father nor my mother had noticed my arm, otherwise, his life might be in danger. How terrible he must feel, loving me and unable to touch me.

Then I remembered how pleasant Sen-Mut was. I was done with the bathing, and I went to bed. I lay there thinking of Sen-Mut, but then I stood up and rushed to the balcony wondering if he might be there. And there he was, looking at me from afar! I stayed on the balcony looking at him. He remained there briefly, but then he left. I went to bed happy. Because of him, it had been a long and glorious day.

CHAPTER 22

PHILAE

Almost a year had passed since I became a woman. I had not seen or spoken to Sen-Mut since my birthday celebration. I had been going to the camp with Aakheperen-Re to be around the armies and practice with the charioteers. We raced against each other and shot arrows. I shot only targets and never killed any animals or went hunting. I didn't like hunting. I loved every little animal except snakes. Snakes gave me the chills. And I loved every human being.

Aakheperen-Re loved hunting since he had gone with our father that first time. We rode horses together and laughed a lot. He had grown to be a very handsome man and drove the women of the palace and the harem crazy. I was happy that he was my big brother. He didn't get sick as he did before anymore. He only got sick when we were in the open desert in the chariot. The dust still bothered him a lot, as it caused him to be unable to breathe.

We were at the beginning of the month of Pachon[25] and Shomu[26] had arrived. Everything was beautiful because it was summer, but it was not yet very hot. Aakheperen-Re and Hapuseneb were very close friends. Hapu always rode with us when he was not in the temple serving Amun. He wasn't here today, but I was glad he was absent because I needed to speak to Aakheperen-Re alone. We had spent the morning riding our horses side by side.

"Let's sail with all our friends tomorrow," I said. "The days are gorgeous, and we are only in the beginning of Shomu. Let's go to the island of Philae. Do you remember when Maat used to take us there to spend a few weeks every summer during the festival of Isis? You can bring your favorite slave. I know who she is."

Aakheperen-Re turned around and looked at me with a smile. "So, you know?"

"Yes, I have known about her for a while. You know how the gossip goes around, especially in the kitchen, when all the slaves are together." I laughed.

He laughed, too. "And who are you inviting?" he asked.

"I am not inviting anyone. You are!"

He stopped, and his horse startled. "What do you mean that I am?"

"I want you to invite Sen-Mut, the future architect and Puyem-Re, Second Prophet of Amun. You see, if you invite them, our father won't be able to express anger at me because he will be your guest, and we will all be together. But first you must speak with Ineni. I don't think Ineni will say no to you, but if he does, tell him it is my invitation. Please tell Hapu

---

[25] April

[26] Summer

to pass the invitation to every one of our friends. I am inviting all of them to this wonderful week of vacation in Philae. It will be a very merry trip, and maybe you can go hunting and bring in the food for the day." I was laughing, and he was too.

"Let's race to the palace, and if you win, I will ask Ineni. But if you lose, I will think about it. Is that a deal?" he asked.

I thought about it because he was a very good friend of Hapuseneb, and if he told him, Hapu would probably tell him not to bring Sen-Mut. And I knew I could win this race, but if I let him win for the first time, it would make him happy, and no matter what Hapuseneb said, he would invite Sen-Mut.

"Let's do it, and I hope my long wig doesn't fall off," I said.

We took off riding very quickly. We were racing the horses very fast, far from the palace. I was ahead, and I started to let him pass me, as I was holding my wig with one hand. I saw him pass me, riding quickly and without looking back. I held back my horse for a while, to make him believe that he could win the race. I finally got to the palace. He was waiting for me, and his horse had been taken away by the stable slave.

"I win! I win! For the first time!" he was screaming, and he looked elated. Then he stopped. "Did you let me win?"

As I dismounted I replied, "No! You beat me for the first time."

I was acting somber, but inside, I wanted to laugh extremely hard, and it was hard for me to hold back the laughter.

"That just means your horse is getting better and faster," I told him.

The guard came and took my horse away, and I came close to him, grabbed him by his right wrist, shook it several times, and told him, "You win! You win!" Inside, I was laughing because he looked so surprised.

"Now, what are you going to do?" I asked him.

"I will go and speak to Ineni and Sen-Mut," he said.

"Yes! It did work," I thought to myself.

As we were walking to the palace he asked me again, "Did you let me win? Because Father gave you the fastest horse in the whole kingdom."

"Yes, I know, but you did beat me!" I smiled at him. "You must be proud of yourself."

"Whoa! I cannot believe that I have beaten you. Yes, I'm proud of myself," he shouted.

"Someday I had to lose, and today was your lucky day. But you beat me because I was wearing a wig and a sheath. Otherwise, I would have beaten you today," I said, with an innocent face and smiling at him, but holding back my laugh.

We walked our separate ways, and I saw him walk toward Ineni's office. "Yes," I again thought to myself. I continued in a hurry as I crossed the garden. When he was out of sight, I started to laugh. I laughed so hard that I had to stop at the bottom of the stairs. I was so happy that it had worked.

I rushed up the stairs to my mother's quarters and told her we were going to Philae. It was her favorite place as well. She looked deep into my eyes and asked me, "Who else is going?"

I told her that all our friends, our slaves, the musicians, the cooks, and Sen-Mut were going.

She smiled, then said, "Well, a lot of people are going. That is good, but do not be alone with Sen-Mut. I don't want Maat to hear that you were alone with him at any time."

"Yes, Mother. Puyem-Re will also be invited," I said.

“That is good,” she said. Then she clapped her hands, and Tuyii, her close servant, came running. She sent for the head of the kitchen and informed him that he needed to prepare everything for our trip. We would sail in the very early part of the morning, before the first rays of Ra.

I kissed Mother and went to my quarters. I was sweating because it was a hot day, and I ran to be bathed. I was extremely excited that I would finally see Sen-Mut again and that I would be able to speak to him without any interruptions.

I determined that I would eat in my quarters that night. I did not see Sen-Mut that night walking beside Hopi. Maybe it meant that he would be coming with us to Philae. I figured I had better go to sleep early because I would need to be awake early. I wouldn’t let T’Queta go to her rendezvous with Hapuseneb either.

The call of the roosters woke me up before Ra had begun to show his rays. T’Queta was still asleep. I heard voices and opened my double doors. I could see slaves carrying many baskets full of fruit, bread, and other foodstuffs. They had been loading the ships since the day before. I closed the doors and woke up T’Queta. I was eager to be bathed, and I wanted her to put a lot of perfume on me. I wanted to hurriedly get dressed and rush to the ship. I was hoping that he would come. “I know he will. He must,” I thought to myself. But then, I started to panic. If he didn’t come, the trip would be boring.

The magnificent rays of Ra started to bathe the land. Everything looked very beautiful. I wore a kilt but planned to wear a white sheath later that night. I loved Philae, and I was hoping that he would like it too.

“T’Queta, don’t forget to bring my bow and arrows,” I reminded her. I rushed to Mother’s quarters and kissed her, and she held my hand and said, “Beloved, don’t be alone with Sen-Mut. Your father has eyes and ears all over his kingdom, and I want you to have a wonderful time. This is the first time we are going to be apart. May the Gods protect you and everyone and carry my love with you!” I hugged Mother and ran out of her quarters. T’Queta was waiting for me. I rushed down the stairs.

"Hurry, T'Queta. Everyone is already on the barge, waiting for us."

"I am behind you, Your Majesty."

We got to the barge, and everyone was there waiting. Hapuseneb approached me with a smile, and he whispered in my ear, "Good morning, Flower of Egypt. Mm, you smell delicious."

He was blocking my view, so I could not see everyone. I forced myself past him and searched with my eyes. All my friends were there on the barge, but Sen-Mut was not. I walked directly to Aakheperen-Re.

"We must speak!" I grabbed him by his arm and walked away from our friends. "What happened? Where is Sen-Mut?" I ask.

Just then I heard a voice behind me say, "Glorious morning to you, Your Majesty." I turned around. He was kneeling with his arms extended, almost touching my feet.

"Rise, Sen-Mut, future architect of Amun. Here, we are all friends, and I would like for you to enjoy these merry days with all our friends and me," I said.

My heart was pounding, and my stomach was full of butterflies again. I could barely breathe because I was so happy to see him. Hapuseneb didn't seem to be happy, however. He was startled when he saw Sen-Mut. But as for me, I felt that the days were going to be beautiful.

"Sail!" I shouted, and the barge started to move. We sailed in Father's barge, and two other barges followed ours. We started to sail south. All the curtains were of white linen with gold accents, and they had been drawn back. The cushions were sky blue with gold trimmings at the edges, and they were everywhere. The musicians started to play. I clapped my hands. "Let's eat breakfast," I said.

I sat down and before I could tell Sen-Mut to sit beside me, Hapuseneb sat on one side of me with Aakheperen-Re on the other side. "Very well, he can sit in front of me, so I can see him better," I thought.

"Sen-Mut, do you hunt?" Aakheperen-Re asked him.

"Yes, indeed. On the farm, we must learn everything," was his reply.

"Hapuseneb, do you hunt with the bow and arrows too?" Sen-Mut asked him.

Laughing as he replied, he said, "Indeed, and guess who taught me?"

"I did! When we were children," I told him, and I laughed about it.

"Have you ever seen her hit her markers?" Aakheperen-Re asked him. "Oh boy, don't make her angry. She can deliver you one in your behind."

Everyone laughed. I knew it was going to be a good sail.

"Sen-Mut, have you ever been in Philae before?" I asked.

"No, Your Majesty."

"You are going to like it. It is my favorite place for vacations. It is going to be a long sail to Philae, and I want you to feel free to walk around and mingle with everyone," I told him.

We were all very merry. I had had several goblets of wine, and I was tipsy. I saw Hapuseneb talking with Tepi and felt a hint of jealousy rush through me. "He is mine!" I thought. I walked to the bow of the barge and looked at the open waters of Hopi. I sure was happy that Sen-Mut had come on this trip. I turned around and looked-for Sen-Mut. When I spotted him, I observed that he was looking at me. I wondered what he was thinking. I smiled at him, and he returned the smile. Then he came closer and stood about a foot away from me, and I became very nervous and could hardly breathe.

"How different everything is from up here," he said.

"Yes, everything looks different from up here," I replied.

He pointed toward a farming area and said, "That is Luny, my town, the farming town where I was born and where I lived with my parents and siblings. It's where I learned how to swim for the first time. I love the waters of Hopi. Majesty, do you swim?"

"Yes, I do, and I do it very well," I said. I noticed how wide the Nile was. It was so immense. I turned around and faced him with surprise. "Did you actually swim across this big river for the audience?" I asked him.

"Yes, Your Majesty. I had done it before. I practiced every Shomu, when the waters had subsided. You can only do it in the summer because otherwise the current will drag you down, and you will drown."

"How did you avoid the crocodiles?"

"My father sacrificed several goats and a bull in the river to distract the crocodiles, and he said a lot of prayers so that I could make it," he told me.

"Sen-Mut of Luny, you are very brave, indeed. Very brave."

My eyes traveled over his well-developed chest and strong arms. Of course, he did it. He certainly looked capable of doing it. I realized that he gave me a feeling of security, like the one Hapuseneb inspired in me.

I clapped my hands and called everyone to the front of the barge. Everyone came, and Hapuseneb stood beside me.

"Everyone! I want all of you to come and see the immense waters of Hopi. And I want all of you to know that Sen-Mut swam across this big river to be heard in an audience. He came with a petition to become an architect, and I granted him that opportunity. Now, seeing the effort that he made to cross the Nile against all dangers, I am amazed that he succeeded and glad that I granted him the wishes of his heart. Let us all raise our golden goblets to him."

Everyone was astonished at his accomplishment and cheered him for it. He was obviously happy, and so was I. He smiled as he looked straight into my eyes.

All of us went back in to eat, drink, and listen to the musicians play. There was lots of laughter. I didn't want time to pass, but Ra was fading away.

When it was time, Puyem-Re started the chanting. We all knelt facing Amun-Ra. The chanting began, and incense was offered. When it was over, it was already dark. The moon was almost full.

We were still sailing. I walked out to the deck to see the beauty of the night. I called Sen-Mut and Hapuseneb, and both came and stood beside me. As did Tepi. I looked at her, and she cast down her eyes, turned around, and went back to her cushion.

I could hear and see Aakheperen-Re laughing very hard, and I smiled at him. He was leaning against several cushions, with his knee bent, holding a golden goblet of wine in his hands. Several of our friends were around him and laughing too. Some of the women from the harem were milling around him, including Isis. I didn't know why I didn't like her, but I didn't.

I turned around and looked at Sen-Mut. We were very close to each other. Then I saw a shooting star, and I pointed it out. "Hapuseneb, have I ever told you about the time when I was in the middle of the universe?"

Sen-Mut's face looked puzzled.

"Yes, but it has been such a long time. We were children then," Hapuseneb said.

"I will tell you again so that Sen-Mut can hear what a beautiful experience I had." I looked at Sen-Mut and smiled.

"I was a little girl of five summers when I was taken by my father to the hills of the Valley of the Dead to test my strength, because when Aakheperen-Re was born, the stars and the Oracle foretold that he would go to the underworld young. How young, they did not know. They told my father that he needed to bear another child to rule his kingdom. The god Amun-Ra took the form of my father, and he covered my mother with his seed. She became pregnant, and I was born. That is why I am divine. The day that I was born, the Oracle and the stars foretold that I was going to be a healthy child and a strong one, and that I would rule Egypt, this land that I love," I said.

Sen-Mut and Hapuseneb were very quiet listening to me. I continued, "To protect me, the Great Maat wanted me to have wisdom, the wisdom of knowledge, kindness, understanding, and the wisdom of foresight. The knowledge of foresight is the wisdom to know who my true friends are and who my enemies are. I can sense danger around me. I can be miles away and hear and know who is thinking of me, or what that person is thinking, or what is being said about me, good or bad."

I smiled at Sen-Mut, and suddenly Hapuseneb started to laugh. I smiled because I knew what he was laughing about, that when he was making love to a slave, he had me in his mind. He looked at me and became embarrassed. Now he knew that I knew his secret. Then I looked at him and laughed.

Sen-Mut was puzzled about our laughter. I didn't enlighten him and instead continued speaking.

“I was put inside of an empty sarcophagus and was left there for three days without eating or drinking anything. My Ka left my body, then traversed the tomb, even though it was very dark inside of it. I could see the guards standing outside the doors of the tomb and the torches burning on the walls. By now my Ka was flying, and I saw the guards posted outside Father’s tent, as well as the horses and the guards gathered around the camp site. It was daytime outside of the darkness of the tomb. Then my Ka flew to Thebes, and I saw my mother and Sitre-In, who is my wet nurse, walking to the temple. My mother was wearing a yellow sheath and carrying white flowers in her arms as they walked to the temple to make an offering for my wellbeing to Amun-Ra. On another day, my Ka left my body again. It was daytime. I saw Aakheperen-Re and Mutnofret, his mother. They were also walking to the temple to make an offering for my wellbeing. Then my Ka returned to my body. My body was cold. I felt like I was floating. My Ka was flying again. This time, I was flying very fast. Suddenly, I was in the middle of all the stars and in the middle of the universe! It was quiet and so peaceful, and it was beautiful. I was amazed by the beauty and by the millions and millions of stars,” I told them.

I became quiet for a moment and was looking at the stars. The silver rays of Thoth were pouring down all over the land. Everything looked so peaceful and beautiful. I was very happy that Sen-Mut was beside me, sailing the Nile so close to me. He made me feel even lovelier.

“Your Majesty, what a beautiful experience. Now I know that only a goddess like thee could experience such beauty like the gods. I would have loved to have been there and see thee in the middle of all the stars. I would have picked up the stars of the universe and made thee a crown of stars,” he said and smiled.

Sen-Mut and I were looking at each other as he said it. What beautiful words he said to me. Then I noticed that Hapuseneb was quiet and lost in thought.

‘Me, too. What a beautiful experience you had. I wish I had been there to dress you with all the stars of the universe,” Hapuseneb said.

I was between the two most important men in my life; the one who loved me and whom I loved, and the one with whom I was falling in love. The music was playing softly, and a soft breeze was moving the skirt of my kilt.

Aakheperen-Re walked up to me and stood between me and Sen-Mut. Putting one arm on my shoulder and the other on Sen-Mut's, he said, "Let's all eat!"

We all ran together and took our places like little children. This time Aakheperen-Re was sitting with a few of the ladies, including Isis. Everyone was laughing and having a great time. My heart was very happy.

"Everyone! Later you can find a place to sleep. There are a lot of cots and spaces to sleep and plenty of blankets," I said.

The hours passed. Eventually, we all became tired. I hated to have to go to sleep, but it was time. I stood up, and everyone rose with me. Sen-Mut knelt.

"Rise, Sen-Mut, future Ptah of Egypt." As he rose, I looked at him, and he bowed his head. I left him with a smile. Then I directed my attention to Hapuseneb. He was standing there quietly looking at me, and I smiled at him. He raised his cup to me.

I walked to my canopy couch, and T'Queta drew the curtains closed around me. She undressed and bathed me. I could hear all of them laughing and talking. Today was a very happy day for me, and I was very tired. I fell asleep knowing that he was close to me and that he would be there the next day.

I woke up full of happiness and energy, knowing that he was there and that no one could tell me not to speak to him. I could jump on my couch with happiness. I ran to be bathed. I could hardly wait to finish being bathed with a wet cloth. I made sure to wear a lot of fragrance.

"Your Majesty, what will you wear today?" T'Queta asked.

"I will wear the white sheath, and a lot of fragrances."

Once I was dressed, I had makeup applied: light kohl on my eyes, very light rouge on my cheeks, and a light touch of red lipstick on my lips. I also wore the mid-shoulder length black wig.

I walked to where everyone had gathered, and everyone rose. At the front of the ship was Sen-Mut, who was looking at me. I saw him kneeling. I nodded my head and he rose. I saw that Hapuseneb was looking at Sen-Mut. Then he looked at me. His look was very serious. He started to walk toward me.

I clapped my hands and shouted, "Let's all have breakfast!"

Food had been arranged on long tables, all kinds of food. Everyone had gathered around the table and started to serve themselves.

Hapu came close to me and whispered in my ear, "Did you bring him to make me jealous? Or should I pull you to me right now and kiss you in front of everyone, so that he will know to stay away from you? Remember the day of your birthday? I was very drunk, but I'm not now. If Pharaoh wants to put me to death, so be it."

At that moment, I did not know what to say, but then I saw Tepi sitting on a couch looking at us. I turned to him angrily. "Did you bring her to make me jealous, too?" He turned around and looked at her, and she was smiling at him.

I walked away from him before he could say anything more. I saw him storming away from the buffet table, and I went to sit down beside Aakheperen-Re. Hapuseneb was saying something to Aakhep'. Then Aakheperen-Re started to laugh out loud, and I smiled at Aakhep'.

I saw Hapuseneb looking for T'Queta.

Later she was sitting beside him, and Aakheperen-Re had Isis in his lap. I saw Tepi's look when she saw Hapuseneb with T'Queta beside him. Why was he doing this? Why was he bringing her here and acting this way?

I didn't care anymore. I walked to Sen-Mut, and I got closer to him. We looked at each other. The rush of butterflies invaded me again, and I was short of breath. I was afraid that he would notice my nervousness when I was with him.

I smiled at him, and he said, "Good morning, Your Majesty. Did thee sleep well last night?" I noticed he was sweating. It was too early in the morning for him to be sweating.

"Yes, I did," I said and smiled again. "I see you have not taken your breakfast yet like everyone else," I told him.

"No, Your Majesty. I was waiting for thee to eat first, and then I will eat."

"First, I don't want you to call me Your Majesty when we are alone. You can call me by a name that you choose. Is that okay with you?" I asked.

He was speechless, and we smiled at the same time. "Everything is so beautiful right now," I said.

He looked at me and said, "Because you make it more beautiful, Maatke-Re."

I started to feel those butterflies again, and I blushed. I was very happy with his words and with the name that he had called me, "Daughter of the Sun." What a beautiful thought.

I clapped my hands, and T'Queta came running.

"Yes, Your Majesty?"

"Bring food for us. You know what I like. Sen-Mut, what would you like to eat?"

He looked at T'Queta. "Your Majesty, may I go and serve myself?" he asked.

"Certainly, you may."

I sat and waited for both to come back. They did, and we started to eat together. From time to time, I looked in Hapuseneb's direction. At that point, he was being entertained by the other girls of the palace. Aakheperen-Re was laughing as everyone else was dancing. I knew that if Hapu kept calm and stayed away, I would be alright.

I had not noticed that Sen-Mut was observing me.

"Maatke-Re, is he someone close to your heart?" he asked.

I was shocked by his question. "Why do you ask?"

"Because he seems like he is, and he keeps looking at thee and at me. Based on the looks he gives me, I'd say that it's likely he is ready to bite my head off."

I laughed. "We have been very close since childhood, and he is just a little bit jealous of you, that's all," I said.

He smiled, and we continued eating. Afterward, we walked inside the ship and sat down with everyone.

Aakheperen-Re looked at Sen-Mut, then said, "Sen-Mut, in here are many beautiful ladies of the harem. You can spend the rest of the day being very cheery with one of them." Everyone laughed, and he smiled too.

The day was almost gone. There was only one more day until our arrival at Philae. I retired early, with all of them still drinking and laughing. I could hear Sen-Mut laughing, too. Then it was quiet.

Later, I was awakened by the men's snoring. I could not believe it, especially the identity of the one who was snoring the loudest. I put my pillow over my ears, and still the snoring was too loud for me to sleep. I got up and walked furtively and quietly to the front of the ship. I noticed that Sen-Mut was asleep, with his left arm under his head. I stood there looking at him under the rays of Thoth. He was beautiful. I looked at his naked chest and arms. I could hardly hear him snore.

The night felt cool. I walked back to my bed and looked for a linen sheet. Next, I walked back and carefully covered him. After I had done so, I returned to my bed. The snoring had finally ceased, and I was at long last able to fall asleep.

I woke up with what I thought was the crow of a rooster. I hadn't realized that roosters were brought on board the ship. I got up off the couch and walked through the protective netting. To my surprise, it was Sen-Mut making bird-call sounds. He was shooting arrows with Aakheperen-Re, Hapuseneb, Ursaramun, and several of our friends from the palace. T'Queta was beside Hapuseneb, as was Tepi. How strange to see both side by side? They were cheering him on as he shoots at the birds.

I clapped my hands. Everyone turned around and stopped what they were doing. T'Queta came to me. All of them fell to the floor, except Aakhep' and Hapuseneb. I smiled at them and said, "Continue! I will join you all in a few minutes."

I ran to be bathed.

"T'Queta, what time is it?" I asked.

"Just a few hours after Ra has shown his first rays."

"Hmm. How long have they been shooting at birds?"

"I believe about an hour, Your Majesty."

"Is breakfast ready?"

"Yes, and no one has eaten yet. They are waiting for thee, Majesty. Early this morning I woke up and went to the bathroom. Next to this tent was a folded royal linen sheet, right at the entrance. It was strange. I am pretty sure that I had not dropped any of thy royal linen," she said.

"Don't worry about it. I will wear the kilt. And get my bow and arrows."

I had finished getting ready for the morning. I took my bow and arrows, and barefoot, I walked to the deck of the ship, where everyone was gathered. There were very many birds already on the deck. I joined the commotion and the laughter.

I saw Sen-Mut smiling at me, and I smiled back. I hit my target every single time, and Sen-Mut was very good as well and had not missed one target. We were all winners.

"Let's eat!" I shouted. I walked to Sen-Mut, and we smiled at each other. Everyone walked ahead of us, including Hapuseneb, which was strange.

"Thank you, Maatke-Re," Sen-Mut said with a soft voice.

I stopped and looked at him. "What are you thanking me for?" I asked.

"For covering me in the middle of the night with thy royal linen," he said.

I was surprised by his words. "Were you awake?"

"No, I felt something over me, and when I opened my eyes, I saw thee walking away and fading into the darkness of the ship."

"You are most welcome, Sen-Mut from Luny," and smiled at him. Then we continued walking to get our breakfast.

Hapuseneb was there looking at us the whole time.

A few hours later, we arrived at Philae, which was beautiful as always.

Sen-Mut was astonished looking at the beautiful temple. We docked at the edge of the banks, and the ramp was deployed. All of us ran out of the ship laughing. It was past the third hour after the high noon. Soon it would be sunset. The other ship was docking behind ours.

"Let's swim!" Hapuseneb shouted.

All of us jumped into the water. We screamed and played in the water for several hours. Our group included Puyem-Re, T'Queta, and Isis.

We raced each other in the water, and Sen-Mut beat us all. That was unsurprising considering his strong arms and legs and considering that he had crossed Hopi.

Eventually, I realized that I needed to get out of the water, or the mosquitos would eat me alive. When T'Queta came close to me, I saw that her long hair was wet. I noticed the way Hapuseneb was staring at her as the long and wet sheath clung to her naked body.

She and I walked to the Pharaoh's bedchambers[27] where everything was already set up for sleeping, including the net around my couch to keep the mosquitoes away from me. I was very pleased by the way that the slaves had set up everything, including the directions of each couch. The one for Sen-Mut had been set up across from mine. All the couches were equipped with nets for the mosquitoes, as mine was.

T'Queta bathed me with clean water from the well and dressed me in the white sheath. I wore a long black wig, rouge, light lipstick, and the coronet of Horus.

---

[27] These days the Pharaoh bedchamber it is known as Trajan's Kiosk, but in my memory, it existed at least a thousand years before Roman Emperor Trajan's rule.

When I emerged, I could smell the wood burning to chase away the mosquitoes and the food that the chef was already cooking.

"T'Queta, I already know who is bedding you," I said. She became quiet. "Do not worry as long you are protecting yourself and he takes care of you as he should. Tell me, what was that all about, you and Tepi cheering him on together as if you were friends? I could not believe he brought her on this trip, knowing you would be here with me."

"He did not invite her. Master Aakheperen-Re did."

"So, it was Aakheperen-Re and not Hapu, hmm? Very well. I am very hungry. Go and bathe yourself well. I will wait here on my couch for you. Did you bring another sheath to wear?"

"Yes, Your Majesty. I have brought a few more from among the ones that thou gave me on your birthday."

"Very well. Make yourself beautiful for him tonight, and you can use my lotus fragrance. I know that he loves it."

I wanted him to be occupied with T'Queta and away from me and Sen-Mut tonight. When she finished, she looked lovely.

"Let's go. They probably are waiting for me." We walked off giggling together.

Sen-Mut was still in the water with Aakheperen-Re, Hapu, and other friends. Tepi was beside Hapu, and they were laughing. I clapped my hands, and they turned around.

"Let's get ready for the procession to the Temple of Isis," I said, and everyone left the water.

"Aakheperen-Re, send your slaves to help Sen-Mut change his wet kilt and make sure he brought several clean ones. Everyone knows where Pharaoh's chambers is except him," I said.

Aakheperen-Re called several slaves, and they all walked together to be changed. I was sitting in front of the water, looking at the beautiful sunset beside the Nile, with T'Queta sitting beside my feet.

"T'Queta I am so hungry."

"Your Majesty, I can run and bring some fruit."

"No, we must wait until after the blessing of the Temple of Isis, so she may bless us all with a pleasant stay on the island," I said.

"Your Majesty!" I was called by a slave. "The Second Prophet of Amun-Ra is waiting to start the procession to the temple of the goddess Isis before night falls."

I stood up and walked to meet everyone. They were all waiting. I saw Sen-Mut, who was very well groomed. He knew the ritual of the temple and how to serve Amun-Ra now that he had trained. I smiled at him, and he smiled back. We all looked beautiful wearing the white linen sheaths which were symbols of purity.

Puyem-Re, the Second Prophet of Amun-Ra, Hapuseneb, and Sen-Mut were at the front. I was behind them; and behind me was Aakheperen-Re. Behind him the priestesses of the Temple of Amun-Ra were carrying burning incense in copper censers. Everyone was carrying palm leaves in their hands. We all chanted to the goddess of love and fertility. I was full of emotions and made petitions for the love of my heart so that we might someday be together forever.

When the ritual was over, we were all hungry, and we started to walk out of the temple. I saw Sen-Mut at the entrance. We greeted each other with a smile. Torches were everywhere, hanging from each pillar on both sides of the temple. Tables full of food were waiting for us, with oil lamps burning on top of the tables. The moon shone above our heads.

I said, "Let's eat!" and everyone sat down. At my right, Hapuseneb took his place, and I called Sen-Mut to sit at my left. I called

T'Queta to sit beside Hapuseneb, a decision which seemed to surprise Hapu.

I looked at him and said, "Remember that for this trip, we are all equal, and we must be pleasant to everyone."

He leaned over and said in my ear, "Ask Sen-Mut how pleasant I was." Then he smiled.

We all started to eat and enjoy ourselves. We were drinking a lot, and I was tipsy. I could not see Aakheperen-Re anywhere around. I stood, and everyone stood.

"If you all have finished eating, feel free to stroll under the rays of Thoth tonight," I said.

I saw that Hapu looked at T'Queta and then looked at Sen-Mut. He apparently couldn't decide what to do: stay with me or leave with T'Queta. But then he made up his mind. He took her hand, and they walked off together.

I looked at Sen-Mut, and quietly we started to stroll around the temple. I still felt nervous whenever I was with him, but it was a nervous excitement. The butterflies were having fun in my stomach, and I was telling him that this temple was built by my ancestors, that my father added to it, and that he had built the Pharaoh's chambers. I added that it was my hope that after his death no one would replace his name, as was done by some Pharaohs in the past to take credit for temples that they had not actually built.

Sen-Mut was impressed with the beauty of the temple, and the full moon made it more beautiful. I suddenly no longer cared about my nervousness.

I had to stop talking because T'Queta was coming up behind me. Behind her were Aakheperen-Re, Hapuseneb, Ursaramun, Tepi, and the rest of the party. My hope that I could be alone with Sen-Mut was gone, but I would make the best of it. We all sat in a circle, and the guards made a fire in the center. Sen-Mut was sitting across the fire from me. Beside me was Aakheperen-Re and Hapuseneb. Tepi was beside Sen-Mut, and they were having a conversation. I became very jealous and I could hardly hold my anger. The slaves were serving wine and beer to him and Tepi. I noticed Sen-Mut drinking wine and looking at me in silence every time he took a sip of his wine.

I stayed and ignored him for the rest of the night. I kept up my conversation with Hapu and with all of them in general. The conversations were very good, and we laughed a lot. But eventually, I became tired. I got up to leave, and as I did, I crossed looks with Sen-Mut. He bowed his head, and I smiled at him.

As I turned to leave, with T'Queta at my side, Hapuseneb said, "I will walk you to the Pharaoh's chambers."

We arrived at the chambers, and Hapuseneb waited outside for T'Queta. She finished undressing me and washed my body well. I wore a white sheath and lay on my couch with the curtains drawn. I saw T'Queta leave, and I was pleased to note that the mosquitos weren't bothering me. I was also pleased with the day, for we had a very good time together, and soon he would walk through the doors to sleep and lie down on his couch which was across from mine.

They stayed for long time, and I fell asleep. I woke up, and no one had returned yet. I noticed that T'Queta had not returned. Then a figure walked through the doorway. By the dim light of the candle, I could see that it was Sen-Mut. He smelled fresh. He had washed himself before bed, as every priest must do. I wanted to speak to him, and I noticed that he was standing in front of his couch looking at me. He did not know that I was awake. I saw him lie down, then everybody came in at the same time. They were trying not to make noise. I remembered the night before and all the snoring. I wondered if it would be another night like that. But to my surprise I was not awakened by snoring at all. Either that, or I was so tired that I simply never heard them snoring because I was deeply asleep.

It was a glorious morning when I woke up, and I was in a good mood. Surprisingly, everyone was already gone, except for T'Queta. She was still asleep. I did not wake her up. I washed myself, put on a kilt, took my bow and arrows, and walked out.

Everyone was swimming except Hapuseneb and Sen-Mut.

"Hat, you overslept this morning, and I am hungry!" Aakheperen-Re shouted.

I laughed and searched for Sen-Mut. I could not see him or Hapu anywhere. I walked to the other end of the island and found him sitting with Hapuseneb. My stomach became cold, and I approached them.

"Good morning," I said. They both turned around and stood; then Sen-Mut knelt.

"Rise, Sen-Mut. Remember that here we are all equal, and you don't have to kneel. What are you two doing this far away?" I asked.

"Sen-Mut was showing me how to fish with a spear."

"Oh! I want to learn, too!" I said.

He smiled at me.

"Your Majesty, you must hold the spear in this way, wait for a medium fish to come near, and don't move at all. When the fish is very near, you must aim at it, then release the spear as fast as you can and with force. There is one!" he said. "Do not move, let him come closer to you."

I waited and released the spear quickly and with force, and to my surprise, I hit it.

"I did it! I did it!" I screamed, and both were laughing.

Hapu said, "I've been trying very hard, but I haven't been successful getting one yet."

I was laughing, and so was Sen-Mut.

"That's because I know how to throw a spear, and you never wanted to learn how to throw it," I told Hapuseneb.

"But you see, I don't like to kill anything. Do you see how the fish is twisting in pain and cannot breathe? That makes me sad," I said.

They looked at each other and started to laugh.

"Your Majesty, what will you do if you have nothing to eat and can only eat fish?" Sen-Mut said.

"That will never happen! Because I don't like fish or chicken, only eggs. Let's walk back and have breakfast. Aakheperen-Re is very hungry. When I was looking for you two, he yelled to tell me that. Let's run to see who makes it back first."

The three of us ran as quickly as we could. Sen-Mut was way ahead of us.

"Look at the way he runs. I'll never catch up with him," Hapuseneb said.

When we got to the temple, everything was set up for breakfast. There were my favorite fruits: watermelons, cantaloupes, grapes, mangos, bananas, and oranges. There were all kind of fruits because the harvest had already begun. There was also juice and hot mint tea, as well as my favorite hot drink, mmm, and warm sweet date cakes.[28]

---

[28] I have read so much misinformation of what we had or did not have in Egypt 3,500 years ago, but what I do remember is drinking some form of hot drink that tasted like cocoa. I have read that the Spaniards discovered cocoa in the Americas and brought it to Spain, but they never traveled to Egypt. How do they know that we did not have cocoa as well? We did have mangos and bananas, but the bananas were small. We traded with other parts of the world.

I noticed that Hapuseneb, Aakheperen-Re, and Sen-Mut were getting along very well. Sen-Mut looked different. I didn't know what it was, but it made me happy that he had won their friendship. And I noticed how much Sen-Mut liked the mango and melon.

We all shared the wonderful breakfast and then went swimming. Later, the slaves brought us baskets with fruit, wine, and juice. I could smell the wood burning, a smell I loved, as the food was being cooked. It made us all hungry.

Sunset was approaching, and I saw Puyem-Re, Hapuseneb, and Sen-Mut get out of the water so that they could be bathed with clean water. They got ready for the chanting in the temple before Ra could fade away. I was very happy that we were here all together.

When all the offerings and the chanting were done, I shouted for everyone to eat, and we ran around like little children. I was having the time of my life because he was with me. There was no more jealousy from Hapu toward Sen-Mut. They spent a lot of time speaking with Aakheperen-Re and Ursaramun and other friends from the palace. We all strolled around the Temple of Isis under the rays of Thoth.

Everything was lovely, but I was never alone with him. There were always a lot of people surrounding us. I loved everything anyway, and I thought he did, too. He didn't speak much when I was around, and I couldn't tell what was on his mind. I wondered if he knew that I liked him. I couldn't tell if he liked me.

We all sat around the fire like the night before, listening to the sound of the harp and the lute. Everyone was drinking, but I was not. Wine and beer gave me a headache, so I just had fresh fruit. Soon it was almost morning, and I could hear the crow of a rooster. The sound made me smile because it reminded me of the sound Sen-Mut made that woke me up that

---

morning two days before, when we were on the ship. We all waited in silence for the dawn. When it came, we rose to face Ra and knelt. It was a beautiful sight when Ra bathed us all with its rays.

Sen-Mut and Hapuseneb would have an hour to bathe and incense the temple. Then they would come back to Pharaoh's chambers and get some sleep. By that time, I would be deeply asleep.

We all woke up late in the afternoon. Sen-Mut and Hapuseneb were not in bed. By the time I had gotten dressed, everyone was waiting for me so that they could have lunch. I called everyone to lunch. I saw Sen-Mut, and my heart leapt. I was very happy to see him. He was walking with Hapuseneb in my direction. I smiled at him, and he smiled back at me with a pleasant smile. I then smiled at Hapu who also smiled back at me. It was so strange that he was no longer jealous. In fact, he seemed at peace.

We all sat together to eat. Sen-Mut sat down beside me on my left, and Hapu sat at my right. I stood and said, "After breakfast, let's all go across the lake to the hills."

Hapu responded, "I pass. I have not slept at all, nor has Sen-Mut. Give us a few more hours to sleep."

"Very well then. After you two rest, we'll all cross the river by boat and walk to the hills."

I saw them walk to Pharaoh's chambers. The rest of the party went to the river and swam.

Three hours later, T'Queta, who was awake, bathed me. I put on a kilt. Sen-Mut was awake and ready to go, but Hapuseneb was still deeply asleep. I decided not to wake him up. The rest of us left, except Tepi and T'Queta.

Sen-Mut, Aakheperen-Re, and I walked up the rocky hill.

“Sen-Mut, someday when you become a Ptah, I want you to build for me a shrine in honor of our god Khonsu, the creator of humanity. He made us out of clay on a pottery wheel. I would like to worship him here every time I come back, as he deserves to be worshipped. He created the universe and everything in it, including the constellations. I love him very much, and I tell him so every morning,” I said.

“Hat, that would be a beautiful thing to do in the honor of the god Khonsu,” Aakheperen-Re said.

“Yes, Your Majesty, I will do it. I will build for thee the greatest temple and the most beautiful one in the whole kingdom, and I will build it so that it will last for all eternity,” Sen-Mut said.

“I am very pleased to hear these words from your lips, Sen-Mut,” I said, looking directly into his eyes.

I felt as if he wanted to kiss me. I became nervous and cast my eyes down and smiled, and for the first time, I noticed that he had fair skin like my mother Ahmose, Aakheperen-Re, Hapuseneb, T’Queta, and Isis. He was not dark as I thought when I first saw him in the audience hall. I had not noticed it before because I only saw him at night and he made me nervous.

“Sen-Mut, have you ridden a horse before?” Aakheperen-Re asked him.

“No, I never have.”

“Well, I must teach you, and tomorrow will be your first lesson,” I told him.

“I agree, so we shall all go riding tomorrow,” Aakhep’ said.

“Aakhep’ are you bringing Isis to ride with us?” I asked.

"No, she doesn't know how to ride. I ordered the guards to bring your horse, Hapu's, my horse, and two more horses. One horse for Tepi, and the other one for Sen-Mut" he said.

"Why Tepi?" I asked him. A rush of jealousy invaded me.

"Because I believe Hapu is starting to like her a lot," he said.

I did not like what I was hearing. What about T'Queta's feelings? I didn't like the way things were going. I thought maybe he was doing this to make me jealous, but we would see who would win in the end. I would win. I will have Sen-Mut's love and Hapuseneb's love, too, I thought to myself.

It was almost sunset when we returned. I saw Hapuseneb strolling with Tepi. He saw us returning from the hills and came to greet us.

"How was the hill? Did you like it, Lotus of Egypt?"

"Very much, Hapuseneb. Sen-Mut has agreed that when he becomes Ptah of Egypt, he will build a shrine there for me in honor of our god Khonsu," I said.

"That sounds like a good idea, and I am sure Khonsu will love you for it, as Amun-Ra does, and the rest of the gods do, because you are the daughter of Horus," he said.

He moved closer to Sen-Mut and put his arm on his shoulder, then said, "It's time for the service in the temple, and you've hardly have any sleep. Tonight, you will sleep like a rock."

Sen-Mut looked at me and bowed his head, then walked off with Hapuseneb to be bathed and serve in the temple.

I saw him come back after the service with Hapuseneb and Puyem-Re, and they joined us for dinner. Sen-Mut was very quiet, and I could see that he was very extremely tired.

"Sen-Mut, you must eat something and go rest," I told him.

He smiled and took a few bites. Then, looking at me, he bowed his head and left. We all finished eating and walked around the island. I could feel the silence surrounding me without his presence. We all sat around the fire and talked.

"Tomorrow, we are going horseback riding. I brought your horse Hapu. You can teach Tepi how to ride, and Hat will teach Sen-Mut. I will ride with you four. It's getting late, and we must go to sleep and rest like Sen-Mut is doing now," Aakhep'said.

We all walked back. T'Queta was walking beside me, and she was very quiet. She was looking at Hapuseneb who was walking with Tepi in front of us and laughing with her. I could see that T'Queta was hurting, but she kept her hurt inside of herself. I did not like what Hapuseneb was doing to her.

"Hapuseneb!" I shouted. He turned around, startled.

"T'Queta go ahead and leave. I want to speak to Hapu by myself. Hapu, come here!" I ordered him. He walked to where I was standing waiting for him. After he approached me, I asked, "What are you doing?"

"What do you mean? I was just having a good time like you are," he replied.

"Why are you spending your time with Tepi?" I asked.

"Are you jealous, Flower of Egypt?" he asked, then laughed.

"Of course not," I said.

"Then why are you so irritated with me? You have been spending your afternoon with Sen-Mut, and you did not wake me up to go with you." Hapu was very serious as he replied.

“I went to get you, and I saw that you were deeply asleep, and I wanted you to rest. Then Sen-Mut came back at the third hour, so we left and went across the water to the hills. Now what’s happening with you and Tepi? I want the truth.”

He became silent, trying to think of what to say.

“Nothing really. Just getting to know her.”

“Getting to know her? I have known for a while that you have been talking to her. Do you like her?”

He started to laugh loudly.

“What is so funny?”

“Laughing at your jealousy,” he said.

I became silent. “Okay, you win. I have been a little bit jealous. But you know what my fate is,” I told him.

“Now, Flower of Egypt, do you believe that it’s fair for me to be forced to remain without a wife or children? Knowing that you will never be mine?”

“I know it would not be fair to you. What about T’Queta?” I asked him.

“I’m still undecided about whether I will take her for a wife or a concubine.”

“She deserves to be your wife,” I said.

“No, because the only one I want for my wife is you. If I take Tepi, she will not be my wife; she will be my concubine.”

I became silent because I had always known what he held in his heart for me. Then I turned to face him. My heart hurt because he hurt.

Looking in to his gray eyes, I said softly, "Do you believe that I will ever be happy, Hapu? Knowing that your heart hurts?"

I started to walk slowly, and he walked beside me in silence. Then he stopped and faced me.

"I know you never will be happy, Lotus of Egypt. And the worst thing is that I love you differently every day, not with a child's love, but with a man's love. I've loved you more and more, ever since that day that you became a woman, and every day you are becoming more beautiful. I don't know how to stop these feelings. I think if I become seriously involved with someone else, my feelings will slow down for you, and I will not be hurting like I hurt now. I am dying to kiss you at this moment, on this beautiful night," he said. He was looking straight into my eyes.

I smiled at him and continued walking. "Have you ever told Aakhep' about your feelings for me?"

"Yes, I have, and he feels the same way that you do, that it's ridiculous that no one can marry the one their heart desires, all just to maintain the royal line. One day he said to me that he didn't care who you love. He wants you to be happy and he wants to be happy himself, with Isis. She is willing to wait, knowing that she will never be Queen, and that both of you may be trapped in a future marriage that you don't want, like Neferu-Bity."

I nodded. "And he is right," I said. After a moment, I continued, "Hapu have you bedded Tepi yet?"

"No, I have not."

"You should marry T'Queta instead."

He became silent. In the meantime, we had reached the Pharaoh's chambers, and everyone was in bed talking. Sen-Mut was sitting on his bed talking with everyone, including Tepi. He had a serious look when he saw me walk in with Hapuseneb. I told T'Queta to bathe me, and we walked outside, and she bathed me. We walked back into the Pharaoh's chambers. Sen-Mut was looking at me, and we smiled at each other. I could tell that he was not too happy seeing me with Hapuseneb.

We all spoke for a while and then fell asleep.

The next morning was glorious. We crossed the river with the horses, and Sen-Mut was in a better mood. We were laughing, very close to each other physically. I started feeling the familiar nervous excitement and shortness of breath. It was terrific being beside him.

Hapuseneb watched us constantly. My horse was not docile with Sen-Mut because he did not know him. My guard was holding the horse, and the horse was moving back and forth. He finally calmed down, and Sen-Mut could sit on the saddle. This was his first time riding a horse, and he was not steady in the saddle. I was afraid that he might fall.

Aakheperen-Re and Hapuseneb walked their horses in front of mine. That helped to make my horse steady for Sen-Mut. I rode beside him at his right. He was not nervous at all. Once the horse had become more accustomed to him, Aakhep' moved into place beside Sen-Mut, and Hapuseneb rode up beside me. I was happy that all of us were riding together.

Once he was ready to trot faster, we started to gallop and then got to the hilltop. We continued riding, and eventually, the morning became hot, so we returned to the island. We had lunch, then went for a swim. Later, we saw the sunset together. I laughed a lot, for I was very happy. He didn't speak much, and when I looked at him, he was looking at me. I still wondered whether he liked me.

I dreaded the return home and the resulting separation from Sen-Mut, but I knew that he would always be there. I knew I would be happy every time I remembered this trip that gave us the opportunity to be together and talk.

We spent the last night of the trip around the fire, and that time I had several goblets of wine. Sen-Mut was across the fire from me, but I wished that he was beside me instead. Hapu, as always, was at my right.

The day finally came for our return to Thebes. We departed at dawn. We spent most of the trip back laughing. I have enjoyed Sen-Mut's company. We were able to talk many times alone, or simply be silent, looking at the stars.

"Maatke-Re, I will never forget these days. They were wonderful, and I will never forget that you were once in the middle of all the stars, and I will always imagine you in the middle of all of them," he said.

"Thank you, Sen-Mut from Luny. I will not forget this trip and the wonderful time we spent together either."

We smiled at each other. I was ready to sleep in my bed, but I was not ready to sleep away from Sen-Mut.

CHAPTER 23

FATHER'S WARNINGS

We arrived in Thebes in the late afternoon. It was almost dark when the barge docked, and the ramp was placed. Sen-Mut came close to me, knelt, and bowed his head to the floor.

"Rise, Sen-Mut future Ptah of Egypt." I said.

"Your Majesty, I want so much to thank thee for the invitation to this wonderful place, for the wonderful time we had together, and for making me feel part of your circle of friends," he said, and we smiled at each other.

"Sen-Mut, I am pleased that you enjoyed yourself as much as I did, and I am pretty sure that we will do it again in the future."

I gave him one last smile and left with everyone trailing behind me. I was walking with Aakhep' and Hapu, and I turned around, and I saw him walking in the direction of the temple. My heart went with him.

I ran to my mother's quarters, feeling very joyful, to tell her what a wonderful time we had and how happy I was. I also wanted to tell her all about Sen-Mut. She would understand.

“Mother!” I exclaimed when I saw her. She was lying on her lounge chair. I rushed to her, and she hugged me, but something was off. She did not look well. She looked pale and tired.

“Mother aren’t you feeling well?” I asked concern. She looked like she did the last time when she was ill. I didn’t like that. I was worried.

“Has the physician come to see you Mother?”

“No, there is no need. I just feel tired.” She said.

I clapped my hands, and her slave Tuyii came rushing. “Go for the physician right away!” I yelled, and she left.

“Daughter, did you have a wonderful time? Come and sit here beside me and tell me all about it.” She smiled at me. “Your face is bright and radiates love. Were you able to spend some time alone with Sen-Mut?”

“No, Mother, I was never left alone with him, even though I wanted to be. We were always surrounded by friends. Aakhep’ and Hapu were always around.

“Very good. We don’t want your father to hear that you were alone with him. Remember, he has ears and eyes everywhere in his kingdom. So now, tell me all about it. I want to hear it all!” she said with a smile.

I told her how I was awakened by the sound of a rooster in the very early part of the morning in the ship and how it was Sen-Mut calling the birds. She laughed, and so did I.

“Do you still have butterflies in your stomach when you are near him?”

“Oh yes, Mother, and I can hardly breathe.”

She laughed, and seeing her laugh made me feel good.

“Mother, he said something very beautiful to me when we were sailing to Philae that night. Thoth and the stars were shining above us. I told him that during my test, of the foresight, my Ka left my body and flew and that I was in the middle of the universe and was surrounded by stars. He was in awe. Then he said that he wished he could have been there, that he would have taken them and made me a crown of stars."

"Oh, that it is very beautiful. Were you alone with him when he said it?"

"No, Hapuseneb was beside me."

She looked as if she was thinking about something.

"And what did Hapu say to this?" she asked

"Well, he was silent at first. Then he said that he wished that he could have been there, too, and that he would have dressed me with all the stars of the universe."

"Those are both beautiful thoughts. But who would not make such offers? You are the most beautiful goddess in the whole kingdom, and your father is Amun-Ra!"

I smiled. "Thank you, Mother. It's because you love me!"

"It's because it's the truth. You are beautiful. I am not telling you all these things because you are my daughter, but because it is simply the way it is. Every day you are looking more beautiful than before."

Then I remembered what Hapu told me that night on Philae, that every day I look more beautiful, and he loved me every day more and more but with the love of a man.

The physician arrived and moved close to her bed. I moved out of the way. He asked her many questions, and I heard her say that she had been very tired recently. She also said that sometimes her chest felt tight, and the tightness caused her pain. He gave her a potion, and she started to relax and eventually fell asleep.

"Is my mother going to be okay?" I asked the physician with some trepidation.

He looked at me and replied, "I believe that she has been experiencing stress since you left for Philae. She was worried about you because you have never been apart from her. Your trip, as I said, caused her much stress, but now she will be fine. She will be able to sleep well tonight now that you are back in the palace. I will be in the next room if she needs me." He bows and left.

I sat on the floor beside her holding her hand for a long time. My thoughts returned to Sen-Mut, thoughts which pleased my heart. Every moment that we spent together replayed in my mind, his smiles and his lovely words: "I wish I had been there. I would have made you a crown of stars." What a lovely thought. I smiled and looked at my mother, who by this point was peacefully asleep.

I left directions for her slaves, specifically Tuyii, to come and get me as soon as she woke up. Then I went back to my quarters. T'Queta was waiting to bathe me. After my bath, I went to bed, and I lay there lost in thought about how wonderful our time together was.

Suddenly, it occurred to me that perhaps he was strolling beside the Nile. I got up quickly and walked to the balcony, pleased to see that he was there. He was looking at me, and when he saw me, he turned around and left. My heart was thrilled that he came to say goodnight to me.

The next morning, I was awakened by T'Queta who was saying excitedly, "Your Majesty, Your Majesty, Master Hapuseneb is here to see you!"

I was puzzled. I didn't know why he would be here. I put on a robe and rushed to the outer quarters, wondering what was going on. He looked at me as I walked into the room.

"Good morning to you, Lotus of Egypt."

"And good morning to you Hapuseneb. Aren't you a bit early to be here? Is something wrong?"

"Yes, Maat summoned me and Aakheperen-Re and all our friends who went on the trip to Philae early this morning, and He just concluded with my questioning. His Majesty asked us many questions about the trip and questioned us about Sen-Mut and you. And let me tell you, he is not in a good mood."

"What do you mean, and what did you told him?"

"Everything, that we were all together at all times, and Aakheperen-Re told him the same. Let me tell you this, he had a great number of our friends waiting in line to be questioned about Sen-Mut and you," he said it with a warning tone in his voice.

I became nervous and remembered my mother's advice not to be alone with him because Father had eyes and ears everywhere in his kingdom.

"I believe he is going to call for you, too, so be prepared. I just came to warn you about it. I don't know what Sen-Mut's fate will be." He said.

I frowned and became alarmed. "What do you mean by 'His fate'?"

"I really don't know why your father is so angry today."

"Is he going to summon Sen-Mut?"

"I really don't know."

The door swung open. It was Aakhep' walking very fast. "Good morning, sister," he said.

"Aakhep', what is going on?"

"I really don't know. I have no idea who told Maat that Sen-Mut came with us to Philae. It wasn't me," he said.

Hapuseneb said, "Nor do I, Aakhep', I told you that it was not a good idea to bring him on this trip, but you said that you won a bet with Hat. You see, this makes me remember when we got that terrible licking by the soldiers when we were younger. Do you remember?"

"Shut up, both of you!" I yelled at them. I was agitated. "T'Queta!" I shouted, then looking at them, I said, "I must reach Father before he harms Sen-Mut." T'Queta approached. "T'Queta, dress me in a hurry!" I told her, and she did.

I ran out through the golden doors. The wind was blowing hard, and it was filled with sand. I covered my face and flew down the stairs, running to the hall of audience.

Father was sitting on his throne. It was clear that he was angry. His face was distorted with that anger. "What's going on?" I thought frantically. Khety was talking to him and to Ineni, and both looked worried.

Father turned his attention to me and said, "I am putting Sen-Mut to death!" His voice thundered throughout the entire hall of audience.

I screamed frantically, "No, Father! Please don't do it! Have you given the order yet?" I was crying and shaking terribly.

"Not yet. But he will no longer live after the high noon today."

"If you kill him, I will kill myself like Neferu-Knib did. I will! I will!" I screamed at him.

The last part got his attention. I could tell I had shocked him. "Guard!" he called.

I was terrified for Sen-Mut's life, but I did not know how to stop Pharaoh. I knew he was going to do it. His words were the law of the land, and he never said something he didn't mean.

The guards came up behind me. "I will kill myself! I will kill myself!" I kept shouting at Father. And then I ran out of the hall.

"Hatshepsut! Hatshepsut!" Father was calling me, but I didn't listen. I kept running away. He continued to call after me until I could not hear him anymore.

The wind was blowing sand incredibly hard. I ran to the stable and jumped on my horse's back. I rode off into the killer storm, a storm that buried cities. I was sobbing. I didn't care anymore. Father is going to kill him.

I rode far away, and then dismounted and hit my horse hard to get him to run away from me. I knelt facing the storm. I didn't want Father ever to find my body. The sand continued to pelt me on my face and body.

"Your majesty! Your majesty!" It was Sen-Mut's voice calling me. He was riding to me on horseback. He jumped down, and grabbing a tapete[29] from the horse's back, he hit it to make him run away. He covered our heads with the tapete.

"Your Majesty, this is a terrible sandstorm. It could bury us and kill us. Do as I tell you to do," he said.

I saw him kneeling on the sand, digging a hole with his hands very quickly. I had no idea what he was doing. He pulled me into the hole with him and said, "You hold the tapete over our heads, and I will dig us out as the sand is covering us!"

We could hardly breathe because we were so choked by the sand. The first time his arm brushed mine, I felt an electrical current over my arm and body. I didn't know what caused it. At the same time, I could feel weight of the sand burying us on our backs. He was shoveling the sand with his hands as fast as he could, so that we could eventually climb out

---

[29] A straw carpet.

of the hole, but the sand was covering us quickly. My arms started to hurt from the weight of the sand over our heads and backs.

Finally, the storm passed us, and he finished digging us out of the hole. When we emerged, we stood side by side coughing and covered in sand. We stood there looking far away as the wind carried the sand away with it. We did not speak to each other or look at each other. We still couldn't breathe normally, coughing because of the sand clogging our airways.

After a while, I started to walk away from him without saying a word. I knew that I would cry if he said anything to me. What could I tell him? That I loved him and wanted to kill myself because Father was going to kill him anyways and that I wanted to die too? I wanted to run away from him as far as I could.

He followed me without saying a word, all the while keeping his distance. After walking for a few hours, Ra was high, and it was terribly hot. I was thirsty. I saw the royal cavalry riding toward us carrying the royal banner.

I panicked! Father was coming. I turned around quickly and looked at Sen-Mut, with tears pouring down my face. I resolved to die with him.

"Sen-Mut, I called. "Run and stand beside me!" I yelled. He ran up to me and stand beside me at my left.

I saw that Hapuseneb and Aakhep' riding beside Father.

"Are you alright?" Father asked.

"Yes, I am. Sen-Mut saved my life!" I shouted.

The disturbed look from this morning was replaced by surprise.

"Guard!" Father shouted.

I panicked and started to shake. I took a few steps and stood in front of Sen-Mut. “Did you hear me? He saved my life!” I shouted at Father again.

Looking at me, Father told the guard, “Bring the horse and give it to Sen-Mut.” “You ride with Hapuseneb, and we will talk in the palace,” he, said.

That was when I knew that I truly loved Sen-Mut.

CHAPTER 24

AHMOSE NEFERTITI

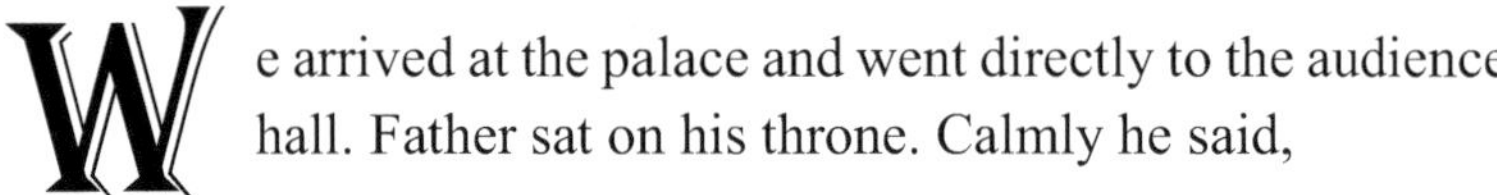

We arrived at the palace and went directly to the audience hall. Father sat on his throne. Calmly he said,

"Ineni, your pupil saved Horus's life. I will grant him his life for now, but he will not come close to my daughter. It's up to you to warn him and keep him away from her. He will remain your pupil for saving her life." Looking at me, he said, "You will not spend any more time with him. Whether he lives, or dies will be up to you. Running into that sandstorm to kill yourself was wrong. You almost killed me again. How did Sen-Mut know that you were running into the storm?"

"I don't know Father. I dismounted my horse, believing that you were going to execute him. I knelt facing the storm, and I wanted to die because you are being unfair. And I didn't want you to find my body if you had killed him. Then I heard a voice calling me. It was Sen-Mut riding toward me on a horse that he could barely ride. He dismounted with a tapete in his hands. He told me to do whatever he said. I saw him digging a hole in the sand with his both hands and fast as he could so that we could have shelter from the storm. We got into the hole, and I was covering our heads with the tapete as he shoveled the sand away with his hands. We climbed out of the hole after the storm passed us. If he hadn't made that hole in the sand, the dust would have asphyxiated us. Sen-Mut and I were never alone in Philae. At all times, there was someone with us."

"Your Majesty!"

We were interrupted by Hapuseneb wanting to help Sen-Mut.

"He told me when we got to the palace how he knew where she was going. He saw her running and crying when he was in Ineni's office, and he knew that there was a bad sandstorm coming. So, he ran after her when he saw her riding into the storm. He turned around, ran to the stable, jumped onto a horse, and rode after her quickly.

Khety spoke up next. "What he did was very brave, Your Majesty. He did it to save her life. He ran into that killer storm. He didn't have a death wish. He just wanted to save her life."

Father looked straight into my eyes and said, "Indeed, very brave." Then he was lost in thought for a while.

"Ineni, I would like to invite Sen-Mut for dinner tonight at the palace so that I can thank him for saving my daughter's life. Now, Horus of Egypt, be at ease and go to be bathed. You have my word that he will not die because he has put his life in danger to save yours. You have my word."

I looked at my father and smiled at him. I then thanked him for sparing Sen-Mut's life. I left his presence feeling both relieved and content. I knew that Sen-Mut no longer had to worry for his life.

That night I was not allowed in the banquet hall per Maat's orders. I was forced to eat in my quarters. But I trusted my father. I knew that he would let Sen-Mut live.

****

"T'Queta, have you heard anything of the banquet dinner last night for Sen-Mut?" I asked.

"Yes, Your Majesty. We were all worried for his life, including Master Hapu and Master Aakhep'. I heard that Pharaoh was kind and that all the priests were there to support Sen-Mut. According to what I was told by Ineni's slave, and that he was happy that everything had gone well for Sen-Mut."

I became more at ease.

I walked to Mother's quarters. She was still lying in bed and didn't look well at all. I came closer to her, and she extended her hand to mine and clasped it.

"Beloved, you look sad today," she said. Then she clapped her hands twice, and the slaves left her quarters.

"Yes, Mother. Father almost ordered Sen-Mut's death, though he changed his mind at the last minute. But he doesn't want me to look at or talk to Sen-Mut ever again, and my heart is broken into tiny pieces. Someone told him that Sen-Mut came with us to Philae, and even though everyone told him that we were never alone with each other, he wanted to kill him anyway."

"It was me. I was startled when he came to my quarters two days after you left and asked me who went on this vacation to Philae with you. I told him Aakhep', Hapuseneb, Ursaramun, Puyem-Re, all your friends and Aakhep' friends, and one guest. When he heard the last bit, he turned around, and looking at me with piercing eyes, asked, 'Who?' I answered him, told him it was Sen-Mut. Your father became very angry, said that you were on the verge of discovery and that Sen-Mut is susceptible to the sexual desires of youth and would want to sow his wild oats. He said that when he was that age, he was the same and that he knew what it felt like to be young and full of life. And then he said that Sen-Mut would not be able to control his sexual urges and would want to have sex every time he could, and that the romantic setting of Philae, would call for it. He said that he knew that you and he are starting to fall in love because of the way you look at each other. He wondered if I thought he hadn't noticed. He was adamant that you not lie with Sen-Mut. But he was concerned that you would be tempted being near him on a full moon, which calls for making love. If I had told him on the night before you left that he was going, he would have stopped him from going.

She continues, "I couldn't hold my tongue any longer. The way the royal women have been treated is an injustice. I was outraged and furious at him. I started to yell at him, and I told him that if he wanted to stop your heart from loving Sen-Mut, he would never succeed because even though my father forced me to marry him so many years ago, I'm still in love with Ineni! And he knew it, too, from the very beginning because they were the best of friends. I also told him that I knew about the woman that he was in love with before our arranged marriage, that I knew she had broken his heart after his coronation when she married someone else and moved away. I told him that I knew he still looked for her when he goes on his military campaigns. And I told him again that he could not stop your heart from loving Sen-Mut."

Mother's mood had apparently changed while she was saying all of that. She looked different. Then she became silent.

"So Ineni is the man," I thought to myself. Her sadness showed in her eyes.

"Thank you, Mother for standing up for me and for telling me all of this. I take it that it's been Ineni who you were in love with before this arranged marriage?"

"Yes," she said sadly. She had tears in her eyes. "I've never spoken of my love for him to anyone, until just now with you. My father, my mother, your father, and Ineni were the only ones who knew of my love for him, and my father kept sending him far away to keep him from me. The talk that I had with Neferu-Bity was the same talk my mother had with me, and I cried about it for months, even years. It's very sad not to be able to share your love with the one you love and who loves you. That is why I do understand your love for Sen-Mut. I wish you so much happiness, my beloved daughter."

Her hand was shaking as she caressed my face, and it was cold. I found that strange.

She continued, "I love you with all of my heart, and I wish my beloved Neferu-Bity had not killed herself for wanting to love someone else. If you ever need help, and I am no longer here, go to Ineni for guidance. He will help you. I know he will.

"I'm sorry that I hurt your father the other day. I learned how to love him very much over the years, but it's not the same as when you are in love with someone. I feel bad for yelling at him. After that talk, he stormed out of my quarters, and I heard that he was fuming all those days until you came back. I thought that he would understand it by now." She had tears running down her face.

"I love you, Mother!"

She looked very tired, but she managed a smile. Then she closed her eyes as the tears roll down at the side of her face. I felt terribly sad for her and for me. I hugged her and kissed her, then knelt beside her, holding her hand for a long time, thinking about everything that she had said to me about her frustrated love for Ineni. I understood that Father must have suffered, too, when he had to relinquish his love for this marriage and see the woman whom he loved marrying another man, and never to see her again. The traditions that caused people such pain where terrible and stupid, I thought.

Then I noticed that Mother's hand was getting colder, unusually cold.

"Mother! Mother! Are you alright?"

She did not move and did not answer. "Mother, are you alright?!" I screamed over and over. I felt panic and terror overpowering me because I realized she was dead. I screamed, "My mother is dead! She was cold like Neferu-Knib!"

"Mother, I love you!"

The slaves heard me screaming and came running.

"Tuyii, Mother is dead!" I scream.

I sat beside my mother's body, held her, and rocked her in my arms as I sobbed. I saw Puyem-Re quickly enter the room. He examined her, then cast down his eyes and said, "Her Majesty, the Queen has gone to the heavens, and her Ka is reunited with the gods."

Father stormed through the golden doors.

"Father!"

I ran to him, and he hugged me. We cried as we walked to my mother's couch. He let go of me, knelt beside Mother's body, and held her hand and cried. I knelt beside him, and we cried together.

"My beautiful mother, with the most beautiful heart."[30]

Khety walked in with several priests and started to chant the prayer for the dead. I turned around and saw Aakheperen-Re who came in running. I ran to him, and he hugged me tightly. Hapuseneb was behind him, and the three of us hugged each other and cried for a long time

---

[30] I am crying as I write this chapter because I had the most lovely, sweet, and loving mother, and since her death, I miss her so very much. At that time, It was very hard for me not to have a mother anymore as my confidant, and someone I could tell about all my sorrows and happiness, someone that was happy for me or would cry with me. (3/15/2016)

together. I walked to my mother's bed and lay beside her. I put my head on her chest, hugged her, and cried.

"Mother I love you. Why did you have to go so soon? To whom I will pour my heart out to now?" I whispered.

I was moved away from her body by Aakhep' and Hapuseneb. I could not stop crying. Incense was everywhere, and the chanting continued for hours for my mother, the Queen. I wished I could run to Sen-Mut and let him console me. The silence covered the whole land. My tears were the saddest tears for the loss of my beautiful mother and for the man that I loved.

The highest priests were all there. They were ready to remove her body and take her to the house of dead. My father did not let the priests carry her body. He lifted her in his arms and carried her like he did for Neferu-Bity. The procession of priests and priestesses followed us to the House of the Dead. I walked beside my father. I could hear him sobbing, and I cried for both of us.

Among the many people gathered, I could see Sen-Mut behind a tree. He was wearing his priestly white robe, and we crossed looks. He whispered, "I am so sorry." He had tears rolling down his face and I cried harder and nodded my head. I saw him join the procession of priests, chanting prayers for the dead.

I could hear Hapu crying behind me as he walked beside Aakheperen-Re, for he has was her favorite of all my friends ever since he was eight years old.

I searched for Ineni, but he wasn't anywhere. I gathered that he wanted to be alone with his grief and sorrow. I cried for him, too, for a love that he could not have.

Sadness covered the whole land, and Father became terribly depressed.

I hadn't seen Sen-Mut, except for late at night when he walked beside the Nile. On those occasions, I could only see the shadow of his body. He would sit there for a while and then leave. Sometimes when I saw him leave, I would lie in bed with tears in my eyes.

A few days passed, and I was called to the hall of audience by my father. T'Queta bathed me and dressed me in the white kilt. Since my mother's death I had not worn a sheath. There didn't seem any point in doing so anymore.

I walked to the audience hall, and all the priests and priestesses were there. That was strange. As I was walking, I could feel the heavy look of someone watching me. It was Sen-Mut, It was the first time I had been this close to him since the day he saved my life. I lowered my eyes and walked straight past him. I was dead inside, and there was no emotion on my face. I continued walking to Father's throne, and I stood in front of my father.

Khety came closer to me and took my left hand. Facing Father, he said, "Hatshepset, daughter of Amun-Ra, as is the custom in our land after the death of a Queen, the princess next to the throne will marry Pharaoh, and you will be Queen of Upper and Lower Egypt. After the seventy days of embalming and mourning are over, the wedding will take place here in the hall of audience.

Holding my left hand, we walked up the steps to Father's throne. Father stood up, and I stood at his left. Then he extended his left hand, and my right hand was placed on top of his. Khety blessed us, incense was passed over our hands, and it was done. The ceremony was over.

Father and I walked to the palace with everyone, and from there to the banquet hall for the dinner that had been prepared for us.

I told Father I wanted to go to my quarters. He excused me since everyone knew that this ceremony was for political reasons only. I walked quickly. I was thinking that I would be Queen of Egypt soon. Then when Pharaoh goes to the heavens, I could marry Sen-Mut. At least there is some hope for both of us, I thought. That if he had not gotten married to someone else by then. But my heart told me that he wouldn't. Sen-Mut, please wait for me, I whispered under my breath as I was walking to the palace.

Those seventy days were the longest I could remember. I missed my mother, and sometimes I panicked. What would I do if I lost Father as well?

The burial ceremonial was a long process. It was painful and full of sorrow for Father and me. Her body was carried on a golden stretcher, which itself was carried on the shoulders of the priests. The procession was headed by the acolytes, who spread incense as they walked ahead of the priests carrying her body. I stood beside Father for the ritual of the opening of the mouth, and the slaughter of the calves. I already knew that we must eat our last meal with her. Many baskets of all kinds of food were brought for her to have plenty in the afterlife.

We stood in front of her gilded coffin, and the final prayers for the dead were offered. Father placed the golden lid over her mummified body, and the coffin was sealed. Dignitaries from all over the land came to pay their last respects as well, for they knew the Queen, my mother. Thousands and thousands of people from all over the land came to the burial. I could see how much she was loved by our people. She would be greatly missed.

Sitra-In died few months after mother went to the heavens, my heart was completely broken, she raised me as if I was her own and I loved her and missed greatly too.

CHAPTER 25

QUEEN OF EGYPT

The processions of my mother's burial was long and very sad for me and my father. It had been several months since she went to the heavens, and I could feel the sadness and the silence all over the land. I never expected to lose her this soon, nor that the god of the underworld would come for her so quickly. She was still young, lovely, and beautiful. I missed her greatly. In a few months, I would be Queen of Egypt. I would be marrying my father because that was the tradition for royal women, but this time would be different. He wanted to transfer his throne to me, as he had promised when I was a small child. Lately, he had not been feeling well. I could see it on his face since mother's death, and that worried me a lot.

I had not seen Sen-Mut since my mother's funeral, and I felt so alone. Hapuseneb and Aakhep' came to visit me from time to time, and they tried to cheer me up. But it was mostly Hapu who camc and stayed longer. Sometimes I forget that she was gone. I heard from Hapuseneb that Father had begun talking to Khety and the rest of the priests in the temple to gain support for me when the time came for me to assume the throne.

One day as I was walking to Father's quarters, and before I reached his receiving area, I heard Father and Khety having a conversation.

"Your Majesty, are you planning to have an heir with Prince Hatshepset?" Khety asked.

My father's reaction was immediate.

"I am not planning to spoil my daughter. This marriage is so that she can have control over my kingdom when I'm gone. You've told me ever since Aakheperen-Re was born, that he would go to the underworld at a young age. But the years have passed, and he is still here. I love my son, I suffer every day thinking that one day he will no longer be here. I want to make sure that I have your pledge, and the pledges of all the priest of Amun-Ra, by tomorrow… that she will be Pharaoh. I want you to gather all the priests in the temple tomorrow morning. I want to hear all of you say it to me, that you will support my daughter when that day comes," Father said.

"Yes, Your, majesty," Khety said.

Hearing my father's wishes, I turned around and left his quarters, thinking that I had a wonderful father.

In the following days after he had spoken with all the priests in the Temple of Amun-Ra, he issued an edict which declared, **"I, Pharaoh of the two lands, summon all of the dignitaries of the King: the nobles, the companions, the officers of the armed forces, the officers of the courts, and the viziers of Lower and Upper Egypt to come into my presence at the palace so that they may pay homage to Horus, my daughter."**[31]

---

[31] According to ancient records those were his words.

The next day, I was sitting on my bed with my legs crossed. I felt relaxed. I was looking at the sunrise and remembering my father's words from the evening before. I was pleased because Father had told me that tomorrow, he would place the Double Crown of Egypt upon my head to show the priests and the dignitaries of the land that he had chosen me as his successor to the throne. Ultimately, I would be Pharaoh when he was gone.

Late tonight, the priestesses will come to depilate the hair from my body and bathe me, for the early ceremony tomorrow morning. I would be ready for one of the most important moments of my life.

First, I needed to have a conversation with T'Queta.

"T'Queta, are you happy with Hapuseneb?"

"Oh yes, Your Majesty. He loves me very much, and I love him too."

I was pleased to hear it, but I was a little bit jealous because slaves could choose who they wanted to be with and love freely. Why couldn't my life be that simple? Why couldn't I love freely? I thought.

After I was bathed and dressed by T'Queta, I left my chambers. As I walked to the audience hall, I could see that there was quite a commotion all over the palace with preparations for the upcoming marriage and coronation tomorrow morning. Music was playing everywhere. I was pleased. Everything looked lovely. People of all stations were walking about everywhere.

I entered the audience hall, where my father had been reunited with his court. Beside him was his Vizier Rekhemire from Memphis and Hapuseneb, who smiled at me as I approached. Lunch was served to everyone in the audience hall.

After we ate, I left the audience hall, and walked to the stable. I went to my horse's stall. He was so beautiful. I caressed his face.

“Your Majesty.” A voice startles me.

I froze and turned around fast. It was Sen-Mut. I became very nervous. I was, in fact, panicking. I looked around to be sure that we were alone. I smiled at him and the butterflies were having fun in my stomach. It was so nice to see him again close to me. We had not been this close since he had saved my life.

“What are you doing here in the stables?” I asked with a smile.

“I come here sometimes and bring him carrots and raisins because he likes them and because…” He became quiet.

“Because why?” I asked. I wanted so badly to hear him say that it was because of me.

“Because he reminds me of the beautiful memories of you and the wonderful time we had on the island of Philae.”

He’d said it. We were so close to each other that I could smell the mint on his lips. I wanted so badly for him to kiss me and my body was trembling. I didn’t know if he had noticed how nervous I was.

Then I felt the presence of someone else behind me. I froze. I was terrified for Sen-Mut’s life since we couldn’t be caught together. I turned around hurriedly. It was Aakheperen-Re, bringing his horse to the stable.

“Aakhep’, you scared me!” I shouted at him.

“There’s no reason to be afraid of me, but you should be afraid of Father. If he finds out that you are here alone with Sen-Mut in the stable, particularly on the eve of your being crowned Queen of Egypt, you could cost him his life. Do you do realize that, don’t you? And I wouldn’t be able to save his life like we did the last time. It’s best for us to leave right now, before the stable slave returns and sees Sen-Mut here with you.” He said.

I looked at Sen-Mut and saw sadness on his face, enough to make him clench his teeth. I wanted to scream with frustration and run away.

"Sorry, Sen-Mut," Aakheperen-Re said to him.

I looked at Sen-Mut and lowered my face because I was so sorry for me and for him. Aakhep' and I walked away in the direction of the palace without turning my back. There were people everywhere.

"Why are you bringing your horse to the stable instead of the servant?"

"Because when I was riding back, I saw you enter the stable followed by Sen-Mut. I told the slave to go to the kitchen and bring me something to drink and that I would wait in the stable. Sending him to the palace gave me the time to get you out of here before Father could find out you were here with Sen-Mut."

I became quiet.

"Hat, if you care that much for Sen-Mut, why are you putting his life in danger?"

"I didn't know that he was behind me." I said.

"How many times have you met with him in the stables?"

"None. This is the first time that I've seen him or spoken to him since the sandstorm when he saved my life."

"Tomorrow, you are going to be the Queen, and I advise you not to come back here again. In fact, you should avoid any place where he might be because if Father finds out, he will have him killed," he said.

"Well, our palace is the size of a big city, far away from the temple, and that makes it impossible for me to meet with him without Father finding out," I said.

He stopped and put his hands on my shoulders. "Sister, be careful. That's all I'm asking for. You already know that when Father goes to the underworld, you must marry me to continue the royal line, and you must provide me with a son to be the heir to the throne."

I felt like I had been punched in the stomach, and I felt trapped with no way out. I looked at him and asked, "Do you think that is fair to me, being trapped in a marriage that I don't want, and loving someone else?"

"I know. I know that it is going to be very hard on you, but those are the sacrifices the royal women must make for us to continue the royal line," he said.

Just then I realized that he didn't know that I would be named heir to the throne the next morning. Thinking about all of this, I walked back to my quarters.

I was sitting on the balcony thinking about his words when I was interrupted by T'Queta. "Your Majesty, the priestesses are here to bathe you and depilate your body for tomorrow morning, and your bath is ready."

I smiled at T'Queta. "Tell them to come in."

They walked in wearing their long, white robes. They knelt.

"Your Majesty."

I smiled at them and said, "Rise." I got out of bed, and they followed me to the bathing pool. The musicians were playing harps softly. The incense was burning, and the very tall lamps were lit, surrounding us with plenty of light. They gently undressed me, and I sat in a chair. One of them shaved my head, and after she was done, I was laid on a table covered in white linen, and she started to depilate the hair from all over my body. Then I was covered with thick honey. They waited for the honey to smooth my skin, then rinsed it off. The pool was filled with goat milk and rose petals, and I submerged myself on it.

I sat there, sad for me and for Sen-Mut. But right now, I had happiness inside of me for seeing him and talking to him, at least a few words. I sat in the tub for a while for the moisture to work on my skin. Later T'Queta brought me dinner, and I ate slowly, thinking of Sen-Mut and about how much he had changed since the last time I saw him. He seemed more mature in the way he carried himself. He was, in fact, becoming a grown man.

After I finished eating, I walked to the balcony, and I saw him, as I saw him every day. He was there in the darkness waiting for me. I wanted to run down the stairs and kiss him, but I knew I must hold back for the time being because if I did so, he would die. We stayed in our respective places for a while looking at each other, and then I saw him leave. When he left, my heart sank and left with him.

Tomorrow, I would be married to Pharaoh and would be Queen of Egypt.

Very early the next morning, I was awakened by the priestesses and was bathed. They brought the golden kilt, a golden cape, golden sandals, and the pectoral Father had given me during my tenth summer. It still fit. Then they put kohl around my eyes and dressed me.

I walked to the golden mirror and looked at myself. I looked like a teenage boy, but with breasts. I put on the small Horus crown and walked down the stairs. In there was waiting for me Aakhep, Hapuseneb, Ursaramun, and the priestesses. They walked with me to the hall of audience. I stood in front of the large doors. They were opened, and I saw the entire court was present. Father was sitting on his throne, and I walked a very long path to stand in front of him. Khety approached and removed the small Horus crown from my head.[32]

Father spokes. “Come, glorious one. I have placed thee before me that thou mayest see thy administration and the excellent deeds of thy Ka in the palace, that thou mayest assume thy royal dignity, glorious in thy magic, mighty in thy strength. Thou shalt be powerful in the two lands. Thou shalt seize the rebellious who should appear in the kingdom. Thy forehead shall be adorned with the double diadem given to thee by him who presides over the throne of the gods, Pharaoh of Egypt.”[33]

I knelt, and Father placed his hands over my head and addressed the court.

“This is my living daughter, Khnemet-Amun Hatshepsut, who lives. Behold. I have appointed her my successor to the throne. She will command the people in every corner of the kingdom. She it is who shall lead you. You shall proclaim her word. Be united in her command.”

Father thundered, “He who shall do her homage shall live. He who shall speak evil and blasphemy of Her Majesty shall die!”

Then looking at me with a short smile on his lips he said, “For thou art divine. For thou art divine, O daughter of a god, for whom even the gods fight, behind whom they exert their protection every day according to the command of her father, the Lord of the gods.”

I felt very emotional hearing my father proclaiming me the successor to his throne in front all the dignitaries of the court. But I wondered

---

[32] I cannot remember clearly whether this ceremony was done in the morning or evening, when my father, the Great Maat choose me to be his heir to the throne. I believe it was in the morning and later that night he chose me as his consort.

[33] The words Father spoke at the ceremony are written on the pylons in the Temple of Karnak. As per ancient records.

how Aakheperen-Re felt, as Father had chosen me to be his heir. I looked at him and saw that his face was in shock.

Then, I expressed myself. "There I saw the majesty of my father and how divine and great was my fashioner. My heart is glad, and great is his crown."

I turned around and faced the court. My father had thundered those words in a loud voice in front of all the priests of Amun-Ra and the dignitaries of the courts. He removed the Double Crown of Egypt from his head for an instant and brought it above my head, saying, "King of Upper and Lower Egypt, Maatke-Re Hatshepsut. May she live forever." He returned the crown to his head.

Next, it was time for me to walk the long path to the entrance of the hall of audience and for the court and dignitaries to kiss the stone floor that I walked upon. I saw Aakheperen-Re, Hapuseneb, and Ursaramun to my left. Hapu and Ursaramun knelt and kissed the floor. I walked over their kisses. Everyone in the hall of audience was kneeling with reverence on the stone floor and then kissing it. There was a sea of people performing these actions.

I walked all the way to the entrance of the hall of audience, and there he was. Sen-Mut was looking at me with a pleasant look in his eyes. He knelt and kissed the floor several times, and I stood over his kisses. A warm feeling of love traveled all the way to my heart. I turned around with a smile and walked to the throne, as the people continued to kiss the floor that I walked upon.

I rejoined my father at the steps of his throne, and he came down the five steps. We started to leave the hall of audience, walking the long path. I heard people praising my name and Father's name, kissing the ground that we walked on together. They were also praising the names of all the gods of Upper and Lower Egypt.

"May Hatshepsut and Aakheperka-Re[34] live forever!" the people were shouting as we walked out of the audience hall.

"May Hatshepsut and Aakheperka-Re live forever!"

We walked to the palace. The dignitaries of the court followed behind. The people on the streets were cheering and throwing flowers over our heads. It was a marvelous sight for me. That night, I became Queen of Egypt!

Leaving the hall of audience, the people went forth, rejoicing. They published his proclamation, and everyone in every dwelling of the court heard these words. They came, their mouths rejoicing. The numbers were swelling and swelling, and they were announcing his name. Soldiers upon soldiers leapt and danced for the double joy of their hearts. They proclaimed the name of Her Majesty as King. "May Maatke-Re live forever. Thou are excellent in your great soul."

Father's words were proclaimed throughout Thebes: "As for any man who shall love her in his heart and shall do her homage every day, she shall shine, and he shall flourish exceedingly. As for any man who shall speak against the name of Her Majesty, the gods shall determine his death."

I felt as if Father was directing his words to my beloved one.

The celebration started with a wonderful breakfast. Everyone was invited, included Sen-Mut. He kept his distance, and sometimes I noticed that he was looking at me. When he did, I would look at Maat to see if he noticed. I kept busy by talking to Hapuseneb, Aakhep', and Ursaramun to keep myself occupied so that I would not look at him. I didn't want Father to unleash his anger on him.

---

[34] This was Father's original name before he became Thutmoses I at his coronation.

At one point, I lowered my eyes and gazed in his direction again, but he was gone. He had probably left with a broken heart, I thought. I became upset and left the banquet hall as well. The marriage would take place in the evening. There would be a celebration all over the kingdom. The next morning, we would sail north to the city of Heliopolis, the Holy of Holies and the city of the gods

Late in the afternoon, the priestesses arrived. They bathed me well, scrubbed my body with sugar cane mixed with cinnamon, then rinsed me and covered me with sweet honey. I was rinsed again, and finally, I was submerged again in goat milk, and rinsed again with water. I was rubbed with my favorite perfume oil, one made of a combination of flowers, specially sent to be made by my mother for my fifteen summers. The smell suited me.

They put makeup on my face, kohl around my eyes, rouge on my cheeks, and red lipstick on my mouth. They dressed me in clothing made of materials from faraway lands: a golden dress, golden sandals, a belt made with precious stones and gold, and a cape of gold material like my dress, with a very long train. Then they put the long-braided wig on my head.

On the other side of the room was Khety, waiting to place the Horus crown on my head. Today, I would begin my journey as Queen, but I would not be wearing any of my mother's crowns yet. I would be crowned in the city of Heliopolis with the gods' approval. Khety was let into my quarters and I knelt, and he placed the small Crown of Horus on my head.

I walked out of my bedroom where Hapuseneb and Puyem-Re greeted me with a smile. I smiled back at them, but something was missing in my heart, my mother and Sen-Mut!

We left, and Father was waiting at the bottom of the stairs with his court. He looked like a god. He was dressed in a long golden kilt, golden belt, and golden sandals. He was wearing the pectoral of the Pharaoh with the Eye of Horus and the Pschent[35] on his head. He looked just as a Pharaoh should look. He smiled at me from the bottom of the stairs, and I smiled back at him.

I searched for Sen-Mut. When I spotted him, he was looking at me, and we smiled at each other. Father noticed that I had smiled at someone, but he was not bothered by it. My brother was also present, waiting beside Mutnofret, his mother, and Hapuseneb joined him after we reached the bottom of the stairs.

I reached the last step, and Father kissed my forehead. We walked to the audience hall. Hundreds of priests, including Sen-Mut, were aligned at our sides. We reached the entrance of the audience hall. The court, dignitaries, and thousands of people were already waiting there. They dropped their faces to the floor as we walked forward along the long path to the throne.

All the elder priests were lined up to the right and left of the throne. Father and I reached the throne taking the five steps up to the golden chairs. Then we turned around to face the court, dignitaries, and the people of Thebes. I was happy, but my happiness would not be complete until I had Sen-Mut. I searched for him again. He was looking at me, so I removed my gaze from him. I did not want anyone to notice that I was looking at him.

Khety approached my father and me, and bowing his head, he turned around to face the people and shouted, "In the presence of dignitaries from all over the land, the court, and the people of Thebes, Aakheperka-Re takes, on this day, take for his consort Khnemet-Amun Hatshepsut, who will rule as his Queen and as Pharaoh when he is no more and rises to the heavens to be with the gods. Her word will be the law of the land."

Then, taking my right hand, he placed it on my father's left hand.

---

[35] The red and white crown of Upper and Lower Egypt.

There was an outburst of cheering from everyone. Sen-Mut was cheering from his place at the end of the aisle, too. I smiled at him and at the people. Father's hands and my hands were not tied with blue ribbon because everyone knew that this marriage was just to transfer the power of his kingdom to me.

It seemed to me that Father had not been feeling well. I could see it on his face ever since my mother ascended to the heavens. Deep in my heart, I believed that he felt guilty for the last argument they had about my trip to Philae, and that I was falling in love with Sen-Mut.

Very early the next morning, we would sail with the court to the city of the gods, Heliopolis, the cradle and birth place of all the kings of Egypt. Father would present me as his chosen one to all the gods and seek their approval to crown me as his Queen with the Crown of Buto, the Lady of Life.[36]

There would be a celebration that night in the land, but it would be an even greater celebration when we returned to Thebes, when Khety would present me with all my mother's crowns.

We had dinner in the banquet hall, and I told Father that I would retired early. I had not seen Sen-Mut in the banquet hall. Father kissed me on my forehead, and I left. I ran up the stairs and ran to the balcony, and there he was, waiting for me. I brought my hand to my lips and kissed my fingers hoping that he could feel the warmth of my kiss and my love. He did not remain their long. It was late at night, and he had a long walk to Karnak. Or maybe he would sleep that night on a mat in Ineni's office.

****

"Your Majesty, wake up. It's time for your bath. Soon Ra will rise, and you must be ready to sail to your glory!"

---

[36] The "Cobra Crown"

I opened my eyes, and I smiled at T'Queta who was smiling at me. "T'Queta, is everything ready to sail this morning?"

"Yes, Your Majesty. I am excited about the trip. I was a small child when we sailed here, and I am looking forward to sailing again. Do you think we will be close to the green sea, where I was born?"

"I believe that we can try to go there and see it again. I will ask Maat tonight. I don't think His Majesty will mind going there." I said.

"Oh, Your Majesty. Thou have made me very happy this morning. Is Master Hapuseneb coming on this journey for your coronation?"

"I believe so, I said, and I smiled, seeing how happy she was.

"All the other slaves are also anxious and ready to go. They have never sailed before, and everything is already loaded onto the ship." She said.

"Okay, let's go to be bathed," I said.

Before I went in to be bathed, I walked to the balcony to see if Sen-Mut had come at that hour to say goodbye. No, he was not there, but he probably would be at the temple before we leave.

"T'Queta, bring me something to eat, some of my hot drink, date breads, and fruit, enough to fill us until we dock somewhere, and breakfast is served."

"Yes, Your Majesty."

She left. Ra was rising in the east. I washed myself and knelt and blessed the God Almighty. I could smell the incense and hear the chanting and the blessings on the other side of the golden doors.

My thoughts turned to Sen-Mut. I felt as if he were looking inside of me, and I suddenly had the feeling that he was on the other side of the doors. I got up from the floor and ran to the doors. I opened them gently.

Yes, there he was! I could hear the prayers coming out of his lips while he swung the incense censor back and forth in front of the golden doors. Then he noticed me and smiled. I smiled back at him and again closed the doors gently. I leaned back against the golden doors. Then I started to dance with happiness. He had come to see me. I was so pleased, and it felt like the journey would not be as long now that I saw him. I was glad that he came to say goodbye to me, for I knew that it was not his duty as a future Ptah architect. Those were the duties for beginner priests.

I was dancing when T'Queta brought my breakfast.

"Your Majesty, you are dancing, and I can imagine why. I saw the young future Ptah leaving your doors. Did you see him?"

"Yes, I did! And I believe that he came to see me and in a small way, to say goodbye."

I was so happy that I took the tray from out of T'Queta's hands, and put it down, and pulled her to dance with me. After we stopped, I look at her. "Dress me. Father will soon be sending his guard to let me know that he is ready."

As she was dressing me, I ate a piece of the date bread. There was a knock on the door.

"Your Majesty, Pharaoh is waiting," the guard said.

"Tell Father that I will be there soon." T'Queta put the golden sandals on my feet. "I am ready. Let's go." I ran down the stairs laughing.

Father was waiting with the court.

"Good morning, Father."

"Good morning, Daughter. You are so cheerful this morning!"

"Yes, Father. It's a glorious day!" And smiling, I kissed his cheek. Then we started to head out. I saw Khety and hundreds of priests walking.

I knew that a fleet of ships were waiting at the dock to sail and that I would have my own ship. My feet were hurting, and it was a long walk to Karnak, but at least soon I would be able to take my sandals off.

Khety finished the blessings for the journey, and we boarded the ships. Father accompanied me to the interior of my ship. Then, he instructed, "Maatke-Re, I leave you in the company of Hapuseneb and all your friends. The slaves will be serving breakfast until our next stop when you will make your first offering to the god of that town and ask for their approval of your coronation. Then we will continue to Abydos, the city of Osiris, then Memphis, the city of Ptah, then Saqqara, Giza and Heliopolis, cities of all the gods. After the first offering, we will eat with the mayor of that small town and then continue our journey. We will visit every shrine along the Hopi until we reach Heliopolis. We need the approval of every deity of Egypt. The Vizier of Memphis has sent orders to prepare for our arrival and for us to stay there. I also want you to enjoy this long journey."

"Father, I will make offerings with all my heart to every god along the way to Heliopolis."

"That is the way that it should be. The gods will bless you with their approval." He kissed my forehead and then left.

Once he was aboard, his ship started to move, the royal blue and gold banner moving with the breeze. His ship carried all the dignitaries, Khety, and all the elder priests to be witnesses to the approval of all the gods for my coronation. And of course, Father's ship carried his harem.

I stood at the front of the ship, for I loved the breeze blowing on my face. There was a multitude of people along the river, throwing white flowers as the ship sailed to the north. I saw Sen-Mut throwing white petals as my ship passed beside him, and we smiled at each other. No one was watching, and I felt free to smile at him. I was very happy all over again.

We sailed many hours to the temple of Abydos, the city where the head of Osiris was said to be buried. There, I visited the temple Father had built in his honor.

All my personal slaves were dressed in white linen. They carried baskets with gold dust, white flowers, roses petals, fruit, goat milk, and sweet cakes made of dates. The High Priest and the other elder priests were waiting on the ground to start the procession to the Temple of Osiris. My personal slaves were in two rows, with twenty-five in each row. I came down from the ship, and they followed behind me.

I danced for Osiris barefoot, and I made offerings to him of gold dust, perfume oils, flowers, and other offerings. I made all my offerings with a clean heart and with love. And he was pleased with my presents. The wind blew inside his temple, a sign that he was pleased with me and the gifts I gave to him. Father and all the priests were pleased with the way I presented to him these beautiful items.

After I was done with the gift giving, Father showed me the wall on which were engraved the cartouches of the Pharaohs before him, there were cartouches of my ancestors who were Kings. I saw the name of my great, great, grandfathers who were Pharaohs in the past. I saw my grandfather's cartouche with Amenhotep engraved on it and my father's cartouche beside his. I was proud to see his name, Aakheperka-Re engraved among the others.

"Hatshepsut, when you become Pharaoh, I want you to add your name to this list, so that your name will live for all eternity among the Kings of Egypt!"

"Yes Father. I will, and it will be beside yours."

He smiled at me, and we returned to the ships.

The trip to Memphis was very long, but finally we arrived at that great city. It was very early in the morning, before sunrise, and Father's Vizier of Lower Egypt came down from Father's ship and welcomed us to Father's palace.

I was bathed, and my body was prepared and covered in gold dust. I was dressed in the short golden kilt. I would make my offerings to Ptah without sandals. Because I was covered in gold dust, as I walked to his temple, the sun was shining on me, and I was bright like the sun and hot. I walked to the large statue of Ptah, and in his presence, I made my offerings one by one as my slaves brought them to me. I paid my respects with a clean heart and with love to the god Ptah, the creator of all things. This continued for hours.

I danced barefoot before him, burned incense and begged for his help to make Sen-Mut the greatest architect in Egypt. I threw a lot of gold dust over him, and I clamored for his acceptance. Then, once again the wind started to blow in strong gusts. Everyone was astonished at his acceptance of my offerings.

Then I danced for his wife Sekhmet. I threw rose petals at her statue in large quantities. I bathed her statue with the finest perfume oil and poured gold dust over her head. I saw her smiling at me, and everyone else did, too. Father was pleased.

Then I started to dance for Nefertum. As I was dancing for him with love, suddenly the burning fire of the lamps shot flames into the air, and the wind was blowing. I could see the faces of the dignitaries, Khety, the priests, and my father. They were clearly in awe at what they had seen. The triad had spoken: they would accept my coronation. I continued dancing for Nefertum until the oil lamps began to burn low. Then it was over.

I was exulted, but I was also exhausted. I walked to where Father was siting and sat beside him. I ate, for I was very hungry.

It was almost morning when I walked to my quarters. I was bathed, and it was very hard for T'Queta to remove the gold dust from my skin. She tried her best with the other slaves to remove it with oils. I could not keep my eyes open. They did their best, and T'Queta put me in a linen sheath. I was carried to the bed, by whom I don't remember. I lay on the bed and fell asleep.

I woke up very late in the afternoon, but I did not want to get up, as I was still exhausted. However, I made myself get up.

"Your Majesty, I brought you your breakfast, and Master Hapuseneb has been here several times to speak with you," T'Queta said.

I wondered what the urgency was.

"T'Queta, after my breakfast, send for him."

"Yes, Your Majesty."

I sat in the chair and started to have my breakfast, looking at the beauty of the large terrace and gardens and the glorious view from afar. Hopi's waters were a beautiful blue color, lighter than they were in Thebes. The long white terraces complemented the view.

I heard steps approaching me. When I turned around, I saw that it was Hapuseneb, and I smiled. He knelt at my feet and bowed his head to the floor. I found that strange.

"Your Majesty."

"Rise, Hapuseneb. Have a seat. Would you like some breakfast?"

"No, Your Majesty."

"Why are you being so formal, Hapu?"

"Well, you are the Queen now, and I must pay you all due respect as Khety told me to. I am coming with a message from your father. He said that from here, you must sail with him to Saqqara, Giza, and then Heliopolis."

"Now sit down, Hapu. I have not changed, and you will always be my dearest friend. You don't have to stand on formality with me. How do you like this part of the country?"

"Well, I believe it is beautiful, especially this palace, and the view is gorgeous. I want to tell you that I was very impressed by the way you made your offerings to Ptah and the way you danced. I'd never seen you dance like that before, shining with the gold dust all over your body. You looked like you were in a trance dancing. Ptah was very pleased with you last night. He has shown all of us that you have his approval to be the Queen. The wind and the fire in the standing oil lamps showed all of us that he was pleased."

"What do you mean?"

"The wind picked up inside the temple, the sand was not blown in, and the fire in the oil lamps became high almost reaching the heavens," he said.

"I can tell you that I felt as though I was in a trance. It was as if the gods were inside of me and were dancing with me. I also felt as if I were floating in the air, as I still feel right now. It was strange, because I hadn't had that feeling since I passed the test of foresight when I was only five summers," I said.

"Well, you are the daughter of Amun-Ra and with the beauty of all the gods. Everything is going to go well for you in Heliopolis. We sail early tomorrow morning."

"Hapu, wouldn't you ever want to see the country of your birth, that beautiful Island of Crete? There is a possibility that we will go there if you want, because we are going to the green sea after my offerings in Heliopolis."

"Flower of Egypt, I would love to go, but I have been keeping something to myself, and I don't know if it's prudent for me to talk to you about it. Yes, I would like very much to go, but not now."

I was puzzled and frowned. "Can you not talk about it?"

"Hmm, well, I guess I can. But please don't be alarmed. Have you noticed that your father seems tired all the time lately?"

I felt as if I had been hit by a stone.

"My father!"

I became silent, but eventually I answered, "Yes," and I lowered my eyes. "He has been like that since Mother went to the heavens. I thought it was because he was sad, but lately he seems withdrawn and doesn't speak to me that much. I wonder if he feels the Anubis getting closer?" I had tears in my eyes. "I don't want my father to die, Hapu. Not for a long time."

"Don't be sad, Flower of Egypt. You see? That's why I did not want to say anything to you before."

"Thank you Hapu. You are right. Therefore, after my offerings in Heliopolis, we must return to Thebes. I was going to visit the green sea, but it would not be a good idea to go now because of Father's condition."

We sailed early the next morning for Heliopolis. I sat beside Father as the ship began traveling north.

"Father, are you feeling well? I've been worried about you lately since Mother went to the heavens."

"Hatshepsut, lately I have been feeling tired a lot of the time. I think time is catching up with me, as are all the wars, the campaigns to other lands, and an excess of wine." He smiled and lowered his head. He had tears in his eyes. I became sad, and I teared up, too. I squeezed his left hand. "I miss your Mother greatly. I could speak with her for hours and laugh. I trusted her completely, and I feel guilty about her death. I should have trusted you more, and I should have not gotten angry with your mother that time when you went to Philae."

"I know, Father. You know, that day she told me about the woman you were in love with who married someone else and moved away. Mother said that she knew that when you went on your military campaigns to other lands, you looked for her. Have you ever found her?"

He was quiet for a moment,

"No, I never did. But your mother also suffered for a love that she could not have."

"I know. She told me that, too."

"Hatshepsut, my beloved daughter, the gods are very pleased with you. I could see it in every offering you made. I believe Ptah is extremely happy with you, because of the signs he gave to all of us when you were dancing. We were all quite impressed. I am sure Amun-Ra will be even more pleased in Heliopolis. I am leaving my kingdom to you. Rule well and with integrity. Keep your eyes and ears attentive to all that is going on in your kingdom. And know your enemies. Put people that you completely trust beside you to help you, and they will protect you and keep their eyes open for you. Have spies everywhere, and spy on everyone including those that you trust. And don't take pity on your enemies, or they can kill you. Do away with them right away but be sure first that they are indeed your enemies. I like Hapuseneb very much. He conducts himself well, and he knows how I run my kingdom in the audience hall. Keep him always by your side and put him in a key position. He has earned my trust."

"I will, Father. I know, too, that I can trust him. Father, if you are not feeling well, will you tell me no matter what? Would you? Please."

He smiled and patted my right hand. "Ra is almost down. Let's go say our prayers to God," he said.

We stood, then washed our hands and faces. We knelt facing the west and recited our prayers, just as Khety and the elderly priests did. Mother Nut cover the land and Thoth was starting to show his silver rays.

Later, we docked, and the ramp was lowered. There were many large tents on display. I could see the Pyramids of Giza far off. The night was beautiful full of stars, and a cool breeze was blowing. T'Queta brought me a warm galabia, a long robe, and covered me with it.

"Your Majesty, may I have permission to meet with Hapuseneb?"

I smiled because I was happy for her. "Yes, you may go. I will have Tuyii bathe me tonight."

"Thank you, Your Majesty," she said, and I saw her leave happy.

I sat there in the peace of the night, and I thought of Sen-Mut. I wondered if he was thinking of me at that moment and if I would ever be allowed to be happy with him. Suddenly, a large falling star crossed the night sky, and I smiled, though I missed him.

Then I saw at a far distance T'Queta and Hapuseneb walking beside Hopi holding hands. I got up and walked to my tent. At least she could be happy, I thought.

I was awakened very early in the morning, and we sailed north. After about six or seven hours, we would arrive at Heliopolis, and this time it would be different. I needed to be ready to present my offerings when we arrived. I would make my final offering, and I would dance for the god of all the gods, Amun-Ra, my father. I would be sure to please him.

"Your Majesty, we must start the special bath." It was the voice of a priestess, accompanied by a few other priestesses. This bath would be different. They would clean my body and shave it, and I would be bathed in the waters of Hopi. They would pass fire and incense around me and rub me with myrrh oil.

When it was done, they placed white linen on the floor of the ship, and I walked to my bed. I lay on the white and gold linen sheets.

We arrived at Heliopolis, and a procession of priests, among them Hapuseneb, and priestesses walked before us. Khety was wearing the long white linen kilt. A leopard skin lay over his shoulders, and a long baton was in his right hand. The acolytes were spreading the burning incense before Khety, and he started the prayers as we walked to the greatest temple, the Temple of Atum. Father was in front of me, and I walked naked, bathed in gold dust from head to toe, behind him.

Behind me hundreds of slaves were carrying baskets of offerings and gold. It was a hot day, and I walked barefoot to the temple. That day, I needed to make these sacrifices to please Amun and Atum and all the deities of the land. We arrived at the entrance of the temple, and at the very end was a large image of Amun, and behind him, the large Sun representing Atum. It was carved in the wall in gold. I had never seen an image that large before. I was pleased to see Amun. Looking at him, I was invaded with an enormous feeling of peace and joy. And then I knew that he was pleased with me. I would be crowned Queen of Egypt.

At his right and left were the all the other deities aligned with him on the temple walls. As I walked and approached the highest, Ptah was smiling at me. In the presence of all the priests of Atum and Amun, the drums started to sound. I knelt and raising my eyes and arms to Amun and Atum, I exclaimed his name and the names of all the deities in the temple. Then I started to dance. I was intoxicated by the sound of the drums, the incense, and the perfumes. The wind started to pick up inside the temple at the end. I threw myself on the floor, rolled over, and crawled in front of him, letting him know that I was nothing without him.

My father approached me, and the slaves dressed me in a golden kilt, and the golden pectoral. Father stood beside me in front of Amun, putting his arms over my shoulders.

"Blessed one, whom I take in my arms, thou art my heir," Father said.[37]

I heard Father speaking, voicing the wishes of all the gods. But then he went into a trance, and his voice changed. I had never heard this voice before, and I knew that the gods were speaking through him. With a thundering voice, he continued.

"She, thy daughter who lived, is here. And we are satisfied with her life, as it has been lived in peace. She is now thy daughter, born of thy

---

[37] Everything my father says to me in the Temple of Atum is based on ancient records.

form whom thou hast begotten. Thou hast given thy soul, thy bounty, the magic power of the diadem to her. While she was in the body of she who bore her, the lands were hers; the countries were hers. All that the heavens cover and that the seas encircle were hers.

"Welcome, daughter of Amun-Ra. Thou hast seen thy administration in the land, and thou shalt set it in order, restore that which has gone to ruins. Thou shalt build monuments. Thou shalt travel through the lands and embrace many countries.

"Thy tribute is a myriad of men, the captive of thy valor. Thy reward is thousands of men for the temples of the two lands. The gods have blessed thee with years. They present thee with life and satisfaction. They praise thee, for thy heart has been given understanding. They shall set thy boundary as far as the breadth of heaven, as far as the limits of the twelve hours of night."

A different voice overpowered my father. It was Thoth, but his voice came out of my father's mouth. The air was thick and heavy, and I felt as if everything was in slow motion.

"Set the diadem upon his head before the gods and crown him the heir to the throne of the two lands."

I saw two high priests walk in, one wearing the mask of Set and the other the mask of Horus. Horus placed the golden cobra Crown of Buto on my head, and they read, one by one, all my mother's titles, which now belonged to me. I felt strange wearing my mother's crown on my head. I still missed her very much.

My father's voice returned to normal. In a booming voice, which was his own, he shouted, "This is my daughter Hatshepsut, the loving one, I put her on my throne. Henceforth, she shall guide you. Whoever obeys her will live, but he who speaks out against her shall die."

The ceremony was finished, and the celebration began with shouts of "Hatshepsut, Queen of Egypt! Hatshepsut, Queen of Egypt!" There were countless people dancing in the temple.

I was exhausted, so Father and I left the temple together along with all the priests and dignitaries.

Hapuseneb came up to me. "Your Majesty," he said and dropped to the floor.

"Rise, Hapuseneb." I said.

He walked with us to the celebration. Later, I told Father that I was very tired, and we left with the court to go back to the ships. Father walked me to my ship, followed by Hapuseneb, T'Queta, Tuyii, and all my slaves.

I was bathed with warm water, still wearing Buto, the cobra crown, on my head and with the gold dust all over my skin. It was very hard to be removed completely, but the slaves did the best they could. I fell asleep.

****

During the sail back to Thebes, I strolled the length of the ship with the Queen's crown on my head. I observed the ibises in the water and flying in the sky. The people along the Nile were waiting and bowed to the ground as I passed them, throwing white petals of lotus flowers as my ship sailed along the Nile. At times, I thought I saw a large bird that looked like a phoenix flying ahead the ship. I stood there and let the breeze blow on my face.

I remembered Sen-Mut and our vacation to Philae and smiled. Now it will be harder for us to be together, and I must be very cautious not to be alone with him in any place. Father would not have mercy on him this time, and I had to protect him.

We sailed for almost two months on the return trip home. The oarsmen had to row hard against the strong current of Hopi. We stopped many times, and tents were set up for dinner. When we did, I would have dinner with my father, the court, and all the priests.

Hapuseneb made me and T'Queta laugh a lot of time during our conversations. I noticed how well he and T'Queta got along together, and I could see so much happiness on her face. I was happy for her. At least she could be happy, and I know. I must accept my faith, and never be with Sen-Mut.

Sometimes, I sailed with Father for hours and returned to my ship when we stopped for dinner. We did not sail at night because Father wanted to avoid embankments as we sailed. It had happened before with trading ships sailed by sailors who didn't know the waters or the region. There are small islands in the middle of Hopi in between the east and the west, and it was best to sail during the day.

The weeks passed, and we were getting closer to Thebes. Father sent a message with his courier, who rode to the palace to announce our arrival. In one more day, we would be in Thebes.

We docked for the last time, and I slept on Father's ship. Everything was prepared for early the next morning. The slaves would be aligned on each side of the ship, dressed in white linen. They would throw white flower petals in the water of Hopi as we approached Thebes.

The next morning, people were waiting along the left side of the Nile and on the islets on the right. I sat beside Father on a golden chair as we sailed home. The view was spectacular. Thousands of people were blessing us and bowing to the ground as they threw petals into the Nile and cheered us on.

I searched for Sen-Mut, but I couldn't find him. Aakheperen-Re was waiting on the dock with Ineni, the priests, priestesses, soldiers, and members of the court who had not traveled with us.

It was going to be a long day, but at least it was the last day of the coronation rituals. I would be given all my mother's crowns. We were greeted by Aakheperen-Re and the court, and the parade started to the Temple of Amun-Ra.

We walked to the temple, and at the entrance, I saw Sen-Mut standing with the other younger priests. He saw the Queen's crown on my head, and then he dropped to the floor with the rest of the priests. He didn't dare smile at me, nor was there any sign of happiness on his face. But I was glad to see him again.

We continued walking until we were in front of the image of Amun. Then Father spoke to Amun.[38]

"I am before you, King of the gods." Father knelt and bowed his head to the floor. "I have prostrated myself. In return for what I have done for thee, do thou bestow Egypt and the red land on my daughter, Maatke-Re, child of the sun, that she may live eternally, as thou hast done for me."

Hearing my earthly father pleading to the image of my heavenly father, Amun, I prostrated myself at his feet and spoke to him. He knew that my heart was clean and pure. The slaves brought me gold dust, and I danced around the large statue of Amun, as I threw the golden dust over him. The acolytes burned incense in front of me as I danced around him. My heart was happy, as it was during my last offerings to him in Heliop-olis. I danced around him seven times and then stopped in his presence.

He smiled at me, and the First Prophet of Amun Khety shouted, "Amun-Ra has consented!"

---

[38] Father's words to Amun are from ancient records.

All of priests, the members of the court, and the dignitaries were jumping jubilantly.

Then I heard my father's resounding voice, expressing his gratitude to the highest.

"My daughter, who loves thee? Who is united unto thee, beloved? Thou hast transmitted the world unto her, into her hands. Thou hast chosen her as Queen," he said.

The two crowns were joined, and Father took them in his hands and placed them on my head.[39]

Then turning, my father and I faced the people. Amun spoke through my father lips. "Behold ye, my daughter Hatshepsut lives. Be ye loving toward her and be ye satisfied with her."[40]

---

[39] What I remember is that two priestesses approached me, one wearing the headpiece of Buto, the cobra head piece on her head, and in her hands was the red crown of Lower Egypt. The other priestesses were wearing the headpiece of Nekhbet, the vulture, and carrying in their hands the white crown of Upper Egypt. Surrounding me were priests wearing the mask of Thoth, the moon. The scribe of the gods and a priestess were wearing the mask of Sekhment, the lioness goddess.

[40] I don't remember much of what followed during my coronation as Queen, but you can be certain that I never was spoiled sexually by my father, as some historians and archeologists have suggested.

CHAPTER 26

PHARAOH'S DEATH

Father transferred all power and control of the country to me, and I did as I promised Amun I would do. I ordered Ineni to start rebuilding all the statues of the gods that had been destroyed or damaged by the Hyksos every time they came to my land to invade us. They had tried many times to occupy my land, ever since my ancestors took it away from them. And Father had been on many military campaigns against them.

I ordered new shrines and chapels to be built to help contribute to the grandeur of the Temple at Karnak. I ordered a large sacred lake to be built in Karnak.

Then I took full control of the two lands, as Father's health was deteriorating rapidly. Soon, I would be seventeen summers, and I felt that I had matured quickly into a full-grown woman, as if I had lived my whole life already.

One day, I walked to Ineni's office, and Sen-Mut was talking to him. I froze, and my heart jumped. Ineni bowed his head, and Sen-Mut dropped to the floor, touching his head to the limestone floor.

"Sen-Mut, rise," I said softly. I was nervous. I had not seen him this close for a long time.

He rose from the floor without looking at me. Then he lowered his eyes.

"Sen-Mut, look at me," I said softly, and he did.

The three of us were alone. Ineni looked at us, then asked me, "Your Majesty, do you wish to give me new building orders?"

"Yes, Ineni."

I knew that he was making conversation to try to break the tension in the room. I smiled at him and at Sen-Mut. Sen-Mut looked at me and smiled back.

I told Ineni, "I would like for you to send Sen-Mut to rebuild the sanctuaries and chapels. Give him all the manpower he needs to do it. Send along the best wines, the best food, the nicest and largest tent so that he can be comfortable while he is working on these projects. Send slaves to attend to him. That will make the journey to the sites more pleasant."

I know that Father has kept him from me before, I thought.

After we all exchanged smiles, Ineni said, "I will leave you two alone," and bowing his head, turned around and left.

"Your Majesty, it's wonderful to see you again. It has been such a long time, a very long time, since we last spoke to each other," he said. He was looking at me tenderly.

"Yes, I remember the last time. It was in the stables before my coronation."

He nodded his head twice. He was sweating, especially on his hands.

"Have you been treated well these long months away from the palace?" I asked him.

"Yes, His Majesty, your father made provisions that I would be treated nicely in the long months that I was away from here."

"Did you miss Thebes?" I asked him, but I was referring to me. He came closer, and I held my breath, dying for a kiss. He looked deep into my eyes.

"Yes, I have missed Thebes terribly," he said.

I felt his words deep in my heart. He has missed me. I wanted so much for him to kiss me. I lowered my eyes, and just then Ineni walked in.

"Your Majesty, I have visited your father, and I know that he has not been feeling well."

"That is true, and I am very much afraid that my father will go to the underworld and that I will be completely alone."

"Don't be, Your Majesty. You will never be alone," Sen-Mut said and smiled. I was startled by his reply.

Ineni was now looking at both of us. "He is right. If Pharaoh goes to the heavens, you will be able to make many decisions of your own without having to ask anyone for their approval," he said.

I knew Ineni was implying I could marry Sen-Mut and no one could stop me. I thought about it and realized that he was right. That thought brought me great joy.

I smiled at them, and I said good-bye, and walked away. As I was leaving, I stopped, turned around, and looked at Sen-Mut. "I will make my own decisions," I said and smiled at him.

Aakheperen-Re and Hapuseneb helped with the day-to-day business of running the palace, especially Hapu who knew so much about government and management. With his help, I accomplished many tasks. I was also helped by Ahmose-Pen-Nekhbet, who, during my childhood, taught me lessons about government. All of them were helping me to direct the country.

In the hall of audience, I was hearing the concerns, petitions, and disputes of people from all over the land. Father was very pleased with how I was handling the affairs of the two lands. Little by little, he stopped coming to the audience hall.

Every afternoon, after the third hour, Father and I sailed the Nile for hours to feel the breeze on those hot days. I could see the look in my father eyes, looking far away into the sunset, and I wondered what was on his mind. Was he thinking that his time to sail to the west was coming closer? Then my eyes would become full of tears. Eventually, he would fall asleep in his golden chair as the fanbearers fanned us, creating a slow-moving breeze.

In the following months, little by little, Father was drifting more and more into a silent reverie. He would not come out of his quarters, so I visited him if I wanted to see him. I did that many times. Sometimes, I would lean against the door to his bedroom and watch him sleep. I knew that his health was slipping away, and I cried. I knew I would feel completely alone on the day that he sailed into the sunset, never to return.

I would lie in bed and wonder how Sen-Mut was doing. I knew from Ineni that he was rebuilding shrines along the Nile and that he was doing a wonderful job. His architectural studies were almost complete. Ineni had given Sen-Mut a piece of land to build himself a home. I was pleased to hear that. But I wanted more for him.

One day, there was a knock on my golden doors, answered by T'Queta.

"Who is it?" I asked her.

"It's Master Aakhep' and Hapuseneb."

I panicked. Father! I ran to the living room.

"It's Father, isn't it?" I said. I was close to tears.

"No, but he is not well. Father wants to speak to you and asked us to bring you to his quarters," Aakhep' said.

I was worried because I knew that he had not been feeling well. I put on a royal blue robe and walked with them to his quarters. Several priests were there praying, including Khety, Puyem-Re, and many others. I was beginning to realize that his time was coming closer, and I was devastated by the knowledge.

I approached his bed and knelt beside him. I grabbed hold of his hand, tears pouring down my face. He opened his eyes and smiled.

"Hat, my beloved daughter, the kingdom is yours. The firmament is yours. You are the daughter of Amun. You have it all. I want your happiness as your heart would choose it. What I am asking you is to please continue the royal line," he said.

I felt the most terrible pain in my heart. Tears formed, then overflowed my eyes.

All the priests could hear Father's petition to me.

I whispered in his ear, "But Father, don't hold me to these promises. Please," I begged him.

He patted my hand. Then he told me, "You must marry Aakheperen-Re and make him Thutmoses II, so that our blood will not die. You must promise me that you will do this and promise me that when the time comes, you will be happy." And smiles.

He was looking straight into my eyes, and I held his hand again.

"What do you mean, Father? I don't understand."

"Promise me, Hatshepsut, that you will keep your promise."

I lowered my eyes, and tears began dropping to the stone floor, and with a broken heart, I said, "I promise."

"It's done, Your Majesty. We heard it all," Khety said.

He called Aakheperen-Re to my side as I still knelt by my father side. Khety came close to me and held my right hand and placed it over Aakheperen-Re's hand in front of my father. Father watched every movement.

"Hatshepsut, Queen of Egypt, as of today you are betrothed to the future Pharaoh of Egypt, Thutmoses II," Khety said.

Afterwards, I cried for hours. I cried for me, for my mother, and for Neferu-Bity. A few hours later, Father went to the heavens.

The seventy days of mourning were harder on me than on anyone else. I missed my father and my mother enormously. They had left me too soon. All my hopes of happiness were gone.

My father's funeral was the most solemn in the whole land. The entire armed forces were present, as were people from all over this land and other faraway lands. I wore dark blue attire and the Horus crown during the funeral. His body was carried by his warriors over their shoulders in the long procession to his final rest. I was devastated. All my hopes were gone. When my father was alive, I was free, but now I am forced to marry my brother. Now I knew how my mother felt when her dreams were shattered.

CHAPTER 27

MARRIAGE TO THUTMOSES II

AND CORONATION

I was nearing my eighteen summers, and in just a few days I would be marrying my half-brother, as I promised Maat before he went to the underworld. I was dreading that day.

T'Queta was no longer seeing Hapuseneb, since he had taken Tepi as his concubine, and had broken her heart. I knew that she had fallen deeply in love with him, and I could hear her cry every night when she believed that I was asleep. My heart went out to her. She had been like a sister to me for all these years.

I was terribly sad because in four days I would be marrying Aak-heperen-Re making him Thutmoses II, Pharaoh of Egypt. I would never be kissed nor bedded by Sen-Mut. I cried thinking about it. I wanted him to have a part of me, but I didn't know what to do. Then I thought I would give him T'Queta as a gift! She could console him and take care of him for me. I had trusted her with my life, and I would trust her with his life, too. She knew of my love for him, and she thought that he loved me because of the way he looked at me. She wasn't sure, but Hapuseneb had told her that he did. I whispered his name, and with the thoughts of him I fell asleep.

The first orange rays of Ra woke me up. T'Queta was still asleep. I could hear the call of a rooster far away. The sound made me smile, remembering the time when Sen-Mut called the birds on our trip to Philae and my eyes became full of tears. I was lying there looking at the end of the balcony and feeling trapped as the rays of Ra started spreading across the Nile.

I heard T'Queta waking up. "T'Queta, go wash yourself and come and sit beside me on my couch," I told her.

"Yes, my Queen."

Once she returned, I said, "You know that I love you as if you were my sister, but now I must ask you to do something for me. I want you to serve and take care of Sen-Mut. As you know, in three days I will be marrying Aakheperen-Re, and I will never be able to be with him, talk to him, be alone with him, or look at him. My heart is broken, but I must be sure that he will be alright and that he finds consolation in you." Tears rolled down my face.

"I will do it for thee, my Queen," she said.

It was strange that she did not object or ask to stay with me. Maybe she agreed because it meant that she would have a home of her own. I knew she would be happy to cook for him. Sen-Mut was a kind man, and she knew that. I knew that she liked him because she had kept the secret of the pink rose left on my makeup table on the day of my fifteen summers and because of the way she spoke of him.

"Bathe me, and bring breakfast for two, and after the priest is finished with the chanting and the incensing of the golden doors, go to his home and tell him that I am coming to pay him a visit after the second hour of high-noon."

"Yes, Your Majesty."

Once the chanting was completed, she brought my breakfast. I asked her to have breakfast with me for the first time, and her face registered surprise.

"T'Queta, as of today, you will reside at Sen-Mut's home. You will cook and taste his food before he eats, anything that is sent to him by anyone. You will bathe him as you did me, and if it is his desire, you will lie with him," I said.

She didn't respond.

"I am giving you all my sheaths so that you will be properly dressed in his presence. After breakfast, run to his house and give him my message, and when you come back, take as many things you like: perfume, kohl, rouge. I don't want anything. My life is over. Leave me only with two white sheaths, my golden sandals, and my jewelry. When you return, bring back some of my slaves to help you carry everything to Sen-Mut's house and call Tuyii, Mother's slave, to come here to serve me. She will take your place. I like her. She loved Mother very much, and she can console me with memories of Mother." My eyes became full of tears.

"Yes, Your Majesty. May I ask you something?"

"Yes, you may."

"Will you be moving to your mother's quarters?" she asked.

"No, I will remain in my quarters, but my brother will occupy the Great Maat's quarters, perhaps with Isis as his concubine. I don't know, and I really don't care!"

"I see… I will miss you greatly. Thou hast been my sister and have been very kind to me since I was a small child. You are the only one that I care about, since you brought me from the faraway land on the green sea. If thou ever desire for me to come back, call upon me, and I will happily return. I am going to miss our long talks in the middle of the night and the way we used to laugh together about the gossip in the kitchen," she said.

Then we finished our breakfast.

"Go and take the message to Master Sen-Mut now," I said.

"Yes, Your Majesty."

She got up with a smile on her face. She knew that she was getting in, some way, her freedom. She would only receive orders from Sen-Mut and wouldn't have to eat with the other slaves anymore. I knew that he would treat her with fairness and kindness.

The time of her departure was approaching, I thought. T'Queta bathed me for the last time, and we cried together. She dressed me in the white sheath and golden sandals and placed a long wig entwined with golden threads on my head. I did not wear a crown that day. She and the other slaves had packed all that I had given her and helped carry all her belongings down the stairs. They were waiting for us. She looked very happy about her new path.

When we reached the bottom of the stairs, I called, "Guards! To Master Sen-Mut's house!"

Several guards walked before us, and we followed them in the direction of his house.[41]

I had never visited his home before, but I remembered when I heard for the first time that he was building his own house, I was pleased. I used to ride my horse and watch him directing the construction of his house from far away, but I don't think he ever knew that I was around and watching him from afar, because he never turned around or looked in my

---

[41] Writing these memories, I remember how sad I felt on that day, and it brings tears to my eyes, thinking that I would never see Sen-Mut again or be his. I was very depressed on that day. (11/12/2014)

direction. The house was constructed out of adobe, built on a piece of land that Ineni had given him out of the kindness of his heart.

We arrived at his house, and I saw that it was very nice. It was very well built with adobe, and it was beautiful. I was nervous to see him or speak to him again. I had not really spoken to him since the sandstorm, when Father had threatened his life three summers ago, and briefly in Ineni's office before my coronation as Queen.

And so much had transpired in almost three summers. Mother went to the underworld, I had married my father for political reasons, and I became his Queen and co-regent of Upper and Lower Egypt. I had managed the affairs of the whole kingdom. I had held audiences. And then Father went to the heavens to be with the other gods. Now, I must marry my brother to make him a full royal blood and Thutmoses II. Overall, I was all alone in this world except for him, and I was not included in his daily schedule. In fact, I seldom saw him anymore since Maat had gone. He lived his life and made me feel that I was not a part of it. I wish I had not made that promise to Maat on his deathbed in front of all the priests and Hapuseneb.

I also wished it were Sen-Mut I was marrying. I had talked to several priests before, trying to figure out if there were a way to marry him, but all the priests were against it. They believed that I must continue the royal line, especially Hapuseneb.

The guards knocked on his door, and the door was opened quickly. It seemed that he had been waiting for me, and finally I was in front of him. We were face to face, and my heart was pounding hard, I felt the nervous butterflies again in my stomach.

"My Queen!" he said softly and knelt.

I closed my eyes and rested my left hand on his head with love. Finally, I could touch him for the first time.

"You may rise, future Ptah of Amun."

“My Queen, you are most welcome. Come in. This humble house is yours.” He spoke with a frank tone of voice as he did when I saw him for the first time in the audience hall.

I walked in, turned around, and told everyone to wait outside.

“Sen-Mut, you may close the door,” I said,

Standing there looking at him, I noticed that he had grown taller. He was three or four inches taller than me. He closed the door behind me.

“Your Majesty, I am most happy that thou are here in my humble home that is yours.”

He was looking straight into my eyes. I was trembling, and he was sweating. He kept cleaning the sweat off his hands onto his kilt. I could tell he was as nervous as I was. He gestured me to a chair, and he sat in front of me and faced me. His eyes were shining, a look of happiness emanated from them. He was evidently very happy to see me.

“I heard from Ineni that soon you will be the architect and builder you always wanted to be. He also told me that these three summers you have dedicated yourself to learn as you promised. I can see that you have grown older and more mature since we saw each other last. Ineni also said that you have grown wiser.”

“He is very kind,” he said.

“How old are you now?” I asked.

“Soon, I will be twenty summers, Maatke-Re,” he said softly.

His words took me by surprise. I never thought he would remember the name he chose for me when we were alone on the way to Philae. I smiled at him.

“I am close to my eighteen summers,” I said. We became quiet, looking at each other. Nothing else existed but us.

He broke the silence and said, "Your Majesty, you are more beautiful today than you were the last time I saw thee. Thou radiate like Ra."

I smiled at him.

"Would you care for sweet lemon juice?" he asked.

"Yes, please."

He left and came back with a cup of sweet lemon juice. He walked to the door to call T'Queta so that she could taste my drink. I told him not to, for I completely trusted him. I drank from the cup he gave me, and he drank from his cup looking at me. We spent several hours talking and laughing about the fun memories we had in Philae. We were very happy again for those moments and no one else existed but us…until I came to the sad reality of why I was there.

I took a deep breath and said, "As you know, in three days I must marry Aakheperen-Re." I was on the verge of crying and I was trembling. "And it's not the desire of my heart! I came to bring you a gift. I brought T'Queta for you. I would like very much for you to accept the gift."

I was not telling him the real reason why I was there, that I loved him and knew that she would take care of him as if it were me. I didn't tell him that. I would probably never see him or be alone with him ever again.

He lowered his face, and said with a sad voice, "Yes, I know, Your Majesty."

I took a deep breath and stood up.

"Be happy Sen-Mut from Luny. Now call T'Queta in," I said, and he did. I was clenching my teeth hard to prevent myself from crying. She came in and stood beside me. I looked at T'Queta and forced a smile onto my face. I pulled my ring from my finger right finger and gave it to her in front of Sen-Mut. Then I took another deep breath.

"This ring will give you safe passage to the palace any time you want to come and visit me. And you may go to any place in my kingdom freely. After all our years together, you have earned my trust and friendship. You must wear it at all times," I said.

"My Queen, I have served thee with love and devotion. I am grateful that I was at your service since we were little girls. I thank thee for being so kind to me always. I will always be in your debt," she said, then she knelt and kissed my feet.

I looked at Sen-Mut and saw sadness in his eyes. T'Queta was crying. She was sad to see me leave and to meet my fate of marrying someone I did not love. I held back my tears as much as I could. I could not continue talking. I turn around walked towards the door.

Sen-Mut opened the door with his eyes cast down to the floor, and without looking at me, he knelt and said in a low voice, "My Queen."

Then I walked off in a hurry. I left the slaves with T'Queta to help her arrange her things. The two guards followed me. I stopped, and without turning to face them I said, "Don't follow me."

I wanted to run away as far as I could and lose consciousness of everything around me and forget the reality of my destiny. I was feeling the same way when Father ordered Sen-Mut's death and I wanted to die.

I started to walk very fast until I reached the Nile. I sat there and buried my face between my knees and cried for hours silently. I felt lost and all alone. I wanted to get lost in the universe and between the stars where only silence would surround me. "Oh, Mother. How much I miss you now. I don't know if Sen-Mut and I will we ever speak again," I thought. Tears were pouring down my face as I thought of Sen-Mut.

****

Mother Nut had covered the land with its mantle. Thoth had started to pour its silver rays upon the land, and I walked to the balcony, searching for Sen-Mut, and saw him walking beside the Nile as always. His heart must be broken as mine.[42]

I would be marrying Thutmoses in three days, and I didn't want to. I was condemned to a life without the love of a man, I thought.

"No, and I will not die without knowing what it feels like to belong to Sen-Mut!"

I rushed out of my quarters and ran fast down the stairs. A guard started to follow me, but I stopped, turned around, and shouted, "Stop! You are not to follow me!" He took one step back, turned around, and left. I waited to be sure that I was not followed, then I walked fast in Sen-Mut's direction. I was praying that he would still be there. The night was warm and beautiful, full of stars. It felt as I could reach out and touch them.

There he was, and my heart was pounding hard. I felt the usual nervous excitement. I kept walking toward him. When he realized who was approaching him, he knelt at my feet.

"Please don't. Rise, Sen-Mut."

He stood up and was quiet. I broke the silence. "Sen-Mut, I've seen you every night for the last three summers walking beside Hopi. Please don't be afraid to talk to me tonight. Now you can speak freely to me, and we can be ourselves tonight. Please, let's walk into the waters of the Nile in case I was followed."

We did as I suggested. I felt as if we were two thieves hiding. We were surround by tall papyrus plants, and the water was up to our waists, with the slow current lapping around us. My heart was pounding.

---

[42] I still remember these saddest moments of looking at him in the darkness walking by the Nile, and they bring tears to my eyes. (2014)

We stopped and faced each other.

Looking into my eyes, he said, "Every night, I walk beside Hopi and pray that one day I'll have the opportunity to tell thee about this feeling inside of me for thee." Bringing his hand to his chest, he continued, "And every night, I see you in the silence of your balcony as if you were waiting for me..."

My heart was full of emotions as I listened to him declare his love for me.

"For many years, I suffered in silence, keeping secret my love for you. I was warned so many times to stay away from you, not to look at you, that if the Pharaoh discovered my love for you, I would be put to death. Sometimes when we exchanged glances, it moved my heart. I have these feelings, deep inside of me, that you love me, too. This morning, when you brought T'Queta as a gift to me, I wanted to pour out my heart to you and tell you of all my feelings. I wanted so much to tell you that ... I love you."

My eyes became full of tears, and trembling when I hear him said, I love You.

"And I love you, too! I have love you since the first time I saw you in the audience hall. That was when my heart started to be awakened by my love for you," I said.

The expression on his face was full of gladness, full of joy. Then softly, he took hold of my left hand and pulled me slowly close to him. I was shaking as his face came close to mine. I closed my eyes, and gently he pressed his lips on my lips. I tasted the mint on his lips. I felt the earth move under my feet. We kissed for a long time, and I responded to his kisses with a passion I had never felt before. I had waited for this moment for such a long time. He held me tight against his chest, with his arms wrapped around my body. His left arm rested across my back, with his hand holding the back of my neck as he kissed me profoundly.

We were lost in the emotions of love and ecstasy, and nothing else existed, only Sen-Mut and I. My arms were wrapped around his neck, locked in this passionate kiss. I could feel his heart pounding hard against mine.

Slowly, he released me and whispered in my ear, "I must stop before I make you mine, which is the desire of my heart and loins right now. It's very hard for me to hold back." He gently pushed me away from him.

I did not want the magic to stop because he had started to awaken this desire and passion inside of me that I never had felt before, and my body was hot. I was intoxicated by his passionate kiss. Then he pulled from a pouch on his waist two rings made of lapis lazuli.[43]

"I sent for these rings to be made for you one summer ago, hoping that one day I would have the opportunity to give them to you," he said.

I was moved by his expression of love for me, and I was very happy that he felt the same way I did. He held my left hand and placed one ring on my left ring finger, and then he held my right hand and put the other ring on my right ring finger.

Then looking into my eyes, he asked, "Will you be my wife?"

I was surprised, but my heart leapt with joy. Looking at him, I said,

"Yes, I will be your wife! A thousand times, my love, and I will love you for all eternity." I happily said.

He pulled me to him with force and kissed me deeply. I responded again to his passionate kiss. My body became hot, very hot. I had never experienced sexual desires before. It was making my knees weak with

---

[43] A bluish-purple stone flecked with gold. And he made me the happies woman in the world. Oh! How much I still love him.

desire for his body. I did not want him to stop. We were intoxicated with passion from our kisses.

But he pulled me gently away from him. He held me by my arms with his hands. I could see his face under the rays of Thoth. His face was elated under the stars above. He looked gorgeous with his tiny little curls hanging on his forehead. I caressed his hair with sweetness, and he smiled. Slowly, I caressed his face with my left hand. He took my hand and kissed it.

Looking into my eyes, he said, "There will be a time for us to be together in the future. The stars have foretold me that we would not be apart for too long. Wait for me, I want you to just wait for me, please. But for now, you must return to the palace. It is very late, and the guards will be looking for you soon. And you know that if they find us together, I will be put to death."

I covered his lips with my left hand, shushed him and then kissed him.

I started to walk away as he held my fingers, then pulling me back again, he kissed me and whispered in my ear, "I have loved you too, since that first time I saw you on your Father's throne."

"I have loved you since that day, too," I whispered back into his ear. Our hands did not want to let go. He held onto my fingers as I walked away.

He followed me through the tall papyrus plants, through the waters of Hopi, until I reached the palace. I turned around, and he was still there between the papyri. I was overcome with joy. My beloved had kissed me. I could scream with happiness. He loved me. He had said it himself, with his own words.

It was a beautiful sensation he left on me, the thought of him and his lips pressing mine. The warm feeling invaded my whole body again.

An inner dialogue with Sen-Mut echoed through my mind: "Oh, my beloved one, if you only knew how long I have waited for this moment. And now I am your wife. Yes, I am married to you, Sen-Mut. How beautiful are these rings?" They are his expression of love for me.

Then I thought of my mother. "Oh, Mother. If you could only see me and feel my happiness. You were always right. He *is* in love with me!"

I rushed up the stairs, and the guards opened the golden doors. Tuyii was waiting for me, lying on her couch. She was about to get up to bathe me. I said, "No, not tonight. Go back to sleep," so she did. I took off my wet sheath and lay in bed naked, thinking that I didn't want the water to wash away the magic and the touch of his hands, the sensation of his skin touching mine, nor his smell, the smell of a man, nor his strong arms holding me, nor his hard chest pressing against mine and the beat of his heart beating with mine. I wanted to remember his lips, his kisses, the taste of the mint on lips. I brought my fingers to my lips, and I closed my eyes, reliving every single moment. The feeling of hot sexual desire that he left imprinted on me rushed over me. I relived those moments over and over until I fell asleep.

On the eve of my marriage to Thutmoses, I was very happy because I didn't care anymore. I was first and foremost Sen-Mut's wife. That joy would last me a lifetime. The next morning would be the dawn of the new year, and I would be crowning Aakheperen-Re, Thutmoses II Pharaoh of Egypt, and it didn't bother me. Sen-Mut belonged to me, and I belonged to him.

I walk to the other end of the palace to talk to my brother, when I heard Thutmoses and Isis having a conversation about me, and I stood there listening.

I heard her say, "Did you know that there have been rumors all over the palace that your sister has been in love with Sen-Mut for a long time?"

"Yes, I've known that for a long time, since before Ahmose went to the underworld. Father knew about it, too, and he spoke to me of her in our first hunting trip before her fifteen summers. He told me that he did not want her to lead a life without love. She is my little sister and has always been kind and loving to me and memories of our childhood make me laugh," he said with a smile.

"It would not be fair to her never to experience love and lovemaking with the one she loves. You know, she could have chosen him, married him and made him Pharaoh, and nothing could have been done to stop her. But instead she continued with the royal tradition to live and die without love," Isis said.

She continued, "You know that nothing could have held her back. She is Queen of Egypt, and the whole land loves her. She must love you very much to keep her word to your father. We have each other, but who does she have? No one to console her in the night or to hug her and kiss her like we do. Life without love is horrible, I think." She said.

He nodded his head several times. "I know that Hapuseneb has been in love with her for a long time, too, and has been suffering for her love," he said.

After that conversation I went to my quarters and sat quietly on the balcony remembering the sweetness and love of Sen-Mut's. His lips pressing on mine, the way he made me feel that night, and the heat of my body that would not go away. I never knew that a kiss could make a person have all these feelings and emotions. I wanted more of his love, a love that it was real for both of us.

Then I remembered Sen-Mut's words: "There will be a time for us to be together. The stars have foretold me this. Wait for me." I smiled because there was hope for us. For the time being, I needed to keep quiet and wait for him until that moment came.

There was a knock on the golden doors, and they were opened. It was Aakhep'. He had grown into a very handsome man. That was why the slaves wanted to be bedded by him. I smiled at him. He clapped his hands to indicate that the slaves should leave and told them not to return until the first rays of Ra were showing. They left. I was puzzled by what all of this was about.

"Hat, I must speak to you."

I went to my couch and sat against the wall leaning on my pillows. He sat close to me on the couch.

"You know, that I've known for a long time that you have been in love with Sen-Mut. And so, did Maat. He did not want you to live a life without love. But I will be Pharaoh tomorrow, and you must behave as my Queen. You will have no more contact with him. You must not be alone with him at any time. I don't want rumors all over the land now. I want you to have one night of love with Sen-Mut, tonight. Run to him. Be his for one night. Be happy tonight, Hatshepsut. Be happy for one night," he said.

He had a sweet smile on his face. I could not believe what I was hearing.

"But when the time comes, you must produce a royal heir to the throne as Maat said, and if you cannot or don't want to, I must produce an heir with a concubine. So now, run to your beloved and live your night of love with Sen-Mut. Be happy, sister." Then he smiled.

"Thank you, brother!" I jumped on him and hugged him.

He left. I was still in shock, and I sat there for a little bit, assimilating what he had just said. I rushed out of my room to look for my beloved Sen-Mut, but just before I opened the golden doors, Sen-Mut rushed through them, and grabbed me by my waist, and pressed his lips hard on mine. He kissed me deeply, and I melted again with desire.

He whispered in my ear, "I don't care if I die tonight. I needed to tell you that I love you and make you mine."

“The guards! How did you get past the guards?” I asked him.

“There were no guards at your doors.”

Then I smiled because I knew why.

“And there will be none tonight, until the first rays of Ra. I was about to run to your arms, when you opened the golden doors,” I said.

He pulled me closer to him and started to kiss my face gently, then my lips and my neck. He was making my body hot, a delicious feeling of wanting him.

“Make me yours tonight,” I whispered in his ear.

He lifted me in his strong arms. My heart was pounding hard and fast, and I was filled with emotions. I knew that tonight, nothing would hold him back. He was kissing me as he carried me in his arms to the bed. He laid me gently there.

The dim light of the oil lamp shined on his face as he removed his kilt. I could see his gorgeous body, the body of a god. Lying beside me, he caressed my shoulders as he kissed them, and kissed my lips tenderly, slowly removing my sheath, and outlined my body with his hands. We were in a gulf of ecstasy, passion, and love. He made love to me tenderly with such love. He made me his, and we became one. Then I knew what love was and being one with my beloved. I felt joy in my heart that I was his and he was mine. Making love with Sen-Mut made me feel whole. We consummated our marriage.

Then he kissed me gently. Moving to my left, he lay beside me, and kissed me again with his arms wrapped around my body. I was content in my heart and body. We were quiet for a while as he held me in his arms. He laid my head on my pillow, holding his own head with his right hand while caressing my chest with his left hand.

“I want you to know that I never fell in love before. I’ve only fallen in love with you. I started to love you the first time I saw you on your father's throne… on that day, you radiated like Ra," he said and kissed me again.

"I have never fallen in love before either. I fell in love with you that same day," I said with a smile, and I caressed his face and kissed his lips, his delicious lips.

We ate and drank wine, and we kissed each other many times. He hugged me and kissed my forehead as he smiled at me. He made love to me all night. We did not stop or sleep since we didn't know when we would see each other or be together again.

When the rooster started to crow, Sen-Mut got up from my bed and put on his kilt. He came closer and kissed me and looked deeply into my eyes. He said, "We must stay away from each other until the time comes. I want you always to remember that I love you." And smile.

Then he kissed me again on my lips and forehead.

As he was leaving, I said, "Sen-Mut! Remember that you belong to me and that whatever happens, I belong to you! And that I love you."

He smiled and nodded his head several times. He walked away, but before he could reach the golden doors, he turned around and said, "Maatke-Re, remember that there will be a time when we will be together. Wait for me. I love you." Then he turned around and walked through the golden doors.

I lay there quietly, remembering how he made me his, giving me the most wonderful pleasure, I ever felt before. He made love to me so many times during the night, and a rush of desire traveled through my body again. He had made me a woman, and now I knew what it feels being taken by the man who loves me. I kissed the two rings he gave me so that he could carry my love with him until we were able to be with each other again.

It was the celebration of the new year, and I was extremely content, feeling the warmth of his lips all over me, and his body inside of me. It was quite a feeling. I closed my eyes and was lost in thought.

Tuyii came in with the other slaves. They were preparing my bath, and Tuyii was pulling the linen sheets from my bed.

"My Queen, your blood came?" she asked.

At first, I did not know what to say, but I slowly answered, "Yes." I walked to the bathing room to be bathed.

When I was done, I was dressed in the royal white sheath. It had a long train embroidered with gold thread and was worn with a golden cape. They made up my eyes with kohl, then put rouge on my cheeks and red lipstick on my lips. They placed the heavy gold pectoral with the turquoise scarab in the center on me. Then they secured the earrings in my ears. They were long earrings with turquoise scarabs. After that, they placed the wig on my head.

Khety had been waiting in the outer chambers while I was getting ready, and when they had finished dressing me, he was called in. He placed the Queen's crown on my head.

We descended the stairs together, and at the foot of the stairs stood Aakheperen-Re dressed in a golden kilt and golden cape, looking handsome and happy. Beside him were Hapuseneb, Ineni, and Mutnofret, who was looking at me and smiling with joy because her son would finally be Pharaoh.

All our friends from the palace were present. Aakheperen-Re looked at me and smiled, and I returned the smile. I looked for Sen-Mut, and when I spotted him, he was looking at me and smiling. He was walking through the inner garden towards us. My smile broke when I noticed that Hapuseneb had turned around and was looking at him. He became serious.

I reached the bottom of the stairs. I thought about Sen-Mut and was please that I was his.

There were many slaves present as well, holding baskets full of white flowers. They began to throw the flowers on the grown as we walked to the hall of audience. The dignitaries from the different parts of the kingdom were assembled.

Thutmoses and I entered the hall of audience and walked to the throne. We walked up the steps, and he stood one step down in front of Father's golden throne and knelt on one knee. I walked up one step above him. Then Khety brought in the Pschent, the Double Crown of Egypt, and proceed with the proclamation, saying, "It's our custom when Pharaoh goes to the heavens that his Queen must choose her consort, and in the presence of the people of the land of Egypt, Her Majesty, Queen Hatshepsut chooses as Pharaoh of the two lands Aakheperen-Re, son of the Great Thutmoses I."

He handed me the Double Crown of Egypt, and I took it in both hands. And raising it high above Aakheperen-Re head, I said out loud, "I, Hatshepsut I, Queen of Egypt, crown you, THUTMOSES II, Pharaoh of Upper and Lower Egypt, in the presence of all the priests, dignitaries, and the people of Thebes!" And I placed the Double Crown on his head.

An uproar of applause came from the people in the hall of audience, and they began to cheer as I proclaimed him Pharaoh of Egypt. The guests started to salute him.

"Thutmoses II! Thutmoses II!" the people shouted.

As we walked down the steps, and smiling at the people, I saw Sen-Mut in the second line behind the most important dignitaries. I was wearing the two rings he had given me, and I smile at him. Everyone else walked behind us.

The armed forces, the palace guards, and the citizens of Thebes were lined up along the streets, cheering their new Pharaoh. They shouted his name. We rode the chariot together all over the streets of Thebes. People were throwing white flower petals as we passed by.

We arrived at the banquet hall, which was very nicely decorated. The food seemed to taste better, perhaps because I was very much in love. The night was long, and from time to time, I sought Sen-Mut. When I would spot him, our eyes would meet, and my heart would be glad and my body full of desire.

Tepi, Hapuseneb's wife, kept her eyes on me all night, and every time Hapuseneb looked at me, she would become infuriated with him. Once, she walked out of the banquet hall, and he did not follow her. He stayed behind smiling at me. She did not return.

Thutmoses II and I celebrated all night with everyone, except Isis, who was nowhere around. He was holding on his head the Double Crown of Egypt, his dream, and I had just made it come true. I was happy for him because he had made my dream come true, too. I was very tired and retired early, walking to my quarters alone. I did not want the guards to follow me, so I dismissed them. I walked slowly. I wanted to be left alone with my thoughts, to think about Sen-Mut making love to me.

I was bathed by Tuyii, and then I rushed to my balcony naked. He was there waiting. I stood there naked looking at him and letting him know that I only belonged to him. We both stood there looking at each other for a while. I wanted him to read my thoughts and see the desires he had awakened in me.

After the coronation, my brother busied himself with the affairs of the kingdom, as I had done. He barely stopped to say hello to me. He had settled in Father's quarters with Isis.

CHAPTER 28

NEFERU-RE'S BIRTH

Two months had passed since I married my brother Thutmoses II and crowned him Pharaoh, and I had not seen Sen-Mut at all since that night. I had not been feeling well lately, suffering from nausea in the mornings. The smell of the food was making me sick. I didn't see Sen-Mut walking beside the Nile much at night. He had to be careful about doing that now.

One day, I was walking to the stables to get a horse to go for a ride, when Hapuseneb fell into step beside me. Suddenly, everything started spinning around me, and I fainted. Hapuseneb carried me to my quarters and sent for the physician.

After the physician examined me and asked me a host of questions, he said, "My Queen, you are expecting a child. Congratulations. There will be a new heir to the throne. I must notify Pharaoh, Your Majesty. He will be most pleased."

I brought my left hand to my belly, and I looked at Hapuseneb, who was looking at me in shock. I wondered what he knew. I lay in bed feeling happy because I was pregnant with my beloved's seed growing inside of me. I knew I must send word to Sen-Mut. I wondered how he would take the news. Would he be happy, as I was? I wondered how Aakheperen-Re would take this news also.

I did not go to the banquet dinner. Instead I stayed in my quarters. Thutmoses did not come to see me all day until very late that night.

I was lying in my bed when he walked through the golden doors. He came closer, very serious. He clapped his hands, and the slave ran out the room.

"Hatshepsut, I did not expect for you to become with child. I'm shocked. I must warn you that if he is a boy, he must die, for I will never allow the son of a peasant to become Pharaoh of Egypt. But if she is a girl, I will see. She will have your royal blood. So, think about it. I warn you. No one, and I mean no one, should know that it is Sen-Mut's child. You must also be prepared to produce a royal heir to the throne after you have this child." His eyes were cast down when he said it.

"I must tell Sen-Mut," I told him.

He became silent.

"Very well, but you must warn him, that if it is a boy, the child must die, and he must keep his silence about the child." Looking at me, he said, "Take care of yourself." Then he walked away.

After he left, I became angry. "Kill my son! He is going to kill my son! I will kill him before he touches my son. I knew I never should have gotten married to him." I hit the goose down mattress several times in rage. I needed to tell Sen-Mut right away.

I got dressed and left my quarters. It was very late at night. I crossed the inner gardens with Mother's slaves. And got into a litter that was waiting for me. The litter-bearers pulled the litter onto their shoulders and started to walk towards Sen-Mut's house. The guards were carrying torches in front of us as they walked in the darkness. The night was warm, and it was very dark when arrived at Sen-Mut's house.

I got down from the litter as the guard was knocking on the door. T'Queta opened the door, and when she saw me she knelt quickly at my feet and greeted me with a smile.

"Your Majesty," she said.

"I must speak to you tomorrow early in the morning in my quarters. Bring Master Sen-Mut. I must speak to him right away."

Sen-Mut came to the door. He was surprised to see me standing there that late at night. He prostrated himself at my feet. He touched them and kissed them, and my heart became warm.

"Rise, Sen-Mut," I said, and he did. I looked in to his eyes, and said with a big smile, "I am with child!" He was stone-still, and his eyes became wide. "I am the happiest woman in the world right now, and I must speak with you, early tomorrow morning in my quarters. I want you to remodel Neferu-Bity's room for my child. Come at the first hours in the morning; we must speak!" I said.

"I will, my Queen. I will be there as Ra rises," he said with a big smile. Then he knelt, touching and kissing my feet several times. T'Queta knelt as well.

I turned around and got into the litter, and the bearers carried me back to the palace. I was happy to see him again. I wanted to rush to him and kiss him with my whole heart.

I could not sleep all night, knowing that he would be here early in the morning. I wanted to be bathed in delicious-smelling perfume. I knew that would please him.

I woke up before sunrise and was bathed. I was dressed in a white-linen sheath and golden robe. I sat in a chair waiting for Sen-Mut to walk through the golden doors. It was still dark outside. Soon Ra would rise. I was eating fruit when there was a knock on the door. It was Sen-Mut.

"Enter," I said.

He was walking rapidly and had a big smile on his face. He crossed the room fast, T'Queta trailing behind him. They came closer to my table and knelt.

"Rise," I said.

I clapped my hands, and Tuyii came to me.

"You and T'Queta go to the kitchen and bring breakfast for Master Sen-Mut and me. T'Queta, you know what your master eats, and she knows what I eat."

I waited until both were gone. We stood up right away, and Sen-Mut pulled me closer to him gently, kissed me with passion, and hugged me tightly. I had my arms wrapped around his neck and whispered in his ears, "You are going to be a father." I said it smiling.

His eyes became misty, and he pulled back gently with a big smile on his lips.

"I am going to be a father," he said, nodding his head several times.

"I could not sleep at all last night. I was full of emotions, thinking about you and the fact that you are going to have my child, the fruit of our love. That pleases me so much!" he said.

"Yes, I must tell you that I did not send word to you right away because after the physician left, he was going to give the news to Thutmoses. I waited for him all day, but Thutmoses did not come until late last night. When he did, he threatened the life of our child. He said that if it is a boy, he will kill it so that your son never will be Pharaoh. But if it is a girl, he will think about it."

Sen-Mut became quiet, and the expression on his face was somber.

"I will kill Thutmoses first, before he harms our child beloved," I said. "I needed to let you know that he is aware that I am talking to you right now. He warned me that no one should know that this is not his child; but I believe Hapuseneb knows," I said.

"And how is that?" he asked.

"I have been sick with nausea, and I thought I had eaten something that was making me sick. I was walking toward the stables to ride my horse when Hapuseneb came and walked beside me. I got dizzy, and I fainted in his arms. He carried me to my quarters and sent for the physician. He was there when I was told that Pharaoh will have an heir to the throne, and Hapuseneb gave me a stern look. I thought that he probably knew that is your child. You know that they are the best of friends."

Sen-Mut's face looked gloomy.

Seeing his sadness, I said, "Let's wait until our child comes into the world and see what we will do, but I can promise you, no one is going to harm our child. For now, let's be happy with this news." I brought his hand to my belly. "I have your seed growing inside of me." We smiled. "I am in my second month," I said.

"Have you bedded T'Queta yet?" I asked him.

He was surprised at my question.

"No, I cannot forget our first time making love, and I don't think she will arouse me as you do, nor do I feel love for her. You are the air I breathe. You are on my mind every single moment of the day. I desire you every night when I go to bed, and it is unbearable not touching you," he said.

I was about to kiss his lips when there was a knock on the door.

"Enter," I said.

It was T'Queta. She knew that she must knock first. She looked at both of us and smiled. Then she and Tuyii set the breakfast on the table.

She said, "My Queen, may I go and visit with the other slaves, and may I take your slave with me?" she asked. I knew she was giving us time to be alone.

"Yes, both of you may go and wait until I send for both of you."

After they left, we stood up again. He grabbed me by my waist and pressed his lips hard on mine as his hands traveled over my breasts and body. I responded to his kisses and caresses. I became aroused, and he made love to me with passion. I responded to his love making with passion until we both screamed in pleasure as we reached an explosive climax. It was wonderful to belong to him again. It was our second time making love, and it felt much better. I felt the ecstasy of love, and I did not want to let him go.

We lay in bed in each other's arms, then he said, "I cannot forget our first time. And I am crazy about you," he said.

I kissed his lips profoundly because he made me very happy.

"Me too, beloved of mine. My nights are long without you too," I said.

I looked at him, and caressing his face with my left hand, I said, "I must tell you this. I don't know when I will be able to see you again, but be sure, I will protect our child. I will find an excuse for us to meet again. Please find a woman who is close to the same number of months of my pregnancy so that her child can take the place of our child if it is a boy. I don't want someone from this area. Find her in another city. Heliopolis, Memphis, or Saqqara. She must stay on the outskirts of the city until my time comes. Please make sure that our plans are kept a secret."

Holding his hands in mine, I continued, "Find two women who know how to induce labor for both of us, at the same time. And find two midwives who are experts on delivering children. Find a home, better yet a farm, and I will ride the chariot there. Thutmoses won't suspect anything because I ride the chariot every day. No one has followed me yet. This woman must be ready to flee with our child a few hours after it's born," I said.

We got dressed and sat to eat our breakfast. During breakfast, I stood up, walked to my makeup vanity, and grabbed the largest jewelry box. I brought it to Sen-Mut and give it to him.

He looked at me and said, "That is too much. We do not need that much gold."

"I want you to give lots of gold to the woman who will be giving up her child, and I also want you to reward very well the ones who are going to help me to induce my labor and deliver our child. I want you to pay all of them well for their silence. Also, we need a wet nurse with plenty of milk in her breasts who will be ready to leave with our son. I will breast-feed my child with the first milk of my breasts, so that he or she will not forget that I am his mother," I said.

Sen-Mut was listening quietly, and he took many large pieces of my gold jewelry.

"I will have my friend the goldsmith who made the rings for you melt these pieces and make them into new small pieces that aren't recognizable, and I will pay them with these," he said.

"Tell them that they must buy a large farm very far away from this city, and they will have much, much gold. They must care for our child very well. Someday, we will come for him. Beloved, we have seven months to prepare for all of this," I said.

He held my hands in his hand then said, "My love, I will do everything as you ask right after I leave, and I promise that we will be together on the day that you have my child. And remember this: It's going to be a day that will mark the start of our lives together. And we will suffer no more, and we will be together forever."

He kissed my hands, and I kissed him. He pulled me against his body. Slowly, he removed my golden robe and sheath and carried me to my bed. He made passionate love to me again and again. I wanted his blood to run in my veins as his seed was growing inside of me. I did not want to be apart from him after he made love to me. After a while, we got dressed and held hands as we walked back to the dining table and started to eat again.

When we finished, I kissed him again and told him, “Beloved one, you may go now. I will send T’Queta back to your house. If you have a message for me, send it with T’Queta. She earned my trust a long time ago. She has the ring I gave her for safe passage to the palace. No one will stop her from coming here.”

“I will, and I love you, Maatke-re,” he said.

We kissed again, and I saw him carrying my heart with him as he left.

A few months passed, and my belly was showing. I had not seen Sen-Mut, nor had I gotten any messages from him. I continued what I was doing: shooting arrows and riding the chariot at a slow pace, and from time to time, Thutmoses came to visit me with Hapuseneb. He didn’t seem as angry as when he made the threat the first time, but I could no longer trust him. I kept seeing him with Isis, who was acting as though she were the Queen of the palace. And that made me furious, so I wouldn’t talk to him.

I was shooting arrows, when Thutmoses walked toward me and asked, “Are you still angry at me?”

“How could I not be angry with you, when you threatened the life of my child?” I snapped at him.

“Hatshepsut, how can I present a child that is not mine as the future heir of the throne? Tell me,” he asked.

“Well, you could give him a name and allow him to grow up. You don’t have to choose him as the heir of the throne as Father did. We had many other older siblings lined up for the throne; but he chose me, and I was the youngest one of all,” I said.

“No, Hatshepsut!” he yelled at me. “All of them died. It is believed that Father ordered their deaths just for you, because he wanted to crown you Pharaoh. He did not count on the fact that I would live this long or that he and I would finally bond together, because I was half of royal blood. I used to hear my mother cry every night and every time one of our siblings was found dead with no sign of what had killed them. She was terrified every single night for me, thinking that I would be next. There were fewer of us. Do you know how I felt when Father made you Horus of Egypt? You were only five summers," he shouted at me again. "And I was nine summers. He made you Prince of Egypt, not me, and he made me feel terrible. I became angry at you because of that."

He lowered his head, and when he resumed, he had lowered his voice. "But when we heard that that test was over, and you probably would not survive, and Ahmose was called urgently, I became very worried for you and went with my mother to the temple and prayed with all my heart to the gods for your well-being. I promised Amun-Ra that I would not be angry at you anymore. And when you came back from the test, you were so sweet. You held my hand and told me that you would make me Horus and that Father had said that you could."

Now he had tears in his eyes. "How could I not love you? You are my little sister. You were always worried about me. I remember when I was sick, I could see you popping your head through the doors just to see me. And you came to cheer me up every day."

Then he started to laugh.

"I can remember when you wanted for me to be brave as our warriors in the training field, and we went to put the trap in the crocodile's mouth. I was so afraid that night. And you became angry at me because I did not want to do it, and you snatched the trap from my hand and told me that you would do it. I held the torch, holding my breath for you. And you did it. You started to run fast after you put the trap on the Sobek. I had never seen you run that fast in my life. I didn't believe that a crocodile could catch you. Ha, ha, ha! You were screaming, 'Run, run. He's going to eat me!' By then the guard had covered my mouth and had doused the torch and taken me away. I knew you were very frightened as the guard was carrying me. I still could hear you screaming, 'He is going to eat me!'"

We started to laugh together.

"And for that we got a good licking that night, do you remember?" We started to laugh again, and he came closer to me and hugged me. He put his two hands on my shoulders, and looking in to my eyes, he said, "You must not be worried. I don't think I will ever have the heart to hurt you or your child. Maybe we can find another solution."

Suddenly, my child moved for first time.

"Thut, my child moved! My child moved for the first time." He looked surprised, so I took his hand and placed in my belly, "Feel it." I said.

He was scared at first, and it moved again. He started to laugh with me.

"It is wonderful. I've never touched a baby in a womb before," he said, then kissed my forehead and turned around and left. As he was walking away, he stopped and said, "Take care of yourself, Hatshepsut, and your child. I will come to visit you in your quarters sometime soon." This time he was smiling, and I smiled back at him.

I wished Sen-Mut was here to feel our child move. I stood there caressing my belly. I was almost in my fifth month. If he only knew how much I missed him, and his lips pressing on mine and being held in his arms. I hoped that he was missing me as much as I missed him.

A few days passed, and I was sitting on my balcony late at night when I saw Sen-Mut walking beside Hopi. He stopped to look at me. It was extremely difficult for both us, not being able to be together and for him not to see his child growing in my belly. And I wondered if he had bedded T'Queta yet. I hoped she could make his heart happy.

Early the next morning, there was a knock on the double doors.

"Enter," I said.

It was T'Queta. She came close to me and knelt at my feet.

"Your Majesty, I came here urgently to talk to you. There is word from one of the slaves who is serving in Pharaoh's quarters that she heard Isis telling Pharaoh yesterday that he must kill your child if it is a boy. That a son of a peasant could never be Pharaoh of Egypt. She also said, though, that if it is a girl, she must die as well. She said that Pharaoh nodded his head several times, and the slave said to tell thee that she will die with this secret."

"Who is the slave who gave you this message? That I may reward her," I said.

"Her name is Menina," she replied.

I took off my golden earrings and bracelets and give them to T'Queta to share with that slave who sent me the message.

"Isis is a cobra! She is poisoning his mind now. Does Master Sen-Mut know of this?" I asked.

"Not yet, Your Majesty. I just heard of it when I was walking beside Hopi to bring thee this message. Menina, approached me as I was on my way here to give it to you."

She pulled out a sealed papyrus and gave it to me. "It's from Master Sen-Mut. I came running to warn you, Your Majesty."

I eagerly broke the seal.

The message read:

The sun is shining, and it's splendid this morning.

I was pleased because this meant that everything was coming along well. His words were comforting to me and warmed my heart. I brought the missive close to my heart and kissed it.

"Tell Master Sen-Mut to send the next missive verbally with you, that I've read the message, and that I am happy to hear that everything is going well. Tell him that our child is growing fine, and it is moving now. Tell him that I wish he was here so that he could feel his child move. Tell him about what that cobra Isis is doing, poisoning Thutmoses' mind. Tell him that Thutmoses had promised me a few days ago that he would not harm our child and that now he seems to be changing his mind because of Isis. Tell him to continue with our plans and that I send him my heart and my love. You may go now."

I kissed the message and gave it back to her so that she could give it back to him. "Tell him to burn the message."

"Yes, Your Majesty," she said, then left.

A few days later, after T'Queta came and warned me about Isis's poisoning tongue trying to turn Thut against my child, I saw Isis strolling like a peacock in the inner garden of my palace, and I was outraged. The wind was blowing, and I looked at the pillars of the palace. They were high and colorful. I was wearing a long black wig, braided with gold thread, and a white pleated sheath. She saw me and walked away as fast as she could. I ran down the stairs looking for Thutmoses. When I saw him, he was walking towards Me. I could see the Nile at my left. I started to shout at him, and he stopped.

"I don't want that cobra of Isis strolling anywhere in my palace or in any of the gardens of the palace either. Do you understand? Otherwise, I will shoot her with my arrows, and I will kill the snake!"

I was so angry at him and her. Suddenly, there was a black asp behind him, slithering about ten or fifteen feet away.

"Asp!" I screamed,

Thut jumped and ran toward me. The guards reacted quickly and killed the asp. Then, looking at him, I give him a dirty look.

"You should send her to the kitchen where she belongs, and the next time she comes to my gardens, she will be dead. I am warning you!"

I turned around and left him standing there. I just saved his life, the ungrateful bastard.

Several months passed, and it had been a while since I last saw T'Queta. I didn't go out as much, for I was in the seventh month of my pregnancy. Thutmoses came to visit me from time to time. He seemed alright with everything. He told me that Puyem-Re would deliver my child and that everything was ready for when my child arrived.

During those days I had received word from Sen-Mut. He had found the pregnant woman, as well as the woman who was going to induce my labor and a midwife. He said that he had found a small house on a farm on the outskirts of the city, and that everything was ready. He also said that he was keeping track of my pregnancy.

****

I was almost eight months pregnant, and I was becoming anxious. I would meet with T'Queta early the following morning, and she would take me to the farm Sen-Mut had bought. He would be waiting for me there. We would be riding in my chariot. I could hardly wait to see my beloved one.

Early in the morning, T'Queta arrived at the golden doors once the chanting had been completed. We left my quarters and before reaching the chariot, we saw Thutmoses walking in our direction. He approached us and looking at T'Queta, he asked me, "Do you have your slave back?"

"Only when I will be riding the chariot. She will provide me company from now on until I have my child. You know how much I like to ride early in the mornings when everything is cool. This pregnancy has made me feel very hot, and I bathe so many times during the day," I said.

He didn't seem concerned that she was with me.

"Very well, Hat. Take care of yourself and the child," he said and smiled.

We said our goodbyes, and he left.

I drove the chariot as fast as I could, for it was a long distance to the place where Sen-Mut was waiting for me. T'Queta kept looking behind us to make sure no one was following. We arrived at the farm, and Sen-Mut rushed to me, hugged me very tightly, and kissed my lips. T'Queta, walked away and left us alone.

His hand protectively at my waist, he ushered me into this small house and then closed the door behind him. He kissed me with a desperate passion, and I responded to his love. I pulled back slowly.

"Why? I must I have you right now?" he asked rhetorically. "These months have been terrible for me without you and my child."

Then he pulled me close slowly, and he pressed his lips on mine again. We had passionate sex several times. I loved his lovemaking and his strong body. He had very strong arms that made me feel safe and protected, especially when he pulled me against his body, like the first time that he made me his. Afterward, we lay in each other's arms.

He kissed my belly, and my child moved. He was startled and laughed. "Our child moved," he said with surprise.

"Yes, Beloved. It has been moving since my fifth month. I wanted so much to have this experience with you, and I am glad that he moved for his father."

Sen-Mut put his head on my belly again, and with a loving voice said, "You are my child, and I started to love you the moment your mother told me that she was carrying you. You have made me very happy, and soon we will see your face. I can hardly wait to hold you in my arms! I will protect you and your mother with my life." He kissed my belly again, then looked at me and said, "I hope the Oracle chooses a good name," he said.

"If the baby is a boy, I want a god's name, but it will be up to the Oracle to choose one. The stars will tell us what the right name for him or her will be, but if it's a girl, I want to call her Neferu-Re like my beloved sister, Neferu-Bity. But it's also up to the Oracle and the stars to decide the name. I will ask Khety if that name is possible," I said.

"Yes, my love. I agree with you that our daughter should have your sister's name if the baby is a girl," he said, and we got dressed.

"Let me show you around the farm. I believe our child will be safe here for a few days. Then they will take him to Heliopolis, and I will be going with them… Senemen, my brother, bought a very nice farm with the gold I gave him. He bought it from a very wealthy farmer and our child will grow healthy and well off. Senemen will accompany them first with his wife to the farm and make sure that our child will be well taken care of. My sister will also go, and she will help. They will be with him all the time, and later my mother and father will join them and live with him. See, my love, we are not alone in this. Now, the woman who will induce your labor has done it many times. She's a midwife as well. She said that she will give you a very powerful beverage, and within two hours, you will be in labor. My mother is happy that she could help. She was the one who went looking for a pregnant woman and a midwife until she found them. I will reward the women very well. The midwife doesn't know who you are. Nor does the pregnant woman. She is married to a man who is fair-skinned, so there will be no problem with the color of the child. She doesn't know to whom she is giving up her child, or whom she is doing this for, only that you are someone wealthy and that I am doing this as a favor for a friend. I told them that they will be very wealthy, with a large farm and her children will be raised in wealth. They will be here three weeks before you are about to have our child."

"Beloved one, does she have other children?" I asked.

"Yes, she does," he said.

"I'm glad. I would not want someone to lose her child. I wish I did not have to do this, but what if I have a girl and she has a boy? What would I do?" I was starting to panic. "Beloved, you know what would happen if I give birth to my child and I come back to the palace without a child in my arms. He will send the army to look for him and will kill him without conscience, because he will believe that I was plotting to kill him and make you Pharaoh and make our son heir to the throne. I wish I didn't have to do this." I was worried.

He replied, "Then we must give him the boy child. We cannot take the chance of him changing his mind and killing our daughter. Anyway, everything is ready right now and waiting for the moment. I have spoken with Ineni. He will help us, and if Pharaoh asks about me, he will say that he has sent me to the building site and that I should not come back for weeks. I will be able to take our child away from here myself."

I caressed his face and gently kissed his lips. Then he said, "Hapuseneb talked to me few days ago, regarding you and our child, and he offered his help. He said that Thutmoses told him that he would kill our child if it was a boy, and Hapuseneb did not like what he was hearing. He told Thutmoses to banish the child from here but not to kill him because doing that would spur your hatred and your wrath, and you could kill his children, too. Hapuseneb told Thutmoses that it would be better to say that the child had died at birth instead and that I could take the child far away from here. But see, I could never leave you. I love you too much to leave and never see you again. It's not possible."

Sen-Mut's eyes were misty. He continued, "Then he said that Thut told him that he would think about it. He also offered his help for whatever is needed. I did not tell him of our plans. I know all too well that he is Thut's best friend, and I preferred not to tell him anything".

I could see the worry in his face, and it hurt me deeply inside that we had to go through all of this to save the life of our child.

"Thank you, beloved of mine," I said and caressed his face. "I know that Hapuseneb means well. The next time we see each other, we will have our child in our arms." I smiled at him.

"I must go now. Ra is very high, and probably someone is wondering where I am. I don't know how much I can trust Tuyii, my mother's slave, right now. Kiss me, my love, as only you can kiss me." I said. We hugged tight and kissed profoundly.

He knelt and kissed my belly, and I caressed his hair. Then he stood up and pressed his lips on mine again and hugged me tightly again. I whispered in his ear, "May Ra keep you safe always, and may He always shine on the path you will take and be always on your back."

With his arms wrapped around me, he said, "May Amun-Ra protect you and my child always. I pray and make offerings every day to the gods for both of you."

He walked me to the chariot, and T'Queta was waiting for me. I rode away, looking back at him. I saw him standing there as I was getting farther away and kept watching until I lost sight of him. I was leaving my heart with him.

After an hour we arrived at the palace, and I was bathed. Then I asked T'Queta to stay with me for a while, and we ate together.

"Has Master Sen-Mut bedded you yet?" I asked.

She was surprised at my question and responded very quickly, "No, Your Majesty."

Then I said, "I would not mind if he does. I want you to know that. We don't know how long we will be apart. I don't want him to be alone all this time. He has man's desires." I held her hand in my hands. "T'Queta, I want to thank you so much for being a faithful servant and for taking care of Sen-Mut all these months for me."

I got up from my chair, got a beautiful golden bracelet, and gave it to her. She was surprised.

"Your Majesty, it is beautiful. Thee doesn't have to do this. All that I do for you is done with love, and I am pleased to do it. You have already given me so much," she said.

"Thank you, T'Queta." I smiled. "You may go now. Master Sen-Mut must be at his home by now. Please take good care of him for me. And never stop telling him how much I love him. Please."

"I will, Your Majesty," she said, then she left.

My time was almost up, and I had been very nervous. Tonight, I saw Sen-Mut walking beside Hopi. The night was full of stars and in three more days, we would have our child in our arms. I stood on the balcony, and we looked at each other for a while. Then he left. I hoped T'Queta kept his bed warm until he is mine again.

The following morning was glorious. I had been waking up every day missing my beloved one. And my child had not let me sleep well for weeks now. It kept kicking me. Today, I felt strange, and my belly looked lower than before. I was in Mother's gardens when I saw Thutmoses walking toward me.

"Hat, how do you feel this morning? In three more weeks, you will have your child!" he said.

He gave me a nice and sincere smile. I really wondered what was on his mind. I had always considered him a very honest man.

"Yes, are you keeping track of my pregnancy? I must speak to you regarding my child right now" I was still feeling strange. My back had been bothering me all night. "Are you going to let my child live?" I asked him. He became quiet and very serious. I froze.

Suddenly, water was running between my legs. I looked down to see what it was. I did not know what was happening to me.

He looked at me and said, "Hat, you are about to have your child right now. I have seen it before when the slaves were about to give birth."

I became terrified. He was there, so I could not go anywhere. The contractions started, and I screamed, terrified for my child. I started to yell at him, "You are going to kill my child! You are going to kill my child! Please don't! Please don't!" I was crying and terrified of him. I continued screaming at him, and another contraction came. I screamed again in pain.

He lifted me in his arms and carried me. I could not get away from his arms. Then he said, "I will not kill your child. I promise! I promise! Please don't' cry."

"Guard! Guard!" he shouted. The guards came running. "Call the High Priest Khety and Puyem-Re and the midwives and scribes to the Queen's quarters. She is having the child right now."

I wanted to get away from him. but I could not. The contractions were too severe.

"If you are not going to kill my child, prove it. Send for Sen-Mut and T'Queta. I want him beside me! I want him beside me! Call Hapuseneb and Ineni also." I screamed again in pain.

He called another guard and said, "Rush to Master Sen-Mut and tell him to hurry to the Queen's quarters. She is having the child. And send for Hapuseneb and Master Ineni and T'Queta, too. Run!"

I felt somewhat more at ease, but I was still afraid. He carried me to my bed. The slaves were happy and excited, and Mother's slave was so happy. She said, "We must bring the chair for her to have her child."

I saw Khety and Puyem-Re coming in to my quarters. Thutmoses said to them, "Send word to me when she has the child and let me know what it is." Then I saw him leave.

I screamed in terrible pain again. My insides were tearing me apart. Khety and Puyem-Re were near me, and I saw Sen-Mut rushing to my side and kneeling beside me. He held my hand, and our eyes met. The look on his face was one of fear.

"Come closer," I said, and I whispered in his ear, "He is not going to kill our child. He promised. I told him to send for you, and he did."

Sen-Mut closed his eyes in relief.

The hours were long. The contractions would go away and come back worse.

Puyem-Reexamined me and said, "She is almost ready. Let's carry her to the chair."

In that moment, I screamed. The expression on Sen-Mut's face was of desperation. He wanted to help to alleviate my pain. I could see Hapuseneb biting the back of his finger every time I screamed. T'Queta was beside me cleaning the sweat from my face and forehead.

Sen-Mut and Hapuseneb carried me to the standing chair. Ineni was at the end of the balcony. The priestesses were chanting and burning incense. I was weak and exhausted. I didn't think I could continue.

Puyem-Re said, "Hang on to the chair arms, Your Majesty, and push hard. Push! Push!"

He was between my legs with his hands extended to catch the child as it was delivered. I was pushing hard, and I was screaming. Then I felt as my child came out of me. I was trembling and ready to collapse. I was weak.

Puyem-Re handed the child to Khety. Khety raised my child in the air and shouted, "Princess Neferu-Re!"

Sen-Mut carried me in his arms and lay me on my bed. He was smiling and kissing my hands. He knelt beside me as Puyem-Re placed our daughter in my arms. She was incredibly tiny, but beautiful. She had a lot of black hair and looked like Sen-Mut.

I whispered in his ear, "Isn't she beautiful?"

He was elated. I yelled to the scribe to write, "I, Hatshepsut, Queen of Upper and Lower Egypt, on this day of the birth of my child, Princess Neferu-Re, I appoint Sen-Mut to be the great nurse and tutor of Princess Neferu-Re. He will be near my daughter always and oversee her care, protection, and education. Let the whole kingdom know that on this day, Princess Neferu-Re was born. So, let it be written. So, let it be done."

Hapuseneb came closer to me. He looked at my daughter with a beautiful smile. I could see a real happiness in his face, as if she were his child.

I could see so much happiness on Sen-Mut face as well.

I become a mother today, and my daughter was beautiful. As I held her in my arms, I looked at her little tiny fingers and toes. I gave her to Sen-Mut so that he could hold her. He looked very happy. I was so tired that I fell asleep with Sen-Mut beside me.

When I woke up, it was morning. My breasts were hurting. Thutmoses had sent for a wet nurse for her. He was sitting beside my bed, holding her in his arms with a smile on his face. I smiled at him.

"Hatshepsut, she is beautiful and so tiny. She looks just like you when you were born. I remember you were that small. I used to come to your crib, and you would hold my finger. I played with you. I would come to see you every day. I am glad I did not commit the stupidity of doing away with her. Will you forgive me for putting you through so much pain," he asked me.

"Yes, beloved brother. And I thank you also for being kind and saving her life," I said.

"Now, be at peace. No one will ever harm her, I promise," he said with a smile.

He stayed for a while visiting with me. He made me laugh. I knew what he was doing. He was making me feel at ease. He kissed my forehead and said, "Hat, take care of your beautiful princess. She even looks like a princess. I will come back from time to time to see her." Then he left.

Sen-Mut came after a while. I could see such happiness reflected in his face. I told him about Thutmoses's apology, which made him feel much more at ease.

There was a knock on the golden doors.

"Enter," I said.

It was Hapuseneb. "I came to see the small princess," he said.

The looks that Sen-Mut and he gave each other sometimes scared me. I knew he was still hurting. He had married Tepi because he thought he would never have me, and things had changed after his marriage. He was still one of my favorite people, and I loved him; but Sen-Mut was the man with whom I was in love. I wished there could be two of me. And I wished I could spare him this pain.

Everything was going well. Sen-Mut was fond of his daughter, and we were very happy. But one day I started to notice that every time he came to visit me and our daughter, a guard also entered my quarters with him. I asked the guard why he was coming inside my quarters without my permission, and he said that His Majesty Thutmoses had ordered it, that I was not to be alone with Master Sen-Mut at any time. I was shocked by his words, and Sen-Mut and I exchanged looks.

I got dressed and went to see Thutmoses. He was living in my father's quarters, as was Isis. When I entered the quarters, she got up and threw herself at my feet.

"Out!" I yelled at her, and she rushed out as fast as lighting. I turned to Thutmoses. "Akheperen-Re, why is it that your guard comes into my quarters when Sen-Mut comes to visit Neferu-Re and me?" I asked.

"Haven't you heard the rumors? Rumors are that she is Sen-Mut's daughter. I had to put to death several of the slaves in the kitchen to stop this gossip. I don't want him to visit you when you are alone. He must visit Princess Neferu-Re in her room from now on, and with her wet nurse present, and I don't want more gossip in the palace nor in the land," he said.

"I am sorry to hear that, but how can you keep me away from him? I love him, and you know that." I said.

"I know that you love him, but I am Pharaoh, and this cannot continue. How must I look in front of my people? Or maybe you will give me no any other choice than to put him to death," he said.

I screamed at him. "No, please don't do that!" I started to cry. "Neferu-Re cannot lose her father," I told him.

"I've already allowed your daughter to live, and we must avoid any more rumors in the palace. I had to swallow my pride as Pharaoh and suffer the embarrassment for you. Is that understood? She is almost six months old, and in another six months, I will pay you a visit, and you must produce an heir for the throne. A real heir. I should have listened to Isis when she told me not to let her live."

He became quiet. He realized he should not have said that. I knew now that the snake of Isis was still poisoning his mind against me.

I came closer to him, and with force, I punched him in the chest. He stumbled and almost fell to the floor. I started to scream at him, "Don't you dare touch Sen-Mut, nor my daughter, or I will poison your little snake, and you would not be able to stop me! Or better, if you bring her to the arena when I am there, I will shoot her between the eyes with my arrows. Is that understood? And from now on, I don't want to see her anywhere in my garden, either with you or without you. You must send her to the kitchen where she belongs because she is not a royal wife and never will be," I said, then I stormed out.

He yelled at me before I could reach the golden doors. "And you had better not be carrying another child of his because if you do, it will die this time! I spared her life because Hapuseneb convinced me not to kill her. That is why she is alive today."

I turned around rapidly and gave him a look of hatred.

"And I thought you had a good heart. But no, you are simply a hypocrite!" I screamed at him and opened the golden doors. I left and ran to my quarters where I changed into my kilt. Grabbing my bow and arrows, I ran down the stairs and to the stables. I ordered my horse to be saddled. I rode my horse as fast as I could. How dare he! I should not have married him. I screamed in anger.

After a few hours of this, I saw a horse riding towards me. "How dare he send a guard to spy on me! I hate him; I hate him!" I thought. I waited for the guard to come closer to tell him to get the hell out of my sight. But to my surprise, it was Sen-Mut. I called to him, and he rode fast to meet me. We both dismounted, then hugged and kissed with passion, our bodies engulfed in this fire of love.

Then I started to cry. He pulled back. "What's wrong, beloved?" he asked.

"Aakheperen-Re doesn't want us to see each other ever again. He said that you can visit our daughter, but from now on, you must not come to my quarters. He said that he had to order the deaths of several slaves from the kitchen because there was a rumor that Neferu-Re is your daughter and not his and that if I see you again, he will order your death. I am terrified again. I don't want to lose you, Sen-Mut. He said that in six months he will pay me a visit and that I must produce an heir, and if I am with your child now, this time he will kill the child. He also said that Hapuseneb was the one who convinced him not to kill our daughter."

Sen-Mut's face showed concern, and he was flushed. "Beloved, are you carrying my child again?" he asked.

"No, I don't think so, my love."

He hugged me again. I realized that I was very thirsty, so I asked him for water.

"We are close to the farm. Do you remember that it is around here? No one is there. I go there sometimes and think of you. We still own it. Let's go there and have some water," he said.

We rode fast and arrived at the small house. He brought me down from my horse, and we walked into the small home. He brought me water and then went to tie up the horses and water them.

When he came back, he hugged me again. We kissed passionately. We had not had each other for a while, only once in the last three months. I could not stop the fire inside of me. I could not stop it. He pulled off my kilt gently, and I did the same with his kilt. He was kissing my throat slowly.

He picked me up in his arms and gently lay me on the bed. A current of ecstasy ran over my body as he made me his slowly with such love, giving me explosions of pleasure and ecstasy that only he could give me. He clung to my body tightly, with his arms behind my back kissing me on my lips. Then he grunted loudly, reaching his own peak of pleasure and ecstasy and giving me all that he had.

We held each other tightly, and I cried in his arms for a while. When the sobbing had subsided, I looked at Sen-Mut's face. He looked concerned, sad, and pained. We knew that today would probably be our last time together, and we lay there holding each other very tightly in silence.

"I am so angry, and I feel so powerless. I wish I never had to let you go but as I said to you before, there will come a time when we will be together, I promise. Then there will be no more pain for us. I want you always to remember this. I will never stop loving you," he said.

We lay there for a long time holding each other, until we saw Ra start to fade away. We were dreading letting go. Eventually, we got up, washed, and said our evening prayers together. After, we got dressed in silence. I did not want the time to pass.

He came to me and hugged me, then slowly pulled me away from him. "Maatke-Re, I hope I didn't get you pregnant today. When I am with you, I cannot control my desire for you," he said.

"Beloved, it happens to me as well, and if I have gotten pregnant today, I would protect our child, believe me. Even if it meant I had to kill him and his snake," I said.

Sen-Mut became silent. We walked out of the house holding onto each other and stopped in front of the horses. He undid the reins of the horses, then kissed me deeply. I got onto my horse, crying the whole time. He mounted his horse as well, and we walked them holding hands, side by side.

The dark night was full of stars. It was beautiful as we rode slowly. We saw the palace from afar, about a mile away, and we kissed. We were both heartbroken.

"Maatke-Re, trust me. I promise you that we will be together. I promise," he said.

"I believe you. It's just very difficult for me to leave you now. We don't know when we will see each other again." I put my left hand on my heart, then placed it on his heart. "Take my heart with you, my love. You have mine, now and forever," I said.

We rode our separate ways. I turned around and could see that he was still standing there, watching me ride away. I left my heart with him.

For two months after that night, I kept checking for signs of pregnancy, but I wasn't pregnant. I sent a message to Sen-Mut with T'Queta, that I was not pregnant.

Six months later, I received a message from Thutmoses, which said he would make that visit that night. He wanted to produce a blood heir that only I could give him.

I started to drink wine early that afternoon, and I was almost drunk when I was bathed by Tuyii. I was not dressed like a queen that night. I wore a simple white sheath.

He walked through the golden doors. He clapped his hands, and all my slaves left my quarters in a hurry. He was drunk. I was sitting in my chair drinking wine. He started to talk.

"Hat, this is not easy for me either, to sleep with my own sister to produce an heir. Maat told me that if you don't produce a male heir, I was not to force you to have another child again," he said. "I have been drinking all day to be able to do this." I could see that he was not happy either, and I continued drinking.

"Let's finish with this, and this is not going to happen again. This will be the last time you come to my quarters looking for an heir."

We walked to a couch near the balcony, and I was as drunk as he was.

I woke up the following morning as Ra was shining on my face. I didn't remember anything, so I must have blacked it out. I had the most horrible headache the following morning, and that is why I don't drink wine.

Two months later, I started to have nausea, and I realized that I was pregnant.

"Tuyii, go and get the physician." I sat on the balcony and waited. She quickly came back with Puyem-Re.

He examined me and said, "Your Majesty, you are expecting a child. I must notify Pharaoh immediately!" I gave him a smile that was barely a smile. He left.

I was going to have another child. I determined that I would put all my attention on Neferu-Re and my new child. They would fill the emptiness in my heart until I could get back together again with my beloved.

It was not too long before Thutmoses came rushing through the golden doors with a big smile. "You are pregnant. Puyem-Re just came and gave me the great news. I hope it is a prince." I saw happiness on his face. It was his first child.

His happiness was contagious and made me happy, because I could see real happiness in him.

"Hat, I want for you to take good care of yourself. I don't want you riding horses, or driving chariots at a fast pace, or going to practice training camp. We must take good care of you and the future Prince of Egypt."

"Brother, I promise I will. Believe me, I will."

His happiness was contagious to me, and I smiled. We spoke for a while about all the things we were going to do with his child. That night, I saw my beloved from afar, as I did every night. By then, he must have known of my pregnancy. I imagined that Hapuseneb had already sent the edict all over the land announcing my pregnancy.

Lately, I had not seen my beloved Sen-Mut walking beside the Nile, as I had every night before. I became worried and wondered why.

"Tuyii, bring one of my door guards into my quarters right away." I was very worried for Sen-Mut's life.

"Your Majesty." The guard approached and knelt at my feet.

"I want you to find out if Master Sen-Mut is alright, but I don't want anyone to know that I am inquiring about him," I said.

"Don't worry, Your Majesty, no one will know. I have friends everywhere, and I will find out if he is okay."

"You may go now but return as soon as you find out."

He bowed his head, rose, and left. He left his post outside the door, and I paced back and forth on the balcony, waiting for news. There was no breeze that night. The months had gone by fast. I was in my seventh month of pregnancy, and the heat was driving me crazy.

Several hours later, Tuyii came into my bedroom.

"Your Majesty, the guard is in the main quarters."

I ran to him, and he dropped his face to the floor.

"Rise," I said.

"Your Majesty, Master Sen-Mut is alright. He has been sent by Master Ineni to rebuild some shrines along the Nile."

"Does your friend know when he is coming back?"

"No, Your Majesty, but he believes it's going to be a long while before his return. My friend heard that it was Pharaoh who requested that Ineni send Sen-Mut to rebuild the shrines along Hopi."

"Tuyii, bring my jewelry box."

I took fifteen gold nuggets and gave them to him.

"For your complete silence. I want you to share it with the other guard at my door and your friend. Tell him to keep you posted regarding when Master Sen-Mut returns. Tell him that there will be more rewards for all of you. You and your friend must keep your lips sealed."

"Yes, Your Majesty, we will."

"You may go now," I said.

I walked to the balcony, feeling very much saddened. Thut had sent him away purposely.

CHAPTER 29

PRINCESS HATSHEPSET'S BIRTH

I was asleep when my water broke, soaking the sheets and the goose mattress. "Tuyii! Tuyii, run. My water broke, and my child is close to showing his face to this world. Run for the physicians and send for Pharaoh," I said.

The contractions started, and I knew I would going through the same pain as the last time. I knew it would be horrible again. My slaves were holding my hand when the golden doors swung open. It was my brother with a big smile. Behind him was Hapuseneb. Thutmoses ran to me, knelt beside me and held my hand.

"Sister, I am so happy right now. I am having a son. I've sent for Khety and Puyem-Re. I informed the Oracle that they should be ready to tell me the fate of our child as soon as he is born. This time there will be a real male heir to the throne, no matter what. I will treat him better than my father did me," he said.

I was listening quietly, for I was in terrible pain. The contractions became more severe, and I took a deep breath. "Brother, remember that we have an agreement. After this child is born, you are not to visit my quarters looking for another child," I said.

He looked at me and lowered his eyes, and as he nodded several times, he said," Yes, I remember that, and I will keep my word."

The contractions continued, and it was not too long before I was put in the chair. I kept thinking of Sen-Mut when I was having our daughter. I heard the voice of Puyem-Re.

"Your Majesty, push hard!"

I screamed and pushed hard, and then he was holding the child. He looked at my brother and showed him the child, then gave the child to Khety. Khety raised my child in the air. I was waiting for him to tell me what the sex was, when he shouted, "Princess, Merit-Re Hatshepset!"

The look on Thutmoses's face changed. When he looked at me, I could see that he was disappointed. It was not a male heir as he wanted. Deep in my heart, I also wanted a male heir to make him happy, but the gods are always right.

Hapuseneb carried me to the bed in silence. Thutmoses had Merit-Re in his arms. He came to me, put her in my arms, and kissed me on my forehead. "Hatshepsut, she is beautiful. She looks like you and will grow up to look just like you. I am very happy with my daughter. Really, I am. And I know that you are very tired. I will be back early in the morning to see you both. The wet nurse is waiting for her, so just rest for the day," he said.

I give him a short smile, knowing that he was hurting. I felt very sorry for him. I saw him walking away, and I know he had a broken heart.

Hapuseneb waited outside of my bedroom as I was being washed well by the slaves and was changed into a new sheath. Everything was changed on the bed, including the goose-down mattress.

There was a light knock in the door.

"Enter," I said.

The door slowly opened to reveal Hapuseneb. "May I come in?"

"Of course, Hapu. You are always welcome. Come and sit beside me."

"The little princess is beautiful. She looks just like you, Flower of Egypt. I believe you will be happy, having her and Princess Neferu-Re running through the palace."

"Hapu, I know that you are fond of Neferu-Re."

"Yes, very much," he said.

"Have you heard anything from Sen-Mut?" I asked.

"No, but I do let Ineni know of Neferu-Re's progress as she is growing, because I know Sen-Mut will be happy to hear that his daughter is growing fine."

My eyes became full of tears when I looked in to his gray eyes and saw the love he felt for me. I knew that it had to be hard for him, trying to be impartial.

"Flower of Egypt, everything is going to be fine, you will see." He patted my right hand twice.

"I believe my brother was disappointed and grief-stricken. I know he wanted so much to have a male heir, and deep in my heart, I did too, since it would have made him very happy," I said.

"Well, in nine months, you can try again."

"No, there will not be another time," I said.

He looked at me, puzzled.

"I made it very clear to him that it wouldn't happen again, and he agrees to that."

Hapu nodded his head several times. "Rest, Flower of Egypt. I will come tomorrow morning to see you and the new princess. I will bring Princess Neferu-Re to meet her little sister. Rest for now and sleep well. Good night," he said.

"Good night, Hapu, and don't take that long walk to your home in the dark."

He turned around and said, "A litter is waiting for me. Good night."

I lay there looking at my little princess, at her tiny hands and feet. She was beautiful. I wanted to squeeze her hard because she was so beautiful, and I kissed her many times. Then I started to think that I had two beautiful little princesses. And I thought of Hapuseneb. What a great man. I wished I could spare his hurt. I knew that it must hurt him so much, me having someone else's child and not his. Then I thought of Sen-Mut and the fact that I loved him.

CHAPTER 30

MENKHEP-RE'S BIRTH

(THUTMOSES III)

Three month later, Thutmoses approached me on my way to the stables.

"Hat, wait! I must speak to you," he said.

I turned around to look at him.

"Good morning brother. You look cheerful and happy this morning. What is it?"

"I just got very good news, and I want for you to know it before anyone comes and tell you!"

I was puzzled, for I always knew everything that was going on in the palace.

"Isis is pregnant!" he said with a big smile. He was very happy, but I was surprised.

"Brother, are you sure that it is yours? I've heard a lot of rumors that she spends a lot of her time in the temple, talking with Puyem-Re." I looked at him very seriously. My gut was telling me that something was not right.

"Of course, it's mine. Don't you think I've had someone following her? I don't believe that either she or Puyem-Re would betray me knowing that they could lose their lives for it."

"Then, good brother, congratulations. Maybe you will have the male child you want. But remember that he will not be of full royal blood and never will be Pharaoh of Egypt," I said.

"That's fine. If it is a boy, I will betroth him to Neferu-Re, even though she is not my daughter and is not fully royal either."

"As you wish," I murmured. I turned around to mount my horse, but then I turned around again. "Bring the child when it is born so that I can see it," I said.

"Hat, we could have another child, a male child, and he would be of full royal blood," he said.

By this time, I was already on top of my horse. "The only children I want are with Sen-Mut." I smiled at him and rode off to look for Hapuseneb. I wanted to know why he had not told me of Isis's pregnancy. But then I thought, "Well, who cares? The child could be a boy."

I rode fast looking for Hapuseneb. He was walking beside the Nile toward his house, and I caught up with him.

"Good morning, Flower of Egypt," he said.

I dismounted my horse as he held the reins. I started to walk beside him along the same path we used to walk when we were children. I smiled at him.

"Why are you smiling?" he asked.

"I was remembering when we were children. One day, you punched me so very hard on my back, and I remember that it really hurt, and it hurt for days."

"Ah, I remember that day. I've thought about it all these years and feel guilty. I should never have punched you, but I was very angry at you because I got a very hard whipping, like Thut."

We started to laugh.

"That night I could heard his screaming and your screaming. I got a whipping as well, by Sitre-In, but she was not whipping me hard enough. I had to tell her to do so; otherwise she was going to be whipped by a soldier," I said.

He stopped walking, and so did I. Turning toward me, he said, "I want to apologize to you now for that punch. That night I could not sleep thinking about what I had done. And throughout all these years, I kept thinking about it, and I wanted to apologize for it. Will you forgive me?"

"Would you feel better, Hapu, if I forgive you?" I changed the subject to ask him the question that I wanted to ask him. "Why haven't you told me about Isis's pregnancy?"

He was startled. "I tried to. I went to your quarters with Thut to tell you, but you were gone. He wanted to tell you himself. He was very happy about it. The guard told him that you had gone to the stables to get your horse, and he walked quickly to meet you there. He also wanted to tell you himself before you heard it from someone else like me. Ha, ha, ha," he laughed.

"I see." I became at ease. "Do you want to swim with me, Hapu, like when we were children? Let's see who reaches the waters first," I said and took off running. He ran after me. We were both laughing.

I jumped into the waters of Hopi. It felt good. I could hear the splash behind me. He had just jumped in behind me. I was laughing.

“Hapuseneb, are you happy with Tepi?” I asked.

He looked in to my eyes and said, “I will never be happy if I’m not with you.”

I lowered my eyes. He always made me happy and at the same time sad.

“But having you around me like right now, makes me very happy!” Then he splashed water on my face, and he took off swimming. I swam after him, and he stopped. He jumped on me and pushed me down under the water. I was laughing underwater, and we continued playing like when we were little kids.

Then I noticed that he was aroused. He was so close to my face, as the water was dripping down his face. He looked so beautiful, and he was about to kiss me. I was tempted to let him kiss me. I was weak. I knew if I let him kiss me what it would lead to because I was lost in the beauty of his gray eyes and his love. I came to my senses, and I pulled back. I walked away in silence and got out of the water, trembling. Then I mounted my horse, noticing that the rays of Ra were fading away. I turned around and saw that he had remained in the water looking at me. I left. At first, I kept the horse at a slow speed, but then I started gallop to the palace.

****

Nine months later, when Neferu-Re was almost two summers and had been walking for almost a year, it was coming close to the time when Merit-Re Hatshepset would also be walking.

One day, I was sitting on my balcony in silence, watching the slow flow of the Nile. It was a cooler day, and I was grateful for that.

I heard the voice of one of my slaves say, “Your Majesty!”

I turned around to see what it was, and there was Thutmoses walking slowly in my direction holding Neferu-Re by the hand.

"Brother, what a nice surprise! You brought my daughter to see me." I walked to her. She looked just like Sen-Mut. I knelt and hugged her closely and kissed her.

"I came to tell you that Isis is in labor, and soon I will know if it's a boy."

"I hope everything goes well with her and that she gives you what you want. Labor is very hard the first time. Go and be with her. In fact, why are you here instead of with her? I don't understand."

"Maybe I am very nervous?" he said.

"Go. She needs you right now."

He left, and I picked up Neferu-Re in my arms and walked to the balcony. I sat with her in my lap, but she did not want to be in my lap. She wanted to play with my Bastet. She was very cute running after the cats.

Five hours had passed when Hapuseneb walked through my golden doors and walked toward me.

"Lotus of Egypt, Isis had a boy."

I became silent. I wasn't happy to hear that. Not at all.

"How is the child?" I asked.

"He is fine, and Thutmoses is very happy. He named him Menkhep-Re and is thinking he will be the next Pharaoh, Thutmoses III."

"And how is that? He is not a full royal blood child, and he knows that. But for now, let him be happy with his child, and in three months bring the child here so that I can see him. And I will know who he looks like. I'll know whose child he is. I am glad that the child is healthy and that my brother is happy, as I am for him."

CHAPTER 31

WAR

I became very restless as the days went by because I have not seen Sen-Mut at all. I had walked to the Temple of Amun-Ra every morning to make offerings for his wellbeing and protection.

Walking to the temple I saw a man's back, whose body reminded me his. It was him. He had returned. He was talking with Khety. I was happy. I wanted so much for him to turn around and see me, but he did not. I stood there looking at him as he walked away with Khety in the opposite direction. Holding back my tears, I quickly walked to the edge of the Nile and buried my face and my tears between my knees.

He looked well. I wondered if he missed me as much I have missed him, his body, and lips. I wondered if T'Queta had replaced me, and I cried harder.

I decided that I would sail the Nile tomorrow and hope that I got a chance to see him swimming. I knew that he liked to swim in the Nile. Maybe we would be lucky, and we could see each other.

I remained sitting beside the Nile for a while, it became dark. I had to run. Maybe he would walk beside the Nile to see me tonight, I thought. I rushed up the stairs.

When I got upstairs, one of the guards said, "Your Majesty, may I have a word with you?"

"Yes, you may. Follow me," and he did.

"Your Majesty, Master Sen-Mut has returned to the palace after many months away, and my friend said that earlier he was in the temple making offerings to Amun-Ra."

"I am pleased to hear that. How long is he going to stay?" I asked.

"My friend doesn't know how long he will remain in Thebes."

I was elated. "Tuyii, bring me gold." She brought me the small box with gold nuggets. I gave him fifteen nuggets. "Share it with the other guard and with your friend."

He dropped his face to the floor. "Thank you, Your Majesty." I was so very happy that Sen-Mut was back, and my heart was full of joy!

After the guard left, I called Tuyii. "Tuyii, bathe me!" I shouted. "And I want my favorite fragrance in the water."

I was full of joy and full of life, overwhelmed with his return. I knew I must wear the perfume that he liked. I was dressed in a white sheath with long, straight, gold lines embroidered in the linen. I wore my golden pectoral and the golden sandals. I walked to the balcony and sat there and waited for him. And waited. The hours passed. And passed. All my earlier happiness started to fade away as the tears rolled down my cheeks. He had forgotten me.

I closed my eyes, tears pouring down my face in earnest, and wondered why. How could he stop loving me? Perhaps he had fallen in love, and the love of T'Queta had done it.

Slowly, I opened my eyes. And there he was, standing there looking at me. I jumped out of my chair. At that moment, I wanted to have wings to fly to him. The tears running down my face were now tears of happiness. He had not forgotten me. No words needed to be spoken between us. Our love spoke for us. We remained looking at each other for a very long time and having a mental conversation.

It was very late when he left, carrying my love with him. My feelings were bittersweet, but I was satisfied. I was pleased to know that at least I was still in his heart.

"Please wait for me, my love. I am still waiting for you," I told him, though he could not hear me. Then I told myself, "I must see him; I must! I walked to my bed and lay there, desiring his body so much that it was unbearable. I wanted to melt with his kisses and into his body. I wondered when it would be time for us to be together again.

I woke up with desire in my heart, desperate to see him, but I didn't know how to when our kingdom was so big. Even if I disguised myself as a peasant, I didn't know how I could find him without Thutmoses knowing.

I decided that I would tell Thut that I wanted my mortuary tomb to be built. There were no other architects besides Ineni and Sen-Mut. Ineni was too old to start a new project, so he would have Sen-Mut build it for me. That's it!

"Tuyii, go and take a message to Pharaoh. Tell him that I am coming to his quarters to speak to him."

"Yes, Your Majesty."

She left, and I waited anxiously for her to return.

"Your Majesty, he will be waiting for you as you wish right now."

"Dress me," I said.

I was dressed as Queen. I had not dressed like this for a very long time. I strolled the very long limestone floors to his quarters. The two guards opened the golden doors, and I entered.

"Hat, it's nice to see you. I can see that you gained some weight after Merit-Re Hatshepset was born. Every day, I am becoming fonder of her and my son because they are beautiful. Your slave said that you wanted to talk to me and I wanted to talk to you as well. What is on your mind?"

"Yes, brother, I have been thinking that it's time for me to build my tomb. Every night, I have these nightmares that the god of the underworld is coming closer to me. I would like to build my tomb since they take so many years to be built, and I don't want Anubis to take me without my last resting place being finished," I said.

He quietly observed me. "Hat, I'm supposed to die before you, but if I can put your mind at ease, let me summon Sen-Mut to start the drawings for your mortuary temple."

Yes! He took the bait, I thought.

"When are you going to summon him here?" I asked.

"I will let you know," he said.

"Brother, if something happens to me and I go to the underworld, will you protect Neferu-Re as if she were your daughter?"

"Hat, nothing is going to happen to you. And of course, I will protect her and raise her as if she were mine. I have been doing so. I have been visiting with her. She is a princess, and it doesn't matter that Sen-Mut is her father," he said.

"Do you promise?" I asked.

"Yes, I promise. Hat, you and I have not talked for a very long time. Have breakfast with me now, for I must speak to you."

I was gratified that he agreed to let Sen-Mut build my tomb. “I will, brother,” I said.

“How long have you been having these nightmares?”

“Since you threatened my child’s life while she was still in the womb. They’ve become worse since the birth of Neferu-Re.”

“Why haven’t you told me anything about it?” He asks.

“Brother, you have stopped talking to me since your coronation. It only got worse when I had Neferu-Re,” I said.

“Very well, I will summon Sen-Mut after you leave, and I will let you know.”

“Good. Can you let Sen-Mut see his daughter?”

“No, I will not!” he said.

“Why not? He is her father.”

“I don’t’ want him to have any contact with her, or the gossip will start all over again. And don’t ask me again!”

I was clenching my teeth. How unjust and unfair he was. But I tried to remain outwardly calm and said, “Let me know when you summon him.”

He looked at me and nodded his head twice. I got up from the breakfast table.

“Aren’t you going to have breakfast with me? I must speak to you. I got messages from our garrison close to the delta that the Hyksos are starting to regroup and are preparing for war. They still cannot accept that our ancestors liberated us from their hands or that we took our land back.”

I listened patiently. “Do you believe that we are going to war?” I asked.

"I am awaiting messages from our spies to let us know how large their armies are. Then we will know."

"Brother, are you ready for battle? After I leave your quarters, I will talk with General D'Jehuty, and our uncle, and all the other generals of our army to discuss the possibility of war. Have you spoken to all of them yet?"

"Yes, an hour ago," he said.

"Then I must prepare for battle, too."

"Hat, I believe you should stay," he said.

"Thut, they are my men, and I have trained with them all of my life. Do you remember when I put the trap in the Sobek's jaws, and they said that they would fight beside me at any time? Well, I must fight beside them now. Let's meet in the audience hall within an hour and start planning for war."

"We will, sister. You've made my blood run again like that night on the Nile when we were looking for the Sobeks."

"Do you still want to build your mortuary temple?"

"Now more than ever. Summon Sen-Mut as soon as possible so that he can start drawing the plans for my temple. I am not hungry any more. Brother, just let me know when he is coming."

I left very quickly to talk to my guards.

"Guard, let me know right away if you see Master Sen-Mut on the palace grounds. I must see him before I go to war."

"Yes, Your Majesty."

Better yet, I thought, I would go to the audience hall and wait to see him cross the gardens.

I waited and waited.

"Lotus of Egypt! What you are doing here?" Hapu's voice startled me and caught me off guard.

It left me stuttering, "I am, am, am… Have you heard that there is a possibility of war?"

"There's going to be war. It's a certainty now," he said. "I was with Thut not too long ago when a soldier arrived with General D'Jehuty and gave him the bad news that there was going to be war."

I felt a rush of adrenaline and thought of Sen-Mut.

"Thut asked me to summon all the generals to the audience hall, and I just did. We will be meeting here soon. I thought that that was why you were here."

"Yes, I knew of the possibility of war, but it is now confirmed," I said and nodded twice. An uneasy feeling took over me.

"Hatshepsut, Thut, told me that you are planning to go to war too. Are you?" he asked, frowning, furrowing his brows, and looking straight at me with his gray eyes. "I advise you not to go to war. War is terrible." He grabbed me by my shoulders and said, "And I can tell you this, if something bad happens to you, I will honestly die. There will be no purpose in my life if I have to live without you."

I sensed the desperation of the plea in the tone of his voice. He was begging me from the bottom of his heart, I could feel it. I lowered my face in sadness. He was still holding me by my shoulders. He shook me hard, and I was startled.

"Hatshepsut! I am talking to you!" he shouted.

I reacted by looking at him.

"Do you understand what I am telling you? War is terrible!" he said.

Agitated, I said, "But my army knows me, and I must fight beside them. They hardly know Thut. How can they trust him when he never took the test with the Sobek? They know that I am brave as they are, and they are willing to fight beside me with all their strength at any time. I must fight beside them!"

"Flower of Egypt, going to war would be crazy. But if you must go, then I will go to war with you."

"No! I will not allow it. You are not to come with me. I will not have peace of mind during battle if you are there. I will be worrying for your life, and for Thut's, Neferu-Re's, Hatshepset's, and Sen-Mut's life. I need for you to stay here to protect my daughters if we lose the war. I know that you and Sen-Mut will protect them with your own lives if Thut and I were to die. You should take them far south to the Sudan, as far as you can, and find a place where they cannot be found. You, Sen-Mut, and my slaves. I will have all of my gold ready for you and Sen-Mut to take with you," I said.

"Flower of Egypt, if Sen-Mut was the one asking you to stay, you would not think twice would you. You would stay, right?"

"You're wrong. I would go to war anyway," I said.

He was startled and pulled back. Frowning he said, "You would still go to war?"

"Yes, I must fight for my land, as my father the Great Thutmoses I did and as my great-great-grandfathers did. Right now, I can hear the Great Tetisheri saying, 'Hatshepsut, this is your kingdom. Go and fight for it!' I remember that sometimes when my father was walking through the hallway of the palace, he would suddenly just start shouting, 'Hail Tetisheri! Hail Tetisheri!' I remember the guards shouting and hailing her name, too, as they raised their spears in the air. Do you think that I can let them come to my land and kill everyone and enslave Sen-Mut, you, and my girls? Well, no. I must fight with my men until the end, and we will win."

He became silent and lowered his head. He was about to say something when we were interrupted by steps heralding the arrival of the generals of the armed forces.

Thutmoses was behind me as the two of us walked to the throne. I sat beside him. Khety and Hapuseneb stood at his right. Thutmoses was wearing his white kilt and leather sandals. He stood up and said, "I've received urgent messages from several garrisons in the north with assurances that the Hyksos are preparing for war against us."

I was quietly listening as he made the announcement which was followed by a clamor from the generals, priests, and commanders. I wondered if Sen-Mut had heard of the threat of war.

My uncle Thutmoses shouted, "Then we must prepare for war immediately! Bring the large tables and the maps of the north."

The slaves brought several large tables and set them in the middle of the audience hall. From our library, Thutmoses had brought the war plans that were used by the Great Amose I, our great-great-grandfather who had defeated the Hyksos and regained our lands. Thut also had several other maps of the northern region and opened them on top of the table. We all gathered together and began to make strategic plans around these very large maps that I had never seen before. We spent long hours around the maps, and food was brought to us. We continued until the late hours of the night.

By this time, the entire land was on alert, and there was a general uproar occurring. My brother ordered the generals to be ready to transport the army, charioteers, archers, and cavalry across the Nile to Memphis to reach Heliopolis from there. The rocky hills made it impossible for the cavalry and charioteers to cross the terrain to the north.

I called for a litter to be brought and ordered the carriers to take me to the Temple of Amun-Ra. When we got there, I opened the two sets of large doors. I looked at the small golden statue of Amun-Ra placed in the shrine. The dim oil lamp was shining on his face.

I knelt and crawled to him. Raising my arms to him, I prayed, "Father, I, your daughter Hatshepsut, the one you fashioned in my father's body and brought into being, I come into thy presence to beg for your help. There are enemies of the land getting ready to attack this kingdom of yours, the one you gave my ancestors to rule in peace. I come to you to ask thee to give us your mighty strength and help us to destroy our enemies. I ask thee to give me the valor to face my enemies in battle and to succeed. Please protect my brother, Thutmoses II, in battle, protect my daughters, Sen-Mut, Hapuseneb, my people, and protect me."

I lay there for long hours talking to my beloved god, then an immense peace took over my heart and my entire body, as before. He had spoken. We would win this war! I kissed the floor in front of him and poured sweet perfume oil and gold dust over his head. I raised the myrrh incense with both hands above my head and offered the sweet smell to my god, the only god of all the gods, my father. I walked around the altar, making the offering with the incense and chanting prayers.

"Father, I hold you in my heart, and you know that I love you very much. You can see what is inside of my heart, and there is no evil within me." I finished my offerings, very gratified that he had spoken. I retired, walking backward and without turning my back to Amun-Ra.

When I opened the doors to exit the temple, Ra was rising in the east. I walked out of the temple. Apparently, many hours had passed, but I had not noticed the time elapsing.

I stood there looking far away at the rising sun, satisfied. He had spoken. We would win this war. I got into the litter and was taken to the palace.

"Tuyii, bathe me."

After I was finished with my bath, I was dressed in a white sheath and lay on my bed to sleep. The fan bearers were around my bed fanning me with peacock feathers as I slept.

****

The following day, early in the morning before Ra rose, I went to the training battlefield and practiced with my men and my charioteers, hitting the target every single time with my arrows. The army was on alert. We were recruiting more men for battle and preparing for war.

The army, Thutmoses, and I were ready for battle. We would march north and cross the Nile early the next morning. We needed to reach the delta before they did for battle. We would march into an area where we could encircle them as the Great Amose did.

That night, I dressed in my white kilt, and we had our last dinner in the banquet hall with my brother, the generals, and the commanders. There was silence all over the land, but we were prepared and ready for battle. There was not one sign of fear on any of our faces.

A caravan was in place and ready to leave for the Sudan if we died in battle. I needed to speak to Sen-Mut tonight before the sun rose. He had not stopped coming to see me since his return. He always stood there in the silence of the night. But this night it would be different: I would rush into his arms.

I saw him holding a torch in his hand. I changed from my kilt into a white sheath, and I didn't care if Thut found out. I would deal with him later.

I ran down the stairs as fast as I could and rushed to Sen-Mut. He was standing there waiting for me, as though he knew that I could not leave for war without telling him how much I loved him. He saw me and dropped the torch to the ground as we ran into each other's arms. Our lips met in a passionate kiss, and he laid me on the ground and in desperation removed my sheath. He possessed my body like a madman, and we made love under the stars and gave into each other with the most profound love. I did not want him to let go of me, nor did I want to let go of him. We kissed a thousand times with passion.

He kissed my hands, and holding me close to his heart, he said, "I don't want you to go to war."

I was startled and became silent.

Looking at me, he said, "Please don't go. You are going to get hurt and very badly." He said.

I was startled again and pulled back. "Will I die?" I asked him.

After a beat, he said, "No, but you are going to get hurt very badly, and I will be afraid for you. I will be here powerless and unable to protect you, only able to make offerings and recite prayers to Amun-Ra and to all the gods, day and night for your safety. Maatke-Re, I am begging you not to go. Think about our daughter Neferu-Re and little Hatshepset."

"Sen-Mut, will you and I be together after this war?"

He didn't answer at first, but then he said, "Yes."

"That's all that matters to me. It means that we will win this war. I know that we will because Amun-Ra told me so, and I will come back to you."

"Still, I don't want you to go. Please!" He said.

He was begging me, and he was completely serious about it. I did not know what to say.

"Beloved of mine, I must go. I am the strength of my army. How can I tell my army that I will not fight beside them?"

He continued holding me in his arms against his chest. Squeezing me against him, he said, "I love you, Maatke-Re, and I will always love you. I only ask of you that you keep very far away from the front line. Promise me that."

I kissed his lips and caressed his face with my left hand.

"I will, my love, I promise. I have a caravan ready for you to leave to the Sudan with my two door guards. All my gold is for you to raise our daughter and my little Hatshepset as your daughter. Promise me that you will raise them both as yours. I told Hapuseneb that he must go with you if I die. Take Tuyii, T'Queta, and your parents with you. Please," I said.

"Hapuseneb has already told me about your plans, but he will not stay. He will go to war with you. He begged me to convince you to stay."

I was speechless, and I frowned. "He is coming to war with me?"

We could hear the rooster crow far away. He pulled me close to him, as the first rays of Ra lay on his naked body. He possessed me again with passion, and we did not let go of each other. I got lost in the most wonderful pleasure only he could give me, and when we were finished, we lay in the green grass.

When it was time for me to go, he silently lifted me from the grass beside the waters of the Nile. The first rays of Ra were reflecting on the waters of Hopi. I stood there as Ra shined on him, and he dressed me with the sheath. The rays of Ra shone on my face. He kissed me deeply and with such love, and I hugged him close to my heart very tightly.

"I love you Sen-Mut of Luny, and I will always love you. Keep my heart with you, and I promise that I will come back to you." I said.

We held hands, and looking in to each other's eyes, he said, "I will always love you, Maatke-Re!"

Our eyes were full of tears, and we did not want to let go of our hands. I took several steps back, and he pulled me fast and pressed his lips so hard on mine as his arms wrapped my body against his chest. I started to cry, and tears were rolling down his face also. I walked off, away from him fast as I could. If I didn't, I would not be able to leave. I turned around and noted that he was still standing there naked. I yelled one last time, "I love you, Sen-Mut!" and ran away from him quickly. I ran to the palace, leaving my heart with him.

I ran up the stairs to be bathed and dressed before walking to the Temple of Amun-Ra for the last blessing of Khety for war. When I entered my chambers, I saw that Thutmoses was sitting on a chair waiting for me. I was startled. I wasn't expecting to see him there.

"Hat, I know you were with Sen-Mut, but I don't care. I came to ask you to remain here. Our daughters need you here."

"Brother, they also need you here. Let's do this together and make the enemy suffer so much that they will never threaten our kingdom again, and our daughters will be safe and free in their home forever."

He didn't answer but simply lowered his face.

"Brother, why don't you stay? And I will go."

"Hat, how can I stay and let you go when I am Pharaoh? I will look like a coward in front of the armies and my people. Hat, I can't change your mind?"

"No, brother. I am determined to go. I must fight beside my men, and we will win this war."

"Yes, we will. Let's go to war then!" he shouted. Then standing up he left my quarters.

"Tuyii, bathe me!" I yelled.

She was crying while she was bathing me, as were my two other slaves. I didn't try to comfort them. I didn't talk at all because I was thinking about Sen-Mut's words and his begging for me to stay. But I could not desert my warriors, which is what I would be doing if I stayed. They didn't know Thut as well as they knew me. They knew that I would die beside them in battle. I stood up in the tub.

"We will win this war," I shouted. "I will finish with every Hyksos as though they were rats, even if they crawl into their holes. I will pull them out and crush their heads. Be sure of that. And I will come back alive to my daughters and for my kingdom!"

I had this complete certainty inside of me. I was dressed in my white kilt, the pectoral, and the Horus crown.

I walked to my balcony to see the beauty of my land and the Nile for the last time. Surprisingly, Sen-Mut was still sitting at the edge of the Nile. I stood there looking at him until he noticed me. He got up from the grass and faced me. I opened my arms and blew him a kiss. Then, I turned around and left the balcony with tears in my eyes. Oh god, how much I loved him.

I went to my daughters' quarters and was surprised to see Isis there crying. She dropped to the floor as I walked in.

"Rise, Isis. I have already made provisions for the possibility that we might die in this war. Sen-Mut and T'Queta will head south to the Sudan. I know perhaps that Pharaoh has also made provisions for your well-being and for that of your child, but my daughters will go with Sen-Mut where they cannot be found. If you want to go with them, you may go with your child. You and your child will be well taken care of by Sen-Mut."

I looked at my girls. I knelt and held my babies in my arms. By that point, Neferu-Re was walking well. I hugged her and kissed her many times, then kissed her again with the love of her father. Next, I picked up Hatshepset. I held her in my arms and kissed her many times. Tears were rolling down my face, as I set her down. I kissed Neferu-Re again, and then I left. However, before I reached the doors, I turned around one last time and said, "We will win this war because Amun-Ra has told me so." I turned around and exited the room. I descended the stairs, and at the bottom, Thutmoses was waiting for me with all the generals of the armed forces.

We rode our golden chariot through the streets of Thebes with legions and legions of my immense armies. The people were all gathered together in the streets cheering us on, but the look on some of their faces was somber. As we rode past them, I could hear some of them sobbing. Some of them where cheering us on, throwing white flowers as we passed them. If they only knew what my father Amun-Ra had said, they would know that we would win the war.

Part of the army was in front of us and the rest behind. However, the larger part of the army was on the west side of the Nile waiting for us to march north to Memphis.

We arrived at the Temple of Amun-Ra for the blessings of the First Prophet of Amun. Khety blessed us, and when he was done, he approached us and said, "I have been consulting the stars, and they foretell that both of you will win this war." Looking at me, he said, "Your Majesty, keep away from the front line." Looking at Thutmoses, he said, "Keep her away from the front line."

Thutmoses looked at me with doubt on his face, but I knew what Khety was talking about. Sen-Mut had also warned me that I would be wounded.

"I will come back," I said.

Our armed forces were waiting across Hopi to start the long journey to war. We needed to reach the northern part of Lower Egypt close to the delta if we wanted to succeed at keeping the Hyksos far away from Thebes. We boarded the very large barge with the horses and chariots.

We crossed the Nile in silence. Thutmoses spoke first. "Khety is right. You must stay away from the front line, and you should have stayed."

“Brother, what would my warriors think if they didn’t see me? It would be a great let down to them. They said once that they would fight beside me. Well then, I must be willing to fight beside them! Have you made provisions for the child that you believe is your son, if we don’t come back?” I asked him.

“Yes, I have. If things go wrong, then my daughters and my son leave for the south to the Sudan with my soldiers.”

“What? There is no way that my daughters are going to be raised by Isis, I can tell you that.” Then I thought it best to be quiet. My door guards knew what to do when the moment comes, if it comes. They were to take my daughters south with Sen-Mut.

“Hatshepsut, we are going to war, and you are going to argue about who is taking our daughters to a safe place? Well, my army is going to take them to a safe place, and if you are afraid for Sen-Mut, I have made concessions that he will go with them, too. I know you love him, but you did not give me any choice before. I had to keep him away from you. I am trying to avoid another pregnancy and to avoid more gossip, as happened with Neferu-Re, that she was his daughter. We know that she is his daughter, and I will betroth her to my son, even though I know that she is not my daughter. But she is yours.”

I snapped at him. “You know very well who spread those rumors, but you did not cut off her tongue, did you? And innocent slaves that we have known since we were children died because of her spiting venom!”

He didn’t answer at first. Looking straight ahead, he finally said, “But I punished her severely.”

“But not enough!” I said.

“Hat, stop! I don’t want to hear it anymore.”

I walked away from him, fuming, to the front of the barge. She would not raise my daughters. Sen-Mut would.

We crossed the Nile. It was a long way to the delta, though I wasn't sure how long. We would first stop in Memphis and meet with the Vizier of Lower Egypt, who was on alert and waiting for us. There, more soldiers would join us. Then we would cross the Nile again to the eastern part of Lower Egypt and wait for our spies to send the message that the Hyksos had passed Heliopolis going south. My braves, the battleground soldiers, would wait to the south as we attacked the Hyksos from the north behind them, then they would attack from the south.

We arrived at the Valley of the Dead, and a platform was already in place. As all the generals and commanders of the different armed forces climbed the platform, their soldiers hailed them.

Then it was Thutmoses's turn to climb the platform with his horse. Again, all the armed forces hailed him. Then I started to climb with my horse, wearing the Crown of Horus on my head. The uproar was loud. They raised their spears, bows, and other weapons. I knew that this was the reason that I had to fight beside my men. They considered me to be one of them since the day I put the trap in the Sobek's mouth, and they loved me as I loved them.

We marched north to Memphis. It took us about fifteen to twenty days to reach Memphis where we were greeted the by the Vizier of Lower Egypt. He had formed a large army that would join us in battle. We remained in Memphis several days. Our generals and their generals gathered together and studied our war plans, and all agreed. We would wait for our spy's message that the Hyksos had crossed through Heliopolis, then we would cross the Nile and attack from the north and south. At that point, we were about two to three days from Heliopolis, and we waited for word to cross the Nile.

Once the message had arrived that the Hyksos had crossed Heliopolis, leaving many casualties in their wake, we got into the barges and crossed the Nile. We caught up with them. When we did, I could see them from afar, though they didn't know that we were behind them.

"Brother, you must stay back here. Don't come closer to the battleground," I said.

"And you must stay here, Hatshepsut. Remember what Khety said, that you must keep away from the front lines."

"Yes, brother." I knew what he meant, but I was completely restless. I was ready for battle, as were the army, archers, charioteers, cavalry, and the red and black army. They were the bravest of the brave. The palace soldiers would remain with us for our protection, since they could kill up to ten or more men at one time.

I looked at my brother. He looked magnificent in his golden armor with the Khepresh[44] on his head. His gold armor was shining as brightly as Ra, and next to him his charioteer was holding the Nemes, the other war crown which was made of cloth with blue and gold stripes for times when the heat of Ra made the golden Khepresh too hot to wear. He was wearing kohl around his eyes and looking straight ahead.

I was in my chariot with my charioteer, wearing golden half-armor that covered my shoulders. It was designed for easy movements and was made especially for me. It looked like fish scales and allowed air to circulate around my body. It looked like my brother's, which was worn by our father. My armor was tied on my back with leather straps, and I wore the Horus golden crown on my head.

Thut gave the order to charge. The archers were the first to engage in battle, shooting their arrows in the air. Then the army attacked. The Hyksos realized that they were being attacked from behind, and their army turned around to clash with our braves.

---

[44] The war crown made of gold and inlaid in blue with gold stars.

I was restless standing there just watching the battle from afar. I wanted to fight beside my men. I got down from the chariot and ran to mount my horse with my bow and arrows hanging on my back.

Suddenly, I was pulled down with force from my horse by Hapuseneb. “Let me go!” I yelled and kicked him in the shin.

“You’re crazy! You kicked me hard. Didn’t you hear what Khety told you? I know what you were planning. Thut told me to keep my eyes on you and to keep you away from the battlefront. When I saw you pacing back and forth like a tiger in a cage, I was glad that I had kept my eyes on you. Otherwise, you’d be gone by now. I have already told you that if something happens to you, I will die!” He was shouting at me.

Thut came running up behind him.

“Take her to the tent and don’t let her leave!” he shouted. “Hat, do you want to die? Is that what you want? That’s what Khety was trying to warn us about. Guards! Don’t let her leave the tent.”

I walked with the guards to an empty tent. When I turned around, Hapuseneb and Thut were standing there looking at me as I was kept away from the battle.

It was a long day on the battlefield, and many of our men were falling as Ra was going down. I was still being detained by Thut in the tent. Hapuseneb walked into the tent carrying food.

“I am bringing you this food with a message from Thut. He will let you come out if you promise that you will watch the battle from his side and the safe ground. Otherwise, you will remain in here. You need to know that we have suffered many deaths and have had many casualties. Tomorrow our army will attack from the south. Now, Ra is fading away, and the battle will stop for tonight.”

I saw many slaves walk into the tent with water to bathe me.

“No, I am going to my tent,” I said.

I walked off with Hapuseneb trailing behind me, and the slaves followed us. We stopped to pay our respect to Ra, as they did for their gods.

I didn't sleep at all, nor did my brother. We were wound up, waiting for the first rays of Ra to show and the battle to continue. After dawn, we heard the first sounds of battle. We could hear the uproar of our army attacking from the south. I ran out of the tent. I was already dressed in my kilt, leather sandals, and armor.

Thut came out of his tent, shouting, "Attack! Attack!"

I grabbed my bow and arrows, ran to my charioteer, and took off with him. When the army saw me, there was a roar that was incredibly loud. They needed my support to fight.

We charged after the Hyksos with the archers who began shooting their arrows again, followed by the infantry and cavalry. I rode my chariot beside my charioteers, and I started to shoot my arrows as we were at full speed.

Suddenly my charioteer held back the horse's reigns. I asked him, "What are you doing?"

"Your Majesty, I must hold back. I cannot endanger your life. Pharaoh will put me to death if something happens to you. I will not allow anything to happen to you."

"You are my soldier, and I demand for you to take me closer to the front!"

He was reluctant, but we started to move. We came closer to the front line when Ra was high, and it was very hot. I had exhausted all my arrows. When arrows started to fall close to us, the charioteer backed up the horse and turned around, heading back to the camp at full speed. Suddenly, I felt a terrible pain. An arrow had pierced my back.

"Your Majesty, you've been hit! Hold on, Your Majesty."

The pain was terrible, and I saw Sen-Mut in my mind, far away, falling on his left knee in pain. This vision was the gift of foreseeing. I could also see T'Queta rushing to him, trying to help him stand.

"Master Sen-Mut, what's wrong?" she asked.

"I feel a terrible, sharp pain on my back. I believe she got hit!"

"Who got hit?" she asked.

"Hatshepsut! Help me to the temple. I must make offerings for her well-being hurry!"

I saw the pain and anguish on his face.

The pain came back to me worse with the movement of the chariot. My charioteer raised the red banner, letting them know that I was hit. I held on to the front of the chariot and collapsed to my knees in pain. The arrow had penetrated the golden armor. I could see the camp far, far away, and with every stone in the desert that the wheel hit, I screamed in pain and remembered Sen-Mut's warning.

My charioteer slowed down, then stopped and got down from the chariot. "Your Majesty, the arrow went through your left side and close to the middle of your back[45]. I must drive us quickly to reach the camp which is still far away. We don't know if the arrow is poisoned. If it is, you will face a slow and painful death, Your Majesty. As I drive, I will pray to the gods for your life. Can you hold on tight? I will try to avoid the rocks in my path."

I nodded my head slowly. The injury hurt terribly from my neck all the way down to my left hip.

The charioteer got up from where he was kneeling and got in to the chariot. "Majesty, hold on tight now!"

---

[45] Picture where I believe is the arrow wound on my back, on page 790.

The horses started to move faster, and with every movement, forward or backward, I screamed harder because the pain was unbearable. But my beloved had said that I would survive this, so then I must take the pain. It was a long way to the camp. When we finally I arrived, they were waiting for me. I could hear Hapuseneb screaming my name, and I could hear my brother screaming, "Sister!" as they ran to me.

Puyem-Re and several other physicians came up to me. "Everyone moves out of the way," Puyem-Re shouted.

"I will try to carry her as gently as I can," Hapuseneb said to him.

"No! Don't move her," Puyem-Re said. "We don't know how deep the arrow is in her back or if it is poisoned. Bring a stool. We must seat her on it. We must cut the arrow first, as close to the armor as we can. I will try to hold the arrow from under the armor. I will try to avoid moving it as it is being cut so that I can remove the armor and then remove the arrow."

I was on the floor of the chariot, kneeling and leaning my body and head against the front of it.

"Your Majesty, I know that it's very painful for you, but you must make the effort to slide yourself toward me so that we can help you to your feet. I need you to sit on this stool, and we must cut the arrow to remove your armor. Please forgive me, Your Majesty, for the pain I am about to cause you," he said.

I slid back slowly, coming close to fainting. I had lost a lot of blood, and the pain was getting worse. I was also burning with fever.

I looked at Thutmoses and said, "I want you to kill them all."

"I will, Sister, I will!" he shouted.

I reached the edge of the chariot, and Hapuseneb knelt beside me with tears in his eyes. He knew that the arrow could be poisoned, and it terrified him. He held me by my waist gently, while I screamed in pain. He sat me down on the stool that was set beside the chariot.

"I am brave. I am brave like my soldiers. I can take it," I kept telling myself to give me strength to bear this horrible pain. Then I started to pray. "Amun, Father, I am your child, Hatshepsut, the one you formed in my father's body and brought into being. Help me to be brave, and please don't let this arrow be poisoned."

I closed my eyes as they were unfastening the leather belts behind my back to remove the right side of my armor. Hapuseneb was still kneeling at my right and holding my right hand firmly.

"Your Majesty," Puyem-Re said and approached me. Kneeling on one knee, he said, "I want you to know that I am very sorry for the pain I will be causing you. You must be as brave as your brave warriors on the front line who are fighting for you."

I nodded my head and closed my eyes in terrible pain.

"Now, Your Majesty, you must bite down hard on this piece of leather." He put it in my mouth.

"Now, bite hard, Your Majesty."

I did what he asked as he pressed the palm of his hand under my armor. I was screaming and at the same time biting the large piece of leather in my mouth. The pain was so unbearable that I let go of the piece leather and screamed in pain.

"Your Majesty, I am holding the arrow with my two fingers under the armor. Now someone is going to cut the wood of the arrow as close as they can to the armor, and I will try to hold it straight the best that I can for it not to move. Believe me, it will not be as painful as it's going to be later."

I felt the terrible pain as the arrow was being cut, and I screamed in agony.

Hapuseneb gently removed the right side of the armor from my back.

"Lotus of Egypt, forgive me," he said.

Thutmoses rushed beside me and held my hand firmly. I could see the anguish on his face. I screamed in pain as Puyem-Re gently removed the left side of the armor from my back. As he did so, I screamed in pain again. Finally, he succeeded, and the remaining piece of arrow was showing where it had pierced my back. I was burning with fever. I wanted it to be over, but the arrow must come out. He must remove it from my back.

"Let's take her to the table inside," Puyem-Re said.

Hapuseneb gently carried me in his arms as if I were a child. I lay my head on his right shoulder. He set me down gently on a long table and helped me lay on my stomach gently. Thut was kneeling in front of me.

"Sister, I am so sorry you are going through this pain right now. This is what we wanted to avoid."

As he was talking, I could see Sen-Mut in my mind far away, kneeling in front of Amun-Ra with his arms up in the air, praying for me.

"Your Majesty."

I looked at Puyem-Re, as he knelt in front of me. He said, "Now comes the hardest part. I need to cut deep inside the wound to remove the arrow, and we don't have anything to numb the pain, only this beverage to make you sleepy. But I don't think it is going to be enough to calm down the pain I am going to cause you. I will try to do it as fast as I can. I am sorry, Your Majesty, but we must hold your arms and legs, so you don't move."

"Put me on the ground," I said.

Hapuseneb gently sat me up on the table as they placed the linen on the ground. He held me by my waist and right arm and whispered in my ear, "Be brave, as I know that you are. I love you." He held me tightly as he helped me to kneel. I was laid on my stomach. By that point, I was completely worn out and wanted it to be over with.

"Thut, sit on the back of her thighs and hold her legs as hard as you can. She cannot move, and you, Hapuseneb, hold her upper arms hard," Puyem-Re told them. I saw many slaves walking in with jars of hot water and lots of white linens. Priests were chanting prayers around me.

"Now, Your Majesty, bite hard on this piece of leather again."

I bit down, and I felt the sharp instrument on my back. As he was cutting into my skin, I began screaming, and I screamed repeatedly, crying in pain, trying to get away as he continued to cut deeper and deeper.

"I got it, Your Majesty! And now I will pull it out."

He pulled the arrow out, and I screamed again.

My throat was raw from screaming, but mercifully, I was losing consciousness. Tears were rolling down Hapuseneb's face, as I was crying in pain. I hadn't lost consciousness yet, unfortunately, and had to suffer the ordeal more.

"Your Majesty, I must look deep inside this wound to be sure that there are no pieces of the tip of the arrow remaining inside of you, and I must cut some tissue from the inside where the arrow was lodged to be sure that no poison remains in there," Puyem-Re said.

I felt as he opened the wound and cut the tissue from within. I was trying to get away because of the pain, but Thut and Hapuseneb held me hard. It was so bad that I wet my loin cloth. I was crying terribly, looking at Hapuseneb, and tears were rolling down his face as he held my arms firmly. Finally, I blacked out.

Suddenly, my Ka was above my body, and I heard Hapuseneb scream, "Is she dead?" From above I saw everything they were doing.

Thut let go of my legs and knelt beside me with tears rolling down his face. Puyem-Re stopped and rush to my side. He brought one of his fingers close to my nose.

"No, she just fainted. I must finish before she comes back to. This time unconscious can help her with the pain I am causing her. Help me put her back on the table, so I may work closer to the wound."

I saw Thutmoses lifting me up from the floor in his arms, and he laid me gently on my stomach. From above, I saw that Puyem-Re continued working on me, and I saw Thut and Hapuseneb walk to the other side of the table toward my right foot and stand there. I could hear the anguish in their voices.

"Thut do you think she is going to die?" Hapu asked.

"I really don't know if she is, but I so hope not. I hope she holds on. She is my little sister, and I don't want her to die. She should have listened to me and not gone to the battlefield, or at least not so close to the front lines. Khety warned us before we left Thebes, and now she is between life and death. We must pray that she doesn't die."

I saw them leave the tent.

Suddenly, my Ka was flying fast. Then I was in Thebes inside the Temple of Amun-Ra. I saw my beloved kneeling down, offering prayers for me, and he had tears running down his face. I could hear part of his prayer: "Beloved God, the god of all god, I pray that you spare the life of my beloved, your daughter Hatshepsut. Take my life in exchange for hers because I could not live without her."

Suddenly, I was waking up in pain and to the reality of my terrible wound. I was on my stomach on a couch inside of Thutmoses's tent, and beside me were Thut and Hapuseneb. They were happy to see me open my eyes.

"The pain is terrible." I said.

"We know, Hat," Thut said.

Puyem-Re brought a golden cup to me. "Your Majesty, you must drink this. It will help you with the pain and will allow you to sleep. It will also bring down the fever. Please, you must not move. We don't want the wound to re-open. I believe I removed all the pieces of stone from the arrow out of your back. I will spend the night beside you, and if you are in pain, I will give you more of this beverage to keep you asleep."

"Hapuseneb and I will remain in here, too," Thut said.

"I must use the bathroom," I said.

Thut clapped his hands, and two slaves brought a chair with a basin underneath. After, Thut helped me to sit down on the couch slowly. Then Thut, Hapuseneb, and Puyem-Re left the tent.

I was undressed by the slaves. My loin cloth was soaked in urine, and I did my necessities with the help of the slaves. I could hardly stand up, and they carefully helped me to stand. "Bathe me," I said. I was washed standing there, shaking badly, and then they wrapped me in clean linen sheets. A new goose-down mattress and clean linen sheets were placed on the couch. They called Thut, and he walked in with Hapu and Puyem-Re. Thut held my right arm and walked me to the couch. I sat at the edge of the couch and looked at Thutmoses.

"What about the war and my warriors?" I asked.

"We are winning the war, as our grandfather and our father did. You must rest now," he said.

"How long have I been asleep?"

"Almost two days."

I was shocked.

"What? Two days?"

"Yes, Your Majesty," Puyem-Re said. "And you must continue to rest on your stomach. We don't want the wound to re-open. And please drink more of this healing beverage. It is helping with the fever and the pain."

"I am hungry," I said.

Thut clapped his hands, and hot lentil soup was brought to me. Hapu fed it to me. After I finished, Puyem-Re handed the beverage to Hapu, and I drank it all. Hapuseneb came closer and helped me lie on my right side, and the pain was terrible. Then I was on my abdomen again.

■■

A few days later, we won the war. I was unable to sit down on my own. I was lying on my right side when Thutmoses walked in the tent with the biggest smile on his face. Trailing behind him was Hapuseneb, who also seemed happy.

"Hatshepsut, we won the war! It's great news," Thut said.

"Brother, help me up. Hurry, and walk me out of this tent. I want to participate in the celebration with everyone, especially with my warriors," I said.

He helped me sit up, then helped me to my feet. We slowly exited the tent. The uproar of my warriors was very loud. A chair was brought for me.

"No, no chair," I said. "I will stand as a brave warrior for my men."

General D'Jehuty walked up to me and knelt on one knee at my feet. He said, "Your Majesty, we are very happy that you are getting better. Your warriors knew when you were wounded on the battlefield, and they fought harder for you."[46]

---

[46] The emotion that I felt on that day was the best. My warriors were happy to see me walking out of the tent, for they knew that I was wounded badly. I was one of them.

"You may rise, D'Jehuty. I want you to gather all our brave warriors that have fallen and gone on to the long journey. And please be sure that they are dead before burning their bodies."

I continued, "Now, for the Hyksos. I want you to cut off their heads and hands and bring them to my brother, your Pharaoh. Later, hang their heads on poles all over their land. I want the ones that survived this battle brought to my brother. They should meet their final fate by my warriors. I want them to know never to come back and threaten my kingdom. Tell my warriors that I am proud of all of them, and I am sorry for their losses. I know that some of them had close family in the battle. Brother, take me inside the tent. I don't feel right. I think I am going to faint."

He helped me inside. I could hear the cheering of my soldiers as I walked away.

I had been having nausea for several days. I didn't know if I was pregnant or if it was the beverage I was drinking for the pain that was causing me the nausea.

****

The next morning, when it was still early, and the rays of Ra were just beginning to show, I thanked Amun that I had survived and was getting better.

I remembered my beloved. And now the nausea was making me feel terrible. I thought I must be pregnant. If I was, I resolved to step down as Queen and leave Thebes and move very far away with Sen-Mut. I didn't want to go through the same pain we went through with Neferu-Re because I knew that this time Thut would kill my child. I was lying there with my hand on my belly, hoping that everything would get better.

"Your Majesty."

It was Puyem-Re. He saw me caressing my belly.

"Pharaoh has sent word that if you would like to be present when they bring the prisoners to be killed, you can be there," he said.

"Yes, I will be there. Call the slaves in to help me into my kilt."

He left, and a few minutes later my slaves came rushing in. I was bathed and dressed in my kilt and leather sandals. Hapuseneb came in to the tent and brought the Horus crown. He set it on my head as I was still sitting on the couch. Then he knelt on one knee, looking up at me and smiling.

"I thought we had lost you, and it was very hard on me and Thut. However, I am very happy that you are getting better, as is Thut. Let me help you stand."

He held my right arm firmly, and we walked out of the tent. A huge, open circle had been formed, and two chairs were set up for us at the edge of the circle, close to the tent.

"Sister, I am happy to see you, and I can see that you are feeling much better. Are you up to seeing what we are about to see?" Thut asked.

"Yes, Brother."

A soldier brought the captured king of the Hyksos, and D'Jehuty shouted, "Kneel to your king!"

The king refused, and the reaction of D'Jehuty was immediate. He kicked him hard behind his knees, and the king fell onto his knees in front of my brother Then he kicked him again with force, and he fell forward at my brother's feet. My brother stood up and pressed his golden sandal on top of his face.

"Did you think that you could reckon with me? That you could come to my land and threaten me? My ancestors defeated you. My father defeated you, and I, Thutmoses II, Pharaoh of these two lands, defeats you. I condemn you to death, and your head will be taken to your land and will be hung high on a pole so that the people of your land will know never to dare to come into my kingdom again or to wage war against me."

As the king knelt, D'Jehuty raised a khopes[47] and cut off his head. I saw the head fall at my brother's feet, the king's body convulsing as the blood was squirting out of his neck and into the sand. I was ready to vomit. I held my jaw closed very tightly, but I couldn't stop it. What I saw was sickening to me. Silently, I got up from my chair and vomited.

Then I remembered that when I was nine years old, I told my father, the Great Maat, that I wanted to see the severed heads and hands of the rival Hyksos, but my mother said that I was too young to see something so terrible.

I continued throwing up until there seemed to be nothing left, but then I turned around and saw growing piles of heads and hands at my brother's feet, and I started to vomit again. I noticed Puyem-Re was looking at me. I wondered again if I was pregnant or if I was throwing up because the sickening sight.

I turned around and saw Puyem-Re whispering something in my brother's ear. My brother turned to me and gave me a serious look. Then he spoke to Hapu, and Hapu came up to me.

"Flower of Egypt, are you ok?"

"I am only sick to my stomach from seeing so much blood."

"Would you like me to walk you back to the tent?"

"Yes, please," I said.

He held my right hand and helped me to the tent. As I was ready to sit on the couch, Puyem-Re walked in with a golden cup in his hands.

---

[47] A curved, bladed war weapon.

“Your Majesty, I brought you this beverage. It will help with the vomiting.”

I looked at him straight in the eye.

“I saw you vomiting not too long ago, and this will help you. It’s possible that the other herbs are making you sick. Drink it all.”

And I did. It was very bitter, and I did not like the taste.

I could hear our warriors celebrating for long hours until late into night with Thut, Hapuseneb, my uncle Thutmoses, the generals, and the commanders.

I left the tent, noticing that the night was clear. I walked to the area where they had a fire burning and were drinking in celebration. I could see Puyem-Re far away, walking among the piles of bodies and burning incense around them. The bodies would be set on fire the following morning after we left. There was no time to bury the dead. The flies were already multiplying fast. We would be moving out early in the morning, heading back to Heliopolis.

I felt more at ease since the war was over, and my kingdom was safe from the war, and my daughters and Sen-Mut were safe now. I felt grief for my soldiers who had fallen. I would compensate their families when I arrived at Thebes. But I was most worried about whether I was pregnant with my beloved’s child.

I fell asleep and woke up to terrible cramps, and the linens on my couch were soaked in blood. I realized that I was not pregnant. I clapped my hands and was bathed. I dressed in a white sheath. I wouldn’t ride my horse today. I still did not feel well from the wound. A litter was brought, and Hapuseneb helped me onto it. It would take several days to get to Heliopolis where the barge was waiting to cross the Nile, and from there travel to Memphis. And then it would be a long journey back to Thebes, to my daughters, to my beloved, and to my bed.

We sailed the Nile south to Memphis.

****

It took several days to arrive in Memphis by ship, and the people welcomed us in the streets. It was a great celebration as we paraded the streets of Memphis. My father's Vizier welcomed us with big banquets, and the nights were beautiful. Thut and my uncle Thutmoses and the generals spoke of the war and how brave I was. I was the only woman among so many men. I was accustomed to this, as I had been having the experience since I was a little girl, but as a full-grown woman and in war, this was my first time. I could see that I was one of them. I was tired and slowly walked the long white terrace of the palace in silence as the celebration continued until late in the night. The night was full of stars and everything looked peaceful and quite lovely. I held my stole across my arms and strolled around the palace, looking at the beauty of my palace, built by my father when he was Vizier of Lower Egypt.

We were leaving the next day back to Thebes, and I was happy going home. I looked at the stars and thought of my girls, grateful that they were safe and grateful that there wouldn't be any more war. Then I thought of my beloved one and wondered if he was thinking of me at that moment, and I whispered, "Good night, my love."

I walked to my quarters, where the slaves were waiting for me. After bathing, I lay in bed thinking about my loved ones until I fell asleep. We left Memphis very early in the morning, and we sailed the Nile south. The oarsmen rowed quickly to Thebes.

It was almost a week before I saw the tip of the Temple of Karnak from afar. I was happy because soon I would have my babies in my arms. I hoped that I could also see Sen-Mut. I was grateful that the war was over. My back was much better, but it still bothered me.

The welcome home was enormous. The streets were overflowing with people as we docked at the entrance to the Temple of Karnak. It was a day of great celebration.

Thutmoses, Hapuseneb, Puyem-Re, my uncle, the generals, the commanders, and I walked into the Temple of Amun-Ra, where Khety waited for us with a great smile on his face, and the rest of the priests greeted us.

As I was getting closer to the large statue of Amun-Ra, I saw Sen-Mut, and our eyes met. I could see the happiness in his face, and he brought his right fist to his chest. I brought mine to my chest in return, letting him know that he was always in my heart.

As I neared him, I lowered my face and whispered, "I love you."

He replied, "Me too."

I looked directly into his eyes. I wanted to run to his arms and kiss him, but I had to hold back. I was immensely happy to see him. Then I saw my babies and wanted to run to them as well, but I had to pay my respects to the God of all gods, my father Amun-Ra first.

Khety blessed us for returning alive and for winning the war. Once it was done, I ran to my babies and hugged them and kissed them with tears in my eyes.

Thutmoses was holding Menkhep-Re his son in his arms, and Hapuseneb was with Tepi. Everyone seemed very happy. When I looked for Sen-Mut, I caught him looking at me. I walked with Neferu-Re to him so that she could see her father. My heart was pounding hard as I stood in front of him. He knelt on one knee and started to talk to Neferu-Re, though she looked at him strangely. I picked her up in my arms, and though there was silence between us, our eyes, full of tears, met with love. Words were unnecessary.

"Are you feeling better?" he asked. "One day while you were gone, I felt a sharp pain in my back, and I knew then that you had gotten hurt, but now you are here, and I am happy to see that you are well."

"I went through terrible pain as you warned me I would. When the arrow hit me, I saw you in my mind falling on one knee in pain. T'Queta was with you, and you told her that I was hit and asked her to help you to the temple. Later, I saw you at the temple raising your arms to Amun-Ra, praying for him to take your life and not mine."

He was startled.

"Remember the test of foresight I took when I was five summers? I told you about it on our way to Philae." He nodded twice. "That is one of the abilities I acquired. To see and hear, even if I am far away."

"Everything that you saw, it happened to me," he said.

"Hatshepsut." It was the voice of Hapuseneb. I turned around to see that he was walking in my direction. I looked at Sen-Mut. We knew that this was the end of our conversation.

"Maatke-Re, there will come a time when we will be together. I love you." He said quickly. I was about to tell him that I loved him too, but there was not time. Hapuseneb was beside us.

"Hello, Sen-Mut. Hatshepsut, Thut is calling you," he said as he took Neferu-Re from my arms.

"Tell him I will be there," I said, but he did not move away. I looked at Sen-Mut, and I could see that he knew that I loved him, too. "May all the gods bless you, Sen-Mut."

I turned around with a broken heart. I was angry and snapped at Hapu. "Why did you take Neferu-Re from my arms?"

"Because Thut told me to bring Neferu-Re and you, too."

Though I was angry at Thutmoses as well, he and I walked out of the temple together. It was time to parade through the streets of Thebes with my armed forces on a chariot. The street was overflowing with my people. As we passed them, they threw flowers at us. Celebrations were taking place everywhere. I was happy to come back alive and that I could speak with Sen-Mut. I wondered when we would be together.

I was tired, but I continued celebrating in the banquet hall. Finally, I stood up, and everyone dropped to the floor.

"Rise, and good night," I said.

I left and strolled through the garden, then went to my room. When I got there, I walked directly to the balcony, and my beloved was there waiting beside the Nile. I sat there for a while until he left. I was bathed and got into my bed. It was so good to be back home and to hold my girls in my arms and kiss them. I was very happy that I got to speak to my beloved.

CHAPTER 32

PRINCESS NEFERU-RE'S DEATH

I was playing with Neferu-Re and Hatshepset in my rose garden, thinking about how fast they were growing. Five summers ago, Neferu-Re was born, and soon Hatshepset would be four summers. Neferu-Re was looking more like her father, Sen Mut, especially in her eyes and the way she looked at me. It was like he was looking at me.

Thutmoses had summoned Sen-Mut six months ago to draw the plans for my mortuary temple when I was not present. It had been three summers since I had seen or spoken to him, and I missed him dearly. Since our return from the war, Thutmoses had Ineni keep Sen-Mut busy and away from me until I went back to Thutmoses and pressed for my mortuary temple so that I could see him again.

I heard the steps of a soldier entering my rose garden and approaching me. Kneeling on one knee, he said, "Your Majesty, Pharaoh said to meet him at his quarters at the second hour after the high noon."

"Tell him that I will be there, and you may go now."

He rose from the limestone floor and left. I wondered what Thutmoses wanted to talk to me about. I was hoping it was about my temple. I continued enjoying my daughters, as I did every morning in my garden. I clapped my hands, and the wet nurses picked them up so that they could be bathed and fed.

I sat there looking at the slow waters of Hopi, and I walked to the edge. I stood there looking at the current of the Nile as far as it went. I had traveled this long river many times, and I loved it every time. I did not think that I could ever be far away from it, nor from my beloved Thebes.

I walked back to my quarters to be bathed and dressed and then went to meet my brother in his quarters.

"What's wrong? You don't look well. Are you sick?" I said.

"I have not been feeling well for a while, ever since we came back from the war. Do you remember how many flies were everywhere in the camp because of all the dead bodies? I think it has something to do with all the bites I got from the flies."

"What do the physicians say about it?"

"That they have never seen anyone with my sickness before, and they hope it can be cleared up soon."

"It's been three summers since we went to war. Have you been feeling ill all this time? I don't understand why you never told me about this. The last few times we've seen each other, I've noticed red specks on your body which I had never seen before."

"I thought it would clear up all this time, but it has not," he said.

"Did you call me to your quarters to tell me about your sickness?"

"No, I called you to tell you that Sen-Mut has finished the plans for your mortuary temple. I was told that it was ready, and we can go to see it if you like."

My heart jumped with joy. Finally, I would be able to see him up close.

"When are we going to see the plans?" I asked.

"Right now, if you want. Let's walk to Ineni's office. He is waiting for us there," he said.

"Okay, let's go."

We crossed the gardens toward Ineni's office. My heart was beating fast at the thought of seeing Sen-Mut again. The guards opened the double doors of Ineni's office, and he was standing there. He looked at me, but then he threw himself at Thutmoses's feet.

"Rise, Ptah of Egypt. From now on you don't have to lower your head to the floor," Thutmoses told him.

"Yes, Your Majesty," he said. He rose from the floor and walked to the long table, where the plans were open. Thut walked to his right, and I to his left. I slid my hand quickly into his hand and squeezed it very hard to let him know that I still loved him, and he squeezed my hand hard in return. Then he continued and explained the temple to us. To my surprise it was magnificent, beautiful, and lovely. He had reflected all off his love for me in it.

"Hat, what do you think of the drawings for your mortuary temple?" Thutmoses asked.

"I think it's magnificent." I wanted to cry seeing such an expression of love in his plans but held back my tears. I took a deep breath and said "Brother, what do you think?"

"I think so, too. Sen-Mut, when are you going to begin with the construction?"

"As soon you chose the area," he replied.

Thut looked at me and asked, "Where do you think it should be built?"

"I believe Sen-Mut can pick the area to build it. He knows the area well," I said looking at Sen-Mut.

"Sen-Mut, choose the area, and let us know when we should be there for the groundbreaking and the blessings," Thut said.

Thut walked away ahead of me, and I looked at Sen-Mut. My eyes were full of tears. I was very moved by how much he had expressed his love for me in his plans.

"I love you," I whispered, and he nodded his head.

I lowered my head and walked out, following Thut.

"Were you happy to see him?" he asked.

I was shocked by his words. "Very much. You know that I still love him." I replied.

"I am sorry that this love is impossible for you. If it was possible, I would have let you be with him a long time ago. But you are Queen and cannot be seen with him. The gossip would spread all over the land, and I would be the laughingstock of my people. Then I would have no choice but to put him to death, and I don't want to do that. Just keep away from him," he said.

He walked off in the direction of his quarters, and I walked to the Nile. I sat there as tears poured down my face. I found myself talking to him in my mind. "When, my beloved, is going to be the day you spoke of? When we will be together?" Then I spoke out loud, "Sen-Mut, your drawings for my temple are magnificent. I could see the love for me reflected there."[48]

Suddenly, the wind blew softly and caressed my face as if Sen-Mut were speaking back to me. I got up from the green grass and took my leather sandals off. I went back to the palace and straight to Neferu-Re's room and hugged her, crying.

"Mommy, what's wrong? Why are you crying?" she said as she wiped my tears away with her hands.

"I am crying out of joy because I can hug you and kiss you and because you are mine."

I smiled at her, and she smiled back. I held her tightly against my body and kissed her many times. I wiped my tears and walked with her to my quarters. I lay in my bed, and she jumped up and down on my bed. Ra was fading away, and I held her hand and showed her how we must wash our hands and faces before prayers. We knelt together facing Ra. I said the prayers out loud, and she repeated after me. It was cute to hear her say the prayers with me.

"Mommy, I am hungry."

"Do you want to eat here with me, or should we go to the banquet hall?"

"To the canquet hall," she said.

I started to laugh; she still couldn't say it clearly.

"Okay, we will go, but first we must bathe. We'll bathe together."

---

[48] Writing this part of our life brought tears to my eyes. It was so hard for us to be together, as it is now.

I played with her in the water, and we laughed a lot. I wore a sheath, while she was dressed in a kilt, and we walked to the banquet hall holding hands.

When we arrived, everyone dropped to the floor, including Tepi and Hapuseneb.

"Rise," I said.

Everyone did. Neferu-Re ran to Thutmoses, and he held her in his lap. I sat beside him.

"What a surprise. You never come to the banquet hall for dinner," he said.

"She wanted to come here to eat, so I did."

Hapuseneb sat down beside me and whispered in my ear, "Lotus of Egypt, you look beautiful tonight, and you smell delicious."

I was looking at Tepi when I said to him, "Doesn't it bother you to leave her alone with her jealousy eating her?"

"No, because I am with the woman I love," he said and laughed.

"You are terrible, Hapuseneb."

We laughed together, and I wondered why men did things they didn't want to do. I could understand his love for me, but once he was deeply in love with T'Queta. He could have married her, as I'd advised him. And now he was married to someone that he didn't love, and he was paying the price for choosing wrong. It would have been easy to fall in love with him and love him if I were not in love with Sen-Mut. We talked and laughed, the three of us, Thut, Hapu, and I.

I sent Neferu-Re with her wet nurse to her room. She loved Thut, and he loved her very much. I was pleased with that.

“Hat, I am betrothing Neferu-Re to my son Thutmoses when she is of an age to be married.”

I nodded twice and smiled. Of course, I didn’t believe the child was his son. I leaned to my right and asked, “Hapu, when I don’t come here to eat, does he bring Isis?”

“He never has. He is always with her in his quarters, so I don’t think he will ever bring a concubine here. You are the Queen, and he would never disrespect you by bringing her here,” he said.

“I see.”

“I can see that you have completely recuperated from the arrow wound.”

“Yes, the wound is healed, but I still feel like there is something lodged in my back. And it does bother me. I haven’t been able to lie on my back since then.”

“Have you told Puyem-Re that?” Hapuseneb asked.

“Yes, I have, but he said that he remembers well that when I was unconscious, he looked deep inside of my wound and made sure to remove every piece of the arrow and very small pieces of stone. But I can no longer sleep on my back because it feels like I have something poking me there and it hurts. I don’t believe I can go through the same pain as that day, even though I would like for him to look inside of me again. Knowing that there is nothing to numb the pain, I don’t think I can go through with it. I took that terrible pain like a brave warrior.” I smiled.

Hapuseneb nodded his head and said, “Yes, you took it like a brave warrior that day. I was terrified that you would die. I suffered so much seeing you go through that horrible pain. And when you fainted, I panicked. We thought you had died. I saw my world collapse. And when Puyem-Re put his finger in front of your nose and told us that you had only fainted, what a relief Thut and I felt. I am very happy that we are here talking to each other right now and that you are well, except for the pain in your back. I gather you must live with it for the rest of your life. Now, let me tell you that I am astonished by how much Thutmose loves Neferu-Re. He's told me so himself. That's an excellent outcome."

"Yes, after he wanted to end her life. You know, I never did thank you for changing his mind," I said.

"I would not have been able to live with my conscience if he had killed your child, and I hadn't tried to save her. I don't think in the end, he would had done it either. Can you see how much he loves her now, and she loves him back?" he said, then smiled. "I believe you should come more often to have dinner with us."

"Why? Don't you see how Tepi looks at me? Her jealousy is eating her alive."

He laughed.

"You are cruel," I told him.

Then I remembered Sen-Mut. He must be beside the Nile. I stood up right away, and Hapuseneb looked surprised.

"Are you leaving this soon?"

"Yes, I usually kiss and hug my daughters before they fall asleep."

Everyone was still prostrated on the floor.

"Rise, and good night, everyone," I said.

I looked at Tepi and Thut, then went quickly to my girls' quarters. They were asleep, so I simply kissed them and left. I returned to my own quarters and went straight to the balcony.

There he was, as always, waiting for me. I sat on my chair for a while as he sat beside the Nile. Then he left.

I needed to see him. I was dying to talk to him, and I knew where he was. I decided that the next day after breakfast, I would ride my horse close to his house. I hoped I could see him. If I didn't, I would go to the temple and see if he was there.

"Tuyii undress me," I told her, and she did. I wore a sleeping sheath and fell asleep. I woke up early in the morning, and I lay there waiting for Ra to show his first rays. Then I got up and washed my hands and face and knelt. I said my morning prayers and thanked Amun-Ra for blessing me and my land. I was full of happiness as I walked to my breakfast table that morning, just thinking that I might see him. On my golden plate were two eggs, bread, goat cheese, my favored hot drink, and fruits.

As I was eating, the golden doors were opened to admit Neferu-Re, who ran to me. I smiled at her, picked her up, and sat her in my lap.

"I love you so much, sweetheart. Every day, you look more and more like your father." I hugged her close to my heart and wondered when it would be time for the three of us to be together.

"Mommy, can we go and play in Hopi's waters today?"

"Yes, my love, yes. When I come back."

"Where are you going?"

I looked at her and smiled. "I am going to the temple, and it's a long way from here, so you must remain here and play with Hatshepset until I come back, OK?"

She nodded he head.

"Now, let's eat," I said.

We ate together, and I held her on my lap. Afterwards, I got dressed in my kilt, pectoral, and the Horus crown. I held Neferu-Re's hand as we walked to her room, and there was Hatshepset. She saw me and came running to greet me. I picked her up in my arms, kissed her, and hugged her. I thought she looked more and more like me all the time, and I smiled.

I told her, “We are going to play in the waters of Hopi today. Would you like that?” She nodded her head twice. I looked at her wet nurse “Has she eaten yet?”

“No, Your Majesty. She just woke up. I will be feeding her soon.”

I smiled at her wet nurse.

“Well, my princess, I will be back later then, and we are all going to spend the day playing in the waters of Hopi!” I clapped my hands several times and smiled. They started to clap, happy. I kissed Neferu-Re and Hatshepset. “I’ll be back soon. I love you both.”

I left and walked the long stone path to Karnak in a hurry. I decided to walk because I might see him walking, too. When I got to the temple, I knelt in front of the small golden statue of Amun-Ra.

“Father, how much longer must I wait for Sen-Mut and our love? This waiting seems eternal.” Suddenly, I saw the small golden statue smile at me, and my heart became full of happiness. “Soon? Do you mean soon?”

I smiled, but then suddenly a terrible pain went through my heart, and I was frozen. My body started to tremble.

“Father, what does this pain in my heart mean? Tell me, please, tell me.”

I panicked and started to cry. The sadness was overwhelming. I stood up and closed my eyes. Something was not right. I could not see anything in my mind, but what was it? I could not breathe, and I blacked out.

When I opened my eyes, I realized I was on the floor. I didn’t know how long I had been out. I got up and hurried back to the palace. My heart was agitated, and I could see a chariot coming in my direction. It was

Thutmoses and Hapuseneb. The chariot stopped beside me. Thutmoses's was flushed, and tears rolled down his face, as well as Hapuseneb's. My heart stopped, and Thut got down from the chariot with Hapuseneb. I started to tremble.

"What is it?" I said.

Thutmoses couldn't get his words out, so I looked at Hapuseneb, who lowered his face. Thutmoses held my hands.

"Neferu-Re was found dead in her bed," he said to me very gently as though I might break.

And I was breaking. Into a million pieces.

"No, no, no, not my daughter, no!" I scream.

I could not stop screaming. He held me tightly against his chest. Hapuseneb was crying. He embraced me, and the three of us cried together as we had when Neferu-Bity died. My beautiful daughter was dead.

I let go of them, got into the chariot, and rode quickly to the palace.

I heard Thutmoses yell, "I sent word to Sen-Mut!"

I turned my head and screamed at him, "What good will it do now?" I was crying terribly.

On my way to the palace, I screamed, "My baby, my baby!" When I got there, I ran up the stairs to her quarters, which smelled heavily of incense. I saw her small body lying in her bed. I screamed again and picked up her body in my arms and cried and cried. I carried her lifeless body and sat in a chair, rocking her body.

Khety, Puyem-Re, and other priests and priestesses were in the room, and Khety was crying.

"What happened to her?" I asked him.

He came up to me and said, “We don’t know, Your Majesty. She wasn’t bitten by a snake, nor was she poisoned.”

At that moment, Thutmoses and Hapuseneb entered the room, and both came up to me and knelt. They were crying. I could see on Thutmoses’s face that he really loved her as if she were his own daughter.

The door opened again, and it was Sen-Mut. I cried harder. Thutmoses and Hapuseneb got up from the floor. Thutmoses clapped his hands, and everyone left the room, leaving us alone. Sen-Mut came and hugged me, and we cried together, holding the body of our daughter. We were alone for a long time.

We spoke few words in our terrible grief. He sat beside me and held us in his arms.

After a while, the doors were opened, and Tuyii came in crying, bringing the dark blue attire of mourning. Sen-Mut held Neferu-Re’s lifeless body in his arms as I was changed into the mourning attire. I sat down again, and he laid her body on my lap, then he knelt facing me, and gently kissed me on the lips. I started to cry again, as did he.

Looking at me tenderly, with tears rolling down his face he said, “There will come a time when we will suffer no more, when we will be happy together. I promise.” He kissed my forehead again.[49]

Thutmoses, Hapuseneb, Khety, Puyem-Re, and the rest of the priests and priestesses re-entered the room. Thutmoses went to Sen-Mut and spoke with him. I could hear him telling Sen-Mut that he was sorry for Neferu-Re’s death and that he loved her as his own. Sen-Mut was silent and did not say anything. I kept holding her body against my chest.

---

[49] The death of my daughter Neferu-Re is a pain that never goes away. I still feel the pain in my heart as I write this chapter. However, this time it’s hard for me because there is no one who can hold me and cry with me. How can anyone understand my pain when I now live in a different period?

I was still holding her when Khety and Puyem-Re came to me and one of them said, "Your Majesty, we are so sorry for your loss, but it's time to take the princess's body to the house of the embalmer."

I looked at Sen-Mut. He was standing close to the wall. He had a strange look on his face, as if he wanted to tell me something.

Thutmoses came and took her lifeless body in his arms, and we walked together to the house of the embalmer. Khety, as the High Priest, walked in front of us burning incense, and behind us trailed Sen-Mut and Hapuseneb. They were followed by her wet nurse, priests and priestesses, and all my slaves.

I was completely broken, and I felt both of our pain: Sen-Mut's and mine. I was sad for him because, even though he was her father, he was unable to carry her body to the house of the embalmer. Thinking about this made me cry harder.

We entered that terrible place, and we said prayers for the dead as our daughter lay lifeless on top of a table covered with white linen. I could not believe that our daughter was dead.

My grief was terrible. I started to believe that someone had killed her because she was Sen-Mut's daughter. I started to question whether perhaps Thutmoses had done it, but he couldn't have because he loved her as his daughter. I noticed the grief on Thutmoses's face. I also noticed that he did not look well. Then I started to think that perhaps it was Isis.[50]

---

[50] Some archeologists and historians believe that my daughter Neferu-Re died when she was twelve or fifteen years old, but, she died at the age of five years old. As I was writing this chapter, I did some research on her death, and I could not believe what I was reading. How could I be so wrong when I remember very clearly holding my daughter's lifeless body in my arms? I spent four days and nights reading every piece of information I could find on the subject. And one night, I found it.

DIGITAL.LIBRARY.UPENN.EDU. "Queen Hatasu, and Her Expedition to the Land of Punt." This historical and important information was taken from inscriptions sculptured on several pylons of the Great Temple of Karnak. The hieroglyph text was copied and translated by the late Vicomte E. de Rouge in 1872. In his translations, I found the following: "Hatasu appears to have been the mother of only two children, both daughters, Hatasu-meri and Neferu-Ra. The latter died in infancy." I was right all along!

CHAPTER 33

THUTMOSES II'S DEATH

It had been six sad months since our precious daughter Neferu-Re died, and my heart had died with her. I missed my little one so much.

One day while I was sitting under a sycamore tree and looking at the slow flow of Hopi, I found myself lost in thought, wondering how much longer I would be without my beloved Sen-Mut and wondering if he had fallen in love with T'Queta. I am sure that I would not be able to cope with that, but I hoped she had made his heart glad.

It had been three summers since we were in each other's arms. That was when I went to war, and I hadn't felt any real happiness since then. I had made my brother Pharaoh, and the death of my beautiful Neferu-Re made it worse. She was my most precious treasure, and my only consolation and connection holding Sen-Mut close to me.

"My Queen."

A guard startled me, and called my attention, then asked permission to come closer. I nodded my head, and he came closer and knelt.

"Speak," I said softly.

“A slave approached me furtively and said that one day, several years ago, she sent thee a message with T’Queta. It was on a day that T’Queta was walking beside the Nile if you can remember the message. She must speak with thee urgently and in private.”

“Tell her to come to my quarters at the late hours, after all the slaves are asleep. Tell her that I remember her, and I will see her tonight.”

He bowed his head, turned around, and left in a hurry. I looked far away south, and Ra was fading away in the west. I got up and walked to the palace, saddened by everything and wondering what was the urgency of this slave that she must speak to me.

After the chanting and the incensing of the golden doors, there was a knock on my door.

“Enter,” I shouted.

It was Hapuseneb. He didn’t look happy, but then again, none of us did. My brother Aakheperen-Re had been very sick for a few months now and had no relief from his illness. His body was full of boils that itched and made it feel as though there were insects crawling inside his body. He hurt, and a terrible odor came from his body. I wondered if the gods were punishing him. Did he have something to do with my beloved Neferu-Re’s death? He swore to me that he did not.

“Hapu, you look very tired,” I said.

“Yes, I am. I came to tell you that Thutmoses is not well, and he is not getting any better. I went to see him this afternoon, and he is worried that this time Anubis, god of the underworld, will come for him. I tried to take his mind off it by talking to him about various topics, like when we were children. I managed to get him to laugh, especially when I talked about that time when you two went down the Nile looking for a Sobek in the middle of the night. He said that he doesn’t sleep at all and that you don’t come to see him anymore, which makes him really depressed. He even asked if you were waiting for his death. I told him no, that you always ask me about him, which is the truth. He swore that he had nothing to do with little Neferu's death, and he told me to tell you that he promised that he would never hurt her, because he loves her, and he keeps his word. He also said that he kept you away from Sen-Mut to avoid another pregnancy and the rumors that would result regarding the child's paternity. Also, he wanted to protect your integrity as Queen of Egypt."

I looked at Hapuseneb. I believed everything he said. I knew him very well and knew when he was telling the truth, but I could also tell that he was keeping something from me. I could feel it.

"What is it Hapu? I know you very well, and I can tell that you are keeping something from me."

His face was startled, and he smiled to hide it. "You do know me well, lotus of Egypt."

"Yes, I do, so there's really no point in trying to hide anything. Tell me."

"I am going to get to the point. Are you planning to get your lover back? Will Sen-Mut warm your bed again if Thutmoses goes to the underworld?"

Finally, I knew what he was getting at. Apparently, the jealousy had started again.

"You must keep away from him for a while because all eyes are going to be on you. You know that I am telling you all of this for your own good, as a friend and for the good of the country."

I laughed at his words. "Don't you mean that you want to keep him away from me and my bed since you cannot have me for your own?"

He laughed loudly.

"Part of that is the truth, but if you are planning to govern this country, you must make sure to avoid being the subject of gossip, especially if you want the support of all the high priests of the Temple of Amun-Ra, the viziers, mayors, and governors, and of the people of Thebes. You don't want to give Isis ammunition to destroy you. Right now, she must be praying to all the gods for her son to be crowned Pharaoh of Egypt. As we speak, she is speaking to the priests of the temple, trying to gather support for her son to be crowned Pharaoh. She has not approached me, for she knows where I stand and that is beside you. As far as I know, there is only one person who agreed with her, but the majority are upholding their promise to your father. Only you should rule Egypt once Pharaoh has gone to the underworld."

"Hapuseneb, I thank you, as always, for your love, support, and kindness to me. The child is only three summers. What she really wants is to rule Egypt through him. She must be out of her mind if she believes that she can get around me. She doesn't realize that I control all the armed forces and my kingdom, not Thutmoses, and she had better start realizing that I can step on her head and smash her like an insect. She doesn't know that my brother has never told me not to hurt her? And she probably believes that I have kept silent because my brother intervened for her. How wrong she is. She doesn't realize that I see her as an insignificant and weak woman, that I can kill her anytime I want to. I have not done it because she made my brother's heart glad and kept him busy. I know she tried to poison my brother against me, and that fact has angered me many times, but what can she do to me? Nothing. Her ambition to become Queen failed with my brother, and it will fail with me because Thutmoses has upheld his promise to our father that he would only give a title of a secondary wife to someone of royal blood, and she is not. That is her punishment from Amun-Ra. She has had these ambitions since my brother took her for a concubine, poor idiot.

"Well," I continued, "you have known all this for the last five summers, and you had better send her a silent message from me. Tell her that she should stop angering me, that there will be no one to protect her if Pharaoh dies, and that if I kill her, I will raise her child as my own, even though I have my doubts that he is my brother's son since he is too dark to be the son of my pale-skinned brother. Tell her that I have not forgotten the way she poisoned my brother's mind when I was carrying Neferu-Re in my womb, and that I believe that she had something to do with Neferu's death. If I prove that she did, I will not send someone to kill her but will do it myself, and I will kill her son, too, as payment for my daughter's death. Send her that message."

"I knew she had angered you considerably. What I didn't understand was why you had never done anything to stop her. I get it now. You saw her as I did, as insignificant woman. She can't rival your strength in any way. You are a warrior. I will send her the message right away through one of my spies who will pass it to her through a slave," Hapu said.

He held my hand and patted it several times. "You know, Flower of Egypt, that your sadness and grief are also mine, don't you? I feel your anguish for the loss of Neferu-Re inside of my heart."

I saw the sincerity in his eyes.

"I know that you do, Hapu. We have been together all our lives, since we were children, and you have been with me through all the ups and downs of my life. Have you seen or heard anything from Sen-Mut? Do you know how he is holding out in this grief of ours?" I asked him.

"No. Have you spoken to him lately?" he asked.

"No, I have not seen him since the burial of Neferu-Re," I said. I became quiet and introspective. I thought to myself, "I only see him at night from my balcony. I am completely dead inside without him and Neferu-Re."

Then a soft knock on the door brought me back to reality.

"Enter," I said.

It was Menina, the slave whom I was waiting for. She came closer with her eyes cast down. Hapuseneb recognized her: she was the one who spied for him in Pharaoh's quarters. She knelt and completely bowed her head down to the cool limestone floor.

"Rise and speak," I said.

"Your Majesty, I've come to inform thee of the way Pharaoh is being neglected by Isis. She does not come to see him or visit him at all. The linens are not being ordered to be changed by her, and there is a terrible smell in his quarters. Even the incense does not help with the smell," she said.

I became enraged with such anger that it overpowered me. I stood up fast and walked to my jewelry box, and I took a heavy gold bracelet and gave it to her for her services.

"You must go tomorrow to the goldsmith to remove my cartouche," I said.

"Yes, Your Majesty." She knelt again and bowed her head to the floor.

"I want you to follow me right now," I told her. I looked at Hapuseneb and could tell that he knew what I was thinking. We left and went to my brother's quarters. I could smell the foul stench as we were getting closer to his golden doors. The guards opened the doors, and the horrible stench that escaped his room made me gag. I almost vomited.

The room was dark, with only the dim light of an oil lamp beside him. He was sitting, leaning against the wall. I could not believe the terrible condition of my poor brother.

"Guards!" I started to scream. "I want twenty slaves, fresh linen sheets, a new mattress, and more oil lamps. I don't want darkness in my brother's quarters." I was so angry at everyone, yelling at the top of my lungs.

I approached him, and he perked up and seemed very pleased to see me. When he saw me, the expression on his face changed. Even though it was dark, I could see him. I came closer to him and sat beside his bed. I had to hold back tears, seeing him this ill and forced to live in these deplorable conditions being Pharaoh. My poor brother. It was as though he didn't have any family. The stench was terrible. I held his hand, not concerned about whether he was contagious.

"Brother, where is Isis? Why isn't she here with you?"

"She said she must be away from me because she doesn't want our child to catch what I have. She and I agreed that my son must stay away from here, and she must protect him."

Then I spoke softly. "Do not worry, Brother. I will protect him. And if she supposedly loves you so much, why isn't she here with you?" I shook my head and got up from his bed in anger. I opened the double doors and started to yell at the top of my lungs, "Guards, bring Isis here. Even if you must drag her out of her bed to do it. Right now! And I want more soldiers guarding Pharaoh's door and leave this door open at all times."

They brought all twenty slaves. I looked at Menina, and I told the rest of them, "From now on, you must follow her orders. I want the golden doors and the balcony doors open until this stench is gone form Pharaoh's quarters! Change the linen sheets right now and every hour. Remove this mattress and bring a new one right now. Guards, carry him to be bathed in warm water with soothing oils." I was fuming about the conditions in which I had found my brother.

"Hapuseneb, order several mattresses to be made in a hurry. I want him to sleep comfortably tonight and every single night from now on," I told him.

The guards lifted him up in their arms and carried him gently to be bathed. While that was going on, the old mattress was replaced with the new one. I could see the slaves redressing the bed with fresh white linen sheets.

"I want four linen sheets put on this bed every three hours when he is a wake. If he is asleep, you must let him sleep. I don't want any noise that could wake him up."

When the guards carried him back into the room, he looked fresh and clean. They lay him gently on his bed. He was alert and full of life again. I told them also to bring the most fragrant flower, the blue lotus, and put them all over his quarters.

"Send for lentil soup, the one that Pharaoh likes, and send for the musicians to play the harp for Pharaoh and make his heart happy tonight," I told Menina, now the master slave.

"Your Majesty."

It was the voice of Isis. Her voice infuriated me, especially her tone of hypocrisy. When I turned to her, her eyes were cast down. She came closer, about two feet away from me, and knelt at my feet.

With anger, I said, "You are not to leave this room anymore until Pharaoh is well. Is that understood?"

She nodded her head several times. "Yes, Your Majesty."

"You are not to eat or sleep away from these quarters. You will feed my brother his food with love and kindness. You will bathe my brother yourself and with love and kindness. You will eat with him in here from now on, and you will sleep beside him in this bed." I was so angry at her that I wanted to do away with her at that very moment.

"Guard, give me the whip!" I yelled.

The guard rushed and gave it to me. I struck her with rage on her face, arms, and all over her body. I unleashed all my fury on her, for her ill will against me, for conspiring to kill Neferu-Re at birth, for the possibility that she had something to do with Neferu's death, for speaking out against Sen-Mut to my brother, for leaving Pharaoh's side, and most of all, for leaving him in this terrible condition.

"I want you to remember that I am Egypt. And I can do away with you any time I want. I have not done it because you have a son," I said and pushed her to the floor with the sole of my sandal.

"Guard," I yelled. "This slave is not to leave this room or go anywhere. If she does, kill her, or you will be killed. Make sure to pass this order to the other guards: she is not to come out of these quarters until I change my orders."

The guard's face showed satisfaction.

My brother remained silent the whole time. He said nothing that might countermand anything I said or any of my orders. The room was clean and full of light from the oil lamps, and the stench was beginning to go away since the mattress and linens had been changed. But the smell remained on his body. I had no idea what sickness was plaguing him or what was causing the stench.

"Guards, in the morning, after Pharaoh has been bathed, carry him to the balcony to get the rays of Ra that he may be made stronger and get healthier."

"Yes, Your Majesty," one said and bowed his head.

"Hapuseneb, send word to Khety to prepare a very strong sleeping potion for Pharaoh, and to bring it to him that he may able to sleep well tonight."

"I will," he said. Then he left.

I sat beside my brother in his bed. It felt clean, but I didn't like the smell of his body. At least the stench was almost gone from the room. I should have paid more attention to him, but because of my grief, I neglected to visit him.

"Brother, how are you feeling after the bath and the change of linens?"

“A lot better, and thank you for coming,” he said. I noticed tears in his eyes as he smiled.

I held his hand and squeezed it. “You are going to get well soon. I know it,” I said, hoping to offer him some hope, but aware that I didn’t know for sure.

I could hear chanting and could smell the incense burning. I knew that it was Khety coming closer. He entered the room with several priests. This time he brought a different incense smell composed of soothing herbals. He started to chant the spell for the sick to chase away sickness. I joined in the chanting, for I knew it well. Pharaoh had finished eating the soup that Isis was feeding him. He looked calm and satisfied.

Then the chanting was over. I sat beside him again, and Khety gave me the potion. I brought the cup to his lips. He said that it had a very bitter taste, but eventually he drank it all. The harpist was playing, and the music soothed my brother to sleep. It was silent in the room.

I left his room quietly. Hapuseneb was waiting for me outside of the open golden doors, and Khety was behind me. We walked away in silence from his quarters and made our way out to the inner garden and sat down on the chairs. I looked to the east. Soon it would be dawn. It had been a long night, and we were tired.

Khety broke the silence that we had fallen into. “It won’t be long before Anubis, the god of the underworld, will be claiming his Ka, and too young to die at the age of twenty-eight summers,” he said.

The reminder made me feel sorrowful, and I was on the verge of crying. “How do you know that?” I asked him.

“His eyes are glossy. I’ve seen it many times when someone is near death. It won’t be too long,” he replied.

During the conversation, I noticed Hapu was very quiet.

“How long?” I asked.

"Maybe a few days or less," he replied.

"Then it's a good thing that I saw him tonight," I said.

I wondered why Thutmoses did not stop me when I was whipping Isis. Khety interrupted my thoughts.

"If he becomes alert in the next few days, it will be within those days that he will die. It's as if the gods give people the chance to make amends or ask for forgiveness, and the body knows of their departure," he said. "Your Majesty, I advise you that in the next few days you should be prepared for what is coming."

He got up, bowed his head, and left.

"Hapuseneb, you've been very quiet. What is on your mind?" I asked."

"I am saddened that my childhood friend will leave us soon. I'm surprised at the way you whipped Isis, too, though she deserves it, I know. I have never see you enraged like that before. I feel bad that I didn't tell you about the stench of his quarters and on his body and that you found out from someone else and not me. I did not tell you before because I wanted to spare you this grief."

"Hapu, don't worry about it. I do understand. I know that you mean well. I love you no matter what, and I know that your heart always wants to protect me from grief. Where is Sen-Mut?" I asked.

He became silent.

"He is in the Valley of the Dead working on your mortuary temple," he said.

"Send word to him that he must come at once, and summon General Nehesi, my uncle Thutmoses, General D'Jehuty, Thuty, Teshi, Hapu the scribe… I mean your father, and the rest of the generals. Ineni must be here, too. Send them the message that the Pharaoh is near death."

I felt in my heart that he did not wanted to hear that I was calling for Sen-Mut.

"Are you sure you want to call Sen-Mut?" he asked. I could see that he was agitated by the tone of his voice.

"Yes, I am," I replied looking at him in the dark. "Hapuseneb, did you notice how tired Khety was tonight? He can hardly walk. He also seems short of breath. I am glad he had a litter waiting for him to take him back to the temple. It's a long walk and he is very old. How old is he?"

I wanted to distract him and make him stop thinking about keeping Sen-Mut away from me.

"I believe that he is about the same age as Ineni," he replied.

"Then he is about two hundred summers?" I said.

Turning his face toward me quickly, he let out a loud laugh. I knew I had redirected his thinking.

By this point, the first rays of Ra were showing against the dark. Dawn, it was a beautiful sight. I was lost in thought. Then I became sad again, knowing that my brother would not see future dawns. Maybe his Ka will be in the middle of all the stars, and I will be able to see him shine in the night. I was lost in thought.

"Lotus of Egypt, I will send word to Sen-Mut right now that you want him here because he is the farthest away. In a few hours, I will summon the rest since they are much closer. Now, let's get some rest," he said.

"I want them all in my rose garden at four in the afternoon, but I will first meet with you and Sen-Mut in private at the second hour after high noon. We must speak first about how I am going to run my kingdom," I said.

"Lotus, remember that I love you, and remember my advice tonight. Now, let me walk you to your quarters."

"Thank you, Hapu, but not tonight. I would like to sit here and see the first rays of Ra rise, bringing me a new life," I said and sighed.

He left, and I stared at him for a long time, until he faded away in the still darkness. "How beautiful is his love for me, and he endures pain in his heart," I thought.

I saw the first rays of Ra far away and waited a while, looking at its beauty, and thinking that soon everything is going to change. I needed to rest. It was going to be a very long day. I wondered if my brother had slept well. I got to my quarters and walked to my tub, and my slave bathed me before I lay down. The thought of having Sen-Mut back in my life made me tremble with desire, accompanied by a great joy in my heart.

"We won't have to wait for too long my love, not anymore," I said, and then I fell asleep.

Ra was high when I woke up. It was almost noon. I walked to the tub, and the slaves bathed me with fragrant water and perfume made with special oils that Sen-Mut liked. After they were done, I went back to my bed.

"Your Majesty, which sheath will thou wear today?"

"I don't know yet. I will lie here for a while. I am tired today. Have you heard if Pharaoh slept well last night?"

"Your Majesty, I hear that he is well this morning. He had his breakfast and is talking to several of the priests of the temple including Master Hapuseneb, High Priest Khety, and Puyem-Re, and Ineni. Early this morning I spoke to Pharaoh's slave, Menina, and she said that he slept well all night last night and was bathed this morning by Isis, as you ordered her. And that he was sat on his balcony for Mighty Ra to bathe him with his rays. He seems full of life this morning. She said that the smell is almost gone, and that Isis slept beside him. And she fed him his breakfast this morning."

"Very well. It's good to heard that he is feeling much better this morning."

I remembered Khety's words last night. Those were the signs Khety spoke of. I was lost in thought when a knock interrupted me.

"Enter," I said.

It was Pharaoh's guard. He said, "Your Majesty, Pharaoh is requesting your presence in his quarters."

"Send word to him that I will be there within an hour."

"Yes, Your Majesty." He turned around and left.

I will dress for Sen-Mut today, "Bring me the white royal sheath, the colorful stone belt, and the colorful golden pectoral. Today, I will wear the Queen's Crown."

I wore makeup, red lipstick, and rouge. Then my slave dressed me, and she placed the long wig braided in gold thread on my head and the Queen's golden crown. I looked at myself in the golden mirror that Father had given me for my fifteen summers, and I looked beautiful for my beloved Sen-Mut.

I walked to Thutmoses's quarters. The door guards were silent and solemn and knelt as I approached them. I walked through the open golden doors and expected to find Hapuseneb and the other high priests with him, but they were all gone. Everything looked very clean inside of his quarters this morning. The daylight shined everywhere, making it easy to tell what had been done for him. I noticed the stench was gone from the room, but some remained on his body.

He was sitting up and leaning against the wall on his goose-down pillows.

"Good afternoon. You are looking much better today," I said and smiled at him.

He smiled back at me. I came closer to him and sat beside him on his bed. I felt the presence of someone behind me, and I turned around. It was Isis, standing there in silence. Her face looked bruised, showing signs of my whipping last night. The marks of the whip were all over her arms and face and body.

"You may go and see your child, but from a distance. We don't know if what Pharaoh has is contagious. Come back after I leave, and everything I told you before stands."

With her eyes cast down, she replied, "Yes, Your Majesty."

I turned my back to her and felt her leave.

"Brother, did you want to see me?"

In a very a low voice he said, "Yes, I know now that I am not going to get better. I feel that Anubis is coming for me, and I am going to the underworld soon, very soon. I spoke to Khety and Hapuseneb this morning regarding his opinion, and he confirmed what my Ka has been telling me all these months. I've thought very carefully for the last few months about what I am to ask you. Soon, you will be free of me. I know you will be looking for your beloved Sen-Mut. I want to make sure that before you do that, you follow our tradition and marry my son Menkhep-Re and transfer the royal blood for him to become Thutmoses III, as our customs dictate, and becomes Pharaoh of Egypt."

I was completely shocked at what I was hearing from his lips. I became angry and shook my head several times, and looking straight into his eyes, I said, "Absolutely not! I have already been miserable in this marriage for the last five years when you kept me away from the man that I have always loved. I am not going to be apart from Sen-Mut any longer."

I found myself shouting at him. I was boiling with anger inside of me. I was so close to happiness, and he could not and would not prevent that. I wouldn't allow him to make me do what he wanted me to do anymore. I am going to do what I always wanted to do, be with Sen-Mut.

"Don't forget that when I married you, I was sure that you were my brother. And remember I was a Queen, and I could have chosen whomever I wanted to marry, including Sen-Mut. However, when I was five summers, I promised you that I would make you Horus of Egypt, and I did just that, and continued the royal bloodlines. I kept my promise to Father, but not anymore, Brother. You can go to the underworld in peace."

"Isis is very afraid of you, and she believes that when I am gone, you are going to do away with her and my son, and there will be no one that can stop you from doing it because you believe that she had something to do with Neferu-Re's death."

"Absolutely yes! And I still believe it. But I am not a murderer, Brother. What makes you believe that he is your son? Tell me. Because I don't believe he is. I've told you that from the very beginning of her pregnancy she spent too much time in the temple and that she was seen many times talking to the Second Prophet of Amun. Look at the child well. He doesn't have your skin color. You and Isis are both fair-skinned," I said.

"Hatshepsut, I am warning you. I have already hired a silent assassin to kill Sen-Mut if you kill my son and Isis," he shouted at me.

I was in shock. I could not believe what I was hearing from his mouth. He was threatening the life of my beloved one?

"Now, you, hear this, Brother. If that silent assassin touches one hair on Sen-Mut's head, I will kill your son and that snake Isis. And in the most painful ways. I will make sure of that. I will use them as target practice or cut off their skin slowly or whatever might be the most painful death. Now, you are also warned!" I stormed out of his quarters, leaving him there in silence. I was so angry at him.

"Guard! Guard," I called from the top of my lungs. He was dying and still ungrateful to me, after all I had sacrificed because of my promise to Maat. And he still wanted me to continue without my beloved one? Well, it was not going to happen.

The guard came running to me. “Your Majesty,” he said breathlessly and knelt at my feet.

“I want fifty of my bravest armed soldiers who are ready to kill. Send them to wait for Master Sen-Mut, the architect, across the Nile. He is coming from the Valley of the Dead to Thebes. Bring him safely to me, to my rose garden, as soon he arrives. Whoever comes close to him, kill them right on the spot. Don’t let anyone come close to him. Guard him with your lives, or you will pay with your own lives.”

I was shaking all over with rage. No one was going to hurt him, no one. I rushed to my quarters, grabbed the Horus crown, then ran down the stairs. I walked hurriedly to my rose garden and set the crown on top of the table. He would be here soon. I waited anxiously for him. My body trembled just thinking that finally we will be together. As I waited, I got lost in memories.

So much had happened. It had been five summers without him, only sharing a few words in all that time. I had tried to find ways to see him. I went sailing the Nile many times, hoping to catch a glimpse of him swimming in the river. I knew that he loved the waters of Hopi, but I never saw him swimming. I walked to the Temple of Amun to try to get a glimpse of him many times. Sometimes I saw him, but he didn’t see me. We had suffered so much being kept apart by my Father and then Thutmoses.

I remembered that this was when I got the idea for my mortuary temple and got Thutmoses to agree and order it to be built. But he summoned Sen-Mut and spoke to him when I was not present. I was happy when Thutmoses sent for me and told me that the plans were completed, and we should go and see them. I was nervous as we walked to Sen-Mut’s office, which used to be Ineni’s office.

We walk into his office, and he was standing there, wearing his white kilt and leather sandals. We looked at each other. I wanted so much to run to him, but I could not. I wanted to smile at him, but I was afraid that I could put him in danger. He opened the drawings on a large table.

Thutmoses walked to his right, and I walked to his left. I moved quickly very close to him, I slid my right hand into his hand, and squeezed it very hard. He squeezed mine in return. I wanted him to know that I still loved him. The plans were magnificent. Thutmoses and I went to the ground-breaking ceremony and the blessing of the four corners of my mortuary temple. Sen-Mut had buried my scarabs with my cartouche and titles and scarabs with the names of all my loved ones, alive and dead.

I remembered that T'Queta was no longer allowed in the palace, so there were no more messages between Sen-Mut and me. Sometimes when we crossed looks, I could see the pain on his eyes.

But there would be no more pain for us. The wait is almost over, beloved one, the wait is almost over.

I could hear the soldiers approaching across the outer gardens, and my heart was pounding. Then the inner gardens. I was trembling, and then he was standing in front of me. Giving me the smile, I had waited such a long time for. Finally, I felt free and smiled back with the biggest smile that came from my heart. He stood there clenching his hands at the sides of his kilt, holding back his emotions, and stopping himself from running into my arms. I could hardly speak because I was holding back my tears.

I took a deep breath and said, "Guards, from now on you will guard Sen-Mut's life wherever he goes. Wait in the inner gardens until I call."

"Yes, Your Majesty," the guard replied and left.

Sen-Mut walked slowly to where I was standing. He was holding back his tears, as was I. My body was trembling with emotions. Slowly, he knelt at my feet and touched them.[51]

---

[51] I had waited for this moment for a long time. Reliving this moment right now has brought tears to my eyes as I remember how full of emotion I was on that day. (3/8/2016)

I closed my eyes as the tears poured down my face. I touched his head gently and with tender love. Sen-Mut closed his eyes, and the tears were rolling down his face, too. I took a deep breath.

"Rise, Ptah of Egypt," I said softly, and he did. We were so close that I could see the tears in his eyes and the smell of mint on his breath. I wanted so much to kiss his lips.

"Sen-Mut, Pharaoh is dying," I said.

Looking straight into my eyes, he said, "I know, Maatke-Re. It won't be long before we can finally be together."

Hearing his voice and his words brought tremendous joy to my heart.

"It may only be a few hours as Khety indicated in his message to me this morning, and the message from Hapuseneb I got last night, telling me that you wanted me here. I felt a great joy to hear that you wanted me here," he said.

I was about to say something when I saw Hapuseneb walking behind Sen-Mut. Sen-Mut wiped his tears, turned around and they greeted each other.

"Sen-Mut, I am pleased to see you again," he said.

They smiled at each other. I sat down and Sen-Mut sat at my right and Hapuseneb was across from both of us. I didn't see any expression on Hapuseneb face, and I knew that this moment was hard on him. Hapuseneb was about to say something when wailing and screaming started all over the palace. Pharaoh was dead. My eyes filled with tears, and I waited for it to be formally announced that my beloved brother had died. I stood up, and Sen-Mut and Hapuseneb followed. A guard came rushing to my garden and knelt at my feet.

"Your Majesty, Pharaoh is dead," he said.

"Rise, and you can go now," I said.

I fell silent feeling an enormous grief over me, as the tears rolled down my face. I love you, Brother. I lowered my head. Sen-Mut and Hapuseneb knelt at my feet.

"Rise, Ptah of Egypt and Priest of Amun."

Removing the Queen's Crown and the wig from my head, I set them on the table. I knelt on one knee, and Hapuseneb placed the Horus crown on my bald head. Finally, no one would ever keep us apart, I thought.

Sen-Mut slammed his right hand on the table, "You must rule now," he said.

"And I agree," Hapuseneb said.

Then looking at Hapuseneb, I said, "Oversee the preparation of my brother's body with Khety. I want the best of everything for the embalming and his burial."

Too young to die at twenty-seven summers, I thought.

"I will, Your Majesty!"

I saw Hapuseneb leave.

Looking at Sen-Mut, I said, "Sen-Mut, follow me."

As I was walking toward my quarters, the slaves noticed the Crown of Horus on my head, and they threw themselves at my feet then Sen-Mut and I walked up the stairs and reached my quarters. The guards saw the crown on my head and lay at my feet as well.

"Rise!" I said. They did and opened the golden doors.

"No one comes through these doors, not even the slaves," I told them.

"Yes, Your Majesty!" they replied.

I rushed to my bed and sat on it, leaning back on my elbows and spreading my legs.

"Now, I am all yours. Take me now," I said.

I wanted his lips pressing mine and all of him inside of me. Looking at him, I said, "No one will ever separate us again."

He came to me like a lion, pulling me by my wrist, and lifted me in the air as though I were a feather. He tore the sheath from my body. I stood naked in front of him, wanting his lips to travel all over my skin. He removed his kilt quickly, grabbed me by my waist, and pressed his open mouth on mine. We were locked in the most profound passionate kiss. The moment we had waited for so long was here. We did not let go of each other. We were engulfed in this passion mixed with ecstasy to possess each other's body.

He pushed me against the wall with his body. We became one.

Finally, he was mine again, and I was his. I was going to collapse from all the pleasure and ecstasy he has giving me. He still pinning my body against the wall.

He rested his head on my left shoulder, breathing heavily. We stayed locked together for a while. Then he kissed my lips lovingly, and, releasing me slowly and lifting me in his powerful arms, he carried me to the bed. Gently and lovingly, he laid me there. He knelt on the floor beside me, holding my left hand between his hands, and looked into my eyes.

"I love you, Maatke–Re, and I love you with all of my heart," he said.

My eyes became full of tears as he continued.

"I have waited for this moment anxiously for five summers. My body is trembling with ecstasy, satisfaction, and elation. It's a satisfaction no one else can give me but you. I can finally caress your face." He gently caressed my face. "And your body, and now I can bury my face in your bosom and get lost in the smell of your skin, knowing that you are mine. Your body, mind, and soul, forever."

He had tears in his eyes as he kissed my lips again. I pulled him by the neck into my bed, and we held tightly onto each other and cried together. We remained quiet for a while, full of emotions that words could not express.

He pressed his lips to my forehead and whispered, "I hope I did not hurt you with these wild desires to possess you that overpower me. I went wild when I looked at your naked body and the hardening of your nipples under your sheath, the spreading of your legs. You make me so wild and full of desire that I couldn't control myself. Now you are mine again and this time forever." He smiled. "I am the happiest man in the world right now," he said, kissing my hands.

"Thutmoses came to my quarters only once in these five summers. He was very drunk, and so was I. I already knew that he was coming to my quarters that night, looking for an heir. He had sent word earlier that day that he was going to visit me. I got drunk, so very drunk. I don't remember anything of that night, and he never came back again because I told him before that was going to be the only time. And he agreed. We drank some more, and then he said that we should just get it over with. I only remember when I was awakened by the sun shining in my face. By then, he was gone. I must have blocked everything out of my mind. I have never spoken about it or even thought about that night until now. Two months later, I was carrying his child. He wanted a male heir, but I had Hatshepset. She's four summers now and beautiful. You will meet her soon. He has kept her away from me since the death of our Neferu. She's been raised by Isis and the wet nurse. But that is going to stop after the seventy days of mourning and after the funeral. She is coming back here. She is my daughter, and I want her beside us."

Sen-Mut silently listened to me. My eyes traveled all over his naked body, the body of a god, and one that I had missed and loved so much. I smiled. I started to softly caress his strong shoulders, and he closed his eyes in pleasure. I drew my open hand slowly down to his chest and caressed it slowly. I became hot again.

And so, did he. He opened his eyes and laid me on my back, kissing me softly. A rush of desire overpowered us, and our bodies locked together in passion yet again. His mouth came to the base of my neck, then his lips traveled down to my nipples, and he started to suck them hard and then gently bit them, making me feel that same electrical current inside my body as before. I welcomed him inside of me again. The sensation was powerful and delicious. Again, he was making me moan. After a while, and in the most romantic moment, full of passion and ecstasy, he made me reach the stars. I heard him grunt as he was making me scream with passion. Then I felt his ejaculation inside of me. I was satisfied, for I knew that he had given me all of himself again.

I rested my head on his chest and smiled because I knew that no one would ever keep us apart again.

"I am still so hot. I want more and more of you," I told him.

He smiled.

"This is just the beginning. I am going to give you more in a few minutes to satisfy the desires of our bodies and to make up for all those years that we were kept apart. And it's going to last for a lifetime," he said.

We started to laugh. He got up from the bed, and I observed, with appreciation, his strong naked body of a god. He walked to the golden goblet and drank water. He brought it to me, and I drank.

Looking at me, he said, "Beloved, you must not get pregnant for now."

Then I realized that I could get pregnant. I knew that he was right.

"Yes, you are right. I mustn't. And I am probably carrying your child right now," I said.

I ran to the bathroom and washed myself and returned quickly to his side.

"Later on, I will ask T'Queta what she takes for preventing pregnancy. I told her I did not want children. The only children I want are with you," he said.

I smiled. He made my heart glad.

"I noticed that you have more sexual experience," I told him.

"Yes, I do, but every time I took T'Queta, or whoever else was under me, it was you who was on my mind. After I was done, I became angry and left Thebes to the field and wouldn't return until I was called by Ineni again. And this time was to draw the plans for your mortuary temple three months ago. I worked hard drawing it, and I put all my love for you into it. When I finished it, I sent message to Thutmoses that it was ready. I did not expect to see you there, and I was surprised when you entered my office with Thutmoses to see the plans. That moment when we exchanged glances, a sharp pain went through my heart. I wanted so much to talk directly to you, but your look was cold and indifferent. That hurt more than anything. I had to swallow my pain again. Then, when Thutmoses walked to my right side and you were at my left, and you held my hand and squeezed it hard, I knew that I did not have anything to worry about, that you still loved me. You made me very happy at that moment."

I covered his lips with mine. We were both crying, and he held me tightly against his chest.

He continued, "Then I had a reason to build for you with love, and when I started breaking ground for your temple, it brought me closer to you. Sometimes in the night, I screamed so hard in anger because I was so powerless, and there was no one that I could run to for help. The only thing that I could hold onto, was your love and the fact that you were my wife.

I kept coming to the temple and hoping that I could get a glimpse of you, and I never did. So, I made offerings to Amun many, many times to help me so that this moment would come soon. I knew it would, and finally it has."

We had tears in our eyes as he spoke about how hard it had been for both of us, all the years of being kept apart by Thutmoses and my father.

"I wanted so much to see you and talk to you, my love. Sometimes I would walk to the temple to see if I could see you. Sometimes I did, and my heart was happy all day long; and sometimes I did not. I went sailing in the afternoon just to see if I could see you swimming in the Nile, but I never saw you. Then sometimes I would go to Ineni's office, and he would tell me of your achievements, and hearing about that brought gladness to my heart. Sometimes he would tell me how much you were hurting inside of your heart for me. I spent those days depressed. One day he said that I should be completely sure that you love me. On those days, I would cry, but they would be happy tears," I said.

Sen-Mut held my hands and brought them to his lips. Then he noticed that I was still wearing the two rings he had given me when he asked me to be his wife.

He looked at me, surprised.

"You still wear them?" he asked.

"Yes, I am your wife, and I always will be," I told him.

He kissed both of my hands and my forehead.

"I love you so much, Sen-Mut."

I pressed my lips tenderly on his lips, caressing his face, and I kissed him with passion.

"And I love you, too, Maatke-Re," he said.

“Beloved of mine, are you hungry?” I asked.

“No, I really don’t have an appetite right now. There is so much going on in my mind,” he said.

I put on a white sheath and a sky-blue robe, then walked to the golden doors and opened them. I could feel the silence all over the land, and I became very sad because my brother was dead. I wished we had not departed in this way, all because of the poisonous snake Isis, poisoning his mind to make her son Pharaoh before he died.

“Guard!” I called.

“Yes, Your Majesty?”

“Send for all my personal slaves to come here at once and tell the rest of the slaves of the palace to go to the hall of audience by the eighth hour of the night. Also, tell Tuyii to bring enough food and drink for two. Send for Menina, the Pharaoh’s head slave, and ask her to come at once to my quarters. I turned around and walked inside my quarters, and for the first time, I noticed how spacious and large my outer quarters were, almost the same size as Pharaoh’s quarters.

Sen-Mut was standing on the balcony, looking at the last rays of Ra. He had gotten dressed in the kilt. I came from behind him and wrapped my arms around his waist, hugging him tightly. He held my arms around his waist with his hands.

“These five summers were the longest and the hardest of my life, but standing here with you, I cannot believe that the wait is over. It seems like I am dreaming, and I don’t want to wake up,” he said.

He pulled me gently by my hand and wrapped his arms around me and kissed the left side of my forehead.

“No more suffering for us, beloved, because this will never happen again,” I said.

"I will make sure that this will never happen to us again. You can be sure of that," he replied.

There was a knock on the doors. I picked up the Crown of Horus, and I placed it on my head and stood beside him. I looked at Sen-Mut and smiled.

"Enter," he said.

More than fifty slaves came walking in two rows of twenty- five, one on my left and the other one at my right. I stood there wearing the Horus crown with Sen-Mut beside me. Everyone prostrated themselves on the floor.

"Rise," I said, and so they did with their eyes cast down.

"Pharaoh is dead. I assume all of you have already heard the news. The land is in mourning, right now, and I have taken my rightful place as Horus of the two lands. From now on, anything that you see or hear in my quarters or anywhere in the palace will remain with you. I want each of you to look to your right and to your left. Look at the person next to you, because between you are all my most trustworthy spies. I have eyes and ears all over the palace and all over my kingdom, and death will fall upon you and your entire family if you speak ill of me or Sen-Mut, either inside or outside of these quarters or in any place in my kingdom. If you hear about plots against me, you most run to Master Sen-Mut. As of today, he is Ptah, Steward of Amun, and Master of the Palace."

All of them bowed to the floor giving Sen-Mut the proper respect.

"Also, bring any information to Master Hapuseneb, who, as of to-day, will be the Vizier of the South. After the seventy days of mourning and the burial have taken place, everything is going to change. It will go back to the way it was before I married Pharaoh. I want music, laughter, and happiness to return to this palace, and to the whole land. At that time, I will summon all of you again into my quarters. My servants who take care of my quarters will remain here. The rest may go now."

I clapped my hands, and they rose from the floor and left. Then I clapped my hands again, and dinner was served for me and Sen-Mut for the first time. We were finally alone, without fears and without worries. Finally, I was with the man I loved and who loved me.

With a wide smile on his face, he said, "Ptah, Steward of Amun and Master of the Palace? You have surprised me, Maatke-Re."

"You deserve it and more, beloved of mine, and I will give you more, my love."

He kissed my hands, and with his right hand, he pulled me by the neck and kissed my lips. His breath smelled as delicious as his kisses. He was a very clean man.

"Guards!" I called.

"Yes, Your Majesty?"

"As of today, Sen-Mut is Ptah, Steward of Amun and Master of the Palace," I said.

Both guards dropped their faces at Sen-Mut's feet.

"Rise," Sen-Mut said.

"Summon Master Ineni, General D'Jehuty, and every general in the armed forces, including the navy, to the audience hall at the ninth hour tonight. Also, summon First Prophet of Amun, Khety, Second Prophet of Amun, Puyem-Re, priest Hapuseneb, and the rest of the priests of the Temple of Amun-Ra. I want fifty soldiers always guarding Sen-Mut wherever he goes. Send twenty soldiers and bring Isis to the audience hall, too, at the eighth hour this evening," I said.

"Yes, Your Majesty." They were on their way.

I was full of emotions. I looked into Sen-Mut's eyes, and softly I said, "Beloved, we have waited for this moment for such a long time, and we have gone through so much pain together, with the death of our Neferu-Re six months ago. That day, you were looking at me, leaning against the wall as I held her lifeless body in my arms. I felt as if you wanted to tell me something or you knew something. What was it?" I asked.

"It's nothing. Sometime later I will tell you, but for now, let us be happy and enjoy our happiness together," he said and smiled.

"When Thutmoses was carrying her body in his arms to the House of the Dead, my heart hurt so much because you should have been the one carrying her body. You were her father, and I cried harder for both of us," I said.

I continued, "I want you to know that Thutmoses really loved her as his own and was wonderful with her since she was born. And I am most grateful to him for that."

He came to me, and held me in his arms, and we cried together just like we did on that tragic day. Then he wiped my tears away and kissed my eyes with the most tender love. I wiped his tears.

"Beloved, I will wear the dark blue mourning sheath and the Crown of Horus tonight. They will not look at me as their Queen any longer. They will look at me as the Supreme Ruler of the Two Lands. And to you, my love, everyone is going to drop their heads to the ground when you walk by, in any place in this kingdom."

Sen-Mut had become quiet.

"Beloved what is on your mind?" I asked.

"I wonder how the priests in the temple are going to react to the powerful titles 'Ptah, Steward of Amun' and 'Master of the palace' that you have just given me," he said.

"Beloved, I want you to know that as of today, I hold the military and the entire power of this kingdom in my hands. And they can't say absolutely anything. I will shower you with all the titles this kingdom can offer, because you deserve them all. For all the hurt you have suffered, and because I love you! No one will dare to say anything. I have held the power of my kingdom since an early age. And they were present when my father passed the power of the whole kingdom to my hands on the day of my coronation when I was crowned Queen and co-regent. Before that took place, all of them had pledged alliance to my father, and to me if Pharaoh died. And by that, they also meant Thutmoses II, for they have known ever since Thutmoses was born that one day the god of the underworld would come for him. And before my father died, he made sure that I would have control of the army and the support of all the priests in the Temple of Amun-Ra, and of the Oracle. We have very powerful people in high places like Amun-Ra and all the gods, too. Beloved, during the seventy days of embalming and the burial, I want you to learn everything that you must do with my kingdom, and I will pass control of everything into your hands. Could someone else continue with the construction of my temple as you learn about the political landscape and the management of my kingdom?" I said.

"Yes, Senemen, my brother. He has been helping me to prepare the ground for the temple; I taught him how to. I am teaching him to become an architect and builder also," he said.

Then Sen-Mut walked to a chair and sat down.

"Very well, my love. I would also like to bring your family to live close to us and build them a wonderful residence close to the palace, so you and I can go and visit them. Would you like that?"

He fell silent. After a bit, he said, "My father Ramose died three summers ago, but my mother is still alive," he said.

I became saddened and silent when I heard that. I approached him quickly with a broken heart, and I knelt in front of him and gently caressed his face. Looking into his eyes, I said, "It's heartbreaking for me to hear that, beloved. And I am so sorry that I was not there to console you through your pain. Please, I would like for you to build the nicest home for your mother, and I want your brothers and sisters to live there, like on the farm.

I want them to take care of her well. Also, send them a few slaves to help them with the chores of the house."

My heart was really saddened to hear about the death of his father.

"I must ask her if she is willing to leave her home on the farm," he said.

"Very well. Send a courier to your mother, and if she decides to stay, make her a lovely home and send many more slaves to help on the farm and with the crops. Also, from now on, buy everything that is produced on your farm for the palace. I don't want you to leave my side from now on, and if you must go somewhere else, you must be accompanied by my most brave soldiers always, until everything settles down. Are we agreed?"

He smiled, nodding his head. "Yes, I don't want us to be apart either." He bent over and gently kissed my lips.

"It is over. No more pain and no more tears for us, my love," I told him.

We walked to be bathed, holding hands "You're still very quiet," I said.

"I am amazed at how everything has changed in a few hours, and we have never bathed together before," he said and smiled.

"Or are you wondering if I don't have any feelings for my brother's death?"

He was startled that I had read his mind.

"Beloved, I want you to know that I am feeling mixed emotions inside of me. But right now, you are the most important person in my life. My brother caused us all this pain for five years, so, though I am heartbroken about his death, I cannot let that interfere with our happiness anymore," I told him.

He kissed me deeply, making me want his body again. He was no longer that nineteen-summers young man when he made love to me for the first time. He was now a man. He looked like a man, and he acted like one.

He clapped his hands, and the slaves left. Standing in the middle of the large pool, he looked deep into my eyes and slowly kiss my shoulders and my neck, while his hands traveled down to my chest. His lips moved slowly all over my body. And we make passionate love and making me his again.

I laid my head on his right shoulder as he held me tightly and caressed the middle of my back with his fingers. I wanted to remain in his arms like this all night. We stayed straddled for a while.

It was very late by now, and the chanting of the golden doors was over. Eventually, I pulled back and kissed his lips with love as I caressed his face. He responded with another passionate kiss.

Looking deep into my eyes, he said, "My wife, you don't know how much I've missed you, how much I love you. I've been dying to make love to you for the last five years. Remembering your smell every night, a memory that made me want you even more."

"I have always loved you, my husband, and I have missed you just as much," I whispered in his ear and kissed his cheek.

We were enveloped in the magic of love. Holding each other, we did not want to lose this wonderful feeling. He lifted me up and un-straddled my legs from him.

He clapped his hands, and the slaves came back to finish bathing us. He whispered again in my ear, "I hope you did not get pregnant." Then he laughed.

I became quiet, my eyes wide open. I had completely forgotten about that, but he was looking at me and smiling.

"I would love to have another child with you, but I know I cannot. We will deal with this tomorrow," I told him with a smile.

He kissed my forehead, and we finished our baths.

"I must go and speak to T'Queta and ask her what she takes and her method to avoid pregnancy." He

"Very well, beloved, but you must change into the new kilt and sandals I ordered for you this morning, and you must be accompanied by fifty of my bravest soldiers at all times."

He held my hand and helped me to get out of the bathtub. I looked at his naked body, the body that I knew and loved and had missed so much. I wore the very dark blue sheath underneath the dark blue mourning robe with gold trim. I knelt on one knee, and Sen-Mut placed the Horus crown on my bald head.

We walked through the golden doors and descended the stairs. Hapuseneb was walking toward us, and he dropped at my feet.

"Rise, Hapuseneb."

He looked at Sen-Mut. I saw how he clenched his jaw, but he hid his emotions and simply said, "Welcome back, Sen-Mut. I did not have the chance to properly welcome you back or to say hello to you today. It's been a very busy day, as you know, and I am pretty sure Flower of Egypt has keep you busy all afternoon."

I was shocked to hear him say that, but Sen-Mut just smiled and said, "Now, since you put it in that way, yes, and in the most delicious ways, and I give her the love that she deserves."

My jaw dropped. I was taken back by this conversation. I realized that I had better do something before they got into a fist fight.

"Let's walk," I said in a loud voice.

I was afraid that Sen-Mut would punch him and send him across the Nile, but neither of them moved.

"Sen-Mut, you and I must talk tonight after the announcement of Pharaoh's death," Hapuseneb said.

"Yes, Hapuseneb. It is about time for you and me to have a long talk."

"Okay, both of you must talk, but tomorrow. I am very tired right now, and I must deal with the edict for the announcement of Pharaoh's death. Tomorrow we will get together and make plans. You must also summon the prophets of Amun-Ra and Ineni. How is Khety feeling right now, Hapuseneb?"

"I don't think he is too well, Flower of Egypt. I must speak to Sen-Mut about what you and I spoke of this morning before the rays of Ra started to show, and he must understand."

"I will hear all that you have to say to me tonight, Hapuseneb," Sen-Mut told him.

Finally, we started to walk. Sen-Mut's blood was boiling, I could tell. Hapuseneb's jealousy was eating him alive.

Sen-Mut stopped walking. He grabbed hold of my wrist with a hard grip and whispered in my ear, "I want you to explain to me what you were doing with him in the early part of the morning before the rays of Ra were showing?"

"I will explain later," I said.

He let go of my wrist, and we started to walk again.

When we arrived at the audience hall, everyone was there, including Isis. She had her eyes cast down. I walked up to the throne, and I looked at Isis. Everyone had dropped to the floor as they saw the Horus crown on my head.

"Everyone, look at me!" I said.

I sat down on the throne. I knew Isis was boiling with anger.

"I have summoned everyone here tonight to announce Pharaoh's death. As many of you know, I have held the Crown of Horus since I was a child. Father crowned me Queen with the Double Crown of Upper and Lower Egypt. Again, I am Horus of Egypt. I want for the whole land to know that I hold the reins of the two lands, Upper and Lower Egypt, and my word is law. As of today, I am no longer Queen of Egypt, but Horus in my brother's place. It was my title before and after the Great Maat's death. I chose to marry my brother to continue the Thutmoses bloodline, and I did. I gave him a daughter, Princess Hatshepset. We are all in mourning, and after the seventy days, I will do the ceremony of the opening of the mouth, eyes, and ears. This will take place in his tomb. I will be the one to do it because I am his only blood relative. Now, I present to you Ptah, Steward of Amun-Ra and Master of the Palace, Sen-Mut."

Everyone dropped their faces to the floor at Sen-Mut's feet, including Isis. He saw how everyone lowered their heads.

"Rise, and I present to you High Priest Hapuseneb, as of today Vizier of the South. His word is also law in this land, second only to mine and Sen-Mut's," I said.

Everyone again dropped to their faces in the floor.

"After the seventy days of the mourning period, happiness will return to the palace as before when my father, the Great Maat, and Ahmose, my mother, were alive. I want the palace to be full of laughter, music, and happiness. Scribe, let it be written, and let it be done. Send the edict to every corner of the country that everyone is to mourn their Pharaoh with respect. All the slaves and Isis must leave the audience hall now. The rest of you should remain here."

After they left, I continued, ‘Tomorrow everyone here will meet with me and Sen-Mut, including the scribes, and Hapuseneb. Thank you for coming, and we will see you tomorrow at the second hour after noon.”

I walked down from the throne with Sen-Mut and Hapuseneb at my side. “Let’s eat and talk, the three of us,” I said.

“Maatke-Re, Hapuseneb and I have a pending talk,” Sen-Mut said with a firm tone of voice. “And after that, I am going to my house to talk to T’Queta. Once that’s done, I will be back because you and I have a conversation to finish as well. Guard!” Sen-Mut shouted, and the palace guard came rushing to us. “Escort Horus back to the palace,” he said.

I looked at both and shook my head.

“Well, I will talk to both of you later,” I said.

I was so hungry and now this. Hapuseneb had always been so jealous of Sen-Mut, and soon Sen-Mut would explode. I waited for Sen-Mut until the early part of the morning, wondering and worrying about the two of them. I waited and waited, until I finally fell asleep. I was awakened by a kiss and a smile.

“Beloved, you came back. Did you eat?”

“Yes. Hapuseneb took me to his house, and Tepi fed us both. He was surprisingly pleasant and explained to me why we must remain apart for a while until he can get all the priests to agree for you to be Pharaoh. He said that maybe you might have to share the throne with the child as co-regent for a few months. Then we will be able to crown you Pharaoh.”

“And what do you think about all of this, Sen-Mut?” I asked.

“I believe he is right, just for few months, but not as separated as we were kept before. I could see you every day and eat with you and make love to you as many times as we want. Only I would not sleep here at night. But soon, my love, soon,” he said.

"This is breaking my heart, this whole situation. Do you know that?" I responded.

"And it is also breaking mine, my love," he said.

"Beloved, we have never slept together. Let tonight be our first night. No one is here. I sent them to sleep in another place, just to be alone with you. I will bathe you tonight."

He smiled.

"I would love that, my love. I need to feel your heart beating close to mine tonight," he said.

"Let me bathe you with cool water. It's very hot right now," I said.

We walked to the tub holding hands, and I washed his hair and body. I did not bathe, for I had already bathed. As I was drying his body, he asked, "Do you really love me, Hatshepsut?"

I looked at him and smiled. "With all of my heart and soul."

He lifted me in his arms and laid me on the bed. I could see how tired he was. We kissed with passion.

"If I were not so tired, I would let you have it." He laughed and held me tightly in his arms. "Good night, my love, and sweet dreams," he said.

"Sweet dreams, beloved one," I said, and we fell asleep.

I was awakened by kisses on my cheeks. I opened my eyes and smiled. I was full of joy and desire, knowing that finally he was beside me. I turned around to face him. He was kneeling behind me, and he had a beautiful smile.

"Glorious morning, beloved," he said.

I sat and smiled. “Glorious morning to you, my love. Am I going to have it now?” I asked and laughed.

I rushed to the bathroom and washed up. I came back with a smile on my face and jumped in the bed naked. I knelt facing him. He pulled me to him gently and kissed me. Then he pulled back.

“I must stop right now and leave, otherwise, I will make love to you. I don’t want you to get pregnant, not now, even though I am so hot. What am I supposed to do now? It’s all your fault. Look at how you have me.”

He had an erection.

Slowly, I came closer to him and started to kiss him softly. He pulled me down with him onto the bed, and we became one. I was as lost in this elixir of love and ecstasy as he was. He was making me scream and made me come to a delicious climax. He was about to explode in ecstasy, but he pulled his member away from my gem and spilled his seed on my belly. He lay on top of me. He looked at me and softly kissed me.

“I am sorry, but I had to do that. I don’t want you to get pregnant yet, but I promise, I will be back with answers, and this will not happen again. I cannot be away from you anymore, and this is not going to work having sex in this way,” he told me.

He got up, and I followed him. We washed each other. Afterward, I opened the golden doors, and the slaves came rushing in with our breakfast. We ate holding hands. We could not believe how happy we were, that finally we were together and that it would be forever. We were so very happy.

He got up from his chair and knelt on one knee at my feet.

“My love, I must go now and find answers from T’Queta. Remember, I am to meet with Hapuseneb and the scribes, and I will see you at the banquet hall for dinner tonight,” he said.

I whispered in his ear, "Tonight we will sail Hopi under the stars. I want to scream with passion, with you inside of me. What you did earlier did not satisfy me completely. Something was missing. The feeling of your seed inside of me, and your explosion of ecstasy. Beloved, I promise that no one will know that we are away. Leave your home from the back in the dark. I will order the barge to be ready to sail tonight. I will give the order as soon as you leave here. It makes me angry that we still have to hide our love."

"Not for too long, my love," he told me.

"We will leave at the seventh hour tonight. It will be the same barge we sailed to Philae."

"That would please me very much. I can relive those moments when I wanted to kiss you under the stars and could not, but this time no one will be keeping me from making you mine and kissing you under the stars tonight," he said. Then he kissed me, and he left.

I clapped my hands.

"Bring me the head slave Menina, the head chef, and Sailor Neb-Ery."

"Yes, Your Majesty." She left hurriedly.

A few minutes later the chef walked into my quarters.

"Your Majesty," he said and dropped to the floor.

"You must prepare the most delicious plates, pastry, the best wine, the best of everything to serve to me and the Ptah, Steward of Amun tonight. I want the musicians to be playing as we arrive at the barge. Decorate the dining area beautifully, with lots of flowers. I want the oil lamps to light up the barge, but later dimmed. I want the most romantic night, and you cannot speak of this to anyone. I want complete secrecy when they load the barge."

"Yes, Your Majesty."

I clapped my hands once, and the slave came to me.

"Bring me my jewelry box," I said.

She brought it to me, and I pulled out a handful of jewelry and gave it to the chef.

"A gift for you, for all the years in our service, and for keeping your mouth closed. In two days, you must go to my goldsmith to remove my cartouche from it."

"Yes, Your Majesty. Everything will be ready for tonight." He knelt and then left.

Then walking in, kneeling, and bowing his head was Neb-Ery, the sailor.

"Rise. Neb-Ery. I summoned you to let you know that from now on, you will oversee my barge. And we sail tonight until the early part of the morning when we will return to Thebes. You will be personal sailor to Master Sen-Mut, Ptah, Steward of Amun. Wherever he wants to go, you will take him. Tuyii, bring the other jewelry box."

She brought it to me, and I pulled gold nuggets from my box, gold that had just been brought from my gold mines. I grabbed a handful and gave them to him

"I want complete silence regarding this sail tonight and forever," I said to Neb-Ery.

"Yes, Your Majesty."

"You may go now. Get some rest for tonight. We are sailing at the seventh hour after the last rays of Ra when Mother Nut covers the land. We will leave when Master Sen-Mut arrives at the barge."

"Yes, Your Majesty." He bowed his head to the floor and left.

I clapped my hands twice.

"Bring Menina, and all of you leave when she gets here."

Menina walked into my quarters. She was an older and heavy woman, with long black hair. She looked like a person I could trust. Maybe with all her life experience, she could give me advice on what I needed.

She dropped her face to the floor at my feet.

"Rise, Menina. I want you to have a seat. I wanted to thank you for all the information you have given me through the years. I want you to keep your eyes and ears open, and I want you to tell me everything that Isis does. Who she speaks to and what she speaks of. I mean everything. Now, for the real reason I called you in. I need some information regarding women's matters. You have known for many years that Master Sen-Mut has been the love of my life, and we have waited to be with each for a long time. Now the wait is over, since yesterday, with the death of Pharaoh. We rushed to each other's arms and made love several times yesterday, and I am afraid that I could be pregnant with our love making. Do you know anything about how to prevent pregnancies in the future? Because I cannot be pregnant at this moment. I have to run this country."

I became quiet, anxiously waiting for her reply.

"Yes, Your Majesty. There is an herb that is of bitter taste and that you can start taking right now for the blood to come down in a few days if you were pregnant. You can make love every day until that day when the blood comes, and you can be sure that it will work. Also, there is a mix of herbs that you must take every day in the morning to avoid getting pregnant in the future, and you can enjoy sex with Master Sen-Mut. But if you stop drinking it, you can get pregnant. This is what the women in the harem and the slaves from the kitchen drink to prevent pregnancy. Also, pessaries of crocodile dung with honey," Menina said.

"What is that?" I asked.

"It's crocodile poop. You place a small amount on a small piece of linen and soak it in honey, then put it inside of you. There are also other methods that men do to themselves. Some of them tie a piece of linen on the head of the penis during the erection to hold the seed from entering deep inside. I believe that the herbal drink will be the best for you, but it has one problem, it could make you sterile and then you will not be able to have babies when you want them, but you can alternate. Use the herbals tea for few weeks then switch to the dung and honey the other times. I can prepare all of this for you. Or master Sen-Mut can climax outside of you. Or use the linen method. If you got pregnant yesterday and don't want to take the bitter herbs for the blood to come, you can say that the child is Pharaoh's, and I can induce labor before your due date. No one will ever know that it was not Pharaoh's child." She said.

"Well, I've learned so much from you today. I did not know that these methods existed for preventing pregnancies," I said.

"I thought that you knew of all these methods before and that you were taking care of yourself after the birth of Princess Hatshepset."

"No, I did not allow Pharaoh to make another visit to my bed, only once. I want you to prepare the bitter herbal right now so that I can have some peace of mind tonight. Will I get sick? Or will I be in pain?"

"Only if you've gotten pregnant. Some cramps will accompany the blood. But if you are not pregnant, you will have a little more flow of blood than usual and a lot sooner than your normal time of the month."

"Thank you so much for helping me. Go and make the potion for me right now, and from now on, you will make a schedule for when I should take it and when I should stop. Now bring me that blue box over there."

I pointed it out to her. She got up and brought it to me. I opened the box and gave her many gold nuggets. I could see the look in her eyes when I gave her so much gold.

"Your Majesty, this is too much," she said.

"It's alright. You have been faithful to me when you ran to T'Queta to warn me about Isis poisoning Thutmoses's mind, trying to get him to kill my child when it was born. I have never forgotten that. I sent you a gift with T'Queta on that day, and there will be more as long you remain faithful to me."

"She gave me the gift, and I will always be faithful to you, Your Majesty," she said and dropped her face to the floor.

"Rise, Menina, and you may go now. I will see you when you return with the beverage, and send my slaves in." She left.

I needed to be bathed with Sen-Mut's favorite fragrances and with a touch of myrrh, bathed with oils to make my skin soft for when he caressed my body tonight. I was being bathed when Menina came back and brought the bitter drink.

"Your Majesty, I made it a little stronger in case it is needed, but that has made the drink more bitter."

I took the golden cup in my hands. It was warm, and I drank it. It was so bitter that I could hardly swallow it.

I looked at Menina, and she said, "It must all be drunk."

I finished it, though I did not like the taste. I clapped my hands twice, and the slaves left me alone with her.

"Are you sure it will not make me sick tonight?"

"I am pretty sure, Your Majesty."

"Menina, you must keep guard of your lips on this," I told her.

"I will, your Majesty. I believe that you deserve all the happiness with Master Sen-Mut."

"Now, I want to know, who spread the rumors that I was pregnant with Sen-Mut's child?" I asked.

"Isis did. She said it in the kitchen one night, as you thought, when you were screaming and punishing her for spreading the rumors two days ago. She was indeed the one who spread the rumors all over the palace. And after Pharaoh ordered the death of several slaves in the kitchen, he ordered an investigation. All of us were called in by D'Jehuty, and he questioned us one by one. He concluded that she was the one who started to spread rumors in the kitchen. D'Jehuty said that the child was Pharaoh's and that if he heard rumors again any place in the palace or in the land, we would all be put to death, even if we all were innocent. He met with Pharaoh and told him the results of his investigation on that same day. Pharaoh came to his quarters, and when he walked in, he took Isis by surprise. He grabbed her by her hair, and in a rage, he slammed her into the floor. I could see the terrified look on her face. It was the first time I'd seen Pharaoh so terribly angry. Really, I had never seen him angry at all. He had brought a horse whip with him, and he punished her with it. He was screaming at her, saying that she had caused the death of innocent slaves, and now because of her poisoning tongue, she had torn you and him apart. I could hear the whistle of the whip falling on her. I could hear her screaming as the whip fell upon her, and I saw that she tried to get away from him but couldn't. When he was done, he dropped the whip beside her and told her to remember the deaths that she had caused. She would not stop crying, but I did not feel sorry for her because the ones who died were also my friends. He left her there and left his quarters. She was in a corner, crying for a long time. When he came back, she was very quiet. He sent her away to the kitchen, and right away he sent for a few women of the harem. Later, Master Hapuseneb and D'Jehuty joined him, and they all drank and talked for long hours, each of them holding a woman of the harem on their laps. After that, a few weeks went by before he sent for her again."

"Do you know if she or my brother killed my daughter Neferu-Re?" I asked.

“I am sure Pharaoh did not, for he got very depressed and was very upset when he heard the news that little Neferu was dead. I could hear him cry. He asked her many times if she had anything to do with her death, and she swore that she did not. Honestly, I really don’t like her. And I really have no idea how far she would go, but to commit murder and harm a royal child? I really don’t know if she did.”

“Thank you, Menina, for your words. They are a relief and are consoling to me. I thought my brother had killed my baby, and I was devastated at the thought of it. Now you have brought closure to my doubts and pain,” I said.

“Your Majesty, I can tell you that he really loved you. You were his little sister, and I never heard anything bad about you from his lips. I never did.”

She was shaking her head. Listening to her words brought tears to my eyes for my dear brother. The only family that I had left lay in the House of the Dead.

Menina saw my tears.

“Your Majesty, remember only the good times with him and remember that he permitted you to know love with Master Sen-Mut. Now it’s finally your time to be happy with Master Sen-Mut and remember that this is a new beginning for both of you. Forget the past and enjoy tonight and the many nights to come when he will be beside you and you will be in his arms.”

It was nice to hear her comforting words. And yes, she was right, this would be a new beginning.

“Dry my body, Menina, and let’s continue our talk in my bedroom.” I put on the royal robe. “I am Sen-Mut’s wife. I have been his wife for the last six years, and no one knows that, only the two of us. And now you. You must guard this secret with your life because it could cause your death and that of your entire family. I will make sure of that. I also know that you are one of Hapuseneb's spies. This conversation must never reach Master Hapuseneb's ears."

I became silent and thought of Hapuseneb and that this would kill him.

"I would never fail you, Your Majesty. I know this would kill him," she said.

I was startled by her response. I looked at her.

"I have always known that he was in love with you, ever since childhood. Also, I know that Princess Neferu-Bity killed herself because she was in love with him, but he was in love with you. She did not want to be betrothed to your brother Thutmoses because she didn't think she could be happy married to him. She wanted to marry Hapuseneb, but he didn't return her feelings. Those were very sad days for all of us when she died, and when Pharaoh ordered the death of her wet nurse. I was glad that I was not the one who prepared the poison for her to kill herself."

I never knew that her wet nurse killed herself. Well, that Father ordered her to kill herself. This explained why she was not at Neferu-Bity's funeral, I thought.

"Do you know who made the poison for Neferu-Bity?" I asked.

"She made it herself," she answered.

I was shocked. "What do you mean that she made it herself?"

"Since she was nine summers, she knew which leaves and herbs were curative and which ones were poisonous. She became interested in plants and their uses," she said.

"I never knew that. We used to spend a lot of time together, and I never saw that she was interested in plants and herbs or making potions. Your answer shocked me, Menina. I still miss her and spending time with her. I never had anyone close to me like Neferu-Bity to talk to. After she was gone, I had Mother, and now she too is gone. Now I understand why, when I was nine summers, on the day she was betrothed to our brother Thutmoses, she told me that if she was forced to marry him, she would kill herself."

"She was far too young to think of death. Her death took all of us by surprise and was the worst of shocks for Pharaoh and Her Majesty, the Queen," Menina said.

"I don't know who was hurting more on that day, Pharaoh, my mother, or me. Since that day, I have had no one close to me anymore, only Hapu and Thutmoses, and they didn't talk about girl things, you know? Thank you, Menina. Speaking with you has clarified many things for me. I still don't know how my child died, and I still believe that Isis had something to do with her death. It was not poison that killed her. She stopped breathing, but she was fine several hours before she died. I heard the story about Pharaoh when Thut was young, and how terrified his mother Mutnofret was every day and night because she believed someone was killing my siblings. There was panic all over the palace, and Mutnofret thought that he was next. However, there was never any sign of poisoning in any of my siblings," I told her.

"There are other ways they could had done it, but it is better for you, Your Majesty, to never know what those ways are. Or you never will be happy. We still don't know if she was murdered," she said.

"In my heart, I know Isis did it. She would have a lot to lose because Neferu-Re was not full royal blood, and her son would never be full royal blood if he was betrothed to her. But Hatshepset is full royal blood."

"Your Majesty, we don't know that she did it. There was no way she could have. Neferu-Re was always with Master Sen-Mut or in the care of Amose-Pen-Nekhbet and her wet nurse. He is a respectable war correspondent and historian, and he has been with the family since Pharaoh Amose. It would have been very difficult for her to do it. Maybe the princess was not feeling well and neither you nor her wet nurse noticed, Your Majesty."

"Perhaps, but Sen-Mut was not allowed to visit Neferu-Re anymore by order of Thutmoses. I hate that woman so much. In my heart, I believe she did it. Maybe she had several accomplices. I think it was her, partly because she wanted Pharaoh to kill my child earlier because it was Sen-Mut's daughter. Yes, Neferu-Re was Sen-Mut's daughter. I became pregnant the first night that Sen-Mut made love to me. It was the night before my marriage to my brother," I said.

"Yes, Your Majesty, I understand."

"Well Menina, we have spent several hours together. I thank you for your help. At what time must I take the first bitter potion tomorrow to prevent becoming pregnant?"

"We must wait until the first blood comes down. If you have gotten pregnant, it will be within three days. The blood will come with some cramps. Otherwise, if you are not, you can start drinking it after three days have passed, the first thing in the morning after you get up from bed and before breakfast. I will personally bring it early in the morning, although I might have to wake you up, Your Majesty."

"Very well. I will wait for three days. Then we will know if I have gotten pregnant. I hope not. I don't want to lose Sen-Mut's child."

"Your Majesty, one word of advice. Do not drink anything brought to you by someone else."

"Thank you, Menina. I would not. I must finish with my bath. Thank you again. Send my slaves in when you leave."

She got up, bowed, and left.

The slaves walked in and followed me to the bath.

I lay on top of the white linen as I was being massaged with fragrant oils and thought all about what Menina had told me, that Neferu-Bity made the poison herself. I was too young to understand love at that time, but she did. How terrible she must have felt when Hapu told her that he was in love with me. "Mother Hathor," I thought. I hope the gods have forgiven her for killing herself. But then I shook my head. I realized I should not think such sad thoughts since they could spoil my happiness with Sen-Mut tonight.

"We are done, Your Majesty," one of the slaves said.

I stood up, and they covered me in the royal blue robe. I clapped once, and one slave came and kneeled.

"Yes, Your Majesty?"

"I want you to go to the audience hall and look to see who is there, so you can let me know. Go. And come back in a hurry."

She left hurriedly.

"Now, I must rest for tonight."

I had my eyes closed when she came back, and I was awakened by the slave's soft voice.

"Your Majesty."

"Yes?" I opened my eyes.

"There were so many priests of the Temple of Amun, many of whose names I didn't know. I saw First Prophet of Amun, Khety, Second Prophet of Amun, Puyem-Re, Master Sen-Mut, Master Hapuseneb, Master Ineni, and other dignitaries whose names I didn't know. I've heard that lunch was brought to all of them, and they have been behind closed doors for hours," the slave said.

"Run back there and take a message to Master Sen-Mut."

I took a small piece of papyrus and wrote:

Beloved, I will bathe you tonight.

“Give it to the guards at the doors and tell them they must give it to Master Sen-Mut immediately and to no one else. Go now.”

When she returned, she said, “Your Majesty, when I got there, they were all leaving the audience hall. I saw Master Sen-Mut, and I give him the message personally. He read it and said to tell you that he is looking forward to that, and he had a big smile on his lips.”

“Bring me my jewelry box. All of you, come here,” I said.

The ten of them knelt at my feet.

“I have had you for so many years, and I want to reward you all tonight, and tonight is very special for me. I want all of you to sleep in my quarters, and no one should leave this room until I return when Ra will be showing his first rays. If you must go to the kitchen or take care of necessary bodily functions, keep an eye out for Master Hapuseneb. If you see him, you must tell him that I am not feeling well and not seeing anyone.”

“Yes, Your Majesty,” they said in unison.

I opened my large jewelry box and let each of them pick out something that she liked. They all were giggling and happy. I trusted all of them. Some had been with me since they were young and were friends with T’Queta, too. They had grown up. They were full grown women.

“And don’t forget, in two days all of you must go to the goldsmith to remove my cartouche from the jewelry.”

“Yes, Your Majesty.”

The chanting began outside of my golden doors, and all of us knelt to face Ra as he was fading away.

“Dress me. I will wear the blue sheath with the golden belt, stole, and the golden sandals that my mother gave me for my fifteen summers,” I said.

I was dressed and put kohl in small lines on my eyes, a small amount of rouge on my cheeks, and a small amount of red lipstick on my lips. I wore a wig made of many tiny little braids of natural hair down to my shoulders entwined with strings of gold. I looked in the mirror, and I looked beautiful.

"Bring me the small gold necklace, the one that looks like a pectoral, and the gold earrings." I said.

The slave brought the necklace, put it on my neck, and then the earrings.

"Your Majesty, you look so beautiful, but today you are more beautiful than usual. You are radiant," she said.

I smiled at her and thought, "All for you my love. I am not Horus tonight. I am just a woman in love." I took the golden stole and put it over my shoulders and walked off through the golden doors.

I told the guards, "No one is to come into my quarters tonight, only my slaves. Whoever might be looking for me is to be told that I am indisposed for the night, and no one is to know that I left."

"Yes, Your Majesty."

"I need a torch bearer," I said, and one of my guards walked with me holding the torch.

The night was not hot as I walked to the barge. Mother Nut had covered the land with darkness, and the beauty of the stars shining made the night clear and lovely. To my surprise, Sen-Mut was standing beside the barge waiting for me in his white kilt and leather sandals.

I stopped and sent the guard away and moved closer and closer to him. We stood there in silence looking at each other, and he kissed me softly and lifted me up in his arms, holding me tightly against his chest. I rested my head on his strong chest.

The barge was very well decorated. There were many candles, flowers, and food, all well-arranged.

"Let me bathe you, my love," I whispered in his ear as he carried me to the couch and gently lay me there and looked at me.

"You look so beautiful tonight. You radiate more than the stars, and your smell makes me want to bite you," he said.

I laughed.

"Beloved, give the order to Neb-Ery to sail."

He shouted, "Neb-Ery, sail!"

The barge started to move slowly. He stood there looking at me quietly, and I smiled at him. Suddenly, sadness overwhelmed me, pressing my chest, and I started to cry. I did not know why I was crying?

He rushed to my side and knelt beside me, holding my right hand.

"What is it, my love? What's wrong?" he asked.

Our faces were so close to each other I could smell the mint on his lips. I caressed his face with my left hand, and I pressed my lips to his with force. He responded to my passionate kiss, putting his arms around me and holding me in his arms.

"Don't cry, my love," he said.

I was sobbing, and looking into his eyes, I said, "Sen-Mut, promise me that we will never be apart ever again. Promise me that."

"I promise. I promise that we will never be apart ever again." He held me tightly in his arms, then he kissed my forehead and rocked me in his arms.

"Are you calm now?" he asked.

"Being in your arms calms me down. Beloved, let me bathe you now. I know that you must be very tired tonight."

He smiled at me.

"Actually, I am not. I am full of life right now and cannot believe that we are free and together again." He was smiling at me.

I removed his kilt, and my eyes traveled over his naked body, the body that I love. Then I removed the sandals from his feet.

He removed my sheath. We walked naked holding hands to an open space under the stars. In that area large clay containers with warm water and the finest oil fragrances awaited us. Rose petals from my garden were floating on the surface of the water. It had been set up for us by the slaves. There was also a small wooden stool. He sat down, and I washed his body, his face, and his hair with love. Gently, he pulled me by the hand and brought me closer to him. He sat me on his lap.

"I have the secret for you not getting pregnant. Now we can make love any time we want, without worrying about that," he whispered in my ear.

Smiling at him, I said, "I've already spoken to Menina this morning. She was Thutmoses's private slave in his quarters, and she gave me a bitter herbal to drink this morning in case I became pregnant yesterday."

I started to feel cold. I dried him fast to avoid his getting cold. He picked me up in his arms and took me to the couch, then covered me with his body and kissed me passionately and with so much love. His hands traveled all over my body slowly. And after long moments of ecstasy, we reached a powerful climax. He made me lose conscious as he made me reach the stars again.

What a wonderful feeling our lovemaking was.

He kissed my forehead and said, "I love you so much, Maatke-Re, and I will never be tire of telling you how much I love you. My profound love for you occupies my entire soul, and there is no room for anyone but you. When we were apart, I felt powerless. I would yell in anger and scream, 'She is my wife, and her love belongs to me!'" he said.

I covered his mouth with my lips and hugged him tightly. My eyes were full of tears listening to what he went through. He held me close to his heart.

"This is love. A love that hurts is real love. No one else can ever occupy my heart, only you, even when I am dead," he said.

We lay in each other's arms as I listened to his words and told him in return, "Never will there be other than you, even if you die. You are always on my mind, in my heart, and on my lips. I breathe through the breath you take. On the night you asked me to be your wife and we married under the stars, and promised to love each other forever, I told you that I would love you through all eternity.[52] That is how my love will last for you, throughout all eternity," I told him.

"Thank you for loving me that way, and I will love you through all eternity as well. Lying here with you in my arms, I feel complete. I don't need anything else, just you beside me," he said and kissed me again.

"Are you hungry?" I asked him.

"Yes, I am so very hungry." He smiled.

He helped me with the royal robe, and I covered his body with a white linen robe, encrusted with gold thread that I had ordered to be made early that morning for him. We walked holding hands and barefoot to an area where food had been set up. I had ordered all his favorite food and wines. We ate under the stars, drank a lot, and talked of the future. We also talked about that day's meeting. He was keen to tell me about it but didn't

---

[52] And I have.

want to spoil the night, so he planned to put it off until the next day. He wanted this night to be only for the two of us and no one else.

After we ate, we walked to the couch that was placed on the bow of the barge. He took off his white robe, and I took off mine. He sat naked, leaning back against the pillows. I sat down between his legs, with my back leaning on his chest. He covered me with his arms.

“I like nights like this. Dark without Thoth so I can see the constellations better, and the stars are brighter. See that one over there? It is the large bull. I have been studying them since you sent me to the temple to train to be a priest. That was before I became an architect. Learning about the stars is part of the training for the priesthood. As I was studying the starts, I learned that within the stars is the figure of a woman who is pregnant and who will bring a light into this world, a great light.”

“What do you mean?” I asked.

“I don’t know what it means, only that she will bring a great light in to this world. The stars speak of the future, like when I knew that your brother would die. Do you remember the night I asked you to be my wife, and we married under the stars? I told you that there would come a day when we would be together forever. Do you remember that?”

“Yes, I do, and I waited for a long time.”

“I’ve known since then that Anubis would come for him, but I did not know the exact day. I made a celestial chart for him and saw the movement of the celestial beings because Khety showed me how it is done. I did it, knowing that it would take some years to come to pass. After the birth of our daughter Neferu-Re, I did another chart because Thutmoses was keeping us apart. And I did not like what I saw. I saw the death of our daughter Neferu-Re. I never told you about it because I didn’t want to break your heart or cause you any pain, so I took all that pain to myself.”

Tears were running down my face, and I turned around and faced him. I caressed his face and kissed his eyes that were full of tears. How could we console ourselves on the loss of our child? It was a terrible pain for both of us.

"That's why, when I was holding her lifeless body in my arms, you were standing there against the wall, looking at me as though you wanted to tell me something? Those were terrible days for both of us. And with the pain from being kept apart. It's been only six months since we lost her," I said.

He squeezed me tightly and pointed to the sky.

"Hat, look. A falling star."

I turned around and watched its slow fall in the night sky. It was beautiful. He was right about the dark night. I could see the stars and the constellations better.

He continued holding me in his arms. We became silent for a while looking at the beautiful night full of stars as the barge sailed. Then I noticed his breathing. He was asleep.

I covered both of us with my royal robe and remained silent looking at the stars. There was another falling star. I wanted to tell him about it, but I let him sleep instead. It had been a long day for both of us.

I found myself offering a silent prayer. "Oh, Mother Hathor, thank you for bringing him back into my life so that I can hold him in my arms, as he is holding me tonight. Thank you for his love."

The barge continued sailing north in the silence of the night. I fell asleep with Sen-Mut holding me in his arms under the stars.

Still dark, I was awakened by Sen-Mut, who needed to urinate. It was so easy for him: he just went overboard. I went to the bathroom, and when I returned, he was standing there naked looking up at the stars. I could see his well-formed body and butt. I came quietly from behind and pinched his butt, and he jumped. We laughed. I was very happy. I was feeling very content. He had water in a golden cup waiting for me, and we sat down and drank. We lay side by side, this time with pillows behind our necks, and looked at the stars.

"I don't know how Pharaoh, I mean my father, could sleep with a neck holder. It's too hard for me. That is why I use pillows," I said.

"The neck holder is to keep the vertebrae in line. I've tried it, and it does help my back and neck," he said.

"Should I order a new couch with one on your side?"

"No, not now. Remember no one is supposed to know that we are sleeping together," he said.

"How much longer do we have to sleep apart?" I asked him.

"More than seventy days. Maybe another week after your brother's funeral. By then, things will be different."

"Beloved, the rays of Ra will soon show," I said.

"Not, for a while. We still have about six more hours left to us," he said. "See, I know the time by the position of the stars and the constellations, and I will teach you how to be able to tell time during the night hours."

"I would like that." I was impressed with his knowledge.

"While we were being kept apart by Thutmoses, and I was at a building site or rebuilding shrines along the Nile, I would remember our trip to Philae when you told me that your Ka left your body, and you were in the middle of all the stars and constellations. I thought that it must have been a beautiful experience to see them up close. I was there all alone in the night looking at stars, and I would picture you floating in the middle of all of them and keeping me company," he said.

I caressed his face and kissed him softly on his lips. I loved the smell of mint in his breath. I started to caress his chest softly. He looked at me with a smile. He pulled me on top of him, and we made love again.

"I wanted to have you like this every night when we were apart," he said.

"And I did too, my love. I love you, Ptah, Steward of Amun. Now, you can have me any time you want to," I said.

He turned me around and was on top of me, pressing his body against mine and biting my lips. We were eating each other's lips. His fingernails were digging into the flesh of my bottom, but I didn't feel pain, only ecstasy. He made me moan as he pressed harder against my body. The moans turned into screams. We screamed together as we reached the most delicious pinnacle of love making.

We remain entwined with each other for a while. Then he kissed my lips and forehead gently.

"I love you, Maatke-Re."

I got up to wash myself with fresh warm water and stopped. I looked at him, thinking that by leaving his scent on me I would always remember him, his smell, and his lovemaking. I wanted him to always remember that he belonged to me. I stayed there looking at him in the dark and washed myself slowly, but I noticed I was sticky. I washed myself again and again in a hurry and wondered if the smell had gone away. I dried myself quickly and walked up to him. I stood beside him and admired his naked form.

My eyes traveled over his body from head to toe and admired the body of a god that was mine. He pulled me gently to him. As I came closer, he noticed the smell on me.

"What did you do to yourself?" he asked.

I was embarrassed to tell him, but I did. He started to laugh robustly.

"You did what?" he said and continued laughing. He held me tightly against his chest. I started to laugh with him.

"Maatke-Re." He said and looking into my eyes. "In this life, no one will ever have my body again. I belong entirely to you. Not only my body," and putting my hand on his heart, "but my soul, too."

He kissed me with such force that I felt pain and tasted blood, and I brought my fingers to my lips. He had bitten my lips.

"That is for you to remember what I just told you," he said.

He got up and pulled me by the hand gently.

"Come with me, and let's do something so that we will always remember that we belong to each other."

We walked to his kilt, and he pulled out a small dagger that he always carried with him. He slashed his left wrist, and blood welled from the cut. I was shocked.

Looking at me, he asked, "Do you love me, Horus of Egypt?"

"Yes, I do."

I gave him my left wrist, and he pressed the tip of the dagger to it and slashed it[53]. I felt a sharp pain, and my wrist started to bleed. He took my bleeding wrist and pressed it on his open cut.

He said, "This seal our love forever. My blood runs in your veins, and yours runs in mine. No one will ever separate us, not even death itself. Never doubt my love for you."

---

[53] Picture of the wrist cut done by Sen-Mut on page 790.

And looking into his eyes, I said, “Not even death will keep us apart, my love.”

Then he kissed me deeply. He tore a piece of linen from my royal sheets and wrapped my wrist with it. I tore another piece from the same sheets and bandaged his wrist with it because his cut was bleeding more than mine. He held me in his arms, and we walked again to the bow of the ship. We lay down holding each other.

He was looking at the stars when he said, “In three more hours, we will be reaching Thebes.”

“Sen-Mut, beloved of mine, you have made me the happiest woman in the world tonight.”

“And you have always made me the happiest man, especially when I make love to you. You have this power over me that makes me tingle all over my body when I am near you and when I make love to you.”

“That is called love, my love,” I said.

I covered our bodies with my royal robe. We became quiet and eventually fell asleep again.

We were awakened by Sailor Neb-Ery.

“Your Majesty and Master Sen-Mut, we are getting close to Thebes. We will be there in about an hour.”

“In forty minutes, stop the ship and draw the ramp. I will walk the rest of the way to Thebes. You can go back now,” Sen-Mut told him.

Neb-Ery bowed his head to us and left.

“Beloved, I don’t want you walking,” I told him.

“It’s only a short distance, and the first rays of Ra soon will be pouring all over the land. I will enjoy the walk, remembering this wonderful night with you, and now it will be nice to see the dawn holding you in my arms. I've wanted to do this since we went to Philae. I wanted to kiss you so badly, but I couldn't. But see? I can kiss you now."

He kissed me, a loving and profound kiss, and gave me a beautiful smile, then held me tightly to his body. The first rays of Ra were starting to show. Sen-Mut and I got up, and he went to wash himself as he must. Afterward, I washed myself, and we both knelt. He chanted the morning prayers and the blessing to Amun. We got up, and I walked behind him to help him get dressed in his kilt. I tied it on his waist.

"Maatke-Re, when are you going to let your hair grow? I believe you would look beautiful with long hair," he said.

I smiled at him.

"One of these days, I will surprise you, beloved. I have never had long hair before. Did you know that?"

He shook his head. He helped me put on a sheath, and we walked holding hands to the edge of the barge. We were getting closer to the point at which he would disembark.

With a serious look, he said, "I would like for you to wear the sheath from now on, especially when Hapuseneb is around you."

"What? Are you jealous?"

"Perhaps," he said.

I smiled at him, but I did not answer. Eventually, I said, "We will talk about that tonight when you come to eat with me in the banquet hall."

"I mean it, Hat. You are my wife, and I don't like the way he looks at you when you are wearing only a kilt."

I was stunned at this sudden jealousy. I held my tongue. He pulled me close to him, holding me by my shoulders with his hands. Ra was shining on his face.

"I will tell you why tonight after the dinner," he said, and then he kissed me.

The barge stopped, and Neb-Ery pulled the ramp out onto edge of the bank.

Sen-Mut kissed me again. "I will see you later today," he said.

He walked over to the ramp, then stood there. I was still watching him when the barge started to move again. We were moving apart as the barge continued its journey. I whispered, "I love you."

He whispered back, "I love you, too," and started to walk to higher ground until we lost sight of each other.

The barge was getting close to Thebes when I noticed a figure standing at the edge of the dock. It was Hapuseneb. He was waiting for me, and I was willing to bet that he had being waiting for me all night long. The ramp was put into place, and I walked toward Hapuseneb.

"Good morning, Hapuseneb," I said.

"Good morning, Hatshepsut!"

Uh-oh. He never called me Hatshepsut unless he was angry with me.

"I have been trying to speak to you since last night. The guards did not let me come into your quarters, and a slave told me that you were indisposed. I assume that you spent all night with Sen-Mut."

I could see that he was ready to explode. He was clenching his jaw, and he was flushed as Ra was shining on his face.

"You look like you're ready to explode. Why?" I asked him.

"Where is Sen-Mut?" he asked, searching behind me.

"Did you look for him at his house?" I said.

"No," he answered.

"Why are you asking me then? Are you spying on me?" I snapped.

"I have not been spying on you. I wanted to tell you about yesterday's meeting, and as I was walking home, I saw the royal barge moving away and assumed you were with him."

He looked at my wrist and grabbed my hand. "Did you hurt yourself?"

"Yes, but it's nothing," I said.

Sen-Mut came up from behind him. I pulled my hand away from Hapuseneb quickly, but not before Sen-Mut saw me.

"Good morning, Hapuseneb." He said it with a very firm voice. Then he looked at me with piercing eyes. "Good morning, Maatke-Re."

"Good morning, Sen-Mut," I said.

"I came to talk to you about yesterday's meeting, but I can see that Hapuseneb beat me to it."

Every time Sen-Mut and Hapuseneb were both close to me, I became afraid, and it made my body tremble.

"Well, let's walk. I was not feeling well at all last night, so I left on the barge. I have returned to hear about the meeting from both of you," I said.

"If you are still not feeling well, we can come back later this afternoon, after the second meeting," Sen-Mut said.

"I agree with him," Hapu said.

"I think that would be much better," I said.

I noticed that Sen-Mut had removed the bandage from his wrist. They both walked me to my quarters, then left together. I clapped my hands, and the slaves came rushing to me.

"Take a message to the chef. Tell him to make a breakfast banquet for the audience hall this morning," I said.

I knew my beloved had not had breakfast, and I was pretty sure Hapuseneb hadn't either. He had probably been waiting for me all night long, his jealousy eating him.

I was bathed, and the slaves removed the dressing from my wrist. One of them put an ointment on the wound for the cut to heal, and I ate breakfast alone.

I was glad the day was cooler. I lay on my bed thinking of what a beautiful night Sen-Mut had given me, a night to remember, making love to me under the stars and teaching me about the constellations. My lips felt sore where he had bitten me, and I smiled. Our blood then ran together, as he said. His love was perfect. And he had better remember that he belonged to me for all eternity.

I wished Hapuseneb and Sen-Mut would get along. The tug-of-war between them scared me. I could see that they got along well when I was not around, but I could feel the tension between them when I was. And Sen-Mut wanted me to wear a sheath all the time? Well, we would talk about it tonight, though I knew what he was going to say. I laughed softly to myself.

I woke up after noon and lay there. There was a knock on the door, and I sent a slave to see who it was. She came back with a message from Khety. I opened it. He requested my presence in the audience hall.

I was quickly bathed and dressed in a kilt. I wore the Horus crown. As I walked to the audience hall, everyone fell to their faces.

"Rise!" I shouted.

I sat on the throne looking at everyone. Sen-Mut stood at my left and Hapuseneb at my right.

Khety walked close to me and stopped about seven feet away.

"Your Majesty, we all present here have been debating the succession to the throne. You are the chosen one since the beginning of this debate because, as you know, Pharaoh's child is too young to rule Thebes," Khety said.

He continued, "I pledged to your father, as have many in here, that we would support you in the succession to the throne. We are debating one detail, though. Because of the constant threat from the borders, we could make the child co-regent with you since he is not of full royal blood. Let's use his male name just for political purposes, and you solely will rule Thebes anyway. Otherwise, we will be in constant threat of war from all directions. Remember the war you and your brother fought? Well, the next one could be worse because they could come from all directions. The enemy and everyone in the whole land knows that you are a woman, and they will test your strength. They also know you are a warrior, and you are not easy to reckon with. But you don't want this beautiful city to be destroyed by invaders."

I stood up, looked at him and at Puyem-Re. Every high priest was present.

"I don't believe he is my brother's son," I shouted.

I could hear murmurs breaking out in the room.

"I will make up my mind after I consult the Oracle tonight. Send a message to the priests and the Oracle that I am coming to consult the stars," I told everyone present.

Khety conferred with Sen-Mut, Hapuseneb, Puyem-Re, and the rest of the high priests. After they spoke, he came back to me and said,

"Your Majesty, we all agree with you. Let's see what the Oracle tells us if there will be threats of war soon."

"Let's all gather tonight in the banquet hall," I said.

As I was leaving, I said, "Khety, Puyem-Re, Hapuseneb, Ineni, and Sen-Mut, follow me to my quarters. Hapuseneb, summon Generals D'Jehuty and Nehesi to my quarters."

Once the meeting was over, we all walked to the outer room of my quarters, a very large room for my privy consul with a large balcony. They gathered around me. A slave served wine to all of us.

"I don't want him to be my co-regent because I don't believe he is my brother's son."

Just then, Generals Nehesi and D'Jehuty entered and walked up to me. They both knelt.

"Your Majesty," they said.

"Rise."

"Your Majesty, even if he is not your brother's son, his name can be used for political propaganda, to ward off the enemy who are a constant threat to the land," said Sen-Mut.

"I agree with Sen-Mut on this. When I pledged to your father that I would see you reach the throne, I meant it. But for now, let's be careful and wise. Don't let anger cloud your judgment. In a few years, we can proclaim you Pharaoh," Khety said.

Nehesi picked up the argument. "Your Majesty, in the meantime we can prepare by building a larger army and reinforcing the border with more garrisons."

"I could start recruiting and training more warriors," D'Jehuty continued.

Suddenly, I started to have terrible cramps. Menina was right. Holding back the pain, I responded, "Let's open the gold mines to start recruiting more warriors and building more garrisons."

I felt another sharp cramp and became pale. I looked at Sen-Mut, and he came closer to me.

"Sen-Mut, carry me to my bed and send for Menina," I said.

Hapuseneb jumped from his seat and came up to me. Everyone was puzzled.

"The meeting is over," I said, twisting in pain. "Khety, we will see each other tonight if I feel better. Otherwise, Sen-Mut and Hapuseneb will be there for me."

Gently, Sen-Mut picked me up in his arms and carried me to my bed. Hapuseneb, Khety, and Puyem-Re followed.

"Your Majesty, since when have you being feeling like this?" Khety asked.

I didn't know what to say, so I settled for part of the truth.

"Almost a week. It's female issues. You all may go now. Hapuseneb, send for Menina," I said.

But Sen-Mut clapped his hands, and several slaves came rushing to us.

"Run and bring Menina here immediately," he said.

"Yes, Master."

I started to feel another cramp. It was horrible. I was bending over in pain, and I was sweating cold. The pain was getting worse. I looked at Sen-Mut. He was holding my hand, and I squeezed it very hard with each cramp. I saw Menina enter and hurry to my couch.

“Master Sen-Mut and Master Hapuseneb, please leave the room. I will take care of Her Majesty from here,” she said.

Sen-Mut looked straight into my eyes. He knew what was happening to me.

Hapu looked worried and started to walk away with Sen-Mut.

After they crossed through the double doors of my bedroom, Menina said, “Your Majesty, this means you were pregnant with Master Sen-Mut’s child, and the blood will come soon.”

I started to cry. I wanted our child.

“Don’t cry, Your Majesty. You will have many other children in the future, remember you must rule this land first.” She got up from the floor, opened the golden doors, and called the slaves. “Bring a lot of white linen,” she said.

After she got what she asked for, she said to the slaves, “You may leave now.”

She folded the white linen.

“Your Majesty, you must put on this right now. The blood should be coming soon.”

I did as she said, then half an hour later, after excruciating pain, I had a severe cramp that made me scream. Then I felt the blood rushing out of my body as she was sitting beside me. I was experiencing cold sweats, felt tremendous pain, and bled a lot. A series of small cramps followed. She wiped my forehead with clear water.

“Menina, how long I will stay like this?”

“Probably one or two more days,” she said.

“When can I start to take the contraceptive again?”

"You must rest your body first for a month before you can take it."

"Ahhhh. A month?"

"Yes, Your Majesty. A month," she answered me, nodding her head several times.

"Can you tell Sen-Mut everything? He is probably worried. And please don't tell Hapuseneb that I was pregnant."

"I will not, Your Majesty, but I believe he already knows."

I was puzzled.

"He's seen it with T'Queta."

"Was T'Queta pregnant?"

I was shocked.

"Yes, several times. I was called on many instances by Master Hapuseneb to terminate her pregnancies. Master Hapuseneb and T'Queta had a long relationship. The last time I was called, she cried her heart out. She wanted the child, and he almost let her have it. But he always had you on his mind. The following day he changed his mind, and I was called to bring her the bitter herbs. The same mixture that you drank. She drank it, crying, while he stood there to make sure she did. That was the last time they were together," she said.

I remembered that day. She was crying all night and for several weeks after that. I cried for her, too.

"I remember. That day, she asked me if she could be out all day with Hapuseneb, and I told her she could. How sad, how very sad. I feel bad for telling her not to get pregnant. After I gave her to Sen-Mut, did she ever get pregnant?"

"No, Your Majesty. She didn't because Master Sen-Mut made it very clear to her that he did not want children, and she knew that. He only wanted children with you, like Master Hapuseneb. During those times, I became very good friends with her, and she shared her feelings with me."

"Is she now in love with Sen-Mut?"

Menina became silent but nodded her head several times. "Yes, she is, but when Master Sen-Mut and you were apart, he seldom came to his house. He kept away by choice, but when he came back to the house and before he had sex with her, he asked her if she was taking care of herself and using contraception. Even though she told him yes and he was having sex with her, his mind was somewhere else. She knew that he was thinking of you. And when he ejaculated, he did so outside of her to be sure that she would not get pregnant. She also told me that Master Sen-Mut has never kissed her on her lips and that he leaves the moment sex is over. It was nothing like she had with Master Hapuseneb. He would kiss her, hug her, and laugh a lot with her. He was also her first sexual experience, and he made her feel wanted and loved. She was deeply in love with him," she said.

"I know that she was, and I know that he loved her, too."

"But he loves you more, Your Majesty. Your Majesty, do you know that he is not married to Tepi? He took her as his concubine. Even she knows that he is in love with you, and she has accepted that because she knows that he will never have you, now less with the return of Master Sen-Mut into your life."

"How do you know all of this?" I asked.

"We slaves communicate with every servant in the kingdom. Some of them started in the kitchen and come for my help from time to time for the bitter herbs. She also told me that they fight a lot, and Master Hapuseneb comes back very late at night, and most of the time, she knows that he was with you. That hurts her deeply. I believe he did not want to hear her nagging."

I noticed my cramps were gone and told her so.

"You must change the linen and let me help you bathe. The blood will continue, but will be less now," she said.

"I want this linen with the blood of my child to be buried."

"I will bury it for you, Your Majesty."

She bathed me. Remembering what she said about Sen-Mut and T'Queta confirmed what Sen-Mut had told me before. I loved him even more.

"I am so hungry, Menina. Stay and eat with me." I clapped my hand and the slaves came running. "

"Yes, Your Majesty?" one of them said.

"Bring food for four, my favorite fruit, and mangoes for Master Sen-Mut. Tell Master Sen-Mut and Master Hapuseneb to come in," I told them.

Both men hurried in.

"Lotus of Egypt, are you okay?" Hapu asked.

I looked at Sen-Mut and answered Hapu.

"Yes, I am fine. For the last few months, I have been having these terrible cramps, and Menina brought me an elixir to help. Sen-Mut, I would like for you and Hapuseneb to meet with Khety and Puyem-Re tonight and consult with the Oracle to see what he says about the future of my kingdom if there will be threats of war. I really don't want a co- regent. I don't trust Isis," I told them.

Then Hapuseneb said, "She has spoken with several high priests. She didn't care that I was standing near them, but they ignored her. What I know is that most of them were on your side. Your father ruled this kingdom for so many years, and all of them were his closest friends. I know that all of us pledged to be faithful to you when the time came. But I believe they are right. You should have the child as a co-regent for now. You will control the kingdom, and, in a few years, we will crown you Pharaoh, as your father wanted, and you always wanted."

I looked at Sen-Mut.

"Steward of Amun, what is your opinion on this?" I asked him.

"Khety and the high priests are right, as Hapuseneb said. Let's be sure that we will not suffer an invasion from all directions. Let's preserve your kingdom and ensure it is free of all danger."

"Hapuseneb, summon everyone, including Isis, and bring the child to the audience hall tonight. Let's get it over with. Also, send for Pen-Nekhbet, the scribe. Anyway, at least it will not be for too long." I said.

"Your Majesty, you must rest. It would not be good for you to wear yourself out," Menina said.

"I can summon everyone for the ninth hour tomorrow morning," Hapuseneb said.

"Hapuseneb, that will work perfectly. We will go to hear what the Oracle has to say about the future of Hatshepsut, and Hatshepsut will rest for the night," Sen-Mut said.

"I will leave now and start writing the summons. I will be sending them out tonight," Hapu told me.

"Then I will rest for tomorrow morning. I believe the rest will help me feel better," I told them.

"Menina, walk with me," Hapuseneb said.

Then, looking at me, he said, "If you don't need her anymore, Flower of Egypt."

She looked at me and smiled.

"Yes, she can leave now," I said.

They turned to leave, but before they left, he stopped and looked at Sen-Mut, saying, "We will meet in the Oracle's temple at midnight."

Then they turned around and left.

Sen-Mut came closer and held my hand and kissed my forehead. He said, "I am sorry that you lost our child. I promise we will have many children. I promise. About fifteen or twenty-five, and we can form a small army of little Hatshepsut's and Sen-Mut's."

We started to laugh. We finished eating, and he lifted me in his arms and lay me on the bed again. Then he clapped his hands, and two slaves came running.

"Yes, Master Sen-Mut?"

"I will bathe now."

He came back half an hour later looking fresh and clean. He lay beside me. "I am very tired right now. I will rest beside you a little bit, and then I will leave to return to the temple of the Oracle."

"I wish you didn't have to go," I said, and he smiled, pulling me closer to him, and kissed me. I rested my head on his chest, and we fell asleep.

I was awakened by the voice of a slave.

"Master Sen-Mut, in one hour, it will be time for you to go."

I looked for him and saw that he was already dressed. He smiled at me.

"You look beautiful sleeping like a little girl," he said.

I smiled.

"I must leave now. I will come for you in the morning to go to the audience hall. Rest now. These are going to be long hours for me and the rest of the priests and for the Oracle tonight," he said.

He came closer and kissed me. Then he left in the dark.

I was awakened early in the morning by Menina.

"Your Majesty, I came very early this morning to bring you these potions of herbs that will help you clean your insides. Also, I wanted to tell you that Master Hapuseneb asked me if you were pregnant last night, and I told him no. I told him that for the last few months when your blood comes, it comes with terrible cramps, and I bring you soothing herbs to lessen the pain. Then he said that he trusted me, that he trusted that I was telling him the truth. He will probably find out that I was lying to him last night and that you were pregnant when they were in front of the Oracle," she said.

"I knew that he was going to ask you about it. Thank you, Menina. I know that all of them know how to read the stars. But no one can change that I am in love with Sen-Mut. Help me bathe and get ready. Master Sen-Mut and Hapuseneb should be walking through those golden doors any time now."

"Yes, Your Majesty. What you will be wearing today?"

"The kilt and the Horus pectoral and the golden sandals. I will wear the red crown of Lower Egypt. He will not have Thebes, and I will not make him co-regent of the whole land."

A slave came running to me and said, "Your Majesty, Master Sen-Mut is walking up the stairs."

"Everyone goes now. We will speak later Menina. Come tonight," I told her.

"I will, Your Majesty."

She left as Sen-Mut walked into my bedroom. I looked at him with a smile.

"Beloved, you look so tired," I said.

"Yes, I am. I can hardly keep my eyes open."

"Beloved, come and lie beside me and sleep. I am Horus, and they can wait all day if I want."

I clapped my hands several times, and seven slaves came and knelt.

"One of you, go to Master Hapuseneb and tell him that I am postponing the audience until tomorrow at the nine hours of the morning. Tell him to send messages to everyone, including Isis. Run to First Prophet of Amun and tell him the same. Another, go to Puyem-Re. Leave now."

They rushed out the doors.

"Beloved, let the slave bathe you," I said.

"Hat, how are you feeling this morning? I was very much worried about you."

"I know that you were, beloved of mine. I am much better now. Now, tell me what the Oracle said."

"They searched the water of the sacred pond and read the stars. Khety was right. They are getting ready to invade. They believe that part of this land belongs to them and that since you are a woman, you will not be able to withstand a strong battle."

"Beloved, how do they know that the eagle in the nest has gone to the underworld?" [54]I asked.

---

[54] The eagle on the nest referred to my brother gone to the underworld.

"They must have spies, as we do in their land."

"Tell Nehesi and D'Jehuty to follow them after the announcement that there is a co-regent. So, let them take the news to Hyksos. When they return here, kill them all." I said.

"I will give the order. It's also foretold by the Oracle that you will be Pharaoh like you always wanted and as your father wished. You will be the first female Pharaoh to rule Egypt, and things will happen as you wish. I can tell you that my dear friend Khety was not feeling well last night and did not remain with us until the end. He only stayed until they announced that there will be peace. Then after he left, the Oracle announced his death and announced that before he dies, he will make sure that everyone has pledged to be faithful to you and that you will have everyone's support for your ascension to the throne." Sen-Mut said as his eyes were closing.

"Beloved, come let me bathe you very quickly, and you can sleep beside me. You've hardly had any sleep since the day before yesterday. Are you hungry?"

"Yes."

I walked with him to be bathed. I bathed him as quickly as I could, and I sent for food. By the time he was patted dry, the food was waiting for him on my bed. He ate a few bites and fell asleep. I ordered the food to be taken away. The linen curtains were closed around us so that the light would not bother him. I kissed his forehead, and he squeezed my hand. I embraced him from behind and fell asleep beside him.

At some point in the night, I woke up, and he was standing on the balcony looking at the current of Hopi. I came from behind him and put my arms around his waist, hugging him tightly against my body. He turned around and, with a smile, kissed my lips.

"How long before I can have you again?" he asked me.

I looked at him.

"One month," I said.

"What? A whole month?" he asked.

"That was exactly what I said to Menina when she told me yesterday."

"What am I going to do with this? See how aroused I am?" he said.

I started to laugh.

"Beloved, we are going to have to wait. We don't have any choice," I said.

"I think I am going back home and complete this punishment far away from you because I know that I will not have control of myself if I am near you."

"Back to T'Queta's arms?" I asked.

"Jealous, my love?" he. said.

"No, but who else is going to satisfy your desires?" I said.

"Only you. I told you that before, that your blood is running in my veins, and I told you that there will never be another woman who will have my body but you. Didn't I say that to you yesterday? And now that we are talking, what are you going to wear to the audience hall? A kilt? I think that would be okay for today, but in the future, wear the sheath, especially when Hapuseneb is around you."

"Beloved, tell me why you don't you want me wearing the kilt," I said, but I knew why.

"Because your breasts are very well formed, and you have a goddess's body. I see the way he always looks at you. I don't want him making love to his wife or any other woman of the harem thinking that you are under him."

I started to laugh because I knew he was going to say that.

"So, you are a jealous man?"

"Yes, only with you. I know he is not the only one who is looking at you. Even my brother Senemen believes that you are beautiful, and I had to stop him from looking. I became very angry and told him that from that day on, he was not to look at you."

I took a deep breath. "I will do as you ask, beloved."

By this time the rays of Ra were showing, and we said our prayers together.

"We must eat and get dressed for the ceremony. I will wear the red crown of Lower Egypt today. I am not going to let him look like a Pharaoh in control of the whole land. Isis will know that she will never have Thebes. I am Horus, and Thebes belongs to me and will always be mine. I will take Lower Egypt back when I am Pharaoh."

"Maatke-Re, I totally agree with you on this. I will always support you in everything, and I will always be by your side," he said.

We ate and got dressed. I wore a kilt and the golden pectoral with the Eye of Horus. There was a knock on the door.

"Enter," I said.

The golden doors were opened, and there was Hapuseneb wearing the ceremonial, priestly, long white robe with golden designs on the edge. He looked gorgeous. My two most beloved men. The one whom I loved and was in love with, and the one who loved me. I saw the look on Hapuseneb's face when he saw Sen-Mut.

Looking at me, he said, "Good morning, Flower of Egypt."

Looking at Sen-Mut, he said, "Good morning, Sen-Mut. You came early?"

"No, I did not come early. I slept here."

Hapuseneb's face flushed. He clenched his jaw and grit his teeth.

"The Deshret[55]!" I shouted. I needed to diffuse the tension between them.

Hapuseneb gave me a serious look.

"The red crown? Why the red crown?" he asked.

"Remember my father crowned me in Heliopolis and in Memphis with the Pschent, the Double Crown of Lower and Upper Egypt? When Pharaoh died, I became Horus again. It is my right to wear it, and I am not going to wear both crowns to give this child the right to control both lands one day and to allow his mother to believe that she has won."

"But you cannot wear both crowns yet either. You are not Pharaoh yet. That will come later. Soon, but later," Hapuseneb said.

"This is not a marriage ceremony, Hapuseneb. And it never will be. If I wear the Horus crown, it's the same as wearing the Pschent, and I am not going to do that. Sen-Mut, send for Nehesi and D'Jehuty and tell them that I want the army to be present at the audience hall. I don't want any surprises from the priests, so I want them to feel the presence of the military. Then they'll know who is in control of the entire army and the land. Sen-Mut, I'll see you in the audience hall," I told him, and he left.

"Sen-Mut, wait!" Hapu shouted. Then he turned around to face me. "Hatshepsut, if you bring the army to encircle the audience hall, the priests will believe that you are threatening them."

---

[55] The red crown of Lower Egypt.

"Isn't this the way it is done? Sometimes we must take measures that show them who is ruler of the land and who is not," I told him.

"Please, give me one more hour. I will talk to all of them about the red crown. I will come back with an answer, and if they say no, then do what you must do."

I looked at Sen-Mut, who nodded.

"Alright. And tell them that this is not a marriage ceremony. Then you must send word to Sen-Mut. He will be waiting for your answer with D'Jehuty, Nehesi, and the army."

They left. I became impatient, but I was firm about the decision I had made.

"Wine!" I shouted.

The next hour was the longest one ever. I drank so many goblets of wine that I became tipsy while waiting. Then the golden doors swung open.

Hapuseneb had a smile on his face.

"Lotus of Egypt, they all agreed with you. Some of them were in the audience hall on the day of your coronation by your father, and they saw when your father placed the Pschent above your head. They also agreed with your decision to wear the red crown of Lower Egypt. Khety said that you have the wisdom that you acquired when you were younger."

"Were all of them in favor?"

"Only Puyem-Re was silent, and he will not go against it."

"Of course. I believe he is the father of the child."

I knelt on one knee, and Hapuseneb placed the red crown of Lower Egypt on my head. He helped me up from the floor, and we walked down the stairs to the audience hall.

When I entered the audience hall, the child who was holding Khety's hand let go, ran to me, and hugged my legs. I knelt and kissed him. I grabbed hold of his hand, and we walked together to the throne, then stood there together with our hands clasped.

I could see the look on Isis's face when she saw the red crown on my head. She lowered her face.

Khety started the ceremony, and he declared Menkhep-Re, co-regent of Lower Egypt, obliged to defend the borders of Thebes when he came of age, and to do so beside the Horus of Egypt. I knelt, and Khety removed the Deshret from my head and placed it above Menkhep-Re head for few minutes, while chanting a prayer to the gods. When he was done, everyone applauded, and Khety returned the red crown to my head again.

I knelt and kissed the child again, and he hugged me. In that moment, my heart moved. I was moved by his expression of love for me.

Khety took the child's hand and walked down the steps to Isis and gave her the child.

"Scribe, as of today the child Menkhep-Re becomes co-regent of Lower Egypt. So, let it be written, and let it be done. This edict must reach the whole land, not later than today," Khety said.

Isis's face was without expression, and she walked with the child, holding his hand.

"Sen-Mut. Hapuseneb," I called. They both came up to me. "Both of you make sure that the scribe wrote everything as I said it."

"We will," said Hapuseneb.

"Maatke-Re, what is wrong?" asked Sen-Mut.

"I wonder if I am being unfair to the child. I wish I could find out if he is really my brother's son, and I wish I didn't hate this woman so much."

"You still can change your mind later and marry him to make him full royal blood," Hapuseneb said.

"No, that will never happen. I will be Pharaoh because it is my birthright. And I have other plans."

Hapuseneb was startled. "What plans?" he asked.

"To rule on my own, with you and Sen-Mut beside me, along with the rest of my trusted ones. Let's make Egypt the most powerful country in the world, and, from now on, Thebes should be the most beautiful city of all. And there will be peace all over my land. Bring the child to my rose garden tomorrow afternoon. I want to look at him again, and I hope I am not wrong or misjudging Isis."

The next day, I was sitting in my rose garden waiting for Sen-Mut and Hapuseneb to bring the child. They seemed to like him, too. His face lit up when he saw me. He ran to me, and I hugged him.

I looked at Sen-Mut and Hapuseneb and said, "Leave me with the child."

I picked him up, sat him on my lap, and kissed his cheeks. I started to teach him words for fruit. He tried to say them, but he couldn't. I gave him fruit juice, and he liked it. I had ordered a wooden ball to be made for him, and we played together.

I was falling in love with the child. I knew I would never harm him nor leave him without a mother. Why was he so dark? He had the same skin tone as Puyem-Re. Could it be my father's color? My mother was pale, while my father was dark, but not as dark as Nehesi, who was from Nubia. I was born golden tan, and Mutnofret was pale-skinned like my brother. Only time would tell when he grew up. Then we would see who he looked like. I continued lying on the grass with him.

"Guard!" I called.

"Yes, Your Majesty?"

“Take the child to his mother and tell her that Sen-Mut and Hapuseneb will be picking him up tomorrow morning and to send Hatshepset with them, too.”

“Yes, Your Majesty.”

I kissed his cheek, and he left walking like a big boy who did not need to hold hands.

****

The seventy days of embalming for my brother Thutmoses II was complete. We had prepared for the burial ceremony that would begin early in the morning the next day.

I walked with Hatshepset and Menkhep-Re, holding their hands, into the tomb built for him by Ineni. I held Menkhep-Re in my arms, and together we held the adze for the ceremony of the opening of the mouth, ears, and eyes of my brother for him to be able to eat, hear, and see in the next world. The child was very strong. He did not cry when the High Priest, wearing the mask of Anubis, walked in, as the other priests chanted the potent spells.

I cried and touched his coffin.

“Farewell, beloved brother. We will see each other in the after-life.”

The women started to wail, and Isis was one of them.

It was a very long day for all of us. We returned to Thebes. I was holding the child on my lap all the way to Thebes, and beside me was Hatshepset on Sen-Mut’s lap. On my right was Hapuseneb. Three large barges were used to transport everyone to the Valley of the Dead and back. It was very late in the evening when we returned.

Sen-Mut and I bathed in silence.

He knew that I was hurting badly, that I really missed my brother. He was the last of my family left.

****

Almost three years had passed since my brother's death and the threats to my borders had stopped. The garrisons were in place in Upper and Lower Egypt. We had formed a mighty army, bigger than that of my father. I continued training with my soldiers. I was learning a new defense: how to pull a dagger quickly and switch it from hand to hand and kick the knees of my opponent, then jump on top of him and stab him in the chest with the dagger. I wore a shorter sheath, split at both sides of my thighs, so that I could ride my horse and train with my soldiers. I did it as a concession to Sen-Mut.

The left side of my back still bothered me where the tip of the arrow went through my golden armor. I could not lie on my back to sleep. Sometimes I wondered if a piece was still lodged inside my back. When I spoke to the doctor, he said that on that day he had removed all the small pieces of the arrow. As he said, the gods were with me on that day because the arrow's tip was not poisoned.

Sitting on my balcony, I was waiting for Sen-Mut to come back from the Valley of the Dead. Sometimes he remained there for a week or two and waiting for him drove me crazy. It always seemed so long. I could go and see him, but he preferred for me to wait until part of my temple was finished.

I loved to sit there on my balcony and see Ra fade away slowly with all its beautiful colors. That day had been very windy. Shomu was showing himself, and it was clear that it was going to be another hot summer.[56]

I had received a missive from Sen-Mut early in the morning, promising that he would be returning that day. He indicated that he had very good news, and I wondered what it was. He was planning to tell me in the presence of Khety and Hapuseneb.

"My love!"

It was the voice of my beloved calling me. I got up from my chair and ran to his arms. He hugged me and kissed me forcefully. I could feel the heat in his loins, and he was making me hot with his kisses.

He was dirty from head to toe from the desert sand. It was all over his face and body.

"Now do you see why I don't want you to come to visit me? You would get as dirty as I am right now. The wind has been blowing sand all day long today, and my head and hair is full of it, so much sand that it feels very heavy on my head. I am going to shave all of my hair tonight," he said.

"No, I don't want you to do that! I love your tiny little curls on your head," I told him.

Holding my shoulders with his hands, he said, "Maatke-Re, Shomu is here. The summers are hard on me and on my men, and on the slaves as well. You can't imagine how my head feels right now. It's so heavy with all this sand on it that it feels as if it weighs a ton. I believe we are going to have several very bad sandstorms this summer. I can feel it in my bones, and I don't want you riding your horse far away from the palace.

---

[56] And it is still the same Sunset after 3,500 years, showing the beauty of God.

I don't want you to be caught up in the middle of one. Promise me!" he said.

I lowered my face, but he raised it with his hands.

"Can you understand that?" he asked.

"Yes, I can, and I promise, I will not ride my horse far from the palace. But about you shaving your hair? Well, maybe I can't understand that because I've never had long hair before, but if you must, you must."

He lifted me in his arms and said, "Now, we must bathe together."

We laughed. I did not call for my slaves. I wanted his body as much he wanted mine. He was aroused. I bathed him, and when I was trying to wash his hair, I found that I could not. There was too much sand in it. I called for my slave and ordered his hair shaved off completely. I had never seen so much sand in someone's hair before.

They returned with a stool for him to sit on. After he sat, he said, "I want you to shave off my hair." They cut and shaved off all his hair. He looked strange to me. I had never seen him bald before.

"Give him a massage with his favorite oils," I ordered. They spread the thick white linen at the edge of the bathing pool as he walked to be massaged. I told the other two slaves to bring the food for Master Sen-Mut to my quarters and leave it there.

When he was finished with the massage, he looked both relaxed and clean. Then he clapped his hands, and the slaves were gone. He walked me out of the pool and looked deeply into my eyes.

"I will not disappoint you tonight," he said.

He wrapped his arms around me and kissed me. He became aroused all over again, and I loved it. I had been waiting for him and for this moment since he left, and it seemed like forever.

He lifted me in his arms.

"Light as a feather," he said.

He took me to our bed and laid me on it. He turned me around, and I was on my stomach. He started to kiss the right side of my neck. It felt mmm…, it felt wonderful. He was slowly kissing my back. His smell was wonderful and, accompanied with his kisses, was making me hot. I could feel that he was aroused all over again. He turned me over and kissed my lips with passionate love. We were entangled in delicious ecstasy, ecstasy that only we could give to each other. He made love to me very tenderly.

How much I loved him. After our love making, we lay there, holding each other.

"Are you hungry, beloved?" I asked.

"Yes, very much."

"Why didn't you say something? We could have eaten before we began."

"How could I eat when the only thing on my mind for a whole week was making love to you. I was so aroused as I was crossing the Nile, thinking of you on the barge. I wondered if Neb-Ery had noticed how aroused I was. I was going to bathe over there, but I preferred your hands bathing me and touching every part of my body." He was smiling as he was telling me all this. "But the wind was blowing so hard, I would not have reached Thebes clean, and I prefer the touch of your hands bathing me."

I had ordered his favorite meal of duck with molasses and his favorite juice, mango. I also ordered cakes made of dates. It was our favorite. We sat down at the table and started to eat, very happy to be together.

"Are you very tired?" I asked.

"Not really. I hardly did any work today. The wind would not let us continue with the project."

"When are you going back?"

"In a few days, after the wind stops blowing. Senemen is there, and he knows what to do, but I would prefer to be the one who directs the construction of your temple. I want to set the foundation firm and strong so that it will last forever, even after we are gone to the underworld. I want for everyone when they see your temple to know that I built it for all eternity and with all my love for you."

I caressed his face and kissed his lips.

"Thank you, my beloved one, but I want for you to stay with me at least for one week. Can you?" I asked.

"I would love to. But remember, if I remain here, the building will slow down, and it will take more time for the construction to be completed. I can hardly wait to see it once it starts taking shape. It's going to be the most impressive temple in the whole world," he said.

"Then I must come to visit you and stay with you for a week. I also want you to build your tomb right next to mine. I want yours to connect with mine. I want you to build a large room made of solid gold and silver. The walls must be made of solid gold and the floors of silver. Have Tuthy send for the gold. Get it directly from my mines so that we can worship Amun-Ra together in there in the afterlife. I will leave it up to you to make my sarcophagus the way you want. I will order a nice sarcophagus for you, too. I want you to take, little by little, of my belongings, including my jewelry, and start putting it away as the construction progresses. I don't want any tomb robbers stealing all that belongs to me, and I don't want anyone ever to find my treasures."

"I will do as you wish. You're very smart to think ahead," he said.

“Beloved, in your missive you said that you have a surprise for me?” I asked.

“Yes, but you must wait until tomorrow morning. I received a message from Khety and Hapuseneb. I summoned Nehesi, D’Jehuty, your uncle Thutmoses, and all the high priests and dignitaries for tomorrow at the ninth hour of the morning to the audience hall. I want for you to wear the kilt and the Horus crown tomorrow morning.”

“Beloved, what is it? Why? I’m confused,” I said.

“Hapuseneb will be here early in the morning to put the Horus crown on your head, and he probably knows that I am here by now. He doesn’t miss one thing with his spies everywhere, and I don’t know when he is going to give up on you. Sometimes, he makes me very angry. I think that one of these days I am going to have it out with him, and I am afraid that I will lose control of myself.”

I covered his lips with my fingers. “Shh, my love. You know that he is very protective of me. Remember, we have known each other since I was five summers. Bear with him, please. Just make the best of it when you are around him. He knows that I am in love with you and that I have loved you since the first day I saw you in the audience hall, and that makes him jealous of you,” I said and smiled.

Sen-Mut looked at me with a very serious expression.

“But sometimes the way you look at him gives me the impression that you are also in love with him,” he said.

I was shocked by what I was hearing from his lips. How do I defuse his thought? How do I respond to this to him? We were interrupted by a knock on the door. I was saved, and I took a breath. I was going to answer the door, and he grabbed my wrist and squeezed it hard.

“Answer me first,” he said, looking at me intensely with his piercing brown eyes.

"You are the only person whom I have ever been in love with." I made this declaration to him, looking straight into his eyes, willing him to believe me, and he realized that I was telling the truth. I caressed his face and kissed him. We stood up and put on our robes.

"Enter," I shouted.

It was Hapuseneb, who looked to be in a cheerful mood. I was relived. I didn't have to deal with another confrontation between them.

"Sen-Mut, you look different. Oh, I can see you have shaved your head before coming from the Valley of the Dead," Hapu said.

"No, my slaves just shaved his head as he was being bathed," I said. His look was piercing, and he give me an angry look.

"Very well, we were going to surprise you tomorrow. The decisions were made by the High Priest Khety and he is going…"

"Hapuseneb!" Sen-Mut cut him off. "Come early tomorrow morning to place the Horus crown on her head. I have kept everything from her, and we should keep it that way until tomorrow morning."

Sen-Mut continued, "Maatke-Re, I will be going to my house after he leaves. It's better this way, until everything comes about as it is supposed to. I don't want to spoil anything for you."

I did not believe what I was hearing from his mouth. Was he going to leave and not sleep with me tonight?

"And I agree with him," Hapu said. He was putting more wood into the fire.

"Should, we leave now?" he asked Sen-Mut.

"No, I will stay here for a while before I go," he told him.

Hapu looked at me. I looked at Hapu, and then I noticed Sen-Mut was looking at both of us as Hapu and I crossed looks. The look on his face was as if he wanted to know if I really did not feel anything for Hapu.

"Flower of Egypt, I will see you very early in the morning then," Hapu said and bowed his head.

"Good night," I said. Then he left.

I turned around fast and faced Sen-Mut.

"Sen-Mut, don't do this to me, not tonight. Please do not leave. We have not slept together for a whole week," I said.

He was standing there looking at me very seriously.

"Maatke-Re, I must, or I will explode right now," he said.

"Sen-Mut, I am not talking to you as your wife. Now, I am talking to you as Horus. I am ordering you to remain in here," I said.

He kept staring at me. I didn't know what I had done wrong or why he was angry with me, but clearly, he was.

"What is it? What did I do wrong? Why is he mad at me?" I thought.

"It will only be for tonight, my love, only for tonight. I need to cool off. I will be here at the first hours tomorrow morning."

He got dressed and walked off.

I started to cry. He had left me standing there, and left without kissing me? We had never had a fight before. Why had he done that? Tears were running down my face. I walked to the balcony and saw that the night was completely clear and full of stars. Then I saw him walking beside Hopi. He stopped and looked up at me.

I turned around and walked off the balcony with my heart broken, leaving him behind. I lay in my bed with tears in my eyes. He had been telling me every day and night that he loved me. But if he loved me, why was he hurting me? My heart was very depressed, and I fell asleep crying.

I was awakened by a kiss on my lips. He was there beside me, kneeling on the floor looking at me. "Sen-Mut!" I hugged him tightly, and he held me very close to his chest.

"I am sorry that I left without kissing you, but I needed to put my thoughts together. I realize that it's not your fault that he has been in love with you for such of long time, and I must live with it. I brought you a gift that I sent to be made a while ago. I was going to give it to you tomorrow, but this night calls for it. I was rude to you tonight, and I am completely sorry. I was feeling hurt in my heart when I saw you standing on the balcony looking at me, then turning your back on me and walking inside the room, leaving me there all alone with a feeling of emptiness. And you did make me feel alone, which has never happened before, not even when we were keep apart. Then I thought that too much hurt has been dealt to both of us, and that after all that we have been through, I realized how stupid I was. I love you, Hatshepsut, with my whole heart. I promise that it will never happen again."

I replied, "How can I breathe without your breath, beloved one. Yes, you did hurt me tonight, and I could not figure out why. I love you so much," I told him.

He came closer and covered my lips with his lips and held me so close, I could feel his heart beating with mine, as one. Then he got up from the bed and came back with an oil lamp in one hand and a box in the other. He sat beside me.

"Open the box," he said.

It was a small, black inlaid box. I opened it and pulled out a necklace. It was made of many colorful mummy bits, and it was beautiful.

Then, I pulled out a bracelet made of the same bits and of the same colors as the necklace.

I was about to close the box. "Keep looking," he said.

I touched the inside of the box. There was a gold ring with different colored stones, the same colors as the necklace and the bracelet.

"How beautiful and lovely," I said.

I pulled him by the neck, and he fell on his back on the mattress. I sat on top of him, came close to his face, and whispered in his ear, "My love, they are beautiful, and you have made me happy again." I kissed him many times. He turned me around, and then he was on top of me.

"The women who has the world in her hands and all the gold mines is hard to give a gift to. I wanted to give you something that no one ever had, something different."

I looked at him in the dim light of the oil lamp that was shining on his face. He was smiling. He kissed me with such tenderness and love, and I responded with the same love. He made me his again and again until we fell asleep.

I was awakened by the rooster's crow. When I turned around to see Sen-Mut, he was gone. I got up, ran, and called the slaves.

"Have any of you seen Master Sen-Mut this morning?"

"I did, Your Majesty. I saw him leaving the grounds of the palace when it was still very dark."

I thought that he probably went to change his kilt. I stayed in bed until the first rays of Ra began to bathe the land. It was still three hours away until time to go to the audience hall. I wondered if the surprise he talked about was what I was thinking it was. Would I be Pharaoh?

I ran to be bathed and wore the white kilt, embroidered with gold thread. Ra was bright, and I picked up the box with Sen-Mut's gift and looked at it again. The sun was shining on it. It was beautiful. I had never seen anything like it. He was so very thoughtful. I put the necklace and bracelet on, but no earrings.

I was looking at myself in the golden mirror when Hapuseneb walked in. I noticed he was looking for Sen-Mut.

"Did Sen-Mut sleep here last night with you?" he asked.

"Why are you asking? When you already know the answer."

Hapu started to laugh. "No, I don't know the answer."

I looked at him. Of course, he knew that he did.

"Then I am going to leave you wondering," I said and started to laugh, and he did, too. I knelt, and he placed the Horus crown on my head. He was holding my hand as I was rising from the floor when Sen-Mut walked in. I smiled at him, and he smiled back.

He looked very handsome, but strange, without hair on his head. He was wearing his priestly long white robe with his white kilt underneath. The robe had designs of the constellations embroidered in gold thread from his left shoulder down to his leather sandals. Hapuseneb was also wearing a white robe embroidered in gold designs. We left and descended the stairs.

I was surprised to see many priests had gathered on the palace grounds. This must be it. I was going to be Pharaoh. I was nervous and full of emotions, happy that I had beside me the two most important men in my life, walking with me to the audience hall. We walked through the double doors of the audience hall, and I saw that it was full of priests. Every one of them was there, including the very old ones whom I had known since I was a child. They all wore the priestly white robe and the long kilt. I walked to the throne and sat. Sen-Mut was at my left and Hapuseneb at my right.

Sen-Mut and Hapuseneb walked down the steps to the place where the priests had gathered. They had formed two lines in front of me. Everyone had taken their place. Then I saw Isis standing there with her eyes cast down, holding Menkhep-Re's little hand, and with Hatshepset, my precious daughter.

Khety came forward.

"Your Majesty," he said, smiling and bowing his head to me.

"It's been three summers since the Pharaoh went to the heavens. After consulting the Oracle and the stars many times during these three summers, they have confirmed that you are the chosen one. You were chosen by all of the gods to hold the Double Crown of Egypt and rule the lands of Upper and Lower Egypt, for you are divine and the true daughter of Amun-Ra," he proclaimed.

I was so happy to hear it from his own lips. Finally, it was confirmed that I would be Pharaoh of Egypt. There was an explosion of applause.

I searched for Sen-Mut and found him in the left line, almost at the end of the line, followed by another younger priest. He mouthed to me, "I love you," and I mouthed back, "Me too." Hapuseneb was in the right line a few steps ahead of Sen-Mut. He was very happy, too, and I smiled at him. I whispered, "Thank you." Both were very happy for me. They both worked so hard for this moment for me.

Khety was happy, too, as he announced it. I could see Ineni clapping his hands in the air, and my uncle Thutmoses the youngest brother of my father also applauded with the audience.

Khety continued, "The Pschent Crown of Upper and Lower Egypt will be placed on your head, Your Majesty, and the coronation will take place in the new year, as every coronation before." He bowed his head and smiled. And in a low voice he said, "As your father always wanted." I smiled back.

Finally, I would be Pharaoh of Khemet[57] And from that point forward, not only men would hold the Double Crown of Egypt, I thought.

I stood up from the throne and looked at everyone, smiling. I was very grateful to all of them. Hatshepset and Menkhep-Re were clapping their little hands. It was cute to see them both doing it as everyone else was. To them, it was fun, and they were looking at everyone.

"I thank you, First Prophet of Amun, and I also thank every priest, priestess, and the Oracle. A special thanks to my most beloved men, Sen-Mut, Ptah, Steward of Amun, and Hapuseneb, Priest and Vizier of the South. During the past three summers, you have consulted the Oracle and the stars many times, and the gods have confirmed that I am the chosen one, that I am the true daughter of Amun-Ra. As the Great Maat, my father, had told me since I was a small child. The right decision has been made. I can promise you that I will rule my land in peace with my neighbors. There will be no more war. You can live your days in peace and prosperity. We all love this land very much," I said, and applause followed my speech.

"Steward of Amun and Vizier of the South!" I shouted. I looked at Sen-Mut and could tell that he wanted to rush to me and kiss me. That was also my heart's desire. Hapuseneb was walking toward me, and I smiled at him. They both stood beside me in their places once the announcement was over. The children ran to me, and I hugged them and kissed them both.

Then I looked over, and I saw Isis talking to Puyem-Re. I ignored them. No one was going to spoil my happiness today. I kept my attention on the children.

---

[57] 3,500 years ago, Egypt was known as Khemet.

"Horus of Egypt," Sen-Mut called to me.

I turned around and faced him, and he whispered in my ear, "My heart is filled with happiness for you. I wanted you to hear it directly from the lips of the first Prophet of Amun this morning. I love you."

"Beloved, I love you, too. I know that you and Hapuseneb have worked very hard for these past three years to help me to reach the throne of Egypt. Without you, I would not be the future Pharaoh, and I thank you with all my heart."

"I have a surprise for you," he said, smiling.

"Yes?"

"I will bathe you tonight, Goddess of Thebes."

"Will you?" I said, laughing. Then I whispered in his ear, "Are your hands going to travel slowly all over my body?"

He threw his head back and laughed so hard.[58]

Then Khety, Ineni, my uncle Thutmoses, Hapuseneb, and many other priests approached to congratulate me.

Sen-Mut shouted, "Everyone is invited to the celebration of the announcement of Horus becoming Pharaoh of Egypt in the banquet hall."

We all started to walk to the banquet hall.

"Beloved, please have Khety come to my quarters first. I must speak with him alone, and I must thank him privately. Also, I want the older priests, friends of my father, to be brought to my quarters. Give the order for the litter-bearers to carry them to the palace and up the stairs," I said.

---

[58] I can still hear his laugh.

Sen-Mut gave the order, and we waited for the litter to be brought for them.

I was sitting and waiting in the outer quarters when the golden doors were opened. Khety walked in, looking tired. I should have ordered a litter for him, too. How could I have forgotten that?

"Have a seat, First Prophet of Amun," I said, and he sat right in front of me.

"Khety, I personally want to thank you for all of the work you have done for me in these past three years, working very hard on the promise you made to my father, that I would reach the throne of Egypt." I stood and walked up to him. I took his right hand and kissed it. He seemed surprised. "This kiss is for being a faithful friend to my father and to me all of your life, and for all the years of service to the highest, Amun-Ra. Is there anything which your heart desires and I can please you with?" I asked.

"The only request that I have is that you will rule the land with fairness, as your father did. Love your people so that when I am gone to the underworld, my Ka will be at peace that I have made the right decision. In my heart, I know I did, as the Oracle said that you are the true daughter of Amun. Don't stain your soul. Keep it pure that you may reach the heavens and be with the gods."

"Be at ease, Khety. I will rule my kingdom with fairness, and I will watch over my Ka. I have another request for you. I need your full support for the future. For when the time comes, I want Hapuseneb to be chosen First Prophet of Amun. I will need the support of the elder priests without any objections."

He lowered his eyes and thought about it.

"Your Majesty, in line for my place is Puyem-Re, Second Prophet of Amun. I know how you feel about him, but you know the line of succession. Still, I will consult the stars, and I will get back to you on this petition," he said.

"Very well, Khety. I will wait for your answer. I want you to enjoy the banquet that Sen-Mut has prepared for me. Wasn't it a lovely thought?" I smiled remembering what Sen-Mut had whispered in my ear.

I clapped my hands twice, and the slaves came running. "Let all the elder priests in," I told them.

My beloved walked in with a big smile, helping some of the very old ones. Also entering were Hapuseneb and Puyem-Re. There were about sixty elder priests present in my quarters. Some of them had survived my father. I kissed the hand of every one of them and told them that I was very grateful for their support and friendship to my father and me. I said that if there was anything that I could do for them to please make the request to Hapuseneb and Sen-Mut, who I would be sending to their rooms, so they could write their petitions.

Sen-Mut and Hapuseneb sent for litter-bearers to take Khety and the rest of the priests to the banquet hall. We spoke in harmony, and I was pleased with all of them. They made me very happy. The litter-bearers carried them in their arms until they reached the last step. Then they placed them in the litters, and we all walked across the inner gardens to the banquet hall.

My beloved was at my left and Hapuseneb at my right. The last rays of Ra were showing signs that they would soon fade away.

Hapu said, "Lotus of Egypt, kissing their hands was a remarkable gesture. I never thought you would show them how grateful you really are to all of them." He smiled.

Sen-Mut was lost in thought, listening to Hapuseneb's words. I stopped walking and looked at the tall pillars of the banquet hall. The hall was beautiful, decorated with yellow and white flowers. I had never seen it decorated with yellow flowers before that night. And I was full of joy.

"All for you, my love. The yellow flowers are my favorite color, and I wanted to make this day bright and beautiful for you," he said.

I whispered in his ear, "Sen-Mut, my beloved one, it's beautiful, and you have made me very happy today. Everything looks lovely, and I am looking forward to being bathed by your hands tonight."

I lowered my face and smiled. And he smiled, too.

I could see that Tepi was looking at Hapuseneb as he was looking at me. We continued walking until we reached the banquet hall. The beauty of all the yellow flowers made my heart very happy. I wanted to turn around and kiss Sen-Mut lips, but I had to hold back. Sen-Mut and I strolled beside the buffet. The table included yellow roses. We didn't have yellow roses in Thebes, and there were so many of them. I only had the pink ones from my gardens and the red and white ones from my mother's large gardens, the ones that we brought from Crete when I was five summers.

I turned around and looked at Sen-Mut's eyes.

"Thank you, my love. Everything is lovely, and I am dying to kiss your lips. Can you follow me to the outer gardens?" I said.

I turned to the hall and shouted, "Everyone, let's eat, and let the music start!"

Sen-Mut and I strolled to the outer gardens. We turned to face each other, and he gently held my left hand and kissed it. I gently caressed his face, and I kissed him. He returned it with passion. I had my eyes closed, lost in ecstasy.

Slowly, he released me. "We must stop, or I will not stop, my love."

I smiled at him.

“Yes, let’s enjoy the dinner and leave as soon as we can. I want to feel your hands travel all over my naked body as you bathe me tonight,” I said and smiled.

He laughed.

“And me too,” he said. Then we went back to the banquet hall.

That night, we all ate in harmony. All the priests were happy and raising their golden goblets to me every time I looked at them.

Hapuseneb did not say too much that night. He was lost in thought.

“Hapu, I want to thank you with all of my heart for being with Sen-Mut in this fight for me. I know that you both fought hard for me to be chosen for the throne of Egypt. I will reward you well, my dearest friend,” I said and smiled at him.

He replied, “I did it for love, Lotus of Egypt. Like he did.”

I lowered my eyes, saddened by his words. I wished I could spare his pain.

Sen-Mut was talking to Ineni, Khety, and Puyem-Re. I whispered to him, “My love, we must leave now.” I smiled. Then, I stood up, and everyone dropped to the floor except the older priests. I looked at Hapuseneb; he was also in the floor. Sen-Mut and I passed behind him.

I stopped at the entrance to the banquet hall and said, “Rise. You may continue with the celebration.”

Sen-Mut and I turned around and strolled through the gardens holding hands. The night was full of stars. As we walked and reached the bottom of the stairs, I leaned against the wall beside the stairs. Sen-Mut put his left hand against the wall and his right foot on the first step.

I spoke first, looking at him tenderly.

"Beloved of mine, I want to thank you for the nice surprise of the banquet for me. Everything was lovely, and you made me very happy to-night."

Looking at me under the stars, he said, "Hat, I did it because I love you." He kissed me. "And now, no one can tell me that I cannot bathe you, or I cannot sleep with you all night anymore," he said.

He lifted me in his strong arms and carried me up the stairs. I was laughing. The guards opened the golden doors.

Sen-Mut stopped and told them and all the slaves, "All of you can go to the banquet hall and join in the celebration for your Queen tonight, who will be crowned Pharaoh of Egypt in the new year. Enjoy the ban-quet!"

They all left, and he carried me to the bath tub. He put me down, and from behind he started to kiss the right side of my neck slowly. I closed my eyes in delight as his lips traveled slowly down my back, and I smiled, enjoying it. He removed my kilt and removed his. I felt the warmth of his body brushing against my body and the heat that had taken over him. He closed his eyes in delight, and I heard him gasp. I turned around, and he opened his eyes. I pressed my lips on his, and he wrapped his arms around me tightly and held me against his chest. We were trembling with desire. I was as hot as he was. He was holding back his desire.

He held my right hand and walked me down to the warm water where yellow rose petals were floating, and perfume was scenting the wa-ter. How sweet was his love for me. He started to pour warm water slowly over my body and bathed me slowly, kissing my shoulder. Then he lifted me in his arms and laid me on my stomach on top of the white linen sheets that he had ordered earlier. He exited the tub, and he knelt beside me. He poured perfume oil on his hands. By this time, I was feeling incredible desire for his body. Then he started to massage my back with his hands and brush his lips slowly on my back. With every kiss, he sucked my skin. The feeling of his warm lips and kisses traveled all the way into my most inner parts.

I heard him say, “Soft, very soft.” As he continued to caress my body gently with his hands, he turned me around to face him. Looking into my eyes, he said, “I love you, Maatke-Re,” as we became one so very slowly.

“I love you too, Ptah, Steward of Amun,” I said.

He made wonderful love to me as always, and after a while, as I laid in his arms, I said, “This is the most wonderful bath I ever had.”

He laughed, and holding me, he said, “Hat, lying beside you, the warmth of your love fills my heart and my entire insides with satisfaction. No one ever could give me this much pleasure. Only you and your love.”

“Beloved, always love me the way you do, because in my heart, there is no space for anyone but you,” I told him.

We kissed again, and I hugged him tightly close to me because I knew that he would soon be returning to the Valley of the Dead and the construction of my temple.

He got up and walked inside of the tub, and he lifted me from the edge of the tub and put me in the water. We bathed each other, and then we dried each other. I looked at him and smile. He now had a bald head like mine.

We walked to our bed. There, we drank some more wine. Then we walked to the balcony holding hands, and he leaned his naked body against the stone wall. He held my back against his chest with his arms wrapped around me. We looked at the night full of stars in silence. And I loved these moments with him holding me.

“Sen-Mut, I want you to hold my body always like this until we grow very old together. Promise me, my love,” I said.

“I promise,” he said, giving me a squeeze. “In seven months, you will be Pharaoh.”

I smiled, and he kissed the back of my bold head. I turned around to face him and kissed him. We walked to our bed holding hands. We lay there in silence, holding each other, and he kissed my forehead again.

"Sweet dreams, beloved," he said.

"Good night, beloved of mine," I said.

We drifted off to sleep in each other's arms.

CHAPTER 34

CROWNED PHARAOH OF EGYPT

My beloved Sen-Mut came back from the Valley of the Dead a few months early because he had advanced in the construction of my temple. Leaving Senemen, his brother, in charge to continue with the construction, he came back to me to plan and prepare for my coronation, a long process, for which he was helped by Hapuseneb, Khety, D'Jehuty, Nehesi, and the priests.

On that day, many priests were preparing for it too, and I heard that it's a long process. Sen-Mut laid out the plans of how the procession would proceed, including details about the position of each of the armed forces and the positions of the priests, priestesses, and dignitaries who would be invited to my coronation. The whole country would be here in Thebes that day. Hapuseneb had already sent out the announcement, and D'Jehuty and Nehesi oversaw all the armed forces following Sen-Mut's directions. There was a great deal of commotion all over the palace for the preparations. I was very pleased.

Every day I woke up very happy because Sen-Mut was sleeping beside me, and because no one could tell us not to be together anymore. We bathed, ate, and made passionate love as many times as we wanted to, with no worry of pregnancy. Menina brought me the bitter herbs every day, and Sen-Mut and I alternated the drinks with other methods of contraception. There was no more hiding or worry. I was immensely happy because I had the love of my life with me. I had Sen-Mut.

Many people came from faraway lands to sell and trade with us. They brought many beautiful items to be traded for gold. Sen-Mut and Thuty managed my gold and gold mines. Sen-Mut had become an excellent administrator during these few years.

A few days before, Sen-Mut had brought Hatnufer, his mother, to meet me. I was happy to meet his mother, his two sisters, and another brother. Now, I had a family, including my daughter, Hatshepset, who was still small.

During her stay, I received many salesmen who came from distant lands, bringing beautiful merchandise. I received every one of them. I did not want to miss anything that was beautiful for me or for the palace. I received them in the large white gazebo, which was surrounded by tall white pillars and hanging white linen curtains, with a pool full of floating pink, white, and blue lotuses in the water. Many of the salesmen knew of the coronation to come and brought beautiful gold material for my kilt and cape. They also showed me other colorful material that came from other far off lands. I was immensely happy to see so many beautiful items. They brought back memories of my mother when we went to Crete, that far away island on the blue sea, where I saw so many colorful materials.

The salesmen showed me many beautiful objects, like large vases from Greece. I got them all. They would be full of colorful flowers everywhere in the palace and on my balcony.

I sat on my chair, and Sen-Mut's mother sat beside me at my left. On my right was my cheetah, Jotham, who now was fully grown. Everyone loved him. Sen-Mut's sisters were afraid of him in the beginning, but then they fell in love with him. He was tame, and he let them pet him and play with him. He roamed everywhere freely in the palace.

Hatnufer and her daughters helped me choose many colorful materials and fragrances, and I was generous with them and gave them many gifts. I also gave gifts to my closest slaves. I didn't look at them as my slaves. I looked at them as family, especially Tuyii and Menina.

I continued inviting T'Queta to join us for dinner in the banquet hall. We all were very happy to be together again. T'Queta knew Sen-Mut's family well, and I was glad for them to meet again.

One morning, Sen-Mut went to his office early and came back in the afternoon. He walked through the golden doors, and I observed the way T'Queta looked at him with loving eyes. But he walked past her and did not look at her. I ran to his arms like a child, and I kissed him on his lips. He kissed me back with a smile. He sat down, and I showed him everything that I got. He thought that all I had acquired was beautiful.

Hapuseneb came in and talked to Sen-Mut. They sat together and drank wine for a while, laughing a lot. Sometimes I would notice the way Hapuseneb looked at T'Queta. She had become more beautiful than before. He should have married her, I thought.

D'Jehuty, Nehesi, my uncle Thutmoses, and Ineni joined them. Trailing behind them was Ursaramun. And from time to time, I would turn around and look at Sen-Mut only to find him staring at me, his love for me showing in his eyes, and I would smile at him. I was so glad that he was mine and that we loved each other so very much. Seeing him getting along with Hapuseneb made me even happier. Then all of them gathered together on my balcony. I could hear him laugh, and I smiled, too. His happiness was mine too, and I was immensely happy.

Menina came every day to bring me the bitter herbs for me not to get pregnant, and I rewarded her well for all her help. I thanked her again for being my ally and for helping us when I was pregnant with Neferu-Re.

We spent several weeks with Sen-Mut's mother and sisters. We took them sailing, and Hatnufer liked the breeze blowing on her face like I did as we sailed the Nile. She told me about Sen-Mut's childhood and made me laugh many times. She told me that when Sen-Mut came for the first time to Thebes, he was only seven summers, and he fell in love with the buildings that were built by Ineni. From that day forward, he kept telling his father that he wanted to be an architect and builder like Ineni.

My land was completely happy, with laughter and music everywhere. Sen-Mut and Hapuseneb got along well. There was no more jealousy between them, and I had peace of mind. Or so I thought. Sen-Mut didn't say anything about Hapuseneb, so I gathered that everything was going well between them. Then he went back to the Valley of the Dead and would come back a week later. We enjoyed each other very much when he was with me.

****

I heard the golden doors opening.

"My love."

It was the voice of my beloved, and as always, I ran to his arms, and we kissed. He held me tightly to his chest and rocked me in his arms. He was happy to see me every time, as I was to see him.

"I have been missing you every single day, my love," he said.

"Why don't you come back then?" I asked.

"Because I want to stay and continue with the construction of your temple. I want everything to be just right. Remember when we were in Philae, and I promised I would build for you the most beautiful temple that will last forever?" He was smiling. "Well, that is what I am doing now. I want it to be the most beautiful one for you, and if I stop and come here every time, which is my heart's desire every day, I will never finish building it."

"Then, beloved, I will come and stay with you for a while," I said.

"No, my love. The heat is intense, and there are flies everywhere. I know you. You don't like mosquitos, and the flies will make you crazy. You would not last one hour there, and I prefer for you to remain here looking beautiful and waiting for me so that when I come home, you can run to me and greet me with your kisses, like right now." He kissed me again.

"Khety sent word to me that he wants to speak to both of us today, and that is why I came earlier. And I am in the need of a very good bath, beloved. Are you ready to bathe my body with your soft hands?" he asked, then he laughed.

I grabbed his hand, and we walked to be bathed. Before we reached the tub, he stopped, held me, and kissed me. And then he made love to me as if it were our first time.

Afterwards, we ate together and then got dressed and walked to the temple to meet with Khety.

Khety was sitting and waiting for us. He did not look well at all. He was very pale. When he saw us, he greeted us with a smile from his chair.

"Horus, I am very happy to see you, and you, too, Sen-Mut. Have a seat, please. I wanted to speak to both of you regarding your upcoming coronation as Pharaoh. The elder priests and I have set the date to begin the bathing ritual." Then smiling, he said, "I am old, and I feel my age. I'm tired. My dearest friend, your father, has gone to the heavens and most of my other good friends have too. I feel that Anubis, the god of the underworld, is getting closer and is roaming my Ka, but my soul is not ready to leave yet. I am asking the gods for a little bit more time because I must fulfill my promise to your father, that you reach the throne of Egypt. I want personally to crown you Pharaoh of Egypt, as I promised your father. I have been consulting the stars with the other priests, and we have chosen the days for the bathing ritual that is done for pharaohs. It is a very long process and a very tiring one. It will last until the day before your coronation. You are going to be exhausted when it is done. I have been consulting the stars for the last few months, looking for the correct time for the purification. It must be done after your blood passes. I also consulted with the spirits of all the gods, and all agree with the chosen days. On those days, the stars will be in the right position. They will be aligned in the firmament, and that is a good omen.

"The bathing will start at midnight on the second day of the week. The priestesses will perform the ritual of the bathing and the shaving of the body to purify it. Everything will begin when Mother Nut is covering the sky. On that night, the priestesses will chant the highest prayers for pharaohs over your head and body. This ritual has never been done for a woman before, especially by virgin priestesses. It has always been done by priests for a man. So, on those days, they will burn incense around and above you. They will chant many prayers over your body. It's a very long process from beginning to the end.

"Sen-Mut, I wanted to talk to you about this. This preparation is a very long ritual, and you cannot be around Hatshepsut during this period of purification and blessings. I suggest you go back to the Valley of the Dead and continue with the building of her temple. I will send word to you a few days before the coronation for you to come back, and you will go through the cleansing ritual of your body as well. When you do come back, it is preferable for you to stay those days in your house and abstain until the morning of her coronation. Then you can be with her, as she is being dressed by the priestesses. Hapuseneb will be there also. You cannot touch her body during the six weeks of blessings," Khety said.

Sen-Mut opened his eyes wide when he heard all of this. I was ready to burst into laughter, seeing the expression on his face.

Khety continued, "Until she is crowned Pharaoh. I know it's going to be hard for both of you to be apart, but it must be done. Her father had to do it. If you want to be present during the blessings of her body with the purified water of the sacred pond and for the blessings over her head, you could be present with us, but you will not touch her, nor will you bathe her. I would prefer for you not to be present because she must concentrate to say the Pharaoh's prayers. I know that with you there, it will be hard for her to concentrate. As I said, the bathing is only done by the elder priests. It will be performed by sixty of them. They will be divided into six groups of ten, and each group will represent each of the elements: Ra the sun, Earth, Fire, Wind, Nut, and the last one will be under the rays of Thoth. The blessings of Thoth are performed on the first day of the full moon. Hat, during the bathing of Nut and the stars, you will sleep under the stars naked so that Mother Nut will always protect you at night and everywhere you go. The stars will always brighten the paths that you take in the night. These blessings will remain with you and with your Ka through eternity. You will always be Pharaoh, now and in the afterlife."[59]

---

[59] And how right he was. In the year 2002, I went to Egypt, fulfilling a wish of my heart that I'd had since I was a little girl. When I arrived in Egypt, I kissed the ground, and I was immensely happy. Finally, I was home, a home that I have missed so much since I was five years old. To my surprise, everyone loved me, too. I was the happiest woman in Egypt. But everything seemed strange to me. Of course, all of this had transpired 3,500 years ago, and my brain had not accepted that everything had age and was in ruins. Nothing was the same. The mix of the old with the new have me confused. Cairo is a modern city now and is beautiful.

I wanted to run and see the Nile and touch the waters of Hopi right away. I wanted to bathe in his waters. It was dark already when I arrived, but I didn't care. I knelt to touch the waters. But I was stop by Amro the owner of the apartment that Jim (Ex-husband) had rented for me in Cairo. I was told that it was not possible because of the bacteria in the waters of Hopi. I wanted to leave Cairo and run to Thebes, now Luxor, and wanted to see Karnak. I had forgotten that it was very far from Cairo. It's about twelve hours by train. I remained in Cairo for a that week, and I sailed the Nile as I used to 3,500 years ago and slept for three hours daily as before, but this time I was not in my barge, nor with the fan-bearers. I was in a small felucca, but I didn't care, I was in my home, and sailing the Nile. I was full of happiness, but there was a great silence within me. I was in another time, without my loved ones.

After a week in Cairo, my chauffeur took me to the train station to check and see what train I was going to take to Luxor the following day. A set of stairs was in front of me. To

"I remember this same talk I had with your father," Khety said. "I was young and full of life then, and we were all grown men. I remember the day you were born, and the Oracle read your future to your father, told him that you would live, that you were a healthy child, that you will rule this land. Your father's face was full of happiness. He was so proud of you, as when you took the test of foresight when you were five summers. I always knew that you would pass it, but your father was terrified because he adored you. You had all the strength that he wanted in a male heir, but you were such a small child to go through that dramatic experience. He knew that your bother Thutmoses would never be able to take that test, even if he wanted to. Your father only wanted him to be well, but he was so proud of you. You were brave and strong."

Then, looking at Sen-Mut, he said, "And you, Sen-Mut, you were in her future too. On the day of her birth, the Oracle foretold of a man that would love her, and she would love him too and rule beside him. The day you two met, during that first audience, she ordered so many nice things

---

the left were the ones going up to the trains, and to the right were the ones exiting the train station.

I started to walk up the stairs to the open field to where the trains were on the tracks, and I saw a group of men. About forty or fifty of them they were coming down the right stairs, and between them was a very old man, wearing white clothing, including a turban on his head, with a white sheath covering his body. He looked at me, and he started to shout, "Faharuk! Faharuk!" The rest of the men follow to shout out loud, "Faharuk! Faharuk!" and raising their fists in the air. I turned around to see who was behind me and see to whom they were shouting at, but there was no one behind me. I realized that they were shouting at me.

I saw a police officer rushing on top of the stairs, looking to see what all that commotion was. He looked at me. When I reached the top of the stairs, I asked him what they were shouting at me. He said, "They were shouting at you, 'King! King!' And I don't know why they are shouting King at you? They should be calling you 'Queen.'" I realized that what the old men saw in me was the Double Crown of Egypt. Then I realize that what Khety told me 3,500 years ago, was the truth, that I will always hold the Double Crown of Egypt on my head, and through all eternity.

for you: a goose mattress, a room of your own, all the best wine, food, a new kilt, and sandals. I wondered if you could be the one the Oracle spoke of. Then that night in the banquet hall, the way both of you looked at each other, I wondered again if you were the one in her future. And it was you. You were that man that would make her heart glad and happy, and she would rule beside you."

Khety nodded several times and smiled.

"Sen-Mut, can you please excuse us? I must speak with Horus alone for few minutes," he said.

"Sure, Khety. I will be in the temple. Hat, meet me in the temple when you finish."

"Yes, beloved." I said, and he left.

"Hatshepset, now I must speak to you about your request for Hapuseneb to be First Prophet of Amun when I am gone to the underworld. I have spoken with the elder priests. They were reluctant when I suggested it in the beginning, as per your request, but at the end they all agreed because there is uncertainty between all of us that the child, Menkhep-Re, is Pharaoh's son. If you are right, as we believe, that Puyem-Re is his father, then this means that he has betrayed the house of Pharaoh and has broken the rules of the priesthood. I had to make sure that on the day of my death Hapuseneb will be chosen First Prophet of Amun-Ra. Be assured that he will be chosen." Khety said.

"Khety, I am pleased to hear that. And I am sorry you are not feeling well, but promise me to hold on and don't depart from this life yet. I am honored that you will place the Pschent, the Double Crown of Egypt, on my head and see that the wishes of my father come true," I said.

"Hatshepsut, remember the time when you came to talk to me after your father's death, regarding you wanting to marry Sen-Mut? I want you to know that at that time, I spoke to all the priests regarding your wishes and they were all against it, especially Hapuseneb."

I did not know that Hapu knew of my request to Khety.

"We all knew why Hapuseneb was against this marriage, and I am sorry that I could not agree with it at that time. We really held Sen-Mut in high esteem, but your father wanted the continuation of the royal blood and that was a must. He made me promise that the Thutmoses's royal blood would continue in the family. Let me explain to you that the man's seed is the one that can produce children and the continuation of the royal blood. I know you know that, but I wanted to clarify it to you. Without a male heir, there is no more royal blood, and you have refused to have another child with your brother. Your Father clearly knew how much you and Sen-Mut love each other," Khety said.

What? Father knew? I said, I had no idea.

Khety continued, "And the proof of that was the day that you ran into the sandstorm to kill yourself when he was about to order Sen-Mut's death, and Sen-Mut ran after you and saved your life, putting his life in danger to save yours. Your father was very aware of his love for you, and he wanted your happiness at all costs, that is why one day he came to talk to me and asked me to speak with the Oracle and see what Thut's future would hold. On that day, I sent word to the Oracle that Pharaoh was coming to consult the Oracle and the stars. That night at midnight, the Oracle told your father that Sen-Mut honestly loved you, and that you loved him too, and that you will have two children. It also said that Thutmoses II will go to the underworld three or five summers after being crowned Pharaoh and that you will be Pharaoh beside the man that you love and that loves you. Your father was very happy. I could see the gladness and satisfaction on his face, knowing that from all the Queens in the palace, at least you would reach happiness. Then on our return from the Oracle on that early part of the morning, as tired as we were from the lack of sleep, he made me pledge to him that I would again speak to the elder priests and that they would keep their pledge and their faithfulness to him, for when he went to the underworld that you would reach the throne of Egypt. And for you to be finally happy with Sen-Mut."

I was surprised to hear all this, that Father was preparing my happiness at the end. Even on his death bed, when he made me promise that I would marry Aakheperen-Re. Now, I understand everything. When he was dying and made me promise that I would be happy, at that moment I did not understand what he was trying to tell me. I then understood the importance of the continuation of the royal blood, and we didn't even know if Menkhep-Re had my brother's blood.

I saw Khety closing his eyes. I stood from my chair and came closer to him and patted his hand.

"Khety, thank you so much for everything that you said," I said.

He did not respond. He was asleep, so I walked to where the younger priests were with Sen-Mut. I told them to carry Khety to his quarters, but Sen-Mut came and lifted him up in his arms and carried him to his room.

"Thank you, beloved of mine, for taking him to his room. In four days, I will begin the sacred bathing." I said.

"Maatke-Re, this is going to drive me crazy for six weeks. And not seeing you for that long? Nor can I touch you at all? OK, this is what we are going to do. Let's start making love as much as we can to make up for all the days that we will be apart," Sen-Mut said.

We started to laugh together, then he said, "I will also go through the bathing rituals the day before your coronation, and I will be purified like all the rest of the priests and you."

I started to laugh, and I agreed with him. I looked into his eyes, and smiling, I said, "Let's have our dinner in the barge tonight, and sail the Nile, and you can make love to me all these days. We can be away for these three days, with no one around us. You and I can swim naked in the Nile, and enjoy ourselves, like that first night we got back together after being kept apart by my brother. That night, you made me the happiest women in the land."

"And you made me the happiest man that night too. Having you all those hours in my arms and under the stars I was immensely happy, as I am right now. Let's re-kindle that night. I want to kiss you all over like that night. And I may bathe your body. Whoa, I am hot already," he said.

I laughed and said, "Let's do it then."

We walked back to the palace and Sen-Mut sent for Sailor Neb-Ery to prepare two barges: one for ourselves and another one for the slaves and the cooks. I sent for the master cook to prepare everything for tonight, as he did three summers ago. I wanted everything to be lovely like that night and wanted all the best wines for Sen-Mut. Only one thing would be different this time, my beloved did not have to go out through the back of his house to meet me.

The night was dark as he liked it and full of stars as we sailed the Nile. He bathed me slowly, and the touch of his hand had me hot. He did it so slowly, and we submerged our bodies in the most delicious ecstasy of passionate kisses. Then he walked to our couch and brought a white linen sheet and spread it open on the floor of the barge. He held my hand and guided me to the center of the linen. We knelt facing each other. Bringing both of my hands to his lips, he kissed them and the two rings he gave me when he asked me to be his wife. Without saying another word, he held me close to him and gently laid me on my stomach. He started to massage my back with aromatic oils and kissed my back slowly. I loved it when he kissed my back and the way he did it. I was becoming hot with desire. He laid on top of my back. He started gently sucking my skin and tenderly biting my back, and he made love to me like that wonderful night. We relived the most wonderful moment again, lost in ecstasy and love.

He lay beside me, putting the back of his hand over his eyes, and breathing heavily. He said, "See how wild you make me? When I am making love to you, whoa! I lose consciousness of everything, and the only thing that matters to me in that moment is this delicious ecstasy you give me and that I am in love with you."

I turn around and laid on my belly with my hands folded under my face, I was looking at him and listening as he was telling me of his sensual experience with me.

"I love the way you kiss my back and made love to me like the last time. Beloved, where did you learn this way of love making?" I asked.

"This way, no one showed it to me, nor the kissing of your body. It is all the desire of my heart to do it to you. I love kissing your soft body and skin, and three summers ago, when I did it for the first time, I loved it. Don't you like it?"

"Of course, I love it, and I love everything you do to me. I believe our love making is wonderful," I said.

"What makes it more wonderful is that we love each other and give ourselves to each other with love. That is why we can make passionate love and enjoy each other's body," he said.

We made love again, and I was very happy because he was mine. We laid there after this wonderful ecstasy, holding each other, looking at the stars.

"I love you, Maatke-Re," he said.

"I love you too, my beloved one," I replied.

He got up from the floor and got a goblet with wine, and we both drink from the same goblet. He went to our couch and brought a large galabia and more wine and food. We drank and ate all night, and we got drunk and laughed a lot, laying on the couch looking at the stars. Then there was a falling star. It was a very long one, and he said, "That is like our love, beautiful like the stars."

"Yes, my love, beautiful like the stars," I said and curled tight to his body, and we fell asleep under the stars. The barge sailed north in the silence of the night, under the stars.

****

The few days left we spent swimming and playing in the waters, and we kissed as many times as we wanted. We laughed a lot and Sen-Mut hugged me and made love to me with passion. We spent these three days very happy and returned late in the afternoon to the palace.

“Beloved, tonight at midnight the bathing rituals start. Stay here and leave tomorrow morning before I get here. And believe me that I am going to miss your body every night until I see you in one week. Are you going to go to your house?” I asked. I was jealous.

“No. I am going back to the construction site of your temple,” he said. I kissed him on his lips, and he hugged me tightly.

“Hat, I have one wish to ask of you,” he said.

“What is it, my love?”

“On the day of the coronation, on that night after the celebration is over, I want to undress you, and I want to make love to you, slowly as you are wearing the Double Crown of Egypt on your head, that I may pay the respect to the body of a Pharaoh.”

Laughing, I said, “And your wish will be granted, beloved of mine.”

We walked up the stairs and slept for a while, and I was awakened by my slaves. Sen-Mut sat on the edge of the bed. I came to him and stood between his legs, and looking at him, I caressed his face with my left hand. We hugged and kissed, and I kissed his forehead.

“Until I see you again, my love, in six weeks,” I said.

Sen-Mut walked me to the golden doors and kissed me again. I turned around and looked down the stairs and could see the torch bearers and the guards waiting, and with them, seven priestesses. The priestesses were all dressed in white, with long white capes and hoods over their heads, which meant that they were all virgins and their faces could not be seen by men. I turned around, looked at Sen-Mut, and smiled at him. He smiled back.

I started to walk down the stairs. There were many torch bearers with the guards and they walked in front of me, and the priestesses followed behind. We had to walk to the temples in Karnak, and it would be a long walk to the priestesses' pool.

It was before midnight when we arrived, and more priestesses were waiting for me. They started to undress me, saying prayers and tearing the sheath in pieces after it was removed from my body, a sign of my rebirth. I was guided into the pool of fresh water, and they scrubbed and scrubbed my skin until it almost hurt. They scrubbed all over my body, head, face, and hands as they said incantation words. The bathroom was full of the nice smell of incense that was only for special rituals. They continued pouring water over my head and saying prayers of cleanliness. Then they walked me out of the pool and lay me on top of a table that was dressed in white linen, and they started to look all over my body for any sign of diseases. Their faces were very serious, and they looked white as porcelain. They turned me around and looked for more diseases and looked inside of my butt.

I was walked again into the pool of warm water and was bathed, and more prayers were chanted around me. I had a feeling as if I was floating. Then they walked me out of the pool again, and I noticed that the table was in the center of a circle of symbols on the floor. They lay me again on the same table with a dry linen sheet and started to shave every part of my body with strings, starting with my head. They took my shaved hair and placed it in a small wooden box. I was then covered in honey. I was told to repeat several prayers with them as they chanted over my body, and I did. Suddenly, I had the feeling that I was floating in the air again. Was it the incantation prayers that were making me feel like this, I wondered? Then my Ka came out of my body, as when I was five summers. Now my soul was above my body, and I could see myself from above on top of the linen table. I could see the priestesses around me, and I saw them wiping away the honey from my body with pieces of linen. Then my Ka came back into my body, and I could see their faces as they were wiping the honey away from my body, then taking the pieces of the white linen and folding them neatly and placing them in a nicely finished wooden box.

I was guided into the warm water of the pool and bathed again as they were saying more prayers over me. I was taken out of the pool again and walked to the clean linen table. They started to pour aromatic herbs and massage my body and began chanting more prayers. They kept the room a nice temperature, so I would not be cold. After they were done, they walked me to a small circle with symbols, and my body was rinsed with the sacred waters of Amun. I stood in there and spread my arms at my sides as they pat my body dry. I was dressed in a white linen sheath covered in gold symbols, then they put a white cape with a hood over my head. They all then fell on their faces to the floor.

A litter was waiting to carry me to the palace so that my feet would not touch the ground. When the doors were opened, I could see the first rays of Ra rising. I was very tired and fell asleep during the long walk to the palace. I was awakened as they carried me up the stairs to my quarters. The golden doors were opened, and I stepped down into my quarters, then to my bedroom. My beloved was gone. Everything was impeccably clean. White linen covered the white limestone floor where I walked, and everything was dressed in white linen. I was given food that was not contaminated with blood by the priestesses. I thought, "I must sleep right now. I am so very tired. The bathing by the First High Priest will start at high noon. He will bathe me with the prayers of the first elements they represent. I don't know what the first element will be."

After eating very little, I still felt that I was floating in the air. I was nauseated and felt strange. I lay in my bed and saw Sen-Mut's side of the bed empty. I missed him beside me. I remembered his petition and smiled. I wondered where he went. Did he go to the Valley of the Dead as he said he would? I was so tired and fell fast asleep.

I was awakened by the priestesses.

"Your Majesty, it's time to wake up and get ready," one said. "We know you are very tired, but we must continue with your preparation for the coronation."

She gave me a sweet smile. I got up from my bed and went to the bathroom. Several priestesses were waiting in there to bathe me, so they did. I was not given any breakfast, for all the blessing must be done while fasting. They dressed me in a white linen sheath that they had made for me to wear, and they covered me with a white cape and covered my head with the hood. A litter was waiting for me outside of the golden doors to carry me to Karnak so that my feet would not touch the ground. We arrived at Karnak, and I was taken into an open and very large patio. Ra was high in the middle of the open patio. I saw the first ten elder priests who had formed a circle in the center, and Khety, First Prophet of Amun-Ra, was one of them. He looked well and full of life, and I became happy. It was good to see him. The priestesses removed my sheath and guided me to the center of the large circle. Khety smiled at me and waited until the rays of Ra were above my head, and then he started to chant in a loud voice:

"I call upon the God of all Gods, Amun-Ra, to descend from the heavens and pour Your rays upon the head and body of Your most beloved daughter, Hatshepset. You, fashioned her in her father's body, and brought her into being into this world as Your own. There is no doubt in any of us, your faithful servants, that she is Your most beloved daughter and Your chosen one. We all seek, Almighty Ra, to pour over her Your blessings that she will rule these lands of Yours as the mighty Pharaoh of Upper and Lower Egypt."

He became silent, and I said the prayers of my heart:

"My beloved Amun-Ra, I, Hatshepset, Your beloved daughter, and daughter and granddaughter of the earthly Pharaohs of the two lands, whom You had chosen before me, come into Thy presence as when I was a little girl to ask that You pour Your blessing upon me, that You always protect me, guide me, give me courage to defend my land, and that You will always be present in me every day of my life. With Your guidance, I will rule well and with fairness this land that I love. Bless me with Your wisdom, kindness, knowledge, understanding, love, and happiness."

Khety started to chant again, and I repeated the chanting words with him. He came closer to me, and he started to pull rays from the sun and place them around my head. As he was chanting around me, he continued pulling more rays from Ra and placing them above my head. Then I understood what he was doing. He was making a crown with the rays of Ra. When he completed the prayers, Khety stepped back and another elder priest came and did the same thing around my body. I continued repeating the chanting prayers of Ra. Each priest had their own different prayers and blessing. Another came and brought incense and walked around me, passing the incense in a circle around my body, chanting prayers of Ra. I continued repeating his chants. Every elder priest did their special prayers of Ra over my head and body. I could see the rays of Ra were fading away, and just before the last rays vanished, the ten of them approached me with a round golden vase in their hands. They poured the water of the sacred pond over my head and naked body. I saw them walking away and standing in their places. Then the priestesses came and covered my body with a new sheath, and I was covered with the same cape and hood over my head.

I looked for Khety and whispered, "Thank you." He nodded his head twice and smiled. By this time, he looked very, very tired, as every one of us was. The litter was waiting to carry me back to the palace, and I got on it. I was completely tired and very hungry, but this time I felt that the interior of my body was completely clean and that I was emanating light from within. The strange thing was that I had the same floating sensation as before.

The first blessing of Ra was over, and the second blessing would continue tomorrow at the same time by another elderly priest of the same group. All of them would be pouring their blessings on me. I walked into my quarters so very hungry and was again given food not contaminated with blood. I ate it quickly, and it felt as if I had not eaten anything. I wanted more, and they gave me a little bit more potatoes, celery, and green onions. I fell into a deep sleep and was awoken again by the priestesses. This time I was more rested, and I was bathed again by them. Again, no breakfast. This time I noticed the left side of my white cape had the symbol of Ra embroidered with golden thread. I continued with the blessing for another five days, and for the next five weeks, I was blessed with every element. On my cape was sewn in gold thread the symbols of every element that I was blessed with.

On the night of the blessing of Mother Nut and the stars, the bathing of my body was to start when the last rays of Ra were gone. I was so hungry I ate everything that I could, for my fasting began that day at noon and lasted until the following morning. I was carried again to the temple where they were waiting for me. I walked into the center of a circle where the symbols of every element were carved into the limestone floor. The cycle was almost completed, and the High Priest was representing Mother Nut and the stars. He was wearing a long, dark blue cape with stars, embroidered in gold thread. The dark blue represented the night, and the golden stars represented the brightness of the stars. He approached me, and, looking into the night sky, he started to summon Mother Nut. Pulling stars from the dark sky, he made a crown of stars above my head, and chanted the prayers of Mother Nut. I repeated after him the prayers for Mother Nut.

It was done. It was almost midnight. I was covered with the cape and hood over my head, and I was carried back to the palace. I walked to my quarters, very hungry and so very tired. I was carried directly to my balcony in the litter. A couch was waiting for me under the stars, so Mother Nut would pour out all her blessings over me, Tomorrow night would be a full moon, and Thoth would shine all its silver splendor. It would be the last blessing by the last ten priests representing Thoth, and the day after tomorrow, early in the morning I would be crowned Pharaoh of Egypt.

I had lost weight from fasting all those days. I lay naked under the dark blue sky and the stars. The night was warm, and it was not a full moon yet. And no mosquitos. I was glad because I must sleep all night naked, but I was missing Sen-Mut. I was so terribly hungry that I could not go to sleep, so I laid there thinking of Sen-Mut, my beloved. I was not given the chance to miss him that much, for I had been so tired every day. Finally, I dozed and fell asleep.

I was awakened by the crow of the rooster, and I got up fast and saw the first rays of Ra rising in the east. I washed myself and knelt and give Ra thanks for bringing me safely to the beginning of this day, and that all honor and glory belonged to thee. I got up from the floor and could now eat.

“Tuyii. Tuyii,” I called to my mother’s slave as I walked into my quarters. She ran to me.

“Yes, Your Majesty.”

“Send for my breakfast right away. Bring a lot of fruits and sweet breads and my favored hot drink. I am so hungry. And bathe me right away.”

I walked to my bathroom and sat thinking of Sen-Mut. He must be going through his ritual bath too, I thought. I would love to see him, but I could not until the morning of my coronation. One more day, my love. I was bathed and sat at my table, ready to eat. There was a knock on my golden doors, and when they were opened it was a priestess. She looked at my table and saw so much food, but nothing contaminated with blood. I thought she was going to say not to eat, but she smiled and said, “Your Majesty, I will wait for you to finish with your breakfast, but don’t eat so fast, otherwise you will get sick to your stomach.”

I ate so much, and she was right. I ran to the bathroom and vomited.

“Your Majesty, are you alright?” she asked.

I walked to my bed and lay there with a sick stomach. She came closer to me, and with a sweet smile said, "You became sick because you have not eaten much during these six-weeks. And I came early this morning to take your measurements for the kilt and the golden cape."

I smiled at her. I really liked her, I thought. She was so sweet to me. I got up from my bed, and she took my measurements. The golden sandals were brought up earlier during the week. I must try them on right now, I thought.

"Tuyii, bring me the golden sandals," I said, and she did. I put them on, and they fit nicely. They had a nice finish and didn't hurt my feet as I walked. There was a knock on the doors.

"Enter," I said.

It was Hapuseneb.

"Good morning, Flower of Egypt. I have not seen you for six weeks. How are you? And how did it go, with all this fasting?"

"I am exhausted, Hapu, and it's very tiring. But it's nice to see you and speak to you. I have not spoken to anyone until today, and you are the first friend that I've spoken with since the bathing began."

He nodded his head and smiled.

"Well, one more day, Flower of Egypt, and your dream and your father's dream will become a reality. I am very happy for you."

"I know that you are, Hapu. Have you gotten through the bathing ritual yet?"

"No, but later today I will be meeting with Sen-Mut there."

"Hapu, is everything ready for my coronation?" I asked.

"Yes, everything is ready, and everything is going to be perfect, just the way Sen-Mut has planned. It's all very well organized. Khety was talking to me yesterday when he sent the message to Sen-Mut to return to Thebes, and I saw him earlier this morning. He had just gotten back from the Valley of the Dead and asked me if I had seen you. I told him no, but I will tell him when I see him today that I have seen you. I know that Khety had asked him to stay away from you for these six weeks. He told me. Is there anything you want me to tell him this afternoon when I see him?"

I became quiet and looked at him. He was clenching his teeth. I smiled and shook my head. I knew Sen-Mut, and I knew he would not like it if I sent him a verbal message with Hapu. I walked to my desk and took a small piece of papyrus and wrote this message

"Beloved of mine, I am looking forward for you to pay your respect to the body of your Pharaoh. I love you."

I was smiling as I sealed it. I placed my seal on it and turned around and gave it to him to give to Sen-Mut. He looked at me and took the missive, and I smiled. I needed to change his mind right away because I knew he hurts.

"You said that everything is ready. Finally, I will be Pharaoh. How do you see Khety? Do you think he will be able to sustain himself all those long hours? I think he is very fragile, and I pray to the gods that he will be strong during the coronation. I need him, and I want him to put my father's double crown on my head, as my father wanted him to do," I said.

"Khety asked me to help him and be at his side at all times during the coronation. He is very old, and he is afraid that he is going to be needing my help. I see that he is fragile, and he is afraid that he won't be able to stand all those long hours of the coronation. He will wait for you at the temple for the blessings, then he will walk with us, heading the procession to the audience hall. It's going to be an exhausting day for him and for you. First, you will be walking to Karnak for the blessing of Amun-Ra, then back to the audience hall for the coronation."

"Hapu, I don't want Khety walking this time, nor any of the sixty elder priests of Amun. Make sure that the litters are ready to carry all of them. I want Khety to place the Double Crown on my head as were my father's wishes."

I noticed that Hapuseneb did not look at the priestess, nor she at him, and I remembered why. They were not allowed to cross words nor to look at each other. Those were the rules of the priesthood. It's to avoid them falling in love. If they did and lost their virginity, both would be put to death, beginning with the priest. If a priestess changed her mind and wanted to leave the service of the highest and get married, they were free to do so. They could still serve in the temple, but no longer as priestesses for Amun-Ra. That is why their places of worship are far from each other. They come together only for high ceremonial celebrations, but always with their eyes cast down to the floor in front of a priest. They could not serve in the Temple of Amun-Ra because of their blood every month, and they are considered unclean during those days. After the blood is gone, they must go through the ritual of bathing. And that is why they cannot be a priest nor serve directly in the services of Amun-Ra.

"Hapu, I am completely happy that I will be Pharaoh tomorrow morning, and that the ritual of the bathing, the hunger, and the lack of sleep is almost over. I am dying to eat a piece of duck with molasses. My mouth is watering right now. I have not eaten real food for weeks."

He laughed. "I see a lot of food on your plate right now, and that you are eating."

"Oh, yes. But real food is what I want. You cannot believe how hungry I am. I could not sleep at all last night. That's how hungry I was. One thing that I was very pleased with was sleeping under Mother Nut and under the stars. It was beautiful. I saw many falling stars and made many wishes. That kept my mind away from the hunger. I know that from now on, and for all eternity, I will be at peace in the nights when I am asleep, and I will always have the shining stars over my head," I said.

He smiled and said, "Flower of Egypt, it will be like you said, and it sounds beautiful and lovely, what you experienced last night." He looked at me with such love. “I will come back very early in the morning with Sen-Mut,” he said.

I smiled at him and saw him leave with my message for Sen-Mut in his hand.

The priestess smiled at me, then said, “Your Majesty, tonight will be your last bathing ritual and blessings, and I would like to tell thee that I was pleased to serve you. I will be back tonight before the first rays of Thoth show, and we will go to the Temple of Amun-Ra for the last bathing. You have done well. Rest as much as you can the rest of the day until we come for you later. We will be here long before Thoth is high in its splendors. After that, we will come back very early in the morning to bathe you for the last time before Ra shows his first rays and blesses the land. We will dress you with the golden kilt and the golden cape for the coronation.”

“Please have a seat,” I told her. She sat down in front of me. “I want to thank you and all of you for the help during these six weeks and the caring and the loving way you treated me.” I smiled at her and she smiled back.

“Your Majesty, it was my duty to serve you as your subject,” she said.

“Will you tell me if there is anything needed in the temple?” I said.

“Your Majesty, we will tell you in the future, but for now, I must run to have the kilt and the cape finished today.”

“Very well. I will wait for you before Mother Nut covers the land.”

She bowed her head and left. I went back to my bed and laid there thinking of the request of Sen-Mut and laughed. Soon, beloved of mine. Soon we will be in each other’s arms again, I thought.

After the priestess left, I lay on my bed but continued to be hungry, so I got up and ate as much as I could until high noon, when I began my last fast. I ate and was satisfied with everything I ate, and I went back to my bed and lay there. My happiness was great, and I could hardly contain myself with so much happiness inside of me. I could not fall asleep for a while, but I finally did doze off. I was deeply asleep when I was awakened by all the priestesses. I was surprised to see so many of them at one time in my quarters They brought the golden kilt and the golden cape. They tried them on me, and all fit perfectly. The cape had a very long train. Everything was beautiful and was in gold material.

They asked me to sit down, and I did. They brought the golden beard to be sure that they could adjust the leather behind my head correctly. This golden beard had been worn by my father and all the Pharaohs before him. It was the sign of a man's power and strength. They also brought the Pschent, the Double Crown of Upper and Lower Egypt. They set it on my head, and it was large for my head and heavy on my neck. I became worried, and I looked at her.

She smiled saying, "Don't be worried, Your Majesty. We have ordered a gold helmet for your head. It will go under the Double Crown and hold it in its place, as it was done in the past for your father."[60] She smiled and that took the worries from me.

They brought the crook and the flail. The crook is the symbol of kingship and has a long stick as a handle with a hook on the top. The flail, a symbol of the fertility of the land, is a stick with three strings with beads. I touched them, and holding them in my hands brought tears to my eyes along with memories of my father, the Great Thutmoses I. He had held them in his hands in the large ceremonies of the palace. I wish he was here to see me crowned Pharaoh as he always wanted.

One of the priestesses put the golden sandals on my feet, and I walked with them several times around my bedroom. The leather was soft,

---

[60] The gold helmet can be seen on my forehead under the Pschent on the cover of this book. This is the way it looked on me 3,500 years ago.

and the gold was not hurting my feet. I started to walk to my golden mirror and was stopped by one of the priestesses.

"Your Majesty, we must wait until tomorrow morning for you to see yourself, radiant and dressed in the splendor of your golden attire," she said.

I looked at her and smiled, and she was right. I would wait for my beloved to see me dressed as a Pharaoh.

They undressed me and walked me to the tub with lukewarm water and bathed me as they chanted prayers. When we were done, they covered me with the white linen robe They had completed the symbols of all the elements that I was blessed with by Khety and the priests. They had embroidered them on the robe with gold thread and on the hood. We walked out together through my golden doors, and a litter was waiting for me. As I climbed into it, I was surprised to see all the priestesses of the temple waiting for me at the bottom of the stairs, about two hundred of them.

It was dark, and I could see Thoth moving slowly. When we arrived at the temple, all sixty priests were there waiting for me. The priestesses removed the cape from me, and I walked naked to the center of the large circle. I noticed that the circle had all the elements that I was blessed with. All the priests started to chant the prayers to summon the spirit of Thoth. They were carrying burning incense in the censers. I turned around in to the left in circles, and they turned in the opposite direction. I chanted the prayers with them, and all of them started to pull silver rays of Thoth and were pouring them on my head and body as they walked in a circle around me. The view of all of them was spectacular, the way all of them shined as the sun.

Then the ritual was over. I was seeing their clean souls, and I felt that I was floating in the air again. I saw Khety, and he smiled at me. I nodded my head and smiled. I was covered with the white robe, but my head was not covered with the hood. I got into the litter and was taken to the palace and into my quarters. I was dressed in a golden sheath to sleep in, had something to drink, and fell asleep.

I was awakened by the sensation that I was floating in the air. I could see my body from above on the bed. It was still three or four hours before they would come back to bathe me and dress me, and my beloved would be here. I lay back on the bed and spoke to my mother Hathor and father Amun-Ra and gave them thanks for allowing me to complete the ritual of the bathing and for being blessed with all the spirits of all the elements. I promised that I would be a good Pharaoh to my people. I dozed off again and was awakened by the feeling that someone was in the room and was looking at me in the dark. I opened my eyes, and Sen-Mut was standing there.

He came quietly and knelt beside me. Whispering, he said, "My love, you look beautiful as Thoth is shining on you. Sorry to wake you up. I came now because I could not wait until this morning to see you. I know that I will not be able to be alone with you this morning, and everyone is going to be here as you are being dressed for the coronation. Also, I wanted to tell you that I got your missive, and that I love you too. Are you hungry? Have you eaten tonight? I brought you warm food that I had T'Queta made for you. I have already tasted it, and it's safe to eat. I got worried about you after hearing from Hapuseneb that you had lost weight and were hungry the night before last. I felt bad for you, and I told T'Queta to make the food not contaminated with blood. I brought it to you because I wanted to see you. You must eat now, right now, while the food is still warm. This will hold you through the coronation tomorrow morning, and it's going to be a long day for you. I could not come earlier because, not too long ago, I finished the bathing ritual, and the pool was full of priests from Memphis, Heliopolis, and Saqqara. All of them are here. I've never seen so many priests gathered together in one place and going through the bathing ritual."

I smiled at him.

"Beloved, I have missed you so much too. I ate a lot yesterday, and, yes, I am hungry right now," I said.

Smiling at him, I caressed his face with my left hand, and he came closer and kissed my lips gently. A current of desire ran over our bodies, and I was hugging his body with a desperate desire for him to possess me. We were so hot and locked in this profound kiss. He abruptly pulled me away from him and stood up from the floor quickly.

"I better leave right now, or I will possess you at this moment. I have been desiring your body for the last six weeks, and I am hot right now," he said.

We knew that we could not give ourselves to the desires of our bodies until the ceremony was over.

"I am going home. I will be here in a couple of hours, and I will see them dress you. Then I will undress you tonight," he said. We laughed together.

"I will see you soon, my love, and I am dying to kiss your lips again," I said.

"If I kiss you, Maatke-Re, I would not be able to stop myself this time."

He came closer and kissed my forehead, and I smiled. I could see the happiness on his face.

"I will be waiting desperately for you, my love," I said, then I saw him leave.

I walked to the balcony and sat on my chair. I started to eat as I looked at the beauty of the night. Everything was so lovely, Thoth and the stars. I went back to my bed after eating, and I was full. And I thought of Sen-Mut and how much he loved me and cared for me, bringing me food not contaminated after all those hours in the temple at the bathing ritual. I could not go back to sleep. I was completely awake. It was not too long before the door of my quarters was opened, and many priestesses walked in.

"Many blessings to you, Your Majesty. Finally, the day of the coronation has arrived, and we are here, ready to bathe you."

I looked at all of them as my slaves were lighting many oil lamps. Everything looked bright with the light of the oil lamps. I walked with all of them to my bath and did my body necessities, and I was bathed with such love. My body was shaved again from my head to my toes including my eyebrows. Special incense used only for coronations was burning, and aromatic herbs were massaged all over my body.

"Your Majesty, you will probably be happy when everything is done. The good thing is that this occasion only happens once in a lifetime. The day we heard that you were chosen to be Pharaoh, we all were very happy for you. More surprising was when Khety, First Prophet of Amun-Ra, paid us a visit and told us that we must prepare your bathing for the coronation. We all jumped in happiness, so he brought us instructions of what to do and how to do it. It was nice to bring you to our bathing pool and do the first bathing for you," the priestess said.

I was as happy as everyone else listening to what they were telling me. I looked at all of them and said, "I want to thank every one of you for making me feel a part of you and for treating me with such love and kindness all these six weeks. And as of today, all of you are invited to the banquet hall to join me and celebrate my coronation."

They clapped their hands and cheered. I was bathed very well, and they helped me come out of my pool and was patted dry. I walked to my bedroom. And was surprise, when I saw the golden kilt, the gold belt of Pharaoh, and the golden cape. The entire room was clear and dressed in gold material, as were the bed covers. The ruffles at the bottom of the mattress were white linen with gold threads.[61] I saw how they had transformed my room, and I was completely moved by the beauty of my bedroom.

---

[61] To the historians and archeologists, the priestesses were the first ones in that lifetime to make the mattress ruffles for my bed.

I could hear Sen-Mut's voice on the other side of the doors. I wanted to run to him, but I had to wait. I heard him talking with Hapu. The priestesses started to put heavy kohl on my eyebrows and eyes and making long lines at the sides of my eyes, as was done for my father before. Then they started to dress me with the golden kilt and the golden belt, then the golden wrist cuff.[62]

I sat down on my chair, and the golden sandals were put on my feet by the slaves. I stood, and they put on me the golden pectoral that Father had given me for being a brave warrior when I became ten summers. Then they put over my shoulders the golden cape, and the train was very long.

"Your Majesty, you look very beautiful, like a god," they said, and brought the golden mirror Father had given me for my fifteen summers. I looked at myself in the mirror, and it was the truth. I looked radiant like a god.

"They can come in," the priestess said, and they were called in.

Sen-Mut and Hapuseneb walked into my bedroom, and Hapuseneb was holding the Crown of Horus. Both became mesmerized, and their mouths dropped open when they saw me. I smiled at Sen-Mut and at Hapuseneb. Sen-Mut was wearing the long white kilt with the golden belt. Over his shoulders, he wore the white linen robe embroidered in golden threads. From his left shoulder all the way down to his sandals, were the constellations. Now I understood that he must have gone through the same bathing ritual as I did when he became a priest, especially in the fields of astrology and astronomy.

---

[62] Now it's June 28, 2016, and my heart and my chest are full of emotions, remembering this moment, getting dressed for my coronation, and remembering my father, the Great Maat, and my mother, Ahmose. Father, I thank you for making it possible for me to reach the throne of Egypt beside the man I love.

Then Hapuseneb approached me, wearing his white kilt and long white linen robe with gold thread designs, and I knelt on one knee. He placed the Crown of Horus on my head. As I rose, everyone fell to the floor, their faces touching the floor, including Sen-Mut and Hapuseneb.

"Rise, everyone," I said.

We walked out of my bedroom, and in the outer quarters were Ineni, my dear uncle Thutmoses, Puyem-Re, and all two hundred priests and priestesses, who headed the procession down the stairs. Sen-Mut was at my left and Hapuseneb at my right, as always. I kept looking to my left at Sen-Mut, and he kept smiling at me. Then gently he pulled me by my hand and said, "You look beautiful, and you radiate as a god."

I smiled at him.

"Thank you, beloved. I feel like one," I said.

He nodded his head with a smile, and we continued walking. Hapuseneb whispered in my ear, "Your Majesty, you look so beautiful, more beautiful than anyone but you."

My eyes filled with tears, because I could see the love for me in his eyes.

We started the long walk to Karnak, to the Temple of Amun-Ra, where Khety was waiting and would do the prayers of Pharaoh. All the priestesses walked ahead of me, carrying burning incense, as hundreds of slaves were spreading petals of white flowers for every step I took to Karnak. Behind me was my little Hatshepset and Menkhep-Re holding the hands of Isis, then Ineni, my uncle Thutmoses, Generals D'Jehuty and Nehesi, as well as every general of my armed forces, then Ursaramun, Senemen, Thuty, Teshi, Sen-Mut's family, the family of Hapuseneb, and dignitaries from all over the land.

The streets of Thebes were full of people and soldiers with banners representing each battalion. The cavalry on their horses aligned on each side of the street, the charioteers in their chariots, the archers, were all along the path to Karnak. Every branch of the armed forces held colorful banners. I walked proudly as I passed my armed forces, and they hailed me. The dignitaries followed by the bravest of the braves, the palace guards. One of them could kill ten or more enemies in a ground battle, and I was very proud of all of them.

We continued walking on the path of stones through the rows of Sphinx until we arrived at the Temple of Amun-Ra. I looked at Sen-Mut, and he was smiling with his eyes very wide open.

“We are almost there, my love. Almost there,” he said.

I smiled back and saw his lips, his beautiful lips, and I wanted to kiss him but held back. I was full of emotions. We walked up the steps of the temple and were followed by everyone else.

The Temple of Amun was the largest temple of worship for the priests and could hold thousands of them and thousands of people. At the entrance door, Sen-Mut and Hapuseneb held back a few steps, and I proceeded to walk in by myself. The view was magnificent. All the priests were in front with Khety, including the sixty elder priests at his right side, and all were wearing long white kilts. It was a beautiful view. Khety looked magnificent, radiant, and full of life. He was wearing a leopard skin over his left shoulder, a golden belt, and holding in his left hand a long baton. He gave me a big smile, and as I came closer to him, he bowed his head, as did all the rest of the priests. By the time I reached the image of Amun-Ra, everyone was in the temple.

I knelt on both knees, and Khety removed the Horus crown from my head. He started to summon the presence of my father Amun-Ra, and the wind started to blow inside the temple. It had happened here before, and I felt the presence of my father. Khety, along with all the priests and priestesses, started to chant over my head the prayers of Pharaoh. I could hear Sen-Mut and Hapuseneb also saying the prayers with them. The incense was brought and passed over my head and over my body as I said my prayers. I stood up, and a golden goblet was given to me with the warm blood of a bull that they had just slaughtered away from the temple. I took it in my hands and took a sip. That bestowed the strength of the bull on me.

The ceremony ended, and everyone exploded in applause. I was full of emotions and so much joy. I looked for Sen-Mut, and he had the biggest smile on his lips as he was applauding. He whispered, "I love you, Maatke-Re."

My eyes filled with tears because he was mine, and I said, "I love you too, Ptah of Egypt."

Then I looked for Hapuseneb. He also had a big smile and nodded his head as he applauded. I took a few steps down, and I saw Hatshepset, my daughter, and Menkhep-Re clapping their hands, and they were looking at everyone as they were clapping. I smiled at both. Ineni was also clapping hard, and he had a big smile on his face too. I smiled back at him. He was as elated as everyone else.

Khety headed the procession out of the temple, followed by the sixty elder priests, and I walked behind them. I reached the entrance of the temple as Khety stood a few steps down and all the priests were waiting in the streets. I stopped at the entrance as Ra shined on me, and my people and the armed forces started to sound the horns and drums. The people were applauding all over and throwing white flower petals, and I took the first steps down to the street. This time I had to walk the path by myself until I reached the audience hall for the coronation. I started to walk down the street, and hundreds of slaves were aligning in two rows in front of me with baskets full of white flower petals, spreading them in my path. Khety and the sixty elder priests were carried in the litters by the litter-bearers in front of me. Sen-Mut and Hapuseneb followed behind me, and behind them the priestesses. Behind them was Hatshepset, Isis, Menkhep-Re, Ineni, Nehesi, D'Jehuty, my uncle Thutmoses, all the generals of the armed forces, Ursaramun, Thuty, Teshi, Sen-Mut's family and Hapuseneb's family, the dignitaries then palace guards.

White flower petals were flowing in the air, and I loved the beautiful view as petals fell on me. I was at peace and full of joy. I could see so many women cheering me on, and I smiled. I love my people, I love Thebes, my beloved Thebes. In just a little bit more, I would be Pharaoh. The long train of my cape and my kilt shined brightly as the rays of Ra were shining on me. I felt strange walking without the Crown of Horus on my head, but today I would be crowned with the Pschent, the Double Crown of Egypt.

I saw the love of my people on their faces, and that made me very happy. Finally, I arrived at the entrance of the audience hall, and I stood there looking at the golden throne of my father awaiting me. Then I saw Sen-Mut standing at the right side of the throne of Egypt, waiting for me, and we crossed looks. The feeling inside me was of love, peace, and happiness. At the left of the throne was Khety, and beside him was Hapuseneb. All the elder priests were behind Khety. They were waiting for me with big smiles.

I started to walk the long path as the slaves spread gold dust for every step I took. I was full of emotions as I walked the long path, looking up at the enormous pillars. I saw them so many times in this audience hall. As I walked forward to the throne, the train of my cape dragged the gold dust with me. I was happy. Finally, I reached the five steps of the throne, and Khety walked down and gave me his hand. I walked up the steps to the golden chair and knelt. I knew that this was it. I heard the loud voice of Khety invoking the prayers for Pharaohs again with both hands over my head. The large gold pectoral with the Eye of Horus was brought. He removed the small pectoral from my neck and placed Pharaoh's pectoral on my neck, the one my father wore and his father before him. The gold beard was brought. He fastened it on my chin and tied it behind my head. The beard represented the power and the strength of a male ruler.[63] Again, he placed his two hands over my head and continued with the Pharaoh's prayers.

---

[63] None of the previous Pharaohs had actual beards. They wore this golden beard in the ceremonies with the leather straps tied behind their head.

"You are the true daughter of Amun-Ra, and He fashioned you in your father's body and brought you into this body of a god. He has chosen you to rule the two lands," Khety said.

Then the Pschent, the red and white crown of Upper and Lower Egypt, was brought and given to him. Khety raised the Double Crown into the air, shouting, "In the presence of Amun-Ra and all the gods, the high priests of the two lands, and the people of Egypt, I, First Prophet of Amun, and server of the Almighty God, Amun-Ra, crown you, Hatshepsut I, Pharaoh of Egypt."

He placed the Pschent on my head.

It's done. I am Pharaoh of Egypt, I thought, immensely happy.

Then he gave me his hand and helped me rise from the floor, and I was guided to the golden throne. I sat there, wearing the Pschent, the red and white Double Crown of Egypt. Another priest approached with a pillow in his hand holding the crook and the flail. Khety took them in his hand, and, shouting, "The crook is the symbol of kingship," and gave it to me. Shouting again, he said, "The flail is the symbol of fertility of the two lands," and he gave it to me too.

Holding both in my hands, I crossed them over my chest. Everyone broke into loud shouts.

"Hail, Hatshepsut I, Pharaoh of Egypt! Hail, Hatshepsut I, Pharaoh of Egypt!" Everyone was shouting.

I turned to my left and looked at Sen-Mut, and he had tears in his eyes, as did I. He said, "I love you with all my heart, Pharaoh of Egypt."

I smiled at him and said, "Thank you, my beloved. Without you, I never would have reached the throne. And I have not forgotten your request."

We smiled at each other again. Then I looked for Hapuseneb. He was looking at me and was very happy. I could see it in his eyes, and I felt his love for me. I nodded my head and smiled and whispered, "Thank you." He nodded his head many times, smiling and applauding.

Khety spoke to Hapuseneb, and he helped Khety take a few steps down. Khety proceeded to unroll a large papyrus and started to read all my kingship titles[64]:

"Horus"

"Mighty of Souls"

"Favorite of the Two Goddesses"

"Fresh in Years"

"Golden Horus"

"Divine of Diadems"

"Sovereign of Upper and Lower Egypt"

"Beautiful God"

Khety looked at me and smiled, then continued.

"Mistress of the Two Lands"

"Maatke-Re, Beloved of Amun"

"King's Daughter"

"Divine Consort"

"Great Royal Wife"

---

[64] From ancient records, public domain.

“Prince of the Two Lands”

“Khnemet-Amun-Hatshepsut”

“She Lives Eternally!”

Everyone exploded in an uproar, clapping and shouting, “Pharaoh! Pharaoh!” Then the other headpieces were brought up and were presented by Hapuseneb.

“Your Majesty, we present you with the following headpieces that you will wear during your lifetime,” he said.

Each priest brought a headpiece, starting with Hapuseneb. He presented me with the Khepresh, the war helmet. It had blue and gold stars and a Uraeus[65] on it. It was made of gold and inlaid in blue enamel with small gold stars. Hapuseneb bowed his head to me as he was presenting the helmet and was smiling.

Next was the Nemes. It was a blue and gold striped war cloth with the vulture and the Uraeus on it. It was to be worn during battle when the Khepresh got too hot on the battlefield.

The Hedjet was the white crown of Upper Egypt.

The Deshret was the red crown of Lower Egypt.

There was also the golden crown of Hathor, followed by other deities’ crowns, and the list of crowns was long.

Then the coronation was over. I stood in front of all my people and smiled at them. The uproar and the applause of the dignitaries and the guests was immense. I could hear the loud hails of my people outside in

---

[65] Cobra.

the streets. It was so loud that I could hear them hailing my name, "Hatshepsut I! Hatshepsut, I! Pharaoh of Egypt! Hatshepsut, Pharaoh of Egypt!"

I looked at my beloved and smiled at him and remembered what Khety had told me six weeks ago, what the stars had foretold my father, that I would rule beside the man I love. I looked at Khety and walked to him.

"Khety, we did it, and we made it together. I want so much to thank you for all your help and for holding strong until now. I know you must be very exhausted." I looked at him with loving eyes as I continued, "And for being a good and faithful friend to my father and to me. I know that he is watching right now with my mother from the heavens. You helped me reach what was written in the stars the day that I was born. Thank you."

"Yes, Your Majesty, it's accomplished. And now I can go to the underworld in peace, knowing that you are going to do good for your people and be protected by the two most important men of the two Egypt's and who love you very much." He said.

I continued walking and personally thanked every elder priest for their help and faithfulness to my father and to me. I walked down the steps of my throne beside my two most beloved men, Sen-Mut and Hapuseneb. We walked the long path to the entrance doors of the hall of audience as the people hailed my name and dropped and kissed the ground I walk. The view was magnificent of thousands and thousands of people from all over the land, aligned and cheering me on as I walked down the street. The golden chariot was waiting for me to ride with the charioteers. The view was magnificent and spectacular. Sen-Mut walked me to the golden chariot, and the general of the charioteers was waiting for me to ride with them all over Thebes.

Looking into Sen-Mut's eyes, I said, "Beloved, I am looking forward to our time together alone." I smiled.

“And I am looking forward to our time alone too,” he said and gave me a big smile.

Sen-Mut and Hapuseneb followed behind me in a chariot. Behind them were battalions of archers and brave soldiers, the bravest of the brave palace guards, then the cavalry. We rode the golden chariot under the hot sun of Ra, and the people were throwing rose petals and lotus petals.

Six hours later we returned to the palace, and, to my surprise, two very large statues of me wearing the Double Crown of Egypt were at the palace entrance. I turned around and looked-for Sen-Mut. He was looking at me with a big smile on his face. He had done it. He did it for me. An enormous desire to kiss him overpowered me, and I got down from my chariot and started to walk towards Sen-Mut. He was walking to meet me too. Everyone stayed back. We came so close to each other, and I was desperate to kiss him. He was desperate to kiss me too.

“I want to undress you right now and make love to you right here,” he said.

“And I am desiring you, my love,” I said.

My body was trembling with desire.

“Beloved, what a wonderful gift you have given me. The throne of Egypt, and now these enormous statues of me at the entrance of the palace. Beloved, I need to kiss your lips right now, and I don’t know what to do,” I said.

He looked straight into my eyes, and, smiling, he said, “Let’s ride your chariot to the palace, and we will have plenty of time to be alone together. They must walk the long way to reach the outer gardens, then through the inner garden to reach the palace. You are Pharaoh, and they must wait for you.”

We laughed as we rode the chariot to the palace. I was between Sen-Mut’s strong arms and body, brushing my body against his, and he was aroused, as was I. Then we stopped, and a guard dropped to the ground.

"Rise," I said, and he did and took my golden chariot away from my gardens. We rushed up the stairs, and my door guards dropped themselves at my feet.

"Rise," I said and smiled at them, and Sen-Mut smiled at them too. They looked so happy to see me wearing the Double Crown on my head.

"No one comes through this door," Sen-Mut said.

We walked into my quarters right away, and I took backwards steps, laughing looking at Sen-Mut who stood there smiling. He followed me with a desirous look in his eyes. I noticed how much he was aroused. Then I stopped, waiting for him to take me. The desire of my body was overwhelming. He knelt and crawled on the floor to where I was standing and slowly removed the golden sandals from my feet and started to kiss my toes, kissing them slowly up to my legs as he slid his hands slowly under my kilt and up my thighs. His head was under my golden kilt. I was laughing, and I closed my eyes in delight and desire. Then he removed my loin cloth from my body and removed my kilt. And slowly kissing my thighs, my belly, all the way up to my lips. We were locked in the most passionate kiss. I was holding him tightly against my body with my arms wrapped around him, then I slid my hands under the robe over his shoulders and removed his robe. The robe dropped to the floor as we were still locked in this most passionate kiss. I was in delight. He continued pushing my body with his body. I could feel all of him. I removed his kilt and loin cloth in a hurry. I continued stepping backwards until we reached the cool stone wall. He pinned me there and we became one. We were lost in ecstasy, and he made passionate love to me as I wore the Double Crown of Egypt on my head. We exploded in the most powerful climax, hearing him grunt aloud in pleasure, giving me all what he has. He rested his head on my shoulder breathing heavily. He had paid his respect to the body of his Pharaoh.

“I could go to sleep right now, beloved. I am so tired,” I whispered in his ear.

He released me gently and kissed my lips. He lifted me up in his strong arms and sat me on the bed, and he removed the Double Crown of Egypt from my head and laid my head on the pillow.

“Close your eyes, my love, and breathe deeply. It will relax you. Sleep a little bit. They still have a long way to get here,” he said, and I did.

I woke up some time later and Sen-Mut was beside me, with his arm over his eyes.

“How long have I been asleep?” I asked him.

“Only about fifteen minutes,” he said.

“I must go to the bathroom and wash myself. I have not been taking the bitter herbs all these six weeks, and I cannot get pregnant at this moment.” I said.

“I agree,” he said.

I ran to the bathroom and did my necessities and washed myself well, and when I came back, he was fully dressed and had fallen asleep on our bed. His left arm was over his closed eyes. I got dressed quietly. I didn’t want to wake him up. I lay beside him and waited twenty minutes. He’d hardly had any sleep either. I kissed his lips gently, and slowly he opened his eyes. He smiled and sat at the edge of the mattress, and I got up from the bed and knelt between his legs.

Looking into his eyes, I said, “My love, you are the most precious thing to me. Thank you for loving me the way you have and for the two large statues at the entrance of the palace. Thank you for continuing to love me when we were apart. I want you to know that this kingdom is yours, with everything in it. Including me.”

I hugged him tightly, and he hugged me back and gently kissed my lips.

"Pharaoh Hatshepsut, I am the one who must thank you for loving me the way you do. I never expected to be loved back the way you have loved me, with the greatest love anyone can imagine, and for trusting me when I told you that there would be a time when we would be together. I love you and I always will, my beloved Maatke-Re." He said with a smile.

He kissed my lips, and I rested my head on his strong chest.

"We must go now, but I wish we could stay here, me holding you in my arms," he said.

"I wish that too, my love. I could sleep forever. But the feast must continue, and we must celebrate my coronation all night long," I said.

He placed the Double Crown on my head, and looking at him, I said, "My love, that was the most delicious respect you have placed on the body of your Pharaoh." I laughed.

"I loved every moment of it as I was making you mine," he said, smiling.

We walked out the golden doors holding hands, and I looked at my two older guards. They dropped to the floor.

"Rise, my faithful guards. You are invited to the feast of my coronation," I told them with a smile.

"Beloved, tell D'Jehuty to send replacements for my door guards so that they may enjoy the feast of my coronation. They have guarded my doors since I was a little girl," I said.

"I will, Your Majesty," he said and smiled.

We were very happy and laughing as we walked down the stairs holding hands. Everyone had just arrived at my inner gardens, and they dropped to the floor as I walked down the stairs. We continued walking to the banquet hall, where there was another surprise from Sen-Mut. Everything was decorated in gold and white linen. All the banquet tables were covered in gold material, all with white roses and white flowers everywhere. Everyone was standing in the banquet hall, including Sen-Mut's mother Hatnufer and his brothers and sisters.

The guard announced my entrance in a loud voice, "Hail, Hatshepsut I, Pharaoh of Egypt!"

Everyone started to clap and shout, "Hatshepsut I! Hatshepsut I!"

Then the guard shouted, "Sen-Mut, Ptah, Steward of Amun-Ra and Master of the Palace."

Then he announced, "Hapuseneb, Vizier of the South, Khety, First Prophet of Amun-Ra, Puyem-re, Second Prophet of Amun-Ra," and continued announcing the names of all the dignitaries of the land that had come to witness my coronation.

Standing at the entrance doors, I smiled at everyone, and everyone dropped to the floor. I looked at the beautiful decorations and settings Sen-Mut had ordered. I sat on the golden chair that was my father's and brother's and was now mine.

"Rise, everyone. Let the celebration begin," I shouted.

The music started, and the dancers started performing for me. Everyone exploded in applause. I was the happiest women in the world. I had become the first woman Pharaoh of Egypt. I celebrated with my precious daughter Hatshepset, Menkhep-Re, my dearest friends, my people, and especially my beloved Sen-Mut and Hapuseneb. The night was beautiful. It was a full moon. Thoth poured his silver rays all over the land, and everything looked lovely, as if he was happy too.

We celebrated until the early part of the morning. The celebration continued all over my land for weeks.[66]

Sen-Mut and I left the banquet hall holding hands, and we could see the first rays of Ra rising in the east.

"Beloved, everything was so beautiful and perfect today. Thank you, my love. You and everyone else made me very happy," I said.

He smiled and said, "You don't need to thank me, my beloved. You deserve everything. It is I who must thank you for the rest of my life for trusting me, loving me, and for being my wife."

He lifted me up in his arms and carried me up the stairs to our quarters, and the replacement guards opened the golden doors. Sen-Mut took me to our bedroom and undressed me. I was very tired and was falling asleep. I made the effort to walk to the bathroom. We were bathed by the slaves. The water was poured over my head and face, and it cooled and refreshed my body and felt good. We were very tired, and our eyes were closing. The slaves finished bathing us and patted us dry.

"Go and enjoy the feast of the coronation of your Pharaoh in the banquet hall," he told the slaves with a smile, then lifted me up in his arms again and carried me to our bed. He laid me gently on the bed and lay beside me as we cuddled in each other's arms. I felt his kiss on my forehead.

I whispered, "I love you, Ptah, Steward of Amun."

"I love you too, Pharaoh of Egypt," he said, and we fell asleep.

****

---

[66] I still feel the emotions of that day, when I became Pharaoh of Egypt beside the most powerful men in my life (Sen-Mut, Hapuseneb, and Khety) as if it happened yesterday. (October 2016)

It was very late at night when I woke up, and Sen-Mut was not in bed. I searched for him and found him standing on the balcony, looking at the stars quietly. He was naked, and I came from behind and wrapped my arms around his waist and hugged him tightly. He turned around with a smile and covered me with his arms.

"My love, did I wake you?" he said.

"No, beloved. I just woke up when I did not feel your body beside me. Then I saw you standing here, looking at the stars."

"This night is beautiful, isn't it?" he said.

"Yes, my love, it is. Aren't you tired from the long coronation and all the celebration?" I asked.

"No, I could not sleep for too long. It's hot tonight and looking at the stars I wonder, sometimes, how do the stars foretell the future? And why can I read them and foretell the future too? It's as if we are mentally connected. You know that someday I would really like to study them. It will take a lot of patience in a room with a balcony surrounding it, so I could walk around in a circle and follow their movements in the dark sky in complete silence to concentrate."

I turned to face him.

"Beloved, I want you to do it. It will please me very much to have you here close to me rather than only see you on the weekends. Sometimes you are gone for two weeks. It will please me very much for you to do as your heart desires. This kingdom is yours, my love. You can send someone else, like Hapuseneb, to inspect the construction sites sometimes. He has some knowledge of architecture. Or you can let Senemen continue with the building of the temple, and once a month we can go together. Or you can go with Hapuseneb, whichever you like," I said.

"My love, give me some time to think about this. Leaving the construction of the temple makes me uneasy."

"Well, beloved, as you wish. Come and let's bathe to cool off our bodies," I said.

We walked, and we bathed each other with cool water. I dried his body, and we went to bed.

"Beloved, do you know that I cannot sleep if you're not beside me?" I said.

"Maatke-Re, it happens to me too. Sometimes, I wake up and watch you sleep. It makes me happy to watch you sleep, and that we are together, and that you are my wife. This means that we will be tied together for the rest of our lives."

He snuggled me, and we fell asleep.

****

I was very much involved in the daily hearings with Hapuseneb in the audience hall. Sen-Mut had gone back to the Valley of the Dead to direct the construction of my temple. He said, "I want this building to last for all eternity, as our love will last." His words always filled my heart with love and joy.

I went to the warrior training camps with Menkhep-Re, and he loved it. He was growing, now six summers, and he loved to come with me and see me training with my warriors. I had a surprise for him. In a few months he would start his own training. I wanted him to be as one of our bravest warriors and to defend our Palace when he grew up.

****

A few months passed. Sen-Mut and I made love every time he returned from the Valley of the Dead. I loved his body, and it stayed imprinted on my mind. I enjoyed our love making very much and desired him all the time.

"Maatke-Re, for a few months I have been thinking of what you said, and to study the stars I must build an observatory. I decided that I will build it," Sen-Mut said.

I sat up quickly in the bed, and smiling at him, I said, "I am very happy to hear that, my love. And that you are going to do what your heart desires. Then I don't have to wait for you to return from the Valley of the Dead to see you. You have made me very happy right now with this decision. How soon can you start building the observatory?" I asked.

I was looking at him full of joy. I could now have him beside me every day and night. He sat up in the bed and pulled his pillow and placed it against the wall. Then he leaned his back against his pillow and said, "I already left Senemen in charge of the construction, and he knows if he encounters any problems to notify me right away. He must follow the plans of the building as I order."

I came closer to him and kissed his lips, and he smiled.

"I have drawn some sketches for you to see. Tell me which one you like," he said and got up from the bed and walked to the corner wall and came back carrying very large papyri.

"Beloved, will you build it on the palace grounds?" I asked.

"No, I must find a place far away from the palace, where only silence and darkness will surround me."

"Let's see the plans you have drawn," I said.

He opened them and laid them on top of the bed.

Looking at the sketches, I saw a very high tower but didn't see stairs to access the top. The top was encircled by a balcony like he wanted. It had three large square doors. The one to the left was facing east, another one was facing west, and the other one was facing north. The second papyrus had the interior design with a bed in the center of the floor and a small dining table with two chairs. On the balcony, he had drawn three very large square tables, facing east, west, and north, where he would lay the papyri as he followed the stars and constellations. The third papyrus showed the back wall behind the bed. There was a door to reach the toilet, which had a seat like the one in the palace. The fecal waste would drop down into a very large basket full of sand. The waste would be picked up every day by the slaves, as was done in the palace. Large jars along the wall of the bathroom would hold water for bathing. Inside, near the dining table, were large jars for his favorite wine. On the balcony, he had drawn a room for Tuyii.

"How are we going to get up to the top and come down?" I asked.

"I will make a special chair to be pulled by ropes to go up and down," he said.

"Will the ropes be strong enough to hold our weight?" I asked, concerned.

"Yes. I will make the chair myself with strong wood. It will be the same wood I use to make the floor. As long we are in there, I will pull you up and lower you to the ground myself. Your palace guards will guard the ropes and will pull me up or down. I completely trust them," he said.

"And me too. Beloved, there will not be another way down?" I asked.

"Yes, there will be. Do you see those dots in the tower drawings? Those will be steps to go up or down in case of emergency. And you must learn how to climb a tree like the goddess Basted."

"I don't understand," I said.

"Those will be retractable steps," Sen-Mut said.

"I still don't understand."

"I will show you tomorrow. I have ordered tree trunks to be cut and brought here. They will be arriving tomorrow, and you will be able to see what I mean with the dots here. I will show the slaves tomorrow what size they should be cut. I want them to be strong enough and safe for you to be able to come down in case of emergency. You will understand it better when the project is under construction," he said then turned the page. The next page was plans for the inside of the tower with the same dots as on the outside of the tower.

"How big is it going to be on the top?" I asked.

"It's going to be large enough, with plenty of room to walk around and for the three large tables. I need to do my drawings on the large tables and have plenty of space where I can take notes easily," he said.

I noticed that he was excited about it. I could see it in his shining eyes and by the way he was speaking to me. I noticed the force within him, one that moved him, and the look on his face was serious as he was explaining his drawings to me.

"When do you want to begin?" I asked.

"At the beginning of Shomu. It will be summer, and I hope we don't have the sandstorms that will hold back the construction of it and of your temple."

I became quiet for a moment, then said, "Beloved, I already saw into the future. There will be no sandstorms this year, and you will be able to finish the observatory as you wish."

He looked at me and smiled.

"Since when can you see the future?" he asked.

"I believe everything started after the bathing and before my coronation. I also find it strange, but I remember when I was five summers and passed the test of the foreseeing. I started to experience certain abilities, like when I could hear a scarab crawling under my bed," I said.

"Hmm. You can hear a scarab crawling? You never told me that before," he said.

"I had forgotten until now. During the rituals of the bathing of the elements, my Ka came out of my body, and I saw everything from above, like when I went to war and was wounded by the Hyksos. This time, I saw my body lying on the linen sheets as the priestesses were pouring honey and herbs all over me. I had forgotten to tell you that too. After my Ka returned to my body and it was all over, I felt as if I was floating in the air," I said.

"Do you still experience going to the middle of the universe as when you were five summers?" he asked.

"I don't know how. It just happens when my Ka comes out of my body, and I don't have control of it," I said.

"Maybe during my studies, you can try doing it. That would help me with the stars map of the constellations. Because you will be in the middle of all of them and be able to guide me. That would be an ability I would like to have. I can imagine it must have been a beautiful experience for you," he said.

"Yes, my love, it was the most impressive experience I ever had, and I like the feeling of flying. I would love to do it again. Beloved, I could see everything from above, and I wish I had wings to fly. Sen-Mut, I also have vivid dreams of the future in my sleep. Weeks, months, or even years can pass, and it becomes reality, that same moment in time. I wonder if my Ka comes out of my body when I am asleep and travels to the future," I said.[67]

---

[67] As I remember this talk I had with Sen-Mut, I still have the same experiences with my Ka in this life. And I remember my dreams. Days, weeks, years, or thousands of years can pass, and I still remember them. I had dreams of the future 3,500 years ago. One morning 3,500 years ago, I woke up with Sen-Mut beside me, and I told him that I had a strange dream in which I was speaking with a strange man that was dressed strangely. We

The following day he got up very early in the morning and kissed me good bye, and I saw him leave. That morning he was meeting with his engineer Min-Mose, and he was carrying under his arm the drawing plans of the observatory. Together they were going to see the cut trees for the building of the floor and the dots in his drawings, and tomorrow we would look for the right location to build it.

---

were beside a big box, and that big box had strange wheels. The strange clothing was a shirt with buttons in the front, and the big box was a car with rubber tires. In 1983, I was talking with a co-worker, and we were beside a car and suddenly I remembered my dream in Egypt 3,500 years ago. It was the same man, with the same shirt and the same car. I know that many of you readers may have had my same experience, of being in a place you have never been before but knowing the place and knowing that you have been there but not knowing when. This is because when you are asleep your soul comes out of your body and travels to the future. Also, I believe that many people are attached to a certain place but don't know why, like my dearest friend, whom I love very much. He had his company in an area with a view of the rocky hills in Albuquerque, New Mexico, and his office had large glass windows facing the hills. The rocky hills looked like the rocky hills of the Valley of the Dead, in Thebes, Egypt.

When I was a little girl, in this present time, I did not know why I kept looking at a lighthouse on the beach. I could stand there and look at it for a long time. There was something strange about it that I could not figure out. I knew that something was missing, but I did not know what it was. One day I walked inside and went up the stairs. It was tiring for me. When I got to the top, something was not right, and I did not know what it was. I realized that it was missing the floor where our bed was. I was puzzled by the lighthouses because of the similarities to Sen-Mut's observatory. Also, the lighthouse was missing the very large balcony around it where Sen-Mut had the large tables.

I never cease to amaze myself with my memories, and the talks I had with my beloved. If he only knew how hard it is for me not having him beside me and hearing him laugh, kissing my lips, putting his arms around my body, and not being able to hear him say, "I love you Maatke-Re."

****

We rode our horses early in the morning south and looked for the correct place, and we found one south of Hopi and far away from the palace and away from the path of the floods.

"Beloved, you look so very happy," I said.

"Yes, I am. Thank you, Hat, for allowing me to build the observatory," he said.

I came closer to him and held his right hand and kissed it. Then looking into his eyes, I said, "Beloved, never tell me thank you again. Everything belongs to you, including me." I smiled.

He brought my hand to his chest and kissed me on my lips. I caressed his face with my left hand.

"I love you, Ptah of Amun," I whispered in his ear.

"And I love you too, Pharaoh of Egypt."

He hugged me as we looked at the current of Hopi. The current was subsiding. Shomu would soon be here, I thought.

We were at the end of the month of Pha-Rmuti,[68] and the Nile had retreated, its waters leaving a silt of rich soil. Soon the peasants would plant the crops, and we would have a good harvest. It was good for my kingdom.

"Beloved Maatke-Re, tomorrow morning I will start the construction of the observatory."

---

[68] The month of March.

I was looking at him as he was washing his face, hands, and arms, getting ready to say our evening prayers.

"I am very happy for you, my love. How long will it take to be built?" I asked.

"I really don't know. Maybe three to six months. I want to make sure that the ground for the foundation of the building is solid, so it will not sink or tilt to one side or collapse. It's going to be very high above the ground, and I can hardly wait to start and finish building it," he said.

I smiled at him with love. He looked very animated, and that made me happy. I walked to the washing vase and washed myself. We knelt facing the west as Ra was fading away and said our prayers. After our prayers there was a knock on the golden doors, and Tuyii announced that it was Master Hapuseneb. We walked to the outer quarters, and I saw an expression of sadness on his face.

I knew it was Khety.

"Good evening, Your Majesty," he said and knelt on one knee.

"Rise, Hapu," I said.

"I am not coming with good news. First Prophet of Amun is dying, and he wants to speak with you before he goes to the underworld."

"If you wait, we will be ready in a few minutes," I said.

My eyes became full of tears. I felt as if I was losing the last part of my father, and I looked at Sen-Mut, who was very saddened too. We got ready, and I wore the Horus crown on my head. We left our quarters, and the litter-bearers were waiting downstairs for us. We got into the litter, and they took us to the temple. We walked to Khety's quarters. His room was very spacious. I had never been in there before. Then I saw him and ran and knelt beside him with tears in my eyes. Sen-Mut was behind me, and Hapuseneb was across from me at the other side of the bed by Khety's feet. All the other priests were around him, chanting prayers and burning incense. His time was coming closer. I held his hand in my left hand, and it was cold, like my mother's hand.

"Khety, I am here," I whispered softly, and he opened his eyes and tried to smile but hardly had the strength.

"Hatshepsut," he whispered. I came closer to him and lowered my ear to his mouth. "Be good to your people. I am pleased that I accomplished your father's wishes, and you reached the throne. And your request will be fulfilled for Hapuseneb. He will take my place after I am gone. Be happy. You have two men that love you very much, and they will give their lives for you."

Slowly his hand lost strength and released mine. I saw his eyes open for the last time, and he went to Heaven.[69]

I cried for my good friend, and Sen-Mut held me in his arms with tears in his eyes. Khety had been good to him since I sent Sen-Mut to him when he was young. I could see the tears rolling down Hapuseneb's face as well. He had given him many years of friendship and teachings. I nodded my head to Hapu, and he came to me. I touched his arms and hugged him.

"I am sorry, Hapuseneb. Now he is at peace. I want the best of everything for his funeral. Please be in charge. He was family to me, and he deserves the best," I said.

Looking at me, he lowered his eyes and whispered, "Lotus of Egypt, thank you. I mean thank you for the request to Khety. For me to become First Prophet of Amun. I heard that it will be done tonight, after

---

[69] Dear Khety, I want to thank you for being my father's friend and for all your help in helping me reach the throne of Egypt. You are greatly missed by all of us, and we all loved you then. (7/15/2016)

his body is taken to our priest the embalmer here in the temple. It's our custom to choose right away a First Prophet."

"Hapu, you are my dearest friend, you deserve to be First Prophet of Amun," I said and squeezed his hand. I turned around and walked to Khety's body, and I kissed his forehead. "Goodbye, my dearest friend."

Sen-Mut looked at me and said, "Beloved, I must stay here tonight with the other priests and continue with the prayer for the dead, and I must postpone the groundbreaking for the observatory for few days. I was surprised when I heard Hapuseneb thanking you for the position of First Prophet of Amun. You never told me that you had spoken to Khety before regarding his position to choose Hapuseneb as First Prophet of Amun. I believe it's a very good idea and a strategic one. I wonder how Puyem-Re will take the news that Hapuseneb has been chosen to take Khety's place."

"I thought about asking Khety a long time ago, and I started to work on that when I was chosen to be Pharaoh. He has been working at it for the last three years. Tonight, Khety confirmed to me that my petition will be granted. And Hapu will be made First Prophet of Amun-Ra by the elder priests tonight. I made the request to him that day he asked you to leave us alone for a moment, on the day he let me know when my first bathing ritual was going to be. Do you remember when he asked you to leave us alone? Then he fell asleep, and I went looking for a younger priest to carry him to his quarters, but you carried him instead? That was very sweet of you. I lost track that day of what I wanted to tell you, and then we sailed the Nile for three days. On that night, I remembered again and was about to tell you, but you were carrying the white linen sheets and placed them on the floor of the barge and made love to me. I forgot all over again until today. Please forgive me," I said.

"Hat, there is nothing to forgive, my love," he said.

The prayers for the dead started and only men were allowed, but I was no longer considered a woman. Among them I was Pharaoh, and I remained with them during the chanting of the prayers for the dead. Sen-Mut, Hapuseneb, and I accompanied his body to the house of the priest embalmer, followed by every priest in a long procession with burning incense. From there we all walked to the Temple of Amun, where Hapuseneb would be chosen First Prophet of Amun.

I stood in front of the statue of Amun, and the fifty-nine elder priests cast their votes in favor of Hapuseneb. I saw the face of Puyem-Re, turn into a shock. He became pale, but he did not object. Then the baton and the leopard skin were brought, and Hapuseneb was dressed by an elder priest. I ratify his position.

"As of today, in the presence of the elder and young priests of the Temple of Amun-Ra, I, Hatshepsut I, Pharaoh of the two lands, declare you First Prophet of Amun-Ra, and you will continue with the title of Vizier of the South. Let it be written and let it be done."

Hapu looked into my eyes with his loving eyes and gave me a smile.

"Thank you, Your Majesty," he said

He remained in the temple talking to all the priests, and Sen-Mut and I left.

"Now, I have the two most powerful men in my kingdom," I thought.

This morning Sen-Mut had gone to the temple as he did every day for prayers for Khety's soul, but today on his return to the palace, he looked different, I thought. He had stopped and visited T'Queta for a while. I still had a hint of jealousy, but I knew that he did visit her from time to time because he told me so.

"Beloved, on the way back from the temple, I visited T'Queta," he said.

I looked at him and smiled.

"When you go and visit her, what do you talk about?"

“Mostly it is about her and if she is alright. I told her that Khety died, and she said that she heard of it. But today was different,” he said.

“How is that?” I asked.

“Well, she came closer to me and held my hand and kissed it and rubbed my hand on her face. I knew what she had on her mind and what she wanted, and I told her that I don’t mind if she has a lover. Then she stopped and let go of my hand. She said that she did not want a lover, that she was missing me greatly. I asked her if she was still in love with Hapuseneb, and she shook her head and said that she was in love with me. That took me by surprise,” he said.

My heart was rising, and my blood was becoming cold, waiting for him to tell me that he laid with her.

“Did you lay with her?” I snapped at him.

He came closer, pulled me by my waist with force, and looked into my eyes, saying, “Are You jealous?”

“Yes,” I said.

“Don’t be. I am in love with you and only with you. I only enjoy making love with you,” he said, and, with a smile, he kissed me.

Then he made passionate love to me. That was his assurance to me that none else existed in his life but me.

Later, we rode our horses to the building site where Min-Mose the engineer had started the groundbreaking, and when we dismounted, Min-Mose dropped his face to the ground, as did all the slaves.

“Rise, Min-Mose”, I said, and he did. “Tell the slaves to continue working.”

He shouted at them loudly, “Continue!”

He had set up the royal tent, and Sen-Mut's plans were on a large table. They spoke for a long time and walked off together. I was sitting there when I started to get sick to my stomach, for it was too hot for me. Not even the fan bearers could cool me down, and I started to vomit. The heat was intense. Sen-Mut was far away from me.

Could I be pregnant again? I was startled at the possibility of it and remembered the day of the coronation he made love to me. I had not taken the bitter herbs for six weeks. I sent for Sen-Mut right away, and he came back.

"Beloved, it is very hot for me to be here, and I am not feeling well. I will return to the palace. Tell Min-Mose that I am taking his chariot and his charioteer to the palace."

"Hat, are you OK?" he asked, and I started to cry. He held me by my shoulders with his hands, and, looking at me, he asked, "What's wrong?"

I lowered my eyes and said, "I believe I am pregnant again."

He had a big smile and hugged me tight against his chest and kissed my forehead.

"Well, I will be a father again. That makes me very happy, my love, and I hope it's a boy," he said.

We smiled at each other. Then kissing my lips, he sent for Min-Mose's chariot, and he rode the chariot carefully until we got to the palace. He carried me in his arms up the stairs.

"Tuyii," he called, and she came running with other slaves.

"Tuyii, send for Menina and the physician right away."

Menina came rushing in and knelt beside my bed.

"Your Majesty, what is wrong?" she asked.

"Menina, I believe that I am pregnant. I had not taken the bitter herbs for six weeks, and on the day of the coronation, Sen-Mut and I made love. And after we had sex, I did not believe that I had gotten pregnant. The following day I started to take the bitter potion again, and we have been having sex since then."

"Well, Your Majesty, if you are pregnant, let's stop the herbs for now. Do you want to have this child?"

"Yes, I do. I want the seed of my beloved to grow inside of me again."

"Very well, Your Majesty. I will call for the physician to check you and to be sure that everything is well with you."

"Thank you, Menina. Please keep it to yourself," I said.

"I will, Your Majesty. Now let me bathe you today. You are full of sand from the desert," Menina said.

Sen-Mut interrupted her.

"I will bathe her today. Have them prepare the bath."

He undressed me and carried me to the tub. I could see so much happiness in his face. He placed me in the middle of the tub and poured cool water over my head. I was silent. He was doing it tenderly as he said, "Hat, you are very quiet."

I took his hand and brought it to my belly and smiled at him. I was happy too.

"Beloved of mine, there has never been a pregnant Pharaoh before," I said.

"No, but you are not just a Pharaoh. You are a goddess. And goddesses can do whatever they want to. Don't be worried about anything. I am at peace and happy right now," he said and kissed me.

After the bathing, I felt a lot better. The cool water had taken away the heat from my body, as well as the nausea. I saw how tenderly he dried my body and put a white linen sheath on me and carried me to the bed, where the physician was waiting for me. He examined me.

"Your Majesty, you are not pregnant," he said.

"What?" I looked at Sen-Mut. His eyes were wide open.

"Why? I was nauseated and vomiting."

"Were you under the sun for too long? You look like you have lost a lot of weight since the last time I saw you," he said.

"Yes, I have, during the bathing ritual before my coronation."

"Well, Your Majesty, the sun and the loss of weight could have made you fragile, and the heat causes nausea and makes you vomit. I see it many times in my patients," he said.

I realized that he was right. I was disappointed.

The physician left, and Menina was standing there quietly. Sen-Mut took the place of the physician and held my hand.

Beloved, we have many years ahead of us, and we will have many children. I promise," he said and smiled.

I knew that deep in his heart he wanted another child, as I did.

The following morning, we rose together and washed ourselves to receive Ra and said our prayers. He was bathed by the slaves, and I was waiting for him at our dining table with breakfast ready when he came back refreshed and clean. He sat beside me. Then looking at me, he held my hand.

"You are so quiet this morning," he said and kissed me.

"I don't know how I could have been so wrong thinking that I was pregnant," I said.

“Well, you had me so happy for a little bit, but we have plenty of time in the future. It is better for you not to be pregnant for now. You just became Pharaoh, and it would be funny to see the male Pharaoh with a growing belly!”

He was smiling, and it was funny.

“You are right. The gods will know when I should have another child,” I said.

We finished having breakfast, and he kissed my lips, then was on his way to the groundbreaking again for the observatory. As he was walking out of our quarters, he turned around, and looking at me he said, “Hat, I love you.”

I smiled and answered back, “And I love you too, beloved.”

I walked to the balcony and saw him riding his horse with several guards behind him.

He was so loving with me and never left without saying, “I love you,” or fell asleep without saying, “Sweet dreams” and “I love you, Maatke-Re.”

****

During the construction, I visited the site many times and watched my beloved at work under the hot rays of Ra. I sat under the shade of the large royal tent, which I had ordered to be set up for Sen-Mut. I was amazed at how he could create things out of stones. I now knew what the dots were in the drawings. They were thick, round pieces of wood cut from the trunks of trees, and they were placed inside holes in the building. They were steps going up around the building, and they were retractable from the inside. I saw him being brought up to the top of the observatory by ropes as the building progressed. I could see him standing way up high on top wearing the red Nemes on his head that distinguished him from Min-

Mose. He would stand on top of the building looking at me, and sometimes he waved at me as they were setting the wooden floor on top of it.

Late in the afternoon, he would come down and meet me with a kiss, and the slaves bathed him with fresh water. We would have dinner with his engineers and sit beside the Nile in the dark of the night, talking with everyone. I ordered the best food for everyone, including the slaves that were building the observatory. I wanted them all to be happy, so they would work with happiness and say prayers of well-being for Sen-Mut's observatory.

"Beloved, when the construction is over, I want you to reward every slave with five gold nuggets, and reward Min-Mose well too," I said.

"I will, my love. You have a beautiful heart. My love, why don't you return to the palace? I will send for you when we are close to finishing the observatory. You spend all day alone under this heat, and when I come back, I am so tired that we hardly speak," he said with a smile.

I caressed his face.

"You are right, beloved, and the mosquitos are eating me alive. I will leave early tomorrow when the morning is still fresh," I said.

"My love, believe me, I want you here, but I hope you can understand that this place is not for you. Me and my crew are adjusted to the heat and the mosquitos and flies," he said.

"I completely understand you, my love. Don't worry. As soon you are done, send for me."

I looked at him, and his eyes were closed. He had fallen asleep. I cuddled next to him as the fan bearers fanned us with large peacock feathers. The net for the mosquitoes was closed around us. The good part was that the nights were cooler, and I liked that.

****

Six months passed, and the observatory was finished. Sen-Mut sent for me and for Hapuseneb. I took with me my personal slave Tuyii and ordered plenty of food and wine to last us for a while, including chickens and goats. Hapuseneb was happy as we rode our horses to the observatory. He came to bless the building. I was amazed at how wonderful the observatory looked. Sen-Mut greeted me with a big smile, kisses and hugs.

"I am happy that you got here, my love," he said, then greeted Hapuseneb. I could see the happiness in his eyes.

"Beloved, it's time for you to come and see your new residence," he said and smiled.

"Beloved, are you sure I will not fall?" I asked.

"No, my love. I made it very strong to hold your weight. And believe me, my love, if you fall, I will commit suicide," he said.

"Sen-Mut! Don't say that ever again," I said.

"It's the truth if that ever happens. I cannot live without you," he said, looking into my eyes.

"I completely trust you, my love. Let's go up," I said.

I had butterflies in my stomach thinking that soon I would be pulled up in the air.

"Hat, I will go up first, then I will send the chair down, and I will pull you up myself with the help of the slaves here on the ground. I want you to hold tight to the ropes as I pull you up, OK?" he said.

Then he kissed me, and I smiled. I saw him sitting on the chair, and the slaves started to pull him up, all the way to the top. Our eyes were locked on each other. He reached the top and returned the chair down, and it was my turn. I sat on it, and Hapuseneb fastened a strong belt on me as he smiled.

"Your Majesty, you will be amazed at the view," Min-Mose said.

He signaled to Sen-Mut that that I was ready. I held the rope tightly as Sen-Mut said to, and Min-Mose began pulling the ropes himself. I was nervous in the beginning, but I was amazed by the view. I could see very far away. I looked up, and there was a large open door in the bottom of the floor. The chair went through that door, then Sen-Mut pulled the chair in and set it on the wooden floor. He removed the belt from my waist and hugged and kissed me.

"Welcome to your home, my love," he said and closed the door on the floor and locked it. Holding my hand, he showed me the view around the balcony. The view was magnificent from up there, from all angles. The floor was a very large octagon, and I felt secure walking on the hard floor. He continued showing me around, holding my hand. Three large tables were set up for his drawings, facing east, west, and north. There was also plenty of space for a few people to walk freely around the balcony, where there were also several chairs.

He then showed me the inside of the house and our bed. The bed had a net around it for the mosquitos. He had set up everything very lovely. Flowers were on top of the small wooden dining table, and I noticed a very small vase with a very tiny lid behind the flower jar, probably a perfume for me, I thought. There were also several golden goblets set on another table. He had installed wooden doors to close the three large openings. He showed me the bathrooms. He had also built a small room for Tuyii to sleep in and had made a kitchen on the ground for her to cook. He had done everything perfectly, and I was happy with the man that I had.

"Maatke-Re, tonight we are spending our first night here, and I already left Hapuseneb in charge of the palace with Ineni. Tuyii is waiting on the ground to come up and serve us and bathe us later. I will bring her last," he said.

I smiled and walked to the bathroom again and noticed how solid the floor was.

“Hat, I am bringing Hapuseneb and the engineer up. Make yourself at home now,” he said and walked around the balcony and disappeared from my sight.

Ten minutes later, Hapuseneb was walking toward me. I greeted him with a smile.

“Lotus of Egypt, how do you like it?” he asked.

“Hapu, I am so impressed with the view. I could see so far to the east, the west, and to the north. I can see the palace from here, and it’s very far away. And from every side of the balcony, I can see Hopi running from south to north,” I said.

“I am also impressed with Sen-Mut’s project. What made him make a home way up in the sky?” he asked.

“It is not a house. Well, sort of it is. It’s an observatory. He wants to study the constellations and the stars.”

We were startled by a scream, and I ran to Sen-Mut. He was laughing. It was Tuyii screaming as Sen-Mut and the slaves were pulling her up. I started to laugh, as did Hapu.

“Oh, Your Majesty! I was so very scared that I would fall. Forgive me for my screams,” she said.

I started to laugh again. Sen-Mut could not stop laughing, and Hapuseneb was laughing too. Then it was time to bring Min-Mose up. He was pulled up, and we all sat together as Tuyii served all of us warm food and wine. She had cooked enough food for the guards too.

Sen-Mut was very happy and smiling as he drank his wine, and he kept looking at me. Then I remembered when we were in Philae, and he was across the fire, looking at me and drinking his wine. I could feel his happiness in my skin, and I was very happy too. He had accomplished one of his dreams, and I was glad to help make it happen.

We continued the celebration as Ra was fading away, and the four of us washed ourselves and said the evening prayers. After the prayers we continued drinking, eating duck, goat meat, breads, grapes, goat cheese, and chives and waited for Mother Nut to cover the sky.

Little by little the stars were showing, and I could see the face of Sen Mut light up. He was mesmerized at the view of the stars, seeing them up close, as were I, Hapu, and Min-Mose. We continued drinking and looking at the beauty of the constellations. Sen-Mut was right. Everything did look better from up here.

I noticed the night was getting colder and the wind was picking up. He clapped his hands, "Tuyii, bring galabias and blankets for all of us," he told her.

"Blankets? How did you know it was going to be cool up here?" I asked.

"Because it is cold in the desert at night, as in the Valley of the Dead. I climbed up the rocky hills in the nights to see the stars up close, and it does get colder in the rocky hills," he said.

"I see," Hapuseneb said.

"Well, it's time for me to go. It's very late, and I still have two hours to reach the palace," Hapu said.

"I must go too. I have not seen my family for six months, and my wife has been waiting for me," Min-Mose said.

I heard Sen-Mut calling down to the slaves on the ground, and they were ready to lower Hapu and Min-Mose. We said our goodbyes, and they were brought down.

Tuyii had prepared warm water for bathing, and Sen-Mut and I bathed each other. He was very tipsy from so much wine, and I was laughing a lot. He looked at me and said, "You look beautiful tonight. Do you know that? Even without hair." He smiled.

He kissed my lips and continued, "When I was drinking the wine tonight, and we were talking, I kept looking at you because I was remembering when we were in Philae. You were across the fire from me, and I wanted to kiss you, every time I took a sip of wine."

"Beloved, tonight I remembered that same moment in Philae, and the way you were looking at me that night. I did not know that you wanted to kiss me?" I said, and we laughed.

"Come and kiss me, Ptah of Egypt, and make love to me tonight. And remember that night, when I wanted so much for you to kiss me too."

He came closer and pressed his lips hard on mine, and we made passionate love under the stars. After our love making, we lay satisfied and held each other in our arms.

"I want you to know that when I was building my humble home in Thebes, with every piece of adobe brick that I put in my home, I had you on my mind. I was building it for you, including the flowers around my home, as I built this observatory too," he said.

"Thank you, my love. When I heard Ineni had given you that piece of land and you were building your home, I rode my horse to see it, and I saw you from afar. You never turned around or noticed that I was looking at you," I said.

Pulling back a little bit from my body, he looked at me.

"No, I never saw you, and I am very sorry that I did not," he said.

He got up from the wooden floor and came back with two galabias made of camel hair, silk, and cotton, and covered me.

"Beloved, it's best for us to sleep inside. It's getting cold right now, and you could catch a cold," he said.

He helped me up from the floor and walked me to the bed. I laid there as he closed the three doors around us.

“Beloved, please be sure that Tuyii will not be cold tonight,” I said.

He walked to Tuyii’s room, then came back and got more blankets and another galabia and took it to her.

“Was she cold?” I asked.

“Yes. I told her to close the window of her small room. She will not be cold anymore. The walls are thick enough, like ours, and I believe she will be fine now.”

“My love, come to bed. I cannot sleep without you. Have you made sure that our soldiers and slaves have warm galabias?” I asked.

“Yes, they do. And blankets. Knowing you, I know you want the best for your men,” he said.

He smiled and lay beside me, at my left, as he did in the palace. I felt cool, and it was very nice. I’d never felt this cool before. We snuggled together, and it felt warm in his arms.

With a groggy voice, he said, “My love, thank you again for being a marvelous woman with me. Holding you in my arms, I feel complete.”

I was about to say something to him, but he had fallen asleep. He had drunk a lot of wine tonight. I covered him very well, and kissed his lips and whispered, “Good night, beloved.”

****

The following weeks we needed to get adjusted to the new schedule of sleeping during the daytime and being awake all night. He started to smoke as he was studying the night skies. I noticed that he had not given me the small perfume on the table, and I took it in my hands to smell it.

A hard scream came out of Sen-Mut’s mouth.

"Stop! It's poison!"

I was startled. He came walking fast and gently took it away from my hand and put it back on the small table. Holding me by my shoulders, he said, "This is poison, my love. Please never touch it again and warn Tuyii."

"Poison?" I said. I was puzzled.

Looking at me, he said, "Yes, I will keep it in here. If one day you are gone forever, I will come here, and I will commit suicide. I don't think I can live without you."

My eyes filled with tears, and I caressed his face and gently kissed his lips.

"That will never happen, my love. Now that I am Pharaoh."

I felt like crying after hearing what he said.

It was dark, and I lit the oil candles, helping Tuyii. I was silent during his sketching and writing.

"Maatke-Re, I cannot concentrate with you around me," he said.

"How is that?" I asked.

"Because I feel guilty that I am neglecting you, and I am not putting much attention towards you with all this work that I am doing. And you have no one to speak to."

"Well, my love, if you believe that it is better for me to go back to the palace and leave you alone here, I will go, and I can come from time to time and visit you?"

"No, and that is not what I want," he said.

"Beloved, it's the truth that I do get bored sometimes, but I love seeing you doing your drawings and love to be beside you as I sit in silence, contemplating the night full of stars."

“Let’s spend a few weeks in the palace and one-week sailing, and then come back here. Would you like that?” he asked.

“Yes, I would love that very much, beloved,” I said.

We went back to the palace, and he got up to date with everything in the palace. Then we sailed the Nile before returning to the observatory again. We were very happy.

****

We spent lots of time in the observatory. By this time, he had drawn the constellations, and he was making the Zodiac. I was amazed by his intelligence. He made an astrology chart of me and told me that I was born under the sign of the Lion, the King of the Zodiac, and I was ruled by the Sun. He said he was born under the sign of the Scales.

I could see how much he was involved in his study of the stars and his drawings. There were many months like that, and it was tedious and sometimes boring for me. But I could not be away from him and leave him there all alone. Looking at him concentrating on what he was doing, I remembered what I always wanted. I wanted him to be Pharaoh of Egypt.

We spent a few years going back and forth to the palace and getting up to date with everything. We eventually returned to the palace for good, and he returned to the construction site of my temple. He believed that he must be there.

On his returns, we went back to the observatory for few days. He has made me very happy all these months, and I know I have made him happy too.

CHAPTER 35

OBELISKS

"Beloved, let's walk beside the Nile. I would like for you to do another project for me. I want the people to see you as their god and know that nothing is impossible for you, that you can do something as grand as two large obelisks for my jubilee, so large and high and close to the sky, that they can be seen from all over the land," I said.

"Hat, your jubilee is in three years. I don't think I have enough time to prepare and do it. First, we must build very large ships to hold the weight and the size of the obelisks. We must cut them and bring them from Aswan. As you know, Aswan is very far from Thebes. And I don't know how long it will take for the stone cutters to cut two perfect obelisks from the quarries of Aswan, hoping that we don't encounter any problem separating them from the granite. Remember, the cutters must also carve inscriptions of your coronation and the offering to Amun-Ra," Sen-Mut said.

Nodding his head several times, he added, "I believe it is a very good idea taking this task. After all, you are marvelous and ingenious, my love. I will summon the engineers tonight."[70]

---

[70] According to archeologists, there were four obelisks of mine in Karnak. The memories of these events are not clear in my mind as of the dates. I believe that this happened in the earlier part of my coronation as Pharaoh, because by ordering the obelisks, I would honor

He smiled and kissed me, and putting his right arm over my shoulder, we continued walking south. Amun-Ra was fading away, and we walked to the waters of the Nile and washed ourselves, knelt, and said our prayers to Amun.

As I remained kneeling, I thought of how happy we were and that our suffering had ended. I loved him so much.

"Beloved, can you wait until tomorrow to meet with the engineers and Nehesi?" I asked.

"Well, what do you have in mind?" he said with a smile,

"Bathe you tonight and have you all for my own, so I can make love to you. I am already missing you."

I laughed and pinched his bottom and took off running to the palace. He chased after me, laughing. We ran up the stairs, and I ran to our quarters and leaned against the cool wall. I clapped my hands twice and said, "Tuyii, take the rest of the slaves with you until I send for you all."

We saw them leave, and he came closer, pressed his warm lips on mine and took off my sheath. I removed his kilt, and we were naked. He smelled my shoulders and kissed them slowly.

"I love your smell, Maatke-Re…mmm," he said.

He made passionate love to me against the cool wall. He gave me all his love and all of him tonight.

After our love making, we walked to be bathed and sat in the tub. I sat between his legs and leaned my back on his chest. We spoke for hours,

---

Amun-Ra and record my coronation as Pharaoh. In the Obelisk, I show Amun-Ra my love, devotion, and appreciation for him being my father.

playing with our fingers, of how I wanted the obelisks to look. The slaves came back carrying large jars with warm water and poured them into the tub.

"Beloved, I want gold on the tip of the obelisk to honor Amun and shine across the land. I want my people to see it from every part of the land of Amun. On the top of the obelisk, I want a carving of my father Amun crowning me Pharaoh that will last for all eternity," I said.

"Yes, my love. I believe that your name will last for all eternity, and I will do as you wish," he said.

****

Sen-Mut got together with Nehesi, D'Jehuty, my uncle Thutmoses, Min-Mose, Hapuseneb, and other engineers in the audience hall the following morning. I listened as he explained my wishes and the project. They all agreed with the idea and how it would be done, and they believed it would be a great achievement and glory for Sen-Mut.

As the talk continued, Hapuseneb looked at me and walked to where I was sitting.

"Flower of Egypt, I believe that this new task you are ordering is a marvelous idea. Your name and Sen-Mut's achievement will be recorded for eternity as one of his greatest," he said, nodding his head twice. I could sense jealousy in his voice.

"Yes. Don't you think it is a great idea? That my obelisk will be beside my father's?" I said.

I was trying to ease his jealousy.

"What else is on your mind, Hatshepsut?" he said with a harsh tone.

Uh oh, he is angry, I thought. It was as if he could read my mind. I looked straight into his eyes, then said, "What else could I have on my mind, Hapu?"

He was clenching his teeth.

"I don't know. Tell me. But if it's what I am thinking that you are trying to do, you will not succeed," he said, and he turned around and walked off.

Sen-Mut was looking at me and then continued talking about the project.

Many hours later, the meeting was concluded, and we all walked to the banquet hall for dinner.

"Your Majesty, we all believe that this is a good idea, and we will celebrate your jubilee," Min-Mose said.

We were all happy.

I walked beside Sen-Mut, and he was silent. Has the jealousy started again? I asked myself.

"Beloved, you are very quiet," I said.

"What were you and Hapuseneb talking about?" he asked.

I took a deep breath.

"Beloved, are you jealous?" I asked. I did not want to tell him about the uneasiness of Hapu.

"It's not that I am jealous, Hatshepsut. It's the way you look at me when you were talking to him. Hapuseneb was flushed, and you have a lost look on your face."

"Believe me, my love, it's nothing. He agrees with this project, and he said that our names will be recorded in history. You know he wants the best for me and that's it."

Sen-Mut looked at me with a very serious look.

"Hatshepsut, I hope you are not keeping anything from me," he said.

"No, beloved. I am not!" I said.

I felt bad for not telling him the whole truth. If I did, it would discourage him.

I ordered three ships to be built in Memphis. Sen-Mut was very busy in drawing the plans for the obelisks, and the ramps where the Obelisk would be pulled and set in place in Karnak.

****

Three years passed, and everything was ready for his journey to Aswan. I had given him all the manpower he needed for this project, including part of my army to help with anything he was going to need. The month of Akhet had begun, and he had to leave soon to use the flood currents to sail to Aswan.

He would be leaving early the following morning, and I could not sleep all night. I kept looking at him as he slept. I am going to miss him, his body, his lips, I thought.

He woke up and smiled.

"How long have you been awake?" he asked.

"I have not slept at all," I said.

"Come, my love. Lay beside me, and let's go back to sleep. And I promise, before I leave, I will make crazy love to you that will last you until my return," he said.

"Well, beloved, we don't have to worry about that, I will sail with you this morning, and I will return to Thebes if I get bored."

He sat on the mattress, looking at me.

"That is a good idea, but I want to warn you, the heat in Aswan is triple the heat here in Thebes. I prefer for you to remain here."

He was right. I had been to Aswan before, and it was terribly hot.

"Beloved, you don't want me to go with you?" I asked.

"Hat, it's not that I don't want you to come with me. It is because with you there, it will take longer for me to do what I must do. Do you remember when I was building the observatory? It will happen again, and your jubilee is getting closer. If I don't finish this project on time, you will not be able to celebrate your jubilee. I'd love for you to come, but not now. I will not be able to work or concentrate as I need to. There is nothing over there, only rocks and the heat," he said.

"OK, my love. I will remain here."

He held me in his arms, and we laid together and fell asleep.

He woke me up with a kiss, when the first rays of Ra were showing. We walked to be bathed, and he dispatched the slaves and made crazy love to me, with the deepest passion, until we were exhausted. I bathed him gently and kissed him many times. Standing facing each other, he raised my chin with his hand and said, "I promise to be back in no time. You will see, my love. Keep very busy for these months that I will be gone. Keep busy in the audience hall and with Hatshepset and Menkhep-Re. There is a lot you can do here. But most of all, remember that I love you."

He smiled.

"And I love you too, Ptah of Egypt," I said, and we hugged each other tightly and kissed me again.

We got dressed, he in his white kilt, and I in a long white linen kilt, the Horus pectoral, golden sandals, and the Pschent on my head.[71]

Everyone was ready to walk to the temple, so we did. The blessings were done by Hapuseneb, and the three ships were ready to sail. I had given Sen-Mut all the manpower he needed to accomplish this task, including part of my army, and they were on the ships. I walked up the ramp to a ship with him and Min-Mose. The ships were enormous and very high above the water.

Everyone was in their place, with the oarsmen ready to paddle. I looked at Sen-Mut, and he smiled, giving me assurance that everything was going to be OK. He walked me down the ramp and knelt and kissed my feet. I placed both my hands on his head.

"May all the gods accompany you on this journey. I will pray every day for your wellbeing and for your crew. Please return to me safely, beloved," I said.

He raised his face and smiled.

"For you, I will. Hat, I love you."

He rose and kissed me on my lips, then walked up the ramp. The horn sounded, and the drums started to beat inside the ship. The oarsmen started to paddle the waters, and the ship started to move slowly south. He stood in the bow of the ship holding tightly to a rope, and beside him was Min-Mose saying goodbye, as was everyone else. I walked beside the ship, smiling at him, until I could not see him anymore.

---

[71] I know that on the murals in my temple I have been shown wearing a short kilt, but I sometimes wore a long kilt or a sheath as well.

"I love you, Sen-Mut. See you soon," I whispered and continued walking.

I was at ease, because he would be close to me. If I wanted to see him, I could go and see him. I knew that he would succeed in this task, as everything he had done before, because he is a mighty Ptah!

Sen-Mut's brother Senemen approached me. I had only seen him a few times on different occasions at the banquet hall, and I knew that Sen-Mut didn't want him around me. He prohibited him from talking to me since he made that remark to Sen-Mut.

"Your Majesty," he said and knelt on one knee.

"Rise, Senemen," I said.

He looked in some ways like Sen-Mut. He smiled at me.

"Your Majesty, just to let you know, Sen-Mut put me in charge of finishing the ramps for the obelisks for when he brings them from Aswan. Also, Your Majesty, your temple is coming along well."

"Thank you, Senemen. I know that you have been helping your brother in the building of my temple for a while. He has mentioned it to me several times before. I would like to invite you sometime for tea or for dinner in the banquet hall when Sen-Mut returns from Aswan," I said.

He was looking at me, mesmerized.

"Thank you, Your Majesty."

He knelt again.

"Raise," I said, and he did, then turned around and left.

Hapuseneb caught up with me, and we walked together to the palace.

"Hapu, will you have breakfast with me?" I asked.

"I would love to," he said.

We arrived at the palace, and he said, "I, want to apologize for what I said to you three summers ago, in the hall of audience, when Sen-Mut announced your wishes."

"Yes, I remember that day. What I wanted to do was to honor my father Amun, but you were jealous, weren't you? And now that you are here, I want to give you a gift. I sent it to be made a while ago."

"A gift for me, Lotus of Egypt? You don't have to give me anything. Being this close to you is the best gift I can have. And yes, I was jealous then," he replied.

"I could see it on your face and you were flushed, but everything is forgotten, shall we? You have been my dearest friend since we were children, and I believe I have neglected you. I have never shown you how valuable and how special you are to me," I said.

I clapped my hands twice, and Tuyii came running.

"Yes, Your Majesty?"

"Tuyii, send the guard with a message to the goldsmith. Tell him to bring the special gift that I sent to be made a while ago," I said.

"Yes, Your Majesty."

Hapuseneb and I were having our breakfast when the goldsmith came in.

"Your Majesty, I brought the gift you ordered," he said.

Kneeling, he placed the inlaid box at my feet.

"Rise, and I want you to return late this afternoon. You may go now."

"I will, Your Majesty."

He bowed his head and left.

The inlaid wooden box was very heavy, and it was beautiful. I picked it up from the floor and give it to Hapuseneb. He was looking at me with those beautiful gray eyes and with a smile on his face.

"So, you sent this gift to be made for me?" he said.

Smiling, I said, "Yes, but it is not the wooden box. It is what is inside of the box, and you can open it."

He was smiling, and he opened the box and pulled out a beautiful solid gold box. It was engraved with his titles of First Prophet of Amun, and Vizier of the South, the name of Tepi, his children, his parents, and my cartouche. He was moved and surprised.

"My beloved Lotus of Egypt, I never expected a beautiful gift like this from you. I don't have words to say how much you mean to me," he said.

Then he stood up and knelt and kissed my feet and then kissed them again.

"Rise, Hapu, and you may sit down now," I said, and we laughed.

"Can I see it? I have not seen it yet," I said.

He handed it to me. It was a very heavy gold box, about 17 inches by 12 inches by 9 inches, and it was well made. It was just beautiful. I was happy to give him this gift.

"Hatshepsut, you have made me very happy today," he said and smiled. "Well. you always make me very happy when I am with you. And I never expected to be First Prophet of Amun, either. That was a big surprise to me, and you made me Vizier of the South as well. Giving me those titles means so much to me, and now this beautiful gold box as a gift."

"Hapu, you have done so much for me. You helped me reach this throne. How can I not be grateful to you? I want you to know that you will be very well rewarded, and nothing will ever lack from your life, for the rest of your life. You will live in wealth, and your family will too. I want you to know that I know that you hurt inside because of me. I can see it every time in your eyes, and you have hurt more because you keep it all bottled up inside of you. But please believe me that it is not my intention, and I hurt too because you are hurting," I told him.

He had tears in his eyes, and I did too.

"Well, no more tears. Let's finish our breakfast. Tomorrow bring your child to play with my daughter and Menkhep-Re. They can be very good friends when they grow up, and we are old," I said.

"Yes, they will be, and now that Sen-Mut is on the way to Aswan, we can take the children to swim in the Nile as when we were children," he said.

"I would like that very much. Bring Tepi and we can spend a good afternoon with the children. I will invite T'Queta, so she won't be so alone. I hope you don't mind," I said.

"T'Queta? Please don't! Tepi will not give me peace of mind. She is always complaining that I spend too much time with you and not with her. She drives me crazy all the time, and sometimes I don't want to go home. That is why I leave the palace late."

"Ok, don't bring Tepi. I will bring T'Queta," I said.

"That is much better," he said, and we laughed.

"But I know much, and why you don't go home earlier," I said.

He frowned, then laughed and said, "So, you are spying on me?"

I laughed.

"No, but the gossip from the kitchen spread all the way up to my quarters. Do you still love T'Queta?"

He was silent for a moment before answering.

"Sometimes I think of her and of how my life would have been with her if I had listened to you. She did give me so much happiness, and we laughed all the time. And she gave me the love I could not get from you."

He smiled, and I sighed.

He stood up and said, "Your Majesty, we will meet tomorrow in the afternoon."

"Wait, Hapu. Bring the golden box here."

I walked to where my treasure was and opened the very large box containing gold nuggets. He stood beside me.

"Open your box and fill it up with gold nuggets," I said, and he did.

"Now, the gift is complete." I smiled at him, and he smiled back at me.

"Tuyii, have my royal litter-bearer take Hapuseneb to his house." And looking at Hapu, I said, "It makes me very happy that you are my best friend."

He smiled and said, "I love you, Flower of Egypt."

He left carrying the heavy golden box. I walked to the balcony and looked south. It had been almost four hours since my beloved left, and I missed him already. In a few weeks, I would sail to see him. I knew he would be surprised and happy. Late in the afternoon, the goldsmith came back.

"Your Majesty, I came back as you requested."

"I would like for you to make a very large gold box engraved with all the titles I have given Sen-Mut. And in the center, on the top of the lid, I want the image of Ptah, and under Ptah, 'Sen-Mut, Steward of Amun and Prince of the Palace.' I want it made and ready for the day he arrives from Aswan. I want to surprise him," I said.

"Yes, Your Majesty," he said.

"Before you leave, I want to thank you for the wonderful gold box you made for Hapuseneb. It was exquisite. I want the same perfect work for Sen-Mut's gift."

"I am very happy that my work pleases you, Your Majesty."

"Tuyii, bring me my jewelry box," I said.

She came back with it in her hands.

"I want to reward you for your wonderful work."

I took several jewelry pieces and a hand full of gold nuggets and give it to him.

"That's for your wife. May she be very happy tonight and make your nights and days merry from now on. Don't forget to remove my cartouche from it. I want you to melt some of these gold nuggets and make a gold necklace and engrave my name on a cartouche. On the back, engrave your name, so that everyone will know that it is a gift from me and that you are one of my favorites in the palace," I said.

"Oh, Your Majesty, these are wonderful gifts. I am so very pleased, and I am in your debt forever."

He was smiling, and that pleased me.

"You may go now," I said.

He knelt and kissed my feet several times, then I saw him leave. I walked to the balcony and thought of Sen-Mut. Now my love, the world will be next for you. The love of Sen-Mut was rooted deeply inside of my heart and filled my chest with infinite love for him.

A month passed, and I missed Sen-Mut so much I paced back and forth all over the palace. I tried to entertain myself with everything, but I could not concentrate on anything. I knew I must hold back my desire to go to Aswan. I had to.

A few more months went by, and I was sitting in the gazebo looking at the lotus floating on the water of the pool and caressing the head of my cheetah, Jotham. I got up from my chair.

"Tuyii, send for the master chef and send for the Capitan to prepare the royal ship. We are going to Aswan," I shouted.

"Oh yes, Your Majesty. I have never been to Aswan before," Tuyii said.

"Well now you are going to see it!" I said and smiled at her.

"There is not much to see, but I must see my beloved. You must prepare everything, including the perfume Sen-Mut loves to smell on me. I want to wear the turquoise sheath the day we arrive and the golden one the evening when I have dinner with my beloved. I want him to find me beautiful, like his goddess."

"Yes, Your Majesty."

"Hurry, I want to leave tomorrow early in the morning," I said.

I saw her leave, running to take the messages. I could not sleep. I was anxious, so I got up and was bathed. It would take us a week to get to Aswan, I thought.

It was a glorious day the following morning and was not raining any more, but the current was strong when we embarked. Everything was arranged perfectly when I walked onto my ship. The wind was moving the large sheer curtains around the ship and the canopies of my bed.

****

We had been sailing south on the Nile for five days. In one or two more days, I would be in my beloved's arms.

"Tuyii, I am ready for my body to be depilated and massaged," I said.

A long table was brought by the slaves in charge of depilating and massaging my body. After removing all the hair from all over my body with honey wax and massaging me, I was bathed with fresh water brought from the palace well. I was very relaxed and fell asleep as the wind blew over me. The following morning, the sky was blue, and it was a glorious day.

"Tuyii, ask the Captain how long before we dock in the quarry."

"Your Majesty, he said in two more hours," she said.

"Tell the chef to have the buffet ready with all the food and wines that Sen-Mut loves. Tell the other slaves to prepare a bath for Sen-Mut with his favorite fragrances and to prepare my bath with the perfume that he loves on me."

The interior of the ship looked beautiful, with the canopy of white curtains with gold accents. The cushions were made of gold fabrics, and pink roses were everywhere in the sitting area. I thought it must be hard for my beloved to bathe properly there, only swimming in the waters of the Nile.

My slaves put makeup on me, starting with lining my eyes with kohl, making double lines around each eye, rouge on my cheeks, and soft, red lipstick on my lips. Then they dressed me in my turquoise sheath with the golden belt and golden sandals and a long wig down to my shoulders entwined with gold. On my head, they placed the Crown of Horus.

I noticed that the ship was slowing down, and the horn sounded. It took Sen-Mut by surprise, and he turned around fast. He saw the ship and dropped everything he was doing. He stood there, looking at the ship moving close to the banks of the Nile. He ran down the hill to meet me. I was standing on the bow with my slaves, and I could hear and see everyone on the ground cheering my arrival.

I saw the red Nemes cloth on Sen-Mut's head breaking through the gathering of the army and slaves at the edge of the Nile to see me. Then the Captain of the Guards sounded a horn, and the guards formed a wall and made a path for Sen-Mut to walk through them. Finally, the ship stopped moving. He stood at the edge of the Nile with a big smile on his lips as the Captain gave the order to place the ramp. Sen-Mut was smiling at me with great joy. He waited until the ramp was placed, then rushed up to the ship, and we hugged and kissed deeply.

"My love, what a big surprise," he said. He had big smile on his face and hugged me tightly.

"I knew that you were coming. I felt it in my heart, and I kept looking at the Nile every day and every time my heart jumped."

He held me and kissed my forehead several times and kissed my lips. I looked at him. I was so in love.

"Beloved of mine, I wanted to surprise you, and I really could not be without you any longer," I said.

"I am very happy that you came to visit me. I have been missing you too." He said then kissed me again.

He was covered in sweat and dust. He had become darker from the hot sun and the quarry dust and sand, but his mouth smelled of clean mint. I held his hand.

"Come, my love, let me bathe you," I said.

"Yes! My love, I need your hands bathing my body… and more."

He lifted me up in his arms, and I was laughing as he carried me near the bed. He stood there looking at me as he removed the Nemes from his head. I was shocked. He had shaved his hair off again. I did not say anything, and I understood. He removed his kilt, and he was completely aroused. He removed my sheath and laid me gently on the bed, and we made passionate love for hours. His body tasted salty from the sweat. I didn't care, and we laughed.

It was late afternoon when I stood up and held his hand and guided him to the bath to bathe him. I bathed the body of the god, the body that I loved so much. And he bathed me and caressed my body and kissed me all over. He was aroused all over again, and we made love again.

Looking into my eyes, he said, "I have missed you so much, do you know that? Do you?"

"Yes, I know, beloved of mine. That's why I came to see you. I could feel the warmth of your love all over my body, desiring me. Those nights you drove me crazy desiring you, until seven days ago when I decided that I had had it and said to myself I am going to him. I knew that I could not be without you any longer."

Sen-Mut started to laugh. He now looked clean and smelled clean. We had dinner with Neb-Ery, Min-Mose, and several other foremen that were working on my obelisks.

During our cheerful dinner, Sen-Mut said, "Hatshepsut, I am afraid that I don't have very good news with the first obelisk that we cut. I made it so large that it almost reached the sky, but it cracked close to the tip. I had to abandon that task and start planning for another one that had less weight. If I had succeeded with that one, I would have cut the other one the same size, but I had to start all over and go back to the drawing board. I recalculated the weight and height and am going to cut them less high, but they will still be very large. You will be pleased with them," he said but did not look happy about it.

Over the next few days, I woke up in his arms before sunrise, and we said our prayers together. I had the cook prepare his favorite plates for breakfast and dinner. Very early every morning I kissed his lips and saw him off to the quarry before the sun started getting hot.

The day before Sen-Mut was to take me to the hills from where he was cutting the obelisks, the heat was unbearable. I didn't know how much longer I could remain there. My beloved returned very tired late in the afternoon, and I bathed him every evening. We had dinner and sailed in a small barge to refresh our bodies from the heat of the day. He always fell asleep quickly. He was so tired from working all day under the sun.

We woke up early before the rooster crowed, and we said our prayers together. Today he was to show me the quarry from where they were cutting the obelisks.

I saw the two large ships that were to bring the obelisks to Thebes anchored near the quarry of Aswan. Sen-Mut was building two ramps packed with sand where the obelisks were going to be dragged onto the ship. They were going to be pulled by the other two ships onto the one that would carry them to Thebes with the help of the army and the slaves. I noticed that on the inside of the ships were large logs to make it easy for the obelisks to roll onto it and to be centered and secured by wooden boards, so it would not tilt from side to side. That would be horrible and could cause great loss of life, I thought.

We had our breakfast and were on our way before the sun heated the land. We rode our horses to the large rocky hill. We dismounted and walked to where the damaged obelisk was. I was impressed by how large it was. I walked on top of it and thought it was so huge that it would have reached the sky. I believed the whole country could have seen it, from one side to the other side of the land.

I looked at Sen-Mut. He was wearing the red Nemes on his shaved head, and he looked good. Then I saw that they had already cut the first smaller one, and it would be taken out from its place. I realized I was keeping Sen-Mut from his work.

"Beloved, I know that I am holding you back from your work. I will be returning to Thebes tomorrow morning," I said.

He looked surprised.

"Hat, you have only been here three days. You are not in my way, and I love to come to your arms after I finish my day. But I do think it's too hot for you to be here. I would love for you to remain a few more days with me if you don't mind." He asks.

"I will, my love, but it's terribly hot here. I've never been in a place as hot as this."

I remained a few more days as he asked. We enjoyed ourselves, and I spent the remaining days swimming because of the heat. My skin became darker from the sun. The day before I would be returning to Thebes, I thought about how much I dreaded leaving my beloved.

Sen-Mut and I spent our last evening with his crew, and then we made love and were merry.

"My love, I am very happy that you came to see me. I want you to send me a missive when you get to the palace to be sure that you arrived safely. I love you, my love. Carry my love with you," he said, and he kissed me.

"I will, beloved, but I don't want you to travel back home in any of the ships carrying the obelisks. I know that you are returning home when the Nile swells again to make it easy for the ships to sail to Thebes, and I want you safe and away from danger. I will be missing you until you come back to my arms," I said.

"I promise I will not sail on the same ship."

He made love to me, and we kissed many times. I left the following morning, leaving my love with him. My ship left the shore of Aswan, and I stood on the back of the ship looking at Sen-Mut. Sen-Mut stood at the edge of the Nile, watching me sail north.

****

Four months had passed since I left my beloved in Aswan when I received a missive from him.

Beloved Hat,

The two obelisks are loaded on the ships, and it was very hard work to load them. We are ready to depart Aswan since the monsoon season is here. The Nile is swollen for us to sail north. We will be leaving tomorrow early in the morning, and it will take more time to sail north carrying these heavy obelisks. We must take our time to make it to Thebes and keep my crew safe. I will not sail with the obelisks, as I promised you. I received a missive from Senemen telling me that the ramps are ready for the obelisks to be unloaded in Karnak. Before I left Thebes, I left instructions with him of how I wanted it to be done. And you will have your obelisks for your Jubilee, I promise, my love.

I believe I will be seeing you in seven days.

I love you, Maatke-Re.

Yours,

Sen-Mut

The week passed, and it was getting dark as I was sitting on my balcony.

"My love!"

It was the voice of my beloved, and I rushed into his arms. We kissed and hugged. I was very happy to see him back home.

"Beloved, you surprised me!"

I was smiling, and he was too.

"I wanted to surprise you as you did to me in Aswan. And I am happy that I am home. I expect the first obelisks to be arriving in a few days. I had the oarsmen of my ship row faster because I wanted to be home and sleep in your arms tonight. Also, I wanted to be sure that the ramps are finished and ready the way I left instructions with Senemen to be done. I want to unload them as soon they arrive here. We must pray that everything goes well as I erect them. It's going to be a hard task. My love, I must summon D'Jehuty early in the morning. We must have all the manpower we can get," he said.

"Yes, my love. You will have all the manpower you need," I said.

We walked to be bathed by the slaves and then ate and made love. I was complete again. Sen-Mut was home. We drank a lot and fell asleep.

Sen-Mut summoned D'Jehuty to our quarters early the next morning and ordered every man to be ready.

"Maatke-Re, I will be gone all day. Keep your eyes on the Nile to see your obelisks passing the balcony," he said then kissed me and left with D'Jehuty.

I kept looking all day at the Nile from my balcony, and it was getting dark when I saw the first ship carrying my obelisk. It was so large. I screamed and called all my slaves to come and see it, and they gathered next to me on the balcony and were cheering me on. It was wonderful to see the first one arriving. What a man I have, I thought. He amazed me with his willpower to achieve such an enormous task. The other ships followed five hours later.

I got dressed and went looking for Sen-Mut. He was talking to leaders of the army, navy, and cavalry and lining up all the manpower he was going to need. I caught the last of his orders: "All of you must follow what my crew is doing. I already told them what to do in Aswan. I want all of you at Karnak early in the morning, at the first rays of Ra and prayers. Follow directions and no one will get hurt."

I was behind Sen-Mut when everyone saw me and dropped to the floor. He turned around, saw me, and smiled.

"Continue, beloved," I said.

"Rise," I shouted, and they did.

I waited for Sen-Mut to conclude his orders, and we walked home, holding hands under the full moon.

"Beloved, let's walk beside the Nile," I said, and we did.

"I want to thank you for everything that you do for me, my love, and I want to thank you in this way."

I stopped and could see his face shining under the rays of Thoth, and I removed his kilt and loin cloth and let him undress me. I kissed him on his lips, and slowly he lay me on the grass. But I sat on top of him and made love to him under the rays of Thoth.

"Whoa! What was that, Hat? It was wonderful to feel you and the way you made love to me tonight," he said.

"After seeing the first obelisk passing by my balcony, and seeing that it was so enormous, I had the same desire to kiss you as when I saw the two large statues at the entrance of the palace on the day of my coronation. You have made me happy tonight, and I had to reward you by making love to you."

"Well, I love it, my love. Do it to me again," he said.

I made love to him again under the stars and under the silver rays of Thoth.

Later that night, I got up from the bed as Sen-Mut slept and sent a missive to the goldsmith to bring me the gift I had ordered for my beloved one, for the day of my jubilee, and to leave it in my quarters.

Very early the following morning, before sunrise, we said our morning prayers and ate breakfast. I dressed as Pharaoh, and the Double Crown was put on my head by Hapuseneb, who came early before sunrise. Everyone was waiting for us, hundreds of slaves with baskets full of white lotus petals and priests, and we walked to Karnak with the army, cavalry, archers, and charioteers. I would sit under a tent where I could see how the obelisks were being unloaded from the ships onto high sand ramps.

The back of one ship was next to the ramp, and thousands of men, horses, donkeys, and camels, all the manpower from all the armed forces, started to pull the obelisk with ropes on Sen-Mut's orders. The slaves were throwing white petals as they pulled. I got up from my chair and took a basket full of white petals and joined my slaves in throwing them under the obelisk. I was happy.

I could hardly see were Sen-Mut was. I only could see the red Nemes on his head far away. A guard approached me.

"Your Majesty," he said and knelt.

"A message from Master Sen-Mut. He said not to be close to the obelisk. It's very dangerous."

"Tell him that I am going back to my tent," I said.

Returning to my tent, I saw Sen-Mut walking in my direction.

"Hat, I don't want you close to the obelisk again. It's very dangerous because that ramp can collapse, and I don't want to lose you. I keep looking for you, and when I did not see you, I became worried and sent one of the slaves to look for you. He came back and told me that you were with the slaves throwing flower petals as the obelisk was being pulled. Beloved, you must stay here. I need to have peace of mind as I complete this task, and it's going to take several days to erect this first one."

He kissed me and left.

I did as he said. It took few days to unload and erect it, and I continued to be amazed by my beloved. He was the best architect and will be the best Ptah of the land for all eternity, and his name will never be forgotten, I thought. I would make sure of that. I ordered a big celebration for everyone and gave them a few days of rest.

We started again until the second obelisk was unloaded and erected, and soon came the day of my jubilee. Hapuseneb blessed the obelisks, and I made offerings to my father, Amun-Ra. It was a happy celebration in Karnak. Everyone from near and far came to Thebes to see the great Sen-Mut's achievements. We all celebrated the glorious day. I gave the order that everyone that worked in Aswan was to be paid with gold nuggets, and that made Sen-Mut happy. He said that they deserved it and that they worked very hard in Aswan.

We celebrated until the early part of the morning, and Sen-Mut and I were tipsy. We left the audience hall, happy and holding hands. We strolled through the gardens, and when we reached the steps, he lifted me up in his arms and kissed me. I had his gift waiting. As we reached our quarters, I walked to the large golden box. Sen-Mut looked at it, and I said, "A gift for you, my love."

He came closer, to look at the gift, it was magnificently and well made. Sen-Mut looked at me and lifted me up in the air, kissing me deeply.

"It's beautiful, my love. Thank you!" He was smiling.

"No, I thank you for your love and devotion and for all the beautiful things you have done for me. For loving me, for helping me reach the throne as Father wanted, and I want you to remember that I will always love you. For all eternity," I said and smiled.

He hugged me tightly, kissed me profoundly, and made love to me. Then we fell asleep in each other's arms.

CHAPTER 36

EXPEDITION TO PUNT

I was awakened by a kiss on my lips. Sen-Mut was leaning beside me smiling, and I smiled back at him. "Good morning, beloved one. Amun-Ra will soon rise," he said.

I saw my beloved rise from the bed and wash himself, as every priest must do before the chanting of the morning prayers. I also washed my hands and face well to receive the blessings of the highest into my body and onto my land. Then I walked beside him, and we knelt together facing Ra, bowing our heads to the floor and rising our faces to Ra as he rose. We chanted the morning prayers together to Amun-Ra.

I was sitting beside him as we ate our breakfast, and he said, "Maatke-Re, I will be in my office this morning inspecting some of the drawings of your temple. Are you going riding this morning? If you do, come and get me. I would like to ride with you. It clears my head, and with so much to do in the palace and at the building site, I could use the break."

"No, beloved. Today I must do something that I have wanted to do for many years, and it is time to do it."

"What is that? You never told me you had something so important that has been on your mind all these years," he said.

I pulled him by his neck and kissed him and smiled at him.

"So, this means you are not going to tell me?"

"I will tell you, but not right now," I said.

He got up from his chair and came beside me and knelt, smiling at me. His eyes traveled over my face.

"You look so beautiful this morning as Ra shines on you, and I desire you now," he said and a current of desire ran over me as well.

He lifted me up in his arms, as always kissing me intensely, and laid me on our bed. We became consumed in the hot fire of love making, so hot and involving the most delicious feelings. I could feel his love for me, deep inside my heart, a love that trespassed my most inner soul and traveled into every fiber of my being. We were submerged in ecstasy until we reached the point of moaning and screamed in explosive pleasure. He made me his again. He looked into my eyes and kissed me.[72]

Lying in his arms, I looked at him and asked, "Sen-Mut, have you ever been in the harem before?"

He looked surprised at the question.

"Yes, I was taken there by Puyem-Re when I was learning to be a priest. I had never had sex before. I kept thinking of when I saw you naked under the silver rays of Thoth, and he had noticed that in every bath I was aroused and asked me if I had taken a woman before. I said no, then he said, 'Tonight, you will become a man.' He took me to the harem, and on that night the women of the harem took my virginity. That night I discovered the most delicious sex. I did not visit them as much as the other priests

---

[72] Sen-Mut, how can I not still love you after 3,500 years when your love is imprinted all over my soul? (3/10/2016)

did, or Hapu, Thut, or Ursaramun and the rest of your friends do. There was this respect of my body for you."

"What do you mean?" I asked.

"After learning the art of sex and reaching many climaxes with the women of the harem, I noticed something was missing inside of me, and I knew it was you. Because I could not get you out of my mind, and that night in the sacred Lake of Mut. Man can get much satisfaction in sex with every woman, but for me love was missing. The love that I feel for you. So, the day that you sent the message with T'Queta that you were coming to my humble home, my body started to tremble with desire for you. When you were in front of me and your smell reached me, and when you placed your hand over my head, I felt a strong current of desire travel all over my body. Then you came into my house and told me to close the door behind you. I looked at you and you were so beautiful, and I wanted to pull you close and kiss you and make love to you like a crazy man. But I had to hold back my feelings, and it was terribly hard to hold back these feelings. That is why I asked you if you wanted lemonade. I needed to compose myself for a few minutes. When I came back with the lemonade in my hands, and looking at you, I could see your love for me in your eyes. I also saw so much sadness in them. Then when you told me that in three days you would be marrying Thut, I could see you were on the verge of crying, and I noticed that you were holding back your tears. I was terribly saddened by it and wanted to hold you in my arms. After that, I could not look at you anymore. I swallowed my tears. That night beside the Nile, when I saw a figure walking fast to where I was standing, I was hoping with my whole heart that it was you. And it was you. I wanted to run to you, but I held back. My heart was pounding very hard. Then you were standing in front of me. I knelt right away so you would not see how nervous I was. Then you said not to do that and to rise. You said let's walk into the waters of Hopi, and I had the opportunity to tell you all that I had in my heart. I could not hold back any longer. I had to pour out my love for you. I told you that I loved you, and when I kissed you, my body was trembling. I had waited for that moment for a long time, and I had to make you my wife. Those two rings that you are wearing now? I wanted to give you a gift that no one ever had." He continued, "I sent them to be made the previous year. First, I had to befriend the goldsmith, because he knew your finger size, and he made the two rings with precious stones that I got from a mine. I traded my services as priest just to get them, and I also befriended the two guards at your golden doors. Both became my good friends."[73]

I was surprised by everything he was telling me, including about my guards.

"Did they know of your love for me?" I asked.

"Yes, they knew that I was very much in love with you and of your love for me. All they wanted was your happiness because they had known you since you were a little girl, and they almost died once, and you saved their lives. I just needed one night with you, that night before your marriage. I didn't care if I died after I made love to you, and I told you that I love you. I wanted your body to belong to me first. Everything was arranged with your guards, and that night I waited at a distance. I saw Thut walk into your quarters, and I saw all your slaves leave, and then Thut too. Then I saw the two guards leaving as well. That was strange to me, and I rushed through the darkness up the stairs and walked through your golden doors. You told me that no one would come back until the first rays of Ra, and that Thut told you to live one night of love with me. I was completely at ease then. That night when I was making you mine, and you were under my body, I thought of your naked body in the sacred Lake of Mut and the water dripping from your head down to your lips and down to your wet breasts. I remember the hardness of your nipples. By then I was inside of you. I never had an explosive climax like that before, and I knew then that I was complete, with your body under me shaking like I was."

He paused and looked at me.

---

[73] 3,500 hundred years have passed, and I still feel that I am wearing those two rings.

"I am aroused all over again, and I must have you right now." he said.

He made me his again, with the same passion he could get from me. After, I lay on his chest as his fingers softly caressed my back.

"I love you, Sen-Mut, and I am very happy that I am your wife. And I am very happy that you made me yours that night." I looked at his face and pressed my lips to his. Then we walk to the bathroom.

We bathed each other, and I bathed the body of a god. I didn't let the slaves bathe his body anymore, for I would become jealous and his body belonged only to me. We got dressed and kissed and walked out of our quarters our separate ways.

I walked north and followed the current of Hopi to Ineni's home. As I walked the path, I was thinking of all Sen-Mut had just told me and of all that he did for my love, and I smiled.

When I arrived at Ineni's home, I noticed for the first time that he had grown very old. He was sitting quietly under his sycamore tree, and he was looking to his right at the current of the Nile in silence. He had grown old and no longer had the same strength he once had. He very seldom came to the banquet hall and shared meals with us anymore. Years had passed since mother's passing, and I bet he missed her greatly. I never told him of my mother's secret love for him, and I believed it would be a perfect day to share it with him as I asked for his guidance.

I needed his guidance in a matter that had been in my heart for a long time, and he was the right person to ask. He had known me well, since I was born, also Khety First Prophet of Amun-Ra. I remembered before Mother passed away, she told me that if I ever needed advises to go to Ineni.

"Good morning, Master Builder of Thebes," I said.

“Good morning to you, Pharaoh of Egypt. What are you doing around here so early in the morning?” he asked with a wide smile.

“I need your wisdom and guidance in a matter that I have had on my mind and heart for a very long time, and my heart is telling me that this will be the right time to do it. For many years, I wanted to talk to you about it, but I did not know how to approach this subject.”

“Dear one, you can count on my silence for whatever your heart desires. I love thee as if you were my own daughter, for I saw you the day you were born. I will try to speak with words of wisdom and hope it will help,” he said calmly.

I was happy to hear his response, and I smiled.

“Ineni, you have known that for so many years I have been in love with Sen-Mut,” I said.

He nodded his head several times and smiled.

“And I always wanted to marry him and was never able to do it because, first, I was warned by my mother that my father wanted to kill him. I would have killed myself if Father had killed him. Then, I was warned by Thutmoses’s II when he was dying. I never told you what he told me. He said that Isis was terrified that I was going to kill her and her son when he was gone to the underworld. He said that he had a silent assassin to kill Sen-Mut if I killed them, but that thought never had crossed my mind. At this point I don’t know who the silent assassin is, and I am always worried for Sen-Mut’s life,” I said.

“The Great Maat, your father, came one night to talk to me about this. He said that probably one day you would come to me for my advice and to help you with everything that I could,” Ineni said.

“I never knew that Father had spoken to you about Sen-Mut?”

"He was very aware of your love for him and did not want to die leaving you all alone and without love, for he knew that someday Thutmoses II would go to the underworld, and you would be left all alone."

"How long did Father know of my love for him?"

"Since your fifteen summers, and the way you looked at Sen-Mut and the way he looked at you. He told me that your mother had spoken to him. When he questioned her about both of you, she told him that nothing was between you, but you were falling in love with him. She said that he was your first love, and it would not be right to leave you alone in this world after both had gone to the underworld, and when Aakheperen-Ra went to the underworld too. He thought about it and knew she was right, and when this time came, he said to give you all the support you needed. That someday you would be Pharaoh, and he had prepared you well to rule his kingdom. I have supported you always when the elderly priests came to talk to me regarding the Crown of Egypt. I want you to know that I never had a daughter of my own, and I am here for you. Whatever decision you make, I am here to support you."

"Thank you, Ineni. You have always been good to me, and I love you for your constant support and kindness. I wanted to talk to you about something that has been in my heart for a long time regarding Sen-Mut," I said.

"Sen-Mut is a good man, and his achievements have won respect in the palace and all over the land, even with all the ups and down between him and Hapuseneb battling for your love. His name is known all over the land as your favorite. I have known for a long time that he had fallen in love with you since that first day he saw you in that audience," he said.

I smiled and said, "I love him so much, Ineni. I don't think I could live without him. I am in my thirty-two summers now, and my life has passed by fast. I refuse to marry Menkhep-Re because I believe he is not my brothers son. And I will not deprive myself any longer from the love of my live to make someone else happy. You have known that his mother has been plotting against me and Sen-Mut for many years, and I could have done away with both, but I don't want to carry their murders on my head. Menkhep-Re is now in his thirteen summers, and I have raised him as my son. I wish I was certain that he is my brother's son. His mother, the conniving cobra, has been plotting against me with some of the priests of the temple. If I married her son, I cannot marry Sen-Mut, the man that I love and who is my all. No, I cannot live without Sen-Mut. That would be a betrayal to his love for me, and I prefer to die first. He deserves to be Pharaoh, and I am ready to crown him Pharaoh of Egypt. I need your advice on how to do it. And here is the other problem, the silent assassin. I don't know who it is so that I can kill him."

"You know that I have always been a friend with the First Prophet Hapuseneb and Second Prophet Puyem-Re. I will try to find out if they know anything of the possibility that there is a silent assassin. It will take a few days to investigate. As soon I get word, I will come to see you at the palace. Does Sen-Mut know that you want to crown him Pharaoh of Egypt?" he asked.

"No, he does not, and I prefer for you not to mention anything to Puyem-Re, for I truly believe that he is Menkhep-Re's real father. And he will not tell you the identity of the silent assassin," I said.

"After Sen-Mut brought the obelisks from Aswan for Amun-Ra and celebrated your jubilee, I thought that was a very good task and achievement. The army admired him for these tasks and bringing the tallest obelisks to Karnak. Now he must do something greater to win the army's approval, as well as the people of Egypt. I must pray and make offerings to Amun-Ra for wisdom and to find the best answer for you," he said.

"Ineni, I would like to tell you something that I have known for a long time and kept silent for all these years since Mother went to the underworld. It's something that she told me when she was dying. She told me that she was very much in love with you, and that both of you suffered greatly when she had to marry my father. And that you loved her so very much too, and that both of you suffered terribly when her father made her marry her half-brother Maat to make him full royal blood and to become Pharaoh. This was the same fate I had with Thutmoses II, with the difference that I married Sen-Mut three nights before the wedding, and he bed me the night before the marriage to Thutmoses II. And with the full knowledge of Aakheperen-Re, who came to my quarters the eve of our marriage and told me to run to my beloved and to live one night of love with Sen-Mut. He had always known that I was in love with him and that he loved me too, and that after our marriage I would not see Sen-Mut anymore. That night I became pregnant with Sen-Mut's child, Neferu-Re, and I believe that Isis had something to do with her death. Even though Thutmoses II said no," I said.

Looking at Ineni, I then said, "I've been meaning to ask you for a long, long time, and I am afraid even now to ask, but I must. You have always been very loving to me. Are you my father?"

I was shaking as I asked him, and he was clearly shocked by my question.

"No. I never bed your mother, but your father knew of my love for her since the very beginning. And I never betrayed him. We were always good friends, and it killed me when she was betrothed to your father and he became Pharaoh. I love her still today. But you are the true daughter of Horus," he said.

"I am very happy that I am Horus's daughter. I'm relieved and very happy. I love my father very much and miss him greatly."

"And he loved you too, very much," he said.

"Very well, Ineni. Bring me news of what you can find out in a week. Come to the palace as soon as you can. And thank you, Ineni. You've always been a great friend. I will see you tonight at the banquet hall for dinner."

I was about to leave when he asked, "Will you have tea with me, Hatshepset?"

"Yes, I will," I said and sat down across from him. I could see the slow current of Hopi at my left.

"You have always called me Hatshepset, and Sen-Mut calls me Maatke-Re. He has called me that since our first trip to Philae. He said that I am the daughter of the sun," I said, smiling.

"Hatshepset is your birth name. I remember the day you were born, the first day of Mesori. Great Maat was very happy and more when Khety the First Prophet and the High Priest of Amun consulted the Oracles, and the Oracles foretold that you would rule Egypt beside a man that loves you and that you love. Khety was always wondered if that man was Sen-Mut, and he was right. At the end of his days, he was happy that it was Sen-Mut because you have a man that truly loves you."

I smiled at him.

"I never knew that Father knew I would fall in love since I was born," I said.

"But your father thought that it was going to be with Hapuseneb, for he always knew that Hapuseneb was in love with you. I think all of us knew that, just by the way he looks at you. But at that first audience when you came to talk to me about Sen-Mut, your face radiated. I knew you were starting to fall in love for the first time."

"Ineni, I love him very much. After Father and Mother went to the underworld, I only have him left. And Hatshepset, but she is always angry at me for not marrying Menkhep-Re and making him Pharaoh, but she knows that I must die first before he can marry her for her to become Queen. How can I put a death sentence on myself and on Sen-Mut when this battle is between me and Isis? Isis also always wanted to be Queen, and she thinks that by having her son be a Pharaoh at that very young age of three summers, she will get to rule both lands for him. But she was left with wanton desire, and the only thing she has is her evil mind and is poisoning my daughter Hatshepset against me," I said.

"Yes, we have known that for a long time. That is what she always wanted. I remember when your father told me of a conversation that he had with Aakheperen-Re, that no harem slave could ever be Queen, only if she came from royal blood. And she does not. That is why he never took her as his secondary wife."

"But I know Thutmoses II really loved her," I said.

"Indeed, he loved her. That is why he treated her as if she was his Queen," he said.

"She and I could have been very good friends. I love her son as if he was my own, and so does Sen-Mut. Even though I have my doubts that he is my brother's child, I would never harm him or her. But conspiring against me and poisoning Aakheperen-Re's mind before he died, and not letting him go to the underworld in peace and causing him to make a threat on Sen-Mut's life? For that I cannot forgive her," I said.

"Does Sen-Mut know about this threat to his life?"

"No, he doesn't know. I have been afraid for his life since before my fifteen summers," I said.

He frowned and said, "How is that?"

"Everything started that day of my first audience, in favor to your friend Ramose to help Sen-Mut, and I told you to invite him to the banquet hall that night. I wanted Mother to give me her opinion, to see if I had used my wisdom correctly, and I wanted Father to be proud that I could make the correct judgments when he came back from his hunting trip. That night Puyem-Re brought Sen-Mut to the banquet hall. Then I saw him at the end of the banquet hall, and then I went and brought him to meet my mother. After the banquet dinner, I left with Ahmose, and that night in her quarters she told me that I was falling in love with Sen-Mut. She also said that I must stay away from him and that if Father found out it would be the end of Sen-Mut's life," I said.

"That is why you stayed away from my office or any place where he could be?"

"Yes. I did not want to bring harm to him in any way."

"Do you remember that morning after the audience? You came and talked to me, and I asked you if the ground moved under your feet?" He started to laugh. "Well, that day your face radiated, and I knew you had fallen in love for your first time. I am glad it was with him. He is a remarkable man, and you deserve a man like him, one who honestly loves you and is beside you," he said.

Ineni continued, "I remember Sen-Mut when he was a lad staring at the window next to the gardens waiting to see you walk to the temple. I could see his heart was going after you. I remember warning him after your father came and talked to me about you and him. It was the day of the sandstorm that your father wanted to put him to death, and Khety and I were so very worried. Then you came in, and he told you that he was putting him to death. You screamed so hard for him not to do it, and your father called the guard to go and apprehend Sen-Mut. I saw the panic in your face, and you screamed at him, crying that if he killed him, you would kill yourself like Neferu-Bity did, and you started to run into the sandstorm. In that moment, it made your father react. Then Khety and I knew that the man in your life was Sen-Mut, and your father knew it too. Then when he found out that Sen-Mut saved your life, your father knew how much he loved you too. That is why he never said anything again against Sen-Mut, but I had to warn him to keep away from you. That day Khety and I had a long talk with Sen-Mut, but we never told him that he was so close to losing his life, and that you ran into the storm to kill yourself. The reason we didn't tell him was, so he would not be afraid constantly and lose his concentration on his studies, because your father had granted his life for saving yours. We opened his eyes to the reality of life in the palace with the royal women, and to be sure that no one would catch him looking at you, that death could be on him quicker that he could even think.

"Maat also talked to the First Prophet of Amun Khety regarding, what? I don't know, but Khety did say it was regarding Sen-Mut and you. He did not elaborate on his conversation, but, since that day, your father never spoke of killing him again. I also became worried for Sen-Mut's life, and I did talk to him again, telling him to stay away from you and that he could not whisper your name anywhere. I told him that the walls had ears, and Pharaoh knows everything that goes on in the palace and out in the whole land. I told him not to trust his feelings to anyone. That is why he stayed away from the banquet hall from that day on, and away from you. He is a very reserved man and trustworthy, and I saw how he had to swallow his love for you in silence. That reminded me of my love for your mother, wanting to hold her in my arms when I could not. I felt sorry for him through all those years without you, as I was without your mother. But everything has changed. Now you two are happy and free to love each other. I am very happy for both of you," he said.

"My beloved Sen-Mut. My beloved one," I whispered. "That is why I have made it up to him, and we will never be apart again. Ineni, I am happy that I came to talk to you. I found out things I never knew. The only thing I knew was my love for Sen-Mut and that his heart was beating for me in silence, because I felt the warmth of his love inside of me. After my marriage to my father, I always felt his love inside me."

"Hatshepset, I believe it's time for you to share your worries with the man that loves you. Tell him to be aware of who is around him and that maybe someone is trying to hurt him, and to be just as alert as every Pharaoh must be. Keep eyes everywhere and trust no one," Ineni said.

"I kept it to myself because the threat on Sen-Mut's life was only if I killed Isis and Menkhep-Re. I knew that I had to keep him safe, that is why on that same day of the threat by Thut, I sent for fifty of my most brave warriors to wait for him at the edge of the Nile and guard him everywhere he went from that day on. I will tell him everything as soon I get to the palace. Let's continue our conversation tonight during dinner. Thank you so much for your wisdom and advice, and I will see you soon. Use the litter when you come to dinner tonight. Thank you, Ineni," I said.

I got up from the chair and walked away toward the Nile. I took off my sandals and walked barefoot. I loved to feel the cool green grass under my feet. I walked to Sen-Mut's office and approached him from behind in silence and hugged him very tightly. He turned around with a big smile on his lips, and the love for me was showing in his eyes.

"I am very happy that you belong to me," I told him smiling.

"What is all this about?" He was laughing.

I held his hand and pulled him close.

"Let's walk beside the Nile. I must talk to you about something that I have keep quiet since Thutmoses II went to the underworld," I said.

The land was covered with the red rays of Ra, and they were fading away. The current of Hopi was slowly moving on my right, and darkness was approaching. Soon Mother Nut would cover the land. We walked holding hands.

"Beloved one, for many summers I have kept quiet about a threat on your life, and the threat was made by Thutmoses II a few hours before he died."

Sen-Mut stopped walking and looked at me.

I continued, "He said that Isis was terrified that when he goes to the underworld I would rush to your arms and nothing could stop me. She was afraid that I would order her and his son Menkhep-Re, who was only three summers at the time, dead. He told me that he had hired a silent assassin to kill you if I killed them. I was in shock. More venom spit from the mouth of the cobra Isis. I got very angry and I told him that thought had never passed through my mind, but if you were to be killed, I would kill them both. And I would make sure it was a slow death. I would use them as arrow practice, or maybe cut them into pieces while they were alive. Whichever death I considered the most painful."

Sen-Mut gently grabbed me by my shoulders and looked at me.

"Why didn't you ever tell me about this?" He had a very serious expression on his face.

Looking into his eyes, softly I said, "Because I did not want for you ever to be worried. I have made sure that no one will come near you to harm you. I have made sure of that all this time. That is why on the day of my brother's death I sent fifty of my bravest warriors to wait for you at the edge of the Nile to bring you to my rose garden. Remember?"

"That is why I was surprised that day, seeing so many guards escorting me to the palace and to your rose garden," he said.

"I always commanded the armies of my father. On that day I gave the orders for you to be guarded always, wherever you go. Also, that is why I sent for Nehesi, the Nubian general, after Thutmoses II's death. Nehesi brought his friends, whom he trusts, and we have ears all over the land, including your brother Senemen. And of course, Hapuseneb. All of them will make sure that any threat spoken anywhere in the palace or out in the land will be known to us, and they will protect you. I have made sure of that. And the greatest part of all is that all of you have become good friends, especially you and Nehesi," I said.

Sen-Mut gently pulled me close to his chest and wrapped his arms around me and hugged me very tightly against his strong chest. He kissed my forehead and whispered in my ear, "Thank you for protecting me all these years. I love you."

He became silent holding me in his arms, then he said, "Now I know why I have loved you since the first day I saw you radiating from your father's throne."

I pulled back and he kissed me profoundly on my lips. He was gently caressing my back, and our bodies became hot with desire. He laid me gently in the green grass and slowly lifted off my sheath. I was naked, lying on the grass, and his hand caressed my body. He possessed my body with this crazy passion. We made passionate love beside the Nile under the stars. We lay there quietly for a while as he held me in his arms then he said, “I can never get tired of making love to you.” He kissed me again.

“Yes, beloved one. I love making love with you. Ineni is waiting for us in the banquet hall. We must be bathed and rush to him,” I said.

“Let’s go,” he said, and lifted me up from the grass and helped me dress, then we walked to the palace.

****

A week had passed when I saw Ineni crossing the inner garden of the palace, coming in my direction.

“Good morning, Hatshepset,” he said. He had a smile on his face.

“Good morning, Master Builder. Do you have any information about the silent assassin, or who he is?” I asked.

“First, let’s go over how you can crown Sen-Mut Pharaoh of Egypt. I believe that he can sail with a very large army and try to find the lost land of Punt like your father did, which brought him much glory. That will make him a great conqueror, as your father the Great Maat was when he found Punt. After your father, no one ever tried to find it again, and the route died with him. Have you told Sen-Mut of the desire of your heart to make him Pharaoh?”

“No, I have not. I was waiting first for your guidance on this matter. I must think carefully about this. I don’t know if I can see him leaving me and going to a faraway land without knowing for how long. I will be afraid for his life and the danger he may encounter in the search of Punt. He is not a marine nor a soldier,” I said.

"Menkhep-Re will soon be sixteen summers, and he's getting very strong and is very close with your armies. From time to time he becomes restless, and within a few years, he could try to overthrow you. My advice to you is to do this as soon as possible or take other alternatives. Isis is constantly pushing him for the throne," he said.

"I know, that spitting cobra. I will talk to Sen-Mut tonight when he comes from Djeser-Djeseru, the holiest of the holies, my funerary temple. He is almost finished. He has been away for almost a week, and he should be arriving before Ra goes down today. Have you visited Djeser-Djeseru yet? Soon it will be completed. It's beautiful. Sen-Mut has become a master builder, like you Ineni," I told him with a smile.

Smiling, he said, "Indeed, a master builder with such innovative ideas. I am very proud of him and all his achievements. I will see you soon, Your Majesty." He bowed his head and left.

I saw Ineni leaving the inner garden in the direction of his home. I walked to the edge of the Nile and stood there looking at the slow current of the water and thinking about what he had said.

Should I let Sen-Mut go that far away? What if he doesn't come back? I would die without him. I clapped my hands, and a guard came running to me.

"Summon First Prophet of Amun-Ra Hapuseneb, General Nehesi, General D'Jehuty, Sailor Neb-Ery, Thuty, Teshi, Senemen, my uncle General Thutmoses, and Master Builder Ineni to the audience hall for tomorrow at the ninth hour of the morning," I said and watched the guard leave, running.

I was sitting on my balcony when the double golden doors opened. It was my beloved walking toward me with a smile on his face. I got up from the chair and rushed to him and kissed his lips. He wrapped his arms around my body.

“My love, I have missed you all these days that I have been away from your arms. The nights are so long without you,” he said.

“Beloved one, I must speak to you,” I said.

I held his hands, brought him to our bed, and asked him to sit down. I knelt between his knees and looked in to his eyes, and with my left hand, I caressed his face.

“There is a desire deep inside my heart, and it has been there for the longest time. It is to make you Pharaoh of Egypt,” I said.

He was surprised at what I had just said.

Then he said, “I never knew that. You never told me, but you don’t have to do that. I like seeing you in your kilt, walking around everywhere, even though I prefer you in a sheath. And let me tell you this, for you to do that you have to step down from the throne and become Queen again. Are you sure you want to that?”

“Yes. For you I want to. I thought about it during the seventy days of the embalming of my father’s body and long before you made me yours. I was so tempted to marry you and not Aakheperen-Re. I was Queen of Egypt and no one could stop me then, but I tried talking to Khety and was told no. They would not support me on this idea. It was also the promise I made to Maat before he went to the underworld, and it kept me from doing it. I had to marry my half-brother to make him Thutmoses II, Pharaoh of Egypt. But now, nothing is going to hold me back. I know Menkhep-Re is in line for the throne, but he is not of full royal blood, nor do I believe he is my brother’s son. I am not going to marry him to make him Pharaoh and have the throne for his mother. I have spoken to Ineni regarding my heart’s desire, and I asked for his advice of what I should do. He suggested sending you on an expedition to find the land of Punt. This will bring you glory. The army will love you and will accept you as their Pharaoh, and the people of the land will look at you as their god. Now, will you give me the pleasure of becoming Pharaoh and I your Queen?” I asked.

“You are my Queen, my Pharaoh. You are my goddess, the Diadem of the Universe, the most precious treasure I have. What else could I want, if all I want is you? You have given me all. My steps are the only ones known in the palace. You have showered me with gifts and given me so many titles and the control of all the land and its treasures. What else would I want when I have it all?”

“Yes, I have given you all. Except the one thing, the right title, ‘Pharaoh.’ You have managed the affairs of my palace and the land. I want everyone to bow their heads to your feet and look at you as their god. That's what I want,” I exclaimed.

He lifted me up from the floor by my shoulders, and looking deep into my eyes, pulled me closer to him. He pressed his body against mine, wrapping his arms around my body, and pressed his lips on mine.

After kissing me, he said, “I must think about it. Now, let’s bathe together.”

He whispered in my ear, “You arouse me when I am near you, like the first time I saw you naked under the silver rays of Thoth, and he was bathing you with his rays. I thought it was a goddess. Then when you called to me and I came near you. Your sheath was wet, and water was dripping down your face and onto your breasts. I could see your wet breasts and the hardness of your nipples, and I became so hot and aroused that my heart was pounding hard, as it’s now.”

He lifted me up into his arms and carried me to the bathing tub. Rose petals were floating on the warm water. Slowly he removed my sheath, and we became one. We were involved in the most delicious ecstasy of love making, and we hung onto each other’s body as he made me his again and again, a pleasure and love only he could give me. After a while, he whispered in my ear, “I am missing your body already, and I am not even gone yet.” I laughed.

He bathed me, and I bathed him quietly. We then got ready for dinner in the banquet hall, and after dinner we walked in the gardens of the palace holding hands. The night was so clear and lovely.

Later that night in bed, I said, "Beloved one, I must have your answer by tomorrow before the ninth hour. I have summoned our trusted ones. I will not tell them of my plans to crown you Pharaoh of Egypt. I won't put your life in danger. I will reveal it to them after your return from Punt, and only Ineni will know for now. I will only speak of the search for Punt and that you will command it."

We lay naked in the bed, for the night was hot, and I saw him fall asleep.

I could not sleep all night long, I saw the first rays of Ra were starting to show. I looked at Sen-Mut, and he was peacefully sleeping. I could hear his breathing. I traced his face with my eyes travelling all over his face and lips. They were well formed. I loved his lips, the crest of his chin, and, well, his entire naked body. I caressed his face gently.

He opened his eyes and smiled.

"Glorious morning to you, beloved one," I said softly and smiled. "I didn't mean to wake you up. I just wanted to caress your face, and have it printed on my mind and in my heart."

He smiled with sleepy eyes. "Glorious day to you, Diadem of the Universe," he said.

He pulled me close to him and kissed my lips.

"It's very early in the morning. What are you doing awake?" he asked.

"I could not sleep all night, thinking of the search for Punt, and if I made the right decision sending you so far away. Maybe it's just better to step down and crown you Pharaoh," I said.

“What do you think will happen if you step down? The high priests and Puyem-Re, the Second Prophet of Amun, will want to crown Menkhep-Re, and you will be the Queen to a sixteen-summers child,” he said.

“You are right, and you still have not given me your answer,” I said.

“I want to give this,” he said and pulled me fast on top of him. I was laughing, then he made love to me. How wonderful it is to make love with my beloved.

We laughed together then he shouted, “Hatshepsut, I love you!”

“I love you, Sen-Mut!” I shouted back, and we laughed again.

The chanting beyond the golden doors began. We washed our hands and faces, and we knelt together facing Ra to the east and blessed the Almighty One, the giver of life. Then after the incensing of the doors was over, we had eggs, cheese, sweet bread, our favorite hot drink, fruit juice, and fruits. I loved fruit in the mornings. It refreshed my insides, I told him as we held hands.

“Beloved, you have not given me your answer yet,” I said.

He kissed me, then said, “I will.”

I became quiet.

“What’s wrong?” he asked.

“I don’t know if I am doing the right thing by sending you far away, to a land that we don’t know, but I must,” I said.

He nodded his head twice, and we walked to be bathed by our-selves.

After, we walked to the hall of audience, and everyone I had summoned was there. I sat on my golden throne. Sen-Mut stood at my left and Hapuseneb at my right.

"I gathered you all together here to inform you that I am sending all of you on an expedition to find the land of Punt. Nehesi, D'Jehuty, and Sailor Neb-Ery must get together and plan the route to Punt. We don't have much information left by my father from when he went there, but the god Amun-Ra spoke to me in a dream and ordered me to find Punt. He wants Sen-Mut to oversee the expedition, and Hapuseneb will accompany him on this trip. Now, you will plan the trip and how many ships are needed and how many of the armies will go. I will leave you all together here with Sen-Mut so that you can work out the plans. You must inform me of the progress and tell me how long it will take to get ready," I said, still not sure if what I was doing was the right thing.

Hapuseneb was as surprised as the rest of them, except for Ineni, for he already knew.

Neb-Ery the sailor said, "Your Majesty, the season of Akhet is almost gone. The waters are starting to subside, and the season of Pha-Rmuti will soon begin. The rich soil will be ready for planting. We can start planting an extra field of crops for the trip. I believe it will take two or three summers to prepare and get ready all the provisions. We can start preparations tomorrow. I will plan the route with Nehesi and see if there is another route to reach the Red Sea. I will begin the construction of the ships after I calculate how many ships and soldiers will come with us on this journey, and I will be inspecting the flotilla of ships."

"Your Majesty, I believe if His Majesty the Great Maat found Punt, we shall find it again," Sen-Mut said with a smile on his face.

Nehesi said, "I will gather the army and the manpower needed as of today. It will be very good for the country carrying out this quest."

They all agreed with finding Punt again, as if they were looking forward to such an adventure. Everyone was smiling and pleased with the news. Everything was being planned for the quest to find Punt. It became a large commotion in my kingdom, everyone talking about this great idea. I received couriers from the Vizier of Memphis congratulating me on the idea and wishing me success on the quest. He offered to help with everything that we would need.

****

A few months passed and Sen-Mut, Hapuseneb, Nehesi, D'Jehuty, Sailor Neb-Ery, and I went to Memphis where the ships were being built. I was proud of my achievement, seeing how everything was taking shape for this quest. There was much excitement throughout my whole kingdom.

****

A few years passed, and all the preparation was done. Five ships had been built and all the soldiers were ready, as was the food, offerings, and gifts for the King of Punt. They would depart in a few days, and I still wondered if Sen-Mut should go. If he didn't go and they returned successfully, the glory would not be his. I didn't have any choice. He must go if I wanted him to be Pharaoh. I started to panic, and the worry overpowered me. The thought of him leaving me did not let me sleep at night. Sending him far away worried me. And always in the back of my mind was the silent assassin, and it terrified me.

Sen-Mut looked happy though. He was looking forward to this adventure, as was Hapuseneb. Now I had two worries on my mind, but I knew that General Nehesi and my soldiers would protect the lives of Sen-Mut and Hapuseneb. Still, I was worried.

The two most important men in my life would be going on this quest. At least I could be at peace knowing that the manpower of the skilled marines, warriors from the army, and some of the bravest of the brave of the palace guard would accompany them, and they would be protecting them very well. I believed Sen-Mut and Hapuseneb would be safe. They must be, I thought.

There was great happiness all over the land, and the following day my beloved would be leaving. I was glad that Puyem-Re, the Second Prophet of Amun, was going with them.

I wondered how T'Queta was taking all of this. She knew that after this quest, Sen-Mut would never go back to his house. He had visited her several times, for she had been faithful to him, and I had kept silent because he said when he visited her they didn't sleep together. I believed him. I knew that she had fallen in love with him. Who wouldn't? I could tell by the way she looked at him. I believed he must have some feelings for her too, but he kept it to himself. She had given him company for five summers, the company that I could not give him when my brother kept us apart after Neferu-Re was born and there was no physical contact between us. We could only see each other in the presence of a guard when he came to visit Neferu-Re. It was very sad for me when we could only share a few words and looks when he started to build my mortuary temple in the Valley of the Dead, and even then, only in the presence of Thutmoses II. How everything had changed since then. Now we were free to love each other as Sen-Mut had told me it would be.

I knelt and asked Amun-Ra to bring him safely back into my arms, and Hapuseneb too, that I may place the Double Crown upon Sen-Mut's head.

The day of the departure arrived, and we were all in the banquet hall celebrating. Sen-Mut was seated beside me at my left, and Hapuseneb was at my right where he always had his place. Tepi was seated in front of us. I noticed that she had been crying. I too had cried several nights wondering if I had made the right decision. How afraid I was for him.

I was lost in thought when Sen-Mut said, "Beloved, you are very quiet tonight. Are you OK?"

I looked at his face, and my eyes became full of tears. I lowered my eyes, then got up quickly. Everyone knelt. I turned around and could barely speak.

I took a deep breath and said, "I must retire. Tomorrow is going to be a long day. Everyone stays and enjoy the celebration tonight."

Everyone raised their golden cups and yelled, "Hail, Hatshepsut! Hail, Hatshepsut!"

I forced a smile and turned around and left beside my beloved. He held my hand as we walked out, mosquitos everywhere. We got to our quarters, and the royal guard opened the golden doors. My slaves were waiting. I clapped my hands for them to leave, and they did.

Sen-Mut sat on the edge of our bed, and I knelt between his knees, resting my head in his lap. Tears were pouring down my face. With his right hand raising my chin, Sen-Mut looked deep into my eyes and said, "Diadem of the Universe, don't worry. I will come back to you. I promise. We will have a long life together, and you can give me more children. Maybe fifteen or twenty-five children?"

I was startled and started to laugh as the tears were rolling down my face. We laughed together, then he sat beside me on the floor at my right, and I held his hand.

"Beloved one, I don't know if I have made the right decision sending you on this quest, and now I am terrified that you are leaving me. I don't know if you will ever come back to me. We don't know how long this quest will take. I was a small child when Maat went on his quest and found Punt, and I don't remember anything about it," I said.

He covered my lips with his hand and said, "His Majesty the Great Maat came back, didn't he? Yes, he did… and I am planning to come back to you. I am just doing this to please you. For me, we can leave everything the way it is."

Studently he got up and said, "I'll be back."

He walked away without giving me time to say anything. He probably went to say goodbye to T'Queta, I thought, and a rush of jealousy came upon me. I waited for a while, remaining on the floor until he came back.

Sweetly, I asked, "Did you go to say goodbye to T'Queta?"

"No, I went to talk to Hapuseneb, and I asked him to stay and look after you. He agreed to do it. Now I feel much better leaving you with someone I trust. I know he will protect you with his own life. I have known for many years that he has been in love with you and that he honestly loves you. I have also known that he married Tepi because he could not have you," he said.

I was surprised that he knew all of that. "Who told you?" I asked him.

"I always knew. Remember, I am a man and noticed all these years the way he looks at you and talks with possessiveness when he speaks of you. Over the years, we finally became friends, and one day we had a long conversation. He told me how he felt about you and that one day he is going to die with this love for you inside of him."

I became sad again and started to cry. Sen-Mut pulled me close to him and lifted me into his arms and kissed me passionately. He held me tight against his chest, and I squeezed him to me as well. I caressed his face.

"Have you fallen in love with T'Queta," I asked him.

The expression on his face changed, and he was startled.

"Fallen in love with T'Queta? Never! I am only in love with you, and in my life and in my heart, there is no space for anyone else but you. I have some feelings for her, yes. I suffered very much when we were kept apart for five summers. I became close to her in those five years, but every time I had sex with her, I thought of you. Your lips, your body, the smell of your skin, and how much I missed you. I care for her, but I am not in love with her. I love her, but this is a different kind of love. It's more like gratefulness to her. It is not like our love. She deserves to be loved. Once she told me that she had fallen in love with Hapuseneb, but he told her that he had chosen Tepi for his wife. I believe that is the saddest part of a slave's life. I said goodbye to her this morning and brought her some gold. I told her that my house is hers now and gave her the deed to the property. I thanked her for all these years of service and companionship. And for her love too."

He became quiet for a second, and I knew it was hard for him too. He took a deep breath, then said, "She started to cry terribly and said that she loves me, that she had fallen in love with me through the years. It was a very sad situation for me because she knew that I only have love for you, and she knew that I would never come back to the house again. I promised to send her a slave to serve her. And I gave her freedom. Is this okay with you?" he asked.

"Oh yes, beloved one. Yes, you may. You have done the right thing with her," I said.

"I never told you that she had several pregnancies by Hapuseneb and that Menina had terminated them because Hapuseneb did not want children with her," I said.

"Hapuseneb told me that himself, and that he felt bad after he did it. He said he did it because he had other reasons, and to avoid more pregnancies, and pain to her, he decided to take Tepi for a concubine. He said he was not in love with Tepi. He did love T'Queta, but not enough to make her his wife. He knew that he would hurt her, and he himself hurt very much after he did it. But he had other more powerful feelings inside of him. I knew that those powerful feelings were for you. Of course, it was you," he said.

I listened to him silently, then I said, "I also love her, my love, and I am most grateful to her for taking care of you all those years for me when we were kept apart by my brother."

He pulled me under his body and pined me down on the floor with great force and kissed me all over. He whispered in my ear, "I love you, Maatke-Re. I love you, and I want to remember every part of your body and your smell, your delicious smell."

Pressing his lips hard on mine, our kisses were eternal. His hands traveled slowly, completely all over my body.

"I will make love to you all night long, so this night will forever be in my mind and in my heart and soul, so that every night that I am away from you, your image will accompany me, and I'll feel you beside me," he said.

We made love deeply and clung to each other's bodies so tightly. I kissed him all over his face, his eyes, his lips, with such tenderness and love, then I kissed all over his body. He was my love and my all.

"Beloved, I love you so much, and I will love you throughout all eternity, as I promised the night when you asked me to be your wife. Please, when Thoth is high and bright in the night, look at him. I'll be looking at him and thinking of you." I kissed his lips gently and said, "And I will be anxiously waiting for your return."

We made love again, and again, and again, all night long. We held onto each other so tightly. I hated to let go of his body, but eventually I got up from the floor and walked to a wooden box and brought it to where he was lying on the floor. I knelt beside him, and I said, "Beloved, this gift is for you, and I want you to wear it today and always."

He opened the box and was surprised.

"It's beautiful," he said.

"I sent for this gold pectoral to be made especially with the body of Ptah for you, and it's blessed by Hapuseneb. Inside the body of Ptah is an amulet for your protection, which has a drop of my blood for you to carry my love close to your heart. I want everyone to know that you are my Ptah, my Architect and Steward of Amun-Ra," I said.

He sat the wooden box on the side of the bed and pulled me up from the floor where I was kneeling. Looking deep into my eyes, he said, "You are the most beautiful goddess." He kissed my lips again, holding me tight in his arms.

There was a knock on the golden doors. It was the slaves coming to prepare our baths and dress us. Several slaves came, and we followed them quietly to be bathed. We walked holding hands and entered the warm water of the tub. I clapped my hands, and all the slaves left us. I was going to bathe his body. Slowly, I bathed him and kissed his body, and he bathed mine and kissed me all over. The oil lamps were lit, and the incense was burning We could see each other's faces in the dim light. I caressed his face with both of my hands, then he took my hands into his and kissed them.

"I want to thank you for your love and for giving me the opportunity to become an architect. You have the most beautiful heart, and without this opportunity, I would never have found love or discovered that I cannot live without you. You are my life, and I remain yours forever," he said.[74]

He kissed both my hands again, and I broke down crying and could not stop. Lifting me up into his arms, Sen-Mut carried me close to our bed, and I stood there crying as he kneeled and patted my body dry.

---

[74] I am crying right now as I remember this moment and dreading seeing him leave for Punt. (3/10/2016.)

He looked into my eyes, and said, "My love, be strong for me please. My heart is also weak. When I walk out those doors, all the eyes of the army are going to be on me, and they will see tears in my eyes. That is a sign of weakness, and you don't want that. And remember that we must walk to the Temple of Amun-Ra before sunrise, and soon it is going to be. I want you to take care of yourself very well, so when I come back you are still as beautiful as you are now."

He had a very sad look on his face. He clapped his hands and several slaves came rushing to dress us. I wore the Queen's golden sheath and not the white kilt. I did not care if the people saw me as Queen that day.

"Is everyone waiting?" I asked the slaves.

"Yes, Your Majesty, everyone is waiting downstairs."

I clapped my hands, and the slaves left my room. I knew this was the moment I had been dreading for days. I knelt, and Sen-Mut put on my head the Double Crown of Egypt.

"You look beautiful, Hatshepsut," he said. I saw tears in his eyes.

He kissed me and said, "Always remember that I'll always love you, and I will come back to you. I promise."

I was trembling, and tears were pouring down my face.

We reached the bottom of the stairs, and the procession started walking. This time I asked Hapuseneb to be on my left, and Sen-Mut was at my right. I wanted to hold his hand but could not. The people of the city were all gathered along the sides of the street. Everyone was cheering us as we walked, but it was so hard to smile. I saw T'Queta wearing the blue attire of mourning. How strange, I thought Then she threw a very large number of white rose petals over Sen-Mut's body as we passed beside her. I don't know if he looked at her, but I did. She was crying hard, and we exchanged looks. I could see the love for him on her face and her pain. I knew it must be very hard for her too. I will send for her from time to time to come and visit me and give her news of Sen-Mut, I thought.

I thought of the years that have gone by. We were in our thirty-seven summers now. I was lost in thought when we reached the Temple of Amun-Ra, and Hapuseneb, the First Prophet of Amun, blessed everyone that was going on this expedition. We then proceeded to walk toward the five ships that were waiting. After a certain point, I ordered the street to be closed. I removed the Double Crown from my head and handed it to one of the guards, who carried it away. I walked with Sen-Mut, holding his hand until we reached the ramp of the ship. I could not hold back my tears any longer. He kissed me deeply as tears poured down our faces.

"May all the gods walk with you on this journey, and may they protect you and your crew always. I love you, Sen-Mut," I whispered.

I placed his hand on my heart and said, "Carry my heart with you, beloved of mine, and come back to me alive. Come back to me safely. Please. And may the rays of Ra be always on your back until you return to me."

He could not speak. I could see how he clenched his teeth, holding back his tears. He turned around, holding my fingers tightly, as I did his. I did not want to let him go. I was sobbing and held his fingers until we were no longer touching. I saw him walk up the ramp to the ship, followed by Nehesi, Teshi, Senemen, and Sailor Neb-Ery. Puyem-Re was already on the ship blessing the inside for the journey. The ramp was pulled back, and my heart sank.

I ordered the guards to let the people come closer. Sen-Mut was on the first ship. The ship started to move. Sen-Mut was standing there, holding a rope, looking at me as the ship started to move slowly south against the strong current. I started to walk beside the ship. The oarsmen began to rower faster at the sound of the drums. I couldn't keep up. I started to run beside him as tears poured down my face, overpowered by the terrible uncertainty of whether I'd made the right decision to let him go away from me.

I ran faster, shouting, "I love you! I love you, Sen-Mut!"

I don't know if he could hear me. I ran until I could run no further. I saw him standing there, looking at me, fading from my sight and followed by the other four ships.

"Amun-Ra, please bring him safely back to me, and bring everyone home to their families. Please," I whispered. I watched the back of the last ship fading away in silence, as the tears poured down my face.

"Aren't you afraid that he will never come back to you alive again."

A voice had whispered close to my right ear. I quickly turned around to see Menkhep-Re standing behind me with a sneer on his face. I became furious and screamed at him.

"You, better pray he comes back to me alive and safe! Otherwise, I will send you to your little war games practice. I will send you a very good meal, and after you finish eating it, I will walk into your tent and ask, 'Did you like the food? Well, you have just eaten your mother.' Then I will kill you," I screamed at him.

The sneer faded from his face fast, and I pushed him hard out of my way. I walked away very fast and sent twenty guards to bring his mother Isis to the audience hall. I then summoned Hapuseneb, Ineni, D'Jehuty, and the priests of the temple and the rest of the court members. I could not contain my anger. When the double doors opened, and she walked in with her eyes cast down, I looked at her with rage. I took a few steps down from my throne, knowing how much she hated not being able to raise her eyes to look at me as my equal. She hated having to prostrate herself at my feet, as she was doing at that moment. She bowed her head down to the floor at my feet. I pushed her shoulder with the sole of my sandal, and she fell to the side. I pressed my golden sandal on the side of her cheek against the floor, and I spoke to her with anger.

"Don't think that I don't know what you have been doing. You have been conniving against me, Sen-Mut, Hapuseneb, and everyone close to me for the longest time. I know you were poisoning my brother's head to kill my daughter, Neferu-Re. I believe you had something to do with her death. And you were the one that spread the rumor in the kitchen that Neferu-Re was Sen-Mut's child. Thutmoses II killed several innocent slaves because of your poisonous tongue. I know you have been conspiring against me all this time. Do you think I don't know that? Don't you know that I can kill you and your son at any time? Yes, I can, but I promised my brother on his deathbed that I would not. But that doesn't mean I can't change my mind any time I want to.

"Don't you wonder why I have not married your son, and made him full royal blood and crowned him Pharaoh of Egypt? Because I believe that he is not my brother's son! I had him as co-regent for political purposes only. And now, pray, and really pray, that Sen-Mut comes back to me safe and alive. Otherwise, I will have a very good meal prepared for you, and after you have eaten it, I will walk to you and tell you, 'You have just eaten your son.' Then I will kill you too. So, get the hell out of my sight now!" I said.

I pushed her shoulder with the sole of my golden sandal, and she fell on her back. She composed herself and crawled backwards all the way to the entrance doors without turning her back to me. Hapuseneb rushed to my side and held my arm. I was trembling with rage. Everyone was talking in the hall of audience. Everyone knew that for years she had been plotting and conspiring against me to put her son on the throne.

I said to them, "For years I have believed that Menkhep-Re is not Aakheperen-Re's son, but I have no way to prove it."

Hapuseneb held my arm and walked me to the palace. I told him what Menkhep-Re had said to me.

He shook his head and said, "We should have done away with him and his mother when Aakheperen-Re died, but you did not want to."

"Because Aakheperen-Re had threatened Sen-Mut's life with a silent assassin if I killed them. The snake Isis had poisoned his mind, and he was so worried until his death. My poor brother. He did not die in peace, and I am glad I gave her that beating in his quarters before he died. Even if we could have done away with them, my soul would not be clean or at peace for when I go to the underworld, and I did not have the heart to do it. I raised him. I loved him as if he was my own son," I said.

We reached my quarters and Hapuseneb said good night and left. I stood on my balcony quietly, looking at the sunset and thinking of Sen-Mut. Soon Mother Nut would bathe the land in darkness, and I sat thinking of my beloved. Our hearts beat as one, as our blood runs in our veins. This great love of ours has made a chain in our minds, and I am glad that we have these mind connections because I know when you are thinking of me, and you know when I am thinking of you. That is the beauty of our love. I am wondering how far you have gone. I wanted to tell you how much I was missing you already, beloved one.

****

It had been almost three months since my beloved left, and I went daily to the temple and made offerings for his wellbeing, Nehesi, and his crew.

CHAPTER 37

SEN-MUT

The first rays of Ra were starting to bathe the land, and sitting at the edge of my bed, a cold chill ran through my body. Suddenly, in my mind I saw someone giving a gold ring that looked familiar to me to another person. I could not make out the ring well, and an uneasy feeling ran through my body. It made me tremble. Then I remembered the ability I had of seeing things in my mind that were happening someplace else at that same moment. What I saw worried me very much because I could not see their faces, and that made me very uneasy. But what was it?

I was thinking of Sen-Mut. Missing him felt eternal and the days without him never ending. It was almost sunset, and I walked to my rose garden and sat down, looking at the fast current of Hopi flowing to the north. I was thinking that the route they had taken to the south would be the one that connected to the large sea and hoping it was the one closer to the land of Punt. After all, Nehesi knew the region well. He knew that the large river did connect to the large sea because his father had told him before, but he has been in that part the region but never gone to Punt. He believed that going south was the correct way, and I trusted him. I was lost in thought when I was distracted by the voice of Hapuseneb.

"Good afternoon, Flower of Egypt," he said.

I looked at him and smiled. He came every afternoon since the day Sen-Mut left, to visit and have tea with me and Ineni. They kept me company and up to date on all the affairs of my kingdom.

Hapuseneb approached me with a beautiful smile, and I said, "Good afternoon to you too, First Prophet of Amun. Sit and have some hot mint tea with me."

"Sure, I will. Soon it's going to be three months since they left. I wanted to tell you that the night before Sen-Mut left, he came and requested me to stay and not go on this expedition. He was worried about you and entrusted your well-being to me. He wanted me to assure you every day that he will come back to you and to tell you that he loves you every day," he said.

My eyes filled with tears. I did not know Sen-Mut had said all these nice things to him. How lovely and caring Sen-Mut was with me.

"Thank you, Hapuseneb," I said, then I squeezed his hand and smiled.

"Hapuseneb, something has been bothering me and worrying me all day long. I had a vision early this morning, and in my mind, I saw a man giving a ring to another man on the ship. The ring looked familiar to me, but I could not see it well. I don't know what to make of this vision, but it does worry me."

"What could it be?" he said.

I shook my head. "I really don't know?" I replied.

I picked up my cup and I was about to take a sip of the tea when in my mind I saw someone giving Sen-Mut a cup to drink. He took a sip from the cup. I stood up and I screamed so hard.

"Sen-Mut! Poison!"

I could not breathe. I was gasping for air and brought my hands to my throat, trying to breathe. I saw Hapuseneb jump from his seat as I was collapsing, and he caught me before I hit the ground. I still could not breathe. I was choking. I could see Sen-Mut far away, also choking, on the floor of the ship. Then I saw Nehesi and Puyem-Re carrying him away. We were both gasping for air. We were dying at the same time, I thought.

Hapuseneb carried me in his arms, rushing me to my quarters and screaming for help. I was fading away into darkness. Death was surrounding me, and I blacked out.

When I opened my eyes and move. I was surrounded by priest and priestesses, and Hapuseneb was kneeling beside me holding my hand almost at sleep. I could hear their chanting prayers around me. I was completely worn out, as if I had battled against an army. I did not have any strength on me. I knew that I had battled the forces of darkness away from Sen-Mut. I felt very cold, I was wet, and soaking in herbs. I looked at Hapuseneb. He looked exhausted. He started to cry when he saw me opening my eyes.

Everyone was shouting in happiness and clapping their hands. I could see gladness on their faces, and all of them knelt on one knee. Ineni was beside me, and tears were pouring down his eyes. I tried to smile at Hapuseneb and Ineni but barely had any strength on me. Then I remembered Sen-Mut and started to cry. I looked at Hapuseneb.

"I thought I had lost you," Hapu, said, as the tears roll down his face.

He continues, "I am so very happy that you are back, and I really thought that I was going to lose you. When you were choking and fainted, I knew that something was wrong. At first, I thought someone had poisoned you, and I need it the help of all the priests and priestesses of the Temple of Amun-Ra to save your life, I carry you in my arms to the palace screaming for help. Sorry I had to tore off your sheath, I need it to poured magic potion made of herbs all over your body, and chanted incantation words to chase death away from you. The priests and priestesses were here days and nights without stopping praying and burning incense around and above your body to save your life." He said, and I was listening and looked at them and nodded all of them had smiles in their faces.

He continues, "I battled death to save your life, because I saw dead all over you, and I order the Book of the Dead to be brought to me, and I opened it. It was the only way that I could save your life. I started reading the magic words and summoned the Anubis the god of the underworld and I plead with him not to take you away from me… finally, I chase death away from you, and I am happy that you are back." He said.

I whispered, "how long I have been unconscious?"

"One week," he said.

"One week?" I could not believe it, it was that long?

I cannot feel Sen-Mut around me as before, and I don't know if he was dead or alive. I thought.

"Hapuseneb, someone has poisoned Sen-Mut." I whispered. "Have you heard any news from Sen-Mut?

I started to panic and cried. Hapuseneb was hold my hand tightly and caress my head.

"Don't cry, Flower of Egypt. You are very weak right now, but you are safe now. You must regain your strength back. And no, we don't know anything of his fate yet. But I am glad that we were able to chase death away from you." He said.

"Hapu, I am very cold." I said.

Hapuseneb lifted my naked body in his arms with such devotion and love, and the slaves came and change the wet linen sheets and mattress, he sat me against the wall, and dressed me with a clean sheath, then covered me with a blanket to warm my body. Kneeling beside me he fed me warm lentil soup.

I started to cry again. I don't want to be alive anymore if he is dead, I thought. I was choking on my tears again.

Hapuseneb's eyes were closing. He was so tired from lack of sleep, and he fell asleep halfway on my bed. The other half of his body was on the floor where he was kneeling.

"Ineni, call the guards in, and tell them to lay Hapu on my bed," I told him.

The guards came in and lifted Hapu and put him on my bed, and he laid beside me. I looked at him as he slept quietly. It felt strange. There had never been a man other than Sen-Mut sleeping beside me.

"He hasn't slept for a week," Ineni said. "The Book of the Dead has never been opened before to summon Anubis to chase death away before for anyone, and he did it for you. During those days that you were unconscious, I told him that he needed to get some sleep, but he refused to leave your side. He kept chanting and praying every single moment. The love and devotion that he has and feels for you is remarkable. Now, Hatshepsut, you must sleep too to gain your strength back. I will be leaving soon and must have some rest as well. I hardly slept at all myself, like everyone else. These days have been very hard on everyone. I have been sitting on the balcony praying for your well-being and for Sen-Mut's life, just as the whole country has. Hatshepset, your daughter, has been going to the temple with Isis and Menkhep-Re. I can assure you that you were not poisoned. We tested your tea with your slaves, and they are all still alive," he said.

With tears rolling down my face, I whispered, "It is not me, it is Sen-Mut. Someone poisoned my beloved. I saw it in my mind, and I don't know if he survived or not. I saw Nehesi and Puyem-Re carrying him as he was choking, and I was choking at the same time too."

I was really sobbing by the time I finished describing my vision.

With a calm voice, Ineni said, “Child, let’s hope he survived this one too. Puyem-Re knows what to do in case of poisoning.” He touched my shoulder and continued, “I will be back before Ra fades away, and then I will go to the temple and say prayers and make offerings for Sen-Mut’s life. Have some rest, child.”

He came closer and kissed my forehead. Tears were rolling down my face as I watched him leave.

“Please, Amun-Ra, don’t take him away from me. Please. Please,” I whispered.

I was still crying, and I turned around to see Hapuseneb sleeping deeply beside me. I knew that he loved me so very much, and he did all that he could to save my life. I held his hand felt asleep.

He woke up after two days. He was happy that I was getting better and left to return to his home. My strength was slowly coming back. I still could not feel the presence of Sen-Mut around me, but my heart felt warm. Was he alive? I cried every time I remembered the image of him choking. It was still imprinted in my mind. Suddenly, I remembered the silent assassin. That must be it. And I would find out who it was.

****

Standing on my balcony and looking at the sunset, I thought and prayed that he was alive. I keep waiting for word on the fate of my beloved one, but there was none. I would deal with whoever had tried to kill him I swear. The only ones that wanted him dead were Menkhep-Re and his mother Isis, and if I found out that they did this, both would be dead. And they knew it.

There was a knock on the door.

"Enter," I said.

Hapuseneb walked in with a wide smile. His black hair was growing back again, and he looked so very handsome.

"Lotus of Egypt, you should not be standing. It's only been a week since you came back to life. Come let me help you to your bed."

I held his hand, but he lifted me up in his arms and carried me to my bed. He sat beside me and smiled, and we spoke for a while. He comes every day and spent all day with me.

"How does Tepi feel about you are staying here all day with me?" I asked.

"She does not complain. She knows better than to say a word, and, as she said, she should not complain because I give it to her every time she wants it," he said and started to laugh. "She has known very well how I feel about you for a long time. That is why I gave her many children to keep her occupied," he said.

He continued, "I wanted to tell you that I arranged an investigation in the palace, and every slave and guard was questioned. What I heard is that on the day that you fainted in my arms and were dying, Isis sent for Menkhep-Re and asked if he had something to do with what was happening to you. He yelled at his mother and said no, then asked her, 'And how about you mother, did you do it?' She said that she did not and they both looked at each other and got very worried. Menina, Isis's slave and my spy, saw them rushing to the Temple of Amun with Hatshepset to make offerings for your well-being. Menina told me that Isis was terrified that you were going to kill them both.

"You mentioned to me in the past that you have been afraid of a silent assassin wanting to kill Sen-Mut. I have investigated and can tell you that I have all my spies looking for him or her since you saw someone giving poison to Sen-Mut. And I am sorry, but we have not received any messenger with good or bad news of Sen-Mut's condition," Hapuseneb said.

I listened in complete silence, with my eyes full of tears, but my heart was calm. A rage came over me.

"I want to kill them both! I want to kill them both!" I screamed.

I hit my goose mattress with my fist.

"I should have killed them both and taken the risk," I said and started to cry again.

He held me in his arms and said, "Really, would you have taken that risk?"

The golden doors opened, and I saw my beautiful daughter Hatshepset walking toward me. Hapuseneb stood and made a place for her to sit beside me.

"Mother, how do you feel today? I came to tell you that there is a rumor in the palace that Sen-Mut is probably dead. I asked Menkhep-Re and Isis if they had something to do with this, and they swear that they do not. Nor did they try to kill you. Isis is praying constantly and does not come out of the temple. I can see real worry on Menkhep-Re face as well. He said that you are like his mother, and he would never try to hurt you. Yes, he would like to see Sen-Mut dead because he is the one who caused him not to be Pharaoh and put you on the throne instead of him, when he is the rightful heir," she said.

"No. I am the rightful heir to the throne of Egypt. That was the will of my father when he crowned me in Heliopolis with the Double Crown of Egypt to take his place when he went to the underworld. And who said I could not rule? Because I am a woman? I have handled the affairs of my land and the armed forces very well. I have fought beside my men, and they love me. I am their god. And it was not only Sen-Mut who put me on the throne but First Prophet of Amun-Ra Khety, all the elder priests of the temple, Hapuseneb, Ineni, Nehesi, Thuty, Teshi, and I have the blessing of Amun-Ra, the god of gods. I did not need the permission of anyone. Now, you can tell them to pray more, a lot more, that Sen-Mut is still alive. I can tell you that, sooner or later, I will find out who sent for Sen-Mut to be killed. And tell Menkhep-Re that he is going to wait until I am dead to become Pharaoh."

Looking directly at her, I continued, "Hatshepset, my dear daughter, I believe he is not your father's son. He doesn't look like your father. He is dark. Your father was fair, and Isis is fair too. I believe he is Puyem-Re's son."

Hatshepset brought her hands to her mouth.

"And I believe that Isis had something to do with Neferu-Re's death. She pushed and pushed until she poisoned your father's head to kill your sister, and he almost did. But later he changed his mind because Hapuseneb convinced him not to do it. He later came and told me himself that he was glad he did not kill Neferu-Re, but when you were born, everything changed. You were a full royal blood princess, and Isis preferred a full royal blood princess for her son. So, did your father. That is why I believe she killed her. But that doesn't change the tradition. You must be Queen first to transfer the royal blood to him to make him Pharaoh, and she never expected that I would become Pharaoh first. Oh, Isis always wanted the throne, but your father could not even make her a secondary wife for she is not of royal blood. She thought that through her son she could rule Egypt, but I have left her with unfulfilled desires on her hands," I said.

"Mother, what makes you believe that she killed Neferu-Re?"

"Because she wanted your full royal blood for her son. Once your father told me something when I was pregnant with Neferu-Re, and I remember clearly what he said on that day. He told me that when I was a very little girl, my siblings in line for the throne were dying, and no one knew what was killing them because there were no signs of how they died. It was not poison. There were no snake bites. They only found them dead.

Your grandmother Mutnofret was terrified that your father would be next, but he was spared. That was the way Neferu-Re was found, dead on her bed. She was only five summers, and there was no sign of what caused of her death. She was not sick at all, and no one can change my mind that Isis had something to do with her death," I said.[75]

She became silent for a moment, then said, "Mother, don't kill them. Please, I beg you. What if you are wrong and she did not have anything to do with my sister death, and they really did not have anything to do with someone trying to kill Sen-Mut?"

I looked at Hapuseneb.

"Let's wait on word from Nehesi about Sen-Mut's fate before making your decision." He said.

Then I looked at Hatshepset, "I will wait until then." I said.

She became happy.

"Very well, Mother. I am relieved that you will wait until then before you make any decisions because they said they are innocent, and I believe them."

She came closer and kissed me on the cheek and left my quarters.

"That is a wise decision, Lotus of Egypt. I believe that they had nothing to do with the attempt on Sen-Mut's live," Hapuseneb said.

---

[75] In this present life, I still believe Isis was responsible for my daughter's death. I met Isis in this life, and I told her about the animosity we had in the past. She said she had always felt that she had lived in ancient Egypt. She apologized for what she had done to me, and we are still in contact from time to time.

CHAPTER 38

T'QUETA

It had been two days since Hatshepset came to visit me. I wondered if she even loved me. Her distance from me had a lot to do with Isis. Her father kept her away from me when she was born and had Isis raise her as her daughter with the wet nurse. He probably believed that I would have harmed my child. Never. She had grown to be a beautiful woman, and she looked just like me. She was betrothed to Menkhep-Re and in line to become Queen, like it would have been with Neferu-Re. (I missed her. I missed my daughter. She had been gone such a long time.) Menkhep-Re was going to have to wait to become Pharaoh. I wished I could find out if he is really my brother's son. I wouldn't be so reluctant to trust him.

****

A week had passed when a very hard knock on the door startled me.

"Enter," I said.

It was Hapuseneb with tears and anguish upon his face. He walked quickly to where I was standing on the balcony. My stomach sank, and I panicked. My body started to tremble uncontrollably. Sen-Mut is dead? I started to cry and scream.

"No! No!" I screamed over and over. "He cannot be dead. Ha-puseneb, he cannot be dead!"

He rushed to me and grabbed me by my shoulders and said, "It's not Sen-Mut who is dead. It is T'Queta."

I looked at him shock.

"What? Dead? Why? How? Why is she dead?" I started to cry. She was so sweet to me, all of her life, and she was like my sister.

"What happened? How did she die?" I ask.

"She committed suicide," he said as the tears were rolling down his face.

"But why would she want to kill herself?" I asked.

"I really don't know why," he said.

We hugged each other and cried together, sitting side-by-side on the bed.

"Who found her?" I asked.

"I did." He said.

I was astonished by his reply, "And how is that you found her?"

"I promised Sen Mut to look after her, and I went to make sure that she was well and being taken care of by the slave I sent, as per his request. I questioned her servant why she was not with her, and she said that earlier she had sent her to the market," he said.

His elbows were on top of his knees, and his hands holding his flushed face. He stood up suddenly. And I did looking at him.

"This is horrible. I cannot believe I am reliving your sister's death," he said.

"Why are you blaming yourself, Hapuseneb?" I asked him sweetly with tears in my eyes.

"Because I hurt her badly several times. Worst, when I took Tepi for my concubine, knowing that T'Queta was in love with me."

"Yes, you did hurt her terribly. I suffered through her agony, and I cried for her when I heard her crying through the night on her couch. I tried to console her, but it was hard. Who can mend or console a broken heart? Only time can heal a broken heart. Those were the worst times she went through. Why didn't you have her as a secondary wife like I told you in Philae?"

"I thought about it, but Tepi was so jealous of you and of T'Queta. I was already having enough of her complaints about you. She would have driven me crazy if I had taken T'Queta with me. And because…" He became silent.

"And because of what?" I asked him.

"Because through her, I could keep an eye on Sen-Mut and you. I got very angry when she told me that he asked her to put a large pink rose from your garden in your bedroom on the day of your fifteen summers."

So, the rose was from Sen-Mut, I thought.

"I never knew that, and she never told me," I said. Thinking how sweet was of her, then tears came back into my eyes.

"That is why on my fifteen summers celebration you grabbed me by my arms and shook me so terribly hard? You left bruises on my left arm that night, and I was afraid for your life if Maat found out."

"Yes. I could not bear seeing him looking at you and you talking to him. Jealousy was eating me. I did not give you a gift, but he did. A stolen rose from your own garden. That is why T'Queta never told you that it was from him. I also believe that she liked him too," he said.

"I want the best embalming for her, with the finest linen. I will do the opening of the mouth ritual. She did not have any family that can do it for her, that she may have after-life. Only you and me. I want her to be buried in a nice coffin with all the jewelry I gave her throughout her life and the gold Sen-Mut gave her before he left," I told him.

He lowered his eyes and nodded.

"She is going to have to be buried in the ground, even though it is not our custom to do that. If I send for a tomb to be dig in the Hill of the Dead,[76] the grave robbers will find it, as they did with my father's Tomb," I said.

"Have they taken her body yet?"

"Yes. I called the guards and sent for the embalmer to take her body to the House of the Dead."

"Did you accompany her body to the House of the Dead?" I asked.

"No, there wasn't time. I came straight here to tell you."

He was flushed from the tears, and I could see the agony on his face.

"We are going to have to bury her in the ground and on our own. Just you and me, somewhere in the Valley of the Dead. Have some peasants from the town of Luny or Memphis come here. You must take them far away to dig the grave for her and be sure no one follows you. I don't

[76] A rocky area near the Valley of the Dead where wealthy people buried their loved ones.

want any tomb robbers to steal all I have given her through the years that she was with me," I said.

"Yes, you are right. I will find a peasant to do it. It must be someone that is from far away from here, who doesn't know this region," he said it with a somber face.

He got up, kissed my hand, nodded and said, "Your Majesty." He turned and left. I had never seen him so somber and sad before.

I walked to my bed and lay there for a long time. With all the good memories of her since we were little girls, I wondered why she killed herself. Could it be because she believes that Sen-Mut is death?

"How sorry I am, my beloved friend," I said in a loud voice and started to cry. I thought about Sen-Mut, and hope he was alive, and cried for him too. I missed him so much. The silence was killing me, not knowing his fate.

There was silence all over the palace. Everyone loved her too. I was distracted by a knock on the door.

"Enter," I said and froze when I saw Menkhep-Re and Hatshepset there holding hands. He approached and knelt on one knee.

"Rise, Menkhep-Re," I told him.

"We came to tell you how sorry we were when we heard the terrible news that T'Queta had killed herself. She was always good to me and kind since I was a little boy. How are you feeling? Hatshepset told me that you were feeling much better, and now this. I have not come before because you were angry at me and my mother, but I can swear to you that we didn't have anything to do with what happened to Sen-Mut. I hope you can realize that," he said.

"Mother, I am so sorry to hear of the death of T'Queta. She was so good to me all my life, and I could talk to her anytime. I went to visit her several times at Sen-Mut's house, and I talked to her just few days ago regarding what you said about Neferu-Re. I found her so depressed, and she did not look well at all, not like the T'Queta that we have always known. She also believed the same as you about Neferu-Re's death," Hat-shepset said.

"I did not know you visited T'Queta at Sen-Mut's house. What else did you two talks about?" I asked her.

"That you believed someone poisoned Sen-Mut and maybe he was dead. When I told her, she started to cry uncontrollably? I felt bad for her. Her slave brought water to calm her down, but I don't think the water did any good. When I left, she continued sobbing terribly. The entire palace is in mourning for her. She was very well loved by everyone," she said.

"Yes, she was," I said.

"We are glad that you are looking better and feel much better, Mother. We will come back tomorrow. I just wanted for you to know that I went and visited her," she said.

I smiled at them, and she kissed my cheeks before they left.

A few days later I went for a walk beside the Nile. Looking at the current of Hopi flowed north it was good for me because it soothed my Ka. I felt such peace inside my heart, even though I had not heard a word on the fate of my beloved Sen-Mut. Could it be my imagination, I wonder? But if it was, why did I collapse, and why was I dying? No, I was right. Amun-Ra had given me the gift of foresight, and what I saw was real.

T'Queta's body was wrapped in the finest linen, I had ordered for her embalming. After the seventy days her embalmed body was brought to her house from the house of the death. I thought of what a wonderful friend and sister I had in her.

Hapuseneb proceeded with the chanting prayers for the dead, and the ritual of the opening of the mouth. I took the adze and touched her lips, so she would be able to eat, speaks, and drink, then I touched her eyes and ears for her to see and hear also in the after-life. A calf was slaughter and we ate our last meal with her. The slaves brought many kinds of foods, for her journey of the after-life, as a farewell.

After everything was done, the slave walked behind us, wailing and crying and throwing dirt over their heads grieving for their friend. We arrive at the edge of the Nile, and the soldiers placed her coffin on the barge and took us across the Nile. The slaves remain behind in Thebes. From here on Hapuseneb and I will go alone to the Valley of the Dead. Two horses were waiting for us. Hapuseneb and I, ride the horses pulling the bulls that pulled the wagon with her coffin to her final resting place. The journey was slow, long, and far. And already the day was very hot.

I thought of Sen-Mut and hoped that he was alive, and my eyes became full of tears. I knew he would have liked to be here with us and help us bury her.

It was terribly hot, Hapu and I arrived at her resting place and we unloaded her coffin with ropes into the grave. I handed him all her jewelry and gold, and he placed the canopic jars by her feet and closed the coffin. He climbed out of the grave and did more chanting for the death. We started to bury her coffin with dirt until we had finished. I could see tears in his eyes, and my heart was broken again. He hugged me tight, and we cried together.

We climbed up onto our horses and started to pull the bulls and the wagon back to the barge. It was very late at night when we arrived at the edge of the Nile. The guards were waiting for us, and we walked onto the ramp of the barge. We returned to Thebes in silence and walked in silence to the palace. We were extremely tired. We had buried her under the severe heat of Ra.

Kissing my hands, he said, "I love you, Flower of Egypt, and thank you for helping me bury T'Queta with your own hands."

He had tears in his eyes again as he said goodnight, and I saw him climb into a litter to be carried to his home. I walked to my quarters and was bathed with cool, fresh water. My two slaves were silent, and I could see sadness on their faces. We spoke of the sweetness of T'Queta, and how much we were all going to miss her. After I was done being bathed, warm food was waiting for me, and I thought of my beloved Sen-Mut. I took a few bites and then laid down.

"Leave only one oil lamp lit. Put the rest out," I told them.

I was so very tired, and I whispered, "I love you, Sen-Mut. I hope you are alive. Come back to me please, Please. You promised."

CHAPTER 39

MESSAGE FROM SEN-MUT

A few days had passed since Hapuseneb and I buried T'Queta's body, and it was almost sunset. I could see the orange rays of Ra fading away as I strolled barefoot over the green grass beside the Nile, holding over my shoulders a white stole made of linen and wool.

I was holding it with my arms crossed, looking at the current of Hopi flowing north, and thinking of my beloved Sen-Mut, wondering if he was alive. My eyes filled with tears.

"Your Majesty! Your Majesty!" I was startled by a voice calling.

A guard was running toward me as he was calling, and beside him was a messenger with a message in his hand. I started to tremble, and I held my breath. I was afraid to take the missive as he knelt and extended his hand to me, so I just looked at it. I was so afraid to take it, and my eyes became full of tears as my body shook. I closed my eyes for a moment and took a deep breath, with trembling hands took the missive. Slowly I looked at the seal and had Sen-Mut's seal. I opened my eyes wide and screamed and jumped with happiness, tears rolling down my face. I could not contain my emotions and broke the seal in a hurry and stated to read.

Beloved of mine,

I could barely read it. I kept wiping the tears from my eyes and started to read again.

First let me

I stopped again and brought the message to my lips and kissed it and pressed it hard into my chest and to my heart. I was crying from happiness and kissed the missive many more times. I continued reading.

tell you that when you receive this message, I hope you are well and radiant, as I have you in my mind. I have not written before until now because my slave tried to kill me by poisoning me, and I was near death. It has taken all this time for me to get well and to have the strength to write to you, my love. I want to tell you that your love saved me. I was sitting with Nehesi, Teshi, Senemen, and Puyem-Re, talking in harmony when tea was brought to us. My slave handed me a cup of mint tea, and as I brought the cup to my lips and was taking a sip, suddenly, I heard your voice screaming aloud, "Sen-Mut Poison!" I dropped the cup, but I had already taken a small sip of the poison. I was choking and collapsed on the deck of the ship. Then darkness surrounded me. I can only remember the agony that I was choking and could not breathe. I was carried by Puyem-Re and Nehesi to my cabin. Later, Nehesi told me that Puyem-Re really worked very hard to save my life.

I am most grateful to you, my love, and to him for saving my life. If I had not heard your scream, I would have swallowed a large portion of the poison and would have died. Puyem-Re said that I was unconscious for almost a week before he brought me back from the dead. The poison left me very weak. It has been almost four moons since we left Thebes. The assassin was one of my slaves who had been at my service for many summers and had helped in my house, and I completely trusted him. He killed himself before Nehesi could interrogate him. Nehesi found a gold ring among his things, and I believe that it was used as payment to kill me.

As I was reading, I remembered everything I saw that same morning in my mind, and I was dying too. I brought the message to my heart. Oh, my love, you are alive. It is going to be a great feast tonight. Your letter brought back my life and happiness. I must pray for your safe journey home, I thought. Then I continued reading.

We continued with our journey to find Punt. Nehesi stopped the ship for the week that I was unconscious, and he thought it would be best for us to return home. After I regained consciousness, he asked me if we should return to Thebes. I told him that we must continue with the expedition, and we must succeed for your glory.

Every night, I looked at the stars and remembered the warmth of your lips and body. I wished I could kiss them and possess your body and hold you so close to me all night. Oh, how much I am missing you right now. Sometimes when I am on my couch in the silence of the night, I can feel your love around me, and I know that you are thinking of me. Beloved, we are still on this journey and hope soon to reach the Red Sea. With the help of Amun-Ra and all the gods, we will find the land of Punt. I can tell you this, if the Great Maat found it, we will too. Nehesi said if we encounter problems through this path to reach the Red Sea, we will take a different route on our return to Thebes. It will be the route from the north. By the time you receive this message we will be a lot farther away from land, and you will not receive another message from me until our return. Please pray that we do not encounter more problems on this expedition. I also wrote to Hapuseneb, and I know he is taking care of you very well.

Beloved Maatke-Re, I send you my love, my heart, and my soul.

Sen-Mut

Oh, my beloved Sen-Mut. How happy you have made me, I thought. Your words of love fill my insides with happiness. I thought I had lost you. I must run and tell Ineni, Hapuseneb, and Hatshepset. How unfair I was with Menkhep-Re and his mother, thinking they had something to do with the attempt on his life. But who else would want Sen-Mut dead, I wondered.

"Guards! Guards!" I shouted.

As I was walking fast, they came running to me.

"Yes, Your Majesty?"

"Run to the kitchen and tell them to prepare for a big festivity tonight! We are celebrating today the re-birth of Master Sen-Mut. Go tell Ineni, Hapuseneb, and my uncle to come to my quarters at once. We must all celebrate together at the banquet hall."

I ran to my quarters full of happiness, carrying his missive in my hands. I read it again as I waited for Ineni and Hapuseneb to arrive, and when I saw them walking together into my quarters, both had a big smile on their face.

"Great news has arrived today. Indeed, very good news," Ineni said.

"I am also very happy for you, Lotus of Egypt. Finally, the good news has arrived," Hapuseneb said.

"I was surprised when a guard rushed to me and said he had a message, and I saw Sen-Mut's seal. I read it right away and indeed was surprised when I read that someone had tried to poison him. I was shocked because you told me that someone was trying to poison him. What a vivid mental connection you both have with each other," Hapuseneb said.

Ineni came closer and hugged me and smiled.

"See, it was good to wait and not put Menkhep-Re and his mother to death," he said.

"Yes, Great Ineni. Always with your good advice and wisdom. But who would want to kill Sen-Mut? We need to find out if he was the silent assassin. Or who paid for Sen-Mut to be killed on this journey. What puzzles me is if this assailant was the silent assassin, he should have gotten paid a long time ago by Thutmoses II and not at this time. Now, I am really starting to worry again," I said.

"Hatshepset, don't be worry anymore, because the danger is over. The assassin killed himself, and now Sen-Mut is safe," Ineni said.

"Let's all celebrate this good news that we have been waiting for tonight," he said.

I was startled when the double doors swung open. It was Hatshepset. She approached me.

"Mother, the news is all over the palace that you received a message from Sen-Mut, and he is alive. This is a very good news. Now, Mother, you must talk to Menkhep-Re and offer him an apology. Isis almost fainted when she heard the good news that you received word from Sen-Mut, and he is alive. The expression of relief that I saw on her face when she heard the news was obvious. She became pale, and the slave had to bring her water. I could see her hands trembling when she took the cup. I think you should apologize to her and to Menkhep-Re," she said.

"Me? Pharaoh? Apologize to them? Never in my lifetime. We still don't know who the silent assassin is, or who paid him to kill Sen-Mut. And she continues plotting against me as she always has. Are you blind to see it?" I snapped at her.

"OK, Mother, have it your way. I can see that I will never be able to change your mind. I must leave now, and I will come back another day. I can see that you are very well now that your beloved is alive and well, and I am also happy that he is," she said.

"Yes, I am, and thank you for coming again," I said and watched her leave.

"She is still very angry at you for not crowning Menkhep-Re," Hapuseneb said.

"He will never be Pharaoh. I have other plans," I said, noticing to late that does words escape my lips.

"What other plans?" Hapuseneb asked.

I did not know what to say.

Ineni looked at me, and reacted, "To crown Hatshepset Queen, but that will come later, so she can transfer the royal blood to Menkhep-Re when Hatshepsut is gone to the heavens."

Oh boy, Ineni saved me, I thought.

"But it will only happen when I am dying," I told Hapuseneb.

"That will be wise," Hapu said.

But the look on his face was one of disbelief. He had known me for a long time and knew that I had lied. That made me feel very bad. I had never lied to him before, and I felt terrible.

"I must go now and get ready for this celebration tonight," Ineni said quickly and left me alone with Hapu.

Hapuseneb had a very serious look on his face. He looked at me angry.

"Why did you lie to me?"

I lowered my eyes, which were full of tears. I should not have lied to him. I never had before.

"Come and sit beside me," I said, and he did. I held his hand and brought it to my heart. "Will you forgive me?" I asked him, begging from the bottom of my heart for his forgiveness.

"Hatshepsut, you have never lied to me, and I have never lied to you. You know that I will give my life for you at any time. Now, tell me the truth." He demanded.

He had only called me by my name a few times in our lives, and I knew that he was very angry at me. I didn't know how to tell him without hurting him.

"The expedition is so when Sen-Mut returns from Punt a hero, I will make him Pharaoh," I said quickly to get it off my chest.

He jumped off my couch.

"Are you crazy? Are you really crazy? he shouted at me.

"This whole expedition is to crown him Pharaoh?" he was flush in anger.

By this point he continued yelling at me. I had never seen him so angry at me before. I was trembling.

"I cannot believe what I am hearing from your lips Hatshepsut. Making him Pharaoh? Do you believe he will reach the throne of Egypt?"

With his finger pointed at the door, he continued, "We don't know who is watching for Menkhep-Re's back, making sure that he will reach the throne of Egypt. I want you to think about what I am about to tell you and take it very seriously. Menkhep-Re is growing and will soon be a man. He is being trained with the best of your army. You put him there. All his friends are also in the army. He has a circle of young men that believe you should be stepping down to let him rule Egypt. Every day he is getting stronger. He is nineteen summers and getting wiser and ambitious. What about in a few years? He could overthrow you, and kill all of us, including you. Remember he blames us for supporting you and crowning you Pharaoh. I have spies all over the land, and I hear what is spoken around every corner of this kingdom and what he speaks with his friends. One of my sons agrees with his opinion. I did not come to you with what I hear every day, nor did Sen-Mut, because we did not want to worry you, and Menkhep-Re was still young. But you must face the truth that he is growing into a man. I am telling you this for your own good. And for all of us too."

I was completely silent. I never realized the danger as he clearly explained it.

"I must go now. I feel betrayed by you," he said and turned to leave.

"Stop," I shouted, and he did. I was ordering him as Pharaoh.

Softly I said, "Can you please come back here and sit beside me?"

He turned around, and his face was blushing in anger. I felt very bad. I did not mean to lie to him. I did not want to hurt him in any way because I knew how much he loved me, and I knew that he hurt because of my love for Sen-Mut. I didn't know how to repair his broken heart and his trust in me again. He approached me with his eyes cast down Oh God, how much I love him too, I thought.

He sat beside me and was silent.

"Did you come back because I ordered it as Pharaoh or because you wanted to?"

He started to laugh.

"Because I wanted too, I could never be angry at you for too long, even if it hurts so bad, and you know that. You are so precious to me."

I rose from my couch and stood in front of him, and he looked up into my eyes.

"Please forgive me," I asked. "Can you forgive me Hapu? Can you really forgive me, Hapuseneb? I did not want to tell you because I did not want to hurt you anymore. I had already hurt you so much. And you are right in all that you have said. I must think carefully. Maybe I am putting all of you in danger, including myself, but I still control all the armed forces. I don't believe he will attempt to hurt any of us because I would order his death."

"Hatshepsut, you must realize that he is not a child anymore. He is becoming a full-grown man and is very strong with the army, and he is well loved by the armed forces. And he has the idea that this kingdom belongs to him. Therein lies the danger," he said.

He stood up and was so close to me that I could smell his breath. It brought back the memories of when we were young, and he was about to kiss me that night under the rays of Thoth. He held me by my shoulders and pushed me away gently.

"I must leave right now before I kiss you. I have been dying to kiss your lips and make love to you for so many years," he said.

I looked into his eyes and said, "I want you to know that I've always loved you too, and a few minutes ago, I thought I had lost you and became so terrified with the thought of not having you in my life."

I took his hand with both of my hands and kissed them.

"Thank you for loving me the way you do Hapuseneb," I said and smiled.

He pulled me close to him and hugged me tightly. It was the first time he had ever hugged me with love and kissed my forehead as a woman. Suddenly slowly he pushed me away.

"Let's celebrate Sen-Mut's re-birth!" he shouted.

I knew his heart was broken. I could hear it in the tone of his voice. He walked away and turning back to look at me.

"I love you, Hatshepsut. I always will." Then he left.

I was standing there in tears and thought what a wonderful man he was. I wondered what would have happened if he had kissed me that night under the silver rays of Thoth, and I had not yet meet Sen-Mut. I stood there in silence for a while thinking of Hapuseneb and how hard it must be for him, carrying this love for me all these years. I laid down on my bed and started to think of Sen-Mut, my beloved one. How happy he had made me today knowing that he was alive. I hoped he came back to me soon. Tonight, I would celebrate this great news, and we will all celebrate that you are alive, my love. I would drink until the rays of Amun-Ra shown. I clapped my hands, and the golden doors opened. Two of my slaves came rushing to me.

"Your Majesty, we all want to tell thee that we are all very happy that Master Sen-Mut is alive and well, and the palace is alive again." They smiled at me.

I was very happy and hugged them. They were surprised and smiled at me. I ran to my makeup desk and opened my jewelry box and gave them each gold necklaces and earrings. They were so very happy with the gifts. I walked to be bathed, and as I was being bathed I started to sing. They sang with me, and I could see happiness on their faces. Life had returned to me and to the palace. I wore a white sheath, a gold necklace, and gold earrings. I felt beautiful. My hair was growing, and I would not cut it off anymore. It would please Sen-Mut when he returned. He always wanted me to let my hair grow. From that day on, my slaves took good care of my hair, and from time to time, they used henna to prevent lice. They also put a very small amount of coconut oil on my hair to make it healthy and shine.

The celebration started. The music and the laughter made me immensely happy. I saw Hapuseneb walking with Tepi. She hung onto his arms, and a hint of jealousy rush over me. Our eyes meet. She seemed very happy today with him. He walked her to where the other wives of the dignitaries sat. He left her there and came walking to me. Our eyes meet, and he had a beautiful smile on his face. He sat at my right, as always, and came close to me and whispered in my ear.

"You smell delicious and look so beautiful with your growing hair. I will finally see you with hair on your head, which I never have." Then he laughed.

“Well, Hapuseneb, you are so cheerful tonight. Did she give you what she always gives you to make you happy?”

I laughed and looked at Tepi. She was staring at us, as always.

Looking into my eyes, “No, I am happy because of what you said to me this afternoon. I never thought I would hear it from your lips, that you always have loved me too. We have been together since childhood, and I always wondered about that night beside the Nile, I should have kissed you that night under Thoth, and I should have kissed you today. I should have made love to you today and made you forget the world around us. But I know you are in love with Sen-Mut. I cannot accept that, but I must live with it. Today you have made me very happy with your words though. And I am also happy that Sen-Mut is alive and well and has continued with the expedition to Punt,” he said.

“Does this mean that you have forgiven me for not telling you the real reason for the expedition?” I asked.

“It took me by surprise, but I had a feeling for a while that those were your plans. I don’t know how to feel about that right now. But forgiving you? There is nothing that you could do I would not forgive you for, Lotus of Egypt. I could never be angry at you for long anyways. But, sincerely, I advise you to think wisely and act with caution in whatever decisions you make from now on. I will always support you, even if I don’t like what you’re doing,” he said and smiled at me.

I stood up and everyone else did as well, then knelt.

"Rise, everyone. I would like to make a toast to the great news I have received today from Sen-Mut, that he is alive and well."

Everyone cheered the news and clapped.

"I would like to make another toast for my most beloved and dear friend. Hapuseneb, First Prophet of Amun-Ra and Vizier of the South, who has been my best friend since childhood and been beside me all these years, in my happiest and most difficult moments of my life. I love him too."

I raised my cup and everyone else did too.

"Let the music begin," I shouted.

The dancers started to dance, and everyone was cheerful, eating and drinking. I thought of Sen-Mut, my beloved one, wishing he was in my bed tonight, and smiled. I drank until the early part of the morning. I was so drunk and drunk of happiness that my love was alive. When I left the party, Hapuseneb walked with me to the bottom of the stairs, and to my surprise he lifted me up into his arms. I laid my head on his chest, and he carried me up into my quarters. The guards opened the golden doors, and he called the slaves, who came running.

He laid me on my bed saying, "Good night, Lotus of Egypt. Sleep well."

He was looking into my eyes, and for one moment I thought he was going to kiss my lips. Instead, he kissed my forehead and walked away. The slaves undressed me and cleaned my body with warm water. They put a sleeping gown on me.

I whispered Sen-Mut's name many times and fell asleep.

Many months had passed, and I had not heard another word from Sen-Mut since the message that he was alive and well. As every night, I sat on my balcony and looked at the stars and thought of my beloved one, wondering what he was doing at that same moment. Was he thinking of me as I was thinking of him? Had he found Punt yet?

CHAPTER 40

SEN-MUT'S VICTORIOUS RETURN FROM PUNT

The first rays of Ra were rising and reflected on my balcony as I lie in bed. It was a beautiful dawn, and I was thinking that the month of Akhet was already upon us. The Nile was swollen, and it rained constantly.

"Beloved, how much longer before I can see you? My heart is at peace, and I know that you are well, but how long will I be without you? These desires of my body are driving me crazy, and the thought of you and the memories of our love making invades my body. I am dying right now to feel your kisses and the touch of your hands caressing my breasts and the curve of my body. The way you make me feel when you possess my body. It's been almost three summers since you left, and my body desires you more and more every day. I miss our talks and our walks beside the Nile and the way you laugh when you pinch my butt," I thought and smiled.

I was startled when the door swung open. It was Hapuseneb with a big smile on his face and a message in his hands. I jumped from my bed.

"From Sen-Mut," he said.

I rushed to him naked, and he handed it to me. He was quiet as I broke the seal as fast as I could, and I walked onto the balcony.

Beloved of Mine,

First, let me tell you that I love you, and I miss you, and I hope when you receive this missive you are well, as is everyone else. I have great news! We have found Punt and are returning home victorious. We are all well, and everything is going well too. I am bringing the King and the Queen of Punt and their family. The Queen has been sick for a long time. Her physicians have done everything they can to help her with her pain, but she cannot find relief from it. They greeted us with kindness, and they are very loving and gentle people. She needs our help, and I offered it. I hope we can give her some relief from her terrible pain and cure it. I am bringing precious cargo for you and all your heart desires as of the myrrh trees for the terrace of your temple. I hope everything is well with you and the kingdom. I am at peace because I am sure Hapuseneb has being taking care of you very well.

What does he mean? I thought.

Soon, my love, I will have you in my arms. I have desired you so much. If you just knew how much I have missed, you. I know you are still as beautiful as *when I left you, and I am dying to kiss your lips.*

The month of Akhet is upon us, and we are sailing the Red Sea and have taken the northern route, as Nehesi suggested, for our return. The south route was harsh on the bottom of the ships. All of us are well and safe. Please make an offering to Amun-Ra for me and for my men and our safe return home. It has been raining hard and is good for our return. This message will take, I believe, three moons to get to you, but by the time you receive it, I will be closer to Thebes and to your arms. If everything goes well, I am sure it will, it will take us about two moons to see you.

I am in the need of a very good bath and to feel the warm water on my skin and especially your skin touching mine. The sweet smell of your body and the warmth of your lips. My love, until we see each other again, I send you my love. My heart, body, and soul are always yours.

Sen-Mut

I brought his message to my lips and kissed it and pressed it against my heart. I turned around and looked at Hapuseneb with the biggest smile, and he also smiled at me.

"It's a glorious day, Hapuseneb!" I shouted.

"It is indeed a very happy day. He also wrote me, but I have not opened the missive yet. The guard was bringing you the message when I saw him, and I took it. I wanted to make you very happy today, so I brought it to you," he said.

"Where is the messenger? I want to talk to him after his rest. Send the best of everything and give him a special room with a slave to please him, and care for him, and don't forget that he must be brought to me after his rest," I said.

"I will," he said.

With these emotions, I forgot that I was completely naked in front of Hapuseneb. He lowered his eyes and did not look at me. He had seen my naked body before when I was dying, but no one else had seen it but Sen-Mut. I rushed and put on a white sheath and the royal blue robe.

"Hapuseneb, would you like to have breakfast with me?" I asked.

"Yes. Today is a very special day. I must enjoy your company as much as I can before Sen-Mut get here, and we will no longer be able to spend time together alone as we did for these last three summers. I did enjoy having you all for my own," he said and smiled.

"Has anyone else seen the messenger other then you?"

"Yes, several slaves, and all were smiling like I was. Lotus of Egypt, the palace will go back to its normal happiness, except for my heart. You have filled my heart with happiness these three summers, and I love looking at you. You look so beautiful as Ra shines on you and on your long hair," he said.

Caressing my face and hair he said, "Sen-Mut is a very lucky man having the Double Crown and the woman I love."

"Thank you. Hapuseneb. Sit by my side, please. I have never thanked you for loving me the way you do, or for saving my life three summers ago. I want you to know that your pain is also in my heart, and I also wonder what would have happened on that night if you had kissed me under the rays of Thoth. Would I have let you make love to me that night? I want you to know that I sincerely love you too, since our childhood. But things did not come out as I expected. I never expected that someone else would walk into my life and into my heart as Sen-Mut did. I did tell my mother that I was in love with you," I said.

His brow furrowed as I continued.

"By this time, you had taken T'Queta, and later Tepi as your concubine, and, yes, I know that you thought as I did that we would never be together," I said.

I took his hand in my hands and brought it to my heart.

"I firmly believe in the afterlife. I hope we meet again in the next life and that your love for me remains the same. Maybe things will be different then, and I can repay you with the same love and devotion you have for me in this life," I said.

The expression on his face was one of surprise. He never thought I would speak to him with my heart in my hands.

"Be at peace, Hapu. I wish there were two of me, so I could love you freely and without restraint and make your heart glad because I love you too," I said, smiling.

He had tears in his eyes and so did I. We were silent, and he brought my hand to his lips and kissed them.

"I understand now. I never thought that you also struggled with your feelings for me. I will always love you, Hatshepsut," he said.

Crying, we hugged each other, and I kissed him on his cheek. We wiped our tears and smiled at each other. A knock on the golden doors startled me.

"Enter," I said.

It was Ineni, walking toward us with a happy face.

"Hatshepsut, I heard that a currier arrived not too long ago. My slave saw him dismounting from the horse. Is it a message from Sen-Mut?" he asked.

"Hapuseneb, can you give the order that music must play all day long until Sen-Mut's arrival? Also, prepare for his arrival. I want several nice quarters on the other side of the palace for the King and Queen of Punt and her family and the chiefs that are accompanying them from Punt," I said.

He nodded his head several times with a smile.

"I will, Your Majesty," he said and left.

I turned to Ineni.

"Yes, Ineni. Life has returned to me, and to the palace, and to the whole land. Sen-Mut is coming home!" I shouted, smiling.

"I am so very happy right now. He said that he should be here in about in two moons. We must prepare for his arrival. He is bringing the King and Queen of Punt and their family. He said he is bringing large treasures and a gift of myrrh trees for the terrace of my mortuary temple. I am the happiest women today. He is finally coming home to me, Ineni. I should get ready and run to the temple and pray for his safe journey home and for his men too, as he asked me to," I said and smiled.

"Hatshepsut, this is very good news to hear. I always knew that he could do it. He is a very remarkable and capable man. I saw it in his eyes the first day I meet him, when he was only a child of seven summers, when I invited my dear friend Ramose, his father, to the palace to the celebration of you becoming the young Horus, I saw this drive inside of him. It reminded me of myself when I was young. Now with the fulfilment of this expedition, no priest can deny your heart's desire. He will be a good Pharaoh, and I know that he loves you very much has since the day he saw you for the first time in the audience hall. I believe he has earned that great title."

"Thank you, dear Ineni. You've always been so good to both of us, and thank you for your right advice about Punt," I said.

We spoke for a while longer, and he left.

The following morning the messengers were brought to my quarters, and they knelt at my feet.

"Rise. Be at ease and have a seat."

I clapped my hands, and my servants approach me.

"Yes, Your Majesty?"

"Bring wine for the messengers!"

"Yes, Majesty!"

"Did Master Sen-Mut give you the message to be brought to me himself?" I asked, smiling.

"Yes, Your Majesty, and when he put it in my hand, he had a big smile. He said to tell thee that he will seeing you soon and was happy to come home," he replied.

I was happy. I wanted to hear more.

"How does he look? Does he look tired?" I asked.

"Yes. Three summers away from home is very tiring," he replied, and I frowned.

"What do you mean? Were you on the ship on this journey too?" I asked.

"Yes, we were. We are the best riders in the kingdom, and Master Sen-Mut brought us on this journey for this reason. To bring you this message personally in or return," he said.

I was surprised. I thought they were coming from our garrison in the delta.

"Tell me about when Master Sen-Mut was poisoned," I asked.

"Those were terrible moments for all of us. We were all worried for his life, and we prayed to all the gods for Master Sen-Mut's recovery. Those were the longest hours and days, waiting to see if he would survive. We were all somber, and when General Nehesi announced that Master Sen-Mut had opened his eyes, it was a great joy for all of us on all the five ships. Then we waited for him to recover, and he decided that we must continue with the journey. Only a brave man like him would've wanted to continue," he said.

I had tears in my eyes as I heard them speak.

I got up from my chair, and they dropped to the floor. I walked to my jewelry box, and picked up a hand full of gold nuggets, and gave them ten each. They were surprised and kissed my feet several times.

"I want to thank you for bringing me this wonderful message. You may go home now. Are you two from Thebes?" I asked.

"I am not. I am from Memphis, and he is from Giza," one replied.

"Very well, I will give orders for you two to be taken back to your homes."

"Your Majesty, can we remain here until Master Sen-Mut's arrival to celebrate with everyone his great achievement?" he asked.

"Yes! Of course! You two were part of this journey, and you will remain here and will be well taken care of until Master Sen-Mut arrives," I said.

I clapped my hands once and Tuyii came.

"Majesty?"

"Tell one of the guards at my doors to take them to the place I ordered for them to rest and have them well taking care off," I said.

"Yes, Your Majesty!"

"You may go now," I said.

They knelt at my feet and kissed them. Then they left happily.

I was very happy that my beloved would soon be home. I sent invitations to Ineni, Hapu, and D'Jehuty to come to my rose garden. The afternoon was clear, and it didn't look like it was going to rain. The four of us sat in my garden, talking about the preparation for Sen-Mut's arrival. We drank wine until late evening and continued with the celebration in the banquet hall until the early part of the morning. Then Hapu walked me to my quarters, and we said our good nights. I walked into my quarters and stood on the balcony and waited for Ra to show its first rays. Then I closed my eyes and said, "I will close my eyes and then tomorrow will be here, and you will be beside me. I love you Sen-Mut." I blew him a kiss.

The next few months I spent in laughter, and in harmony, waiting anxiously to hear news from the garrisons of signs of Sen-Mut's ships. There was joy all over my country, and my people were getting prepared to receive their loved ones that were returning with Sen-Mut as well.

Dignitaries and their families were arriving at the palace from different parts of the country to see his marvelous achievement. My palace had accommodations for all of them, and we spent our time merrily, swimming in the Nile and eating in the banquet hall, just waiting for the moment to arrive. I was anxious to see my beloved one.

It was early one morning, and I was in my mother's garden smelling the roses when I heard shouting.

"The ships are coming! The ships are coming," a few horsemen were yelling.

I ran to the outer gardens. Hapuseneb and Ineni rushed beside me and Menkhep-Re, Hatshepset, Isis, and all my slaves ran to where I was. The palace slaves gathered behind me. A messenger and two soldiers dismounted in front of me and knelt on one knee.

"Your Majesty," they said.

"Rise soldiers," I told them.

"Your Majesty, the ships are almost here. They are about a day away, and I believe they should be here past high noon tomorrow," the messenger said, short of breath.

My heart was pounding, and I was full of joy and happiness. Finally, the wait was almost over.

"How long have you three been riding?" I asked.

"Two days, Your Majesty."

"Guards, take them to be fed and give them a place to rest and sleep, food, wine, and slaves to make their hearts happy. They have brought me the greatest joy," I said.

There was a large commotion in the palace.

"Finally, your beloved will be here, Hatshepsut. Do you still believe that my mother or I had something to do with wanting to kill Sen-Mut?"

It was the voice of Menkhep-Re. I turned around and looked at him. His tone of voice did not sound very happy, knowing that Sen-Mut would soon arrive.

"Why do you have to sneak up behind me every time?" I snapped at him.

"Menkhep-Re, do you remember the words you whispered behind me on my hear on the day of Sen-Mut's departure? Your words were 'Do you believe that he will come back alive?' Do you remember that? Who else would want him dead? Your mother is constantly conniving against me, and I will only believe that you and your mother are innocent when Sen-Mut tells me and shows me something he wants to show me," I said.

I could see Isis listening behind us. She had her eyes cast down when I looked at her.

"I wish there was peace between you and me, Hatshepsut," he said.

"We could have peace between you and me if your mother would stop conniving against me."

Looking at her, I said to him, "You know I can do away with her at any time if I wanted to, but I am not a murderer. And she is your mother. I promised my brother that I would not do away with either of you, and I have kept my word. Maybe someday you will inherit the throne. How can I kill you if I raised you and love you as if you were my own son? Just be patient."

My daughter Hatshepset came close to me and hugged me.

"Mother, the waiting is almost over," she said.

"Yes, my precious, the waiting is almost over. It has been almost three Shomus since he left, and he is almost back home," I said.

"Yes, Mother, he is almost home. These three summers have been hard on you," she said.

I caressed her face, and she smiled.

Looking at Hapu, I said, "Hapuseneb, is everything ready? Did General D'Jehuty organize the welcome for Sen-Mut and his crew?"

"Yes, Your Majesty. Everything is ready for tomorrow," he replied.

"I want lots of flowers where Sen-Mut walks, and I want the streets closed near the ships. Hapuseneb, I want you to greet him on the ship. Give the order to General D'Jehuty for the soldiers to turn their backs as his feet touch the ground, so I can welcome him in privacy and that I may speak with him alone. I will give the order to D'Jehuty for the soldiers to turn back around," I said.

"Yes, Your Majesty," he said.

Why was Hapuseneb acting like this, saying "Your Majesty" every time I said something to him? I wondered…no, I knew. He was hurting.

Ineni was very happy. I could see a grin on his face, and he walked closer to speak to me.

"Your Majesty," he said, with a smile on his face and nodded his head.

"Finally, one more day and the land will be filled with happiness as before. I have missed him too," Ineni said.

"Yes, Ineni. One more day and I will be a happy woman again."

That evening from my balcony I could hear music playing all over my kingdom.

"Oh, Amun-Ra, Father Almighty, I thank you so much that you are bringing Sen-Mut safely back to me, and that the time of his arrival is almost here. Soon I will have my beloved in my arms," I thought.

My body was prepared to be depilated, and I was being massaged with the aromatic oils that Sen-Mut liked to smell on my skin. My body was submerged in goat milk to nourish and soften it. I would radiate for him tomorrow when he lay his eyes on me and touched and kissed my skin. I was lost in my thoughts of him, and just thinking about his body made me hot.

Removing every hair from my body took long hours. It was done with strings and honey wax. They massaged my body well with fragrant oils from foreign lands. It was a delicious smell, and it would be pleasing to Sen-Mut.

The goldsmith had brought two gold boxes, one with gold dust to be thrown at Sen-Mut's feet as he walked into the hall of audience, and the other box was a special gift for my beloved one.

It was very late in the night, and I could not sleep with these emotions. Then I heard a soft knock on the door.

"Enter," I said.

It was Hapuseneb. He came closer and sat at the edge of my bed and was quiet. I smiled at him. I knew what he was feeling, and I held his hand tightly as tears started to roll down my face.

"I wish I had kissed you that night," he said, nodding his head several times.

"Yes, I wish you had too. It's so very hard for me to see you hurting this way, Hapu, and my heart is never fully happy," I said.

"I want you to know that I will die loving you, Flower of Egypt, and maybe in the afterlife I will have you all for my own." With broken words, he continued, "Because this love will surpass eternity."

I noticed that he was drunk, the smell of wine on his breath. It seemed that he had been drinking all night. He had tears in his eyes. I knelt on my bed and hugged him very hard from behind his back, and we both cried. He kissed my right hand and left the room.

I lay on my bed with mixed emotions. Happy and waiting to see my beloved one, and sad because Hapuseneb was hurting terribly and I hurt.

I had a few hours of sleep, and my emotions were still high. I lay there until I could see the first rays of Ra. I heard a knock on the golden doors.

"Enter," I said.

It was Ineni. He had a serious look on his face, and I panicked.

"What is it, Ineni?"

"Tepi just came to my home. She said that Hapuseneb did not return home last night, and General D'Jehuty is looking for him everywhere. He must speak with him before Sen-Mut's arrival. Tepi said she thinks that you were probably the last person he was with last night," he said.

I knew what she was implying, and she was wrong.

"Ineni, he came and talked to me late last night, but he left."

I became worried that he would do something stupid because of the way he had spoken to me.

"Ineni, send all the guards to look for him immediately," I shouted.

Please, Mother Hathor, don't permit him to do something crazy and don't let anything happen to him, I prayed. I rushed to my balcony and saw him sitting at the edge of Hopi, very far away.

"Ineni, there he is! Look! Guards! Guards!" I yelled.

My two door guards rushed inside my quarters to where I was standing on the balcony and stood beside me.

"Look over there," I said and pointed out with my finger toward the Nile.

"There is Master Hapuseneb. Go and get him on a litter and take him to his home to be bathed. Tell him that General D'Jehuty is looking for him and that I will be waiting for him too. Leave now," I said, and they rushed out from my quarters.

"Ineni, can you go with them please? See that he is OK for me? Sen-Mut is almost here, and he must be prepared to receive him," I said.

"Yes, I will, Hat. I have always known that he is in love with you and suffers terribly with this feeling. I will talk to him. I wonder what happened to him last night," Ineni said.

I saw Ineni leave and a few hours had passed when the first horn sounded, announcing the view of the first ship. My beloved was still three hours away, I thought. I clapped my hands and a slave rushed to me.

"Yes, Your Majesty?"

"Bathe me now. Prepare the golden kilt, the golden sandals, and the golden cape. And for tonight, I will wear the golden sheath. Then, as I am bathing, you must dress the bed in the golden linen, and place vases with pink roses and many oil lamps all over my quarters. For when Master Sen-Mut arrives, I want him to find this room beautiful. Be aware when we leave the audience hall to light up all the candles, and you must prepare a warm bath with the finest oils for Master Sen-Mut tonight," I said.

"Yes, Your Majesty. I will do it all as you ask. Your Majesty, I want to tell you that we are all very happy, and I hear that everyone in the land is too, that Master Sen-Mut will be here today. We miss him too," the slave said with a smile.

I was happy to hear her words.

"Bring me the two largest jewelry boxes."

Two slaves rushed to my makeup table and brought me the golden coffers. I opened my jewelry boxes and let my twenty-five personal slaves pick a piece of jewelry as a gift. I had so much gold jewelry, and it made me very happy to share it with them. Everyone took their piece and were happy with the gift. All at once, they prostrated themselves on the floor and kissed my feet, one by one.

"In a few days, all of you must go to the goldsmith and have him remove my cartouche," I told them.

They thanked me and continued with the orders I had given them. I was immensely happy as I walked to be bathed. The musicians were playing the harp and the lute as I was being bathed with a lot of fragrances. Incense was burning, and rose petals were floating on the water.

I walked out of the bathtub, stood with my arms extended from my sides, and they pat my body dry. We were happy and singing songs of love. I walked to my bedroom, and the second horn sounded loudly. Now the ships were coming closer. I could hear everyone cheering everywhere, and I smiled. I wanted to run to my balcony to see the ships, but they were coming from the north, but my balcony faced southeast, it was not possible. I could hear the harp being played in my bedroom. My heart was pounding. He was almost here. In one more hour. A slave started to put makeup on my face, kohl on my eyes, rouge on my cheeks, and red lipstick on my lips. They raised my hair into a bun on top of my head and tied it securely. I was trembling with emotions. Oh, how happy I was! I wondered if he had changed. Would he find me beautiful again? Oh, how much I love him. They wrapped the golden kilt around my waist and put on the golden belt and my golden sandals.

There was a knock on the golden doors.

"Enter," I shouted.

It was Hapuseneb, and he took my breath away. He looked gorgeous with his wavy black hair, gray eyes, and long black eyelashes. He was wearing a long, pleated white kilt with gold trim and a leopard skin across his shoulder. He looked serene, and we smiled at each other. I could still see the pain in his eyes and wished I could spare him this pain.

Tuyii opened the large box and pulled out the Pharaoh's heavy golden pectoral with the Eye of Horus and two heavy gold cuffs defining the Ankh in the center. I wouldn't be wearing earrings. I turned around and faced Hapuseneb. He was in awe when he saw me.

"A goddess so beautiful," he said and knelt.

"Rise, First Prophet of Amun and Vizier of the South," I said and touched his head with my left hand.

He rose from the floor, and I handed him the Pschent, the red and white crown of Egypt. As I knelt on one knee, he placed the Double Crown on my head. Kneeling brought back memories of when I was crowned Pharaoh of Egypt by Khety, and all the emotions were running through my body as on that day. But today they were different. My beloved one was returning home, and I was immensely happy.

Hapu gave me his hand and helped me rise from the floor. I heard the last horn, and I got goosebumps. My heartbeat quickened with emotion. My personal slaves lined up in front of me in two rows, ten on each side, and five in the center in front of me. This was it. The golden doors opened, and I handed Tuyii the golden box full of gold dust to be thrown over Sen-Mut's body and at his feet as he walked in to the hall of audience.

Hapuseneb held my hand and helped me walk down the stairs. The soldiers started to cheer, and everyone else did too. I could see the happiness on their faces, and I smiled because of the joy and happiness that they brought me. It reflected on their faces. Then the band started to play. The priest and priestesses, holding censers in their hands, spread the burning incense as they walked ahead of the military. Two lines of hundreds of slaves, dressed all in white sheaths, held baskets full of white petals, and the band played as they all marched ahead of me. I started to walk to the Temple of Karnak where the ships would soon dock, and I would welcome my beloved and his crew. Hapuseneb was at my right as always, Ineni, Menkhep-Re, Hatshepset, and Isis were behind me. Behind them were viziers, governors, mayors, and every dignitary from all over the land as far as Heliopolis and Alexandria who had come to welcome the arrival of the expedition.

General D'Jehuty was at front with the other generals of the military, including my uncle Thutmoses, who had grown very old, followed by the charioteers, archers, battle ground soldiers, palace guards, and cavalry. Every armed force was present, and we all walked through the

Avenue of Sphinxes to the Temple of Amun-Ra where the first ship would dock in Karnak.

The streets were full of people, and many of them had come from all over the country to welcome Sen-Mut and his crew and their loved ones in this victorious return. Soldiers were lined up on each side of the avenue to Karnak. Archers, charioteers, and all the armed forces were present, holding banners representing their battalions at their sides. Seeing the immensity of my military forces made me very proud of all of them and of my kingdom.

I saw the ramp for the ship, and my heart pounded. I was eager to see Sen-Mut and to be in his arms. Then I heard the thundering voice of General D'Jehuty giving the order to the soldiers to make a human shield between me and my family and my people. The soldiers turned their backs to me and Hapuseneb.

Hapuseneb stopped and looked into my eyes.

"It was my pleasure to be with you and to serve you these three last summers, Your Majesty," he said and bowed his head.

I was about to say something, but he walked away fast toward the ramp. I saw the bow of the first ship moving slowly, and I started to tremble with happiness. All my emotions were in the center of my chest. Then I saw him standing on the bow of the ship, and our eyes met. My eyes filled with tears, and butterflies fluttered all over my body. I wanted to run to him, but I stopped walking. Looking at him, he took my breath away, as when we were young and full of life and saw each other.

Hapuseneb continued walking. The soldiers placed the ramp on the ship, and the last horn sounded. The military turned around and lined up on each side of the ramp, holding their spears in their hands.

I saw Hapuseneb walk up the ramp and welcome Sen-Mut. They greeted each other with wide smiles and talked for several minutes. Another horn sounded. Many of the soldiers rushed up the ramp and on to the ship, making a human shield with their bodies and blocking the view of the inside of the ship to me. The soldiers on the ground turned their backs to me. A double horn sounded again, and Sen-Mut started to walk down the ramp. A loud cheer erupted, by my people on the streets and the soldiers started to hit the ground with their spears as they shouted, "Sen-Mut! Sen-Mut! Sen-Mut! Sen-Mut!"

I could also hear people all over shouting, "Sen-Mut! Sen-Mut! Sen-Mut! Sen-Mut!"

Emotions were running inside of me until I could not hold my composure anymore, and we ran to each other's arms and kissed so profoundly and hugged so tightly. We kissed again and again. There were no words spoken, only love and tears of joy as we kissed for a long time. He held me against his body.

"Maatke-Re, my beautiful and beloved Maatke-Re. How much I have missed you. I love you. I love you!" he said and rocked me in his arms.

Tears of happiness were running down our faces as we held each other. I could not believe that he was finally home. I was so very happy. I pulled back and caressed his face. I pressed my lips gently to his lips again and gave him a heartfelt kiss of love, as he held my body tightly to his. Looking into his eyes, I caressed his face again.

"Ptah of Egypt and Steward of Amun-Ra, I welcome you to Thebes."

"I love you. If you just knew how much I have missed you and waited for this moment with all my heart," I said and hugged him.

We kissed with passion. He was fully aroused, and I became full of desire.

“See how much I have missed you? I have missed your body so much, our love making, your smell. Let me smell you again,” he said and buried his face in my neck and took a deep breath.

“My love, let’s finish with all of this as soon as possible, so I can make love to you. Your smell is making me crazy right now. I am very hot, and I don’t think I can hold back. I want to be inside of you at this moment,” he whispered in my ear as he rocked my body in his arms.

“My body and heart desire you as much, my love,” I whispered back, and we smiled at each other.

Looking at me he said, “I have brought so many gifts for you and for your kingdom, you are going to be surprised and very, very happy.”

We kissed again, and looking at him, I wanted to eat his lips, his beautiful lips, the lips I had missed so much, and the taste of mint from his mouth was left on my lips from his kisses.

“Beloved one, you have made me the happiest woman in the whole kingdom and in the whole world. I have dreamed of this moment every single day since the day that you left.”

He knelt on one knee, and looking up into my eyes, he smiled saying, “My King, my Queen, and my wife!”

I caressed his face with my left hand. I smiled at him and bent down and kissed him again.

“Rise, Ptah of Egypt, Steward of Amun,” I said.

We smiled at each other and kissed and hugged again. I did not want to let go.

“D’Jehuty!” I shouted.

A horn sounded, and the soldiers turned around to face us. They started to shout, “Sen-Mut, Ptah of Egypt! Sen-Mut, Ptah of Egypt!” as they hit the ground with their spears. We turned around and saw Hapuseneb walking down the ramp. Beside him was the Second Prophet of Amun-Ra Puyem-Re, and behind them were General Nehesi, Master Sailor Neb-Ery, Senemen, Teshi, and the procession of the court of the King and Queen of Punt. Drums played and there were dancers with feathers of different colors as they walked down the ramp.

Then the wall of soldiers started to open, and I could see how happy Hatshepset was, smiling at me. Menkhep-Re looked very happy too. Ineni and Tepi were also happy to see Sen-Mut back. We had a long walk to the Temple of Amun-Ra. The people were lined up beside the avenue to have a view of Sen-Mut and his crew. Slaves were throwing large amounts of white lotus and rose petals for every step that we took, and the people in the streets were throwing flowers at his feet and all over his body, shouting, “Sen-Mut, Ptah of Egypt! Sen-Mut, Ptah of Egypt! Sen-Mut! Sen-Mut!” as we passed them. He waved at them and smiled. I could see the happiness on his face every time he looked at me.

We arrived at the Temple of Amun-Ra, and the double doors of the chapel were opened by two guards standing beside each door, and they hailed me and Sen-Mut. Sen-Mut and I walked into the first entrance of the shrine of Amun-Ra, then the second double doors were opened by the guards, and we were in front of the god of all gods, Amun-Ra. Only one oil lamp was burning, and the light reflected on the gold statues of Amun. We knelt together holding hands and prostrated ourselves on the floor, and he started to chant his prayers of thanks. We made offerings to Amun-Ra. We burned incense around the altar and poured perfume oils and gold dust over the statue of Amun-Ra. Holding hands, we walked around the altar chanting more prayers of thanks for bringing him and his men safely home.

Then he stopped. Turning me around, he grabbed me fast by my waist and kissed me deeply. We could not contain ourselves. We were burning with desire. We were going crazy kissing and touching everywhere. We were completely hot, so hot. I took off the Double Crown and lay it on top of the altar as he was taking off my kilt as fast as he could, and then the loin cloth. I removed his kilt and loin cloth, and he pulled me to him fast and embraced my body. I loved his strong arms around me, and kissing me with passion, he gently lay me down on the cool floor. We were lost in the most wonderful passion and ecstasy as we became one in our love making. His lips were locked on mine, and we moaned, lost in pleasure, a pleasure that only he could give me.

"Sen-Mut! Sen-Mut!" I whispered in his ear, and I hung tightly to his body, lost in the most wonderful feeling under his body. We reached a powerful climax together, and I felt his explosion like a hot river inside of me. We remained lost in ecstasy, holding each other on the cool floor.

The dim light of the oil candle shined on his face as he looked at me and caressed my forehead and cheek. Finally, he was mine again. He kissed my lips deeply and moved slowly to my left and held me in his arms against his body. I rested my head on his chest with the thought that I was his again.

"I needed to have you, Hat, or everyone would have noticed how aroused I was as we walked to the hall of audience. I have waited for this moment for such a long time, wanting to feel the brush of your skin against mine, and the smell of your body. I have missed all of you, and now I am at peace and finally home. I cannot believe that you are beside me again. You would not believe how much I have waited for this moment to have you like this in my arms and to make love to you."

He pulled my body against his and pressed his lips hard on mine again.

He continues, "I could just stay in here, laying with you in my arms, with no one around us, so I could continue making love to you all day and all night long and sleep holding you close to me. You don't know how much I have missed you and your body. There were many nights that I lay on the deck of the ship, looking at the stars and wondering if you were looking at the same stars and Thoth as I was. And if you were thinking of me, as I was thinking of you at that moment. Sometimes I felt the warmth of your love, right here in my heart."

He brought my hand to his heart. I listened to him quietly as he expressed his love to me. I held his body tightly.

Caressing his face, I said, "Beloved of mine. Yes, every night I looked at the stars while sitting on my balcony and thought of you, wondering the same, if you were thinking of me at that same moment. My heart felt the warmth of your love, and my insides became warm. You are home, beloved Sen-Mut, and that is all that matters to me now. You must never worry again about leaving my side nor ever again going to any far away land. You have made me very happy right now. Your seed is welcome inside my body. I hope it grows, and we have a child produced of this happiness."

We kissed again. He helped me rise from the floor and helped me dress. We gave thanks again to Amun-Ra for this victorious expedition. And for our love.

We walked out of the shrine of Amun-Ra and left the temple, smiling. I could see how happy he was, and I was too. We met with Hapuseneb and with the rest of the court. Sen-Mut and Hapu were talking in harmony, and both walked beside me toward the hall of audience. I was immensely happy having my beloved back and beside me. Every time I looked to my left, he was looking at me, and we smiled. I could not believe that he was home again and beside me. I was full of butterflies all over again, and full of emotions. I could have exploded from happiness. We looked at each other so many times and smiled as we walked the Avenue of Sphinxes on the way to the palace. We brushed our hands every time we could. An electrical current ran all over my body, and we laughed.

The people in the streets were throwing petals of white lotus over him, and shouting, "Hail, Sen-Mut! Ptah of Egypt!" as we passed beside them. The armed forces saluted him, and the archers raised their bows toward the sky as we passed by them on the streets of Thebes. We walked far to reach the audience hall, and when we finally did, the double doors where opened by the guards. They saluted Sen-Mut, and the slaves started to throw gold dust on the stone floor and to him, in every step he took. I walked to my golden throne and sat upon it. Hapuseneb looked at me and smiled, then stood at my right. Sen-Mut stood at my left.

I looked at Sen-Mut, and his body glittered as a god from the golden dust. General Nehesi stood on the left of Sen-Mut, my uncle General Thutmoses at Hapuseneb's right, Sailor Neb-Ery, Senemen, Teshi, and Puyem-Re, Second Prophet of Amun sat on the first steps going down in front of me. Everyone was already inside the hall of audience. In there were dignitaries from all over the land, and thousands of people from Thebes. All came to see and cheer Sen-Mut.

Sen-Mut took several steps down and walked to the right. Turning to face me with a big smile, he shouted, "Beloved King of Egypt, I present you the King and Queen of Punt, and the seven chiefs of Punt and their families."

The double doors were opened. Drums were playing and dancers from Punt were dancing to the rhythm with large colorful feathers, holding in their arms baskets full of dried, colorful flowers. They threw them in the air as they danced. At end of the dance, the drums stopped, and the dancers threw themselves on the limestone floor, leaving space in the center for the King and Queen of Punt to walk between them. I saw the King and the Queen pass them, and the dancers continued throwing dry flowers over them. I could see that the Queen was walking slowly and limping, holding into the King's arm. She was very, very heavy. It looked as though she was deformed, and the shape of her body caused me sadness. They approached me and bowed their heads. I smiled and ordered chairs for them. They stared at me with a marvelous look, and I smiled back at them.

Sen-Mut clapped his hands and said, "A gift from the King and Queen of Punt for you, Your Majesty."

He bowed his head to me, and I smiled at him. The double doors opened again, and many large bags full of gold rings were carried in by my guards and were emptied at my feet. There were many bags full of large gold rings. They continued bringing them in. There were also many large baskets, so many that I lost count of them. Large baskets of myrrh resin came in, and the smell awakened me. I stood up and walked down the steps and took a handful of myrrh resin. I brought it to my nose and was delighted for the offerings in the temple for my father Amun-Ra. Then came bags and bags of gold nuggets, green gold, gold dust, ivory, and dark ebony wood.

Many hours passed, and Mother Nut had covered the land in darkness. I stood up and everyone knelt on the floor.

"Hapuseneb," I called, and he came beside me. I whispered in his ear, "Order the largest litter they can find, and send for a dozen of the strongest bearers to carry the Queen and the King of Punt to the palace. Make sure that all of their people have a place to rest and eat as well."

"Yes, Your Majesty."

He looked indifferently at me and walked off. I wished I could have spared his sadness.

I looked for Tuyii, and she approached me.

"Send message to my slaves and musicians to prepare Sen-Mut's bath, and you go and light all the oil lamps. Be sure that the bed is dressed in gold sheets and pink roses are everywhere, as I said this morning," I told her.

"Your Majesty, the bed is ready, and the roses are everywhere, just as you requested. I will light all the oil candles right now," she said, then left.

I observed the pain on the face of Queen Ati. She must want to be bathed and, on a bed, resting from this long journey on the ship, I thought.

"Ptah of Egypt," I called to Sen-Mut, and he came close to me. I whispered, "Beloved of mine, all the gifts are beautiful, and we must continue tomorrow. I can see that you are very tired also. The scribe and Thuty will do an inventory of all these gifts of the first shipment. Tell the King and Queen that they are most welcome, and I thank them for such wonderful gifts. I can see that the Queen is in so much pain, and I'm sorry that she had to endure it during all those months on the ship. Tell them that we will continue with the gifts tomorrow and our slaves are waiting in the palace to bathe them, as well as the physician to alleviate her pain. Tell them that they are invited to the dinner celebration later in the palace banquet hall, but if she is indisposed, I will understand. Tell the rest of her family that they are invited to join us in our dinner festivities tonight. She will be brought food to her quarters and won't have to walk to the palace. I already sent for a litter and the bearers to carry her to the palace."

Sen-Mut whispered in my ear, "Only you, my love, with the most kind and loving heart, would make a beautiful gesture like this. That is why I have fallen in love with you and love you so much."

He smiled.

"I love you too, Ptah of Egypt," I whispered back with a smile of my own.

I saw him walking toward the King and Queen and relaying the message.

Queen Ati looked at me and nodded her head and smiled, and I returned the smile.

Hapuseneb came back and whispered to me that the litter was waiting outside. I stood up and everyone knelt.

"Rise!" I shouted.

"Make space for the litter for the King and Queen of Punt," I said, and everyone moved aside.

A dozen of the strongest litter-bearers came and helped her sit on the litter. They lifted her up, carrying the litter on their shoulders. Then I saw King Parihu climb onto his litter, and the bearers lifted it onto their shoulders and waited for me and Sen-Mut and my court. We started to walk toward the palace, and the litter-bearers followed behind us. The

Queen and King of Punt had never seen such a big and beautiful city, with its large temples. They were amazed at the structures. Torches were lit everywhere, which we never had done before. I was in awe looking at the beauty of my Thebes. It had been a glorious day because he had finally come home and was with me.

Music was playing everywhere. Sen-Mu was looking at me, and our eyes met again. My body got hot all over again, and we smiled at each other. Everyone walked to the banquet hall. Sen-Mut and I rushed to our quarters. My door guards looked at Sen-Mut and smiled at him, and they dropped to the floor.

"Rise," Sen-Mut said, and he smiled back at them. They opened the golden doors.

"Guards, send replacements for your post, and take the night off and join the celebration at the banquet hall. Celebrate this glorious day tonight," he told them.

Sen-Mut and I walked into our room. It was full of lit candles and pink roses. Everything looked so lovely and bright, and all was dressed in gold, including the curtains around our bed.

He stood there looking at the room.

"Beautiful!" he said.

He pulled me by my wrist and pushed me against the wall and pressed his body and lips against mine. I closed my eyes and wanted more.

"Beloved, wait," I said.

I knelt, looking up at him.

"Beloved, would you remove the Double Crown from my head, please?"

He gently lifted the Double Crown from my head, and I pulled the golden ribbon holding my hair up. My hair fell to my shoulders. His eyes became enlarged and shined. I saw an expression of surprise and gladness on his face. He knelt beside me on the stone floor and looked at me.

"You look so beautiful, Maatke-Re. I've never seen you with long hair, and after all these years of me begging you to let your hair grow, you finally did it. This is a very nice surprise for me," he said.

"Beloved of mine, I told you that one day I would surprise you. Remember?" I smiled.

He pulled me gently by the neck and kissed me again. He helped me rise from the floor. Kissing me with passion, our bodies started to get hot. I asked him to please remove the pectoral from me, and I removed the golden cuffs from my wrists. He kissed the back of my neck. I started to undress him slowly. He removed my kilt, and we were completely naked. I held his hand and walked him to the bath. The slaves were waiting for us, and the musicians were playing their harps and lutes. They looked at Sen-Mut with smiles.

I clapped my hands and told them, "All of you may go to the banquet hall and enjoy this glorious day and be merry tonight."

"Thank you, Your Majesty." They said and left.

When they left, we walked into the warm water of the pool.

"This is so wonderful, this silence, just you and me alone," he said.

I was washing his body with the warm water. I washed his hair, and I put a lot of oil in my hands and started to massage his back. He was enjoying my caresses all over his body. Then he stood, lifted me up in his strong arms, carried me to our bed, and laid me gently on the golden sheets. He lay on top of me and kissed me with passion, kissing every part of my body. We were entangled in passionate kisses. Whoa, what a wonderful sensation he was giving me, I thought. I grabbed the golden sheets and was gasping for air. He took me to the highest peak of pleasure, and we screamed. We got entangled in the most wild and powerful love making and were immensely happy. I had my husband again with me. I laid on his chest as he breathed heavily.

He said, "I dreamed of this moment, my love, all these three summers that I was gone, missing the smell of your skin, the softness of your body and your lips. I wanted so much to kiss you. I kept remembering the first time I saw you naked under the rays of Thoth in the sacred Lake of Mut. I had not taken a woman yet, and you were like a goddess. You were a goddess in front of my eyes. I had to swim several times that night to cool off and quench the heat inside of me, but nothing I could do would release the desire for your body. Nothing satisfied the desires of my loins that night for you. And the thought of you brought back those desires inside of me.

"I remember when I made love to you for the first time. I was thinking of that and of the night at the lake. I relived the moment I first had you under my body. I had the most explosive climax of my entire life. It was the same explosion of ecstasy that only you can give me, and it overpowers my entire body with pleasure. It happens every time I take you," he said.

He pressed my body against his, and I hung tightly to him. I was very pleased to hear of his desires for me since that first night at the Lake of Mut.

"I never told you that I could see it in your eyes that night, and that opened a warm desire inside of me I had never felt before. I wanted the taste of your lips and to know how it felt being taken and made love to. I wanted you to kiss me that night too. I don't know what would have happened if you had kissed me though. I think I would have let you make love to me. I got into my bed that night without bathing. I did not want to wash away that moment. I wanted to feel this magic that I feel right now with you and when you made love to me for the first time. I also remember you when you were standing in front of me calling me a goddess," I said.

He kissed me gently and pulled me to the side and stood up. I could see his gorgeous naked body, the body of a god, walking around the bed. I was full of joy and he had made me the happiest women in the world tonight, with so much desire inside of me. Then he brought a leather pouch to the bed and sat beside me.

"I brought you these gifts," he said and pulled out a large red rock from the leather pouch and put it in my hand.

"This one is called a ruby," he said.

Then he pulled a large green rock from the leather pouch.

"And this one is called an emerald."

I was amazed at the green color and loved it.

"I have never seen such a beautiful green rock before," I told him.

He put it in my other hand. Both were big, heavy, and very beautiful.

"The emerald is very rare in that land, and we don't have it here," he said.

Then he pulls out a gold ring. And I was in shock.

"And this is the ring that was used to pay the assassin to kill me." He said.

I took it in my hand and was in shock. Completely in shock.

"This is the ring I gave to T'Queta for safe passage to the palace. I cannot believe this! This means that she was the one who paid to kill you!" I shouted.

"Oh, Mother Hathor! Now I know why she was wearing the blue mourning attire on the day you were leaving for Punt. I found that odd. I almost ordered the death of Menkhep-Re and Isis, believing they were the ones that had something to do with the attempt on your life," I said.

I sighed and looked at the ring again.

"You don't have to be worried about her anymore, she is dead," I said.

"What...? Dead...? How? Why?" he asked in shocked.

"She committed suicide." I said, "She poisoned herself. She was very depressed when you left, and I thought that it was because you had said goodbye to her forever. I knew that she had fallen in love with you and maybe realized that she never would have you again. Now I know why she killed herself. She thought you were dead," I said.

Looking at him, I said, "Hapuseneb and I buried her by ourselves. I did the ritual of the opening of the mouth since she did not have any family, only us. Now I understand she must have thought that if she could not have you, you were not going to be mine either. Oh, Mother Hathor. I thought I could trust her. And I thought she was my faithful friend," I said.

"Why is it that in your message you did not tell me that the ring was the one I gave to T'Queta for safe passage to the palace?" I asked.

"Because I wanted to talk to her first and ask why she tried to kill me and if she was the silent assassin. I wanted to get to the bottom of this and find out if there were others in the plot and who was behind it. I knew if I told you, you probably would have ordered her death," he said.

"Yes, I would have. Beloved, I am so sorry to give you this bad news. I was going to tell you tomorrow morning because I did not want to spoil this happiness of ours today. But you showed me the ring, and I thought it better to tell you right away," I said.

He pulled me closer to him, and looking deep into my eyes, he said, "No, you did not spoil our happiness today. I will not allow her death to spoil this glorious day with you. I love you and you make me the happiest man in the world, today I received the most beautiful welcome home and I am so happy right now having you beside me," he said and kissed my lips.

"Did you think of T'Queta on your journey?" I asked.

"I thought of her once or twice in the three years that I was gone. I thought of you every day, and I wanted you every night. The only one who was on my mind and in my heart was you. Let's celebrate tonight. Everyone must be waiting for us," he said.

We hugged and kissed again, and he kissed my forehead. He helped me get dressed in the golden sheath, the golden necklace and earrings, and the golden sandals. I wore my long black hair down to my shoulders. I put on my own makeup, rouge, and red lipstick. He wore the new golden kilt I had sent to be made for him. I walked to the larger golden box, and I walked back to where he was standing.

"This is my welcome home gift to you, Ptah of Egypt," I said and kissed him.

He opened the golden box and looked inside of it, then he looked at me and sat the box on the side of the bed and walked toward me.

"It's beautiful, my love, but the most beautiful gift is what the gods have given me, you," he said, hugging me, then kissing me softly.

I looked at him and smiled. I walked to the golden box and pulled out a very large golden pectoral.

"I sent this to be made specially for you to wear tonight and always, until you become Pharaoh," I said with a smile.

I removed the pectoral I had given him with the amulet and placed the new one on his neck. Then I took the two large golden cuffs, and he put them on his wrists. I looked at him and was in awe. He looked the way I always wanted him to look, like a god, a Pharaoh. He radiated tonight, and he looked very handsome. I noticed that he had grown older on his journey and looked wonderful.

He looked at me in awe as he said with a smile, “You radiate as the stars of the universe, and I am happy that you are mine. He pulled me by my waist, hugged me tightly, and rocked me in his arms. He whispered in my ear, “I love you, Maatke-Re, and I will never be tired of telling you how much I love you and that you are my life.”

He gently kissed me, and we walked out of our quarters, down the stairs, and to the banquet hall, where all the dignitaries of the court and all our people were waiting for us.

We walked holding hands to the entrance of the banquet hall, and the guard announced us.

“Hatshepsut I, Pharaoh of the Two Lands and Sen-Mut, the Great Ptah of Egypt,” he shouted.

Everyone fell on their knees, including Hapuseneb.

“Rise, everyone,” I said.

Everybody started to shout, “Hail, Ptah of Egypt! Sen-Mut! Sen-Mut! Sen-Mut! Ptah of Egypt!”

He was smiling, and all of us were full of joy. I saw Hapuseneb looking at me in awe. I called him to come and sit beside me, as always at my right hand, but this time I asked him to bring Tepi. This was the first time I let her sit with us. Ineni looked at Sen-Mut with a big smile. He was very happy to see him back too, and then he noticed the pectoral on Sen-Mut’s neck and looked at me. He smiled and nodded his head several times. I knew that he meant he looked like a Pharaoh.

My daughter Hatshepset and Menkhep-Re were siting with us. Hatshepset was across from Sen-Mut and looked happy talking to him. I could see the anger in Menkhep-Re’s eyes, and it was eating him. He saw the pectoral on Sen-Mut’s neck. Then he noticed that I was looking at him.

He raised his golden goblet to me. He was now twenty-one summers and very strong with the army, I thought. After a short while, he excused himself.

I leaned over to Hapuseneb and said, “Follow him.”

Hapuseneb looked at one of our spies and signaled for him to follow Menkhep-Re.

I ordered that Ineni, Senemen, Teshi, General Nehesi, Sailor Neb-Ery, General D’Jehuty, Thuty, Puyem-Re, and the King and Queen of Punt join us, and they all did.

I stood, and everyone knelt on one knee.

Looking at Sen-Mut, I said, “I welcome you Sen-Mut, Ptah and Steward of Amun, and beloved of Thebes, General Nehesi, Senemen, Sailor Neb-Ery, Teshi, and Puyem-Re, Second Prophet of Amun, and the King and Queen of Punt to my kingdom, the mighty land of Egypt. Rise.”

I clapped my hands and looked at Sen-Mut again.

“A gift for you, my love,” I said.

“Har-Mose and his lutes,” was announced.

Sen-Mut was surprised when the name of his favorite singer was called. He was smiling at me and leaned over and whispered, “Only you, my love, could do things as lovely as this.”

Har-Mose bowed his head to me and stood in the middle of the banquet hall facing us he started to play his lute and singing Sen-Mut’s favorite Song.

Everyone clapped their hands. Sen-Mut was so happy, and I was enjoying his happiness because it was mine too. After Har-Mose was done, Sen-Mut stand up and applauded hard as everyone else.

I clapped my hands and stood up, and everyone knelt.

"Rise," I said.

"Bring in the gifts!" I shouted.

Guards came carrying heavy wooden boxes and set them on the floor.

I started by calling, "General Nehesi, Guardian of the Royal Seal, in recognition of the splendid expedition and acting fast and saving Sen-Mut's life, I give you the title of Commander in Chief of all the armed forces in Egypt. Here is a token of my appreciation for your faithfulness to your King."

Several male slaves placed a large wooden box at Nehesi's feet and opened it in front of him. He was surprised when he saw what was inside of the wooden box. It was full of gold.

"So that you may live the rest of your life in peace, in riches, in happiness, and in health," I said.

He rushed to my side and knelt and kissed my feet several times.

"Your Majesty, Your Majesty, I am most grateful for this wonderful gift," he said.

I placed my right hand on his head and blessed him for acting fast and saving Sen-Mut's life. I was most grateful to him. It was not our custom for the Pharaoh to touch anyone, but I wanted him to know how grateful I was.

"Rise, Nehesi."

I smiled at him, and he rose and returned to his place.

"Puyem-Re, Second Prophet of Amun," I said.

He rose, then knelt at my feet.

"For doing everything in your power and expertise in medicine to save Sen-Mut's life," I said and smiled at him. I was so happy that the knowledge he had of medicine had saved Sen-Mut.

"Slaves!" I shouted.

The slaves brought in another large wooden box full of gold and placed it at his feet.

"So that you may live your life in peace, and in riches, and in happiness, and in health," I said with a wide smile.

I called the rest of the crew and rewarded each of them with smaller boxes full of gold as a token of my appreciation for their service on the expedition. I then clapped my hands again, and everyone continued talking. I walked to my place beside Sen-Mut. I squeezed his hand and whispered in his ear, "And for you, the Double Crown of Egypt, my love."

He smiled, and looking into my eyes, he said, "Let's talk about it later."

I noticed that Hapuseneb had been very quiet all night. I believed he was hurting terribly, and it was best not to make him any sadder. I started to talk to Tepi and have a conversation with him too.

I could see Queen Ati, and she was feeling much better. The King and their family were having a merry night like everyone else. She was sitting at the left, beside my beloved, and she whispered in his ear. He related her words to me.

"Queen Ati said that you are most beautiful and kind. The hot bath with the aromatic herbs and medication has calmed down her terrible pains. The massage over her body was wonderful and made a big difference in her pain. She is most grateful to you for the invitation to join the celebration of our return. She is enjoying herself very much, with the food, the view of the gardens, and the beauty of your palace. And she said to thank you very much in the name of her family," Sen-Mut said.

"And I love you, my love. You have made this welcome unforgettable," he said.

"I waited for a long time for you, my love, and my nights were long and unbearable without you," I whispered in his ear.

He squeezed my left hand.

"Maatke-Re, my nights were unbearable also, and just thinking about it makes me want to kiss you right now."

"Me too. Let's stroll through the gardens so that you can kiss me, and I can get lost in the elixir of your love," I said.

I was about to stand up, but he held me down, holding my wrist very firmly.

"I cannot," he said.

"Why not?" I looked at him strangely.

He laughed and said, "I am aroused, and the people will notice if I stand up."

We laughed together. We looked at each other smiling. I did not want to lose the magic of the moment, and I held on to his hand. I leaned my head forward past Sen-Mut's to look at the Queen, and she was smiling at me. I nodded my head and smiled back at her.

"Beloved, ask her if she finds the quarters accommodating for her and her family."

He asked her, then he said to me, "She said she likes it very much, and it's lovely and to thank you. She has never seen so much beauty before."

I clapped my hands and the Egyptian dancers came and started to dance to the beat of our drums. They also presented their dancers and music from Punt. It was very pretty and had lots of drums.

I looked around everything and all was so beautiful. There were all kinds of food and flowers. I clapped my hands and called Tuyii, who leaned close to me.

"Yes, Your Majesty?"

I whispered into her ear, "Turn off most of the candles in my quarters and leave only one lighted on my night stand beside the bed. Redress the bed with white linen and fill it with red rose petals."

"Yes, Your Majesty," she said and left the room.

Far from us, at the other end of the banquet hall sat Menkhep-Re, Rekhemire, and a few other friends, talking. Menkhep-Re was furious at me because Sen-Mut was wearing the pectoral with the Eye of Horus and looking like a Pharaoh. Then Isis approached them. I saw her in my mind.

Then I heard her say, "Don't you see she that she has dressed him like a Pharaoh. I believe those are her intentions, to make him Pharaoh over you. You cannot allow that. You must stop her. You should be the next Pharaoh of Egypt."

Menkhep-Re got quiet, "I know, Mother. I know."

As always, she was conniving against me, the snake. If I could only know who the silent assassin was. My thoughts were interrupted by the spy approaching Hapuseneb. He leaned over him and said something, and Hapu excused himself from me and left. Something must be going on, I thought. Tepi was left sitting there alone, so I started a conversation with her again. We only had cross few words before. She seemed pleasant now.

About an hour later, Hapuseneb came back and whispered in my ear, "Tomorrow, I will tell you. Enjoy this night, and don't be worried."

I had trusted him all my life He said that he would tell me tomorrow, and I would wait until then. I didn't want this night to be spoiled by anything. The feast continued in the banquet hall, all over the city, and all over the land, and the conversation continued all night about the expedition. Some of the women from Punt came back with the sailors as their wives.

During the night, Sen-Mut spoke of the route to the south. He said that it was very rough on the ships. He spoke of large fish that jumped out of the water and were beautiful, and of all the different species of fish and how colorful they were. He was in awe of the immensity of the vast sea and of the blue water. It was wonderful to hear of all his marvelous experiences.

The celebration continued until the early part of the morning. We had a very merry night, and there was happiness everywhere in the palace and across my whole land. Everyone was celebrating the return of the crew. All came back alive from the expedition, and they and their families rejoiced as we did.

I arose and smiled.

"We must retire now. Tomorrow will be a very long day. Everyone is invited to see the wonderful things that Sen-Mut has brought from Punt, and there is still large cargo to be unloaded from the four ships," I said.

I smiled at Ineni. He knew why we were retiring. Looking at him, I whispered, "Thank you."

He bowed his head. I looked at the King and Queen of Punt and smiled at them. They both nodded their heads.

My beloved and I left the banquet hall holding hands, and when we reached the bottom of the stairs, he lifted me up in his arms and carried me up the stairs to our quarters. The golden doors were opened by the new guards.

Sen-Mut undressed me gently. I smiled.

"You look beautiful tonight, just as I had pictured you in my mind every night, but the biggest surprise was you long, black hair. You look gorgeous with long hair. It is soft like your entire body," he said and kissed my chest.

I undressed him, and he carried me again to our bed and laid me down gently. He lay down beside me, and I put my head on his chest. He kissed me deeply again.

"Beloved, the love making that you did to me earlier this evening, where did you learn that?" I asked softly.

"Did you like it?"

He smiled. I was embarrassed and smiled at him.

"On the ship, during this journey, I heard so many sex conversations between sailors and slaves. On those nights, looking at the stars, I laid on the deck of the ship, thinking of you, and how much I wanted to make love to you in those ways, and to experience this form of love making I never had before," he said.

He brought my hand down to his member, and he was aroused, kissing me profoundly. He made love to me, this time with such tenderness. After the ecstasy of our love making, he whispered in my ear, "I love you Maatke-Re." We fell asleep holding each other and my heart was glad that he was finally home.

Soon, the rays of Ra were shining in our faces, and I woke up. He was still deeply asleep. I lay there just looking at him, and my eyes travelled over his naked, strong body, over the solid muscle of his chest and well-formed legs and thighs. This was the body of a god, and I had missed it and loved it so much. I did not move, for I did not want to wake him up. Looking at his lips, I wanted to kiss him again. I was completely inebriated with this love for him. He had made me his so many times and I never got tired of his love making. I felt that I was a realized woman and felt protected by him. What more could I want when I had it all and him by my side?

"RRRRR!"

He jumped at me and started to tickle me. I could not stop laughing.

"Stop! Stop!" I said, laughing.

He was completely awake, and we were so happy and laughing with each other. Then he held me close and rocked me in his arms, and I loved it. The feeling of being protected by him made me feel secure and wonderful.

Looking deeply into his brown eyes, I said, "My beloved Sen-Mut, I love you so much." I caressed his lips with my finger and kissed him.

"Beloved one," "I had the strangest dream. In this dream I was standing somewhere, talking with a man. He was dressed strangely, wearing something that covered his body and had a long opening in the front, which was closed with several little round things. We were talking beside a very large box, and this box had strange wheels. I was in a strange place I had never been before. I don't know where I was, but it was not Thebes.[77]

"Yes, indeed. That is a very strange dream," he said.

I clapped my hands, and several slaves came into our room. Sen-Mut and I walked to be bathed holding hands. The water was nice and warm, and he held me on his lap as if I was his child. He talked about the ships and the huts where the people of Punt lived. He knew that the King and Queen of Punt had never seen such a beautiful city as Thebes before.

"Beloved, how long did it take to load everything onto the ships for your return home?" I asked.

---

[77] This dream was in the future of 1982 A.D. The strange box was a car, and the wheels were the tires of the car.

"It took us about four weeks. Everyone wanted to return home soon, and they made the effort to load the ships faster. With the help of the Puntuties, we made it. It was difficult to load some of the animals, so we loaded them last. The ones that gave us the hardest time were the giraffes. They were very restless. I knew that you had never seen many of these animals before, and when I saw the giraffe for the first time and saw that they were amazing and gentle, I thought of you and your gentleness. I wish you were there with me to see the amazing views of this land. There was green grass everywhere for miles and miles. And because you were not with me to see the beauty of this land, I brought it to you."

"What do they eat?" I asked.

"The giraffe eats leaves," he said.

"What does it look like?"

"It is a very tall animal with a long, long neck, and long legs. They look sweet to me. I know you will like her as I do when you see her. Did you like the gifts I brought you?" he asked.

He spoke with an amazed look on his face.

"I can tell you that the King and Queen of Punt received us with pleasure, and they spoke of his father meeting your father. Then I knew I was in the right place. I placed a statue of Amun-Ra and one of you in their land. King Parihu with a group of elder chiefs worshiped you and Amun beside me and my men. I brought you thirty-one myrrh trees for your temple. I brought you many different fragrances that smell lovely, and I know you will love them," he said.

How thoughtful of him, I thought. I hugged him and gently kissed him on his lips. He responded to my kiss.

"Beloved, did you remember me every day?" I asked him.

"Every single moment of the day you were in my mind and in my heart. When they took us to see the jungle, I saw the lions, the hippopotamuses, and the giraffes, and I wanted you to be there with me in that moment to see so many animals that we had never seen before. I was impressed with this enormous land, and so much greenery," he said.

He was smiling, and I could see so much happiness on his face and hear it in the tone of his voice as he was telling me everything.

"My love, we must get ready to leave. My men are unloading the ships. They have been doing it since the early part of this morning. I want you to see all the gifts I brought for you from Punt, and they must bring them to the audience hall. Now, all the rare animals and the wild ones will remain in cages. You will decide what to do with them. I brought a male and female of each, but I don't know if they will survive in this dry heat because they will not have the humidity of the jungle in which to roam," he said.

Sen-Mut and I ate holding hands, and my heart was pleased. How happy I was beside him, I thought. We were so very happy looking at each other, and I was amazed listening to him talk about the blue sea, the high waves, and all that was new to him and now to me. He also said that they were not as advanced as we were, and he really hoped that Queen Ati would find the cure for her pain here. He said that they were wonderful people.

I was dressed in my golden kilt, golden sandals, and Pharaoh's pectoral. Sen-Mut wore the white kilt, the pectoral, and the gold cuffs I had given him as a gift last night. There was a knock on the golden doors.

"Enter," he shouted.

It was Hapuseneb. He did not look directly into my eyes as before but knelt on one knee at my feet.

"Your Majesty."

"Rise, First Prophet of Amun," I said, and I smiled at him, and he smiled back. Sen-Mut stood there silently looking at both of us.

Hapuseneb turned around and looked at Sen-Mut with a smile.

"Sen-Mut, good morning. It's good to have you back again. We did not have a chance to talk much last night with all the celebration. I was going to ask you how you felt being back home again, but it was almost morning when you left the banquet hall. Did you sleep well?" he asked.

"Yes, indeed I did. It was wonderful to sleep beside Maatke-Re's body last night. I have missed her so much," he responded with a smile.

I became tense because Sen-Mut had touched an open wound on Hapuseneb's heart. I called Hapuseneb immediately, and he turned around and came to me. I knelt, and he placed the Double Crown on my head. I looked at him with tenderness and could imagine the pain that was in his heart now that Sen-Mut was back.

"I will wait for both of you downstairs, as everyone else," Hapuseneb said and bowed his head to me.

"Your Majesty," he said and left.

Sen-Mut looked at me seriously, and we walked down the stairs.

Everyone was waiting, and I could see how happy Ineni was, as were Queen Ati and King Parihu, and the chiefs, and all their families. We were walking toward the hall of audience when I stopped. Sen-Mut looked at me, puzzled.

"I want to see that gentle animal, the one with the long neck," I said.

Instead of walking to the audience hall, we all walked toward the ships in Karnak. I was amazed looking at all that he had brought for me and for my kingdom. Then I saw the giraffe and was amazed by her.

"She is beautiful, my love. And yes, she is gentle too. I cannot imagine how they caught her and put her on the ship," I said.

"She was hard to load onto the ship, and it was hard to make her enter the cage. That was an ordeal. After that, she was easy to feed. Not like the wild cats. We had to feed them wildlife during our return, and they only eat fresh kills," he said.

I looked at Menkhep-Re, and he seemed happy. I could see how amazed he was looking at all the live animals, just like Hatshepset and everyone else. Sen-Mut showed me every wild animal. In a large cage was a very large black cat with golden eyes, and it seemed angry. He was pacing back and forth.

"Beloved, we must return some of them back to their jungle. I am afraid of this one because if it gets loose, it can kill someone or my cheetah Jotham. You know that he roams all over the palace, and the slaves love him," I said.

"I agree with you on that. When we take the King and the Queen back to Punt, we will take them back too," Sen-Mut said.

I turned around fast and looked at him.

"No, you are not going back to Punt. Send Nehesi to take them back," I said.

"Yes, my love. I will send Nehesi to take them back. In the meantime, I will order very large cages made of bamboo for the wild ones, so they can have a large place to roam, and the people of the land can come and see them before I send them back home," he said.

We walked for a while and saw the many long horned and short horned cattle.

"I believe they will get adjusted to our land," I told him.

"I believe so too. Now, I want to show you my friends here," he said.

We came closer to a large cage with apes. I saw Sen-Mut's big smile when he saw a chimpanzee, which came close to the edge of the cage and started to scream when he saw Sen-Mut. He smiled at him and it became animated with happiness. Sen-Mut went closer to the beast, and it reached its hand out to Sen-Mut, who held its hand.

"Beloved one, I can see that you have made a friend on this trip," I said.

"Yes, we became friends during the journey back home. Every day I sat down beside his cage and fed him bananas, mangoes, all kind of fruits, and I really liked him. Sometimes I shared my meal and vegetables with him."

I looked at Sen-Mut with such love, seeing his gentleness with these creatures. I could really see happiness in him, and we were complete.

"Beloved, I like him too, I want you to know that everything that you brought back from the journey is also yours. You can keep them in the palace, or they can roam in our trees. Do you think he will like me?" I asked.

"I am pretty sure he will not only like you, he will love you, as I do," he said.

Then Sen-Mut clapped his hands, and a guard brought him fruits. Sen-Mut started to give it to the chimpanzee, and the rest of the apes came closer to us with their hands out for him to feed them too. I took some bananas and started to give to them too, and we were laughing. One of them grabbed my hand, and I screamed out loud. It would not let go of me, and a guard was about to chop his hand off when I screamed for him to stop. At that same moment, the ape released my hand. Sen-Mut grabbed my hand and looked at it worried.

"Did he hurt you? Did he bite you?" he asked.

"No, beloved. He just scared me that's all."

Sen-Mut kissed my hand.

“He is a male. I bet he likes you too,” he said and started to laugh. I laughed with him.

“And I don’t share you with anyone,” he said, and I was startled by the tone of his voice. Was he trying to tell me something?

“I want to feed the big, tall one,” I said.

Sen-Mut clapped his hands, and the guard came. Sen-Mut gave him the order to bring tree leaves for the giraffe. We walked back to where she was, and I started to feed her. How lovely and gentle she was. I really liked her too and wondered if she would survive here, in the middle of the desert in this heat.

“Mother, isn’t this one beautiful?”

I turned around and smiled at Hatshepset.

“Yes, she is. I really like her too. Let’s all walk and continue looking at the animals,” I said.

“Mother, that big black cats scare me.”

“I know what you mean. I am planning to return them to their land when the Queen and King of Punt leave,” I said.

“Why don’t you put the black cat and the leopard together in a very large cage and see who kills who first? Then you don’t have to send them back. Whichever wins the fight you can let it loose, so my friends and I can go and hunt him down,” Menkhep-Re said.

I was startled by what he was saying.

“Menkhep-Re, you only have violence inside of your head?” I snapped at him.

“Who wouldn’t?” he said.

Sen-Mut got angry.

"How about I put you inside one of these cages with one of them, with a dagger in your hand, and see who wins? Then you can show us how brave you are," Sen-Mut said.

Menkhep-Re was startled and got quiet and turned his face away.

I looked at Menkhep-Re in anger.

"Soon, I will be sending you on a military campaign to check the borders to see if the heat of the desert will take away all this anger bottled up inside of you," I told him.

"Mother, don't do that," Hatshepset pleaded.

"Yes, I can, and I will do it. I want him to be very far away from my sight," I said.

"Mother, I am pregnant," she said.

I looked at her. I was surprised and so were Menkhep-Re and Sen-Mut. I hugged her and touched her face.

"I am very happy for you, sweetheart. You are making me a grand-mother? I am too young for that," I said, and we all laughed.

The news took Menkhep-Re by surprise, and he looked pale, as if he was going to faint.

"I hope that in a few months I will be pregnant too with Sen-Mut's child, and you will have a little brother or a sister," I told her.

Menkhep-Re was startled and in shock, and I saw the anger in his eyes.

"Very well. He will remain in Thebes until your child is born," I said with a smirk and walked off holding Sen-Mut's hand, leaving them both standing there.

"Beloved, he will never be Pharaoh during our lifetime. You will hold the Double Crown and then our children will. I wish I could find out if he is my brother's son. If I could, I would make some concessions for him, but every time I look at him, he looks more and more like Puyem-Re. Do you see how dark skinned he is? He doesn't look like my father nor my brother by the color of his skin. My brother had light skin, as does Isis, his mother. Now you see why I cannot believe that he is my brother's son. Beloved, our children will reign after us, I promise you that," I said.

Sen-Mut was quiet, then said, "How did he behave when I was gone?"

"Well, he said something that startled me on the day your ship left, and I had lost sight of you. He came from behind and whispered something in my ear that really made me angry. Then later you were poisoned, and I believed that it was he and his mother that were trying to kill you," I said.

"What did he tell you?" he asked.

"He asked me, if I believed that you would return alive. I became outraged and turned around fast and told him that he better pray that you came back to me safe and alive. Otherwise, I would send him to a war game and would personally kill his mother. I told him I would send her body to be made into a meal and send it to him. I would wait until he finished eating it, and I would walk into his tent and ask him if he liked the meal. Then I would tell him that he had just eaten his mother. And then I would kill him."

"You told him that?"

"Yes, I did. And I did not stop there. I sent the guards to fetch Isis. When she was brought to the hall of audience and knelt at my feet, I pushed her with the sole of my golden sandal, and she fell on the floor. In front of all the ones that I had summoned, I stepped on her face, and I told her that from now on, she must pray that you would return to me alive and safe. Otherwise, I would kill her son, have him prepared into a meal, and send it to her. After she had eaten him, I would tell her what she had done, and then I would kill her too. I was in such a rage that day with her. That was the reason I believed they had something to do with the attempt on your life."

"I am sorry that you have gone through all this anger. Now, my love, I am here, and you don't have to worry about anything anymore. Soon I will be meeting with Hapuseneb, Senemen, General D'Jehuty, Ineni, and my other right hands to put me up to date on everything in the palace and throughout the whole kingdom. I noticed last night you whispered something in Hapuseneb's ear, and he had one of our spies follow Menkhep-Re," Sen-Mut said.

"I did not know you were watching me. Yes, I had him followed. I know he is very angry at me and at you, and I wanted to know what he was up too. In my mind, I could see Isis telling him that I wanted you for Pharaoh because of the way I had dressed you as one," I said.

"I should have done away with both a long time ago, when Nehesi suggested it many summers ago, but you did not want me to do it," he said.

"At what price, beloved of mine? Your life? Do you believe I can live without you?" I asked.

He stopped walking and turned around and faced me. He hugged me very tightly against his chest and held me in his arms quietly, and he kissed my forehead as he always had done. I could see Menkhep-Re looking at us.

"Please my love, no more talk of the past. You are here now and let us enjoy this beautiful day," I said.

We held hands and started to walk again, looking at the rest of the animals.

"Beloved, this horse is beautiful. I have never seen a white horse painted with black stripes before," I said.

"Neither had I until I saw him," he said.

Sen-Mut turned around and looked at me and started to laugh.

"They are called zebras, and they are born that way. He is a male. I also brought a female, she is probably still on one of the ships. I also brought some of their skins and a leopard skin. I like their skin very much, and I brought a leopard skin as a gift for Hapuseneb and for Ineni too. Did Hapuseneb take care of you well when I was gone?"

I was startled at the question. He was looking at the zebra when he asked me. What was he implying? Was he jealous?

"Oh, yes. He is a great friend. He came and visited me every day, and we had tea every afternoon with Ineni. He kept me informed of everything in the palace and throughout the kingdom. And I kept sending Menkhep-Re away to keep him busy on his war games that he likes, and at the same time to keep him away from his conniving mother," I said.

Why didn't he ask me up front if I had crossed the line with Hapuseneb, I wondered? I could see that he was clenching his teeth. He was silent as we continued walking.

He showed me a cage with a hippopotamus and her baby. They were so very large, and the baby was fat and cute, big for a baby. There was so much to see, and only one ship had been unloaded. It was past high noon, and the heat was unbearable, with no breeze to alleviate the swelter.

"Beloved, let's stop for now and have lunch. We can sleep on the barge, so we can be all alone with no one around us. I can have you all for myself," he said.

The soft breeze of the Nile was moving the canopy curtains on the barge as we sailed north, and the breeze caressed his face as he slept. The wind was blowing softly, moving the tiny curls of his hair. I noticed he was snoring. I held his body as I lay in his arms and watched him sleep. He woke up and made mad love to me. He was insatiable, as was I. Our love making was wonderful. It had been only one full day since his return, and I wanted more of him.

The next day, everything was unloaded from the ships. I was around when the gold dust was being weighed, and I took the part that was to be offered to Amun-Ra. There was a lot of gold, and it was a nice gift from the King and Queen of Punt.

Two weeks had gone by since Sen-Mut's return. I felt complete, and we were very happy. Everything had gone back to normal in the palace as before, and music played everywhere, as I liked it.

CHAPTER 41

QUEEN ATI

It had not been long since Sen-Mut's return from Punt, and Queen Ati still did not feel well. Our physicians could sometimes help ease her pain, but sometimes they could not. I could hear her screaming in pain sometimes all the way in my quarters. I wished I could do something for her. She and I had become friends, and she was very sweet. I invited her to my rose garden and to my quarters, several times, and she liked it very much, especially the pink roses. I told her that we brought them from a faraway island called Crete when I was a child.

Then she said, "Your kingdom and the buildings are beautiful, like you."

She smiled at me, and I smiled at her. She was sweet, and I could see that we were close to the same age. I noticed she was looking at my solid gold jewelry box.

"It is beautifully made," she said.

After our visit, she walked to her quarters, limping and hanging on to her daughter's arm and assisted by several of her slaves. After she left, I clapped my hands and asked my slave to bring another jewelry box. I would fill it with jewelry and give it to her the next time she came to visit. The following day, I invited her and her family to the ceremony of the offering of the myrrh trees to my father Amun-Ra and my mother Hathor in my mortuary temple. The ceremony was for the planting of the myrrh trees that Sen-Mut brought from Punt for my terrace and for the delight of the gods.

"We must be ready before the first ray of Ra shows, but I see that you are in pain. You can stay, and your family can come with us," I told her.

"Even in pain, I will be there," she said and smiled.

"I know you are a very strong woman, and I will be very happy if you can come," I said.

****

It was still dark when Sen-Mut and I were bathed by the slaves. They started to dress me in the golden kilt and golden sandals. I was watching Sen-Mut's gorgeous naked body being dressed, and a rush of desire overpowered me. I came close to Sen-Mut and rubbed my body against his and gave him a passionate kiss. He laughed.

"You just made me so hot with that kiss," he said and laughed again.

"I desire you right now, my love," I said.

I clapped my hands, and the slaves left in a hurry. He started to push against my body with his body, and I was taking steps backwards as he was kissing me with passion. I stopped by the edge of our bed. He laid me on the bed. We became one, and I loved it. We were lost in the most delicious passion and ecstasy of love. We reached a powerful and explosive climax, the most delicious feelings that only he could give me.

We lay there, so in love with each other. The moment was beautiful. He moved onto his side and whispered in my ear, "Maatke-Re, I love you, and you are so bad for making people wait." He got up laughing.

"I want to have your child, beloved!" I said, smiling.

He looked at me and with a smile he said, "That will make me very happy. I hope you have just gotten pregnant right now."

"I hope so too. I remember you told me once that you wanted fifteen or twenty children."

I was smiling at him, and he started to laugh.

"Yes, and I still do. We can form a small army." He was laughing as he said it.

I did not wash myself as before. I wanted with all my heart to have his children. We got dressed, and there was a knock on the golden doors.

I knew it was Hapuseneb, who came to set the Double Crown of Egypt on my head.

"Enter," I said and Hapuseneb walked to us and knelt at my feet.

"Your Majesty," he said.

"Rise, Hapuseneb."

He did and walked toward Sen-Mut.

"Good morning, Sen-Mut. It's going to be a very long and hot day today."

"Yes, it's going to be a very hot day. I can feel it already," Sen-Mut replied with a smile.

Hapu walked to where I was standing. I knelt on one knee, and he placed the Double Crown on my head. We smiled at each other.

"We will be waiting downstairs, Your Majesty," he said and walked off.

After he left, Sen-Mut said, "Did he treat you with such formality while I was gone?"

I didn't know what to say. Was he jealous? I wanted to change the conversation, and I noticed he was wearing the white kilt.

"Beloved, you must wear the golden kilt today," I said.

"Hatshepsut, I will wear the white kilt!" he said.

I was stunned by the harsh tone of his voice. He had never called me by my name, and he was looking at me very seriously.

"I am making offerings with Hapuseneb under the very hot sun today, and I prefer the white kilt for now. It is cooler, so I can walk freely under the hot sun. The golden kilt will make my body too hot, and I will sweat terribly under the rays of Ra," he said.

I noticed the tone of his voice was different. He walked to where I was standing and grabbed me by my arms with a tight and firm grip.

"You have not answered me."

He was looking at me with his piercing brown eyes. I denoted jealousy in him, and I was trembling inside. I had never seen him like that before. I could feel the pressure of his fingers on my arms.

"You are right, beloved. No, he did not treat me with such formality as right now. Don't forget, he has been my friend since childhood, and

I believe that he is doing it out of respect for you. He has been a faithful friend to both of us, and he saved my life when you were gone," I said.

He became silent and released his grip from my arms. I just then realized that he was jealous. I ran to my jewelry box and grabbed two golden cuffs to cover the bruises that he'd left on my upper arms.

It was still dark when Sen-Mut and I reached the bottom of the stairs. There were hundreds of torches everywhere, and that would be the only light we would have until the first rays of Ra rose in the east. That wouldn't be for several hours.

I could see Hapuseneb's face, and he seemed at peace. He was wearing the new leopard skin over his shoulder, the one Sen-Mut brought for him as a gift from Punt. Puyem-Re, Ineni, General Nehesi, Hatshepset, Menkhep-Re, Isis, General D'Jehuty, Thuty, Senemen, Teshi, the priests and priestesses, and the Oracle of the Temple of Amun-Ra were all waiting for us in the Temple of Karnak.

We arrived at the Temple of Amun, and the statue of Amun-Ra was carried to the sacred barge. I believe there were more than five hundred priests and priestesses, all in white kilts and white sheaths. I was pleased to see Queen Ati and King Parihu, and the seven chiefs and their families. I could see the shining golden loops in their noses as the light of the torch shined on the face of the King and his children.

We boarded the ships. Three ships were used to transport everyone to the west side of the Nile. We sailed behind the sacred barge across the Nile in the dark and docked on the other side of the banks to the Valley of the Dead. There were several wagons waiting to transport the statue of Amun-Ra, Queen Ati, King Parihu, and the trees to my mortuary temple. The cooks and slaves were already there, as were the guards and part of the army, who had set camp with the royal banner on the outskirts of my temple a few days earlier. We would remain there for several days and celebrate.

"Hatshepset, I will ride with Sen-Mut, Hapuseneb, Menkhep-Re, General Nehesi, and General D'Jehuty. You ride with Isis and the charioteer, and I will see you there. I love you, daughter," I told her.

We rode fast before the first rays of Ra had shown, then we arrived at Djeser Djeseru.

By the time we arrived, the rays of Ra were shining directly on my temple. We dismounted, and I was in awe seeing the beauty of this magnificent temple Sen-Mut had built for me. Then I remembered his words when we were very young and were on our first trip to Philae: "I will build for thee the greatest and most beautiful temple in the whole kingdom, one that will last for all eternity." My eyes became full of tears seeing such a magnificent temple and because he accomplished his promise.

"My love, what are you thinking of?" he asked.

"I am remembering our first trip to the island of Philae, and your beautiful words that have become a reality."

"I will build for thee the greatest and most beautiful temple in the whole kingdom, one that will last for all eternity," he said.

My eyes filled with tears again.

"And yes, I remember that moment, and I meant it. I wanted to be an architect so bad and build it just for you, right there and then," he said and squeezed my hand.

I looked into his eyes.

"Sen-Mut, beloved of mine I love you so much. You can't even imagine how much I love you."

"I love you too, Your Majesty," he said, nodding his head with a smile.

Hapuseneb had gone in front of us, as had Puyem-Re. We continued walking toward the temple. Menkhep-Re was behind us. I turned around and said to him, "Menkhep-Re, you can walk beside me. Hatshepset and your mother should be coming soon."

"I know," he said and walked at Sen-Mut's side. "Sen-Mut, when I become Pharaoh, I would like for you to build something this magnificent for me. I had no idea that you had finished this temple."

I was in shock because of his daring words. I wanted to laugh.

"Menkhep-Re, you're going to have to wait for a long, long time before you become Pharaoh of Egypt. You don't have to wait for me or Master Ineni to build you a burial place though. But I can tell you this for sure, it would not be as magnificent as this one because I built this temple with all my love for Hatshepsut, your Pharaoh."

I did not have to say anything else. Sen-Mut had said it all.

The ceremony began. The acolyte with burning incense walked ahead of the procession, followed by the statue of Amun being carried up to my temple. Following behind was the First Prophet of Amun, Hapuseneb. Beside him was Sen-Mut, followed by the Second Prophet of Amun, Puyem-Re, followed by many other priests and priestesses, each carrying a silver and gold incense censer in their hands. As the procession started, priestesses walked up the ramp. They would split to the left and to the right at each terrace of my temple, and each one would stand in front of a statue of me and represent me in the elevation of the offering of the burning myrrh to Amun.

I started to walk up the ramp, looking at the most impressive view of the priestesses lined up, all in their white sheaths facing Ra. I was followed by Menkhep-Re, and after him, Hatshepset. Isis followed her and then Ineni. I felt so happy. I knew in my heart Amun was very pleased, and Mother Hathor was too.

I walked into the Shrine of Amun. The incense was waiting for me to make my offerings to Amun. Menkhep-Re followed me, and then Hapuseneb, Sen-Mut, and Puyem-Re. The chanting began to summon Amun-Ra. I felt his presencc and threw myself on the floor. I gave complete thanks to Amun-Ra and presented him with the myrrh trees and the gold dust. After that, I did the same for Mother Hathor. Behind me, Menkhep-Re was making offerings with the incense censer. Everyone started chanting. The ceremony was long.

After the ceremony ended and we walked down the ramp, I stood in front of the first myrrh tree as it was planted with prayers to Amun-Ra by Hapuseneb. Then the other trees were planted. By the time all was finished, it was late afternoon just before the sunset, and we celebrated for a few days there. My tent was blue with gold trimmings with the royal banner on top, as was Father's. My beloved was with me at my side every single day. We slept together, and I clung tightly to Sen-Mut's body every night as we slept. His love showed in the way he looked at me. I am a very happy woman. I have it all, I thought.

The amazed expressions on the faces of Queen Ati and her family when they saw the beauty of my mortuary temple were obvious. She wanted to know who my builder was. She wanted him to build one for her in Punt and to build a beautiful city as well. I smiled at her.

"It was Sen-Mut," I said.

She was surprised that he had built my temple.

"Is he your beloved?" she asked.

I smiled at her.

"Yes, he is my beloved one, and he is my Ptah, my architect and builder."

"That is why your mortuary temple is so beautiful, it was made with love. Indeed, with much love for you," she said, and we smiled at each other.

****

A few days after the ceremony in my temple, I sent Queen Ati the jewelry box with several gold necklaces, gold earrings, and gold bracelets. My slave Tuyii came back with word that she was very ill. Later she sent her sweet daughter to thank me.

Many days later she had gotten better, and we ate in my rose garden and spent a lot of time together. I had not had another real friend since T'Queta's death, and I really missed her, even though she did what she did. Queen Ati and I became friends quickly. There were times she was so sick in pain that she could hardly talk and had to remain in bed. The King was always with Sen-Mut, who showed him all over our land. We took them all sailing along the Nile, and they liked that very much. We spent good times together.

Hapuseneb seemed more adjusted to the presence of Sen-Mut again, and Sen-Mut became calmer regarding Hapuseneb. He had not asked me again about Hapuseneb. I could see them laughing together sometimes, and that made me feel better, because having two men being jealous towards each other for the love of me, scared me sometimes. Sen-Mut was calmer and more collected now that he spent all day with Hapuseneb. Sometimes he came back to our quarters with a look on his face as if he wanted to ask me something, but he did not. I wondered if he thought that Hapuseneb and I had crossed the line while he was gone. We had not, and I don't know what they spoke of when they were alone together.

After seeing Hapuseneb and Sen-Mut, my two most beloved men in harmony, I invited Tepi more often to eat with us, and she and I became closer, but not all that close. I could still see and feel the jealousy on her face when Hapuseneb spoke or looked at me.

Early one morning, when Ra was not yet showing his rays, we were awakened by the sounds of people crying, and there was a knock on the doors. Sen-Mut and I got up.

"Enter," he said. It was our physician giving us the bad news that Queen Ati had died in her sleep. Sen-Mut and I became very sad, and I started to cry as he tenderly held me in his arms.

We spoke to the King of Punt and knew that he would like to take her body back to Punt, but there was a problem. The month of Akhet was almost over, and the waters of Hopi were at the normal level. We needed the rain to swell the banks for the ships to sail and take her body back to Punt. We did not have any other choice but to bury her here.

Speaking with Sen-Mut, we agreed that her body would be placed in the tomb of my wet nurse Sitre-In. I ordered her body to be taken to the House of the Dead and prepared for embalming. I also ordered the finest linens for the Queen.

When the seventy days were over, we embarked on the barge, and sailed across the Nile to where wagons and bulls were waiting to carry her body to be buried in the tomb of Sitre-In.[78]

---

[78] The body found in the tomb of my wet nurse Sitre-In is that of Queen Ati from Punt. It is not my body, as has been speculated by Egyptian archaeologist Zahid Hawass.

CHAPTER 42

COUP D' ETAT

The edict of the coming coronation of Sen-Mut was published all over the land. Ineni suggested to do it in a hurry. At the beginning, it was an uphill battle with Hapuseneb, but the elder priests agreed with me that Sen-Mut had all the qualifications to be Pharaoh. He had found Punt and had built shrines for Amun-Ra along the Nile. Sure, he could rule Egypt. I felt the jealousy and angriness of Hapuseneb. He had distanced himself from me, which hurt.

Isis was in a rampage, as was Menkhep-Re. He and I had terrible arguments regarding my decision to marry Sen-Mut and crown him Pharaoh, but neither could do anything about it.

Suddenly, I learned of another tragedy.

"Your Majesty!" Tuyii said and approached me. "We have received terrible news."

My heart froze.

"What is it?" I ask.

"Master Builder Ineni died in his sleep last night," she said.

I was frozen by the terrible news, and I started to cry. He was my support, after Father went to the heavens, I looked up to him for advice as if he was my father. I felt lost. I ran to my bed and lay there crying. The golden doors opened, and it was my beloved. He sat beside me on the bed and held me, and we cried together for a long time.

Hapuseneb came and we spoke for a long time and cried together. Sen-Mut oversaw his funeral. It was terribly sad hearing of his dead for me.

When the seventy days of embalming were done, we carried his body to be buried on the west bank of the Nile in Sheikh Abd el-Qurna. It was a day of terrible sadness. From that day on, Hapuseneb came around as before, but I could still see the pain in his eyes of my coming marriage to Sen-Mut.

****

Sen-Mut and I continued with preparations for his coronation. On the day of the coronation, I would step down as Pharaoh and take him as my husband. At that moment, he would become divine and of full royal blood. Then the ceremony of his coronation would follow.

It was a glorious morning, and Sen-Mut and I were very happy. In less than twenty-four hours, I would formally marry him and happily step down as Pharaoh. I would crown him Pharaoh of Egypt, the desire of my heart for years, and no one would ever keep us apart again.

Sen-Mut and I were in his office when Thuty approached me.

"Your Majesty, good morning. I bring you your seal. Tomorrow is going to be a wonderful day for all of us. I know Master Sen-Mut was very happy when I saw him this morning."

"Yes, we both are," I said and smiled at him. Then I looked at Sen-Mut, who was smiling at me.

"Thuty, remember I want lots of gold dust to be thrown as we walk into the Temple of Amun and when we come out of the temple too," I said.

"Will do, Your Majesty."

He bowed his head and left. I saw him leaving, and he was so happy.

Sen-Mut showed me on the papyrus how the procession of priests and priestesses would be walking to the Temple of Amun-Ra. Hundreds of slaves holding baskets of white flowers would throw them as we walked to the temple. The ceremony would not be held in the audience hall as before, but in the temple. I ordered a gold kilt, gold cape, gold sandals, and golden cuffs to be made for him to wear tomorrow. I would surprise him with them tonight. I was very emotional at that moment. I wanted the whole land to know that he was my husband, and that he has always been my husband. I wanted Ra to shine all over him and for his image be printed in everyone's minds as he radiated as a god.

I was so happy, when suddenly a cold chill invaded my insides, and my chest froze. I had never felt that way before, and my body started to tremble. I became silent, and in my mind, I could see Menkhep-Re in a state of a rage, talking to his friend Rekhemire. I did not like what I was feeling.

I looked at Sen-Mut and said, "Sen-Mut, have you spoken to D'Jehuty and Nehesi this morning? I want to be sure that our armed forces are ready for any surprises by Menkhep-Re."

"I personally spoke with D'Jehuty and Nehesi early this morning. They are ready. D'Jehuty said that Menkhep-Re is still away and should be arriving tonight for the coronation tomorrow morning. D'Jehuty said that Menkhep-Re is very angry but accepting your wishes, but I still have this uneasy feeling inside of me," he said.

"And I have the same feeling. Have you seen Hapuseneb this morning?" I asked him.

"Early in the morning. He will come and join us soon. He went to the temple to say some prayers. He also said that he feels something in the air that he doesn't like. Last night, when I went out for a walk, he met me beside the Nile and spoke of you. He said that throughout his life he has always loved you and only you, and that I knew that. I agreed. I have always known that he married Tepi when he could have married T'Queta. He loved her too but not as he has loved you. But he needed T'Queta to keep an eye on me. I could not believe what he was telling me. I could smell wine on him. He was drunk. Then he said that now that he knows he has lost you forever, that your heart was only mine, he wanted me to protect you always with my own life as he has done all his life. I had the feeling as if he was saying goodbye. I thanked him for his sincerity, and I told him that I will always regard him as a good friend too."

"Beloved, have you made a chart of the stars to tell us about the future?" I asked.

"No, I have not. It takes a long time to do a chart, and I have been so busy since my return with everything, and the coronation preparation, I did not have time," he replied.

"Beloved, are you sure that our army is ready for battle on my orders?" I asked him again.

"Nehesi and D'Jehuty said that they are," he said.

I looked at Sen-Mut and said, "Something is not right. I have felt it inside of me for a few days. There is too much silence around us."

"I feel it too. There is something I don't like either. All of our army and the very bravest guards are posted everywhere," he said.

Suddenly, a terrible scream rang out, and there were more screams everywhere. I saw our guard rush to the site of the screaming. Sen-Mut and I looked into each other's eyes. We knew what was happening. Menkhep-Re!

"Stay in here," he said and picked up the fake Crown of Upper and Lower Egypt and placed it on my head.

"I was going to bring the real one tonight for the ceremony tomorrow. You were right, my love, when you ordered this one to be made. I want you to wear it always. No one can touch you. I will be back with our armies," he said.

He hugged me very tightly and kissed my lips.

"I love you, Pharaoh of Egypt," he said.

Walking to the door, he turned around and stood there for a moment looking at me the same way he looked at me on the day of Neferu-Re's death when I saw him standing silently against the wall. I froze and became terrified for his life. He was wearing the long white robe trimmed in gold, and looking directly into my eyes, I watched him turn around and leave. He was walking fast as he passed the large window, and I saw him cross the gardens.

No one would dare mess with me or my army, and Menkhep-Re better not, I thought. I wanted to go and confront the rebellious soldiers, but I didn't know who was fighting at his side.

I was wearing a long white sheath, split on both sides of my legs, and I remembered that I did not bring my dagger. I didn't have my bow and arrows with me to find and kill Menkhep-Re. I shouted aloud, "Amun, Father, please keep my beloved Sen-Mut and Hapuseneb safe, and everyone that I love Please!"

There was more screaming everywhere. My guards had left their posts and were fighting in the outer quarters. The smell of blood was making me sick. I was terrified for Sen-Mut's life.

"Sen-Mut, my beloved, if you can hear me, save yourself! Save yourself. Please," I said. I was in such a panic and on the verge of crying when Teshi came running in.

"Your Majesty! Your Majesty!" He was almost screaming. "Master Sen-Mut said to place your seal on this order for all the armies to come and fight against Menkhep-Re."

Trembling, I placed my seal on the five papyri without reading them, and he rushed out so fast that I felt something was not right. I was about to tell him to tell Sen-Mut that I loved him, but my words remained on my lips.

I waited for hours. I could not feel Sen-Mut within me, and he had not come back. I feared the worse.

"Please, Amun, let him be safe. And Hapuseneb too. Please. I beg you."

I sat somberly and continued hearing the screams of the dying everywhere, and I did not care anymore. If Sen-Mut was dead, I wanted to be dead too. It was almost dark, and I heard many footsteps. I saw from the large window it was not Sen-Mut but Menkhep-Re. I was shaking all over and could hardly breathe. When he walked through the doors with his soldiers carrying torches, I was so outraged I stood from my chair.

"Where is Sen-Mut!" I screamed at him.

He came closer.

"He is dead. As is every one of your closes friends," he said.

"You cannot kill Sen-Mut!" I screamed back at him.

My body was shaking terribly. Menkhep-Re came closer to me.

"You killed him. You signed all their death sentences," he said, slamming a blood-soaked papyrus on my chest.

I knocked the fake crown from my head and picked up the papyrus from the floor. Tears were rolling down my face, and my body was shaking out of control. I saw Sen-Mut's name soaked in his blood and read:

I, Hatshepsut, Pharaoh of Egypt, Order the Apprehension and Death of Sen-Mut, Ptah and Steward of the Palace, to be Executed on the Spot.

I saw my seal.

"And I showed it to him too," he said.

I started to scream and scream. I rushed upon him and pulled his dagger from his waist and swung it at him fast and hard. He skipped to the left, and I cut his right arm. The cut was large and poured blood. Now I was facing him with his dagger in my left hand. Quickly, I went upon him like a lion and kicked his right knee, and he fell to the limestone floor. I jumped on top of him and straddled his waist, pressing the dagger with force, pushing it with my body as hard as I could, trying with all my might to drive the dagger into his chest. He was holding my wrist trying to push away the dagger from his chest. I wanted to kill him so badly and wanted to die at the same time. He swung my wrists to his right side, and he was on top of me in a flash, smashing my wrists against the floor. The dagger flew from my hand. He straddled me and began strangling me hard with both hands. I could not breathe. I was blacking out when I heard D'Jehuty scream.

"Stop! You need her, or you will never be Pharaoh," he said and pulled him off me.

I got up from the floor, my throat hurting terribly, and gasped for breath. I held my throat with both hands. Then I saw Teshi being held by the soldiers. He had tears in his eyes and lowered them.

"Forgive me, Your Majesty" he said.

A soldier pressed a small spear into the left side of his neck. His blood splattered on me as he collapsed to the floor on his knees, dead.

I looked at D'Jehuty and closed my fist and punched him in the face as hard as I could, screaming, "You Traitorrrr! You Traitorrrr! You Traitorrrr!!" I scream and scream, I could not believe that he had betray us.

I started to run away from there, back to the palace. I was crying and screaming. The pain inside my heart was horrible.

"You will never find his body. Never! You hear me?" Menkhep-Re screamed at me.

I turned around, and with hatred and tears rolling down my face. I yelled back at the top of my lungs, "And you will never be Pharaoh!"

It was dark. The rays of Thoth were starting to bathe the land, and I continued running to the palace. There were bodies everywhere. The pain in my heart was unbearable. My beloved, my beloved is dead? I screamed and screamed, sobbing, thinking I needed to find Sen-Mut's body. Menkhep-Re's words rang in my ears: "Sen-Mut read his death sentence."

"My beloved could never believe that I ordered his death. Never!" I screamed.

"Please, Amun, kill me! I want to die with him," I screamed, running across the gardens.

When I reached the first steps of the palace, I found Menina dying. I knelt beside her. Crying, I held her hand. She was barely alive.

"I tried to reach you, to warn you, but they caught up with me and stabbed me many times," she whispered.

I heard footsteps running behind me and turned around, expecting Menkhep-Re's soldiers, but it was two of my bravest soldiers. They rushed to me and knelt.

"Your Majesty, we held them back as much as we could. His soldiers are right behind us."

I saw them coming. I looked at my brave men, and with tears rolling down my face, I whispered, "Thank you."

Crying, I closed my eyes as Menkhep-Re's soldiers cut their throats in front of me. Their blood splattered on my face. I saw the soldiers walk away, and I was numb with so much pain. I turned to comfort Menina, but she was dead. With tears running down my face, I took large steps up to my quarters, screaming in agony at the loss of my beloved. I tore off my sheath, screaming, and collapsed on the floor in sorrow. I cried and cried lying there. I crawled to Sen-Mut's side of the bed and hugged the mattress, grasping it and the sheets. I could not stand up from the grief.

I must find my beloved's body before the jackals do. I was in so much grief and so full of rage that I felt powerless. I grabbed my dagger and chopped off my hair in chunks, which fell to the floor. I ran and washed the blood from my face and put on the mourning cape and tied it in a knot on my left shoulder. I was completely naked underneath. I took the gold Crown of Horus and put it on. Then I grabbed my bow and arrows and my dagger and rushed down the stairs, running through the palace looking for Menkhep-Re and his mother. I wanted to kill them both. He was not around, nor was his mother or my daughter Hatshepset.

I screamed again and called out the names of my slaves. I didn't know how many were still alive, but some of them came from their hiding places, including my two old door guards. We all crossed the Nile in the barge, and we brought my horse too. I believe between all of us, we were fifty or less.

We arrived at the area where I believed Sen-Mut may have been brought to be killed. My heart froze. We formed a parallel line, and we all lined up together with torches, leaving five feet between us and started the search for his body in the dark. We looked for hours. Then I thought of Hapu. Menkhep-Re would not dare to touch him. He is First Prophet of Amun, and his son may know where Sen-Mut had been taken to be killed. I left my slaves there searching for his body. In the meantime, I went to look for Hapu.

I returned to Thebes with my two guards. They helped me cross the Nile. Thoth was bright, and the night was beautiful and horrible at the same time. My beloved Sen-Mut, my beloved Sen-Mut, I thought over and over, rocking my body and sobbing. I whispered his name many times until we reached Thebes. I rode my horse as fast that I could to Hapuseneb's house.

I saw Hapuseneb's dead body in Tepi's lap, and I screamed and screamed. I dismounted and ran to him and pulled her away with force from his body. I kept screaming at the top of my lungs. I held his body in my lap and noticed that he was still warm. I held his body against my chest and rocked him in my arms, crying. I kissed his forehead, and whispered in his ear, "And I love you too," hoping that he could hear me. I remembered how many times he told me that he loved me.

I thought of my beloved Sen-Mut and held Hapuseneb's body against my chest. I kissed him and whispered, "I love you, Sen-Mut." I was screaming out of control, holding him in my arms, when I heard Tepi scream.

"It is all your fault! It is your fault! Menkhep-Re's soldiers came into the house and pulled him out and told him that all of you were dead. I saw how his face changed in shock. He became silent, as if he was giving up his life as well. They told him that Menkhep-Re was willing to spare his life because of our son, who was his friend and part of the revolt, if he vowed to serve him from now on. I cannot believe what he did, he looked straight at me, then said, 'If she is dead, I want to be dead too.' And they cut his throat. He only has loved you! He always knew that I have known that, and how much I have suffered because of his love for you, and he didn't even care. I waited all these years for him to love me, but he never did. Now your Sen-Mut and your Hapuseneb are dead. You hear me? They are dead because of you!" she screamed at me.

I heard a galloping horse approach. It was Hapuseneb's son.

"You Traitorrrr!" I yelled at him.

He dismounted and was shocked to see his father dead in my lap. He ran to his mother, and they held each other. Tepi was crying out of control.

"Maybe all of you can meet in the afterlife," he told me sarcastically.

"How dare you? Killing your own father," I screamed at him.

"My father knew for a week that this was coming!" he shouted.

I was shocked to hear what he was saying. Hapuseneb knew? That was why when I talked to him several times this week he was lost in thought, as if he was keeping something from me. I remembered that he never told me what he saw that night of Sen-Mut's return when his spies followed Menkhep-Re.

I got up from the grass slowly, laying his body on the ground, devastated with what his son had said. He had kept this terrible secret from me so that I would not kill them and his son and spoil this massacre, I thought.

Numb with so much pain, I screamed at him, "You are not worthy of the love of your father, and you do not deserve the ceremony of the opening of the mouth on his burial. If I see you anywhere from now on, I will shoot you with my arrow. And I swear I will kill Menkhep-Re too. He will not be able to save you either because I am still Pharaoh."

He kept silent, holding his mother.

I ran to my horse, jumped upon it, and charged at him with such anger that he ran away scared and locked himself in the house.

"I will kill you! I will kill you! You hear me?" I screamed.

Devastated, I rode fast, sobbing, towards the barge where my guard was waiting.

How could Hapuseneb have done this to me? Was he afraid that I would kill his son? Was my life threatened and that was why he told Sen-Mut to protect me with his life last night?

He thought I was dead, and he preferred to die than to live without me. Oh! My dear friend, I thought.

I galloped fast and sobbing to the edge of Hopi where my guard was waiting. We started to cross the Nile again to continue looking for Sen-Mut's body. I could see the first rays of Ra rising far away. It was the saddest dawn ever. I covered my face with my hands and cried and plead, "Please, Amun-Ra, let it be that Sen-Mut escaped and is alive somewhere far away. Please, Father." Closing my eyes, I begged Amun-Ra for his life.[79]

When we arrived across the Nile, everyone was waiting. We continued looking on the opposite side and still did not found my beloved's body.

Ra was high in the blue sky. It was hot, and I was very tired and could hardly stand. I looked at all of them with sadness, many of whom had lost loved ones, mothers, husbands, bothers, sisters, and wives in this massacre.

Looking at them, I said, "My advice to you all is to leave Thebes and go to another city, as far away as you can, and start a new life there. Don't tell anyone that you came from Thebes because Menkhep-Re will hunt you down and kill you all. He knows that you were my faithful ones, and he would want to kill you all, wherever you go. I have lots of gold. I want each of you to have part of it. I will bring it and share it with you, but you must remember to remove my cartouche. Otherwise, he can trace you through it. Remain here and wait until I return."

---

[79] Writing about the most horrible moments of my life, being betrayed and losing Sen-Mut and Hapuseneb on that same day, brings so much grief and tears to my eyes.

I saw my personal slaves. They had survived the massacre and were walking closer to me.

"Your Majesty, I will remain here with you. I don't have a family anymore. They are all dead," one of them said, and she started to cry. "And you are the only one left who I consider my family."

Then I heard the voice of Tuyii.

"Me too, and I am willing to die for you, Your Majesty," she said.

I started to cry and shook my head.

"No. He can order both of you to be killed. No, I cannot allow that. Save your lives. There has been too much killing, already," I said, crying.

"We are all very sorry that Master Sen-Mut died, and we are so very sorry that we could not find his body," they said.

I started to cry, and I could hear them weeping with me.

"First Prophet of Amun is also dead. They cut his throat, …and it's terribly sad for me," I said.

Some of them wept. I could hear their sobbing, and I wept with them.

All of them came closer and hugged me. Then I looked across the Nile and saw thousands of my army riding away from the palace with the royal banner. Menkhep-Re was riding with the cavalry. He knew very well that now I would hunt him down and kill him, and his mother too.

I looked at my two guards. I knew that it was safe for them to return with me to the palace.

"Both of you come with me to the palace. I believe he is not coming back for a while," I said.

We left the Valley of the Dead, leaving my people behind to wait for my return. We crossed the Nile in the barge with my horse. The water of the Nile was so serene. I could not stop crying.

When I arrived at the palace, all the bodies had been removed from the inner gardens, but blood was still everywhere. I went up the stairs crying, my body trembling with grief with exhaustion. I walked through my golden doors and saw Sen-Mut's golden kilt, golden cape, and golden sandals laying on top of the chairs where the seamstress had left them. The goldsmith had brought the pectoral and wrist cuffs. I stumbled to the chair and knelt, pulling his kilt and cape to me and lay on the floor crying, hugging and kissing his clothing. I fell into a deep sleep and started to dream that I was in a desert, and I could see Sen-Mut far away walking away from me. I called to him and was running after him, but instead of getting closer, we were getting further apart. He could not see me or hear me calling his name. He was walking further and further. He never turned around to see that I was calling him. I was crying terribly and running as fast as I could to reach him. "Sen-Mut! Sen-Mut! Sen-Mut!" I was calling to him.

I woke up sobbing and into this horrible reality that he was assassinated by Menkhep-Re, and I would never see him again. I lay on the floor for a long time. How could I live without him? How? I started to scream and scream, pulling my hair. I want to die, I want to die, I thought. I will kill myself, but first I must kill Menkhep-Re and his mother. He will not get away with it, I swear! He will never be Pharaoh either. Then I remembered the two guards and ran to the golden doors. They were on the floor. I screamed, and they moved. I thought they were dead, but they were just asleep. I sighed in relief.

"Your Majesty," they said, kneeling.

"Rise, my dear friends, and come into my quarters," I said, and they did.

"One of you go to the kitchen and find something to eat and bring it to me," I said, so one did.

He came back and said, “Your Majesty, there is no food made in the kitchen.”

“Go and find me fruits then.”

He returned with many fruits, and they began eating. I tried to eat, but tears were pouring down my face, and I could not swallow. I was drowning in my tears. I took one bite and no more.

When they finished eating the fruits, I said, “Take all the gold that is in all these coffers and put it on the barge to take back across the Nile. But before we go, go back to the kitchen and take whatever you can for the journey to share with everyone. I will cross the Nile with you and distribute this gold.”

They ran to the kitchen and took whatever they could find as I had told them. I sat in the barge in silence, remembering Sen-Mut and the night when we sailed the Nile together, and he showed me the constellations. Everything was so lovely then and peaceful that night, and he bit my lip and drew blood. He cut both of our wrists and brought them together for our blood to flow into each other’s body, so we would never be apart from each other.

I brought my wrist to my heart and whispered, “I am glad, beloved, that we cut our wrists. I am carrying your blood in my veins, and no one can ever keep us apart. I swear to you on my own blood, that I will not rest until I kill them both.”

I was sobbing terribly, and I could not bear the pain.

We arrived at the edge of the Valley of the Dead. They were all waiting for me under the heat of the sun.

I saw despair in their faces.

“Your Majesty.”

They gathered around me and cried, kneeling at my feet.

“Rise,” I said.

I distributed my gold equally to everyone. Then I said goodbye to all of them. Crying, I turned around and started to walk away when my two slaves ran beside me.

“We are going with you, Your Majesty. We will cook for you and serve you as before,” one said.

I stopped and said, “You both could get killed by Menkhep-Re.”

“We know. We have talked it over between us. We will die serving you. Neither of us have families left, and the only place we know as our home is the palace and serving you,” Tuyii said.

Then one of my two guards said, “Your Majesty, we have guarded your doors since you were a child, and we too will remain with you.”

More tears rolled down my face. How wonderful these people were, willing to serve me, knowing that they could be facing death. I remembered, as a child, kicking them on the backs of their legs for not letting me come out of my quarters to talk to Maat. I was nine summers then. I would try to protect them for as long as I could.

We returned to the palace. All was deserted. The two slaves ran to the kitchen, looking for food to cook. I galloped to the House of the Dead in Karnak where the body of Hapuseneb was taken. The undertaker priests knelt when they saw me. The smell of blood made me sick, and I vomited. I was looking for Hapuseneb’s body, and the undertaker took me to where his naked body was getting prepare for embalming. I stopped and looked at his body from a distance, crying. I walked slowly to where he was laying. Many priests were there chanting prayers for the dead over his body because he was one of them.

I got close to his naked body and took off my mourning tunic and tore it in half and covered his body with it. I knelt at the base of his head and placed my hands over it. I cried for a long time over the memories of our friendship and for me not loving him the way he wanted me to love him. And for choosing to die for me, believing that I was dead.

I cried harder for his betrayal and for Sen-Mut's death. I stayed kneeling on the floor for a long, long time and said many prayers of forgiveness, for I knew that after I left this place, I would never see him again. Now, I knew I was all alone. I rose from the floor, came closer to his body, and looked at his face. He looked as if he was merely asleep. I kissed his lips, the kiss he always wanted, and my tears dropped onto his face. I hugged his body, holding his cold hand, and held onto his fingers as I walked away sobbing.[80]

I walked away from the house of the embalmer, crying uncontrollably. It was sunset, and I was stumbling as I walked beside the Nile, carrying the most terrible pain in my heart and soul. I screamed and screamed and screamed for my beloved one. I collapsed in the grass crying beside the Nile as the sunset faded away into darkness. I laid there crying in the darkness, looking at the stars as they started to show their sparkles. Thoth was pouring his silver rays over me and all over the land. I am not going to get up from the ground, I wanted to die.

I saw torches coming in my direction from afar. It was my guards and my slaves looking for me. My guards came close and knelt beside me and lifted me up in his arms and carried me to the palace. I started to cry again, and I could see his tears rolling down his face as he carried me. We

---

[80] So much grief and pain were bottled up inside of me in this life from the past which I had blocked out for thousands of years. They were brought back to me with the last regression by Leo Sprinkle in 2015, memories I did not want to remember. I have relived every single moment of that part of my life as I wrote this chapter of death. Remembering the deaths of the two most beloved men in my life, and losing them both on the same day, has killed me today with grief. I cannot control my tears. I did love Hapu too, but not the way I should have loved him or the way he wanted me to love him. Even if Sen-Mut was not in my life then, maybe I would have suffered the same fate as my mother. Or maybe not. She loved Ineni but was unable to be with him. Sen-Mut saved my life and had the guts to wait for our love at all costs. (10/28/2015)

sobbed together. I could hear my slaves sobbing behind us as he carried me to the palace. He took me to my bath and left me there for my slave to bathe me. I sat there feeling dead but alive, feeling the water being poured over my head and listening to them sob, crying for me and for their dead.

"Shave my head," I said, and they did.

They prepared warm food that I liked, but I was not hungry. They tried to convince me to eat, but I could not swallow. My tears were drowning me. I told them to call the guards to eat with us, and they came and sat on the floor. I told them not to sit on the floor anymore, to sit with me at my table and to eat with us. They said there was no one in the palace and no sign of my daughter Hatshepset. Everyone was gone. I started to cry. Did she know what was coming, I wondered and cried more.

"Sen-Mut was told that I ordered his death," I said. The slaves screamed and brought their hands to their mouths. "I was betrayed by Teshi, D'Jehuty, and who else? Maybe Nehesi?"

I started to cry all over again and got up from my seat and walked to the balcony. It was dark, and I looked for Sen-Mut's silhouette walking beside the Nile. There was only darkness. This silence and the emptiness inside of me was horrible. The land was completely silent, as if she felt my pain.

"The bastard is going to come back. I will be waiting for him. He wants to be Pharaoh, and without me he cannot be. He needs me, or he has to kill me first and usurp the throne to become Pharaoh," I thought.

I stood there for hours until my body could not stand anymore and was completely numb. I was held up by one of my slaves, and we cried together as she helped me to my bed. I lay on Sen-Mut's side of the bed and held his pillow against my body, pressing it against my nose, looking for his smell and crying.

"How can I live without you? Tell me how. I love you, Sen-Mut," I whispered and fell asleep, still crying.

It was high noon when I woke up and realized that he wasn't with me. I stayed in bed crying. I would not eat. I wanted to be close to him, and I got up from the bed, covered myself with a mourning tunic, and walked out of my quarters. I saw the slaves and the guards washing the blood from the stairs and from the ground. Flies were everywhere. I looked at my servants and thought, "This is the only home they have known."

I walked by them and along the same path Sen-Mut used to walk beside the Nile at sunset, and I screamed in pain. I collapsed crying in the grass again, and I lay there looking at the sun fading away and how Mother Nut began covering the land with darkness. The stars were all over the black sky. Thoth was looking down at me. I could not bear Sen-Mut's death. And after him, what? I was not eating, and I was getting weak.

I saw the guards looking for me. One carried me to the palace and to my quarters again. I could tell by the look on their faces that they wanted to tell me something but could not.

"Do you have something to tell me?" I asked one of them.

"Your Majesty, I don't want to bring more grief and sorrow to you." He said.

"Speak, please."

He lowered his eyes to the ground, and almost holding back his words he said, "This morning I walked the grounds searching for places that needed to be washed of blood. I walked to the stables."

He got quiet.

"Speak."

"I found Master Sen-Mut's horse dead. They have killed it too."

I got up from where I was sitting and walked to the balcony. More tears, another sorrow. My father had given me that horse, and I had given it to him as a gift. The best horse in the kingdom, and the fastest. I cried standing there looking at the current of the Nile.

"Tell the embalmer to embalm Sen-Mut's horse with the finest linen before he takes any other body to be embalmed. And after they finish, I want you two to go to the Valley of the Dead, where Sen-Mut was building his tomb close to mine and bury the horse there.

"Yes, Your Majesty."

I heard their sandals as they went away. My tears stopped. I did not have any more tears to shed. I was empty inside.

****

A month of trying to cope with Sen-Mut's death had passed when my guard came running to me.

"Your Majesty, Menkhep-Re is returning to the palace," he said.

"Bring me my bow and arrows right away. Run. And let him come to my quarters without stopping him. I will be waiting."

After my guard returned, I stood there aiming an arrow at the door, my body shaking badly from the lack of food. When Menkhep-Re walked in, I shot at him fast, but I missed. He was startled and ran towards me, and we fought over my bow and arrow. He snatched them with force from my hands and threw them over the balcony.

"Hatshepsut, I didn't come to fight with you," he said. "I am willing to spare the lives of your two guards, since they have been with you since you were a child, and the lives of your two slaves."

I was looking at my slaves and searching for my dagger. I saw it, but it was too far away from me. He noticed what I was looking at and walked over to it and picked it up.

"I will take this with me. You are very dangerous to me and to everyone right now. I came here to make peace with you," he said.

"Peace? How can there ever be peace between you and me? Don't you have remorse for what you did?" I yelled at him.

He became silent. He looked like he had not slept for a month. Then he shook his head.

"Remorse? No, I did what I had to do to protect what was rightfully mine. How could you want to make him Pharaoh when it is my birth right?" he snapped at me.

"No, you are not my brother's son. Ask your mother the prostitute who your father is. I believe that Second Prophet of Amun Puyem-Re is your father, but I cannot prove it. Well, let's see. Even if you were my brother's son, you are not of full royal blood. You need to become full royal blood to wear the Double Crown of Upper and Lower Egypt. A Queen must transfer to you the other half of the royal blood, and Hatshepset can't do it. I am Pharaoh, and I sure am not going to step down and become a Queen to make you Pharaoh. That is for killing Sen-Mut, Senemen, and Teshi. And Hapuseneb," I said.

"Hapuseneb chose to die himself. I myself was shocked when my soldier told me that he preferred to die with you. I was not going to kill him. I just wanted to make him believe that you were dead and agree to continue being First Prophet of Amun for me because he carried too much power over the land. He had all the priests of the temple at his side. I was going to tell him later that you were alive, but things did not turn out the way I expected," he said.

I was staring at him with anger.

"I can swear to you that you will never be Pharaoh! You are going to have to kill me first and usurp the throne. Now I remember who the naked woman was in D'Jehuty quarters that day I walked in. It was your mother. Selling her body for him to betray me. I wonder what else you promised him to help you in this massacre. Now, tell me where Sen-Mut's body is!"

"Oh, do you mean the pieces of his body after the horses tore him apart?"

A sharp pain stabbed my heart. I could not breathe.

"They were scattered all over the land. By now the jackals must have had a feast with his body," he said with such coldness.

I screamed and charged upon his face with force and punched him hard with my fist. I kicked him, but he did not try to defend himself. He stood there as if he wanted to be punished, then he took one step back, turned around, and left.

He had wounded me so terribly. I ran to my bed and threw myself down on the mattress screaming, kicking, and sobbing. I screamed until I could not breathe anymore. It hurt so bad, thinking of the horrible death and pain my beloved had felt as he was being torn apart by the horses. I screamed and screamed, covering my face and sobbing terribly. "Sen-Mut, beloved, forgive me!" I screamed, remembering the many times Hapuseneb warned me about Menkhep-Re and that this day would come. "Please forgive me for not reading those decrees!"

Sobbing, I held my face, swollen from so many tears.[81]

I told myself that I was the only one to blame for all of this. I should have killed them both after my brother Thutmoses II died, but how could I have when Sen-Mut's life was threatened by my brother? I only wanted my heart's desire, for Sen-Mut to be Pharaoh. I am going to kill

---

[81] And my face is swollen from crying right now. This has been the hardest chapter for me to write. (11/13/15)

Menkhep-Re, I thought. I screamed loudly in a rage until I couldn't scream anymore.

"Tuyii," I called to my slave, making the effort to talk. I was drowning in my tears. "Go and bring me my bow and arrows. Menkhep-Re threw them over the balcony. Run. And then go to the kitchen and bring me several of the smallest and sharpest knives you can find. Don't let anyone see that you are taking them. But first bring me my bow and arrows. Run."

She came back without my bow and arrows.

"Where are they?" I asked her.

"Your Majesty, when I got there, they were gone. But I ran to the kitchen to get the knives and noticed that they had brought many new slaves, and they are cleaning everywhere. I took these two knives because I know they are the sharpest ones, for I have used them before," she said.

"Now, I must wait until he comes back. I will eat and become very healthy and strong again. I am too weak now, and that's why I missed him with my arrow. I have never missed before. I was so angry at him for what he did to my beloved. I will kill him, I swear," I thought.

A week had passed since his return. Hatshepset had not bothered to visit me. One morning, I was sitting on the edge of the bed when the golden doors opened. It was her walking into my quarters holding my grandson Amenemhat's hand. He was beautiful, and he ran to me and hugged me tightly. I held him in my arms and kissed him. He was always so sweet with me. Every time he saw me, his face lit up.

"Good morning, Mother. I have not come to see you before because of your grief. I thought it was better for me to wait until your grief and anger subsided some. You probably think that we knew of the coup, but we did not know. I can assure you of that. I wanted to tell you that neither Isis nor I knew of what was going to happen that day. We were awakened in the middle of the night when it was still dark, and Isis and I and my children were taken away from the palace in silence," she said.

"How could she not have known? When all she has been doing is conniving against Sen-Mut and me all these years and putting you against me since you were a little girl. All of that was your father's fault, keeping you away from me and having her raise you. And the worst was him believing her. Do you think she did not hate Sen-Mut? Of course, she did. She wanted her son to be Pharaoh, knowing that he is not your father son," I said.

"Mother, I can only tell you that I am so very sorry for what has happened. I really liked Sen-Mut and Hapuseneb, and I feel very bad for his death as well. Mother, I came to see if you were feeling better after all this grief, and I know it must be very hard losing Sen-Mut and Hapuseneb on the same day. I know how much you have loved Sen-Mut. We all believed that Menkhep-Re was accepting your marriage to Sen-Mut and that he had accepted not being Pharaoh. It was strange to me. And I can tell you that now Isis is scared to death that you are coming after her. Are you planning to kill her? Please don't do it, Mother. She has always been good to me since I was a little girl."

"But she is a cobra against me. And yes, I am coming after them both. And Rekhemire. And Puyem-Re. And D'Jehuty. I want them all dead," I said in anger.

"Mother, please don't. I don't want to lose you. You are the only family I have left."

"Don't you think he had planned this all along? How long do you think I would be alive if I marry him? Tell me," I said.

Suddenly, an intense cramp took over my womb. The pain was terrible, and I held my womb with both hands.

"Mother, what's wrong?" she asked nervously.

"I don't know. The pain is terrible. Tuyii! Tuyii!" I yelled. I kept screaming in pain, and she came running.

"Tuyii, run for the physician. I don't want Puyem-Re in my quarters. Run," I said, twisting in agony.

"Mother, I will be back right away. Hold on. Let me take my child to the wet nurse," Hatshepset said and left.

I was lying in bed twisting in pain and holding my belly. I felt as if something exploded inside of me, and I screamed in pain. Blood began gushing out of my vagina. I was startled. Was I pregnant? Oh, no. I was pregnant with Sen-Mut's child. Our child. I started to cry uncontrollably and laid holding my belly.

"Beloved, you were going to be a father again," I whispered as tears poured down my face. This child would have been my happiness now that you are gone. Now what? After you, what? I screamed and sobbed terribly, lying there in great pain. The physician came running to me.

"Your Majesty," he said, holding my hand.

"Everything is over. I believe that I was pregnant without knowing it," I said. Tears were rolling down my face.

"I must examine you, Your Majesty," he said.

After he finished, and I was completely cleaned by Tuyii, he sat beside me and looked into my eyes with kindness.

"Yes, you were pregnant Your Majesty, and I am so very sorry for all that has happened to you. And for losing Sen-Mut. All this stress has taken a toll on you and your pregnancy. I want you to know that we all loved the Steward of Amun, Sen-Mut. He was one of us. But for now, you must rest because you have lost a lot of blood, and I notice that you have lost a lot of weight as well. Aren't you eating?" he asked.

"No, I have not been eating since his death."

"But you must, Your Majesty. You are going to continue ruling this land. We, all the priests in the Temple of Amun Ra, promise you that. And we are still supporting you as our Pharaoh, like our dear Khety, Hapuseneb, and Sen-Mut did. I can assure you that all the priests in the Temple of Amun are outraged by this massacre, and believe me, Menkhep-Re went the wrong way by doing this. He is still young and could have waited to be crowned, as all Pharaohs before him have done. I want you to know that a deed as terrible as this one has condemned him to eternal damnation. He killed two servants of God, Sen-Mut, Steward of Amun and Hapuseneb, First Prophet of Amun Ra, and that is the worst, terrible sin there is. He will never have peace in his soul for killing two men of God who never threatened his life. Now he is in the Book of the Damned. He will not have an afterlife. Hapuseneb, Sen-Mut, and you will have an afterlife. Menkhep-Re can do all the offerings he wants to the gods, but they will not hear his pleas. And when the time comes, he cannot erase from the eyes of the gods what he has done," the physician said.

"But Sen-Mut didn't believe in the afterlife and that worries me," I said.

"Now that he has gone to the underworld, he has found out that there is an afterlife and that it is all true," he said, patting my hand.

"We all knew that you could have done away with him and his mother when your brother, His Majesty Thutmoses II, went to the heavens, but you did not. And we admired you for that. After hearing all the conniving words Isis said to make her son Pharaoh, that puzzled us. Why didn't you do away with them? We also knew all that was going on in the palace, but not of the coup," the physician said.

"I did not do away with them because there was a threat to Sen-Mut's life made by Thutmoses II to me before he died. He said he had hired a silent assassin to kill him if I killed them. Hapuseneb was aware of that threat, and he was also aware of this terrible massacre that was coming. He knew of it and did not say anything to me," I said crying.

He was surprised.

"What? He knew of the massacre? That is terrible, Your Majesty!" he said.

"Yes, he did. The night before, he came looking for Sen-Mut, and they walked beside the Nile. Hapuseneb was very drunk and asked Sen-Mut to protect me well with his own life. Sen-Mut was completely puzzle by Hapuseneb's plea. Sen-Mut told me that he had the feeling that he was saying goodbye. I became very worried for Hapuseneb life. I thought maybe he wanted to commit suicide because I was marrying Sen-Mut and making him Pharaoh. I had always known of his love for me, and I loved him too. But life took me down a different path, and I fell deeply in love with Sen-Mut."

Tears rolled down my face.

"We all deeply feel your grief, Your Majesty. We have been making offerings and prayers for Sen-Mut's Ka to be received by the gods and for him not to suffer the second death, since there is not a body to be buried," he said.

Sobbing, I said, "Menkhep-Re told me that he tore his body apart with horses."

He brought both hands to his mouth in shock.

"How cruel he was, and what a terrible death Sen-Mut suffered. Now I know how terrible you must feel, Your Majesty. I am deeply sorry to hear all of this. He will probably kill all of us in the same way when he comes and asks for our support for the throne and we tell him that you remain our Pharaoh. We would support him only if you changed your mind and wanted him to be our ruler, but he must be a full royal blood first anyway. Your Majesty, we want you to know that we believe that Puyem-Re, Second Prophet of Amun, is his father," he said.

"There is a rumor between us priests that he is. Hapuseneb came to me and told me once of his doubts. I also heard it from your own mouth in the audience hall that day when you were yelling at Isis, the day that Sen-Mut departed on his quest to find the land of the Punt," he said.

"Did Hapuseneb ever tell you why he married his young daughter to Puyem-Re?" I asked.

"I knew Hapuseneb very well. He kept his eyes open and spies on everyone to protect you. I believe he did it for that reason and to find out what was going on with Puyem-Re and Menkhep-Re," he said.

"I want you to tell the other priests that I don't want Hapuseneb's oldest son to do the ceremony of the opening of the mouth at Hapuseneb's burial. He was one of the conspirators in the coup against us and caused his father's death," I said.

"He would not, Your Majesty. He feels very guilty for his father's death and for the deaths of so many people. He told us," he said. "Are you feeling a little better, Your Majesty?"

"Yes, the cramps have almost gone away," I said.

"You must drink an herbal potion that I am sending for to be made by your slave. It will clean your insides, and you will feel much better in a few weeks. In the meantime, you must eat to get your strength back. Tomorrow morning, I will come back to check up on you again," the physician said.

"I will," I said. "Tuyii, follow the doctor and do as he ask."

"Yes, Your Majesty," she said and followed the physician.

The doors of my bedroom opened again. It was Hatshepset.

"Mother, what did he say, and what is wrong with you? Why were you in such pain?" she asked.

I became silent and held back my tears. I wanted to be alone with my loss.

“I was pregnant with Sen-Mut’s child, and I had a miscarriage. It would have been the most precious gift he left me,” I said, as the tears poured down my face.

“Oh, Mother, I am so sorry to hear that.”

She came close and sat down beside me. She hugged me and held my hand.

“I don’t want any of them to know that I was pregnant. Promise!” I said.

“Mother, I promise. I will not tell anyone of your miscarriage. I promise.”

****

I continued getting better and got my strength back for only one reason, to kill Menkhep-Re and his mother. He would not get away with the killing of my beloved Sen-Mut.

I hated him so much.

****

A year had gone by since the death of my beloved, and I walked along the edge of the Nile, dead inside. Every night, I kissed his pillow and cried. I felt so guilty for not reading those decrees. I miss you so much, my love. I thought.

I stood on the balcony as I did every night, the silence of the land my only companion, and I started to plan the death of Menkhep-Re in my head. I would wait for the right moment to kill him.

****

Another year had passed since Sen-Mut's death, and Menkhep-Re had not returned to my quarters. I knew he would come here soon, though. I heard from a priest that he was having problems with the armed forces. He didn't have any power to command my army, and D'Jehuty was the one controlling them. And he needed me to become Pharaoh.

I stood on the balcony, lost in my thoughts. I had not seen Isis anywhere either. She knew that I was going to kill her. I didn't need an arrow or a dagger to kill her. I would do it with my own hands. Both had earned my deepest hatred. I turned around and walked into my living room. I was startled to see Menkhep-Re standing in front of me. He looked more mature and not too happy.

"What are you doing in my quarters?" I snapped at him.

"I came to talk to you. I have waited for almost two years and left you with your grief. I can see that you look well since the last time I saw you," he said.

"What do you want?" I asked.

"I came to offer you my peace. I want peace between you and me. We cannot continue in this way. You are like my mother. You were always kind to me, and I miss talking to you and going to the practice field together, racing the chariots, and having target practice. I want it to be the way it used to be. There is no more music or happiness anywhere in the palace. I want us to marry and for you be my Queen, as is our custom. You will control everything in the palace as before," he said.

I had so much anger inside of me, I did not want to hear his voice.

I snapped at him again.

"No. What you want is to be Pharaoh. OK! I will marry you," I said.

He was startled, and his eyes opened wide.

"You will?" he shouted with happiness.

"Yes. There is no point not letting you rule. I think you are ready, and if I have control of my kingdom, why not? Have the priests of Amun-Ra and Puyem-Re pay me a visit," I said.

Joy spread across his face.

"I will right away. I love you, Hatshepsut!" He said with a big smile. He bowed his head and said, "Your Majesty," then left in a hurry.

His words sounded dead in my ears. I didn't care what he said. I would have no pity on him, as he had none when he tore Sen-Mut's body apart.

As soon he left, I clapped my hands, and Tuyii came running to me with the other slave.

"Tell the guards to come into my quarters right away. Tuyii, you stay here," I said.

The other slave ran and brought the two guards in.

"Once I asked all of you if you were willing to die for me and with me. Are you willing to die with me and for me now?"

They became quiet and looked at each other.

“I am planning to marry Menkhep-Re, and on that day, I will kill him. I want vengeance for my beloved one and for Hapuseneb and for all your loved ones who were killed that terrible day,” I said.

“We will, Your Majesty. We will die for you,” the two guards said.

Tuyii and the other slave agreed.

“I believe that if I don’t fail killing him, I will rule my land freely again. But if I do fail, they will kill you all. And me too. We must prepare for that day,” I said.

“Yes, Your Majesty.”

“Leave now, before Puyem-Re and the other priests walk through those doors to confirm what I have told him. Go and take your posts before they get here,” I told them.

The two guards walked away, and my two slaves were silent.

I looked at Tuyii and said, “If you two feels that you cannot go through with this, I understand. I would like for you to think it over and let me know very soon. You are the only ones I can trust. I will set you free on that day, but you two must go far away from here.”

“I will stay, Your Majesty. They killed my whole family,” Tuyii said.

“And I will stay too,” the other slave said.[82]

“You know what will happen if I fail. They will kill us all.”

“Then, Your Majesty, we will die with you.”

---

[82] Unfortunately, I cannot remember the other slave name nor the physician.

We were interrupted by a knock on the golden doors.

"They are here. Let them in," I shouted.

Puyem-Re was now First Prophet of Amun-Ra after Hapuseneb's death, the title given to him by the other priests. He walked in with fifteen priests from the Temple of Amun-Ra. I recognized them all, including the physician who came to attend to me after my miscarriage two years ago. All of them bowed their heads to me. Puyem-Re was giddy.

"Your Majesty, we came to confirm what Prince Menkhep-Re has told us, that you agreed to a marriage and to transfer the title of Pharaoh to him," Puyem-Re said.

I got up from my chair and looked at each of them. My physician furrowed his brow.

"Yes, I agreed to marry him and transfer the crown. Prepare the ceremony as soon as possible," I said.

"Your Majesty, are you sure you want to do this?" the physician asked.

I smiled at him.

Yes, I want to do this," I said.

"Now, it is confirmed. We will have a new Pharaoh," Puyem-Re said.

"Thank you, Your Majesty. We just wanted to confirm that this is your decision. We must start preparations for the coronation. It will bc held in one month. If you agree, Your Majesty," Puyem-Re said.

"Tell him only under one condition. My guards and my slaves must be with me during the coronation," I said.

"Your Majesty, I believe Menkhep-Re will be so happy that he won't mind your request," he said.

“Then I agree,” I said.

I saw them walk away, some with somber faces, others in silence. I walked to the balcony and looked at the stars.

“Soon, my love, I will avenge your death, and I will be coming to you,” I said.

****

There was commotion all over the palace with preparations for the coronation. I did not leave my quarters.

“Tuyii, where are the two sharp knives you saved for me?”

“I have them here, Your Majesty,” she said.

I saw her walk to her couch and cut the seams of the small mattress. She took them out and brought them to me.

“Call in the two guards right now,” I said, and she did.

They came back with her and knelt at my feet.

“I want you to cut these two knives and make them a lot shorter to fit in the palm of my hand, and then sharpen both sides. I want them very, very sharp. With these knives, I will kill Menkhep-Re on that day,” I said.

“We will do so, Your Majesty,” a guard said.

They walked away after bowing to me.

The coronation was getting close, and I was anxious.

"Tuyii, the day of the coronation is approaching, and some of the priests will come to my quarters. The priestesses will come to dress me. On that day, you will get one of the small daggers, and she will get the other one. As we leave to the hall of audience, you will hand me yours. She will keep the other one in case I drop yours," I said.

"I will do it, Your Majesty."

It was a few days before the New Year, and the coronation was about to take place. I was at peace. It had been two years since Menkhep-Re had killed my beloved Sen-Mut and Hapuseneb. Everything would be over soon.

The priestesses came and shaved my body, as was the custom, and bathed and dressed me. They were the same priestesses at my coronation as Pharaoh.

I would wear a new Queen's dress today, and I would not wear any perfume, I thought. I heard the voices of the priests waiting for me on the other side of my bedroom doors. How strange everything felt without my loved one and Hapuseneb. The priestesses finished dressing me, and I saw somber looks on their faces. They did not smile at me or speak to me at all, not even to wish me well. Did they know what I was about to do? They probably did and had seen it with the Oracle. I wondered if they had told Puyem-Re of my intentions. Finally, I was dressed, and the double doors were opened. I walked in front of Puyem-Re and looked at him with the deepest hatred and desire to kill him too.[83]

I forced myself to kneel, and he placed the fake Double Crown of Egypt on my head. The memories of my coronation as Pharaoh came rushing back to me, and I remembered my beloved Sen-Mut and Hapuseneb

---

[83] At this moment, as I am writing this paragraph, I still have such an anger inside of me, wanting so badly to kill the S.O.B., and eager to kill Menkhep-Re.

when they saw me and looked at me in awe. I came back into the reality that they were no longer here with me. My eyes filled with tears.

The procession started, and every priest and priestess walked in front of me. Tuyii and the guards followed me. When it was time, Tuyii quickly handed me the very sharp, small dagger. He will be dead today, I thought.

Finally, I arrived at the audience hall. The golden chair was waiting in silence at the end of the path. The sight of it brought me such sadness. I had not come back here since that terrible day. I heard that Menkhep-Re had not dared to sit on it, and he never would, I thought.

I stood in front of my throne and turned around. I saw Isis with a smile on her face, as if she was daring me. She looked as though she believed that she had won. Beside her was my daughter Hatshepset and my grandson Amenemhat. I looked at all the priests of the Temple of Amun-Ra who were gathered. None of them had satisfied looks on their faces, only Puyem-Re and Isis. I saw Menkhep-Re walking closer, taking the steps up to reach me.

I waited and thought, "Come closer, much closer." And he did. My guards were standing beside my throne. Tuyii and the other slave were sitting on the floor at the foot of my golden chair. Finally, Menkhep-Re was close to me with a big smile on his face, and I forced a smile in return. I jumped upon him, swinging the sharpened dagger and aiming at his chest.

"Die, bastard!" I screamed. "Die!"

We fought for my dagger, standing at the edge of the steps. His soldiers jumped and pulled me back by my waist, and I kicked Menkhep-Re in the chest. He fell backwards down the steps. My guards killed the soldier that was holding me, and many of Menkhep-Re's soldiers came and engaged in the fight. I jumped on the back of one and killed him, cutting his throat, and then jumped behind another one who had cornered my guard and killed him the same way. I was full of rage and could hear people screaming.

"Don't touch her! Don't touch her!" Menkhep-Re screamed.

"Don't kill my mother!" I heard my daughter Hatshepset screaming.

I saw many of his soldiers falling dead. Others came running and pulled me away from the back of another one, taking the small dagger from my hand and slamming me against the floor. There were so many that they cornered my loyal guards.

"You are not my brother's son, and you are never going to be Pharaoh! You hear me? Never!" I screamed at Menkhep-Re.

I got up from the floor and again jumped on the back of one of his soldiers. I was pulled back with force by D'Jehuty. Menkhep-Re was standing at the bottom of the steps, completely shocked. I was furious and turned around and saw Tuyii dead on the floor, as well as my other slave. My two guards, they were my bravest, were still fighting fiercely. I tried to force myself free from D'Jehuty's grip, then I saw my dearest ones fall to their deaths beside my throne, taking with them many of his soldiers.

I heard D'Jehuty yell, "Take her to her quarters."

A few soldiers came, but they didn't seem to know if they should touch me or not. Then one of them grabbed me by my wrist. I kept trying to pull away from him and get back to Menkhep-Re.

"You are going to die! I swear I will kill you!" I screamed at him.

They did not let go of my wrists until we were on the way to the palace. As I was walking, I cried for my slaves and for my guards. They were my dearest friends. Then I cried harder because my attempt to kill

Menkhep-Re had failed, and I was not able to avenge my beloved's life. Now I was completely alone. I would miss them greatly.[84]

After my attempt on his life, Menkhep-Re ordered a smaller room to be built right beside my rose garden and moved me from my quarters into there. My daughter Hatshepset moved into my quarters. I hardly saw her or my grandson anymore since that day. I had two new slaves, though they were prohibited from speaking to me. They bathed me in silence and brought my food in silence. They brought new slaves to serve me every month, so I could not to become friendly with any of them.

At night, I walked beside the Nile under the sky full of bright stars to the area were Sen-Mut used to stand and look up at me. His memory made me cry, and I looked at the stars and told them, "I wish he knew just how much I missed him and still loved him as if he were here."

I continued having bad dreams about Sen-Mut. In my dreams, I could see him walking away from me. I could not see his face. I would run after him, calling as loudly as I could, but he never heard me. I became more depressed every day because he died believing that I ordered his death. I believed that he was angry at me, and that is why he didn't turn around to look at me.

"Beloved of mine, I am innocent. We were betrayed, and I wish I had died with you on that day. Please, if you can hear me, believe me," I said looking at the stars as tears rolled down my face.

Later, I started to plot another attempt on Menkhep-Re's life, but how? I didn't have access to a dagger or anyone that I could trust. I will behave and wait, I thought. He needs me to be Pharaoh.

---

[84] I've never forgotten how brave and how hard my guards fought for me on that day. I don't know who you are in this life, but I want to thank you for giving your lives for me. I missed my guards very much, as well as Tuyii and my other slave. I wish I could remember her name. (2/8/2018)

****

Another summer and winter passed, and Menkhep-Re could still not sit on the throne as he wanted. I believed that the priests were telling him that they already had a Pharaoh. He knew that he would never be Pharaoh as long I was alive, but he also knew that he needed me.

CHAPTER 43

AKHELA

It had been three summers since my beloved's death, and I still hadn't been able to put my hands on another sharp dagger. I had not seen my daughter Hatshepset nor my grandson since my attempt on Menkhep-Re's life.

I walked at night beside the Nile and looked at the stars, my only companions.

One morning, while sitting on my bed, a child walked up and stood there looking at me. She was very small and about ten summers, I guessed.

"Who are you?" I asked her.

"I am Akhela, your new slave, Your Majesty."

"So, you speak, and they let you talk to me?" I said.

"No one said that I cannot speak to you, Your Majesty,"

"What has happened to the other slaves?"

"I don't know, but I was sent by Princess Hatshepset to be your companion and to bathe you and help you in everything," she said.

I smiled. So, she remembers me after all, I thought.

"So, Akhela, where is that name from?" I asked.

"I don't know. I was brought up here from the green sea, and it was a long journey to get here."

I smiled.

"Once, when I was a little girl, I had a dear friend that we brought from the green sea too. Her name was T'Queta," I became quiet and my eyes became full of tears.

I noticed that I could hear myself talk. It was the first time in a long, long time that I was talking to someone, and it sounded strange hearing my own voice again.

"Do you know who I am?" I asked her.

"No, Your Majesty. I was told to refer to you as 'Your Majesty,' so I believe you are someone very important. What I don't understand is if you are someone very important, what are you doing in a terrible room like this?"

"Well, I hope you remain here for a while, and one day I will tell you all," I said and smiled at her.

Akhela has served me well. Now they let her sleep in my room, on a mat on the floor.

****

It had been two summers since she came here for the first time. I became fond of her and taught her how to read and write, but she could not tell anyone. Soon she would be thirteen summers, and she was not feeling well today. Her blood came for the first time. I told her that I would bathe myself today and to come and lay in my bed. She was very surprised.

A few days passed, and her blood was gone. She was feeling better and back to her normal self, and back to sleeping on her mat on the dirt floor. She didn't tell me anything of what was going on in the palace, but I had a good idea that Menkhep-Re and Puyem-Re were getting the other priests to agree to make him Pharaoh over me. And this couldn't happen as long I was alive.

After my dinner, Akhela bathed me, and she had learned to do it well. Not like the first time she tried with her little hands. I saw her light the oil candle and walk to her mat on the dirt floor.

"Your Majesty, once you told me that one day you would tell me who you are. It's been two summers since then. Can you tell me now?"

"Come to my bed," I said.

I patted the mattress twice, and she came and lay beside me with a sweet smile and brushing her long black hair to her back.

"I am Pharaoh Hatshepsut," I said.

She became surprised and brought her hands to her mouth. She got down from my bed and prostrated herself on the floor and bowed her head to the floor.

"Your Majesty, I did not know. Forgive me." she said.

I smiled.

"Rise, Akhela. Come back to bed," I said.

She climbed back into the bed.

"I thought you were in the palace."

"No, Menkhep-Re ordered this room to be made because I tried to kill him."

"Why did you try to kill Prince Menkhep-Re?" she asked.

"Let me start from the beginning so that you may understand," I said.

Over several months, I told her of my beloved, and how we were betrayed, and how he was killed by Menkhep-Re. We cried together.

Then she said, "I would have tried to kill him too, Your Majesty."

Every afternoon, she and I walked beside the Nile, and I related more of my life story. We laughed when I told her of the Sobek. It had been such a long time since I laughed. I looked across the Nile, and my eyes became full of tears. It had been such a long time since then. We walked back, and I was bathed. I lay in silence thinking of Sen-Mut and how I used to wait for him to come back from the Valley of the Dead, and I could hear his voice calling me, "My love!" I used to run to him, and he would hold me in his arms and kiss me with passion. I remember his hair needed to be cut because of the weight of the sand that had blown into it.[85]

I was teaching Akhela how to swim. She needed a few more lessons. Soon Akhet would start, and the Nile would swell with rain. One

---

[85] I sit here on 12/28/2016, writing these memories, and they bring sadness and tears to my eyes. Those were very hard times for me, losing him in that terrible way. I still miss him so much and the way he loved me then, and hearing his voice telling me, "I love you, Maatke-Re." And I would say, "I love you too, Sen-Mut, Ptah of Egypt." I am crying right now because those days of happiness will never come back again. It would have been a consolation for me if I had fallen in love with someone else in this life, but my love for him has not let me.

afternoon, I was sitting beside the Nile, and as I started to walk to my room, I looked up at my balcony. Menkhep-Re was looking at me. I turned my face away from him. It must be eating him alive, unable to be Pharaoh. I continued walking, when suddenly I heard a scream and turned around. It was Akhela, and she was drowning. The current was dragging her north. I ran as fast as I could beside the Nile and caught up with her and jumped in the water, but the current dragged her and me. I could not grab her. I swam hard and fast and finally grabbed her by her hair and held on as hard as I could. The current was dragging me with her further north. I swam hard with one arm, and with the other arm I pulled her close to me, holding her tightly, and finally I came close to the shore and grabbed a papyrus plant. I pulled both of us out.

I was trembling badly and was so very tired. I could barely catch my breath. I had thought for a moment that I was going to have to let her go. I was drowning with her. Finally, I had to pull strength that I did not know I had to reach the shore. I could hear her coughing and throwing up the water she had swallowed. I hit her back several times and saw her spit out so much water. I held her in my arms and she cried and cried.

"Don't cry my dear. It's over. You are going to be fine, and no more lessons for you now until the next Shomu. If I am alive," I said and smiled at her.

She frowned.

"Let's go to be bathed. You will go first," I told her.

We had to walk a long distance down the Nile because the current had dragged us far, past Hapuseneb's house.

She finished bathing herself, and later, she bathed me.

"Your Majesty, I owe you my life, and I am most grateful to you. And when I tell my parents that you have saved my life, they are going to be most grateful to you as well," she said.

I looked at her.

"Your parents? You never told me that your parents are here too," I said.

She became silent, and in a low voice, she said, "Yes, Your Majesty. They brought them here too. My mother works in the kitchen. I told her in secret that you are Pharaoh Hatshepsut, and that you are lovely, kind, and loving to me. That is why she makes those delicious plates of food that you like. I was warned that you should never know that my mother works in the kitchen."

I became silent and thought she could get me a sharp knife.

"Tell your mother that her food is most delicious," I said.

The following morning, Akhela came back with a tray in her hands, bringing me my breakfast.

"Your Majesty, I told my mother that you saved me from drowning yesterday, and my father and the other slaves heard it too. They were happy that you saved my life," she said.

I smiled at her.

"I've learned to love you, child," I said.

****

It was late one night, and I was falling asleep when she said, "Your Majesty, my parents said to tell you that they are in debt to you for saving my life, and they thank you."

"It's nice to know that. I've come to love you over the years. If I had not saved your life, I would be here all alone with no one to speak to. Good night, Akhela."

"Good night, Your Majesty."

I was having my breakfast the following morning, and it was delicious. Her mother made for me my favorite hot drink, and the bread was warm. The eggs, the goat cheese, and the fruits were all good. Then I was startled by the voices of several priests who had come to visit me. They were clearly disturbed when they saw where Menkhep-Re had put me, and there was no place for them to sit down. I invited them to walk with me beside the Nile.

"Your Majesty, we did not know that he has done this to you. When did he put you there?" one of the priests asked.

"I have been there since I tried to kill him," I said.

"Over two summers ago then?"

"Yes," I said.

"I am so sorry that you failed to kill him," one of them said.

"The gods will not punish you for it. He has done a terrible deed to you, to Sen-Mut, and to Hapuseneb. We came to tell you that Puyem-Re and Menkhep-Re keep coming to the temple for our support to remove you from your crown, and we keep telling them that it is not possible, that you are Pharaoh for life. We are here to talk to you because we are afraid that he will try to kill you. He is going crazy and desperate to call himself ruler of the two lands. He knows that as long you are alive, he will never be Pharaoh because you have already sworn to him that he never will be. He knows that he needs you, and he needs that marriage to be a full royal blood," another priest said.

"He doesn't even have the other half of the royal blood either," I said.

"We believe you, Your Majesty, and we have questioned Puyem-Re about this. He swears that Menkhep-Re is not his son, and that he is married to Hapuseneb's daughter," they said.

"Give Puyem-Re this message: 'I, Pharaoh of the two lands, in two months will give him my decision if I change my mind to marry Menkhep-Re.' But first, I must get my quarters back," I said.

"We will give him your message, Your Majesty."

I saw them leave.

Later that afternoon, I was taken back to my quarters in the palace, and I walked up the stairs and felt the silence around me. I became full of sadness. I miss you so much, Sen-Mut, and it will not be too long, beloved, until I avenge your death, I thought.

The new guards opened the golden doors, and I walked in.

"Your Majesty, this is a beautiful room," Akhela said as she walked into my quarters.

Menkhep-Re was standing in the middle of my living room. He had grown older and more mature. He was looking at me very seriously.

"Hatshepsut, I come to make peace with you again. I am willing to forget that you tried to kill me. See, I have given you back your quarters. Now, you can see your grandchildren, and we can be a family again. After the marriage, we can have children of full royal blood," he said.

I was looking at him seriously. How wrong he was, I just wanted him dead.

"I had rethought the marriage arrangement when I sent you the message with the priest this morning. And if I agree with the marriage and crown you Pharaoh, of course we could have children with real royal blood," I said.

I saw his face light up with happiness.

"I want my bow and arrows back too," I told him.

He was puzzled.

"Hatshepsut, I don't think that will be possible. You're not going to need them, and you are not going to the practice field anymore. My mother is terrified of you, and she believes that you will try to kill me again. I cannot let you have any weapons. But for now, be happy. You are back to your quarters, and I am sending a few slaves to take care of you too."

"Can I keep Akhela? She has been with me since she was a small child," I said.

"Yes, you can keep her. Finally, there's going to be peace between you and me. Hatshepset will feel more at ease, and she can come and visit with you," he said.

"After our marriage, what place will she have in your life?" I asked.

"She will be my secondary wife, like in the past when Pharaohs would marry their sisters and take them for secondary wives and have children with them, as my grandfather did with my grandmother Mutnofret," he said.

I became silent and thought of my poor daughter. I wanted her to be Pharaoh, not him.

"What quarters is she staying in now? And in what quarters are you?" I asked.

"She is in the quarters next to yours, the one that was your sister's before, and I have not moved to my father's quarters yet. Not until I am Pharaoh. I hope that will be soon. Hatshepset was happy that you were coming back to your quarters. She was in here before, but when I told her that she must move to the one next door, she was happy to do it because you were coming back, and she could speak to you. She will come to visit with you soon, I promise. I will see you in the banquet hall tonight?" he asked.

"We will see," I said.

"Then I must go for now, Your Majesty," he said.

He bowed his head and turned around and walked off.

I walk to my bedroom, and everything was there including the fake double crown of Egypt.

Later, Hatshepset walked through the golden doors, very happy, and hugged me tightly.

"Mother, I am very happy that you are back here. I have been very sad these few years I was not allowed to come see you or visit with you. Now I believe everything is going to be fine, and we will be happy again," she said.

I smiled at my beloved daughter. She looked just like me when I was her age, but I was determined that he would pay for Sen-Mut's and Hapuseneb death's.

CHAPTER 44

MENKHEP-RE

Right after Hatshepset left my quarters, several slaves came to serve me. They shaved my head and depilated the hair from my body and massaged me. They put perfume in the bathing waters. I was bathed well and felt very clean. I felt like my old self, but I was dead inside. Everything seemed strange.

Now, I must plot how I was going to kill him, I thought. I needed to have him very close to me.

"Akhela," I shouted.

She came running.

"Yes, Your Majesty?" she said.

"Let's walk beside the Nile," I said, and we did at sunset. Once we had walked very far away from the palace, I turned around to be sure no one had followed us.

"Akhela, I need something from you, your mother and father. I need your help in getting something for me," I said.

"What is it, Your Majesty?"

"This must be a secret between you and me and your parents."

I became quiet and lowered my eyes.

"What is it, Your Majesty?"

"I need a sharp dagger, preferably a very small one to fit in the palm of my hand. If there are none in the kitchen, tell your father to make one for me. Tell him it must be a very small one and very sharp on both sides of the blade, and he must keep silent. No one should know."

She was silent for a moment, then asked, "Your Majesty, what do you want a small dagger for?"

"I will tell you later, and you must keep this conversation to yourself. Otherwise, they will take you away from me and put me back in the room beside my rose garden," I said.

"When I go to the kitchen, I will tell my mother," she said.

"But remember, she cannot tell anyone, only your father. And when you come back, don't tell me anything in front of the other slaves," I said.

"Yes, Your Majesty."

"We will walk every afternoon. Then you can tell me everything you want to tell me regarding this. And tonight, we are going to dinner in the banquet hall," I said.

"We? You mean me too?" she said and became very happy.

"Yes, you too. You will be beside me as always, and you will taste my food and drink as always." And I smiled.

"Oh, Your Majesty. I have never been in a place like that. Mother said that it is very big and is decorated beautifully, and in there is all kind of food," Akhela said.

"Yes, it's the truth. So tonight, you will enjoy the food too. Let's go back. Remember everything I asked of you today," I said.

"Can I go and talk to my mother tonight?"

"No, not tonight. Tomorrow, when no one is around her. Or on her day of rest."

"I will, Your Majesty," she said.

We got to the palace, and the golden doors were opened. It felt strange that my guards were no longer standing at my golden doors. It brought great sadness to me and I still miss them. They were my family. I walked inside my quarters and clapped my hands. Two slaves came running and knelt.

"Yes, Your Majesty?" one said.

"Bring a small sheath for Akhela and help her dress. You, bathe me. I will dress as Pharaoh tonight," I said.

I walked to be bathed, and I was dressed as Pharaoh with the kilt, the Pharaoh pectoral, and golden sandals.

Akhela looked very clean and lovely. She and the other slaves were in awe when they saw me dressed as Pharaoh, and wearing the Double Crown of Egypt, and they dropped to their knees at my feet and kissed them.

Akhela and I walked to the banquet hall, and she followed behind me. Everyone became silent, including the musicians, when they saw me, and all dropped to the floor.

"Rise," I shouted.

There were many people I had never seen before, and Isis looked very surprised. Then Hatshepset came to greet me.

"Mother, you came. Menkhep-Re said that maybe you would come and have dinner with us. I want you to know that I am very pleased that you have come tonight. I want to tell you that in all these years Menkhep-Re has never sat in your chair here nor in the hall of audience," she said.

I smiled at my daughter and looked around. From where I stood, I saw the faces of Rekhemire and D'Jehuty looking at me and raising their goblets to me. I hated them so much, the traitors. I ignored them. I searched for Nehesi but did not see him. Was he one of the traitors too?

Menkhep-Re came and greeted me too and sat across from me. He would not stop talking all night of what he wanted to do when he became Pharaoh. I just wanted to scream at him to shut him up, but I bit my tongue and smiled.

"Mother, tomorrow I will bring my children to your quarters. They are growing up. In the beginning, Amenemhat kept asking for you, but tomorrow you will be able to see him again," Hatshepset said, and smiled at me.

I could see that she was very happy seeing me there.

"I look forward to seeing him. I have missed him and you too very much," I said.

I looked at Akhela, and she looked very happy.

"Akhela, bring me something to eat and drink," I told her.

"Yes, Your Majesty."

I saw her leave and come back with my food on a golden tray.

"Now you can go and get something for yourself to eat, and bring it here to eat beside me," I said.

She brought her food and sat at my right, in Hapuseneb's place. And I remember him and brought tears to my eyes.

Everyone was looking at me and at Akhela. They probably wondered who the girl was. Isis was staring at me, and I stared back at her with anger. She lowered her face. I was shocked to see Hapuseneb's son there, the traitor and killer of his father. I give him an ugly look, and he lowered his face too. I was surrounded by traitors and enemies. I finished eating and stood. Everyone stopped talking, and all dropped to the floor with their faces on the floor, including Isis.

"Mother, are you leaving this soon?" Hatshepset asked.

"Yes. I don't want to be surrounded by traitors," I said and walked off with Akhela, leaving all of them facing the floor.

I never went back again.

****

A month passed and one afternoon Akhela came from the kitchen.

"Your Majesty, can we walk beside the Nile?" she asked.

"Yes, we can," I said.

We left the palace and walked beside the Nile. I turned around to be sure that no one was following us, and she did too.

"Your Majesty, my mother spoke to me today. She has spoken to my father, and she said that father said to tell you that he will make it for you. And that he knows of the consequences that will follow, but he and my mother will give their lives for you for saving mine," she said.

She became quiet, and I was silent too as we continued walking.

“I told my mother your whole story, and she was saddened by it. She said that she had never heard of all these killings, only that something must have happened because there were rumors that a big silence came upon this land. And she thought before that you were a man, and not a woman.”

We laughed.

She continued, “Mother was shocked the first time I told her that you were Pharaoh Hatshepsut.” Akhela looked down to the ground, and then she said, “Will I die, Your Majesty?”

I stopped and looked at her.

“Yes, all of us will die if I fail, because they will know that your mother had given you the sharp knife and that you had given it to me,” I said sincerely.

She became silent, and I felt sad for her possible fate and being too young to die. Not for myself though. I was ready and had wanted to die since my beloved’s death. We walked back in silence.

A few days later, she came back from the kitchen.

“Your Majesty,” she said and looked around us, then whispered, “Father said that it is ready.”

“Later, when you go to the kitchen, tell your mother to tell your father to wait until I tell you when to send it with you. Tell him that I want it on the day I will be crowning Menkhep-Re Pharaoh,” I said.

“Your Majesty, now I understand everything, and I want you to know that I will also give my life for you, as my parents will.”

I caressed her face. She was so young.

“If I kill him, I still don’t want to live anymore, not without Sen-Mut. Akhela, when we get to the palace, go and talk to your mother and give her my message. Be sure no one is around her, then take this message to Puyem-Re, First Prophet of Amun-Ra to come to my quarters with Menkhep-Re, Rekhemire, D'Jehuty, and Hapuseneb's son," I said.

"Yes, Your Majesty."

It was not very long until Menkhep-Re, Puyem-Re, D'Jehuty, Rekhemire, and Hapuseneb's son walked through my golden doors. Menkhep-Re had a happy look on his face, but the rest were serious. I waited for all of them to approach me and kneel and bow their heads to the floor.

"Menkhep-Re, rise," I said, leaving the rest of the traitors facing the floor at my feet.

"I have made my decision, and it was the hardest decision for me to make. You killed Sen-Mut and my loved ones, and you and the rest of you betrayed me. I want all of you to know that very deep inside my heart I have this enormous hatred for you all. I curse all of you once, I curse you all a second time, and I curse you with all my heart a third time that none of you will ever have peace in your heart and will never reach heaven," I yelled at them. As I walked around them, I continued, "And that all the gods will curse you too, and your families, now and in the afterlife, and for all eternity, that they may never have peace, and that they be hunted like animals and killed like you have killed my beloved Sen-Mut, Hapuseneb, my slaves, and their loved ones."

I was screaming at them.

"Now, to you Puyem-Re. Deep in my heart, I hate you, and I believe very strongly that you are Menkhep-Re's father. I will go to my death believing that you are his father."

Menkhep-Re's face was distorted, hearing the curse I was throwing at them.

"Rekhemire, your father was a faithful vizier of my father. I believe he must be turning in his grave for you being an accomplice in this massacre and maybe the one who encouraged him to do it. I curse you!

"D'Jehuty, you ate at my table many times. Sen-Mut, Hapuseneb, Nehesi, Senemen, Thuty, and Teshi trusted you and believed in you, and you betrayed all of them. You conspired against me and my loved ones. Believe me, if right now I could kill you all, I would. Traitors," I said.

I looked at Hapuseneb's son and stood beside him.

"And to you. You killed your father. I cannot believe that you have not committed suicide yet. You have no conscience," I screamed at him with anger.

Looking at Menkhep-Re, I continued with anger. "I raised you as if you were my own son, even though in my heart I believe that you are not my brother's son. I could have done away with you and your mother a long time ago, when you were a small child. Hapuseneb warned me so many times about you. Nehesi also advised me to do away with both of you many times. But I could not. You were like my son. Sen-Mut never advised me to kill you but warned me many times that one day you would try to kill me and my loved ones. I could not kill you… but you did. You have a terrible heart, not like my brother's heart. He was kind. That is one of the reasons I believe you are not my brother's son.

"I want to finish this war between you and me. I will marry you and transfer the crown to you. Let's do this as soon as possible. We don't need to wait for the new year, and you don't need to have the Pharaoh's bath. It would take too long, and I could change my mind," I said.

He turned around and looked down at Puyem-Re.

"Puyem-Re, could it be done?" he asked.

There was silence, then I heard Puyem-Re's voice, "I must consult with the other priests before I can answer that."

"Puyem-Re, send word to me as soon you have an answer. Now, leave my presence. I don't want any of you rats in my presence or in my quarters!" I screamed at them.

I saw them leave, crawling backwards without raising their faces from the floor or turning their backs to me.

Three days later, I received word from Puyem-Re that it could be done. I told the messenger to tell him that the end of the month would be fine for the marriage and the transfer of the crown to Menkhep-Re.

"Yes, Your Majesty," he said and left my quarters.

****

The end of the month was upon me. It was late in the night, and I was lying in my bed and thinking that this would be my last attempt to kill him.

The Sun was rising on the east, and I woke up very early and thought of Sen-Mut. I wanted everything to be over with as soon as possible. I was very anxious, and to calm down, I walked in silence south beside the Nile, thinking that tonight I must prepare for death. And tomorrow I will have my vengeance. Lost in thought, I had walked so far down the Nile, that without noticing, I was in front of Sen-Mut's observatory. My heart contracted with sadness.

I looked up and saw the chair hanging above, the one he made himself for us to reach the top. It was tied up high by the long rope. I went around the observatory, looking for the bottom entrance and went through the door. Wooden beams were on the outside of the building. I walked out the door, looking for the way to go up, and walked around and reached the wooden beam. I tied my sheath above my thighs and started to climb up the beams like a cat. After the long climb, I reached the top and opened the small door in the wooden floor and walked onto the wooden floor. I walked around the balcony and reached the east double doors. They were all open. Everything had decayed in four years. We never came back here after he had finished his study of the stars and made the celestial map and the Zodiac. Sadness overpowered me.

I looked straight ahead, and against the wall was a small wooden table and on top of it was the small bottle where he kept the poison. I walked to the table and remembered that day when he screamed at me for picking it up when I thought it was perfume for me. I could hear his voice screaming, "No, stop its poison!" He came right away to me and took it away from my hand and set it back on the table. Holding me by my shoulder, and looking deep into my eyes, he said, "I got this poison to kill myself if you ever die. I know that I cannot live without you." He hugged me against his chest that day. I closed my eyes, and tears poured down my face. I was about to drink the poison. I came back to my senses and thought, I must keep myself alive for one more day until my vengeance is complete.

I turned around and saw the linen curtains, filthy with sand and dust, moving slowly with the breeze. I looked to my left. There was our bed, sitting in the silence of the room and covered with sand and dust. I didn't care. I lay there and cried for hours, until it was dark. I did not want to leave because I knew that maybe I would not come back. Only if I succeeded tomorrow in killing Menkhep-Re would I return. I will come back and drink this poison, beloved, I thought. I cannot continue living without you any longer. My daughter, Hatshepset, will rule Egypt. I thought. And I would leave Akhela and her family well off for their help.

I climbed down the beams like Bastet, and I hung tight like a cat to a tree coming down. I walked north back to the palace in darkness, listening to the sound of the current of Hopi at my left. It had been about an hour since I left the observatory when I saw many torches from afar. They were looking for me. And brought a horse for me to ride back.

Very early in the morning just before the first rays of Ra was showing, I was awakened by Akhela.

"Your Majesty, the royal guards are here. They are going to come into your quarters," she said.

"Why?" I asked.

"They coming to search your quarters."

She looked scared.

Dozens of guards abruptly walked into my bedroom without my orders. I was glad that she had not brought the sharp dagger yet. I got up and put a galabia over me.

"Akhela, right after they leave go for the dagger, and come here right away," I whispered in her ear.

Several palace guards with no reverence enter my bedroom and searched everywhere. They cut and tore open my goose mattress and pillows. Feathers were strewn everywhere. They cut open Akhela's mattress too. They continued searching everywhere and did not find anything. Then they went to my bathroom and continued looking, and they still did not find anything.

When they left, a new mattress was brought up. Ten slaves came in and cleaned everything and left my bedroom very clean, as it was before. I knew he must be afraid that I may try to kill him again. Right after they left, the priestesses came in and bathed me. They were not the same ones as the last time, and they were very quiet. Do they know of my plans again, I wondered? They patted me dry, and I was dressed as Pharaoh. I wore a white kilt, the golden pectoral of Hours, and the golden sandals.

"Leave me now," I said, and they left.

"Akhela, come here. Did you get it?" I asked her.

"Yes, Your Majesty."

I looked at her and became sad. I knew she was going to die too.

"Akhela, I want to thank you with all of my heart for being my companion these years. I learned to love you as my own. I hope that you and your parents can understand why I must do this. Otherwise, I will never have peace in my heart, and I would never be able to avenge the life of my beloved one."

She lowered her eyes, which were full of tears.

"My mother and father said to tell you that they hope you accomplish what you are about to do. Mother gave me something to drink to calm me down right now and something else that I must drink for the guards not to take me alive. They are going to do the same," she said.

I pulled her close to me and hugged her tightly against my chest, and I kissed her, tears rolling down my face.

"This is it, Akhela. May all the gods bless you in the afterlife, and may we meet again. Thank you."

I kissed her forehead again. And took a deep breath and wipe off the tears on my face.

"I am going to call Menkhep-Re to come here to my quarters before we walk to the audience hall. Then when we are leaving together, you will be at my right side, and you will quickly hand me the dagger. You will then step back and do what your parents told you to do. Thank you so much. I love you, Akhela."

My adrenaline was high. The time came, and I asked a slave if everyone was downstairs waiting.

"Yes, Your Majesty," she said.

"Send the guard to give a message to Menkhep-Re to come up here to my quarters. I must talk to him right now."

She left, and soon after, Menkhep-Re walked into my quarters. The golden doors were left wide open. He was well groomed and was wearing the golden kilt, the golden belt, and golden sandals, but no pectoral. I was wearing it. I was standing in the middle of my quarters when he walked in.

"Do you want to speak with me before we go to the audience hall?" he asked.

He was full of happiness, and I did not feel sorry for him.

"Sit down, Menkhep-Re, and let's have some of your favorite wine together," I said.

He laughed.

"Hatshepsut, do you want to poison me right now, before the marriage? Do you believe that I would drink anything coming from you today?"

I gathered that he had been warned. I smiled and clapped my hands twice, and one of the slaves came running.

"Yes, Your Majesty," she said.

"Bring me wine right now. I will show you that I am not trying to poison you," I said, and I laughed.

"What do you want to talk to me about?" he asked.

"After I crown you Pharaoh today, are you planning to assassinate me right away?"

He was shocked by my question and started to laugh.

"Of course not. I want children with you, for my children to be of full royal blood," he said.

I saw the slaves bringing two golden goblets and the wine on a golden tray. I took a goblet in my hands and took a big swallow.

"As you can see, it doesn't have poison," I said and smiled.

"Let's get it over with," I said and walked to his right.

My heart was pounding hard, but I was serene as I walked beside him toward the golden doors. Akhela followed close behind me to my right. I remembered my beloved Sen-Mut and how much pain he must have gone through when the horses were tearing him apart. I felt the dagger being pressed into my right hand, and I turned around fast and screamed, "Die!"

I stabbed him with force right in the center of his chest.

"I want you to die, bastard, for killing Sen-Mut!" I screamed.

I screamed again and pushed the dagger deeper into his chest. He was standing, looking down at his chest in shock, then collapsed to the floor. His body convulsed as he gasped for air. The guards at the door pulled me away from him, holding me by my arms.

Puyem-Re, D'Jehuty, and Isis ran up the stairs. She was screaming. I pulled myself free from the guards and grabbed Isis by her hair and threw her to the floor. I sat on top of her stomach, strangling her as hard as I could with both of my hands. I was not letting go of her throat.

"Die, cobra, for killing Neferu-Re and conspiring to kill Sen-Mut. Die, cobra!" I kept screaming at her hard. Not releasing the grip of her throat.

Suddenly D'Jehuty yanked me hard from Isis's throat. I left fingernail scratches on her neck. D'Jehuty was holding me by both arms. Isis looked terrified, trying to sit-down holding her throat, and trying to breathe, and I kicked her hard in the face with so much anger. She was on the floor again trying to breathe, and I continued screaming.

"Die, all of you! I want all of you dead!"

I turned my screaming toward Menkhep-Re who was laying on the floor with his eyes closed.

"And die, you bastard! Did you think I was going to marry you? I swear to you that you will never be Pharaoh nor will have the royal blood! You will never be Thutmoses III! Not the son of a whore and a murderer!"

I was screaming at him as he lay unconscious on the floor, bleeding from his chest. I could see the dagger still lodged where I stabbed him. Puyem-Re was beside him and screamed for help. Many guards came running up the stairs. Then D'Jehuty pulled me away from his body, and I kicked Menkhep-Re's right thigh. His mother was screaming beside his body.

As D'Jehuty dragged me inside my quarters, I saw the body of Akhela lying on the floor. She was dead. He pushed me into my bedroom, and they placed two guards outside my bedroom doors. There was a commotion everywhere throughout the entire palace, then a deep silence. I walked to the balcony and saw that it was still early. I heard the horn marking high noon. Then I walked to my bathroom and got into the water of the tub, fully dressed in my kilt, sandals, and pectoral.

"I hope he dies, and I will wait for my death," I said. "Beloved of mine, I hope he dies, so I will know that I avenged your death."

I remained seated in the water for many hours, and I felt no sorrow for him. I cry for Akhela and her parents, who give their lives for me.

CHAPTER 45

DEATH

Three months had passed since I tried to kill Menkhep-Re, and I had not heard if he was alive or dead. He must be alive, I thought. I wished he would die. And I felt asleep.

I was awakened by soldiers, and they took me out of my quarters to a very small mud hut, with a mud floor, and a mat on the floor for me to sleep. The hut was beside the Nile, and I could hear the current flowing. The sound did soothe me in the nights. They had posted two guards at the entrance of the door to block me from going out. I didn't care anymore. I just wanted him dead. I would die as a Pharaoh, and he would die as an assassin and a bastard. He was not my brother's son, and he would never wear the real Double Crown of Egypt. Sen-Mut had buried it with all the crowns and my treasures, and he died with this secret.

I could hear the soldiers saying that Menkhep-Re was still near death, and I prayed all day long to the gods for his death. Even if he died, his death would not console these pains inside of me, nor console the pain of my people who lost their loved ones in that terrible and horrible massacre. Over five hundred slaves and thousands of brave warriors died defending me and the palace. I only knew that I wanted him and his mother the cobra dead.

A slave brought me food every day and just left it there. No words were spoken to me, and I had not bathed for several days. The nights were warm, and I tried to wash myself as much as I could with the little water they brought me. My daughter Hatshepset had not come to see me. I wondered if she was alright. I had not spoken to anyone for three months.

Anger invaded me, knowing that Menkhep-Re and that snake Isis had gotten away with the deaths of Sen-Mut and Hapuseneb. One thing she would never forget for the rest of her life is when I had her face under the sole of my golden sandal, and I pressed her face against the floor. Everyone saw it in the audience hall. She would never be Queen of Egypt, and they would never reach heaven for they were murderers. One thing I know is that my heart and soul are completely clean, and I will see the face of god.

In the silence of the night, I spoke to almighty God Amun-Ra, "Father, in the next life, allow me to meet with Sen-Mut that I may tell him the truth and how much I love him and how much I miss him." I said.

Tears were pouring down my face. I felt so guilty for his death, and for Hapuseneb's, and for not reading the death sentence before putting my seal on it. I could not believe how we were betrayed by D'Jehuty, and who else? I didn't know. My heart was completely dead.

"I love you, Sen-Mut. I love you, Sen-Mut. It hurts so bad inside of me, and I feel so empty without you," I said.

As I rest my head on the pillow in the mat on the mud floor, the memories of his return from Punt came back to me, and I smiled, remembering that very happy day, and his lovely words, "My King, my Queen, my wife." And how he hugged me and kissed me with such love. I started to cry and sobbed, "I should have died with you, my love. I should have." Crying and sobbing, I fell asleep.

I was deeply asleep when suddenly I was awakened by two hands grabbing me roughly by my wrists and pulling me up from the mat on the floor. The soldiers dragged me outside of the mud hut where many young soldiers with torches were waiting. In silence, they put me on a barge, and we sailed across the Nile to the Valley of the Dead. I knew that I would finally meet my death.

I was not afraid. I was at peace. I had waited five summers for my death. The night was beautiful and so clear. Thoth was pouring out his silver rays on me and over the land. The night was full of stars, and I remembered the first time I saw Sen-Mut's face. He was standing in front of me in the hall of audience for the first time, with a petition he held in his heart for such of long time, wanting to be an architect. We were so young then and full of life. How much we loved each other. Then looking to my left, I could see Thebes as I was taken farther and farther away from her.

"My beautiful Thebes, how much I have loved thee. I hope you will always remember me. I can promise that I will carry you in my heart and in my soul into the next life," I whispered.

Finally, I will be reunited with my beloved Sen-Mut and Hapuseneb, I thought. And with my beloved father the Great Maat, my beloved mother Ahmose, my daughter Neferu-Re, and my sister Neferu-Bity. See, Neferu-Knib, I finally said your name correctly, I thought and smiled.

"Oh, Great God, the only regret I have, and I ask for your forgiveness, is that I should have made the obelisk of solid gold for you. The gold was used to build a shrine of gold for you in my tomb, so I could worship you in the afterlife with Sen-Mut."

Then I noticed the barge had reached the other side of the Nile, and there were many soldiers waiting with torches and horses to ride. My wrists were tied with twine, and I was barefoot. I was put on top of a horse.

"I want all of you to know that I am Pharaoh Hatshepsut!" I said.

There was a commotion amongst the soldiers.

We started to ride fast. I could see the hills in the distance, and soon we arrived at the base of the hills. They dismounted and pulled me off the horse. I could barely walk without sandals on the rocky terrain. I was taken to the entrance of a tomb with gravel stairs going down. The bottom of my feet was hurting terribly as we walked down the steps. I fell on my right knee and I felt a terrible pain all the way down my leg and felt blood dripping down my knee. The soldier grabbed me by the twine on my wrists and began dragging me over the gravel. My thigh was in great pain as he dragged me along the path.

Not one tear will he get from me, I thought. I will die as a Pharaoh and as a brave soldier. The soldier stopped and pulled me up from the gravel. I stood in front of him, watching as he cut the twine from my wrists. He then pushed me inside a dark, empty tomb. It was very dark, but I felt the presence of something. I did not move for a long time.

I stood still for a while as I heard them sealing the door behind me. I noticed a torch in the right corner of the small tomb once my eyes became adjusted to the dim light. Underneath it was a large, empty basket on the floor, and near the basket was a king cobra, ready to strike. I moved, and it struck me on my right thigh[86]. I hit it very hard on the head with my left hand, and I lost my balance and fell against the sealed door. It came back and bit me again on the right side of my face[87]. I hit it again with my left hand. By this time, the venom was taking effect on me. I watched the cobra slither away. I lay there against the sealed door. The pain was terrible. Then my soul was leaving my body. And from above, I saw my body leaning against the sealed door.

---

[86] Picture of the cobra bite on thigh. Page 791.

[87] Picture of the Cobra bite on my face, on page 791.

It's dark, and darkness surrounds me...

It's neither hot nor cold but a feeling of being... But where?

Then I remember my beloved Sen-Mut.

"Sen-Mut!" I scream.

And my voice is lost through the echo of eternity.

Suddenly my soul was flying fast as the speed of light, then it stopped. I came into the presence of this very bright being. His entire body was so bright, I could only see His feet. I knew I was in the presence of the highest. I threw myself at His feet and touched them. I begged Him to let me go back to earth so that I may find Sen-Mut and tell him the truth that I did not order his death, nor the death of Hapuseneb or anyone else. I don't know how long I was in this place because time stands still in heaven.

One moment in time and my soul came back to earth... My soul came close to a woman who was about to have a baby. And looking down from above, I saw the woman giving birth to a child. Then as the baby came out from her womb and took her first breath, my soul was pulled into this body, and I was born again.

The End

THE BODY THAT IS ON DISPLAY IN THE CAIRO MUSEUM IS THE BODY OF QUEEN ATI FROM PUNT.

Epilogue

Sen-Mut's Expression of Love

I was a noble, beloved of my Lord Hatshepsut, who entered upon the wonderful plans of the mistress of the two lands.

She exalted Me.... appointed me to be the chief of her estate ...I was the Superior of Superiors, the chief of chief of the works... I was in life under the Mistress of the two lands, King of Upper and Lower Egypt, MAATKE-RE living for Ever.

I was one, whose steps were known in the Palace, a real confidant of the King HATSHEPSUT His beloved...

I was the greatest of the great in the whole land; One who heard the hearing alone in the privy council. I was the real favorite of the King HATSHEPSUT, acting as one praised by his Lord every day. I conducted offerings to the GODS every day for the sake of the Life, Prosperity and Health of the King HATSHEPSUT.

I was who entered in love, and come forth in favor, making glad the heart of the King every day, The companion and Master of the Palace.

SEN-MUT.[88]

Research by Evelyn Wells from the ancient record.

---

[88] In 1979, I read his expression of love for me for the first time in Evelyn Wells book "HATSHEPSUT." I could not stop crying on the bus on my way home that day. Also, looking at pictures of the star map in his tomb, I noticed he had put me in the middle of all the stars. How lovely it is that the wall of his tomb speaks of his deep love for me, a love that transcended space and time. I love you Sen-Mut. (3/18/2018)

Pictures of wounds from the past.

Wrist cut done by Sen-Mut between mole and upper cut.

Arrow wounds area, where I believe the arrow went through my back.

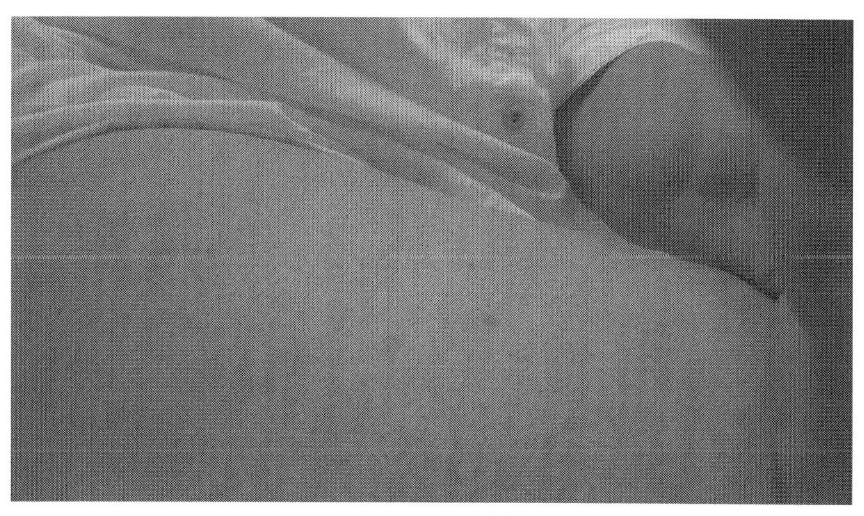

Cobra bite on Thigh.

Cobra bite on my face.

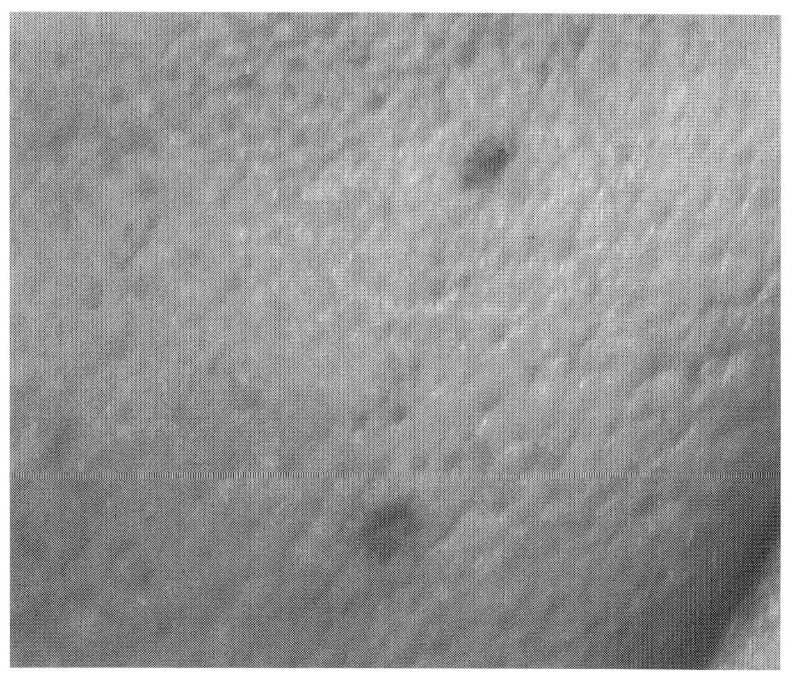

Ancient Names and Terms

AAKHEPERKA-RE: My father's original name before becoming Thutmoses I.

AAKHEPEREN-RE: Birth name of Thutmoses II, my brother.

AAKHEP': Short name for Aakheperen-Re.

ABYDOS: Where the head of Osiris was buried.

ADZE: An instrument used in the ritual of the opening of the mouth to allow the dead to eat, see, and hear in the afterlife.

AHMOSE NEFERTITI: Queen and my mother.

AKHELA: A young slave who give her life for me.

AKHET: Rain, flood.

AMETHU: Vizier of the South and Ursaramun's father.

AMON-HOTEP I: Pharaoh and my grand-father.

AMOSE I: Pharaoh.

AMOSE-PEN-NEKHBET: War correspondent and teacher in charge of teaching Neferu-Re.

AMENEMHAT: Second son of Thutmoses III and Hatshepset.

ANKH: an amulet to ward off evil.

ANUBIS: The jackal god of the underworld.

ATI: Queen of Punt.

BASTET: The goddess of homes and sensuality and represented by a cat.

DESHRET: Red Crown of Lower Egypt.

D'JEHUTY: Commander of the army.

DJESE-DJSERU: The holy of holies, my temple.

HAPUSENEB: My best friend, Vizier of the South, and First Prophet of Amun-Ra during my reign.

HATHOR: Goddess of feminine love, fertility, and joy.

HATNUFER: Sen-Mut's mother.

HEDJET: White Crown of Upper Egypt.

HELIOPOLIS: City of the Gods on the delta, close to the Mediterranean Sea.

HOPI: Nile River.

HORUS: God of the sky, son of Osiris and Isis, and takes the form of a falcon.

HYKSOS: Asians of Greek descendant, invaders of Egypt.

INENI: Master Architect and builder.

ISIS: Goddess of love and fertility, wife of Osiris.

ISIS: Slave and mother of Menkhep-Re (Thutmoses III)

KA: Soul, spirit.

KIOSK: Pharaoh's chambers in Philae.

KHETY: Priest, First Prophet of Amun-Ra.

KHONSU: God of creation.

KOHL: Black powder used to underline the eyes.

MAAT: BULL.

MAATKE-RE: Name given to me by Sen-Mut meaning "Daughter of the Sun."

MEMPHIS: City of the god Ptah the Architect on the west bank of the Nile.

MIN-MOSE: engineer who worked closely with Sen-Mut on all construction, including the obelisks.

MENINA: a slave and expert on herbs and potions, and a spy for Hapuseneb.

MENKHEP-RE: THUTMOSES III

MUTNOFRET: My aunt, my mother's sister, my father's half-sister, and Thutmoses II's mother.

NEB-ERY: Sailor.

NEHESI: General in in the armed forces.

NUT: Mother Night.

OSIRIS: God.

PARAHU: King of Punt.

PHILAE: Island in Aswan.

PTAH: God of architecture.

PUNT: Land of the gods.

PUYEM-RE: Second Prophet of Amun-Ra.

RA: the Sun.

RAMOSE: Sen-Mut's father.

REKHEMIRE I: Vizier of Upper Egypt during Thutmoses I's reign.

REKHEMIRE II: Son of my father's Vizier who later became Vizier under Thutmoses III.

SEKENENRE III: Pharaoh who carried out the first rebellion against the Hyksos, losing his life.

SENEMEN: Sen-Mut's brother and an architect.

SEN-MUT: My beloved, Ptah (architect) and Steward of Amun-Ra.

SET: Evil brother of Osiris.

SOBEK: Crocodile.

TEPI: Hapuseneb's Concubine.

TESHI: One of Sen-Mut's trusted friends.

TETISHERI: My father's great-grandmother.

THEBES: City in Upper Egypt, also known as Waset in ancient times.

THOTH: Moon.

THUTMOSES: General in the armed forces and my father's brother who loved me very much.

THUTMOSES I: Name chosen by my father Aakheperka-Re upon becoming Pharaoh.

THUTMOSES II: Name chosen by Aakheperen-Re, when he became Pharaoh.

THUTMOSES III: Menkhep-Re's chosen name as Pharaoh.

T'QUETA: My personal server and best friend since childhood.

TUYII: My mother's slave, then later mine.

TUTHY: Treasurer and my seal bearer, who also controlled all my gold mines with Sen-Mut.

URSARAMUN: Son of Vizier of the South Amethu, and my friend.

Egyptian Months

AKHET

Inundation of rain for four months.

AUGUST: THOT

SEPTEMEBER: PHAOPI

OCTOBER: ATHYR

NOVEMEBER: CHOIAK

PERET

When the flooded Nile retreats, leaving a silt of rich and fertile soil for planting crops.

DECEMBER: TYBI

JANAUARY: MECHIR

FEBRUARY: PHAMENOTH

MARCH: PHARMUTI

SHOMU

Harvest season. I love Shomu. It was always such a big festivity in the palace and all over the land.

APRIL: PACHON

MAY: PAYNI

JUNE: EPIPHI

JULY: MESORI

About the Author

NELY EMILIANI, before coming to the United States, work for the government of Panama Republic of Panama as a Protocol. Held one of the most sophisticated job of the Country and in the world. 1969-1973.

Work in the United States for 45 years. Retired.

Had the pleasure to meet dignitaries from all over the world, as Kings, Queen, Presidents, Ambassadors, Consuls, Secretary of State, Senator, Astronauts, Movie Stars and Singers and the list is long. Campaigned for Ronald Regan, was invited to the Inaugural ball in Washington D.C.

S.E. General Omar Torrijos, Panamá.

S.E. President Demetrio Lakas, Panamá.

S.E. King Hussein Bin Talal, of Jordan.

S.E. King Faisal Bin Abdulaziz from Saudi Arabia.

S.E. King Shah of Iran, Mohammad Reza Pahlavi.

S.E. Queen Farah Pahlavi.

S.E. Prince Charles of England.

S.E. Former Secretary of State Henry Kissinger.

Former Senator George McGovern.

Former President S.E. Salvador Allende of Chile.

Astronauts: Neil Armstrong, Buzz Aldrin, Michael Collins.

And from behind the scene, help the American Hostage in Iran.

Made in the USA
Monee, IL
23 June 2021

71973642R00448